The Political Economy of Poverty, Equity, and Growth

Series editors
Deepak Lal and Hla Myint

A World Bank
Comparative Study

*The Political
Economy of Poverty,
Equity, and Growth*

Nigeria and Indonesia

**David Bevan
Paul Collier
Jan Willem Gunning**

Published for the World Bank
Oxford University Press

Oxford University Press

OXFORD NEW YORK ATHENS AUCKLAND BANGKOK
BOGOTA BUENOS AIRES CALCUTTA CAPE TOWN CHENNAI
DAR ES SALAAM DELHI FLORENCE HONG KONG ISTANBUL
KARACHI KUALA LUMPUR MADRID MELBOURNE MEXICO CITY
MUMBAI NAIROBI PARIS SAO PAULO SINGAPORE
TAIPEI TOKYO TORONTO WARSAW
and associated companies in
BERLIN IBADAN

Published by Oxford University Press, Inc.
198 Madison Avenue, New York, N.Y. 10016

Manufactured in the United States of America
First printing April 1999

Library of Congress Cataloging-in-Publication Data

Bevan, David.
  Nigeria and Indonesia / David Bevan, Paul Collier, Jan Willem Gunning. —
New York : Published for the World Bank [by] Oxford University Press, c1999.
        p. cm. — (A World Bank comparative study. The Political economy
of poverty, equity, and growth.)
  Includes bibliographical references (p.) and index.
  ISBN 0-19-520986-5
  1. Nigeria — Economic conditions. 2. Poverty — Nigeria. 3. Income
distribution — Nigeria. 4. Nigeria — Economic policy. 5. Indonesia —
Economic conditions. 6. Poverty — Indonesia. 7. Income distribution —
Indonesia. 8. Indonesia — Economic Policy.   I. Collier, Paul. II. Gunning,
Jan. III. World Bank comparative studies. Political economy of poverty,
equity, and growth.
    HC1055.B38   1999

Foreword

This volume is the seventh of several emerging from the comparative study "The Political Economy of Poverty, Equity, and Growth," sponsored by the World Bank. The study was done to provide a critical evaluation of the economic history of selected developing countries in 1950–85. It explores the processes that yielded different levels of growth, poverty, and equity in these countries, depending on each country's initial resource endowment and economic structure, national institutions and forms of economic organization, and economic policies (including those that might have been undertaken).

The Scope of the Comparative Study

The basic building block of the project is a coherent story of the growth and income distribution experiences of each country, based on the methods of what may be termed "analytical economic history" (see Collier and Lal 1986) and "political economy." Each country study provides both a historical narrative and a deeper explanation of how and why things happened. Each study also seeks to identify the role of ideology and interest groups in shaping policy.

Our comparative approach involved pairing countries whose initial conditions or policies seemed to be either significantly similar or significantly different. Although initial impressions of similarity or difference may not have been borne out on closer inspection, this binary approach offered a novel and promising way of reconciling in-depth case studies with a broader comparative method of analysis.

To provide this in-depth study of individual cases, a smaller number of countries was selected than is conventional in comparative statistical studies. We have serious doubts about the validity of inferences drawn from such cross-sectional regression studies about historical processes (see Hicks 1979). Therefore this project, by combining qualitative with quantitative analysis, has tried instead to interpret the nature and sig-

v

nificance of the usual quantifiable variables for each country in its historical and institutional context.

To provide some unifying elements to the project, we presented the authors of the country studies with several provisional hypotheses to be considered in the course of their work. These concern the determinants of growth, the importance of historical and organizational factors in determining alternative feasible paths of growth to redress poverty, and the relative roles of ideas, interests, and ideology in influencing decisionmaking.

The following list of the country studies and their principal authors suggests the range of the overall comparative study:

Brazil and Mexico	Angus Maddison and Associates
Colombia and Peru	Antonio Urdinola, Mauricio Carrizosa Serrano, and Richard Webb
Costa Rica and Uruguay	Simon Rottenberg
Egypt and Turkey	Bent Hansen
Five Small Open Economies: Hong Kong, China, Singapore, Malta, Jamaica, and Mauritius	Ronald Findlay and Stanislaw Wellisz
Malawi and Madagascar	Frederic L. Pryor
Nigeria and Indonesia	David Bevan, Paul Collier, and Jan Willem Gunning
Sri Lanka and Malaysia	Henry Bruton
Thailand and Ghana	Oey A. Meesook, Douglas Rimmer, and Gus Edgren

Several of these volumes have been published in this series by Oxford University Press. In addition, a volume of special studies on related topics has been published (Psacharopoulos 1991).

Deepak Lal and Hla Myint
Series editors

Contents

Tables

Figures

Introduction

This book analyzes economic development during the period 1950–85. The question we address is why, during this period, Indonesia was so much more successful than Nigeria. We argue that, far from being deep-rooted, the reasons for divergent performance reflected temporary and chance conjunctions of circumstances. This has been borne out by the sudden reversals of the late 1990s: at the time of writing (March 1998), Indonesia was experiencing severe economic decline, whereas the Nigerian economy had stabilized.

Nigeria and Indonesia lend themselves naturally to comparison. Both are large, populous developing countries in which an initially agricultural economy was transformed by the discovery of oil. Following the oil windfalls, economic performance diverged dramatically. Living standards in Indonesia grew rapidly—by 8 percent a year—whereas Nigeria experienced an absolute decline in standards. By the late 1980s, on a purchasing power parity basis, per capita gross national product (GNP) in Indonesia was double that in Nigeria. Furthermore, by that time Indonesia was much the more equitable society: the expenditure share of the poorest 40 percent of the population was around 21 percent compared with an expenditure share of only 15 percent in Nigeria. This difference in the share of the poor was accounted for by an offsetting difference in that of the richest 20 percent of the population. Thus, only Indonesia succeeded in achieving growth with equity during the oil windfall.

The central question explored in this book is why equitable growth did not take place in Nigeria after 1972 when, at least superficially, it had the same opportunities as Indonesia. Since both countries received an enormous oil windfall during this period, it is tempting to focus on differences in the handling of the windfall as accounting for the differences in outcomes. Indonesia turned oil income into productive investment, whereas Nigerian oil income was either siphoned abroad or used for prestige projects. However, Indonesian performance was not

1

remarkable compared with that of several nonoil economies. We suggest another possible explanation for Indonesian success: that the country established an environment conducive to growth in the nonoil economy, whereas no such environment was established in Nigeria. Indonesia began implementing a policy of economic liberalization in 1967 and sustained it, whereas Nigeria delayed liberalization until 1986 and subsequently reversed it.

Regardless of the balance between these two explanations of divergence—windfall management versus liberalization—a deeper question arises as to why the countries adopted different policies during the period. A premise of this book is that history matters. That is, to understand policy divergence after 1972, it is necessary to consider events and social structure prior to 1972. Historians sometimes offer explanations in terms of centuries-old causes. At the other extreme, economists often analyze outcomes purely in terms of contemporary events. Here we take an intermediate position, focusing on the period since 1950.

Potentially, policy divergences might reflect either deep-rooted differences in the structure of interest groups or the happenstance of events. We suggest that for the comparison of Nigeria and Indonesia, both are important. For example, with respect to events, in 1966 Indonesia experienced a traumatic episode of hyperinflation that has influenced policy priorities ever since. With respect to the structure of interest groups, we argue that a major influence in Nigeria has been that the politically dominant North has feared that economic liberalization would threaten its position vis-à-vis the South.

Although we argue that differences in performance after 1972 can be related to pre-1972 characteristics, the differences in performance were not in themselves of long standing. In both countries performance during the 1950s and 1960s was similar: although there were episodes of growth, living standards were broadly stagnant over the two decades. We therefore have to explain why the characteristics that generated post-1972 divergence did not do so earlier. There are several reasons. First, Nigeria did not become independent until 1960, so the capacity of interest groups to influence policy was restrained. Second, the new government inherited large accumulated reserves, and thus it was temporarily possible to reconcile conflicting claims. Third, Indonesia's hyperinflation did not occur until late in the pre-1972 period. Fourth, scarcely any developing country adopted a manufacturing-export strategy prior to the 1970s. Interest groups were almost everywhere insufficiently strong to trigger such a strategy, so its merits became apparent only during the 1970s. Finally, the oil windfall was only realized in the post-1972 period. Thus, differences that were unimportant in the 1950s and 1960s became crucial in the changed environment of the 1970s.

Because of the focus on history, detail matters. Thus, although the purpose of the book is comparative, most of the text is taken up with separate analyses of each country—part I focusing on Nigeria and part II on Indonesia. The first chapters in each part provide a narrative of the political economy, focusing on the various phases since 1950. This is followed by a chapter summarizing the effects on economic growth and poverty. The large divergences in outcomes must, to a large extent, be attributed to differences in economic policies. We first consider policies in the factor and product markets that mediated between factor endowments and the growth and distributional outcomes. We then turn to the broader array of economic policies. Finally, we attempt to relate policies to the underlying political processes and interest groups that generated them. Each part concludes by explaining the salient economic outcomes as a result of both policy and the underlying politics.

In part III we use these economic histories to compare the two countries. First we examine the outcomes: similar until the 1970s, divergent thereafter. We then compare the policies. Both liberalization and windfall management policies differed markedly. Indonesia liberalized nearly 20 years before Nigeria, and although both governments had high investment rates during the oil booms, Indonesian investment was more productive. Finally we contrast the political processes and interest groups that we suggest account for these important policy differences.

In the 1950s policymakers in the two countries had a common vision of growth through import-substituting industrialization. By the late 1970s, visions were starkly different. The Nigerian vision was unaltered, whereas Indonesia had shifted to a non-oil-exporting orientation. Central differences in exchange rate policy followed from this vision. Why did the Indonesian vision change but not the Nigerian? Partly, the technocratic advice differed: the Nigerian government disbanded its core of international economic experts in the late 1960s just as Indonesia was establishing one. Partly, too, the neighborhoods differed: Indonesia was on the edge of an area that was rapidly expanding its nontraditional international trade. None of this turned Indonesia into Hong Kong: much oil money was used for import substitution. However, expert advice and proximity to East Asia did gradually build a group with a concern about international competitiveness that provided a rival to the old vision. This group gained power, albeit precariously, from the hyperinflation crisis of 1966, which did much to discredit the old vision.

The Indonesian oil windfall initially strengthened the appeal of import substitution, since the state now had the resources with which to implement it. However, because of the Pertamina crisis of 1975, in which the state oil corporation was exposed as having grossly misused borrowing power and funds, power shifted back to those concerned with international competitiveness. Importantly, this group came to see a potential conflict between the oil windfall and the growth of the nonoil economy. By contrast, Nigerian policymakers saw the windfall not as a potential danger to be navigated, but as an opportunity to implement their vision of an import-substitution strategy. Nigeria had its equivalent of the Pertamina crisis but with very different consequences. President Yakubu Gowon was exposed in the act of suppressing a report that revealed gross misuse of the oil windfall. Unlike in Indonesia, the inference drawn was that the military government was excessively corrupt: President Gowon was toppled, and an interim government set in motion the transition back to civilian rule. The civilian government cannot be said to have had an economic policy vision. Its objective was patronage.

The difference in visions was reflected in different exchange rate strategies. By the late 1970s Indonesian policymakers chose to sacrifice part of the public investment program to achieve exchange rate undervaluation, thereby protecting competitiveness. Because Indonesian nontraditional exports grew rapidly in response, the policies were vindicated by success and became more secure. By contrast, not only did the Nigerian government allow the exchange rate to appreciate during the oil boom, with dramatic consequences for nonoil exports, but also, as the boom receded, the government chose to maintain the exchange rate at its now overvalued level. A task force on inflation, which reported in 1982, recommended this as an appropriate counterinflation policy.

Whereas the old vision had failed early and spectacularly in Indonesia, in Nigeria it failed only gradually. It was not until the crash in the oil price in 1986 that the Nigerian government perceived continuation of the old policies to be unsustainable. Even then, the government was only persuaded to embark upon radical reform by the World Bank, which advised a massive devaluation. The economic shock, of which the public was aware, was therefore associated not with the old vision but with the new. After 1986 the Nigerian middle classes looked back on devaluation in something of the same light as the Indonesian middle classes viewed the hyperinflation episode. As a result, the Nigerian elite was hostile to liberalization, whereas the Indonesian elite was hostile to fiscal deficits.

By the late 1980s Indonesian society was substantially more equitable than Nigerian society. This was partly the indirect result of export-oriented and therefore labor-intensive growth that tightened the labor market, and partly because of direct, distributionally focused policies. From the late 1970s the Indonesian government committed large resources to measuring and identifying poverty and implemented strategies to reduce it.

Why did the Indonesian government attach much greater priority to targeted poverty-reduction policies than Nigeria did? We suggest that this was a matter of differing government aspirations and public expectations. The Indonesian government's concern with poverty dated back to the early 1950s and applied to both the president and the army. President Sukarno, then one of the world's most charismatic leaders, expounded prominently a view of government that emphasized its role as a socially unifying force. As such, the government was expected to tackle great inequalities. The army, too, had aspirations of poverty alleviation, which came from its experience in fighting a war of liberation. Unlike its Nigerian counterpart, it was a mass army that saw part of its role as improving rural infrastructure. Indeed, the army defined itself as having this dual function of military and social service.

Poverty was of much less concern to the Nigerian government. Not only did the army define its role more narrowly, but both Northern and Southern elites tolerated inequality. The Northern elites came from a society in which wealth was justified by hierarchy, whereas the Southern elites saw their wealth as justified by achievement.

President Suharto was probably much less committed to Indonesia's social unification than his predecessor. However, President Sukarno's populist oratory had created expectations in the population that constrained the succeeding government, which was initially a counterrevolutionary government. Nigerians had no equivalent expectations of their government. An example of these differing expectations, and their consequences for policy, is the response to rising food prices. Both countries experienced periods in which the price of staple foods rose in real terms. In Indonesia such increases triggered riots. The government treated these riots as legitimate protests and made great efforts to avoid increases in food prices by ensuring rising supplies. In Nigeria much larger increases in food prices did not lead to protests, let alone to supply-enhancing policies. Indeed, even in the run-up to an election, the civilian government chose to restrict food imports to create rents for its campaign fund. That such a strategy was seen as a net electoral asset illustrates the contrast with Indonesia: the population did not hold expectations that restrained government choices.

In conclusion, the comparison of Nigeria and Indonesia provides a dramatic and relatively straightforward illustration that economic policy matters. Less obviously, it affords an opportunity to trace policy divergences back to their origins. Inevitably, this is a more speculative task. The inappropriateness of historical determinism has been amply illustrated by the record of growth forecasts based on social structure. Diagnoses of some social structures as intrinsically inimical to growth have repeatedly been shown to be wrong. Forecasts in the 1940s condemned Japan to stagnation. The Republic of Korea was similarly condemned in the 1950s, as was Indonesia itself as late as 1966 (Myrdal 1956).

Our interpretation of the effect of social structure and history on growth stops well short of such a diagnosis. We are not claiming that Nigeria's social structure and history will prevent future economic growth. The differences between Nigeria and Indonesia in 1950 were not so marked as to warrant a prediction of divergence. Indeed, in the first two decades of the period 1950–90, social structure and history in both countries were such as to inhibit growth. Yet the changed circumstances of the 1970s, such as the East Asian successes and the oil windfall, together with accidents such as the Indonesian hyperinflation, were sufficient to move Indonesia from stagnation to a phase of rapid growth. There were no fundamental changes in Indonesian society but rather a conjunction of circumstances and incidents that were relatively modest individually.

The East Asian crisis of 1997 suggests that Indonesian policies deteriorated during the 1990s to the point at which growth was jeopardized. Just as this has demonstrated that there is nothing automatic about the maintenance of good policies, so poor policies may also be subject to rapid change. Nigerian policy may be transformed, as occurred in Indonesia at the onset of the Suharto regime. The globalization of the 1990s, so much more pronounced than when Indonesia changed visions in the 1970s, may itself be a circumstance sufficient to induce the adoption of policies promoting growth and equity in Nigeria.

I Nigeria

1 *The Colonial Period*

About 1,000 years ago, Berber tribes invaded the northern part of what was to become Nigeria from the east and northeast. There they established the state of Bornu and seven small Hausa states. These city-states, each centered around a walled capital, had well-developed fiscal, judicial, and administrative systems. Much of these systems was borrowed from Islam, which, however, was never wholly accepted as a religion. In the fourteenth century the Fulanis infiltrated the Hausa states from Senegal. The two groups mixed peacefully until a Muslim fundamentalist, Usuman dan Fodio, started a holy war (jihad) of the Fulanis against the Hausa states (1804–10). The Fulanis overran the Bornu and Hausa states and took over their political structure, modifying it to make the emir an absolute ruler. Dan Fodio established himself as "commander of the faithful" at Sokoto. By the mid-nineteenth century the authority of the sultan of Sokoto had been completely eroded (other than in matters of religion), and the Fulani emirates became independent ministates. The invasions that swept the North did not reach the South; they were stopped by the coastal rain forest and the tsetse fly.

The Yoruba people were dominant in what was to become the Western Region. They set up kingdoms, starting in the sixteenth century, with the alafin of Oyo as the most important king and the oni of Ife as spiritual leader. Early in the nineteenth century these states began to disintegrate. When the British arrived on the scene the Yoruba were a defeated people, having lost a considerable part of their territory to the Fulanis. In the future Eastern Region the Ibos never had a central authority; the dense forest prevented the formation of states comprising more than a few villages.

The North had always been in touch with the outside world through active trade across the Sahara. The South was opened up from the coast when the Portuguese arrived in 1485. Slave trading, involving not only the Portuguese but also other European nations, flourished in the seventeenth and eighteenth centuries. The British explored the Niger in the first half of the nineteenth century, which stimulated commercial interests, and British missionaries established themselves on the coast in the 1840s. In the case of Nigeria, however, the British were the most reluctant of imperialists. To check the slave trade at Lagos, the island was annexed to the British Crown in 1861. But a House of Commons committee advised the government in 1865 to give up all West African colonies except Sierra Leone. Although the government decided to keep Lagos, it declared its intention not to extend its rule beyond the city. However, missionary and trading activities continued to extend inland, particularly along the Niger.

The Colonial Economy and the Growth of Agricultural Exports

Clashes with the French and the Germans, combined with continued government reluctance, led to privatized colonialism: the main trading company, the forerunner of Goldie's United Africa Company, obtained a royal charter and administered, as the Royal Niger Company, law and justice on behalf of the British government. Following the Berlin Conference on Africa in 1885, the British declared the establishment of the Oil Rivers Protectorate, later renamed the Niger Coast Protectorate. In 1906 the protectorate merged with Lagos to form the Colony and Protectorate of Southern Nigeria, which was subsequently extended inland until it included all of Yorubaland. In the meantime the military forces of the Royal Niger Company, commanded by Frederick Lugard, extended the company's territory in the North. Finally, in 1879, the royal charter was revoked, and the Protectorate of Northern Nigeria was formed (1900) under Lugard as high commissioner.

The two protectorates were not united until 1914 and even then continued to be administered separately. In the North, Lord Lugard (as he now was) developed the system of indirect rule that left much of the authority of the traditional rulers intact (except, of course, for the inevitable loss of prestige from the imposition of the colonial superstructure). Indirect rule was later extended to the West and the East of the country, which, in the case of the Eastern Region, led to ludicrous situations: since there were no chiefs, the British had to create them to make indirect rule feasible.

After the conquest of the North and the brutal suppression of uprisings in the century's first decade, close cooperation between the British and the traditional rulers developed. Lord Lugard liked the aristocratic society of the North, and the British became not agents of development but defenders of a stagnant, feudal structure. The traditional check on unjust rulers (assassination of the emirs) was now removed, and the British tolerated gross scandals. Colonial officials found the North much more congenial than the South, no doubt in part because Nigerians with

Western-style education (typically the products of mission schools in the South) tended to be more critical of the British. The Islamic civilization in the North was considered superior and its superiority was explained in racist terms (the Hamitic hypothesis of white invaders).

It is important to stress that the administrative divisions instituted by Lugard and his successors were to a considerable extent artificial. Particular ethnic divisions were largely a creation of the British; people began to see themselves in ethnic terms because the British insisted on seeing them in this way.

Once "pacification" was complete, the government reverted to light administration; the British saw themselves as no more than "great white umpires." British commercial interests were held in check by Lugard's concept of the dual mandate. This involved "trusteeship for the native peoples," which meant that outside investors were not allowed to buy land. For example, William Lever of the Africa Company was repeatedly rebuked when he tried to establish oil palm plantations in Nigeria. The dual mandate also meant an open-door policy: there were no restrictions on non-British imports or direct investments. In marked contrast with British policy in East Africa, expatriate mining concerns or plantations were not allowed to become dominant. In West Africa, to use the terminology of Hopkins (1973), the frontier was dominated by the traders rather than the settlers. Thus, for Nigeria, the arrival of the British did not involve a sharp break with the past. Since the British did not settle, the trading firms (buying palm oil, palm kernels, and, later, cocoa, rubber, and groundnuts) continued to form the main external influence in Nigeria.

Agricultural exports grew rapidly in the early colonial period, as a result of smallholder activity. Growth took place from an extremely low base: at the turn of the century the "recorded value of Nigerian exports totaled only about £2 million, probably less than 2 percent of gross domestic product if anyone had known how to calculate it at the time" (Helleiner 1966, p. 4). At that time, head portage was still the main means of transport; there was not a single highway, and railway construction had only just begun in 1898. From 1900 to 1929, exports grew by 5.5 percent a year in real terms. The colonial government encouraged an indigenous class of independent export producers, intervening very little except in transport, which Lugard saw as central to African development. A railway line from Lagos to Kano, a distance of more than 700 miles, was completed in 1911, and a line from Port Harcourt to Kaduna was completed in 1926. Road mileage increased from 2,000 in 1914 to 6,000 in 1926, communication facilities were extended, and harbors improved. These infrastructure investments were financed largely by external loans; as a result, the government was heavily indebted in the 1930s.

There was little innovation in peasant agriculture in this period. Helleiner's (1966) thesis is that the technology was characterized by fixed coefficients; surplus land was brought into cultivation (and labor inputs increased at the expense of leisure) in response to improvements in the peasants' terms of trade. These improvements were the result of the government's massive investment in infrastructure and a long run of favorable changes in world prices.

The expansion of infrastructure was reflected in the changing composition of exports. Palm oil and kernels (produced in the fairly easily accessible rain forests of the South) accounted for more than 80 percent of exports in 1900. The Kano railway and road building in the cocoa areas led to the rapid growth of exports of cocoa (produced in the West) and of groundnuts and cotton (from the North). At the end of the 1920s palm products accounted for only half of exports, with cocoa and groundnuts constituting another quarter. The development of groundnuts in the North marked the end of that region's traditional, north-facing, preoccupation with trade across the Sahara—the North now became linked to the outside world via the South. Ironically, the railway to Kano had been intended to stimulate not groundnuts but cotton growing.[1] Although the British tried unsuccessfully to convince farmers in the area around Kano to grow cotton, Hausa traders got them to grow groundnuts—an activity that was ultimately to involve some 9 million farmers. The spectacular success of groundnuts not only belies the notion that Africans were unwilling to enter into commercial agriculture but also casts doubt on Helleiner's thesis that no technical change was involved:

> The massive increase in groundnut production was achieved partly by reducing the amount of land under other foodstuffs and cotton, but mainly by introducing minor, though highly effective, changes in technique, which made more efficient use of existing land and labour resources. These changes involved shorter fallow periods, increased manuring, and a greater degree of interplanting. It was only in the 1920s and 1930s, with the advent of the motor car and better roads, that expansion took the form of increasing the amount of land and the number of labourers employed in the industry. (Hopkins 1973, p. 220)

From 1911 to 1937, 1 million acres around Kano were brought under groundnuts, attracting thousands of migrants. The European trading firms got some competition from Levantine migrants, mainly Lebanese, early in the century. The Lebanese, however, diversified from crop buying into transport and hotels (and later also into manufacturing). The European firms were dominated by the gigantic United Africa Company, formed in 1929 after a series of mergers. Lever, the genius of the company, had lobbied unsuccessfully for permission to establish plantation agriculture. Governor Clifford's reply in 1920 to one of Lever's many requests is worth quoting:

As agricultural industries in tropical countries which are . . . in the hands of the native peasantry (a) Have a firmer root than similar enterprises when owned and managed by Europeans, because they are natural growths, not artificial creations, and are self-supporting, as regards labor, while European plantations can only be maintained by some system of organized immigration or by some form of compulsory labor; (b) Are incomparably the cheapest instruments for the production of agricultural produce on a large scale that have yet been devised; and (c) Are capable of rapidity of expansion and a progressive increase of output that beggar every record of the past . . . I am strongly opposed to any encouragement being given . . . to projects for creation of European owned and managed plantations. (Cited by Forrest 1981, p. 224)

Significantly, the possible positive conclusion—that peasant agriculture was worthy of support—was not drawn. The colonial policy against plantations developed only gradually, as a response to the opposition to Lever's plans from other traders, the failures of the plantations that were established, and the probably unexpected success of peasant agriculture. Because the government limited itself to the maintenance of law and order and the provision of infrastructure, the colonial economy reflected individual responses to economic incentives. The period 1900–29 is one in which colonialism and trade brought cohesion:

During these thirty years Nigeria outgrew its original status as a collection, accidentally enclosed within artificial, foreign-made boundaries of "traditional," largely self-sufficient small, agricultural communities possessing a few, relatively insignificant trading links with North Africa and Europe; though still far from an effective national unit, it now emerged as a group of much larger Regional economies, each increasingly tying itself to the world economy. (Helleiner 1966, p. 6)

Instability: Trade Shocks before 1945

The period 1911–45 was one of considerable volatility in world prices (table 1.1). For example, the barter terms of trade index fell by more than 70 percent between 1913 and 1921. In a much shorter period, 1919–21, the index dropped by 41 percent and then increased by 48 percent in the next two years. The 1930s and the war period are of special interest. The terms of trade index (1953 = 100) fell from 74 in 1930 to 48 in 1934, recovered to 75 in 1937, and then fell back again partly as a result of wartime price controls.

Two things may be noted from the data in table 1.1. First, import volumes mirror terms of trade movements surprisingly closely—for

Table 1.1 Exports, Imports, and Terms of Trade, 1911–45
(1953 = 100)

Year	Export volume	Import volume	Barter terms of trade	Year	Export volume	Import volume	Barter terms of trade
1911	19	22	138	1928	44	32	86
1912	19	24	141	1929	49	29	78
1913	21	27	169	1930	49	25	74
1914	21	24	141	1931	46	15	52
1915	20	20	105	1932	51	16	52
1916	23	21	88	1933	49	14	54
1917	27	26	87	1934	57	12	48
1918	27	29	74	1935	60	15	58
1919	31	39	78	1936	67	18	69
1920	34	40	54	1937	77	21	75
1921	23	29	46	1939	60	13	45
1922	28	26	62	1940	58	16	42
1923	32	28	68	1941	75	15	37
1924	40	30	68	1942	64	21	38
1925	51	27	64	1943	62	18	30
1926	43	32	80	1944	56	22	35
1927	50	26	72	1945	59	21	39

Source: Helleiner 1966, table IV-A-2, pp. 494–95.

example, falling by more than half between 1930 and 1934 and expanding by 75 percent in the next three years. Second, export growth continued in the 1930s, even when export prices fell dramatically. However, the previous rate of growth was no longer attained (5.1 percent a year between 1914 and 1930 compared with 2.5 percent between 1930 and 1939).

The surprising lack of stability of import volumes reflects the colonial government's fiscal and monetary system. Under the West African Currency Board (founded in 1912), an independent Nigerian monetary policy was impossible. The money supply expanded and contracted automatically during booms and slumps. The Nigerian pound was backed 100 percent by sterling. The fiscal stance was extremely conservative; the budget had to balance since the colony was supposed to be self-sufficient. Because the bulk of government revenue was derived from trade taxes, and because more than half of government expenditure went for outlays that could not be adjusted easily (expatriate salaries and pensions and debt service), domestic public expenditure was extremely unstable; it had to contract disproportionately during a slump. Thus, the colonial economy had a self-regulating system of adjustment to external shocks, much as under a gold standard. The familiar problem of a boom followed by a balance of payments crisis (as a result of a ratchet effect in public expenditure) simply could not occur.

The period 1930–45 was one of very great strain for Nigeria. In a few years the real producer price for the four main export crops dropped by more than half (table 1.2). Real wages dropped sharply. Foreign firms went bankrupt on a large scale: of 197 firms existing at some time between 1921 and 1936, only 14 survived as independent firms. Even the United Africa Company retrenched, reducing, for example, its outstations in the Kano area from 80 to 20. This was a period of rising African dissatisfaction with the open economy and with colonialism. In 1944 the first political party, the National Council of Nigeria and the Cameroons (NCNC), was founded. Labor unrest grew during the war, and a month-long general strike took place in 1945.

Constitutional Change

The postwar colonial period (1945–60) was marked by constitutional change, rising expectations, and an important change in the government's own view of its role.

The constitution introduced by Sir Arthur Richards in 1946 foresaw a slow movement toward self-government. The constitution quickly became outdated when nationalism, fueled in part by the experiences of Nigerian soldiers returning from service abroad, proved much stronger than the British had expected. The constitution provided for regional houses of assembly and strengthened tribalism at a time when the NCNC (although drawing its support mainly from the South and in particular from the Ibos) still reflected pan-Nigeria idealism. In 1951 a new constitution established a quasi-federal system with three regions (Northern, Eastern, and Western, which now included the former colony of Lagos).[2]

In the 1951 election one party was dominant in each of the three regions: the Action Group in the West, the Northern People's Congress (NPC) in the North, and the NCNC in the East. In this election both the Action Group and the NPC favored strong regional governments. For the NPC this position reflected resentment of Southern progress, the well-founded suspicion that the South considered the North as backward, and the fear of dominance by the South, which in a unitary state would be able to occupy most civil service posts. When "self-government by 1956" was proposed in the central House of Representatives, the North actually threatened secession.

The resulting constitutional breakdown led to a conference in London in 1953. This led to constitutional changes that strengthened the regions in 1954: each got its own governor, premier, civil service, and judiciary; the marketing boards were regionalized; and the principle of derivation in the allocation of revenues was adopted.

Table 1.2 Real Producer Prices for Export Crops and Real Wages, 1930–60

Year[a]	Real producer price indexes (1948 = 100)					Nominal wages[c]	Cost of living[d]	Real wage index (1948 = 100)[e]
	Cocoa[b]	Palm oil	Palm kernels	Ground-nuts[b]				
1930	132.5	126.1	121.1	205.9		—	—	—
1931	96.1	57.7	140.6	130.6		—	—	—
1932	91.7	98.6	124.3	205.3		—	—	—
1933	51.6	71.3	83.5	170.3		—	—	—
1934	84.1	51.9	63.3	81.8		—	—	—
1935	97.5	117.9	290.1	211.7		—	—	—
1936	96.1	107.9	108.2	231.6		—	—	—
1937	150.0	126.7	146.0	177.8		—	—	—
1938	76.3	60.7	82.3	86.2		—	—	—
1939	74.7	56.7	84.2	111.1		—	—	—
1940	48.0	50.3	66.6	99.7		39	32	108
1941	45.3	39.8	46.9	80.3		42	42	89
1942	28.7	36.2	42.3	64.5		68	47	129
1943	32.2	40.2	37.4	83.0		77	64	107
1944	47.2	48.5	57.5	107.4		77	57	120
1945	55.2	48.9	53.1	120.8		84	69	108
1946	78.6	50.9	55.0	109.2		100	71	125
1947	100.0	46.6	50.1	100.0		100	90	99
1948	189.2	100.0	100.0	115.9		100	89	100
1949	102.3	113.7	119.9	132.6		100	90	99

Year							
1950	147.9	111.8	117.5	95.6	103	91	101
1951	216.4	116.9	115.7	180.3	116	116	89
1952	241.8	126.1	130.3	203.3	129	112	103
1953	224.7	258.5	130.6	219.9	132	100	127
1954	258.1	121.5	120.0	225.1	145	105	123
1955	244.4	115.6	108.3	212.4	181	109	148
1956	177.7	93.4	102.0	194.3	181	127	138
1957	188.7	93.4	100.8	217.9	181	119	135
1958	185.2	91.0	99.7	186.5	181	119	135
1959	189.5	84.1	96.1	202.2	281	124	130
1960	149.9	94.1	94.3	195.2	181	132	122

— Not available.

a. 1930–38, calendar years; 1939–60, fiscal years (1939/40–1960/61).

b. 1947/48 = 100 for cocoa, groundnuts.

c. Minimum wage to that for general (unskilled) labor in federal government employment (Lagos); the index has been recalculated from the figures in shillings per day in table I-B-6, since Helleiner's index is inconsistent.

d. 1953–60 Lagos consumer price index (1953 = 100), from table III-B-3; 1949–53 Lagos wholesale price index (1948 = 100) of imported goods from table III-B-1, converted to 1953 = 100; 1940–48 index of landed cost of printed cotton piece goods from table III-B-1 (based on Bauer 1954, p. 421), converted to 1953 = 100.

e. From the previous two columns.

Source: Helleiner 1966, tables I-B-6, II-B-1 to II-B-4, III-B-1, III-B-1, III-B-3. Consumer price indexes used differ between crops.

17

These safeguards provided the North with the security it had sought, leading to the unanimous decision of the House of Representatives in 1957 to demand independence in 1959. Nigeria became independent on October 1, 1960, with Sir Abubakar Balewa (a Northerner and one of the founders of the NPC, but not a Fulani aristocrat) as prime minister.

Superficially, the process of constitutional change in the 1950s may suggest a loss of national unity. This interpretation would be erroneous. Nigeria started out as an artificial collection of people and territories, and the British presence did little to transform this collection into a nation, partly because this was a colony of traders rather than settlers and partly because of the decision to adopt indirect rule. Also, the potentially unifying force of a struggle for independence was absent in Nigeria. The constitutional changes in the direction of federalism represented to some extent a return to the precolonial situation.

Lack of national identity is not, of course, in itself a sufficient reason for federalism. In Nigeria two other factors contributed. First, part of the country, the North, stood to lose from a unitary constitution. Second, the relative size of the three main ethnic groups prevented any of them from imposing its will.

The constitutional changes of the 1950s had two important consequences, which we discuss in subsequent chapters: the transformation of the marketing boards into fiscal instruments (chapter 7), and the negative effect of the focus on the allocation of revenues between regions on the development of a satisfactory federal fiscal system (chapter 8).

Economic Conditions and Policies

Agricultural policy in the postwar colonial period resulted mainly in failures. Before the war the state had proved its inability to pick winners—for example, supporting cotton instead of groundnuts. However, the state's involvement in agriculture was minimal (at the end of the 1920s the Department of Agriculture had a staff of only 56 officers), so that a vigorous extension policy intended to establish mixed farming had little effect. Of those who did accept mixed farming, in 1935 half were classified as emirs, native authority officials, or village heads (Shenton 1986, p. 105). After the war there was much enthusiasm for mechanization, which in the case of oil seeds led to the Niger Agricultural Project at Mokwa—a spectacular failure. "When the Colonial Development Corporation withdrew from its partnership with the Nigerian government in 1954, less than 80 settlers were involved and a loss of £123,473 was sustained" (Forrest 1981, p. 233).

Agriculture was heavily taxed through the marketing boards (discussed in chapter 7). Although intended as price stabilization devices, these boards came to be seen as useful fiscal instruments: through their monopsonistic power, cash crop production could be taxed by increasing the wedge between producer prices and world prices.

More important than what the government did to support agriculture is how little it did. Only tiny amounts were allocated to primary production in the two development plans of the colonial period, which provided not much more than project lists. Only 6.5 percent was allocated to primary production in the 1946–56 plan and 11.9 percent in the 1955–60 plan (table 1.3). The development plans mark an important change in the role of the state in the economy. "Colonial government, whose responsibilities had been conceived primarily as maintaining justice and equal rights and preventing abuses, came in the 'forties to be regarded also as an instrument for raising living standards and promoting social welfare" (Rimmer 1978, p. 146). The state gave up its referee role and adopted an activist stance, very much in line with development thinking at the time and in particular with British thinking during the Attlee government.

Although the public sector remained remarkably small relative to gross domestic product (GDP), it grew rapidly in the 1950s, with the share of public consumption in GDP rising from 3.4 percent in 1950/51 to 7.1 percent in 1959/60. There was considerable growth, especially in the first half of the 1950s. Per capita consumption (1950 = 100) rose to 114 in 1955. It subsequently fell back to 108 in 1960 but appears to have remained well above its initial level.

Table 1.3 Allocation of Funds under Nigerian Development Plans, 1946–74
(percent)

Sector	1946–56	1955–60	1962–66	1970–74
Primary production	6.5	11.9	13.4	12.9
Trade and industry	0.5	1.7	13.3	10.5
Electricity	2.9	5.6	15.1	4.4
Transport and communications	21.0	27.6	25.8	27.9
Education	10.0	14.8	10.3	13.5
Health	12.4	—	—	—
Water and sewerage	15.1	7.7	4.0	5.0
Defense, security, general administration	3.7	7.6	14.5	—
Other	31.2	18.2	—	6.1

— Not available.
Note: Data are for federal and regional allocations combined.
Source: Olatunbosun 1975, table 4.10, p. 70.

Real wages rose much more—by more than 40 percent between 1950 and 1960—and reached a level far above rural income levels. Thus at independence the urban labor market was characterized by a wage premium. The share of gross fixed investment doubled in this period, rising from (a dismally low) 6.9 percent to 13.8 percent (table 1.4). The prewar priority given to infrastructure investments was maintained: transport and communications accounted for 21 percent of investment in the 1946–56 plan and 28 percent in the 1955–60 plan. But now there was also considerable investment in education (10 percent and 15 percent in the two plans), especially in the South. The gap that already existed between the South (exposed to Western-style education through mission schools) and the North (where schooling remained largely limited to Koranic teaching) widened. In 1952 in the Kano area, out of a

Table 1.4 National Accounts, 1950/51 and 1959/60

| | 1950/51 | | 1959/60 | |
| | Millions of | | Millions of | |
Item	1957/58 naira	Percent	1957/58 naira	Percent
GDP at factor cost				
Agriculture, forestry,				
fishing	456.8	66.5	613.0	65.3
Mining	7.0	1.1	6.6	0.7
Electricity, water,				
manufacturing	3.9	0.6	30.6	3.3
Transport,				
communications	31.3	4.0	35.4	3.8
Government	15.0	2.2	36.3	3.9
Marketing boards	41.0	6.0	11.6	1.2
Other	131.5	19.1	205.0	21.8
Total	687.1	100.0	938.5	100.0
GDP at market prices				
Private consumption	609.4	87.1	830.0	84.0
Public consumption	24.0	3.4	70.0	7.1
Gross fixed investment	48.4	6.9	136.7	13.8
Change in marketing				
board stocks	–7.3	—	—	—
Exports	99.9	—	163.0	16.5
Imports	75.1	—	212.0	21.5
Total excluding				
imports	699.3	—	987.7	100.0

— Not available.
Source: Stolper 1966, pp. 94–97.

Table 1.5 School Enrollment by Region, 1957

Area	Primary	Secondary	Total[a]
Northern Region	205,769	3,651	212,684
Eastern Region	1,209,167	12,242	1,231,280
Western Region	982,755	16,208	1,009,888
Federal District (Lagos)	50,182	4,087	55,840
Total	2,447,873	36,188	2,509,692

a. Includes the Nigerian College of Technology (enrollment 684), technical and vocational schools (2,388), and teacher training institutions (36,188, of which only 10 percent were in the North).

Source: Smythe and Smythe 1960, table III, p. 62.

population of 3.4 million, only 23,000 were literate in English and half of those were Southerners.

By 1957 the South, including Lagos, contained about half of the population but accounted for more than 90 percent of primary school enrollment (table 1.5). Both Southern regions announced bold schemes for early universal, free, and, in the case of the Western Region, compulsory primary education. The resulting enormous increase in enrollment quickly increased the share of education in total (current and capital) regional expenditure to 33 percent in the West in 1954/55 and 43 percent in the East in 1956/57. In a period (1950–61) when farm incomes fell by 30 percent whereas government wages trebled, schooling was seen (and would continue to be seen well into the 1960s) as the route to a well-paid, nonagricultural wage job.

In 1948 the colonial government accepted the recommendations of the Nigerianization Commission that a position could not be filled by an expatriate if a suitable and qualified Nigerian was available, and that scholarships should be given to train Nigerians to fill responsible positions. Shortly thereafter Nigerianization was also adopted in the private sector.

The rising nationalism of the 1950s led to a shift in British support for Nigerian elites when it became clear that power could not be handed over to traditional rulers:

> The train carrying the chiefs and elders into the future, as well-subsidized bearers of colonial authority, suddenly had to be shunted onto a siding to make room for the fast express of nationalism. Many of the less well-educated chiefs were at a loss to explain the new policy. They could not understand why the British, seemingly committed to their support, would so soon want to withdraw that support in favor of upstarts. (Bretton 1962, p. 12)

The upstarts were a new elite consisting of educated politicians, bureaucrats, and would-be industrialists, the group preparing to take control of independent Nigeria. The top of this elite was completely Yoruba- and Ibo-dominated. For example, out of 944 students enrolled at University College in Ibadan in 1959, Yoruba was listed as the tribal classification for 408, Ibo for 333, Fulani for 6, and Hausa for 3.

Foreign firms, including the United Africa Company, allied themselves with this new elite, which moved out of its traditional trading activities and into manufacturing. Above all, the economy became politicized in the 1950s. This was not just because both the central and the regional governments adopted the activist development ethos of the time. What was special about the Nigerian case was the combination of huge resources (the marketing board surpluses), the transfer of control over those resources to the regional governments, and the erosion of national appeal of the three main parties. In each region one party became dominant, and party and government finances were no longer clearly separate. According to Rimmer (1978, pp. 147–49), development funds "were used primarily to secure political loyalties, repay political debts, and build personal fortunes." In the regional governments the "welfare and public works powers . . . offered huge opportunities for patronage and went far to consolidate the power of each governing party." Governmental favor (or disfavor) became important. "Farmers were subjected to marketing monopolies because governments required control of surpluses extractable from their labour. Wage-earners were raised up from time to time because their votes were believed marketable and their hostility dangerous." The government was no longer a referee but an active participant:

> Thus economic life in Nigeria became politicised: less through imposition of colonial rule than its withdrawal: the result of a process inspired by the cause of development, financed by improving terms of trade, mediated by decolonisation and a federal constitution.

The relative neglect of agriculture in the 1950s was reflected in stagnant productivity for export crops, with the notable exception of cocoa. Cocoa productivity rose by more than 50 percent during the decade. This was caused in part by new planting (in response to the rising world prices) and thus improvement in the age distribution of the stock of trees. The more significant reason for increased productivity was the increased use of insecticides, fungicides, and improved seedlings. As a result, when the producer price fell by more than 50 percent (between 1952/53–1955/56 and 1961/62–1963/64), cocoa farmers suffered a real income loss of only 11 percent.

For palm produce and groundnuts, however, there was no change in production techniques. Palm produce continued to come predominantly from wild trees, and although groundnut production rose enormously (export volumes almost doubled between 1950 and 1963), the gain appears to have been caused entirely by an increase in acreage. Until mid-1950 there was little official interest in industrialization, but this changed with the gradual transfer of power to Nigerians. At the end of the decade there were tariff increases that amounted to sharp increases in effective rates of protection. Industrialization did not, however, lead to a surge of quantitative restrictions. Quantitative restrictions had existed since the war but were almost completely dismantled by 1954. At the very end of the period under consideration, government (federal and regional) equity participation in manufacturing increased sharply, but, for the most part, government intervention took the form of incentives for foreign direct investment. However, throughout the 1950s the modern industrial sector was tiny, accounting for less than 3 percent of GDP.

Conclusion

In contrast to Nigeria, many African countries enjoyed considerable continuity in policy, and decisive changes did not occur until well after independence. In Nigeria the break with the prewar colonial past occurred earlier. During the 1950s the state adopted an interventionist philosophy, the public sector expanded enormously, commercial and political power began to be transferred to Africans, agriculture was taxed heavily through the marketing boards, and the first steps were taken to build up a modern industry through incentives to foreign investors. More important, perhaps, the probability of the country surviving as a unitary state was already in doubt well before independence. The 1954 regionalization was an outcome of interregional tensions, but it also reinforced those tensions as the power base of political parties became increasingly regional.

2 *From Independence to Chaos: 1960–66*

Nigeria became independent on October 1, 1960. Independence did not involve a sharp organizational or institutional break with the past. The system of government, modeled on the Westminster example, was kept intact. The more important effect of independence was on expectations: politicians now came under intense pressure (as in many other newly independent countries) "to deliver the goods" in terms of jobs, wage increases, and promotions for Nigerians.

In two respects initial conditions were favorable. Foreign exchange reserves had peaked in 1955, but in 1960 they still amounted to almost a year of imports. Oil exports had started in 1958. In 1960 they amounted to only N£4.4 million, but it was already clear that oil would soon become an important source of both foreign exchange and government revenue.[1] In other respects the situation at the time of independence was problematic. Population pressure (especially in the East) and rural-urban income differentials had led to considerable migration, to urban unemployment, and, most important, to resentment toward outsiders. This applied in particular to the Ibos in the North. At the end of the colonial period the position of the Ibos had become very strong, in part because of their educational achievements. They were now seen increasingly as a group that threatened to dominate the country.

Political Developments

The preindependence federal election held in December 1959 had shown each of the main three parties firmly in control of a region. The NPC won 142 of 320 seats in the House of Representatives in the North; the NCNC, in alliance with the Northern Elements Progressive Union, won 89 seats in the East; and the Action Group won 73 seats in the West. The two Southern parties had enough seats to form a coalition, but the NCNC decided to join the NPC instead, thereby ending the traditional Southern

24

cooperation and forcing the Action Group, led by Chief Awolowo, into opposition.

As leader of the opposition, Chief Awolowo managed to make the government's position uncomfortable. He succeeded, for example, in raising enough popular support for his attack on the British-Nigerian defense pact to get the pact abrogated (1962). He also campaigned for large-scale nationalizations but was, in that respect, completely ineffective—the minister of finance made it clear that potential foreign investors should not be frightened away. His support for minority movements and his attacks on corruption were more dangerous to the government. They forced the reigning coalition into a counterattack that involved the declaration of a state of emergency in the Western Region (1962), the trial of Chief Awolowo for treason (he was sentenced to 10 years), and creation of the Coker Commission to examine the finances of Western political parties and government corporations.

On the heels of this crisis followed the census controversy of 1962–64, described by Kirk-Greene (1971) as the beginning of the gunpowder trail leading to the civil war. Since revenue and seats in the house of representatives were allocated to regions on the basis of population estimates, the census became a prime political issue. The initial results implied a population increase since 1952–53 of 30 percent in the North and, implausibly, increases of 71 percent and 70 percent, respectively, in the Eastern and Western Regions. Verification attempts strained the NPC-NCNC coalition. Finally, a recount was ordered that showed population increases of 67 percent in the North, 65 percent in the East, and 100 percent in the West. The old hope of the Southern regions—that the census results would enable them to break Northern dominance—was dashed when the Northern figures turned out to be as inflated as the Southern ones. The old North-South conflict became a North-East conflict, with the Western government supporting the North, on which it depended for its survival.

The federal election, first held in 1964 and then repeated in 1965, was marked by harassment of politicians campaigning outside their own region, by a threat of the East to leave the federation, and by anti-Ibo publicity. Violence and ethnic tensions carried over to the 1965 elections for the Western House of Assembly. These elections became the stage for a national power struggle between two groups: the Nigerian National Alliance, consisting of the Northern NPC and a faction of the old Action Group led by Chief Akintola, versus the United Progressive Grand Alliance, consisting of the Eastern NCNC and the remainder of the Action Group. Chief Akintola's party blatantly abused its control over the state in this election, raising producer prices for cocoa by 50 percent to attract the votes of farmers, promising to establish a hugely expensive steel mill, and declaring some of its candidates unopposed in spite of protests in the courts. The election was marked by considerable violence, including the murder of electoral officers. Both sides claimed victory, but Akintola's followers formed a government and imprisoned their opponents. Large-scale looting and killing of political opponents then followed, until the army intervened and put down what had become an open rebellion. The considerable power given to the regions in the constitution exacerbated ethnic tensions. The NCNC lost much of its national appeal and became increasingly an Ibo-dominated Eastern party.

A first step on the road to creating new states to satisfy minority groups was taken in 1963, when the Midwestern Region, consisting of the non-Yoruba Benin and Delta provinces, was carved out of the Western Region. The increasing identification of political parties with particular regions and ethnic groups was accompanied by a blurring of the boundaries between the finances of the state, political parties, and individual politicians. In the Western Region this was documented by the Coker Commission. Its report showed that part of the marketing board funds (the revenue from a tax on agricultural exports) had been misappropriated, and another part had benefited Action Group politicians and their supporters more indirectly, through excessive profits on contracts for regional development projects financed from the funds. Rampant corruption and the election and census frauds combined to undermine confidence in parliamentary democracy.

At the same time the army became more politicized. Even before independence there had been a debate on whether army recruitment and promotion should be based on regional considerations or on educational qualifications and merit. The North had won that debate; the NPC succeeded in getting a quota system adopted. The Northern Region's quota was 50 percent, with the Eastern and Western Regions allotted 25 percent each. The issue surfaced again during the 1964 election. Meanwhile, tensions developed within the army, in particular between the top officers, who had been promoted rapidly in the process of indigenization, and the group below them—the captains and majors of 1965 who realized they would not have the same opportunities.

Exogenous Economic Changes

Two important changes during 1960–66 were deterioration in the terms of trade and the rise of the oil sector. World prices of Nigeria's traditional agricultural exports had started to fall after the end of the Korean war commodity boom. The slide continued in the 1960s, and by 1966 the barter terms of trade had fallen by about one-quarter compared with 1960 (Aluko 1971, pp. 435–36). Agricultural exports continued to grow in the early 1960s, but they stagnated thereafter; the effect on the balance of payments of the decline in the terms of trade was, from about 1962, no longer offset by volume growth.

The rise of the oil sector can be treated as an exogenous change, since in this period the role of the Nigerian government was limited to granting concessions to foreign oil companies. Production in 1960, still only 17,000 barrels per day, quickly rose to 415,000 in 1966. The contribution of the sector to total government revenue (mainly in royalties and rentals) rose to 17 percent in 1967, and its foreign exchange contribution then amounted to about one-fifth of the value of total exports (Pearson 1970, tables 2, 5, and 7).

Macroeconomic Developments

According to the national accounts data (table 2.1), investment in Nigeria rose extremely rapidly until 1967. Gross fixed capital formation grew at 10 percent a year in real terms from 1960/61 to 1966/67, rising from 10 to 15 percent of GDP. (Table 2.2 gives the change in composition of gross fixed capital formation for this period.) Although public investment expanded, the investment boom was dominated by private, largely foreign investment. The government attempted to attract foreign investors with generous incentives that included import duty relief, accelerated depreciation allowances, and easy remission of profits. Some of the trading firms active in Nigeria in the colonial period now switched to manufacturing. The United Africa Company, for example, became involved in textiles, brewing, plywood, and vehicle assembly. The policy was successful—(nonoil) private investment rose from N£24.9 million in 1960 to N£49.2 million four years later. Private investment then started to decline, however, reflecting concern about Nigeria's political stability and about the continued efficiency of public institutions. The trade balance improved enormously—from –N£44.3 million in 1960 to N£30.1 million in 1966—an improvement caused entirely by oil exports, which, at the end of the period, accounted for a third of the total. However, the improved trade balance was more than offset by a N£140 million increase in the deficit on the services balance, reflecting external borrowing and repatriation of profits. The adjustment mechanism (until 1964) was to draw down the reserves accumulated in the 1950s. Net external reserves declined from N£174.3 million in 1961 to N£81.2 million in 1964.

Government expenditure rose enormously without a commensurate rise in revenue. Between 1960 and 1966 recurrent revenue of the federal and regional governments combined rose by only 35 percent in current prices, whereas recurrent expenditure rose by 65 percent. Because of the high level of foreign reserves, there was initially little pressure to impose fiscal discipline. However, in 1964 a tight money policy was adopted

Table 2.1 National Accounts, 1960/61 and 1966/67

	1960/61		1966/67	
Item	Millions of Nigerian pounds[a]	Percentage of total	Millions of Nigerian pounds[a]	Percentage of total
Private consumption	1,200.9	89.8	1,340.9	77.3
Public consumption	79.5	5.9	114.9	6.6
Private GFCF	77.7	5.8	174.6	10.1
Public GFCF	70.6	5.3	87.4	5.0
Exports including NFS	151.4	11.3	303.4	17.5
Imports including NFS	−243.1	18.2	−285.7	16.5
GDP at market prices	1,337.0	100.0	1,735.5	100.0

Note: GFCF, gross fixed capital formation; NFS, nonfactor services.
a. 1962/63 prices.
Source: World Bank 1974, p. 211.

when it was becoming clear that the balance of payments position was unsustainable. Money supply growth dropped from 16 percent in 1964 to 8 percent in 1966. This was the only time in Nigerian history that a ceiling was placed on Central Bank credit expansion to the government (which in 1964 increased by more than 300 percent).

The economy grew rapidly from 1960 to 1966, at about 5 percent a year (table 2.3). Oil, public utilities, manufacturing, health, and education grew the most compared with other sectors, whereas agriculture was beginning to grind to a halt. The First National Development Plan (1962 to 1968) was an attempt at comprehensive, integrated planning, unlike the colonial plans (the Ten Year Plan of 1946 and the 1955–60 plan), which both amounted to shopping lists of government departments. The development plan aimed at an aggregate growth rate of 4 percent a year, an increase in the rate of investment from 11 to 15 percent of GDP, and an increase in the "directly productive component" of

Table 2.2 Composition of Gross Fixed Capital Formation, 1960/61 and 1966/67
(percent)

Item	1960/61	1966/67
Land and agricultural development	8.4	15.1
Buildings	35.5	23.8
Civil engineering works	21.5	21.9
Plant, machinery, and equipment	25.8	31.1
Vehicles	8.8	8.1
Total[a]	100.0	100.0

a. Excludes payments to foreign oil contractors.
Source: World Bank 1974, p. 210.

Table 2.3 Gross Domestic Product, 1960/61 and 1966/67

| Sector | Millions of Nigerian pounds, 1962/63 prices | | Increase (percent) |
	1960/61	1966/67	
Agriculture, forestry, fishing	799.9	869.5	9
Oil	5.5	102.4	1,769
Other mining	10.3	13.4	30
Manufacturing	57.0	113.4	99
Public utilities	4.2	10.1	140
Construction	55.4	81.3	47
Trade	154.7	200.9	30
Transport and communications	53.9	64.7	20
General government	39.9	51.1	28
Education	32.1	55.1	72
Health	6.3	12.5	98
Other services	25.3	41.4	64
Total GDP (factor cost)	1,244.5	1,615.8	30

Source: World Bank 1974, p. 208.

government investment. The plan allocated almost 70 percent of the budget to the economic sectors (table 2.4), which in 1955–60 had received only 50 percent. Investments in infrastructure continued to dominate this subtotal. Less conventional was the substantial allocation (more than 10 percent) for education. It was assumed that half of public investment would be financed by foreign aid. This turned out to be wildly optimistic—only a third of that amount was received during the first four years of the plan, before the civil war made nonsense of the whole exercise.

The constitutional arrangements meant that the plan was little more than a collection of regional plans, with little attempt to check their consistency. Politicians used the planning exercise as a basis for making promises. The regions acted as rivals, each government facing pressure for industries to be sited within its territory. A striking example of this was the decision in 1964 to split the proposed iron and steel industry into two parts, one to be sited in the North, the other in the East. The industry would have been split into three parts if the political position of the Western Region had not been weak at the time. The plan contained several big projects other than the iron and steel complex, including the Niger Dam, which alone accounted for more than 10 percent of the planned public investment. Some of these large investments were appraised carefully, but other projects were not even identified. Since the headings used in the plan did not correspond to administrative categories, it was unclear how the amounts allocated were supposed to be spent.

Table 2.4 The 1962–68 Development Plan: Composition of Planned Public Investment

Item	Percentage of total
Economic sectors	67.8
Primary production	13.6
Trade and industry	13.4
Electricity	15.1
Transport	21.3
Communications	4.4
Social sectors	24.4
Water supply	3.6
Education	10.3
Health	2.5
Other	8.0
Administration	7.8
Total (₦677 million)	100.0

Source: Nigeria 1962.

Agriculture

The government's role in agriculture was modest. Although the 1962–68 development plan claimed top priority for the agricultural sector, during the plan's first five years only 7 percent of total government spending (capital and recurrent) went to agriculture (Wells 1970, pp. 251–52). In the South investment went largely to settlement schemes and government plantations—both costly failures—and in the North to irrigation projects, which might have been successful but on which only ₦1.4 million was spent. The North undertook a major extension effort, but this does not seem to have much affected farming practices.

The use of improved seeds and fertilizers remained at very low levels, and yields of the major crops remained constant or even declined (Wells 1970; Oluwasanmi 1971; World Bank 1974, p. 239). Agricultural growth was based not on changes in production methods but on expansion of the area under cultivation. This involved substitution of farm work for leisure and became less attractive as producer prices declined and rising wages made rural-to-urban migration an attractive alternative (Helleiner 1966; Aboyade 1971).

The government viewed the sector largely as a source of foreign exchange and government revenue. Its main intervention continued to be the use of marketing boards as instruments for taxation. The marketing boards did not control rubber and food crops, but they were the monopsonies for cocoa, cotton, groundnuts, and palm produce. The boards set prices far below the level of the free on board (f.o.b.) price minus transport and operating costs of the boards; the resulting surpluses were channeled to the government. This implicit export tax reduced producer prices by 20 to 30 percent (Nelson and others 1972, pp. 332–34; Helleiner 1966). Given the urban bias in government expenditure, the policy of keeping producer prices low to generate government revenue can be seen as a huge transfer from rural to urban groups. In addition to the distributional effect, the tax caused allocative losses, both among sectors and within the agricultural sector: farmers had an incentive to switch to crops not controlled by marketing boards. Although the export tax already existed before 1960, things got worse during 1960–67: world prices of the main export crops, other than rubber, fell by only 3 percent but producer prices fell by 18 percent.[2]

Industry

The 1960–67 period was one of rapid industrial growth (more than 10 percent a year). This expansion took place from a low base: manufacturing accounted for less than 5 percent of GDP in 1960. Industrial activity in the beginning of the 1960s consisted largely of the processing of agricultural products for export. The emphasis in this period shifted toward import substitution, especially consumer goods and simple intermediate goods like cement.

The expansion was financed largely by foreign direct investment. At independence, Nigeria represented a large and rapidly growing market. As a result, the merchant firms that had traditionally dominated the importing of manufactured goods into Nigeria found their position threatened by new competitors. They reacted by setting up local production and lobbied successfully for protective tariffs.[3]

Domestic value added in the new industries was low: their products had a high import content and profits could be freely repatriated. Firms with a prior interest in the market accounted for the major part of Nigeria's import-substituting industrialization (Kilby 1969, pp. 75–79; Dina 1971, p. 393). Public investment decisions (usually taken by state governments) were not guided by economic criteria; such decisions involved pork-barrel politics and almost invariably led to loss-making operations.

The government's role as investor was modest: in 1967 the share of the federal and regional governments in paid-up capital in the manufacturing sector was 18 percent (World Bank 1974, p. 244). The government intervened in the sector largely by according incentives to private, predominantly foreign investors: accelerated depreciation, import duty relief, and tariffs. It appears, however, that many of the investment projects that benefited from these concessions would have been undertaken anyway; the main effect of the incentives was to create rents. These rents increased as tariffs were raised, not for protective reasons but for revenue and balance of payments reasons. At the end of the period, part of these rents was transferred to the government budget, when excise taxes were introduced to offset the tariff increases.

Trade Policies

The main instrument of trade policy in this period was the tariff; Nigeria made remarkably little use of quantitative restrictions. The system of quantitative restrictions used in the 1950s (which discriminated between sterling-area imports and other imports) had disappeared by the 1960s; in 1963 the government declared that physical controls would be used only as a last resort. Except for restrictions aimed at South Africa in 1961, the licensing policy was liberal (Fajana 1977, pp. 509–11). Nominal tariff rates in 1960 averaged about 25 percent. Domestic suppliers lobbied successfully for tariff increases (especially for consumer goods), but to an important extent the protection offered by tariffs can be seen as an unintended side effect of tariffs that were set to restrain import growth and to generate public revenue. Import duties, then, accounted for some 60 percent of federal recurrent revenue.

The balance of payments position deteriorated sharply in 1964, with the current account deficit rising to N£92.3 million from N£55.5 million in 1963 (World Bank 1974, p. 219, table 18).[4] Tariffs were raised in response, reaching an average of about 50 percent in the mid-1960s (Kilby 1969, pp. 25–29). Import duties rose from ₦61.3 million in 1953 to ₦84.8 million two years later (World Bank 1974, p. 226). Import rationing was introduced only at the end of the period considered (Onitiri 1971, p. 246).

Wage Employment

At the time of independence only about half a million people were employed in the formal sector. Wage employment expanded thereafter at less than 2 percent a year, from 520,000 in 1960 to 585,000 in 1967 (including agriculture). Wages rose by almost 50 percent in that period, or by about 20 percent in real terms. Both developments bypassed agriculture: wage and employment growth was concentrated in the urban sectors.

As in many other African countries, wages were set at high, non-market-clearing levels. The government acted as wage leader in this period; the private sector followed the real wage increases awarded in the public sector. A general strike by 750,000 workers in 1964 began as a dispute about wages but developed into an antigovernment demonstration that included the unemployed, domestic servants, and nonunion members. It reflected what Isichei (1983, p. 470) has called "disappointment with the fruits of freedom"—a beginning awareness that politics favored a small group of rich Nigerians and that "labour unity had to be achieved before the bulk of national wealth was spent in conspicuous consumption, transferred to overseas bank accounts, or dissipated on wasteful and ill-conceived governmental projects" (Cohen 1974, p. 90, quoted by Isichei 1983, p. 470). Thus the general strike, ostensibly a conflict about wage levels, can be seen as a symptom of discontent that reflected general disillusionment with parliamentary democracy.

Social Services

The government's role in the provision of social services, other than education, was extremely modest. For example, the allocation for health in the 1962–68 plan amounted to only ₦17 million, and only about half of that was actually spent (Ahimie 1971, p. 700). About ₦70 million (10 percent of the total budget) was allocated to education. Primary school enrollment stabilized in the South, where retrenchment followed the large enrollment increases of the late 1950s. In the North, however, enrollment increased rapidly, from 250,000 in 1959 to 410,000 in 1963. This still left enrollment exceedingly low (less than 10 percent of the relevant age group) in the North, where Western-style primary schools continued to be resisted as a threat to traditional Islamic education. Higher education expanded in the country as a whole (four new universities were established), and secondary school enrollment (including vocational and technical training) rose from 115,000 in 1959 to 250,000 in 1963.

Conclusion

Five developments during 1960–66 set the stage for what was to follow. First, macroeconomic discipline suffered from the favorable initial conditions (the huge foreign exchange reserves) and from the oil bonanza. Second, apart from the implicit taxation of export crops and the government's role in raising wages, expanding employment, and granting tariff protection to industrial firms, there was little microeconomic intervention. Third, agriculture was—apart from some ill-conceived projects—neglected, whereas industrial investment, especially by foreign firms, was actively encouraged. Fourth, regional tensions—which were already strong at the end of the colonial period and which had made it difficult to find a constitutional arrangement for independent Nigeria—grew. This occurred because the regions had unequal access to positions in the federal state and because the old political equilibrium was upset by disagreements within the Western Region and the intervention of the federal government there. Fifth, the political process became discredited, having failed in the face of important issues such as the census controversy and the corruption associated with the political parties.

3 Civil War and Reconstruction: 1966–73

By late 1965 Nigeria's political system was in disarray. The government's legitimacy had been undermined by its inept handling of the general strike of 1964. It had used the army and police to suppress a demand with which they were not entirely unsympathetic, and their support was now in question.

Ethnic and regional conflicts had been growing and were brought to a head by two factors. One was the action of the national government, dominated by the North, in taking advantage of disputes among the Yoruba in the Western Region to rig the elections there. This interference by one region in the affairs of another threatened the political stability of the federation.

The other factor was economic and concerned the allocation of revenue among the regions. This had long been a source of contention, but the discovery of oil in the East and in the delta areas of what became the Midwestern state raised the stakes, and caused shifts in the different regions' preferred method of allocation.

Against this background, military intervention came as no surprise. The first coup, on January 15, 1966, was organized by junior officers who saw themselves as rescuing the country from the corruption of the political elite. In his maiden broadcast, Major Nzeogwu, the coup leader, said:

> Our enemies are the political profiteers, the swindlers, the men in high places who seek bribes and demand 10 percent; who seek to keep the country divided so that they can remain in office; the tribalists, the nepotists, who make the country look big for nothing before international circles; who have corrupted our society and put the Nigerian political calendar back by their words and deeds.

This radicalism was never put into practice, however, because the coup leaders did not actually take power but contented themselves with assassinating the "arch-enemies" of the people. In the ensuing chaos the remaining political leaders handed power to a senior officer, General Ironsi, who ostensibly knew nothing of the plot and certainly did not share the radical and populist beliefs of the plotters.

To many Nigerians this was an Ibo-sponsored coup intended to install an Ibo-dominated national government. In May General Ironsi decreed the abolition of the regions and the promulgation of a unitary state, coupled with unification of the country's civil services. This was widely felt to favor the Ibos and confirmed growing suspicions of ethnic preference. In retaliation, many Ibos were killed in the North; in July Ironsi and the governor of the Western Region were assassinated.

The July coup-makers were largely rank-and-file Northern soldiers who demanded either a repeal of the unification decree or Northern secession. The Yoruba chief of staff, Brigadier Ogundipe, was unable to restore order; he resigned his command and left Nigeria. Control passed to Lt.-Col. Gowon, who assumed power on August 1 and quickly restored the federal system. For the Ibo elite the July coup was a decisive setback; many now advocated secession of the East, and Lt.-Col. Ojukwu refused to recognize Gowon's authority. After more massacres in the North in September and October, thousands of Ibo refugees fled to their hometowns, and the demands for secession grew.

The military leadership held talks in early 1967 at Aburi, in Ghana, to patch up some kind of settlement of the crisis. Gowon was flexible and prepared to settle for a loose confederation. But the talks failed, secession became inevitable, and Ibo officers abandoned their units and returned to the East.

Gowon now shifted his position, attempting to achieve greater unity by more diversity. In May 1967 the government replaced the four regions with 12 states. One aim of this change was to gain the support of minority peoples in the northern and southeastern parts of Nigeria who wanted to be free from the domination of large ethnic groups. (Only about half of the population belonged to the Hausa-Fulani, Ibo, and Yoruba groups, despite their political dominance.) The other aim was to dilute the regional power that had bedeviled the country's politics since independence, and in particular to undermine support for the imminent secession.

Days later the Eastern Region seceded as Biafra, but there was little military activity until July. The motive for secession was control of the oil reserves, but the onshore oil and oil facilities were not in areas indigenous to the Ibo people. Biafra lost control of its ports and oil facilities early in the war. Foreign corporations stopped paying revenues into Biafra's accounts and paid them instead into the federal government's accounts, leaving Biafra desperately short of revenue. Lack of funds, combined with the blockade the federal government mounted, prevented Biafra from obtaining the munitions and eventually the food that were vital to its survival. On January 12, 1970, Biafra surrendered, and the civil war was over.

One consequence of the federal government's early resumption of control of the oil facilities was that oil production, although severely curtailed in 1967 and 1968, was restored in 1969. It reached nearly 200 million barrels that year, compared with 150 million in 1966. In 1970 production doubled to nearly 400 million barrels, and by 1973 it had reached 750 million, a plateau at which it remained for the rest of the decade.

A direct consequence of the war was the massive expansion of the military from an army of 10,000 in 1966 to 250,000 in 1970. No substantial demobilization was undertaken until the late 1970s, despite the high priority Gowan gave to rationalizing the armed forces. It has been argued with some justice that Nigeria could not afford the threat to peace and stability that would be posed by a large number of discharged soldiers without jobs, whereas with growing oil revenue, the country could afford to maintain them in uniform.

Another consequence of the war was a switch from the relatively liberal exchange and trading regimes of the 1950s and early 1960s to a much more interventionist state. The federal government's need for foreign exchange with which to prosecute the war induced it to adopt import controls and direct allocation of foreign exchange. These measures fostered considerable growth in domestic industrial activity during the war. They also created a lobby that would fight to retain import restrictions when the government set out to relax them after the war (and when oil revenues had made foreign exchange plentiful).

In 1970 Nigeria faced two principal tasks: postwar reconstruction and the design of a program to return to civilian rule. In October 1970 Gowon announced a nine-point program on which the Supreme Military Council would need to be satisfied before it would hand over control. These points included reorganization of the military, implementation of the National Development Plan, repair of war damage, eradication of corruption, a national population census, and a variety of constitutional, political, and administrative reforms. The original goal of the military had been to return the country to civilian rule by 1969, but the war made this impossible. Gowon's new target was 1976.

When the states were created in 1967, regional allocations of revenue were simply subdivided among them. The criteria for subdivision were arbitrary and aroused considerable resentment, particularly among the most populous states in the Northern Region. At their inception, Gowon had promised a more equitable formula, but it was not until 1970 that the federal military government moved to alter the system of revenue allocation. The new system was embodied in Decree No. 13 of 1970, retroactive to April 1969. The alterations involved an increase in the revenue accruing to the distributable pool account, from which allocations to the states were made, and a partial equalization of the basis on which the account was shared. One-half of the account was to be equally divided among the states and the other half apportioned according to relative population. The population figures used by the authorities and the revenue shares of the states are presented in table 3.1. Following the changes, around three-quarters of states' revenue came from the account.

In the early 1970s Nigeria entered a period of political calm, and the economy boomed. The massive program of reconstruction embodied in the 1971–74 development plan was made feasible by the growing oil revenues, even prior to the oil price increase in 1973. The people, impressively led by Gowon, showed a remarkable capacity for reconciliation with little vindictiveness or bitterness.

In 1973 the government announced it would carry out a census. Despite its determination not to repeat the debacle of 1962–63, that is precisely what happened. The national population was recorded to have risen by an implausible 44 percent over the inflated figures of a decade earlier; two states apparently nearly doubled their populations. Claims of fraud and ethnic domination were again heard. This was a bitter disappointment to Gowon and probably central to his decision the following year to suspend the timetable for restoring civilian rule and renege on the target year of 1976.

Table 3.1 Allocation of Federally Collected Revenue and Population Distribution since 1967, by State

(percent)

State	May 1967–April 1969	After April 1969	Share of population
Benue-Plateau	7.0	7.8	7.2
Kwasa	7.0	6.3	4.3
Kano	7.0	9.3	10.4
North-Central	7.0	7.8	7.3
North-Eastern	7.0	11.3	14.0
North-Western	7.0	9.3	10.3
East-Central	17.5	10.6	11.2
South-Eastern	7.5	7.4	8.2
Rivers	5.0	5.6	2.8
Western	18.0	12.7	17.0
Lagos	2.0	5.5	2.6
Midwestern	8.0	6.4	4.5

Source: Oyovbaise 1978, p. 229.

The Role of Civilians in the Military Government

All political offices were abolished after the coup of January 1966, and the civil service was made directly accountable to the military. However, it was recognized that some mechanism was needed to mediate between the military leadership and the civilian population. Several institutions were accordingly set up and staffed preponderantly with civilians, many of whom had previously been active politicians. These institutions included informal advisory bodies such as the Ad Hoc Constitutional Conference, which met in September 1966, and the Leaders of Thought within each region, who met frequently until August 1967. Opinions differ on whether any of these organizations had much influence on policy. In one view, they had little: it was the military leaders and their civil service advisers who made the decisions that culminated in civil war (Luckham 1971). Nevertheless, they did constitute forums that allowed politicians to meet and to address the public under the auspices of a military regime. Awolowo, for instance, used the Leaders of Thought in the West as a platform for a number of important political statements, including the announcement that if the federal government, by "acts of commission or omission," induced the secession of the East, then the West would follow suit (Kirk-Greene 1971).

The reliance of the military authorities on civilian political institutions is well illustrated by the handling of the Agbekoya riots in the Western Region, which had a long history of peasant unrest. Large-scale riots broke out in 1968, and farmers refused to pay increased taxes; tax collection virtually ceased in some areas. Attempts to resume collection in 1969 induced further riots, and collection was not fully restored until well into the 1970s. The military government chose not to crush the revolt by force, and it lacked the will and the institutions to negotiate a solution. As a result, these negotiations fell to the civilian leadership, notably Awolowo.

In June 1967, following the division of the four regions into 12 states and the secession of the Eastern Region, the co-option of politicians into the administration was formalized when the system of commissioners was instituted. The commissioners were civilians, appointed to take charge of ministries and departments and given seats in the executive council or cabinet.

There are always tensions between ministers and civil servants, but relations between the commissioners and their administration were complicated by the pressure of the military leadership and by the lack of electoral legitimacy of the commissioners. In this three-cornered relationship, the civil service appears to have been a substantial beneficiary. This was certainly the view of the politicians interviewed by Bienen and Fitton (1978):

Some suggested that the civil service had struck a bargain with the military. The military would get what it wanted on interest group demands, e.g. barracks, salary and hardware. The civil service would determine substantive policy in areas outside of narrow military interest group concerns.

It was certainly true that the civil service became much more politically visible after 1967. Senior civil servants regularly made speeches on specific questions of public policy and also on the general nature of the regime. For example, in 1973 the permanent secretary at the Ministry of Education delivered the presidential address to the Nigerian Economic Society (reported in Bienen and Fitton 1978). He discussed several sensitive issues, such as the creation of more states, the allocation of revenue, and the nature of the pressure groups determining policy after January 1966. He distinguished five categories: public officers (civil servants), political appointees (civil commissioners), members of the armed forces, the private establishment (church leaders, trade unionists, and employers), and personal friends and confidants. He concluded that the basis of civilian participation in the military administration was obscure, even to civil commissioners, and he noted that "commissioners and senior civil servants are fellow advisers to the powers-that-be who sometimes receive their advice from outside the two groups, to their mutual frustration and suspicion." He also remarked that "the political reality in Africa today is that the elective basis of government will not, ipso facto, remove the ultimate sanction in the hands of the military."

It was also true that some civil servants became linked with military officers in factional alliances. When Gowon fell from power, it was inevitable that several high-level civil servants would not be acceptable to the incoming Mohammed regime. But the general perception of the civil service as a political actor associated with a corrupt regime meant that removal from office was not restricted to these higher echelons but was widespread through lower ranks as well.

The Economy

Nigerian data are generally poor, and they are particularly so for 1966–73 because of the impact of the war on data collection. Many series do not include the three states that made up the Eastern Region for the years 1967/68 to 1969/70, and there is no accurate way of estimating the national trend during these years.

The composition of GDP during the period presents a picture of considerable stability, with the exception of three sectors (table 3.2). First, the mining sector, consisting almost entirely of oil, grew dramatically, from 7 percent of GDP in 1966/67 to 17 percent in 1972/73. This was before the oil price rise and reflected mainly growth in the sector's physical output. Second, agriculture declined steadily as a share of GDP. However, these are among the least reliable of Nigerian statistics, and it is not clear whether the sector was in absolute decline. This issue is considered further below. Third, general government expenditure more than doubled as a percentage of GDP over the war years. This category accounted for more than one-half of all public expenditure in 1970, reflecting the growth of military spending.

Fiscal and Monetary Policy

The years 1966–73 were characterized by balance of payments crises and threatening inflationary pressure. Import duties accounted for well over half of government revenue; measures to restrict the flow of imports to meet the balance of payments problem induced a decline in revenue at a time of rapidly expanding recurrent expenditure. The federal budget swung into a relatively large deficit in 1966 that was financed mainly by credit from the banking system. Credit to the private sector was severely curtailed, and the economy appeared to be moving into a recession at the end of the year. The war exacerbated the deficit; by 1970 it had reached a staggering 75 percent of total current revenue. Over the next three years the budget was heavily in surplus. In 1971 this reflected a sharp cutback in recurrent expenditure, due to the end of the war, as well as a marked increase in revenue caused by higher oil taxes and the increase

Table 3.2 Composition of GDP by Sector, Selected Years
(percent)

Sector	1966/67	1970/71	1972/73
Agriculture and related activities	51.9	44.6	37.0
Mining and related activities	6.9	12.0	16.8
Manufacturing and related activities	7.4	7.5	7.6
Electricity and water	0.7	0.6	0.7
Building and construction	5.3	6.3	8.5
Distribution	12.8	12.2	10.7
Transport and communications	4.7	3.3	3.6
General government	3.4	7.4	8.2
Education	3.6	2.7	2.9
Health	0.8	0.9	0.9
Other services	2.7	2.7	3.0
Total	100.0	100.0	100.0

Note: At 1962/63 factor cost.
Source: Olaloku 1979, chapter 1.

in indirect taxes following measures to relax import controls. In 1972 and 1973 expenditure increased rapidly—particularly development expenditure, which trebled—but the increase of oil revenue was sufficient to maintain the budget in surplus.

In contrast to the strengthening of the federal fiscal position, the states continued to run deficits through these years, with revenue (including statutory allocations from the federal government, which accounted for around 70 percent of the total) barely sufficient to cover expenditure. The consolidated budget for the public sector as a whole, therefore, remained fairly heavily in deficit throughout the period.

The reliance on deficit financing, particularly during the war years, placed a heavy burden on the monetary authorities. The Central Bank was equipped with wide powers of monetary control, particularly after amendment of the Central Bank Act in 1968. Despite this, it relied solely on credit guidelines and entirely neglected other monetary techniques. It could not, of course, have used open market operations in the absence of appropriate institutions; but neither the treasury bill rediscount rate (after May 1968) nor the liquidity ratio of the commercial banks was changed. The credit guidelines themselves were detailed and designed to favor investment in productive facilities over consumption. But the main impact was to squeeze the private sector to free credit for the government. The percentage change in credit to the private sector in 1966, 1967, and 1968 was 14 percent, 8 percent, and 0 percent, respectively, compared with 61 percent, 81 percent, and 85 percent to the public sector in those same years. The increase in internal public debt was mainly in the form of treasury bills.

The excess liquidity of the commercial banks at the end of the war, coupled with the sharp improvement in federal government finances in 1971, meant that credit expansion could be geared almost entirely to rehabilitation and to the private sector activities that had been hampered during the war. Over the two years following the war, credit to the private sector expanded at nearly 30 percent a year, whereas total credit grew at only 5 percent a year. This expansion far exceeded the guidelines, which were rendered ineffective by the extent of the excess liquidity of the banking system.

The effect on prices was more ambiguous than the extent of credit expansion would suggest. Although the money supply grew at 15 percent annually during the war years and stabilized in 1971, food prices (which dominate the overall price index) actually fell during the war as the food-deficit Eastern parts of the country withdrew from the national economy. However, prices rose sharply during 1969–72 (10 to 16 percent a year), as demand rose following reintegration. Nonfood prices were somewhat stabilized after 1970 by the progressive liberalization of imports and the consequent competitive pressure on domestically produced goods.

Agriculture

As noted earlier, the statistics for agriculture are poor. One index of major food crop production shows a fall of 20 percent between 1964/65 and the last full year of the war, 1968/69. A recovery in 1969/71 to around 90 percent of the 1964/65 level was reversed in the drought year 1972/73 to around 70 percent. This is broadly consistent with the rapid rise in food imports and food prices during the period, although the timing is different. The real increase in these two series occurred during 1968/71, with much slower increases in the following two years. Also, there is no upward trend in food as a proportion of total imports. Finally, the main imported food items were wheat, sugar, fish, milk, and rice, which are not traditional Nigerian staple products. Hence the food deficit appears to reflect an inability to diversify to meet urban tastes rather than a failure to match demand for these staples.

As for agricultural exports, a rapid decline coincided with the rapid growth of oil exports after 1969. Comparing the years immediately before the war with those immediately after it, the export volume of timber and groundnuts each fell to around a third of its previous level, palm kernels halved, and palm oil disappeared; of the major crops, only cocoa beans remained stable.

The national accounts provide data on agricultural exports and total exports as a percentage of GDP, as well as an index of world commodity prices, weighted with Nigerian export quantities (table 3.3). That agriculture's share of export value declined from 62.3 to 13.7 percent over the period is partly a consequence of the rapid growth of nonagricultural exports relative to GDP after 1970, reflecting oil revenues. More important, the decline in the share of export value reflects a dramatic decrease in the volume of agricultural exports. If anything, the decline is understated since the GDP series probably underestimates the growth of national income of the former Eastern Region. Therefore, the fall was

Table 3.3 Exports, 1966–73

Year	Agricultural exports (percentage of GDP)	Total exports (percentage of GDP)	Export price index (1960 = 100)
1966	10.5	16.8	89.3
1967	11.0	17.6	91.6
1968	11.2	15.9	94.1
1969	9.2	17.7	108.0
1970	6.3	16.6	104.7
1971	4.2	19.3	96.9
1972	2.8	19.8	91.8
1973	3.5	25.6	190.6

Source: National accounts.

probably more continuous than appears in the table, with the acceleration after 1969 being less dramatic. Nor can the drop in value be fairly laid at the door of declining world commodity prices. The 1966 and 1972 values of Nigeria's export price index are much the same, and the 1973 figure is dramatically higher, reflecting the oil price increase of the Organization of Petroleum Exporting Countries (OPEC) late in the year. Thus the culprit was the decline in volume already noted.

This decline was largely a result of the heavy taxation of export crops, originally in the form of marketing board surpluses and later through overt export duties and sales taxes. By 1970/71 the boards were operating at a loss even though producer prices were only about one-half of realized export prices for groundnuts, palm kernels, and palm oil and two-thirds for cocoa. In 1973 the military government undertook a reform of the marketing board regime, transferring to itself the power to fix producer prices and lowering and eventually abolishing the taxes. Partly in consequence, producer prices doubled in 1973/74.

Apart from the long-run effect of pricing policies, there are two other possible explanations for the decline in agricultural exports during this period. One is that some productive capacity may have been lost because of neglect during the war. The other is that more production was being diverted to home markets, partly following the expansion of purchasing power and partly as a consequence of an overvalued exchange rate.

Balance of Payments

In 1966 Nigeria's balance of trade moved into surplus, reflecting the growing importance of oil, which had become Nigeria's most important foreign exchange earner, accounting for nearly one-third of the total value of exports. The trade surplus also reflected the wide range of fiscal and monetary measures instituted in 1964 and 1965 to curb the growth of imports. The balance of trade remained in surplus during the civil war, largely because of stringent import controls and, afterward, because the growth of oil exports more than matched that of imports following the relaxation of controls.

The current account remained in deficit until 1973. This posed little problem for the authorities, however, since the surplus on capital account was sufficient to maintain the basic balance in surplus or a small deficit. This net inflow of capital reflected the potentially large Nigerian market and the policy of import substitution behind protective tariffs.

Conclusion

The period after 1965 opened with Nigerian politics in disarray, corruption rife, and a real prospect of the disintegration of the federation. Following military intervention and a civil war, the period ended with the military firmly in control of a much more centralized federal government, but with the underlying ethnic conflict far from resolved.

Although the human cost of the civil war was undoubtedly great, and the material damage in the war-affected areas was considerable, the strife does not appear to have caused any lasting damage to the economy. A period of rapid economic growth followed the war, and it is hard to imagine that GDP would have been much higher in the mid-1970s if the war had never taken place. Even in 1969/70, GDP was higher in the federal territories than it had been before the war for the whole economy. Real growth in 1970/71 was exaggerated by the inclusion of estimates for the three Eastern states for the first time since 1966/67. However, growth was undoubtedly rapid, and continued so in 1971/72, when investment increased by a third, exports by 20 percent, imports by 22 percent, and consumption by 11 percent. This rate of expansion could not be maintained because it included a large element of catching up, and in 1972/73, growth fell back toward the long-term trend. The speed of the recovery was caused both by the oil expansion and by the resulting rapid expansion of government spending. If there had been no increase in oil output, recovery would probably have been slowed considerably, and the large overhang of liquidity in the economy after the war would have been a powerful destabilizing influence.

4 The First Oil Cycle: 1973–79

Nigeria experienced a large, temporary trade windfall beginning in 1974 and ending in 1981. The estimated (undiscounted) value of the windfall during these years was almost double annual GDP just prior to the boom. In this chapter we estimate the magnitude of the windfall and discuss the aggregate asset choices made for its use. We then examine the powerful general equilibrium effects and the political contest that arose from the windfall. Because the economics of the first oil cycle are about the boom phase, which coincided with the first phase of the second oil cycle, it is convenient to take the analysis through to 1981. By contrast, the political story breaks more naturally at the end of the first oil cycle in 1979, since this coincided with a regime change. Therefore, this chapter takes the economic story two years further than the political story. Discussion of the outcomes of these processes for poverty, equity, and growth is deferred until chapter 6.

Oil earnings were distinctive in two respects in addition to their transience: they accrued as foreign exchange and they accrued to the government. Because the earnings accrued as foreign exchange, the extra income could be spent only on tradable goods unless domestic resources were reallocated to the nontradable sector. This is the phenomenon of Dutch disease (see Corden 1984 for a survey).[1] Further, the accrual of earnings to the government significantly disturbed the status quo of the public sector budgetary decision process. It was suddenly possible to increase the public command over resources and public transfers to favored private agents and to reduce taxation. Between 1972 and 1974 federal government oil revenue rose fivefold to form more than 80 percent of total revenue. Oil revenue continued to grow more modestly until 1978, when a contraction occurred as Nigeria priced itself out of the market. This change in the political equilibrium gave rise to further general equilibrium effects generated by the particular expenditure pattern adopted by the government.

l Asset Choices

>f choices because of the oil
vhether to retain the income
e private sector. Of the part
nption and saving. Finally,
mong assets. To measure
res the specification of a

horough analysis to date
income between public
d investment uses. He
income directly by 23
to accumulate foreign ex-
a reduction in the rate of
of extra nonoil GDP remained
More than the entire amount was al-
vestment, and 31 percent was allocated
on. Private consumption grew only at its
rms, whereas private investment declined rela-
oy nearly 10 percent of nonoil GDP. Thus the public
ed more than the entire oil windfall.

Gelb's results are remarkable, they rest upon assumptions
actual performance that are open to question. To check their
robustness, we set out an alternative that to us seems more reasonable—
for example, making better allowance for the effects of the civil war. The
boom had three components: the increase in oil output in the early 1970s
and the 1973/74 and 1979/80 price shocks. Rather than disentangling
the effects of these shocks, we take them together. We take 1970 as our
base year, defining 1971–81 as the boom period. In the counterfactual
scenario we assume OPEC away; the pre-1970 oil output growth would
have continued, but relative prices would have remained unchanged.
We assume that GDP (both oil and nonoil) would have grown at its prewar rate of 6 percent a year, that consumption (public and private) would
have been the same proportion of GDP as its prewar average (85 percent), and that the resource deficit (the excess of imports over exports)
would have remained constant as a percentage of GDP. Given these assumptions, investment follows from the GDP identity.

We show the actual GDP and its components in table 4.1 and the difference between the actual outcome and the counterfactual case in table
4.2. The first three columns of table 4.2 show the differences for oil GDP,
nonoil GDP, and total GDP. Oil GDP is considerably higher than in the
counterfactual case, so output responded to the price increase in spite of

Table 4.1 Actual GDP and Its Components, 1970–81
(billions of naira, 1970 prices)

Year	GDP Factor cost	GDP Market price	Consumption Private	Consumption Public	Invest- ment	Exports	Resource inflow
1970	15.9	16.3	12.4	1.3	2.6	1.9	1.9
1971	17.4	17.9	12.8	1.4	3.5	2.7	2.5
1972	18.0	18.2	12.4	1.5	3.6	2.9	2.2
1973	19.5	20.0	13.2	1.9	4.3	3.3	2.7
1974	22.7	23.1	16.6	2.3	4.4	3.2	3.4
1975	22.9	23.3	16.4	3.2	6.6	2.6	5.5
1976	25.3	25.7	18.0	3.1	8.9	2.9	7.3
1977	26.8	27.2	18.9	3.8	9.9	3.3	8.7
1978	25.7	26.1	20.8	3.2	7.3	2.8	8.0
1979	26.8	27.3	21.6	3.2	6.1	3.2	6.8
1980	27.1	27.5	21.1	3.6	7.0	3.1	7.4
1981	27.3	27.7	21.8	4.2	7.6	2.0	8.0

Source: Bevan, Collier, and Gunning 1992, p. 9.

the OPEC-imposed restraint on oil production. Nonoil GDP is initially higher than in the counterfactual case (1974–77), but by 1981 it is lower. Even total GDP is more than 10 percent lower. This is a remarkable result: in spite of the massive investment program financed by the windfall, output was considerably lower than it could plausibly have been in the absence of the shocks.

The next three columns in table 4.2 describe gross domestic expenditure and its consumption and investment components. During the period of the military government there was a large increase in investment, a trend that was abruptly reversed by the civilian government. In the early phase of the boom the government's savings effort was so substantial that, in addition to domestic investment, foreign assets were also accumulated. As a result, consumption was lower than in the counterfactual case.

The final column shows the increase in the resource inflow (that is, the increase in the excess of imports over exports measured at constant prices). The resource inflow changed for two reasons: changes in the terms of trade and changes in borrowing. In the first four years of the boom most of the extra oil income was used to acquire foreign assets, so that the extra resource inflow was unimportant. However, by the late 1970s the extra inflow was augmenting expenditure by around 15 percent.

It is useful to have a summary measure that describes responses over the whole period of the boom. This is particularly important since sev-

Table 4.2 *Differences between Actual Effects of the Oil Shock and Those Expected under the Counterfactual Case, 1970–81* (millions of naira, 1970 prices)

Year	Gross domestic product			Gross domestic expenditure			Increase in resource inflow		
	Oil	Nonoil	Total	Consumption	Investment	Total	Due to windfall	Due to extra capital inflow	Total
1970	0	0	0	0	0	0	0	0	0
1971	553	48	602	-430	828	397	-204	-70	-134
1972	863	-987	-124	-1,666	825	-841	-717	-153	-564
1973	535	-35	500	-1,455	1,352	-103	-603	434	-1,037
1974	1,002	1,483	2,485	1,376	1,286	2,662	177	4,602	-4,426
1975	238	1,169	1,407	972	3,317	4,290	2,882	3,257	-375
1976	649	1,828	2,478	1,415	5,362	6,777	4,299	4,408	-108
1977	592	1,997	2,589	1,799	6,202	8,002	5,413	5,310	103
1978	195	-147	49	1,868	3,352	5,220	5,171	3,465	1,706
1979	433	-806	-373	1,317	1,894	3,211	3,584	4,825	-1,242
1980	38	-1,801	-1,763	-125	2,595	2,470	4,233	5,794	-1,560
1981	-976	-2,887	-3,344	-328	2,953	2,625	5,969	4,443	1,526
Total[a]	3,068	881	4,131	1,671	16,000	17,671	13,540	17,968	-4,428

Note: See text for assumptions about the counterfactual case.

a. Totals reflect value in 1970 using a discount rate of 10 percent.

Source: Bevan, Collier, and Gunning 1992, p. 10.

eral of them, such as GDP and borrowing, change sign. We therefore consider the bottom line of table 4.2, which shows the discounted totals. For
example, although GDP was sometimes higher and sometimes lower, the
net effect on this measure was a small increase of ₦4.1 billion, of which
₦3 billion was caused by the rise in oil output. Nonoil GDP was altered
very little by the boom. Total expenditure, by contrast, rose by almost
₦18 billion, more than total expenditure in 1970 (₦16 billion). Reflecting the bureaucrats' priorities, less than 10 percent of the increase was
consumed and more than 90 percent invested.

The increase in expenditure of ₦18 billion had three unequal components. As we have seen, only ₦1 billion of it was accounted for by extra
nonoil production. Extra oil income (resulting from both price and quantity increases) amounted to ₦21 billion, but ₦4 billion of that was used
to acquire foreign assets rather than augment expenditure. When these
foreign assets are added to the large increase in domestic investment,
we find that the total savings rate from the windfall was an astonishing
97 percent, the asset accumulation being split between ₦16 billion of
domestic investment and ₦4 billion of foreign assets. Why Nigeria had
such a high savings rate out of a windfall that might at least initially
have appeared long-lasting is one of the key political-economy questions this book addresses.

General Equilibrium Effects of the Foreign Exchange Influx

Dutch disease is a story of resource reallocation between sectors. Referring to it as a disease can be misleading, for the reallocation may be
entirely desirable. The oil windfall raises expenditure on both interna-
tionally tradable and nontradable goods but enhances only the supply
of tradables (through imports). This imbalance is equilibrated by an increase in the relative price of nontradables, thereby attracting resources
away from the nonoil tradable sector. In developed oil economies (such
as the United Kingdom), this declining sector is manufacturing. In Nigeria the nonoil tradable sector is primarily export-crop agriculture. In
the 1960s crops such as cocoa, oil palm, and rubber were the principal
source of export revenue. In addition to the export activities, import
substitutes are part of the sector. Potentially this includes both food-
producing agriculture and manufacturing; however, food imports were
so restricted by import quotas that they are best regarded as quasi-
nontradable. (At their peak, food imports met around 8 percent of calorie requirements, but the domestic price of rice and maize, the principal
imported crops, was generally around three times the world price.)

In table 4.3 the national accounts data are reaggregated into tradable
and nontradable categories. The relative prices shown in part A of the
table are sector-specific GDP deflators and thus denote the prices received

by producers for value added, rather than the prices paid by consumers for commodities. Taking 1970–81 as the period during which Dutch disease effects were potentially most pronounced, relative to pure nontradable services such as construction, the prices of tradable goods, export crops, and manufactures fell substantially, as predicted by the theory. Turning to part B, we look for signs of the resource shifts we might expect to be induced by this change in prices. As expected, the production of export crops collapses in the most spectacular fashion. The shift of resources out of cocoa and allied activities is Nigeria's analogue of deindustrialization, though it is far more pronounced. The factor mobility implied by the relative (and absolute) decline in production is evidently considerable.

Manufacturing production, however, increased relative to all other sectors. This appears to be explained not by rising protection but by the nonmarket allocation of resources, a theme that we take up below. If the

Table 4.3 Prices and Quantities by Sector, 1970–83
(index values)

| | Market | | | | | Nonmarket: |
| | Nontraded | | Traded | | | government |
Year	Services	Food	Export crops	Manu- facturing	Consumer imports	services
A. Relative prices[a]						
1970	1.00	0.86	1.19	—	0.95	—
1973	1.00	1.00	1.00	1.00	1.00	1.00
1981	1.00	1.21	0.71	0.76	0.77	0.63
1983	1.00	1.22	—	0.66	0.76	—
B. Relative quantities[b]						
1970	1.00	1.00	1.00	1.00	1.00	1.00
1973	1.00	0.89	0.66	1.00	1.00	1.15
1981	1.00	0.63	0.11	1.83	1.83	1.60
1983	1.00	0.71	—	1.33	1.33	1.83
C. Absolute quantities[c]						
1970	1.00	1.00	1.00	1.00	1.00	1.00
1973	1.33	1.18	0.88	1.27	1.33	1.54
1981	2.15	1.36	0.22	3.20	3.92	3.45
1983	1.87	1.33	—	2.87	2.48	3.43

— Not available.
a. Relative to services in 1973 = 1.00.
b. Relative to services in 1970 = 1.00.
c. 1970 = 1.00.
Source: Collier 1986.

behavior of manufacturing production does not accord with Dutch disease, food production is even more bizarre. The price of food appears to have risen even relative to pure nontraded services, and yet its production declined compared with all other sectors except export crops. Clearly, the resource shift out of food production was not induced by this relative price change; rather, the price change was presumably induced by the production shift. But this raises the question of what caused the production shift, which we discuss below.

The price changes derived from the sector-specific GDP deflators are corroborated by reference to the consumer price index (CPI). Between 1970 and 1981 the price of food doubled relative to other goods. This shows the prices urban consumers faced rather than those producers received, but it is likely that with such a large price change, food producers enjoyed higher relative prices. A common proxy for changes in the relative price of tradable and nontradable goods is the real exchange rate, as measured by comparison of the domestic CPI with the world price of tradable goods expressed in domestic currency. There are many variants of the latter concept. Here we use the U.S. wholesale price index and the dollar-naira exchange rate. Over the period 1970–81 the real exchange rate thus measured appreciated by nearly 120 percent. Although other measures would yield somewhat different numbers, they would all show a large appreciation, indicating a rise in the price of nontradable goods relative to tradables as implied by the GDP deflators.

We now turn to the employment implications of these general equilibrium changes. Unfortunately, no satisfactory data exist on changes in the sectoral composition of the labor force. Therefore, changes in sectoral employment can only be inferred from the production series. Suppose that the quantity changes described in part C of table 4.3 are correct and that real product wages and productivity had stayed constant. Given these assumptions, the demand for labor would have depended on the initial distribution of the labor force over the various activities. Using 1981 as our base year, applying the trends of table 4.3, part C, yields the employment series shown in table 4.4. These figures make no allowance for the greater labor intensity of export agriculture relative to food agriculture. Since the former sector collapsed, the decline in employment demand is therefore understated. However, even without allowing for this, it is evident that the contraction in tradable crop employment could have accounted for the bulk of agricultural labor shedding during 1973–81.

On the basis of the constant productivity assumption underlying table 4.4, labor demand in aggregate would have increased by 2.6 percent a year. By contrast, the labor force is estimated to have grown during the 1970s at 3.1 percent a year, decelerating to 2.7 percent in the 1980s. We therefore conclude that after the onset of the oil boom in 1973, aggregate labor demand would scarcely have kept pace with labor supply had the

Table 4.4 Sectoral Distribution of the Labor Force on a Constant Productivity Assumption, Selected Years

(millions)

	Agriculture						Total
	Food	Export		Manu-	Public	All other	labor
Year	crops	crops	Total	facturing	sector	sectors	force
1970	17,128	1,686	18,814	1,795	0,432	2,823	23,864
1973	19,697	1,484	21,181	2,280	0,665	3,754	27,880
1981	19,526[a]	0,371[a]	19,897[b]	5,744[c]	1,490[d]	6,069[c]	33,200
1983	21,068	0,371	21,439	5,152	1,481	5,279	33,351[e]

Note: For assumptions, see text.

a. From agricultural production and exports data, plus the assumption that cash crops and food crops have the same labor intensity per unit of output.

b. Residual.

c. From World Bank 1985a.

d. From Suebsaeng 1984, p. 1.

e. Olunsanya and Pursell (1981, chapter 7, table 5) predict the labor force in 1983 at 29.9 million (constant fertility model) or 29.8 million (reduced fertility model). Therefore, although our labor force figure is far below the official figure, it roughly agrees with these independent predictions.

real product wage in each sector been constant. This cautions against the thesis that in aggregate the labor market tightened significantly during the oil boom, unless the residual employment in food production is substantially wrong.

As a token exercise in sensitivity analysis, consider the implications if employment in the food sector had increased significantly during 1973–81, instead of stagnating as implied by our series. If the employment series is revised, then either we must postulate a significant decline in labor productivity in the food sector or the production series must be revised upward. If the production series is revised upward, per capita food consumption would have risen or stayed constant in 1973–81, instead of declining as our figures suggest. But if per capita food consumption was maintained despite a substantial increase in its relative price, then there must have been a large rise in per capita real incomes. Such an increase should be visible both in wage series and in real private consumption, neither of which is the case. Therefore, table 4.4 is taken as representing a set of employment changes consistent with other evidence, contingent on corroborative data on sector-specific real consumption wages. We now turn to these implications for wages.

Recall that table 4.4 is predicated upon an assumed constancy of real product wages. Supposing this to have been the case, then had living standards for labor of a given quality been common across sectors at the start of the period (1970), living standards would have diverged according to the pattern of relative commodity price changes set out in table 4.3, part A. For example, by 1983 food growers would have been earning around 40 percent more than those in nontraded services. Such a scenario is incompatible with the little we know about earnings differentials. Furthermore, incremental labor shifted out of the food sector into all the other sectors except export crops; yet if food were by far the highest-paying sector, it would have attracted labor.

Our analysis of the food sector is set out as a series of knowns and inferences: (a) employment was roughly constant in 1973–81; (b) the relative price of food increased substantially; (c) technology was roughly constant; therefore, (d) *the marginal revenue product of labor must have risen in line with (b)*. Furthermore, (e) the small farm labor market is competitive and wages appear to approximate to marginal products (see the evidence set out in chapter 7); therefore, (f) *the living standard of wage earners in the food sector must have risen*. But (g) the incremental labor force shifted out of the food sector; therefore, (h) *real wages must initially have been lower than in other sectors and tended to converge*.

Of the three inferences d, f, and h, only the last two are testable given present data, and both are substantiated in chapter 7. There we show that at the start of the first oil cycle, unskilled wages were around 60 percent higher in nonagriculture than in agriculture. From 1973 to 1981 real wages in agriculture rose by up to 50 percent, while in other sectors they declined by up to 15 percent. This differential corresponds roughly to the changes in relative product prices shown in table 4.3, part A. It is therefore consistent with our initial assumption that real product wages (and hence marginal physical products) stayed constant between 1973 and 1981 in the food and manufacturing sectors, so that wage differentials changed in line with product prices. If unskilled wages in the two sectors were equal in 1981, part A of table 4.3 suggests that wages would have been 60 percent higher in manufacturing than in the food sector in 1973.

Recall that a puzzle concerning the product market was why the food sector, despite large price increases, had contracted so markedly compared not only with traded goods but also with other nontraded goods. A related question was why the agricultural labor force declined (relatively) despite rising rural wages and falling urban wages. The trajectory of the government-induced unskilled wage distortion is germane to these puzzles. The existence of such a differential in the early 1970s would imply that at that stage the nonagricultural labor market was rationed on the supply side. The expansion of urban employment opportunities consequent upon the oil boom progressively relaxed this rationing, attracting labor out of agriculture. This shift back in the agricultural labor supply curve caused the price of food to rise relative to the prices of other nontradable goods. This effect was then compounded as the price of all nontradable goods rose relative to that of tradable goods because of Dutch disease. Finally, the persistence of a differential until the early 1980s accounts for the ease with which the other sectors bid labor away from agriculture despite the seemingly paradoxical wage trends.

One consequence of the changes in relative product prices could have been a "boom famine" among export crop producers as a result of the massive deterioration in the relative price of their product (Sen 1981). However, this potential effect was mitigated by a mass exodus of labor from the sector, evidenced by the collapse in production shown in parts B and C of table 4.3. The cultivation of low-productivity land was abandoned; for example, vast tracts of rubber trees went untapped. Real wages in the sector actually rose between 1973 and 1981, suggesting that as a result of labor shedding, the marginal physical product of labor rose by so much that it more than offset the price change.

Boom famine was avoided because of a very high degree of intersectoral labor mobility, which was probably made possible by two factors. First, farmers could switch their labor into food production. As we have seen, the relative price of food was rising, and food sellers were enjoying rising real incomes. However, we have also seen that resources were diverted out of food production, so it is unlikely that this was the main escape route followed by the export-crop labor force.[2] The second, probably dominant, factor was that during the boom urban employment was expanding rapidly in cities proximate to the export-crop sector (notably Lagos and Ibadan). This expansion reflects not so much Dutch disease as the behavior of the government.

The Politics of Oil Revenue

In its negotiations with the oil companies, the federal government was successful in acquiring for itself the gains from price and quantity increases. This left the issue of savings versus consumption, and the distribution of extra savings and consumption, directly in the hands of a small group of ministers and civil servants.

As noted earlier, relative price changes caused by Dutch disease transferred income from the traded sector, notably agricultural exporters and manufacturers, to the nontraded sector—food producers and construction and service activities. Additionally, there was a transfer from all other groups to food producers. If the preboom period represented a political equilibrium, this equilibrium was disturbed both by these transfers and by the accrual of oil revenues in the public sector.

Political Actors

It might be expected that in a society numerically dominated by peasants, peasant interests would be paramount. This was not the case in Nigeria. Neither the military nor any of the political parties articulated peasant interests—not that peasants represented a homogeneous interest group. In the Southwest, cocoa growers had, as we saw in chapters 2 and 3, suffered from high taxation. They now faced a further massive decline in their internal terms of trade because of appreciation of the exchange rate. The cocoa-growing population, though geographically concentrated, was characterized by considerable stratification. Income inequalities among cocoa farmers were much more pronounced than among other food farmers (see chapter 6), and there was a large group of wage laborers, many of whom were migrants from other regions. However, all these groups had an interest in a higher cocoa price.

Food-growing farmers, concentrated in the North, benefited from the substantial increase in food prices in proportion to their capacity to generate a surplus. Food growers, however, typically received considerable income from nonfarm sources—income that accrued to groups with distinct interests, particularly women as opposed to male household heads.

Peasants had few means of promoting their political interests. The 1968–69 riots of cocoa farmers had achieved little and were not repeated during the oil boom. The first election in the period, in July 1979, lagged behind the important oil-related policy choices.

The actor in direct control during the period was the army. Having fought and won the civil war, the army was relatively large, nationalistic, youthful, and confident. It did not, however, have a grassroots political or social network. Military leaders tended to see their role as temporary cleanup, combining anticorruption drives with constitutional changes needed to make politics work without returning to civil war.

Politics had failed in Nigeria in two ways. Most obviously, political differences had produced a civil war costing some 2 million lives. Much of the blame for this could be attributed to the federal constitution providing for three regions and the consequent alignments of two against one. This could be remedied by constitutional reform. More worrying for the long term was the tendency of the political process to produce predatory rather than representative organizations. Parties in office dispensed patronage to supporters; parties out of office had nothing to offer. A rational expectation was that tenure in office would be brief and interrupted by military rule rather than alternating between parties.

The military had assumed office because of the failure of the civilian political process. Although the military usurped the politicians, it enhanced the power of senior civil servants. These civil servants were conscious of Nigeria's position as the largest black African state and naturally saw their role as being in the vanguard of African development.

They also had the resources to implement their aspirations. This induced an emphasis on growth, particularly growth of readily measurable outputs and especially those that the civil service could be involved in producing or that were at least African owned.

Urban wage earners, whether in the public or the private sector, were not well organized into effective interest groups. The trade unions were weak and divided and had inherited an untenably favorable wage level. Likewise, the population of Lagos lacked political power, having supported the opposition party in the 1979 elections.

In summary, the broad mass of the population, whether peasants or wage earners, was largely quiescent during the first oil cycle. Under the military regime they had few channels of day-to-day representation. As a result, the bureaucrats of the civil service experienced a period of relatively unconstrained power at a time when vast new resources became available to the state.

The Political Contest for Oil Revenue

The oil boom initially benefited the federal government almost exclusively. The government reacted with a massive spending increase, most of it investment expenditure. Public investment doubled in a single year (1974). The emphasis on investment was so strong that its share in public expenditure rose from about one-quarter to more than half. Although expenditure rose substantially, it did not outpace revenue during the first oil cycle as a whole. Oil revenue rose from 5 percent of GDP in 1967–73 to 19 percent in 1974–79, whereas expenditure rose from 17 to 25 percent.

However, this average conceals a deterioration during the cycle. Federal expenditure doubled between 1973 and 1974 and doubled again the next year. As a result, despite the rapid growth in federally retained revenue, expenditure soon outpaced revenue. In the pre-bonanza, postwar fiscal years of 1971–73, there was an annual surplus that averaged 18 percent of retained revenue (Kirk-Greene and Rimmer 1981, table 14). In 1974 this surplus increased to 46 percent following a 183 percent increase in retained revenue. Thereafter there were four successive years of deficit, averaging 24 percent of retained revenue.

This swing in expenditure—from 82 to 124 percent of revenue—indicates that in the deficit years, one-third of expenditure was not directly attributable to a change in revenue. In real terms, federal expenditure in 1975–78 was on average 3.23 times greater than in 1973 (using the nonoil GDP deflator). Normalizing on 1973, if expenditure had remained at 82 percent of revenue, it would have risen to 2.13, the increase in expenditure relative to revenue raising it to 3.23. Thus, half of the increase in federal expenditure ($1.1 \div 2.23 = 49.3$ percent) is attributable not to an increase in revenue but to the practice of spending a greater proportion of revenue. To some extent this was a policy decision (to spend reserves, borrow foreign currency, and impose an inflation tax), but it also reflected a loss of control over expenditure following the decision to increase it in line with revenue. The state governments experienced a similar increase in expenditure relative to revenue, with the deficit growing from 72 percent of revenue (1971–73 average) to 100 percent of revenue (1975–79 average).

The large budget deficit—the consequence of a decision made perhaps by default—could be financed by an inflation tax or a payments deficit. Inflation, which had averaged 5.5 percent in the decade prior to 1973, averaged 20 percent between 1973 and 1979. This did not fully finance the budget deficit but was nevertheless seen as a political problem. There were attempts at price controls, and in 1976 an anti-inflation task force recommended using the exchange rate to dampen the price level. Between 1975 and 1977 trade was liberalized significantly through piecemeal relaxation of import quotas. As a result of the combination of trade, monetary, and exchange rate policies, the reserves accumulated in the early years of the boom were depleted, and resort was then made to foreign commercial borrowing. By the end of 1978 Nigeria had ₦3.3 billion of external debt.

The Third National Plan, inaugurated in 1975, is a useful indication of the balance of interest groups and their preferences. Ostensibly, the plan sought to reduce inequalities in living standards by means of public expenditure. Overall, private consumption per capita in real terms rose more or less consistently with its previous trend between 1973 and 1979, reflecting remarkable determination by the public sector to control incremental resources. Thus public services were the main instrument for improvement in current living standards. Despite the near-total direct control of incremental resources, there was no attempt to extend control over the entire economy. Development planning amounted to nothing more than a listing of items of public expenditure. Within this list, however, the government gave priority to capital formation rather than to recurrent expenditure, and to human and physical capital-producing sectors.

The suggestion of public sector profligacy in the imbalance between revenue and expenditure is tempered by this pattern of public spending. The share of capital expenditure in federal expenditure rose from 24 percent in 1973 to 52 percent by 1978 (table 4.5). This preference for public capital formation reflected the civil service's commitment to growth. The investment boom was remarkably large, given that the government for a long time treated the oil boom as permanent. In 1974 government documents suggested that as a result of the oil money, "foreign exchange is unlikely to feature as a major problem" for the rest of the decade (Central Planning Office 1974, p. 8, quoted by Oyejide 1991).

Not until after oil revenue fell in 1977–78 was the transiency of the shock recognized. Thus the high investment rate was not an appropriate response to a positive shock correctly seen as temporary.

Recall that in real terms there was little of an oil bonanza as far as private consumption was concerned. The government preempted the windfall for its own expenditure and, in Gelb's (1985) analysis, actually augmented this income by diverting existing income from the private sector. The contest for oil revenue was not, however, simply one of public versus private expenditures. The existence of large central government revenues magnified the old problem of how to allocate revenue to the states. In aggregate the federal government succeeded in retaining an increased proportion of public revenue. Transfers to states fell from 42 percent of revenue in 1970 to 23 percent by 1978. Nonetheless, in absolute terms the amount of revenue transferred to the states increased massively, which intensified the contest among them for a share of the distribution.

In effect, the distribution was based on the formula $y_i = a + bx_i$ where y = share of state i in revenue and x = population of state i. The first term

Table 4.5 Distribution of Government Expenditure, 1973–78
(percent)

Expenditure	1973	1974	1975	1976	1977	1978
General public services	20.2	—	15.9	12.8	13.5	11.7
Defense and public order	36.1	—	23.6	18.9	17.9	23.5
Education	5.4	—	15.5	21.0	9.6	4.5
Health	2.6	—	2.2	2.7	2.2	2.5
Other social services	4.8	—	6.2	8.4	6.3	9.2
Economic services	20.0	—	24.2	32.4	45.8	32.3
Other	11.0	—	12.4	3.8	4.8	16.4
		—				
Current expenditure	76.0	—	53.8	48.2	57.5	47.9
Capital expenditure	24.0	—	46.2	51.8	42.5	52.1
Total expenditure (millions of naira)	1,165.0	2,127.9	4,944.9	5,492.3	7,061.4	5,117.3

— Not available.

Source: IMF, various years.

created a financial incentive for states to subdivide into multiple new states; the second term created an incentive to falsify population estimates. Each of these incentives produced a response. In 1973 the government attempted a census as a prelude to a constitutional settlement that would include restoring civilian government according to the previously announced timetable. But the census provoked and aroused the old ethnic hostilities and had to be nullified in the face of riots. Alarmed by these rivalries, and perhaps with aspirations to permanent rule, Gowon announced in October 1974 that the return to civilian rule would be delayed. He had bought off the public sector labor force in the previous week with the Udoji pay award, which nearly doubled public sector salaries. Because this sparked resentment in the private sector, the pay award was extended to cover all formal sector wage earners.

The incentive to create more states coincided with the only viable means of reforming the constitution. The three-region federation had been a recipe for civil war, and the attempt to introduce a unitary state in 1966 had provoked a coup. But a federation of many states would strengthen federal control and also satisfy local aspirations, particularly among the smaller tribes. Thus in April 1976 the number of states was increased from 12 to 19.

The Gowon regime, however, was becoming increasingly undermined by corruption. Although data on corruption are intrinsically difficult to obtain and interpret, the Lockheed investigation of 1976 provided some insight into the standard practice of foreign companies seeking contracts in Nigeria. During the preceding five years Lockheed had signed contracts with the Nigerian government worth $45 million and had paid bribes to Nigerian officials at the rate of 8 percent of the total contract amount (Turner 1978, p. 174). An attempt by Gowon and one of his permanent secretaries to suppress a document prepared by technocrats at the Nigerian National Oil Corporation and highlighting gross mismanagement was the direct antecedent to an internal army coup in 1975. A countercoup the following year failed but did kill the head of state.

These internal army coups probably undermined the legitimacy of the regime. The new government had no mandate and was severely constrained in its ability to condemn its predecessor, since many participants in that regime remained in power. To justify its existence, it had to take on the role of temporary custodian, the role from which Gowon had been withdrawing. Such a role entailed both a timetable for the return to civilian rule and constitutional reform to make democracy work, and both were undertaken. A timetable for a return to civilian rule was adopted and adhered to. A constitution was enacted that attempted to create interethnic political parties by requiring that all parties eligible to run in elections have a genuinely multistate organization and that any government win at least 25 percent of the vote in at least two-thirds of the states.

As part of the process of reducing the autonomy of the states, the federal government retained an increasing share of federal revenue, as noted above, and became virtually the sole source of funds for the states. By fiscal 1978/79 less than 3 percent of state expenditures were met by state-raised revenue (Kirk-Greene and Rimmer 1981, table 15). The state governments thus became actors in the expenditure lobby.

One form of expenditure was "tax expenditure." Of the four state taxes existing in the early 1970s—taxes on export sales, herdsmen, and personal incomes as well as a poll tax—the first two were abolished during the 1970s, so that revenue was the same in nominal terms in 1978/79 as in 1971/72. This further reduced state autonomy and benefited export-crop-growing peasants, who, as we have noted, suffered from the exchange rate effects of the oil boom, as well as the politically powerful Fulani tribe, who were chiefly herdsmen.

To summarize, the federal government chose not to pass the oil windfall on to the private sector, and it passed on much less to the state governments than their prewindfall share of revenue would have implied. Whereas the federal government imposed tax expenditures on the states that almost eliminated their nonsubvention revenue base, it did not impose tax expenditures on itself. Although by the mid-1970s oil-based revenue constituted some 77 percent of total federal revenue, nonoil revenue increased substantially—by 4.2 times between 1970 and 1977.

Pattern of Federal Expenditure

The pattern of federal capital expenditure changed significantly during the first oil cycle. In 1973 defense and administration accounted for 36 percent of spending. By 1980 this had fallen to 15 percent. Thus the military and the civil service, although jointly in power, took a declining share of expenditure. In this they were assisted by the reduced need for military expenditure after the end of the civil war and by the rapid growth in absolute expenditure permitted by even a declining share. The share of the other major item of capital expenditure in 1973, transport, fell from 30 to 24 percent. The largest increase in share was that of federal manufacturing investment, from 12 to 27 percent. The most substantial decline, other than for defense and administration, was in capital expenditure on agriculture, from 7.8 to 4.4 percent.

The most dynamic component of federal expenditure was thus industrial capital formation, which by 1980 accounted for 20 percent of federally retained revenue. The philosophy that motivated this expenditure was a mixture of beliefs—that racial equality was important, that some activities were strategic, and that such sectors should be publicly controlled. Behind this lay a fascination with large-scale heavy industry and resentment at a commercially successful racial minority—Lebanese and Syrians—who owned many small establishments.

The Nigerian Enterprise Promotion Decree (1972) scheduled 22 activities reserved for nationals and another 33 in which foreign enterprises were excluded unless they were 40 percent Nigerian owned and above a certain size, thus primarily excluding Syrian and Lebanese entrepreneurs. In 1977 the two schedules were broadened, the 40 percent requirement was raised to 60 percent, and all unscheduled enterprises were required to have 40 percent Nigerian ownership. More than 1,800 companies were affected.

The program, started in 1972, created a massive equity divestment problem for foreign companies and matching asset bargains for Nigerians with liquid wealth or the ability to borrow. A publicly funded bank, the Bank for Commerce and Industry, was established to provide such finance. By 1977 there was concern that these assets were very narrowly held by a new Nigerian elite, and rules were introduced attempting to widen future share ownership. In addition to private equity holdings, the state bought equity in strategic industries and itself established two massive projects, one in steel and the other in petrochemicals.

Steel Project Proposal

The steel project was first conceived in the 1950s. Since it was a massively expensive decision, it is worth detailed consideration. It began with the building of a Russian steel mill, Ajoakuta, in the middle of the country. Without nearby fuel or ore supplies, both are imported and then transported by truck. The original plan included a rail network to bring in these inputs and to use the steel. Nigerian ore, and some coke, could then have been used. But the rail network plan was soon abandoned because of its immense cost. An alternative means of transporting the ore was then investigated, and a river link was planned. However, this would have involved moving more than 50 oil pipelines and would have cost $2 billion; it was therefore abandoned. The feasibility report on Ajoakuta is 21 volumes long and has never been translated from Russian. Few Nigerian decisionmakers are likely to have read it.

Because of delays in the completion of Ajoakuta, pressure mounted for a second steel mill, Delta, this time of West German and Japanese design. If all planned steel projects had been completed, the total cost of the two mills would have been $10.8 billion (at ₦4.2 = $1). If the plants were then run to produce steel, the cost would be higher. This is because the unit cost of steel in Nigeria greatly exceeds the world price. Prior to the 1986 exchange rate reform (discussed in the next chapter), the cost per ton was $400 against $150 world price. Even at the postreform exchange rate, unit cost is still $360 because of high import content. The plants cannot run efficiently below 30 to 40 percent capacity, but it is doubtful if the market will permit more than 20 percent capacity. At 40 percent capacity, the net present value of running the mills is around –$3 billion, so the total cost of steel mills is $13.8 billion.

Project Rationale

How did the decision to establish two steel mills come about? Both the Russians and the West Germans were thoroughly interested parties. Both feasibility studies were undertaken by, and only understood by, agents with a strong financial interest in selling steel mills. The commissioning of the feasibility studies either was naive or, more likely, reflected a prior belief in the desirability of steel mills that transcended numbers. The prosteel lobby was within the civil service in the Ministry of Steel and Industries. An antisteel lobby eventually developed in the Ministry of Planning, as it became aware of the opportunity cost. However, the prosteel lobby was so strong that the funding for steel was set up as a prior claim on oil revenue before it ever reached the budget, the oil companies paying around 80,000 barrels per day of oil into a London bank escrow account reserved for the payment of steel mill suppliers. This protected the project from the budgetary cuts that all other projects suffered in the 1980s.

The prosteel lobby in the civil service was apparently motivated initially by grandiose and naive visions of development. The two role models were Japan and Russia (thus the designs of the two mills). The Japanese model was based on the perception that Japan had industrialized because it had acquired heavy industry. There was also the grand scheme of linkages between local iron ore, local coal (largely unsuitable for coking), and the construction of a national rail network. Steel was to make Nigeria the industrial giant of Africa.

The pattern of resource allocation in the colonial era was perceived to be an outcome of colonial policy, not an outcome of comparative advantage resulting from market forces. The lack of industry was interpreted as an imperial decision to retain industry in the metropolis; the natural role of an independent national civil service was to promote industry.

Finally, the industrial planners revealed preferences (in the 1975 development plan) for "glamorous" industrial activities with a high-technology, real engineering, or high value added component, and they offered fiscal incentives to favor such activities over low-technology projects, light industry, and elementary industries such as textiles and foodstuffs. In part these preferences reflected a notion of what the pattern of activities in a developed economy should look like. To follow that pattern was to become developed. The private sector would do only the "easy" (profitable) activities, leaving the public sector to do the "difficult" (unprofitable) activities. In part these choices reflected a preference for low import intensity of production, misspecified as the "value added maximization principle"—the notion that those activities should be chosen that have the highest proportion of value added to output. Neither criterion had any economic foundation.

Beneficiaries of Public Expenditure

The infrastructure programs—transport, power, and housing—expanded in this period partly in response to such highly visible problems as endemic power cuts. The programs were constrained by the inability to construct and administer them rapidly rather than by a lack of finance; in the mid-1970s the Nigerian economy appears to have encountered the proverbial bottleneck. Budgets were underspent in sectors such as telecommunications, where there was clearly excess demand for services, and spectacular administrative incompetence led to the cement scandal, when so much cement was ordered that the ships carrying it to Lagos were kept waiting at sea for long periods because of a lack of unloading facilities. Infrastructure expenditure was also directed to prestige public consumption, notably the building of a new capital at Abuja.

The nearest the government came to giving oil revenue to the majority of Nigerian households was in expanding primary education and making it free. Primary enrollment increased from 37 percent in 1970 to 79 percent in 1978; secondary enrollment increased from 4 to 10 percent. Higher education was, however, given priority; almost as much capital was spent on universities as on the universal primary education program. Overall, education's share of recurrent expenditure increased from 2 to 17 percent.

Education was, in many respects, ideally suited as a recipient of public revenue. First, it benefited primarily the politically strong but educationally backward Northern states. Second, as an investment in Nigeria's future, it suited the development aspirations of the army and the civil service. Third, although it directly benefited children (a group without influence), the family structure in rural Nigeria is such that parents can expect to receive remittances from their employed offspring (Caldwell 1982) and, because of the disequilibrium wage premium that persisted during the 1970s, education enhanced entry to wage employment. Farm household heads could see the expansion of education as a welcome, state-financed diversification of economic activities away from agriculture. Fourth, education was a publicly provided activity and thus involved the federal and state bureaucracies not just in funding but also in administering a simple and easily expanded activity. Finally, education was probably the most promising investment for the Nigerian economy, which needed to invest the proceeds of a depleting natural resource in long-term, sector-unspecific capital.

However, education as an investment did not confer immediate benefits. The first beneficiaries of the increase in public expenditure were not primarily recipients of public services but rather new public sector employees and a corrupt elite. Public employment approximately tripled—from 0.5 million to 1.5 million—between 1973 and 1981. As chapter 7 shows, in 1973 urban wages for the unskilled were considerably higher than earnings in agriculture. Thus the mobile, mainly the young, wished to gain entry into the urban wage sector. Furthermore, because of the rural family structure discussed above, parents were keen for their offspring to relocate. Therefore, the expansion of public sector employment opportunities was popular irrespective of whether it was productive.

Judging whether existing public sector workers benefited from oil revenue requires speculation about what wage trends would have developed in the absence of oil. Wages rose in 1974 by 60 to 100 percent as a result of the Udoji award and thereafter declined rapidly. However, we suggest that at the start of the period, urban wages were in disequilibrium and tending to fall. In this interpretation, existing wage earners benefited from a delay in this adjustment process. This delay was only for a few years, because by the mid-1980s the adjustment had been largely completed.

Public sector pay policy to some extent mirrored the financial fortunes of the government, with large pay awards following the increase in the oil price. By 1979 the impetus behind expenditure increases had led to a substantial budget deficit and an exercise in retrenchment.

The government had long had some control over private sector wages through fair-wage clauses in government contracts, with the reference level being pay in the public sector. However, although a national minimum wage was introduced in 1981, from 1973 to 1979 the government showed relatively little responsiveness to the interests of wage earners, whether public or private. There was also no direct attempt to control or subsidize escalating food prices.

In response to rising food prices, the government attempted to increase food supply without increasing the budget allocation to agriculture, which we have seen was small and in relative decline. To encourage foreign companies to set up large farming operations, the government changed the legislation concerning land tenure (the Land Use Decree of 1978). Agricultural policy thus ran precisely counter to industrial policy, where foreign capital was being displaced.

Conclusion

The windfall of oil revenue gave rise to general equilibrium effects that transferred income from the politically weak Southern cocoa, rubber, and oil palm interests to the politically strong food producers of the North and also massively expanded the traditional relationships of gifts and patronage. The increase in government expenditure enhanced the opportunities for corrupt fortunes—in the private sector by excessive profits on government contracts and by favorable terms on foreign equity acquisition, and in the public sector by kickbacks on contracts and import licenses. The scope for patronage was so large that it provides a possible explanation for why control of the government was so contested within the army.

Since during the boom the government acquired and spent the oil revenue, per capita private consumption on average did not rise significantly relative to the trend. However, the average case obscures the fact that there were both winners and losers:

- New urban wage earners, who acquired their jobs because of boom-enhanced government expenditure, gained because for most of the period urban wages (though falling) were higher than rural wages.
- Food producers gained because of the rising relative price of food combined with a fairly constant marginal physical product of labor.
- Existing urban wage earners lost because money wages did not keep up with rising food prices (which form about half the cost of living).
- Producers of tradable agricultural goods could have lost heavily because of the drastic decline in the relative price of nonoil tradable goods. Their losses were mitigated, however, by the ability of labor to exit into more remunerative activities, notably urban employment opportunities that were expanding throughout the South.[3]

Had it not been for the war, the group that stood to gain most from the oil boom was the Ibo elite. It was the most commercially sophisticated of the large ethnic communities, and it dominated the region in which oil was based (under the original three-region boundaries). The Ibos should therefore have gained both from the commercial opportunities arising from rapid growth and from regional public revenue under the old derivation principle. However, their position was undermined by the war (since they were the losing group) and by the abolition of the derivation principle.

The Hausa-Fulani elite, which held power during the windfall, had the opposite characteristics. Although by no means cohesive, it did have a common interest. Having deliberately retarded non-Koranic education in its own region, it was at a disadvantage in commercial activity and so wished to channel the windfall through an expanded public sector. Since general equilibrium effects happened to reward the Northern population, this was consistent with the Northern elite's desire to satisfy its own constituency. It also meshed with the desire of the federal civil service for a commanding-heights strategy. This civil service goal was not, however, supported by economic sophistication. The corps of international economic technical assistants had been discarded in the late 1960s, and the investment program was not subjected to economic criteria. This conjunction of a powerful political impetus to public investment and a lack of civil service skill is what makes Nigeria's economic history in this period so spectacular: almost the entire windfall was invested, and yet, as will be seen in chapter 5, there was nothing to show for it.

5 The Second Oil Cycle: 1979–87

The fiscal and balance of payments difficulties into which the Nigerian economy was descending after 1976 were transformed briefly by the second increase in the oil price in 1979–80. This increase ended the incipient fiscal disequilibrium of the first cycle and created a further impetus to expenditure. However, the second cycle was not itself rescued by a further boom until the economy had fully adjusted both to the decline in oil income that began in 1981 and became more severe in 1986, and to the need for debt repayment consequent upon borrowing early in the 1980s. In this chapter we continue the economic story from 1981, measuring the magnitude of the shock, the slump, and its repercussions. The last section of the chapter takes up the political story after 1979.

The Magnitude of Shocks and Asset Choices: 1981–90

Because of a major policy break in 1986, it is convenient to divide the decade into two periods. During 1981–86, income declined massively and an economic control regime was created. During 1986–90, there was an eventually aborted liberalization of this regime combined with further shocks.

The Slump: 1981–86

The slump of 1981–86 is remarkable for its scale and for the distinctive policy choices made by the three governments that presided over it—first the Shagari regime and then the two military governments of Buhari and Babangida. We begin by measuring the scale of the crash, distinguishing between its two components, oil income and borrowing. We then turn to a question that the shocks forced on the Nigerian government and the private sector: should assets be depleted?

Oil revenue started to collapse during 1981 as a result of two policy errors. The oil ministry adopted an overoptimistic pricing strategy (Nigerian oil was more expensive than North Sea crude by $4 a barrel), and the government reneged on its long-term contracts to sell on the spot market during 1980 (which caused a backlash in the oil community). The market collapsed further in 1986 as a result of the price fall, although this was mitigated slightly by the opportunity to increase production.

As in our previous analysis of the boom period, to quantify these shocks we need a counterfactual case. For the boom period we assumed that OPEC would not have been formed. The counterfactual scenario we adopt for the slump is conversely that the OPEC pricing position of 1981 would have been sustained at the 1981 volume of Nigerian oil exports. The scale of the loss of export income is shown in table 5.1. Over the whole period, export income (by this time essentially the same as oil income) more than halved because of crashes in 1982 and 1986, with a partial recovery in the intervening years.

The oil shock was compounded by the unsustainability of the previous borrowing. Not only could the flow of borrowing not be sustained, but also the accumulated debt had to be serviced. By 1986 this had changed the country into a net capital exporter. This swing from borrowing to repayment was so large that it was of the same order of magnitude as the oil shock. We quantify it by taking as a counterfactual continued borrowing at the 1981 level (in constant prices). Table 5.2 sets out this reduction in borrowing and compares it with the oil shock.

Cumulatively, the losses from these two sources during the five years were 120 percent of gross domestic expenditure (GDE) in 1981. Although both the oil shock and reduction in the net capital inflow were volatile, in combination they followed a steady path of deterioration, as shown in the last column of table 5.2. The terms of trade deterioration caused by the fall in oil prices implied that gross domestic income (GDY) would

Table 5.1 Loss of Export Income, 1981–86
(1981 = 100)

Year	Export volume	Terms of trade	Export income
1981	100.0	100.0	100.0
1982	94.0	77.1	72.5
1983	100.0	68.2	68.2
1984	105.1	78.0	82.0
1985	115.7	78.3	90.6
1986	115.6	37.4	43.2

Source: Bevan, Collier, and Gunning 1992.

Table 5.2 Reduction in Resource Inflow, 1981–86
(billions of naira, 1984 prices)

Year	Export loss	Reduction in net capital inflow	Total reduction
1981	0	0	0
1982	12.8	0.9	13.7
1983	14.8	11.4	26.2
1984	8.4	25.9	34.3
1985	4.4	32.0	36.4
1986	26.5	17.2	43.7

Source: Bevan, Collier, and Gunning 1992.

fall relative to production (GDP); the reduction in the net capital inflow implied that expenditure (GDE) would fall relative to income. The three series are compared in table 5.3.

Two features of the table are noteworthy. First, the scale of the decline in real expenditure is extraordinary. If anything, the fall of more than one-third during only five years understates the human impact because population increased by 15 percent over the period; thus, per capita expenditure was nearly halved (declining by 44 percent). Second, production of the nonexport (in other words, nonoil) economy was stagnant or declining.[1] This can be seen either as disappointing, in view of the high rate of investment during the boom and the rapid growth of the labor

Table 5.3 Production, Income, and Expenditure, 1981–86
(1981 = 100)

Year	Nonexport gross domestic product[a]	Gross domestic income	Gross domestic expenditure
1981	100.0	100.0	100.0
1982	100.6	88.6	89.8
1983	93.7	82.8	77.0
1984	87.8	85.3	68.1
1985	96.3	93.8	70.5
1986	96.1	73.4	64.8

Note: The construction of the series is discussed in Bevan, Collier, and Gunning 1992. The data do not correspond to published series because some major adjustments have been made in order to value output and expenditure at approximately equilibrium relative prices, instead of at the highly distorted prices used in all official series.

a. Total GDP is not shown because it followed nonexport GDP closely.
Source: Bevan, Collier, and Gunning 1992.

force, or as demonstrating resilience in the face of such a severe slump in demand.

Policymakers and private agents were thus faced with a precipitate decline in expenditure brought on partly by a loss of oil income and partly by a decline in the scope for borrowing. A crucial decision concerned whether these losses would be borne predominantly by assets or by consumption. To the extent that the crash was temporary, a reasonable strategy would be to shed assets. However, the weakening of OPEC and the manifest unsustainability of borrowing at the 1981 level suggested that the bulk of the expenditure losses would be long term.

Since the decline in expenditure was rapid and could to some extent be regarded as temporary, there was a case for cushioning consumption. However, the savings effort could not be reduced by extra foreign borrowing because the initial borrowing propensity was itself unsustainable. Therefore, the only means of extra dissaving open to the economy was to consume the existing capital stock by failing to replace it as it depreciated. Offsetting this, the shocks implied a large rise in the relative price of nonoil tradable goods. In turn, this indicated that if the capital stock had been correctly allocated between the tradable and nontradable sectors on the basis of relative prices during the boom, then the allocation would now no longer be optimal. Since capital once installed is sector specific, the main way of relocating it is through investment. A change in relative prices with an initially correctly allocated capital stock therefore raises the real rate of return on investment.

The chosen strategy, as shown in table 5.4, was asset depletion: of the fall in expenditure, 53 percent was accounted for by investment and only 47 percent by consumption. As a consequence, investment was reduced far more dramatically than consumption. By 1986 consumption had declined by a quarter and investment by 60 percent. Although on the credit side of the asset position (investment) there was a collapse, on the debit side (borrowing) the asset position moved from rapid debt accumulation to debt repayment. The net effect of these changes is the savings series shown in the third column of table 5.4.

The savings rate was highly erratic. In 1981 it was only 17 percent, which is very low considering that the economy was in the late stages of an unprecedented income boom. The Shagari government failed to use the opportunity of the windfall to accumulate assets. During 1982–83 the savings rate crashed to 10 percent. Thus, the government's response to adversity was consistent with its behavior overall, which tended to be profligate. Arguably this was because the Shagari government was peculiarly ill suited to address painful economic choices. Its very design was that of a patronage system responding to the central issue posed by the oil windfall of the 1970s: how a geographically concentrated resource windfall should be distributed in the wake of a civil war. The political contest had been about which patronage network controlled public expenditure. Like any patronage system, the government needed a continuous flow of resources to maintain itself. This need was accentuated by the general and presidential elections scheduled for late 1983.

The strategy of dissaving, though economically unsound, was politically successful: the Shagari regime survived the elections despite facing an economic decline that would have unseated most governments. However, allegations of fraud were sufficiently widespread to raise questions about the government's legitimacy, and it was immediately toppled by a military coup. The subsequent Buhari regime followed the practice of previous military governments in Nigeria by claiming it had seized power temporarily to clean up the government. This gave the regime license to take drastic action and to make a dramatic break with past policies. The centerpiece of policy change concerned assets and can be understood by looking at table 5.4. The Buhari regime was fortunate in benefiting from a substantial improvement in export income, yet it retrenched domestic expenditure. As a result, the government succeeded in its first year in doubling the savings rate to nearly 25 percent.

The policy position of the Buhari regime was politically unsustainable. The combination of fiscal stringency and failure to liberalize the economy relied on a highly repressive and authoritarian stance by the government and offered no obvious route to resolution of the economy's structural problems. It was not surprising that the regime's policies generated another coup in August 1985. The new government under Babangida was in an extremely weak political and economic position. Politically, it could not pose as a military clean-up regime since it was displacing just such a government. Economically, it was immediately faced with the crash in the oil price so that in its first full year of office, 1986, real income fell by more than 20 percent—an unprecedented decline even by the harsh standards of preceding years. The short-term

Table 5.4 Investment and Consumption, 1981–86

Year	Investment (1981=100)[a]	Consumption (1981=100)[a]	Savings rate (percentage of gross domestic income)
1981	100.0	100.0	16.9
1982	76.3	95.9	10.0
1983	52.7	87.9	11.7
1984	44.0	78.9	23.2
1985	38.5	84.9	24.9
1986	40.5	75.8	14.2

Note: See note to table 5.3.
a. 1984 prices.
Source: Bevan, Collier, and Gunning 1992.

solution chosen was to revert to asset depletion: between 1985 and 1986 the savings rate crashed by more than 10 percentage points. Asset depletion bore the brunt of the income decline; the rate of dissavings was 63 percent. The choices of the Babangida regime at this stage were similar to those of the Shagari regime. Its lack of legitimacy appeared to make it as vulnerable to popular discontent as a civilian regime facing an election would have been. Yet, as we will see below, the Babangida regime subsequently implemented far-reaching policy reforms.

So far we have considered asset behavior only at the aggregate level. We now distinguish between the behavior of the government and other agents (tables 5.5 and 5.6). During the Shagari phase of the slump (1981–83), most of the fall in income was borne by the public sector. In response, public consumption was protected by reducing the public savings rate from 32 to 6 percent. Despite this public asset depletion, the investment collapse was markedly more pronounced in the private sector.[2] Arguably, the private sector recognized the public policy stance as unsustainable and wished to avoid irreversible capital expenditures.

During the Buhari phase (1984–85) both public and private incomes recovered modestly. The remarkable rise in the aggregate savings rate, noted above, was common to both the public and private sectors; the public turnaround from 6 to 35 percent was extraordinary. Whereas private consumption was maintained, public consumption was savagely reduced, thus reversing the priorities of the Shagari regime.

Table 5.6 shows that the Babangida government was able to protect its own income, passing the shock on to the private sector. The taxation device used by the government to achieve this shifting of the shock was devaluation. This occurred in late 1986 and forms the focus of our analysis of the reform period in the next section. The public sector savings rate was thus halved despite a maintenance of income. The private sector

Table 5.5 Public and Private Consumption and Investment, 1981–86
(1981 = 100)

Year	Consumption		Investment	
	Private	*Public*	*Private*	*Public*
1981	100.0	100.0	100.0	100.0
1982	95.9	96.1	55.8	95.1
1983	86.7	95.0	37.9	65.6
1984	79.2	77.6	53.9	40.3
1985	86.1	78.9	30.6	44.8
1986	76.2	73.5	39.3	39.3

Note: See note to table 5.3.
Source: Bevan, Collier, and Gunning 1992.

Table 5.6 Public and Private Income and Savings Rates, 1981–86
(billions of naira, 1984 prices)

	Public sector			Private sector		
Year	Income	Savings	Savings rate (percent)	Income	Savings	Savings rate (percent)
1981	30.1	9.7	32.1	78.6	8.8	11.1
1982	26.6	10.5	39.5	69.7	−0.9	−1.2
1983	20.3	1.3	6.2	69.8	9.3	13.3
1984	20.0	4.5	22.3	72.8	1.7	23.4
1985	23.6	8.2	34.6	78.5	17.2	21.9
1986	22.3	4.2	18.5	57.5	7.2	12.5

Source: Bevan, Collier, and Gunning 1992.

savings rate also fell sharply, presumably in an attempt to cushion consumption.

The ultimate device the public sector has for taxing the private sector is inflation. Surprisingly, despite the fall in public income, annual inflation averaged only 16 percent during the slump. There were, however, two distinct phases. In 1981–84 the rate averaged 24 percent and was accelerating, whereas in 1984–86 it averaged only 6 percent. The growth of currency holdings was similarly dichotomized, with nearly all the growth occurring during the Shagari government. A measure of the considerable fiscal achievement of the Buhari regime is that currency holdings increased by a mere 4 percent between 1984 and 1986. However, even during the Shagari period, inflation was somewhat contained because of the choice to reduce investment rather than print money. Given the general ambience of waste during the Shagari years, this self-denial is noteworthy. It suggests that the government was much better at controlling broad aggregates than the detailed content of its expenditures. The central failure of the Shagari government was not that it spent too much (although it did) but that its expenditures were so unproductive.

Abortive Reform: 1986–90

Despite the austerity of the Buhari regime, the economy continued to deteriorate as the government failed to address many of the dysfunctional policies it had inherited. In particular, it was unwilling to undertake many of the reforms pressed on it by the international agencies, such as trade liberalization, exchange rate devaluation, or elimination of the domestic petroleum subsidy. It had, however, established a credible record of fiscal reform that was to prove important for its successors.

The incoming Babangida government saw more clearly that austerity was not enough and that it had to be accompanied by more positive reform measures. A public debate was initiated on the merits of accepting an International Monetary Fund (IMF) adjustment package. Babangida lost this debate because it became clear that an overt deal with the IMF would be bitterly resented. The government then proceeded, idiosyncratically, to adopt a program that was fully approved by the IMF, while keeping that institution at arm's length and accepting no IMF financing.[3] The program was adopted in July of 1986—a year in which world oil prices were halved and oil revenue again fell dramatically.

The structural adjustment program (SAP) was wide ranging, but its centerpiece was the adoption, in September 1986, of a market-determined exchange rate system and the elimination of import licensing. The new exchange rate system initially had two components. The second-tier foreign exchange market covered all trade transactions and included an auction for official foreign exchange receipts and an interbank market based on autonomous inflows of foreign exchange to the private sector. The official (first-tier) exchange rate was maintained for foreign debt service obligations. In July 1987 the two rates were unified, but downward pressure on the rate because of expansionary fiscal policies in 1988 led to a reappearance of the differential between the exchange rate on the auction where the depreciation was partially suppressed and the interbank rate, which was market determined. Table 5.7 gives these nominal exchange rates for the reform period and the years immediately preceding it.

As the reemergence of a variable, but sizable, differential between the official and parallel rates demonstrates, the original intention of achieving a unified and market determined exchange rate was undermined through frequent policy changes and increasingly direct foreign exchange allocation. Firms and other users of foreign exchange were not allowed to bid directly at the auction but had to work through the banks. Strict

Table 5.7 Nominal Exchange Rates, 1982–90

(ratio of U.S. dollar to naira)

Year	Official rate	Parallel rate	Differential (percent)
1982	1.485	0.880	68.8
1983	1.382	0.553	149.8
1984	1.308	0.311	321.0
1985	1.121	0.265	322.9
1986	0.743	0.259	186.9
1987	0.250	0.212	17.6
1988	0.223	0.155	43.8
1989	0.136	0.093	45.6
1990	0.125	0.104	19.5

Source: World Bank data.

limits were placed on the maximum allocation to any one bank, greatly inhibiting the incentive to compete. Partly in consequence, the banks were able to operate a very successful cartel, obtaining substantial rents from their foreign exchange dealings. The government tacitly connived in this arrangement, presumably because of its concern to slow the depreciation of the rate. Since it was a net seller of foreign exchange on the auction, this artificial lowering of its naira receipts exacerbated the budget deficit, thus increasing the pressure for more rapid depreciation of the rate by fueling inflation.[4]

Despite the incomplete reform of the exchange rate mechanism, it was substantially better than the previous arrangements. First, there was no sign that the extreme overvaluation of 1983–86 was reemerging. Second, although the government reverted to a system of foreign exchange allocation to banks that was direct and relatively insensitive to price, the allocation to ultimate users of foreign exchange was now market driven. The direct allocation did generate rents, as before, but it did so in a way that had far less malign consequences for resource allocation. Since private agents acquired foreign exchange at the parallel rate, the effect of the auction was not a relative price distortion but a loss of government revenue.

The other central component of the SAP was trade liberalization. This included lowering tariffs, reducing the import prohibition list, and abolishing import licensing and virtually all price controls. Average nominal rates of protection initially fell from 33 to 23 percent. Following the completion of a tariff study, a new tariff regime was announced in the 1988 budget, with rates specified for a seven-year period, thus providing producers and consumers with a relatively stable long-term structure to reduce uncertainty. The new schedule was higher than the interim ones, and nominal protection averaged around 28 percent. However, this underestimates the real reduction in protection, which was determined prior to the reforms by the restricted availability of imports under license more than by tariffs.

Although the late 1980s were characterized primarily by policy reforms, the economy experienced further external shocks. Table 5.8 updates the information given in table 5.2 and charts the change in resource inflow for the period. Compared with the already bad outcomes for 1986, there was further deterioration in oil receipts during 1987–88, followed by a recovery peaking in 1990, when more than 40 percent of the ground lost after 1981 was temporarily recovered. This gain was the result of the Gulf War and was understood to be temporary. The government announced that it would treat the increase in revenue as a temporary shock that should not have a long-term effect on the level of government spending. To that end, it began setting up stabilization funds. However, in the aftermath of this windfall the government lost control

Table 5.8 Change in Resource Inflow, 1986–90
(billions of naira, 1984 prices)

Year	Change in export income	Change in net capital inflows	Total change
1986	0.0	0.0	0.0
1987	–0.2	–7.8	–8.0
1988	–2.6	–5.9	–8.6
1989	4.4	–12.1	–7.7
1990	11.3	–16.4	–5.1

Source: Bevan, Collier, and Gunning 1992.

over expenditure more egregiously than ever before, with the fiscal deficit approaching 10 percent of GDP. In response, the government again resorted to overvaluation of the official exchange rate. By 1994 the configuration of macroeconomic policy was back to that of 1984; the liberalization of the late 1980s had proved abortive.

To a large extent, the resource flow in the reform period had become endogenous, since it reflected the rule adopted by the government of broadly limiting total debt service to 30 percent of export earnings. The increase in export income then generated an increased rate of actual debt service. Compared with 1986, the total annual reduction in resources was fairly stable from 1987 to 1990 and, cumulatively, about 35 percent of 1986 GDE.

Table 5.9 is the analogue of table 5.3, covering the SAP period. One feature that distinguishes the period is that nonexport GDP resumed growth. Although there was little change between 1986 and 1987, growth averaged 9 percent a year from 1987 to 1990. Many factors make it difficult to interpret this recovery. Even given the highly deteriorated state of the economy in 1986 and the prevalence of excess capacity, the growth rate was high by any standard, and extraordinarily so by the standards of Nigeria over the previous 15 years.

The growth rate is the more surprising when set alongside the investment figures. Despite the rapid growth of nonexport GDP over 1987–90, GDE did not surpass its 1986 level until 1989. This was because of the substantial reduction in the resource transfer between 1986 and 1987. In consequence, resources available for domestic absorption declined by 9 percent even though GDP was stagnant. Subsequently, GDE followed a relatively similar path to GDP, growing at 8 percent a year on average.

One implication of these calculations is that the problem of aggregate domestic adjustment was by no means over in 1986; a further sharp decline in absorption had to be managed before any amelioration started. How were these changes in absorption divided between investment and

Table 5.9 Production, Income, and Expenditure, 1986–90
(1986 = 100)

Year	Nonexport gross domestic product[a]	Gross domestic income	Gross domestic expenditure
1986	100.0	100.0	100.0
1987	100.9	100.4	91.2
1988	112.3	105.9	98.6
1989	119.8	120.3	104.8
1990	129.3	136.1	114.6

Note: See note to table 5.3.
a. Total GDP is not shown because it followed nonexport GDP closely.
Source: Bevan, Collier, and Gunning 1992.

consumption? As table 5.10 shows, the severe compression of consumption that took place between 1981 and 1986 was not compounded further: aggregate consumption remained stable from 1986 to 1987. In consequence, all of the downward adjustment was borne by investment, which fell by more than 40 percent to less than one-quarter of its 1981 level. Not until 1990 did investment share in the recovery that subsequently took place. As for consumption, it grew at a steady rate of a little under 7 percent a year during 1987–90. The savings rate, which had been sharply depressed in 1986, remained at a very low level until 1989, when it recovered to more normal levels. In 1990 it rose to 24 percent.

Two conclusions from these figures are worth noting. First, the strong recovery in growth cannot be attributed to aggregate investment, which remained at an extremely low level; the increase in 1990 came too late to have influenced output in that year. It is possible that the national accounts figures fail to capture all investment occurring in the relatively new, informal, post-SAP urban activities, but several other possibilities also suggest themselves. The level of capacity utilization at the start of the period was extremely low, as already noted. Much of the previous high level of investment was unproductive or even faked, so there was plenty of scope for allocational efficiency gains within a smaller total. Also, the post-SAP capital intensity is likely to have been lower, partly because import substitution tends to raise capital intensity and partly because overvalued exchange rates make imported capital goods artificially cheap.

The second conclusion to draw is that consumption was protected from further compression early in the SAP and then permitted to grow steadily at the rate of expansion of total resources. As table 5.11 shows, the slight fall in aggregate consumption between 1986 and 1987 involved

Table 5.10 Investment and Consumption, 1986–90

Year	Investment (1986 = 100)	Consumption (1986 = 100)	Savings rate (percentage of gross domestic income)
1986	100.0	100.0	14.2
1987	58.5	99.1	15.3
1988	60.8	107.7	12.8
1989	63.6	114.7	18.2
1990	91.1	120.3	24.2

Note: See note to table 5.3.
Source: Bevan, Collier, and Gunning 1992.

a sharp contraction in public consumption (by more than 15 percent) and a modest increase in private consumption of 2 percent. Thus private consumption was protected from the considerable fall in resources in 1987. Public consumption remained at its new lower level until 1990, when it recovered to its 1986 value. Private consumption, by contrast, grew at around 7 percent a year. As for investment, it was again the public component that bore the brunt of the contraction. From 1987 to 1989 public investment was halved from its 1986 level, whereas the private component fell only by one quarter. The recovery in 1990 was shared by both sectors, with private investment surpassing its 1986 level.

In table 5.12 aggregate income and savings are partitioned between the public and private sectors. There is a marked contrast between the two sectors. In the private sector, income grew continuously during 1986–90 at a little more than 5 percent a year. The savings rate was also relatively high (averaging nearly 18 percent) and, except in the difficult adjustment year 1986, relatively stable. The public sector path was very different. Income fell by 17 percent in 1986–88 and then more than doubled in 1988–90. The savings rate was highly volatile but also highly procyclical. During the trough year of 1988, the public sector dissaved at nearly 11 percent; during the peak year of 1990 it saved at nearly 30 percent. After the massive decline in private sector income during 1986, the private sector appears to have been reasonably isolated from the extreme volatility of the government's circumstances.

General Equilibrium Effects

Faced with such a large external shock, relative prices were bound to change substantially to preserve market clearing. These price changes were largely in the hands of private agents, who accepted them. The government, however, intervened in some important markets; in particular, it fixed the price of foreign exchange and the ex-factory price of many manufactures.

Table 5.11 Public and Private Consumption and Investment, 1986–90
(1986 = 100)

Year	Consumption		Investment	
	Private	Public	Private	Public
1986	100.0	100.0	100.0	100.0
1987	102.0	84.3	69.8	54.9
1988	111.5	88.3	79.3	47.7
1989	120.5	85.3	75.0	55.0
1990	123.9	102.2	105.1	83.7

Note: See note to table 5.3.
Source: Bevan, Collier, and Gunning 1992.

The Slump: 1981–86

Although there were small devaluations during the period, the exchange rate became massively overvalued until the auction was introduced in September 1986. As a result, there was huge excess demand for foreign exchange, which the government rationed. This gave rise to patronage and to trade restrictions. As Gelb and associates (1988, pp. 228–29) aptly note:

> In effect, this strategy redistributed part of the oil revenue from the government to favored importers . . . and so severely aggravated the fiscal problem caused by falling oil revenues. Nigeria's prices moved more and more out of line with those of its trading partners. The result was a vicious cycle of rising distortions, declining efficiency, falling non-oil output, fiscal deficits, inflation, and disruptive cuts in public spending.

Table 5.12 Public and Private Income and Savings Rates, 1986–90
(billions of naira, 1984 prices)

Year	Public sector			Private sector		
	Income	Savings	Savings rate (percent)	Income	Savings	Savings rate (percent)
1986	22.3	4.2	18.5	57.5	7.2	12.5
1987	20.8	1.0	5.1	59.4	11.3	19.1
1988	18.5	−2.0	−10.8	66.0	12.8	19.5
1989	26.9	6.7	25.1	69.1	10.7	15.5
1990	38.0	11.2	29.3	70.6	15.1	21.4

Note: See note to table 5.3.
Source: Bevan, Collier, and Gunning 1992.

Whereas during the oil boom the main mechanism of patronage had been public expenditure, during the slump this source declined and was replaced by rents from foreign exchange allocation. An indication of the growth in such rents and the implicit tariff rates generated by import restrictions is given by the evolution of the parallel market premium over the official rate. At the start of 1981 the premium was only 37 percent; during 1983 it surpassed 200 percent, and by 1986 it was 330 percent. The refusal of the government to devalue more rapidly before its eventual policy reversal in 1986 is a highly visible policy error. Its consequences were to reduce the income of the export sector and to impose cumbersome and rationed access to imports, thus handicapping firms that depended on imported inputs. Since most of the export income accrued to the government, the main loser from the policy was the government itself.

Four factors encouraged overvaluation. First, macroeconomic policy was not high on the government's agenda, and foreign exchange rationing was the automatic consequence of inertia. Second, the rents from administered allocation, which accrued disproportionately to the political elite, were a disincentive to its removal—if not the initial motive for overvaluation. Third, the economic consequences of devaluation were not well understood. Devaluation was seen as inflationary both by the popular press and within the central bank, which was surprised when it proved not to be so. Fourth, there was a degree of "exchange-rate fetishism" in Nigeria and a concern that the naira should remain at least as valuable as the dollar.

The policy of ex-factory price controls was motivated in part by a desire to restrain inflation. Even had it been effective in holding down the consumer price of domestic manufactures, the policy would not have succeeded because the given monetary demand would have pushed up other prices more rapidly. However, because the price controls were usually enforced only ex-factory and not at the consumer level, the primary beneficiary was the distribution sector. The main exception was in the pricing of automobiles, where the beneficiaries were upper-middle-class consumers.

Between 1981 and 1986 real aggregate demand fell by 35 percent. This inevitably changed the relative prices needed for market clearing—the relative price of nontradables needed to fall. Unless actual relative prices responded accordingly, we would expect an income decline of this magnitude to cause a collapse in production. In particular, in most economies real wages would be unlikely to fall by such a large amount over such a short period, causing rising real product wages and consequent unemployment and falling production. We have seen that those prices controlled by the government diverged from market-clearing levels. Private agents thus had to adjust not only to the external shock but also to the disequilibria created by government pricing policies.

Contrary to expectations, nonexport production declined by only 4 percent during the slump. The dip was temporarily more acute during 1983–84—most likely because of the drought of those years. At first view, a mere 4 percent fall in production in response to a 35 percent fall in demand implies considerable product and factor market flexibility in the private sector. This has to be qualified somewhat because the labor force grew over the period by approximately 15 percent. Some of this labor force was accounted for by higher unemployment, but the extent of unemployment was limited. Although the unemployment rate rose sharply in urban areas, in rural areas it remained low, so that nationally it rose only from 2 to 6 percent. Thus the employed labor force increased by around 10 percent despite the slump. This was achieved because real wages fell rapidly. Evidently, the labor market was highly flexible, but the decline in output relative to employment suggests that product markets may have been somewhat less responsive to changes in demand.

The apparent decline in output despite employment growth might, however, be an artifact. Output might have been shifting between sectors in such a way that, at 1984 official relative prices, output declined even though the resource shifts were presumably value enhancing at prevailing prices. More generally, for given factor availability, resource shifts in response to relative price changes mean that real output rises when measured at ex post relative prices but falls when measured at ex ante prices. In Nigeria, where relative prices changed substantially because of the large shocks, this point deserves emphasis. We are able to get some indication of its importance by comparing the change in GDP over the period 1981–85 at two different sets of relative prices—those prevailing in 1977/78 (approximately ex ante prices) and official 1984 prices. GDP fell by 9.5 percent when measured at 1977/78 prices but by only 2.1 percent at 1984 prices, suggesting that measured output growth was highly sensitive to the relative prices used. Although the official relative prices prevailing in 1984, which were used to construct the constant-price national accounts series for the slump period, were far out of line with market-clearing prices for the reasons discussed above, they can still be expected to give some downward bias to the measured production trend.

In analyzing how relative prices changed during the slump, we use open economy macroeconomic theory to guide disaggregation. First, the distinction between tradables and nontradables is basic to the analysis of trade shocks. A negative trade shock such as Nigeria experienced reduces domestic expenditure. This spending effect changes the relative prices of importables and nontradables. In the absence of quantitative restrictions on imports, the domestic price of importables is determined by world prices, the exchange rate, and tariff rates. If all these variables are exogenous, then reduced demand for importables will lead to a reduction in imports at an unchanged domestic price, whereas for nontradables the reduction in demand can be accommodated only by a fall in the price. Thus the price of nontradables declines relative to importables. Mobile factors (typically labor) will be drawn out of the production of nontradables and into the production of importables.

Second, when trade restrictions rise in response to the shock, as they did in Nigeria, a further distinction must be made between protected tradables (import substitutes) and unprotected tradables (exports). Third, we distinguish between import-dependent industries and those using mainly domestic inputs, since the former suffered from foreign exchange rationing. This changes in a substantial way a central result of Dutch disease theory: a negative trade shock may now reduce industrial output if it is determined directly by the availability of foreign exchange for the import of intermediate inputs. Fourth, since investment fell substantially relative to consumption, we assume that the demand for nontradable capital goods is likely to have fallen by more than that for nontradable consumer goods. Finally, since per capita incomes fell sharply, we distinguish between luxuries and basic consumer goods.

For concreteness we have chosen illustrative examples of the key aggregates that result from this classification. Among the tradable goods, cocoa was an important nonoil exportable, cars were protected luxury goods with a high import intensity, and textiles were protected luxury goods that relied more on domestic inputs (cotton). Among nontradables, food crops were basic goods, services were more likely to be luxuries, and the construction sector was supplying nontradable capital goods.

We now consider the impact of the shock on these sectors. First, as discussed earlier, total private consumption fell by around a quarter in real terms between 1981 and 1986, or by about one-third in per capita terms. This spending effect should have reduced the output of nontradables through a fall in their relative price. This in turn should have affected not only consumer nontradables (services and food) but also cars and textiles, which were still protected by quantitative restrictions in this period. Therefore the spending effect should have led to a fall in the output of cars, textiles, services, and food. Second, the shock reduced the availability of imported inputs, which affected import-dependent industries such as vehicle assembly over and above the spending effect. Thus the production of cars should have been particularly hard hit.

Third, the decline in per capita income should have led to a relative decline in the demand for luxuries. In this instance we expect demand for food (with a relatively low income elasticity) to fall less than demand for luxury consumer goods (cars, textiles, and services). This should draw labor, released from shrinking urban activities, to rural areas. Fourth, the growing overvaluation of the exchange rate should have depressed domestic cocoa prices, so we should expect a shift of labor from cocoa to food production, reinforcing the positive effect on food output of return migration. Finally, because capital formation fell much more sharply than consumption, this should be reflected in the demand for the output of the construction sector. We therefore expect that sector to have suffered most from the fall in real expenditure.

We can now compare our theoretical predictions for 1981–86 with the actual outcomes for both prices and outputs shown in table 5.13.[5] Production of luxuries (cars, textiles, and services) fell sharply, as predicted, and the decline was most marked in import-dependent industry, with production of cars falling by almost two-thirds in the five-year period. The change in the construction sector is very much in line with the fall in investment demand: both declined by 60 percent. We have predicted that basic goods (food) would gain relative to luxuries under a fall in demand. The combination of labor shedding in urban activities and the relative increase in the demand for basic goods shows up as an increase in food production. In per capita terms, food production rose by 6 percent over the period. Since there is no reason to expect that factor productivity increased, this presumably indicates an increase in the rural labor force as a result of return migration. Finally, cocoa suffered from exchange rate overvaluation, and the domestic price fell by two-thirds relative to import prices between 1981 and 1984. This was reversed in the final year, 1986, as a result of the devaluation. These price changes were (with some delay) reflected in the output series. Cocoa production fell by 40 percent over the period. Again, this should have raised food production as rural labor shifted from cocoa to food crops.

We now turn to evidence on factor movements. Although there is no direct evidence on rural-urban labor shifts, the labor force surveys of December 1983 and June 1985 indicate that within both the rural and urban economies, labor shifted into agriculture. The proportion working in agriculture increased from 66 to 71 percent in rural areas and from 12.5 to 15.6 percent in urban areas. The only indicators of sectoral investment are the data on the sectoral distribution of loans and advances made by commercial banks, including loans to agriculture, manufacturing, and trade. These data are a poor proxy for changes in fixed capital since the loans may have been used largely for working capital requirements. However, they show that the share of agriculture doubled between 1981 and 1986.

Reform: 1986–90

In 1986–90 the government temporarily abandoned its previous resistance to relative price changes. We therefore expect relative price changes to be important for two reasons: the devaluation and the additional external shocks. First we consider the spending effect of the shocks. Recall that for 1981–86 the theory explained the fall in the output of importables (cars and textiles) as a response to the fall in private consumption. Despite the increase in consumption after 1986, the theory does not predict an increase in output, because of the change in the trade regime. With a removal of quotas, a rise in consumption demand should be reflected in imports rather than domestic output. Therefore production of cars and

Table 5.13 Quantities and Prices, 1981–86
(1981 = 100)

Item	Cocoa[a]	Cars[b]	Textiles[c]	Con-struction[d]	Services[e]	Food[f]
Quantities						
1981	100.0	100.0	100.0	100.0	100.0	100.0
1982	89.7	316.2	121.4	79.8	100.8	104.7
1983	80.5	119.7	68.0	70.3	94.8	90.7
1984	80.5	39.9	48.8	57.3	77.7	114.4
1985	92.0	77.8	51.7	39.5	74.5	114.0
1986	57.5	36.4	44.0	39.4	77.5	138.1
Prices						
1981	100.0	—	100.0	100.0	100.0	100.0
1982	100.0	—	107.2	113.3	99.2	109.2
1983	107.7	—	180.8	115.7	119.7	128.4
1984	115.4	—	284.4	120.5	166.3	176.8
1985	123.1	—	298.6	141.0	162.1	166.3
1986	269.2	—	390.6	175.9	169.6	153.8

— Not available.

a. Quantity from CBN 1990, p. 79. Central Bank data (annual reports) on producer prices paid by the marketing board were used to construct the price index.

b. Quantity from the Central Bank's index of industrial production (IIP) (vehicle assembly); no price series available.

c. Quantity from IIP (cotton textiles); price from CBN 1990, p. 93 (price index for clothing in the composite—rural and urban—CPI). The sharp drop in quantity for 1984 is not genuine but due to a nonresponse problem.

d. Quantity from national accounts (GDP in building and construction in 1984 prices); price from national accounts (implicit GDP deflator).

e. Quantity from national accounts (GDP in repairs and other services in 1984 prices); price from national accounts (implicit GDP deflator).

f. Quantity from CBN 1990, p. 78 (total production in tons of maize, millet, wheat, acha, beans, cassava, potatoes, yams, cocoyams, plantains, vegetables); price from national accounts (implicit GDP deflator).

Source: Bevan, Collier, and Gunning 1992.

textiles should not be affected directly by the spending effect, but only indirectly, as labor is drawn into other sectors such as construction. Nontradables should gain from the spending effect, and, as a result, output of services and food should rise. Again we should expect the output of the construction sector to follow the path of investment, and we should therefore expect stagnation of construction output with an upturn in the final year.

In the pre-SAP period, trade policy relied heavily on rationing of foreign exchange and import licensing. This was supplemented by a wide array of quantitative restrictions (QRs), including import bans for many agricultural and manufactured products. As already noted, the import licensing system was abolished when the second-tier foreign exchange market was introduced. Trade reform should have reduced the profitability of import-intensive industries, including assembly operations such as car production. The effect should have been negative for sectors that lost QR protection (cars), but not for textiles, where QRs remained in force although they were often evaded. The automobile industry should also have been negatively affected by the rise in the cost of its imported inputs because of the devaluation.

We now compare the predictions with outcomes (table 5.14). As expected, output of cars fell catastrophically: in 1990 output was less than 12 percent of what it had been in 1981. Recall that we chose cars as a proxy for import-dependent production of import substitutes. The decline of that sector was an important achievement of the SAP. For construction we find, again as expected, that there was rapid growth. Despite the continuing investment slump, the devaluation radically cheapened structures relative to equipment, shifting the composition of investment toward construction. For cocoa, production increased by more than 140 percent between 1986 and 1990. The nontradables—services and food—gained as predicted. The effect was modest in services, whereas food production rose sharply—by about one-third in per capita terms—although some of this may have been caused by an improvement in income distribution. Food output should have risen as a result of the spending effect, and this gain may have been reinforced by relatively higher demand for basic goods, but food production would have been competing for labor with both cash crops (cocoa) and urban activities.

In the absence of sectoral employment data we cannot be sure what the net effect on urban employment was of the contraction of import-dependent production such as cars and the expansion of other sectors (including government employment). The analysis suggests that the negative effect must have dominated, causing labor to shift from urban to rural areas: only an increase in the rural labor force can explain the expansion of both cocoa and food production. Although no data support this, there is general agreement that significant "ruralization" took place.

What can be concluded from this analysis of relative prices and re-source reallocation and the preceding analysis of asset behavior? The period 1981–86 is sometimes characterized as "stabilization without adjustment," the implication being that asset behavior was satisfactory whereas resource reallocation was not. On neither count is this descrip-tion accurate. The asset story is one of debt accumulation and invest-ment collapse. Given the investment decline, the resource reallocation process was bound to be severely handicapped since the capital stock became virtually immobile. Yet resources did evidently move and in a direction consistent with our simple macroeconomic analysis.

Such an analysis cannot be expected to account for the entire range of price and output changes in the economy. However, it does appear that many of the substantial changes in the composition of output were broadly explicable in terms of the slump. Some of these, notably the growth of food production, were an efficient response to adversity, indi-cating prompt redeployment of resources by the private sector. That is, there was considerable efficient adjustment prior to the government's

Table 5.14 Quantities and Prices, 1986–90
(1986 = 100)

Item	Cocoa[a]	Cars	Textiles[b]	Con-struction	Services	Food
Quantities						
1986	100.0	100.0	100.0	100.0	100.0	100.0
1987	104.9	57.7	149.5	109.4	100.9	94.6
1988	229.9	38.7	151.6	120.6	102.1	120.9
1989	255.8	33.0	137.0	125.6	103.5	126.7
1990	243.8	32.4	148.2	131.7	105.5	127.5
Prices						
1986	100.0	100.0	100.0	100.0	100.0	100.0
1987	121.8	118.4	104.0	109.7	160.1	108.6
1988	128.6	121.9	107.0	116.6	225.4	165.2
1989	139.6	206.6	160.5	124.4	249.5	230.1
1990	121.8	—	172.5	136.4	289.1	307.5

— Not available.

Note: For calculations, see notes to table 5.13.

a. Data on world cocoa prices were adjusted both for changes in the 1991 par-allel exchange rate and for a slight increase in the ratio between domestic and world prices between 1986 and 1987. This procedure implies that after 1986 the domestic price is assumed to follow the world price (converted at the parallel exchange rate).

b. 1986 data not available; set at average of 1985 and 1987 data.

Source: See notes to table 5.13.

policy reform. However, other changes, notably the contraction of the cocoa and construction sectors, were arguably the consequences of inappropriate government responses. Finally, the industrial sector probably contracted in an inefficient fashion brought about by input rationing instead of by price incentives. The allocative implications of the market were put to the test only in the final period of our analysis.

The Politics of the Second Oil Cycle

The constitution under which the 1979 elections were fought had been designed to introduce cross-ethnic parties. To be registered, a party had to demonstrate cross-regional organization in the short period between legalization of political activity and the start of the election campaign. Inadvertently, the short time frame had the effect of seriously limiting the number of participating parties: only five were able to meet the organizational requirements. Because three of these had an uncontested ethnic base and all five had a distinct regional base, people continued to identify with an ethnic or regional group rather than with cross-ethnic classes—precisely the opposite of the intended effect.

The distinction between ethnic and regional loyalties was somewhat blurred because the tribes were fluid. The three largest (Yoruba, Hausa-Fulani, and Ibo) constitute only half the population and are themselves consortia: the Ibos have been losing membership since their defeat in the civil war, and the Yoruba are largely a creation of the last century. The electoral system thus created contestable natural monopolies at the regional level for a party credible as the local victor.

The political process was therefore more a matter of capturing the dominant party than of parties competing for votes. To win the backing of the locally dominant party, an aspiring politician needed to build a personal following of active workers rather than a wider constituency of passive support, and this encouraged patronage rather than representation. Because of the resulting loyalties, each party tended to win its regional base, and there were genuine contests within only two of the three major ethnic groups. The only chances of a political contest not dominated by regional and ethnic loyalties would have been through a two-party contest or a contest of multiple parties at the regional level. As it was, because each party was assured of winning control of the patronage system within its region, the prospect of patronage reinforced the tendency to support the "natural" party. In the 1979 elections for the House of Representatives, 78 percent of the votes went either to the winning party in each state or to the winning party federally; parties unable to dispense patronage attracted only 22 percent of the votes.

The Shagari Regime: 1979–83

As a result of the election, at the federal level control shifted from the army—and from the small group of civil servants behind it—to a political party, the National Party of Nigeria (NPN), led by Shagari. Although the NPN contained many former politicians and was predominantly Northern, it lacked identity as a cohesive group with regional or class interests or with national goals. The NPN was an artifact, characterized by a set of rules designed to build a coalition that would win the election. The Northerners at the core of the party recognized that to win, they would have to share power with other regional groups. The party constitution was therefore a carefully designed system of patronage. For example, the vice presidency, which was combined with the economics ministry and had enormous power over a large portion of the capital budget, was given to an Ibo. Forrest (1986, p. 8) suggests that "a more appropriate name for the party would have been the Party of National Patronage." The presidency was to rotate among the three major linguistic groups, and at midterm the cabinet was enlarged to 45 with at least two members from each state. The party became a loose amalgam of baronies, each with its personal network.

Usually, a national party elected after a period of increasingly unpopular military rule enjoys a honeymoon period. Unfortunately, the legitimacy of the NPN's accession to power was seriously in doubt. The constitution had carelessly stipulated that the winning presidential candidate must have 25 percent of the vote in two-thirds of the states, although the number of states (19) was not divisible by three. The NPN candidate met this criterion in only 12 states, and so the constitutional ambiguity was whether the attainment of two-thirds of 25 percent of the vote in a thirteenth state would suffice. This vital ambiguity was decided in favor of the NPN by a judicial process that was reasonably perceived as partisan. The losing participants saw the NPN government as having usurped power though a civilian coup d'état. This lack of legitimacy immediately undermined NPN authority and the capacity of its leaders to think beyond personal survival. The perception of illegitimacy was self-fulfilling: in an attempt to secure its position, the party developed close links with the police and relied on them to help rig subsequent elections (Forrest 1986, p. 12).

The combination of a party constitution that effectively guaranteed a regional dispersal of power with the failure to establish enforceable rules of democratic conduct encouraged regional baronies. The barons needed the support of their local police and an entourage, and they looked to national office as the means of financing these requirements. No one had sufficient power independent of patronage obligations to be able to pursue national objectives. President Shagari was thus constrained by the implicit constitution of his party from imposing discipline on the barons. In the midterm cabinet reshuffle, only two ministers were replaced despite evidence of extensive corruption and incompetence.

The federal character of the government also fueled the creation of new states, since every state was entitled to its share of top federal appointments. Even within states, revenue sharing and the federal system operated as forces propelling an increase in the number of local governments. Between 1979 and 1983 their number roughly tripled.

The return to democracy thus represented a massive shift of players away from the small coterie of permanent secretaries and generals who had managed the first oil cycle and who were devoted to national growth through public capital formation. The objective of government became the maximization of its support.[6]

Despite the discontinuity in policy formation generated by the return to democracy, the new president and his advisers were conscious of the failings in the management of the first oil cycle. In his 1980 budget speech the president said, "The mere fact that we are currently experiencing rising crude oil prices should not be taken as a signal for the kind of import liberalization of 1975–77." However, good intentions at the top were no match for bad intentions elsewhere in the political system. Four types of pressure for public expenditure can be distinguished. First, there were direct expropriations made by elected officials in their own favor. Second, there was intense lobbying to break into the distributive network. Third, there was an incentive to generate public contracts, because of their output but also because of the opportunities for corruption. Finally, there was continued desire for the national prestige projects that had characterized the military regime.

It is unusual for elected officials to vote themselves large payments because of the obvious resentment it arouses in the electorate. Nigeria had a network of mass-circulation newspapers that the government was not able to control, which ensured hostile publicity for such payments. Yet this did not inhibit Nigeria's elected officials. The tone was set from the first meetings of the 1979 parliament. The priority of members of parliament was to vote themselves large increases in salary and to divert newly completed public housing from the civil service to their own use. A similar pattern occurred in the states. For example, in Kwara the governor made payments of ₦100,000 each to 42 legislators and awarded himself ₦2 million.

Two possible explanations exist for such behavior. If politicians recognized it as suicidal, they were choosing to snatch short-term gains, perhaps suffering from a collective action problem that it was not in the individual's interest to adopt the standards of behavior that were necessary to keep the NPN in office. More likely, politicians did not recognize that the military would shortly return to power. They therefore made enormous expenditures to win votes in the 1983 election and assumed the electorate would tolerate their behavior. They must have taken for granted the voters' acceptance that the political contest had been largely about which patronage network controlled public expenditure and not primarily about government.

Given that both the national and the NPN constitutions controlled the distribution of expenditures among the states, the easiest way for an area to increase its share of revenue was to divide itself into more states. The proliferation of states was also a natural way of extending patronage: by ensuring the fair geographic dispersal of public expenditure, the constitution in effect protected patronage. President Shagari described state creation as "the single most important desire of most Nigerians," and by 1983 the Senate had authorized 30 requests for new states. There was an analogous increase in the number of local government authorities.

Meanwhile, the mechanisms the constitution provided to reduce patronage rather than direct it were allowed to wither. Perhaps the leading example was the requirement that all public officers declare their assets. Although this was an article of the constitution, the legislature never passed the enabling bill.

The principal momentum behind public expenditure was probably the opportunity it provided for kickbacks on contracts and public employment. For example, the contract for a major dam construction project that the military government had approved for $120 million was renegotiated by the new administration for $600 million, with the difference allegedly distributed among the parties to the contract. The River Basin Development Authority Program provided a clear instance of the priority of rents on contracts over preferences of voters. For example, the Bakalori project incurred costs per irrigated hectare that were apparently 15 times greater than those in similar projects in Côte d'Ivoire. Although displaced peasant farmers staged mass protests in April 1980, the protests were suppressed at the cost of several lives.

There was little centrally determined reallocation of expenditure in the second oil cycle. A few massive national projects inherited from the military government were maintained, the two major ones being the steel mills and the new capital at Abuja. However, these expensive decisions were entirely consistent with the two influences that we have suggested were dominant in this period—the opportunity for patronage and the NPN constitutional imperative of regional evenhandedness. The pressures for public expenditure could be accommodated without a budget deficit only while revenue was rising rapidly. The 1981 budget was expansionary, but more telling was the budget of 1982. By this time the second oil boom had clearly ended, the pumping rate having been sharply reduced after March 1981 in an attempt to defend prices. As a result, the budget had already run into massive deficit during the second half of 1981. Government indebtedness to the financial sector rose from ₦2.3 billion in June 1981 to ₦6.8 billion by February 1982. Yet in the 1982 budget the estimates for current expenditure were almost double their 1981 level. The pressures for continued expenditure growth were evidently overwhelming.

In the absence of a domestic bond market, the decision by default to run a large budget deficit could be financed only by an inflation tax or a payments deficit. However, inflation was perceived as undesirable, and a government task force endorsed the policy of moderating it by means of exchange rate appreciation. The government chose instead to borrow abroad through syndicated loans for specific projects. External debt, which had been $2.7 billion in 1978, was $14.4 billion by the end of 1983. The participants in this scramble for debt included the state governments, which were responsible for $2 billion of this total. After 1979 they had been permitted to borrow abroad on their own behalf. This move is again consistent with our characterization of the NPN government as a consortium of regional baronies. Both state and federal governments displayed the same degree of financial irresponsibility, generated by the free-rider problem that characterizes baronial politics.

By April 1982 a foreign exchange crisis existed, and during the year the final IMF entitlement was drawn. By the end of the year, aggravated by the Mexican debt crisis, Nigeria had become quantity rationed in the world credit market. In just three years the public sector had so inflated expenditure that the country had passed through the phases of revenue surplus, reserve depletion, and foreign borrowing.

The Shagari government—faced with a decline in both federal and state revenues through the automatic revenue-sharing formula in the constitution—was now forced into choices. The budget deficit could be closed (implying a choice between tax increases and expenditure reductions) or financed by inflation, an option rejected earlier. The latter step would require QRs on imports or tariffs (in each case with export subsidies as an optional extra) or devaluation. The choices the government made reflected not just the balance of interests within the government but the near vacuum in national policy formulation and the absence of centralized budgetary planning. During the public revenue bonanza, decisions had not reflected thought-out national objectives, and the same could be expected of the intrinsically more difficult political problems encountered during the second oil slump.

We would expect, for example, that the policy variables that would change in response to a decline in oil revenue would be confined to automatic responses. We would also expect the states to be the first to encounter cash constraints and to curtail expenditure; the federal government would be better able to avoid expenditure cuts through its control of the Central Bank.[7] We would expect, finally, that expenditure would be curtailed only by a random process of failures to pay for contracted purchases, such as defaults on loan repayments, defaults on supplier credits, and delays in paying wages.

This expected response pattern broadly characterizes developments until the end of the civilian government. By late 1981 seven states had defaulted on teachers' wages, and many projects were halted by contractors because of nonpayment. At the federal level, emergency stabilization measures began in April 1982. Planned cuts in expenditure of 40 percent were made across the board with no attempt to prioritize. Revenue was increased through excise duties, and gasoline prices were raised though still kept low. The constraint at the federal level was foreign exchange, and the principal response was the direct control of foreign exchange allocation. Given the fixed exchange rate and the policy nexus, this was the most automatic of the possible responses: foreign exchange became scarce and so it was rationed. Import licenses were restricted, duties were increased, and an import deposit scheme was introduced. When these measures proved insufficient, the payments deficit was financed by the only means available—the involuntary accumulation of trade arrears, which increased during 1983 by $4.7 billion.

Delay did not make adjustment easier, because the legislative and presidential elections were due in August and December of 1983. In January 1983 there was a large extension of import licensing, but the continuing budget deficit was now financed mainly by inflation; bank credit to the public sector grew 50 percent in 1983, and inflation was more than 50 percent. The election increased the need for patronage expenditure just as the previous significant source of funds—kickbacks on public contracts—was in decline. Import licensing provided the required alternative, although this was probably fortuitous. Many imports were channeled through presidential task forces, with some of the profits going into party funds. Licenses were even distributed to the states and then sold by governors. Without reference to the committee supposedly in control of licensing, licenses permitting ₦682 million in imports were issued during 1983. If these licenses are valued at the black market rate prevailing in 1983, the rents on them were worth more than ₦1 billion.

Some attempt was made at policy coordination, because economic decisions were dispersed over three ministries (finance, industries, and commerce), the Central Bank, the Budget Bureau, and the Council of Economic Advisers. The coordinating body, the Economic Stabilization and Implementation Committee, was established within the Office of the President. The committee's report avoided any discussion of the exchange rate (a key issue by 1983). Forrest (1986, p. 15) considers that it was "commissioned to give the impression that something was being done, and that it was never intended that [it] should provide a serious critique of government economic policy."

The Buhari Regime: 1984–85

The civilian regime fell to a military coup in January 1984. Organized by the "Kaduna mafia," which represented Northern concerns, the coup was induced by a convergence of interests and events. First, the principal bulwark of a democratic government, its legitimacy, was forfeited by the Shagari regime, which had used its connections with the police for extensive ballot rigging. The opposition, still a majority of the electorate, did not find the results credible. Second, the government's manifest profligacy had coincided with a decline in private living standards. According to table 5.5, by 1983 per capita private consumption in real terms was almost 15 percent below its 1981 level. In a normal democracy a government presiding over such a fall in living standards would be unlikely to be reelected. The Shagari government succeeded at the polls partly because of rigging and partly because of the tribal-cum-patronage nature of the contest: disaffected electors had nowhere else to go.

A third trigger for the coup was that the NPN constitution required rotation of the presidency after Shagari's second term. The North, which had for the most part controlled the government since independence, was reluctant to forfeit control for what could be 16 years. Finally, there were rumors of an impending junior officer coup. Recall that in January 1966 Nigeria had experienced such a coup by radical populist young officers who themselves did not take power. Since then such coups had become common in other West African states. The basis for radical populism was present, given the sharp decline in the living standards of urban workers and the blatant corruption of the elite. However, it was not in the interests of any of the major contenders for power. The possibility of a radical populist coup encouraged senior officers to stage a preemptive coup as a defensive strategy.

The new Buhari regime was heavily weighted toward the North. The military elite and its allies had all been supporters of the NPN, and the government's stated aims were indistinguishable from those of the second Shagari administration. The Buhari economic policy was to continue the automatic controls that had come into force under Shagari in the absence of policy reform. However, this policy vacuum was disguised by an application of simple military "virtues"—discipline, hardship, and nationalism. The official policy stance of the Buhari government was a "war against indiscipline," but stringency was applied selectively. The balance of payments was to be dealt with by a three-year period of acute austerity when imports would be regulated by QRs (tariffs were actually reduced). Austerity indeed ensued: private per capita consumption fell by almost 10 percent in 1984, with much larger reductions in public expenditure (table 5.5). Nationalism meant the maintenance of the exchange rate, which in turn meant no deal with the IMF. (The IMF had become such a bête noire that the government may have maintained the exchange rate to avoid dealing with the organization.)

The maintenance of the exchange rate and its corollary of import licensing suited both the small group who acquired the licenses and the much larger group—broadly the urban middle classes—who benefited from cheap imports. During civilian rule (1979–83) capital flight had amounted to ₦18 billion (Ogunsanwo 1986, p. 2). This illegally held wealth was evidence of illegally earned income, of which the largest source had probably been rents on government contracts. As the Lockheed investigation in 1976 showed, such rents were not new but probably increased greatly under the civilian government. However, the decline in oil revenue during the Buhari period probably induced a switch from rents on government contracts (which, as we have seen, were massively reduced) to rents on trade, which was becoming more restricted. Trade rents had begun in the civilian period but were confined largely to food. The task force that had the monopoly on rice imports during 1983 incurred a landed cost of ₦14 per bag, whereas the retail price was ₦120 to ₦150. Some of the rents had allegedly financed the election campaign of the NPN. However, from 1984 until the devaluation of 1986, overvaluation was so severe that it presumably became the locus for rents.

Finally, in keeping with its penchant for quantitative regulation, the government introduced price controls on a limited range of items. These controls were, however, enforced only ex-factory, not at the retail level. The data show that at the retail level, goods subject to ex-factory price controls experienced, if anything, more rapid price increases than unregulated goods, so the benefits of these controls accrued entirely to those able to make purchases at ex-factory prices.

The Price Intelligence Unit (PIU), which administered ex-factory price controls, identified for us eight items for which it believed such controls had been effective. The staff of the PIU claimed that the controls were largely a facade and that not a single firm had ever been prosecuted under price control legislation. The PIU had difficulty getting firms to comply with its information requirements, and the unit had no desire to penalize firms that did provide price information by requiring them to set lower prices.

The unit did not regulate retail prices, and the staff believed that, except in rare cases (cars and cement), ex-factory price controls had no effect on retail prices but merely on distribution margins. The staff claimed that in several instances the managers of firms lobbied for the imposition of low ex-factory prices on their products, since this increased the rents in distribution and provided an opportunity for the managers to acquire some of these rents. Fortunately, seven of the eight items were covered by the CPI, and by using the raw price observations, an index could be constructed for price-controlled items. Table 5.15 compares the prices of these items with those for importables (also indexed from raw price observations). Until the onset of controls in 1984, the group of subsequently controlled products tracked the price index for importables very closely. However, by July 1986 the relative price of controlled products appears to have risen by 12 percent since the immediate precontrol year of 1983.[8]

The one exception to this failure of price controls was the retail price of cars, for which the ex-factory price was enforced. To a considerable extent, the consumer of the locally produced Beetle, typically a car for a middle-rank civil servant, was the constituency the Buhari regime saw as its own. For example, despite severe retrenchments in the private sector, there was only negligible civil service retrenchment during the Buhari period.

In addition to defending this constituency, the Buhari regime attempted to secure its power by constructing the apparatus of a police state. The secret police, the National Security Commission, was expanded rapidly and used to intimidate and scrutinize military officers as well as opponents of the regime. Strikes were banned, a wage freeze was imposed, and trade union influence much reduced. The press was regulated and journalists imprisoned. Yet the leading politicians of the Shagari regime, especially those from the North, were treated with considerable leniency. The Buhari regime was thus perceived as regionally partisan and nakedly nonparticipatory in a way that had not been true of the previous military regime. Recall that during 1966–79 the military had been desperate to avoid the appearance of rule by the gun.

Table 5.15 Price Indexes for Price-Controlled Manufactures and Importables
(1980 = 100)

Year	Price-controlled items[a]	Importables	Relative price of controlled items
1980	100	100	100
1981	—	113	—
1982	117	121	97
1983	164	161	102
1984	234	238	98
1985	—	255	—
January 1986	284	274	104
July 1986	340	298[b]	114

— Not available.

a. Evaporated milk, Omo detergent, Elephant cement, Star beer, Fanta orange soda, Volkswagen car ("Beetle"), and tires.

b. June.

Source: Calculations based on unpublished Bureau of Statistics data.

The Babangida Regime

The overthrow of the Buhari regime by an internal army coup in July 1985 continued the downward spiral into political illegitimacy that became even more acute during the first half of the 1990s. However, in economic terms the coup was initially the most successful regime change in Nigeria's history. The Babangida regime palpably had no mandate to replace the Buhari regime and could not accuse its predecessors of corruption without implicating its own members. To justify its existence it had to return to the participatory style and temporary custodial role of the 1966–79 military regimes.

The first attempt at this, a national debate intended to reach agreement on a deal with the IMF, was a near disaster. The regime sought to avoid responsibility for an agreement while clearly seeing it as desirable, but failed to orchestrate a media campaign. As a result, the media were inundated by massive opposition to the deal: critics associated the IMF with the austerity that inevitably followed the fall in income, many feared the surrender of sovereignty and status, and some were hostile to international capitalism. The government lost the debate by default during the autumn of 1985. However, the need for an agreement was heightened by the collapse of the oil price in January 1986.

At this juncture the government took political and economic action. To protect itself politically, it announced a timetable (which it did not adhere to) for the return to civilian rule, and it created a commission of nonmilitary advisers to oversee the transition. As in 1975, these measures reduced the tension associated with illegitimacy by declaring the government temporary. However, if military rule was not to be permanent, what was its purpose? The 1975–79 regime had justified its temporary existence in terms of the design of a workable constitution. Shorn of this, the Babangida regime had little option but to claim as its role the management of an emergency economic transition, which implied some economic policy initiative.

One initiative was the introduction of substantial fiscal retrenchments. The government also started to depreciate the exchange rate below the psychological threshold of parity with the dollar. This, though by itself an inadequate response, at least signaled to the population that a time of enforced policy changes had arrived. The government also invited the World Bank to draw up an adjustment program that was then submitted for IMF approval. The IMF offered a loan as part of this program, which for form's sake the government declined. The key elements in the program were the floating of the exchange rate, trade liberalization, and fiscal and monetary stringency. Upon floating, the exchange rate initially fell from ₦1.27 per dollar to ₦4.60, which indicates the magnitude of the policy change.

The devaluation changed relative prices rather than the price level: the postdevaluation inflation rate was one of the lowest in Nigeria's history. The most marked increase in prices was for previously controlled consumer luxuries such as cars and airline tickets. The sharp increase in the price of cars became a rallying cry for the elite. Air travel had also become a significant component of the elite lifestyle. Such travel had been at least self-financing through the capacity to import at the official exchange rate. After the devaluation, air travel dropped by 80 percent.

The devaluation provoked protests from other interest groups. Import-substituting manufacturing firms, many of which could not survive trade liberalization at any exchange rate because they were operating at low or zero value added at world prices, responded by retrenching workers. They had already suffered prolonged decline caused by shortages of imported inputs, and the devaluation merely replaced this constraint with a demand constraint. Other firms, however, were net beneficiaries. Therefore, there was no sharp break in manufacturing performance overall, and the government could console itself with some evidence of expansion.

Another interest group, the North, had little to gain from the devaluation because the remaining tradable crops were grown elsewhere. Furthermore, the North had lost power with the Babangida coup and a failed countercoup, and its capacity to influence policy—previously considerable—was now limited. As for the civil service, it suffered relatively little. As shown in chapter 7, public employees were dramatically better protected from layoffs during the slump than other workers, and since the net impact of the devaluation and liberalization was scarcely inflationary, their real incomes were also largely protected. Public sector workers in the state corporations were, however, threatened by privatization. The marketing boards were abolished, costing employees their jobs.

The changes of mid-1986 were by far the most substantial and abrupt shift in Nigeria's economic policy since 1950. Other than the high rate of public investment during the first oil cycle, the reforms were perhaps the only large, conscious intervention motivated by a perception of national economic benefit. The change was feasible because key interest groups were either weakened or protected, the fall in the oil price created a sense of immediate crisis requiring urgent action, the government had the precedent and little choice but to adopt publicly the role of temporary economic reformer, and there was an awareness that the oil windfall had been a missed opportunity. Unfortunately, these conditions were largely temporary. Offsetting them was the continued decline in private per capita consumption because of the collapse in the oil price and the need for debt repayment. The synchronization of the economic shock and liberalization by a government perceived as illegitimate tempted the government's many opponents to blame the policy change, and hence the government, for the decline in consumption.

The government itself was, at best, ambiguous toward liberalization. The Northern interest groups that reasserted themselves to prevent the transition to democracy had the same fundamental reasons to be hostile to a liberalized economy as during the first oil boom: the North was educationally backward and would lose the commercial race on a level playing field. And whereas during the boom the increase in food prices caused by the general equilibrium effects of Dutch disease had benefited the Northern constituency, during the slump this went into reverse. Household budget survey evidence, discussed in the next chapter, shows that during the liberalization there was a powerful redistribution of income from Northern to Southern households. Thus, while the opposition was hostile to liberalization because it chose to misinterpret the causes of consumption decline, the government had its own reasons to regret its policy and to reverse it.

6 Economic Growth and Living Standards: 1950–92

In this chapter we review the evidence on Nigerian living standards and economic growth from 1950 to 1992. For much of the period the data are inadequate, but a few remarkable findings are reasonably secure.

Living Standards, Poverty, and Inequality

The data base from which to construct long-term trends in the level and distribution of living standards is unusually inadequate for Nigeria. Although there are a large number of village studies, the first national survey from which a distribution can be calculated is for 1992. As a result, many pertinent questions are unanswerable, and the inferences we draw are little more than speculation. Our key conclusions can be summarized as follows:

- Mean private consumption was lower by the mid-1980s than in the early 1950s, by around 30 percent. This did not reflect a steady negative trend but rather two distinct phases: mean living standards rose around 1.5 percent a year before the mid-1970s and then over the subsequent decade declined by around 7 percent a year. During the aborted liberalization of the late 1980s and early 1990s, living standards again rose rapidly and the incidence of poverty declined.
- The distribution of income among social groups fluctuated over the period. The North gained relative to other regions during the 1950s but lost during the liberalization of the late 1980s. Cities were better-off than rural areas for most of the period, but this favorable situation was eroded and possibly reversed during the 1980s. Within the cities wage earners enjoyed higher incomes than the self-employed, but this differential was eroding during the 1980s. In the rural areas the evidence on long-term trends in inequality is mixed. There is some indication that landownership was becoming more concentrated, but the increase in food prices relative to cocoa prices from the mid-1960s to

the mid-1980s must have reduced two major inequalities: in the 1950s cocoa farmers were better-off than food farmers, and cocoa income was more highly concentrated than other income components.

In this section we discuss trends in mean private consumption, present snapshots of the incidence of poverty, and describe patterns and trends in inequality among significant social groups.

Long-Term Trends in Mean Per Capita Private Consumption

Until 1980/81 there was no published national household budget survey from which either incomes or expenditures could be estimated. The scope for constructing estimates of long-term trends in living standards is therefore severely limited. Collier (1983) compares the results of the many village studies, but any temporal inferences from such a data set are highly precarious. In table 6.1 we use a series of urban and regional surveys to provide an approximate guide to changes in living standards. A good baseline is provided by surveys of Lagos in 1953 and the rural Western Region in 1951/52. From 1953 onward there is a CPI (based on Lagos prices) that serves as a deflator for subsequent observations. The Lagos survey was repeated in 1959/60, 1979, and 1980/81. The latter two surveys covered all urban areas, although Lagos was reported separately. Surveys for 1974/75, 1978, 1981/82, and annually thereafter report data for all urban areas without usually breaking out Lagos. As a result, we have two chains of data on urban income—one for Lagos and the other for all urban areas. These are linked using the 1980/81 survey, on the assumption that the changes in Lagos incomes are representative of the changes in average urban incomes in the period before 1980.

The rural series rests on point observations of the Western Region in 1951 and 1965 and national (rural) observations in 1963, 1974/75, 1980/81, and annually thereafter. For 1963 and 1980/81 the data can be broken down by region. Whereas for the urban series a common concept of income could be used, for the rural series there were compelling reasons to adopt expenditure rather than income as our measure of living standards. Some of the surveys reported only expenditure, and income fluctuations with associated high variations in savings rates make expenditure a better guide to permanent income; the authors of the 1951/52 survey note this point particularly. The expenditure data include subsistence consumption and are for a consistent set of items, as far as can be discerned.

The urban and rural series are linked through a comparison of per capita expenditure in 1983/84, obtained from the most thorough published national survey data. However, no allowance is made for differences in rural and urban price levels. As of that year, the urban cost of living would have needed to be 55 percent higher than the rural cost of living for living standards to be equal—a not unlikely differential.

Table 6.1 Urban and Rural Living Standards, 1950–85

Year	Urban	Rural	All[a]	Year	Urban	Rural	All[a]
1950/51	—	—	100	1968/69	—	—	84
1951/52	—	104*[b]	104	1969/70	—	—	86
1952/53	—	—	108	1970/71	—	—	94
1953/54	104[c]	—	108	1971/72	—	—	—
1954/55	—	—	113	1972/73	—	—	—
1955/56	—	—	114	1973/74	—	—	120
1956/57	—	—	110	1974/75	135[g]	144[h]	146
1957/58	—	—	110	1975/76	—	—	140
1958/59	—	—	109	1976/77	—	—	133
1959/60	103[d]	—	106	1977/78	—	—	124
1960/61	—	—	114	1978/79	125[i]	—	133
1961/62	—	—	108	1979/80	113[j]	130[k]	127
1962/63	—	—	114	1980/81	107[l]	104[m]	141
1963/64	—	125*[e]	115	1981/82	92[n]	104[n]	133
1964/65	—	—	115	1982/83	83[n]	98[n]	135
1965/66	—	146*[f]	105	1983/84	70[n]	87[n]	106
1966/67			104	1984/85	52[l]	73[o]	73
1967/68	—	—	88				

— Not available.

* Denotes observations for the rural Western Region only. This series is spliced with that for all rural areas using data for 1980/81, which provides data for both the Western Region and all rural areas.

Note: Data are index values for real per capita income or expenditure as specified below. The first observation in each of the rural and urban series serves as the base, but instead of being set to 100, it is set to the national accounts index number for that year.

a. Whereas the other series are derived from budget surveys, this is derived from the national accounts series on private consumption at current market prices. The sources for this series are Stolper 1966, table 2, for 1950–58; World Bank 1974, table 11, for 1958–70; and FOS, *Statistical Abstract 1985*, table 11.5, for 1973–84. The Stolper series is in constant prices; the others are deflated by the CPI. To get the data onto a per capita basis, a population growth rate of 3 percent a year has been assumed. The 1952/53 census estimated the population at 30.4 million; the Centre for Population Studies at the University of Ibadan regarded this as an underestimate of 11.7 percent and put the population at 34 million. The Centre estimated the mid-1962 population as 45.3 million, implying a 3 percent growth rate for the period. This is also a reasonable figure for the more recent period (see Collier 1986 for a discussion).

b. Derived from Galletti, Baldwin, and Dina 1956. Expenditure per household per year on all goods and services is reported as £134. Expenditure (including for subsistence) is used rather than income because with unusually high cocoa prices, transient income was positive. Galletti, Baldwin, and Dina noted an unusually high savings rate but considered expenditure to be normal. Household size can be deduced as 8.63. There is no CPI between the date of the survey, 1951/52, and the start of the Lagos CPI in 1953. We assume constant prices despite the modest inflation rate subsequent to 1953, because Galletti, Baldwin, and Dina reported that certain nonfood consumer goods were still falling in price as a result of postwar trade recovery.

c. From a consumer budget survey of Lagos households, as reported in Nigeria 1963. An income concept is used, which can be replicated for all the other urban surveys.

d. From a consumer budget survey of Lagos households, as reported in Nigeria 1963.

e. From FOS, *Rural Economic Survey of Nigeria 1963/64: Rural Consumption Enquiry Food Items.* This survey covered only expenditure on food items. The regional comparison is made on a per capita basis.

f. FOS 1966. This survey included all items of expenditure. It is linked to the 1963/64 observation for the Western Region by a comparison of food and drink expenditure deflated by the CPI.

g. From an unpublished national household budget survey, derived from ILO 1982, tables TP3.1 and 3.3. For all urban areas, the concept of "total income" is comparable with the 1980/81 concept of total income and so linked from that year.

h. From an unpublished national household budget survey, derived from ILO 1981, tables TP3.1 and 3.3. The expenditure concept is comparable with the 1980/81 rural survey. No household size was given, so it is assumed to be the same as in 1980/81.

i. From a household budget survey in all urban areas, comparable to FOS, *Report of Urban Household Surveys 1979,* and cited therein (p. 14); FOS, *Report of Urban Household Surveys 1982.*

j. Same source as (i).

k. From FOS, *General Household Survey 1980/81,* tables 3.5a and 3.5b. These tables give per capita income in 1979/80 and 1980/81. The comparison is then chained to the 1980/81 observation.

l. From FOS, *Report of National Consumer Survey 1983,* table 15A. This report provides data both for Lagos, from which comparisons with 1960 and 1953 are made, and for all urban areas, from which comparisons with 1978, 1979, and subsequent years are made.

m. From FOS, *Report of National Consumer Survey 1983,* table 11B. However, because the household sizes reported there are clearly erroneous, household sizes were taken from FOS, *General Household Survey 1980/81,* appendix table 1A, which was based on the same sample of households. Since state-level expenditure data were reported, the weighted regional average data were derivable. The expenditure per capita for the Western Region was then compared with the 1965/66 observation.

n. FOS, *Report of National Consumer Survey 1981–84,* gives total household income data that are comparable with the income concept reported in (i) for 1980/81. This series was then used for both rural and urban households. Household size for 1983/84 is taken from the *General Household Survey* for that year and applied to each of these years. The 1983/84 expenditure per capita data are used to link urban and rural living standards, though no allowance is made for differences in the cost of living.

o. Unpublished FOS data.

Table 6.1 suggests that between the early 1950s and the mid-1980s both urban and rural living standards declined substantially. Urban living standards are shown as falling slightly during the 1950s. This is, however, a compositional effect: households headed by laborers, artisans, and clerks all experienced increases in real income, but the proportion of laborers increased relative to the others. There are no further data until 1974/75, when urban real income peaks because of the Udoji award, though it is not massively higher than in 1953. From then on, the decline is rapid and substantial until 1985.

Rural income (or expenditure) shows growth in real terms between 1951 and both 1963 and 1965. The data suggest annual per capita growth of 2.5 percent from 1951 to 1965 and 1.6 percent between 1951 and 1963. However, the evidence is confined to the Western Region—the cocoa belt. Since 1951 was a relatively good year for cocoa prices, the most likely bias in the survey's estimate of income is upward, and thus the likely bias in growth rates is downward. The next observation of rural income is not until 1974/75. Although there is only a national figure, the implication is that rural income stagnated starting from the mid-1960s, although it was still above its 1951 level. Between 1974/75 and 1980/81, income fell at an annualized rate of 5.2 percent. This is consistent with the Dutch disease general equilibrium effect discussed in chapter 4, whereby export agriculture contracted. By 1980/81, income in the Western Region had reverted to its 1951 level, implying a decline of 2.2 percent a year after 1965. From 1980/81 until the mid-1980s, rural income declined at an annual rate of 8.5 percent—still less than the decline experienced in urban areas.

As for urban per capita income, at the start of the period (1950) it was 56 percent above rural income, without allowance for differences in the cost of living. By the end of the period (1985) it was 37 percent higher.

The "All" column of table 6.1 matches the previously mentioned household budget survey data with national accounts estimates of per capita private consumption. As discussed in note *a* of the table, this requires an assumption about the rate of population growth. There are two large discrepancies between the data sources. In the mid-1960s two rural surveys suggest that expenditure rose substantially more than implied by the national accounts. For 1979–81 the surveys suggest a decline, but the national accounts indicate an increase. The former discrepancy is not critical, since both sources show a significant increase in living standards between the early 1950s and the mid-1960s. The latter discrepancy is probably more likely to lie in the survey comparisons. Other than these discrepancies, the two series are in broad agreement. In particular, the national accounts data support the key result that by the end of our period per capita private consumption was substantially below its level at the start of the period. Both series also suggest that living standards rose from the start of the period to a peak around the mid-1970s, and that this was succeeded by a decade of decline despite massive oil revenues. However, the national accounts data imply a significantly smaller fall in living standards than do the budget surveys.

For the final period of aborted liberalization, the provisional national accounts agree closely with new data from the household survey. A comparison of National Integrated Survey of Households (NISH) data for 1985/86 and 1992/93 shows an increase in real per capita expenditure of 26 percent. The (provisional) national accounts for 1992, when compared with those for 1986, show a 25 percent rise in per capita private expenditure at constant prices.[1] For the liberalization phase, therefore, we can say with some reliability that living standards were at last rising strongly.

Changes in Poverty

The data series of table 6.1 are already somewhat ambitious, even though they are confined to sample means of budget surveys. However, for distinct statements about poverty we would need the frequency distributions around these means. Unfortunately, distributions are not available on a comparable basis prior to 1981. The Galletti survey of 1952/53 (Galletti, Baldwin, and Dina 1956) reports in appendixes its raw data for the 187 surveyed households, and we have used these data to generate a distribution of per capita income. Although this is of some interest, it is not comparable with later surveys. An alternative source on the trend in absolute poverty is the per capita consumption of calories. Although we have data only on mean consumption, because the income elasticity of demand for food is low, its consumption will be more equally distributed than for other items. Therefore, the mean gives some guide to the food consumption of the poor. Galletti, Baldwin, and Dina (1956) found per capita rural calorie intake of 2,559 per day in 1952/53 (derived from table 110). At the peak of the second oil boom, 1979–81, the Food and Agriculture Organization (FAO) estimated that per capita calorie intake averaged 2,378 nationally. Both these figures were well above the 2,080 that the World Health Organization (WHO) suggests is required for adequate health, but the decline is consistent with the hypothesis that the incidence of poverty increased.

Stewart (1985) reviews other survey evidence on nutrition and concludes that "the national estimates do not suggest any trend over time . . . [and that the evidence] from micro-nutrition studies, from hospitals and from the impression of well-informed observers is that the food

Table 6.2 Regional Inequality, Selected Years

Item and year	West	East	North
Urban and rural nonfood expenditure			
Nigerian pounds per capita per			
year at 1957 prices			
1950	8.95	4.18	2.26
1957	14.84	7.13	4.07
Normalized on the North			
1950	396	185	100
1957	365	175	100
Rural food and drink consumption			
Naira per capita per year			
1963/64	120	97	100
1980/81	143	128	100
Percentage change from			
1963/64 to 1980/81	19	32	0
Urban per capita income			
Naira per month			
1979	38.9	37.9	28.7
1980/81	39.4	37.7	29.2
1981/82	34.2	30.8	43.8
1982/83	45.4	49.1	41.4
1983/84	43.2	30.7	51.4
Normalized on the North			
1979	134	132	100
1980/81	135	133	100
1981/82	78	70	100
1982/83	110	119	100
1983/84	84	60	100
Rural per capita income			
Naira per month			
1980/81	23.0	19.7	16.2
1981/82	24.7	21.7	12.9
1982/83	29.0	13.3	14.0
1983/84	29.5	23.6	14.4
Normalized on the North			
1980/81	142	122	100
1981/82	191	168	100
1982/83	207	95	100
1983/84	205	164	100

Source: For urban and rural nonfood expenditure, Okigbo 1960, table IX.2, and 1952 census, with no allowance for population growth. For rural food and

and nutrition situation has not improved over time" (p. 119). Four micro studies found the incidence of severe malnutrition among children to be 1.6 percent (rural North), 7.6 percent (remote rural North), 4.0 percent (rural East), and 3.5 to 18.8 percent (the districts of Lagos). Only for the period 1985/86 to 1992/93 is there a basis for estimates of changes in poverty. This period is, however, of some interest in that it was the time of the abortive liberalization during the oil crash.

Inequality among Social Groups

The lack of frequency distributions makes summary measures of distributions, such as the Gini coefficient, infeasible as indicators of inequality. Nor would such a measure, even if available, reflect satisfactorily how distributional issues have mattered in Nigerian society. The most significant inequality observed has been interregional (or its close correlate, interethnic) inequality. Table 6.2 assembles data on the level of and changes in regional inequality. The administrative regions of Nigeria have, of course, changed substantially over time, from 3 to 19 states. The table retains the original three-state aggregation.

For the 1950s our only source is the national accounts as regionalized by Okigbo (1962). This suggests that the North, although the poorest region, was gaining relatively during the period. Although regional accounts were not maintained, budget survey snapshots that can be reaggregated on a regional basis are available after 1962. The first national survey of 1963 published data only for rural food and drink consumption. This can, however, be compared with the same data for 1980/81. This confirms Okigbo's finding that the West was the richest region in per capita terms, with the North the poorest, and suggests that the North-South divide widened during the 1960s and 1970s despite the political dominance of the North. The latter's growing economic inferiority may have been at the root of the reluctance of the Northern elite to rely upon market mechanisms or to relinquish control over the distribution of oil revenue.

Additional information comes from a comparison of village surveys. There have been a substantial number of such surveys dating back to 1930. Because the surveyed villages differ, as do survey methodologies, differences in income cannot be attributed solely to differences in sur-

---

drink consumption, 1963/64 data from FOS, *Rural Economic Survey of Nigeria 1963/64: Rural Consumption Enquiry Food Items*, table 1; 1980/81 data from FOS, *Report of National Consumer Survey 1980/81*, table 11B, using household data from FOS, *General Household Survey 1980/81*, appendix table 2A. For urban and rural per capita incomes, data are derived from FOS, *General Household Survey* (various years), using the 1980/81 survey weights by state.

vey dates, and so comparisons may be of no value. With this proviso, the 11 studies of cocoa farmers suggest that real household income declined substantially over time. Fitting a time trend to the data cited by Collier (1983) yields a significant negative trend for the log of real household income: –2.3 percent a year from 1930 to 1974. When all those studies conducted outside the cocoa belt are pooled, there is a significant positive trend of 1.9 percent a year. Experimentation with disaggregation of this group into smaller groups of contiguous states by means of dummy variables failed to identify any significant differences. The results are:

$$\ln Yc = 5.95 - 0.023t$$
$$(0.68) \ (0.010)$$
$$[8.71] \ [2.24]$$

$$r^2 = 0.31, DW = 1.42, F = 5.05$$

$$\ln Yf = 3.12 + 0.019t$$
$$(0.52) \ (0.008)$$
$$[6.04] \ [2.33]$$

$$r^2 = 0.14, DW = 2.19, F = 5.43$$

where Yc = log of cocoa farmers' income and Yf = log of food farmers' income.

After 1978, data exist to construct an annual series for urban areas, and from 1980 the same applies for rural areas. During 1979–1983/84 Northern cities were the most favorably placed group, and Northern rural areas were the least favored. The success of the Northern cities in that period coincides with the interval of civilian rule under the NPN, a party dominated by Northern city interests. The rural North suffered from less rain than normal during this period, although relative prices were, if anything, moving in favor of its net export—grains. For the liberalization period 1985/86–1992/93, NISH surveys can be compared, although data are only available for a different regional grouping North, Middle, and South. In 1985/86, per capita mean expenditure in the Northern and Middle belts was virtually the same, and 20 percent below that in the South. By 1992/93 there had been no change in the North, whereas the Middle and the South had increased expenditure by 30 percent. Thus regional inequality increased during liberalization, with the already more prosperous South gaining compared with the North.

A second important inequality, touched on above, is between rural and urban areas. Unfortunately, there is no estimate of rural-urban differences in the cost of living, although we know that foods are cheaper and manufactured goods dearer in the countryside. The nominal differential is shown in table 6.3. It appears that between 1950 and 1980 there was a considerable differential in favor of urban residents, but this was massively eroded during the 1980s. It seems likely that by the end of our period, allowing for cost of living differences, the differential had been reversed.

This important change is discussed in our analysis of the labor market during the oil slump (chapter 7). Several commentators have attempted to measure rural-urban differentials from assignments of GDP components. Jamal (1985, table 5) summarizes 10 estimates that range between 170 and 460 percent for various dates between 1960/61 and 1977/78. However, it would be unwarranted to interpret differences between estimates as indicating changes over time, and all the estimates portray greater inequality than implied by table 6.3 (once allowance is made for cost of living differences).

Intraregional rural inequality is probably best approached through the village studies. Table 6.4 summarizes such information for food and cocoa farmers, showing the distribution of income and expenditure on a per capita and household basis. This range is unfortunately necessary because of differences among studies. By recomputing the original data for cocoa farmers in the Galletti survey, we are able to present all four distributions for this survey. The first point to note from table 6.4 is that the extent of inequality is acutely sensitive to the measure used. The measure that most

Table 6.3 Rural and Urban Per Capita Expenditure Differential, Selected Years

Year	Expenditure (naira)		Differential (rural=100)
	Rural	Urban	
1952–54	—	—	181
1974/75	—	—	163
1979/80	—	—	151
1980/81	22.45	40.18	179
1981/82	26.71	40.18	150
1982/83	27.83	40.98	147
1983/84	31.43	43.80	139
1984/85	36.14	43.80	121
1985/86	39.51	47.41	120
1992/93	—	—	113

— Not available.

Source: 1980–1986 data from FOS, *Report of National Consumer Survey* (various years). Since these do not report household size, data from FOS, *General Household Survey 1980,* were adopted. For pre-1980 data the 1980/81 figures are scaled back according to the data of table 6.1. For example, the implicit rural per capita expenditure for 1974/75 is (135/107) × 22.45.

closely corresponds to living standards—per capita expenditure—shows a far more equal distribution than the more commonly used household income. Second, on virtually all the measures, there is more inequality among cocoa farmers than among food farmers. Third, rural inequality is not considerable. The average differential between the bottom quintile and the top decile in per capita expenditure is only 1:4, even among cocoa farmers, and must be substantially less among food farmers.

The trend in rural inequality is largely unresearchable, for there are too few snapshots of distributions of income or expenditure. The only related variable whose distribution has commonly been measured is land, the major rural asset. Collier (1983) compared the distribution of land among food farmers identified in the village studies. He found that the land share of the bottom 40 percent of households decreased significantly both over time and with higher population density. Conversely, the land share of the top 10 percent of households increased. This may indicate that inequality in rural areas has been increasing among food farmers, but any such inference must be highly tentative.

From 1980/81 onward we can use the NISH surveys to construct a limited time series on broad socioeconomic groups (table 6.5). Finally, for 1992 there is at last a household survey from which a national distribution of expenditure over persons can be constructed. This is presented in table 6.6.

Our conclusions on poverty and equity outcomes must necessarily be tentative. Private living standards rose about 1.5 percent a year from the

Table 6.4 Intrarural Inequalities
(percent)

Category and group	Share of bottom 20 percent	Share of bottom 40 percent	Share of top 10 percent
Per capita expenditure			
Cocoa farmers	10.22	23.96	20.44
Household income			
Cocoa farmers	5.03	14.66	36.44
Food farmers	—	20.62	23.50
Household expenditure			
Cocoa farmers	6.93	18.23	26.79
Food farmers	—	18.50	33.50
Per capita income			
Cocoa farmers	6.22	17.31	32.38
Food farmers	—	21.75	19.75

Source: For cocoa farmers, recomputations of data collected by Galletti, Baldwin, and Dina 1956; for food farmers, 17-village survey reported in Collier 1983, table 70.

Table 6.5 Real Household Income by Socioeconomic Group, 1980–86
(rural self-employed in 1980/81 = 100)

	Rural			Urban		
Year	*Self-employed*	*Wage earners*	*All*	*Self-employed*	*Wage earners*	*All*
1980/81	100	178	105	150	203	166
1981/82	103	160	107	124	177	142
1982/83	95	147	99	106	164	129
1983/84	86	135	89	94	140	109
1984/85	73	92	74	69	101	80
1985/86	74	95	84	69	101	80

Source: NISH surveys and consumer price index.

early 1950s to the mid-1970s. During the decade of the oil slump they fell about 7 percent a year, and by the late 1980s they were some 30 percent lower than at the start of our period. Given this decline in mean consumption, it is probable that the incidence of poverty rose. The pattern of inequality among social groups has shown long cycles. The North first gained and then lost relative to the other regions. Urban-rural differentials probably emerged during the 1940s and 1950s and were eroded during the 1980s, as were differentials between wage earners and the self-employed. Within the rural economy, cocoa farmers, who became the richest group in the first half of the century, fared worst. This pattern cannot be reduced to a statement that inequality in the aggregate increased or declined. The snapshot for 1992 shows inequality greater than that in Ghana, a country that remained dependent upon cocoa, but similar to that in Zambia, another natural resource economy.

Growth Outcomes

Twenty years after Helleiner (1966) wrote that "Nigerian national accounts in recent years are clearly in a state of mild disarray," his understatement still applies. To examine growth outcomes we use data from the national accounts, but they must be considered extremely fragile.

Table 6.6 Distribution of Expenditure over Population, 1992

Income group	*Share of expenditure*
Lowest quintile	5.1
Second quintile	10.1
Third quintile	14.8
Fourth quintile	21.0
Fifth quintile	49.0
Top decile	34.2

Source: World Bank 1995, table 30, based on NISH survey, 1992.

Table 6.7 GDP and Investment, 1950–90
(1950/51 = 100)

Year	GDP in aggregate	GDP in agriculture	GDP in manufacturing	Investment
1950/51	100.0	100.0	100.0	—
1951/52	107.5	108.2	100.5	—
1952/53	115.2	109.9	110.1	—
1953/54	117.9	114.0	112.7	—
1954/55	126.6	120.0	120.1	—
1955/56	129.9	123.0	124.9	—
1956/57	126.9	118.7	141.3	—
1957/58	132.1	121.5	146.0	132.1
1958/59	130.6	133.3	229.6	154.6
1959/60	136.3	131.8	254.5	154.6
1960/61	142.4	137.6	279.9	170.5
1961/62	147.2	140.2	292.6	166.8
1962/63	155.6	149.2	303.7	186.3
1963/64	170.2	161.8	387.7	186.3
1964/65	177.5	161.2	412.8	239.9
1965/66	189.5	162.2	504.0	280.1
1966/67	183.4	147.3	506.3	263.4
1967/68	154.9	126.4	433.3	221.2
1968/69	153.2	124.6	475.9	193.9
1969/70	194.3	142.5	599.8	223.1
1970/71	254.1	175.8	725.2	330.4
1971/72	284.0	184.8	702.4	456.8
1972/73	294.7	173.3	868.9	545.9
1973/74	320.0	167.1	1,078.4	545.9
1974/75	357.1	184.4	1,042.6	530.1
1975/76	346.4	165.3	1,289.1	774.4
1976/77	384.1	162.7	1,589.9	1,083.4
1977	398.1	168.2	1,639.3	1,151.0
1978	374.6	153.7	2,807.5	832.9
1979	400.5	149.0	4,462.8	728.4
1980	408.0	156.5	5,797.7	828.0
1981	375.3	130.6	9,199.8	837.9
1982	371.9	134.2	10,039.5	701.9
1983	346.8	133.6	6,940.0	532.6
1984	331.3	127.0	5,062.9	404.9
1985	360.6	148.2	5,248.2	328.5
1986	367.4	162.2	5,124.7	338.5
1987	364.7	157.0	6,109.5	265.0
1988	400.9	172.2	7,004.8	265.5
1989	426.8	180.7	6,390.5	305.1
1990	449.0	187.9	6,331.8	351.6

— Not available.

Note: The constant prices series were chained using prices of 1957/58, 1962/

Table 6.7 provides a series on GDP, 1950 to 1990, and investment, 1957 to 1990. GDP grew in three broad phases. From 1950 until 1977 growth was sustained with a brief interruption during the civil war. From 1977 until 1987 there was a fairly continuous decline of nearly 10 percent overall, representing a severe loss in per capita output. Finally, from 1987 until 1990 growth was rapid. Investment follows the same path but with much greater changes between phases. From 1958 to 1977 investment rose as a share of GDP (at constant prices), whereas from 1977 to 1987 it collapsed. Estimates of the capital stock, based on an assumption of 10 percent depreciation, suggest that investment peaked relative to GDP in 1981.

The GDP series is extraordinary in that an absolute decline in output begins well before the second oil boom and persists through it, with the nadir reached in 1987. Growth then resumes and is rapid. Within GDP, agriculture reached an absolute peak in 1971/72, which was not regained until 1990, with a phase of decline lasting until 1984. This path of agricultural decline and recovery is most obviously explicable in terms of Dutch disease. Manufacturing, which is the more obviously tradable activity in the absence of policy-induced restrictions, followed a different path. It reached a peak in 1982 and thereupon collapsed; it was still nearly 40 percent below that peak in 1990. Evidently, during the oil boom not only was manufacturing heavily assisted by the government, but much manufacturing activity proved unsustainable. To the extent that the oil revenue was not wasted on unproductive investment, it was wasted on subsidizing unsustainable output.

Investment reached a peak in 1977, and by the late 1980s it had fallen to the levels of the mid-1960s. The Nigerian statistics are of little help in studying investment in detail; a sectoral breakdown of investment, for example, is not available. Investment totals are, however, disaggregated by type of asset, which gives at least some indication of the composition of investment. These data are shown in table 6.8. We use three aggregates: building and construction (which includes housing, nonresidential buildings, road building, and dams, for example); a rough proxy for

---

63, 1977/78, and 1987. The three Eastern states are excluded for 1967/68–1969/70. There is a break in the series for manufacturing between 1957/58 and 1958/59. The investment series is scaled so as to be the same as the GDP index in the first year for which it is available. There are breaks in 1963 and 1973, when the series is assumed to be the same as in the previous year.

Source: For 1950–62, Helleiner 1966, pp. 412–16; for 1963–69, FOS, *Annual Abstract of Statistics 1966*, pp. 156–57, and *Gross Domestic Product of Nigeria 1958/59–1966/67*, pp. 25–30; for 1969–73, FOS, *Statistical Abstract 1975*, pp. 148–49; for 1973–77, FOS, *Annual Abstract of Statistics 1985*, pp. 157–58; for 1977–90, World Bank 1994b, annex table 2.

Table 6.8 Level and Composition of Investment, 1958–84
(millions of naira)

Year	Building and construction[a]	Land improvement[b]	Transport equipment, machinery	Total
1958	118	28	71	217
1959	148	24	83	254
1960	144	22	88	254
1961	140	55	86	280
1962	154	45	76	274
1963	162	59	86	306
Total 1958–63	1,566	566	233	490
Percent	100	55	15	31
1963/64	221	55	102	359
1964/65	238	64	199	501
1965/66	300	68	217	585
1966/67	296	55	189	550
1967/68[c]	252	49	160	462
1968/69[c]	217	43	145	405
1969/70[c]	292	26	148	465
1970/71	366	25	299	690
1971/72	544	25	386	954
1972/73	685	29	427	1,140
Total 1963/64– 1972/73	6,142	3,411	460	2,272
Percent	100	56	7	37
1973/74	3,360	64	795	4,219
1974/75	3,150	85	862	4,097
1975/76	4,163	81	1,741	5,985
1976/77	5,052	93	3,228	8,373
1977/78	5,918	105	3,398	9,421
1978/79	5,787	110	2,942	8,839
1979/80	5,557	107	1,892	7,556
Total 1973/74– 1979/80	32,987	645	14,858	48,490
Percent	68	1	31	100
1980	6,112	113	—	—
1981	6,408	117	—	—
1982	5,349	116	—	—
1983	4,624	112	—	—
1984	3,368	112	—	—
Total 1980–84	25,861	570	—	—

— Not available.

Note: Data are in 1957 prices for 1958–63, in 1963/64 prices for 1963/64–1972/

infrastructural investment—land improvement; and transport equipment and machinery. After independence the high proportion of investment that went into building and construction was maintained. During the oil booms, transport equipment and machinery continued to account for one-third of total investment, agricultural investment virtually stopped, and the share of building and construction soared to more than two-thirds of the total. Since output of other services at the end of the 1973–83 period was virtually the same as at the beginning, the efficiency of investment must have fallen dramatically.

In table 6.9 we measure the efficiency of investment (crudely) as the ratio of investment to the increase in nonoil GDP over the same period. Until the early 1960s (from 1951 to 1963), the data suggest an incremental capital output ratio of 3:4. The ratio almost reaches 5 in the next decade. After the first oil price increase, the ratio more than doubles, reaching an incredible 12.6 for 1973/74–1979/80. In 1977/78 prices, investments totaling ₦86.5 billion (1973–84) correspond to a GDP increase of only ₦1.4 billion; the minor growth of the 1970s was largely offset by the fall in output during the early 1980s.

Two effects are operating here, which unfortunately, by their very nature, are impossible to disentangle. One is the spending effect of a resource boom. The spending of boom income raises the relative price of nontradables, and, to the extent that capital formation involves a demand for nontradables, this lowers the efficiency of investment. The peculiar composition of Nigerian investment—with a very high proportion spent on building and construction rather than on tradables such as machinery and transport equipment—reinforces this effect. The other effect is corruption. Kickbacks on investment projects added to total costs. Although the scale was new, the phenomenon itself was not. Corruption was evident, for example, in the investment program (especially road building) of the second half of the 1950s. The unit cost of civil engineering works rose by 64 percent in 1954–58, but the unit cost of vehicles rose by only 18 percent.

The growth that did occur between 1950 and 1964 was largely agricultural, and this growth had little to do with capital formation. It consisted mainly of an increase in the production of export crops in response

---

73, and in 1977/78 prices for 1973/74–84.

a. Buildings and civil engineering works in the first series; buildings and other construction, except land improvement, in the other series.

b. Land and agricultural and mining development in the first series; land improvement and plantation and orchard development in the second series; and land improvement and breeding stock in the third and fourth series.

c. Excludes the three Eastern states.

Source: For 1958–63, FOS, *Annual Abstract of Statistics 1975*, p. 160; for 1963/64–1972/73, FOS *Economic Indicators*, September 1976, p. 47; for 1973–84, FOS, *Annual Abstract of Statistics 1985*, p. 165.

Table 6.9 Efficiency of Investment, 1951–84

Period	Investment (millions of naira)	Increase in nonoil GDP (millions of naira)	Ratio of investment to increase in nonoil GDP	Price year
1951–57	746	169	4.4	1957
1958–63	1,586	483[a]	3.3	1957
1963/64–1972/73	6,142	1,292	4.8	1962/63
1973/74–1979/80	48,490	3,833	12.6	1977/78
1980–84	38,020	–2,392	–15.9	1977/78

a. Increase from 1958/59 to 1963/64.

Source: For 1950–62, Helleiner 1966, pp. 412–16; for 1963–69, FOS, *Annual Abstract of Statistics 1966,* pp. 156–57, and *Gross Domestic Product of Nigeria 1958/ 59–1966/67,* pp. 25–30; for 1969–73, FOS, *Statistical Abstract 1975,* pp. 148–49; for 1973–77, FOS, *Annual Abstract of Statistics 1985,* pp. 157–58; for 1977–90, World Bank 1994b, annex table 2.

to favorable world prices. Output increased not only as a result of increases in the cultivated area but also through the introduction of new varieties and, in the case of cocoa, through spraying against capsids, which raised yields by 20 percent.

In 1964–73 the oil sector and (nongovernment) services accounted for the bulk of GDP growth (37 percent and 30 percent, respectively). Agriculture, as already noted, stagnated in this nine-year period, and manufacturing grew rapidly (by 160 percent in constant prices over the period) but from too small a base to have much effect on the total. Finally, from 1973 to 1984 there was no growth in aggregate. Two sectors grew— manufacturing, which trebled in size, and government, which more than doubled—but nongovernment services stagnated and agriculture declined.

It is hard to avoid the conclusion that the oil boom derailed an economy that was previously growing well, and that growth could resume only once the boom had ended and liberalization was implemented. The investment that took place during the boom either produced no output or was more than offset by a decline in the productivity of the existing capital stock.

7 _Factor and Product Markets_

In this chapter we consider first the markets for capital, labor, and land. Within the capital market the formal sector was subject increasingly to financial repression, which started in the early 1960s and reached a peak in the early 1980s. During the oil slump modest moves were made toward decreased regulation. We show that the informal rural credit market is extensive, but that the amounts loaned are small and the loan durations short. In the formal labor market, government intervention preceded that in the capital market by a decade, as did deregulation. A premium for unskilled urban wage earners emerged in the 1950s and probably peaked in the late 1960s. The erosion of this premium was modest during the oil boom but rapid during the oil slump. In the informal rural labor market, labor allocation appears to be quite efficient and the market is substantial. Finally, the land market is shown to be flexible despite government attempts to restrict the marketability of land.

The remaining sections of the chapter are devoted to product markets. Here our focus is on the development of the marketing boards, the main channel for government intervention in agriculture.

The Capital Market

We consider first formal sector financial markets. Until the mid-1960s, government intervention in the banking system was confined to reducing the risk of bank failures by legislating the liquid asset ratio. Licensing of banks was introduced, but no formal criteria were laid down for the award of licenses. Various money market institutions developed during the 1950s, such as treasury bills and a stock market (both in 1958). However, Brown (1966, p. 169), the major analyst of the formal capital market in this period, concluded that markets were by no means fully integrated: "There is ample evidence that such continuous relationships do not yet exist in Nigeria." Indeed, Brown described the market in long-term government securities as "irrational."

In 1962 the Central Bank acquired powers to regulate interest rates. Initially this was apparently seen as part of the apparatus of overall liquidity control: Brown, for example, discusses the matter only in the context of intervention to raise the level of interest rates. Central Bank powers over interest rates were gradually increased. In 1969 the interest rate structure of each bank was made subject to individual approval by the Central Bank. In 1976, following a recommendation of an anti-inflation task force, differential interest rates by sector were introduced in favor of the "productive" sector. This sector was construed to include residential housing, for which the maximum interest rate was fixed at 6 percent.

Real interest rates began to fall during the 1960s. The rate on long-term government bonds fell from 6 percent in 1962 to 2 percent in 1972. However, with the onset of the oil boom, real interest rates became heavily negative. Even on advances to nonprime borrowers between 1973 and 1981, the real rate averaged –10 percent.

In addition to interest rate controls, the Central Bank acquired the power, in 1964, to direct the quantity of credit to specific sectors. This move was a response to balance of payments problems: private credit was restrained overall, but specific sectors thought to be important to the growth process were favored. As a result, the banking system became progressively constrained by a plethora of regulations and direct controls designed to funnel credit to preferred sectors. At one stage, banks were required to allocate their credit among 18 sectors of the economy, based on stipulated criteria. During the oil slump this was simplified to eight sectors in 1984, to four in 1986, and to two in 1987. As of 1987, half of bank lending was allocated to two priority sectors—manufacturing and agriculture. Although agriculture was classified as a priority sector, its share of formal credit was modest relative to its role in the economy: manufacturing was awarded a minimum of 35 percent against only 15 percent to agriculture.

During 1986 nominal interest rates were permitted to rise, and real rates became positive again. This action was taken largely because of a reduction in inflation following credit controls and a reduced budget deficit.

After independence, the indigenization of the banking system became a central aim of government intervention in financial markets. Indigenous banks were subsidized and encouraged. The foreign banks that dominated the sector during the colonial period were "mutualized": 60 percent of their equity was to be held by nationals. Although the government was not hostile to private financial institutions, its interventions were motivated by a belief that the market seriously misallocated capital. A series of government development banks were established during the 1960s and 1970s to direct long-term finance to favored sectors. Onoh (1980) comments: "The humiliation experienced during the operation of the colonial financial arrangement and subsequent abuses and indifference to local economic conditions largely explain the systematic state intervention in the financial system since political independence."

Nevertheless, private capital markets did develop. The stock market, established in 1958, had 93 companies quoted on it by the 1980s. The private return on investment has been estimated for the period 1966–71 by Equere and Longe (1975) and for the period 1977–81 by Akimtola-Bello and Adedipe (1983). The former study provides data in nominal terms separately for 128 companies. Averaged and expressed in real terms, the post-tax earnings return on capital employed (at historic cost) was 11 percent a year. The second study calculated the post-tax earnings yield for 60 quoted companies as a proportion of the market value of the equity. In real terms this was 22 percent. The period studied by Equere and Long coincided with the civil war, whereas the other study period was during the oil boom, a change that presumably affected both the performance of firms and the demand for financial assets. Since in the second period the economy was experiencing windfall income, it is surprising that the increase in asset demand did not depress the return on equity (not including capital gains) below the level identified. However, during this period it was easy to acquire financial assets abroad, and many Nigerians did so illegally. The high return may reflect the lack of confidence of the Nigerian elite in the future of their own or other domestic companies compared with the relative safety of foreign holdings; in other words, their assessment that domestic investment was a high-risk activity because wealth might be confiscated in the future.

The informal credit market is pervasive in Nigeria. Matlon (1977, p. 322) found that 55 percent of his sample of Northern farmers had borrowed during the preceding year. More than 80 percent of the loans were purely in cash, with an annual interest rate of only 11.4 percent.[1] The security on loans can be based on pledging land or trees or on a reputation acquired through regular transactions with a trader. In land-pledging contracts, the loan is made in return for the use of some of the debtor's land during the period of the loan. This contract can thus be viewed as a tenancy for which the tenant pays a bond repayable upon return of the land, with the rental payments being the forgone earnings on the bond. In Matlon's survey, land-pledging was not extensive: only 3 percent of the land was held as pledges.

In the South, pledging takes the form of a claim on the cocoa harvest by the creditor. Adegoye (1983) describes a formal process in which the parties hire a letter writer or a lawyer to draw up a document and sometimes hire a surveyor to draw a map. As many as five people sign as witnesses, and the document may have a postage stamp affixed to it as a means of implicating the government. Agreements vary in their formal legal validity, and the above ritual suggests that enforcement is regarded as a serious problem. Interestingly, the sanctions provided by shared kinship or residence networks play no part in enforcement. Adegoye notes, "It is not necessary for the pledgee to come from the same village or even the same state as the pledger. In fact, studies have found that better business relations occur when the only contact between the pledgee and the pledger is brought about by pledging" (p. 270). Interest on the loan is not paid in cash; rather the pledgee is given permission to harvest the cocoa crop of the pledged trees. This is liable to create severe problems of moral hazard since the pledgee has an incentive to overpick and undermaintain the trees. Presumably, the contract is drawn up in this way, rather than as a promise of the proceeds of the sale of the crop by the pledger, because permissions cannot be revoked until the loan is repaid, whereas promises can be broken. This inefficiency again indicates the enforcement problems associated even with collateral-backed credit contracts.

The main assets other than land are livestock, farm tools, nonfarm capital, and grain stores. Matlon found the combined value of these to be 30 to 40 percent of annual income for the average household; this proportion did not vary systematically with current income.

The extent to which credit and liquid assets overcome a capital constraint was assessed by Matlon through an analysis of fluctuations in intrayear consumption. His data, on which table 7.1 is based, reveal symptoms of a cash constraint: cash expenditure followed closely the peaks and troughs of cash income, and the share of food in expenditure was at its lowest during the income peak and at its highest during the income trough. The credit market, despite being extensive, was evidently not up to the task of smoothing expenditure. This is confirmed by the limited value of credit—never more than 7 percent of expenditure in any quarter.

Table 7.1 Intrayear Fluctuation in Cash Income and Expenditure

Item	February–May: land preparation	May–August: planting	August–November: harvest	November–February: harvest
Mean income (naira)	4.36	1.97	6.63	13.83
Mean expenditure (naira)	7.32	3.15	7.74	12.99
Food expenditure as a percentage of total	24.5	36.1	24.4	15.7

Source: Matlon 1977.

The Labor Market

We distinguish two phases for the formal sector labor market in the period 1950–87. During a long episode (1950–80) unskilled workers in privileged sectors of the economy (public and large-scale urban enterprises) succeeded in acquiring rents in the form of a wage premium. Subsequently they were unable to maintain this premium. These two episodes are considered analytically in chapter 8. Here we establish the factual basis for that analysis.

The Acquisition and Loss of Rents: 1950–80

At the start of the 1950–80 period, wage rates probably reflected in large part local labor market conditions. Prior to 1938 there had been no organized industrial relations. In that year unions acquired legal status, but even by 1950 union membership had reached only 110,000. In 1941 the governor was empowered to set minimum wages in industries where collective bargaining did not exist. In 1942 the Department of Labor was created, and in 1946 a union division was established within it, staffed by British trade union officials who set about creating British-style trade unions.

Real wages in large urban and public enterprises rose sharply. A consumer price index is available only from a 1953 base, but the magnitude of nominal wage increases prior to that date suggests that the growth in real wages started earlier. For the period 1950–53 there is an implicit GDP deflator for consumers' expenditure (Helleiner 1966, table III-B-2). Using this as the deflator, the real minimum wage paid by the government to general unskilled labor rose by 19 percent between 1950 and 1953. The rise in real wages may predate 1950, but, since there is no satisfactory deflator for the period 1946–50, it is not possible to investigate the question. However, for the earlier period 1939–46, for which there is a CPI, the minimum wage paid by the government rose in real terms by 18 percent.

Between 1953 and 1965 real wages rose at an average annual rate of 4.2 percent (table 7.2). Recall from chapter 6 that during this period private per capita consumption was rising at only around 1.5 percent nationally. Thus, even had there been no differential between urban wage earners and all other groups in 1953, by 1965 the premium over other groups enjoyed by wage earners would have been around 37 percent. Including the 19 percent increase between 1950 and 1953, real wages rose by 95 percent between 1950 and 1965, suggesting a 56 percent premium for wage earners by 1965 had there been no premium in 1950. Table 7.2 also shows that over the long term, European firms matched increases awarded by the government to its own staff.

Table 7.2 Formal Wages, Selected Years, 1938–65

Year	Real wage (1953 = 100)[a]	Government minimum wage as a percentage of wage paid by European firms
1938	—	86
1945	—	114
1950	—	78
1953	100	—
1957	126	98
1959	121	—
1960	—	96
1962	124	—
1964	—	85
1965	164	100

— Not available.

a. Defined as a simple average for four major urban centers.

Source: Kilby 1969, tables 75 and 76.

What was the motivation behind the emergence of these rents? Although the government had created two institutions, unions and minimum wages, either of which might have accounted for the surge in wages, it seems likely that the cause of wage growth was more complex. Kilby (1969) argues that during this period the industrial muscle of unions was limited, but that they were effective in bringing political pressure upon the government. The government was keen to become an attractive employer, and the unions increased the cost of not doing so. Foreign firms were politically vulnerable during Nigeria's independence phase and susceptible to pressure from unions to match the pay settlements awarded by the government, which had, in any event, been their previous practice.

The rise in wages was, therefore, not the outcome of conventional collective bargaining, nor was it directly imposed on firms by the government. Rather, the government wished to purchase the political benefit of rents to its employees, and firms could not afford to resist the unions' desire to maintain wages comparable with a traditional peer group.

The substantial premium for unskilled labor in the urban formal sector coincided with the emergence of urban unemployment. The first national urban survey of 1963 found an unemployment rate of 14 percent; 89 percent of those unemployed were males aged 14 to 30 (Kilby 1969, p. 208). The high rate of unemployment may have been the result of the urban-rural wage differential, as hypothesized by Harris and Todaro (1970), or of temporary errors in expectations caused by rapid changes in selection criteria, as hypothesized by Collier and Lal (1986).

The rapid subsequent fall in the unemployment rate to 8 percent at the time of the next survey in 1966 suggests the latter explanation. However, high unemployment probably contributed to a change in the government's perception of the desirability of a wage premium. The increase in the wage paid to unskilled labor also had the effect of squeezing differentials with skilled labor. The ratio of the top artisan class 1 grade to the bottom unskilled grade fell from 6:1 during 1947–49 to 3.5: 1 by 1964–65.[2]

Fajana (1975) similarly found a high degree of compression in the premium for skill among wage earners; he reports that during 1953–70 the minimum wage for unskilled labor in Lagos rose from 57 to 77 percent of the skilled artisan rate. This relative increase in the minimum wage corresponds to changes in average earnings by skill. The employment and earnings reports (covering 1956–60) show an increase in the mean earnings of unskilled wage earners as a percentage of the mean skilled wage from 42 to 52 percent. Similarly the industrial survey (which covered the period 1963–67, after which the survey ceased to break out wages by skill) shows an increase from 49 to 66 percent. In government employment there was a similar compression because of wage awards in 1954, 1959, and 1964. Fajana concludes that these changes in skill differentials cannot be explained by the changing pattern of supply and demand for skilled and unskilled labor, and he instead attributes them to government intervention.

Interestingly, in Northern Nigeria the large increases in unskilled wages appear to have occurred some years later than in the rest of the country. It was not until the late 1960s that federal employment policy (like other federal policies) began to be implemented in the North, so the wage lag probably supports Fajana's thesis.

During the 1970s the government continued to increase its interventions in the labor market through three important pressures for higher wages. First, during the oil boom, public recruitment increased enormously, tightening the market. Second, in 1978 a national minimum wage was introduced at a level above the going rate for unskilled labor. Third, even before this the government had increasingly influenced wages through fair-wage clauses in government contracts. This practice dated back to a directive from the British Colonial Office in 1946. The criteria for "fairness" had not been specified but naturally tended to become the rates the government itself paid as an employer. The expansion of government contracts after independence, and especially during the oil boom, increased the leverage of this control enormously.

Despite these influences for higher wages, the trend changed. The trend is difficult to discern because there are no adequate wage surveys and because pay awards were large but infrequent in the public sector. Hence real wages show violent fluctuations. However, to the extent that there is any trend, it appears to be downward. The International Labor Organisation (ILO) found that the unskilled urban wage in 1979 was 5 percent lower in real terms than in 1973 (ILO 1981). The open market rate for construction workers, perhaps a good indicator (Altaf 1985, table 6), shows a statistically insignificant trend of –2 percent a year for 1973–81.

The largest single shock to the market was the Udoji award of 1974, confined initially to government employees but extended throughout the formal sector following demonstrations and unrest. The inflationary consequences of this award were lessons learned during the oil slump and particularly during the experiment with the second-tier foreign exchange market, when compensatory pay awards to government employees were rejected with explicit reference to the consequences of Udoji.

The modest decline in urban real wages probably coincided with continued growth in the living standards of other groups, although we have seen (table 6.1) that there is some discrepancy for this period between the national accounts and the rural survey data. Direct series on rural real wages are for the most part nonexistent. Oyejide (1986) constructs an index spanning 1970–82 that shows a growth rate of 7.3 percent a year in real terms. Collier (1986) fitted a time trend to wage rates on rubber plantations for which there are annual data for 1973–81. He found a significant increase in real wages of 5.4 percent a year.

However, according to the national accounts, between 1965 and 1981 per capita consumption rose at an annual rate of only 1.3 percent. Taking urban real wages as stationary between 1965 and 1973 and thereafter falling at 2 percent a year, and assuming that rural incomes rose at 1.3 percent from 1965 to 1981, then the rural-urban differential would have narrowed by 30 percent over that period. We suggested above that had there been no differential in 1950, by 1965 the differential would have amounted to roughly a 56 percent urban premium. The foregoing analysis implies that as of 1981 this premium would have been reduced to around 8 percent.

In the urban economy the average wage of unskilled labor in five activities spanning manufacturing and nontradable services was ₦0.83 an hour in October 1981 and ₦0.87 an hour in October 1982.[3] In small-farm agriculture in February 1983 the wage for male labor was ₦0.56 an hour (FOS, *Labourforce Survey 1983*, chapter 6, p. 3), and in "modern holdings in agriculture" the hourly wage during 1981/82 was ₦0.99 for permanent labor and ₦0.88 for casual labor. These figures suggest that by the early 1980s earnings differentials for unskilled labor in agriculture and other sectors of the economy were not substantial. On the basis of the labor force survey, agriculture paid around 35 percent less; on the basis of the modern holdings survey, it paid between 6 and 19 percent more.

Retrenchment: 1980–87

The period 1980–87 is characterized by a sharp reduction in urban employment. The deep recession generated layoffs, return migration to rural areas, unemployment, and large reductions in real wages. Because this was such a major testing time in Nigerian history we devote substantial attention to it. We begin with an account of layoffs, termed "retrenchments" in Nigeria. We then show how the fall in labor demand affected workers in terms of unemployment and outmigration. Finally, we investigate the responses of urban real wages and the incomes of other groups of workers.

The major data source on retrenchments is the Shuttle Survey, conducted during January 1984, which documents employment changes from October 1982 to October 1983. This survey covered about a quarter of formal sector employment.[4] Retrenchments were found to be heavily concentrated in the private sector, which accounted for about 70 percent of retrenched workers. In fact, because response rates were skewed in favor of public sector establishments, the data understate the true extent to which retrenchments were a private sector phenomenon.

A better guide is the propensity of each type of employee to be retrenched, which can be derived from the data in the survey. An employee in either the federal government or a federal parastatal risked a 0.40 percent chance of being retrenched during the period. For an employee of a state government or a state parastatal, the chance was 1.69 percent, and for a private (formal) sector employee, 9.75 percent. Thus, although on average during the year an employee ran a 3.38 percent risk of retrenchment, workers in the private sector ran risks 25 times as great as those of federal employees.

Within the public sector this low rate of retrenchment was more than offset by recruitment. The survey found a net increase in employment of 3 percent during 1983. For 1984 Khan (1985) reports aggregate data on the public sector. Within this sector the federal civil service expanded at 3.9 percent at a time when GDP fell sharply.

The government was highly conscious of retrenchments as a politically sensitive issue, especially in view of the rise in unemployment with which it is assumed to be closely related. Although the inference that retrenchments contributed to unemployment seems natural and obvious, it is mistaken. An indication of this comes from breakdowns by state of the retrenchment rate during 1983 and the unemployment rates in 1982 and 1984. The *General Household Survey 1982/83*, published by Nigeria's Federal Office of Statistics (FOS) in 1984, reports data from which a state-specific unemployment rate can be derived. Although the survey was conducted over 12 months, its midpoint was October 1982, and so it provides a picture of unemployment rates for the six months prior to the retrenchments observed in the Shuttle Survey. Our next state-level breakdown of unemployment is for December 1984. We can therefore regress the change in the incidence of unemployment upon the incidence of retrenchments to see to what extent the latter have increased unemployment.

What we observe is a *negative* relationship between retrenchments and the change in unemployment: the more severe the incidence of retrenchments in a state, the less unemployment rose. This relationship is too weak to be statistically significant. The important point is not that the relationship is negative but that there is no support for a positive relationship. This remains true if the incidence of retrenchment is related not to the change in unemployment but to its 1984 level. States with high retrenchment rates in 1983 did not have high unemployment rates in 1984.

In unraveling this seeming puzzle, it is useful to decompose the observed unemployment rates by location, gender, age, and education. Location is particularly important because survey estimates of rural unemployment are notoriously suspect (in Nigeria they are in any event reported as very low). We therefore confine our analysis to the urban labor market. Urban unemployment for the period 1966–86 fell steadily until the peak of the oil boom in 1980 and thereafter rose rapidly (table 7.3).

The *Labourforce Surveys* do not break down the unemployment rate by age and education. However, they include data that can be combined with other survey data to provide reasonable estimates that reveal an extraordinary picture of unemployment during the oil slump. The overall urban unemployment rate rose from 7.3 percent in 1983 to 11.9 percent in July 1986. However, this average conceals radically divergent experiences for different groups (tables 7.4 and 7.5). Males aged 25 and above (84 percent of the labor force) and workers with less than secondary education (73 percent of the labor force) had low unemployment rates throughout the period. For example, even in July 1986 those with no education had an unemployment rate of only 3.6 percent, and those aged 25 to 44 had a rate of 3.7 percent in June 1986. By contrast, those with secondary education and those less than 20 years old had unemployment rates of about 40 percent by July 1986.

The unemployment problem was thus almost entirely one of young secondary school leavers. These were not the people who suffered the severe private sector retrenchments noted above, which were heavily concentrated in construction and manufacturing. Retrenched workers in these sectors are likely to have been among the less-educated 70 percent and the older 85 percent of the urban labor force. Despite suffering retrenchments, the unemployment rates for these groups remained low.

Table 7.3 Urban Unemployment Rates, Selected Years, 1963–86
(percent)

Year	Male	Female	Both sexes
1963	—	—	14.0
1966	10.4	4.3	8.0
1974	5.8	6.9	6.2
1976	4.7	3.5	4.3
December 1978	—	—	2.3
December 1979	—	—	4.1
Average 1980	—	—	1.5
Average 1982	—	—	2.8
December 1983	5.8	10.6	7.3
December 1984	6.9	9.9	7.9
June 1985	(8.5)	—	9.7
December 1985	9.8	—	—
March 1986	(7.9)	—	9.1
June 1986	(10.4)	—	11.8

— Not available.

Note: The male unemployment rate for 1985 and 1986 is estimated on the assumption that it stayed constant relative to the rate for both sexes observed in December 1984.

Source: FOS, *Labourforce Survey* (various years); Nigeria, Ministry of Labour, *Quarterly Bulletin of Labour Statistics 1983*, tables 1.3 and 1.4; FOS, *General Household Survey 1982/83*, appendix table 3B; FOS, *General Household Survey 1983/84*, table 7.

Table 7.4 Urban Male Unemployment by Age Group, Selected Dates
(percent)

Age group	Distribution of labor force, Dec. 1983[a]	Distribution of unemployed				Unemployment rate			
		Dec. 1984	Dec. 1985	March 1986	June 1986	Dec. 1984	Dec. 1985	March 1986	June 1986
15–19	5.9	21.2	26.2	24.0	27.1	20.8	30.6	32.3	39.0
20–24	10.2	54.6	40.3	38.7	39.5	31.0	27.3	30.2	32.9
25–44	60.2	15.6	22.1	26.0	26.0	1.5	2.5	3.4	3.7
45–54	19.3	5.7	6.0	9.3	3.1	1.7	2.1	3.8	1.4
55–59	4.3	2.9	5.4	2.0	4.3	3.9	8.7	3.7	8.5

a. We assume that the shares of each age group in the labor force stayed at their observed December 1983 levels between then and June 1986.

Source: FOS, *Labourforce Survey 1983*, for the age distribution in the labor force; other data from FOS, *Labourforce Survey* (various years).

Table 7.5 Unemployment by Education (Both Sexes), Selected Dates
(percent)

Education	Distribution of labor force, Dec. 1983	Distribution of unemployed				Unemployment rate				
		Dec. 1983	Dec. 1984	June 1985	March 1986	Dec. 1983	Dec. 1984	June 1985	March 1986	July 1986
None	41.3	8.8	10.5	12.4	4.8	1.6	2.0	2.9	3.3	3.6
Primary	31.9	22.1	31.1	20.1	19.4	5.1	7.7	6.1	5.5	6.0
Secondary	16.6	67.7	54.4	61.1	59.2	29.8	25.9	35.7	32.5	46.4
Postsecondary	10.2	1.5	4.0	6.5	6.6	1.1	3.1	6.2	5.9	7.8
University or polytechnic	—	—	—	—	—	—	4.7	—	—	8.7
Other	—	—	—	—	—	—	2.1	—	—	—

— Not available.

Note: We assume that the shares of each education group in the labor force stayed at their observed December 1983 levels between then and June 1986. The major bias in this assumption would be for postsecondary graduates, who were increasing rapidly in number. The figure of 8.7 percent unemployment for university or polytechnic graduates in 1986 corrects for this by allowing for a 30 percent increase in the stock of graduates. This in turn is calculated by estimating the total stock of graduates in December 1983 and the flow during the period. The former estimate is derived from the Shuttle Survey, which gives proportions of graduates by type of employer, and from Khan 1986, tables 2B and 3, which give total employment by type of employer. This procedure yields a stock of employed graduates of 114,000; applying the graduate unemployment rate observed in 1984 yields a total stock of 120,000. The flow of new graduates in 1984 and 1985 is taken from data on degree awards in FOS, *Annual Abstract of Statistics 1985*, table 5.1.

Source: Educational distribution from a NISH survey, FOS, *The Nigerian Household 1983/84*, table 8; other data from FOS, *Labourforce Survey* (various years).

128

There are two possible explanations for this phenomenon. First, retrenched workers might have been given preference (because they had experience) over new labor market entrants in competition for new vacancies. In this case the group from which retrenched workers were drawn (older, less-educated workers) would continue to have a low unemployment rate at the expense of the young and the more educated. Alternatively, retrenched workers might have migrated back to the agricultural sector. In this case retrenchment would not only be consistent with low unemployment for older and less-educated workers, but it would also be unrelated to the high unemployment rates of the young and educated. There is probably some truth in both hypotheses, but we will suggest that the second is much more important. For this we have four pieces of evidence.

First, there is no correlation between the geographic incidence of retrenchments and the incidence of unemployment—indeed, there is a statistically insignificant negative correlation. Yet if retrenched workers were merely bumping new entrants out of vacancies, high retrenchments would be associated with high unemployment. Second, there is evidence of a shift back to agriculture. Although the *Labourforce Surveys* cannot be used to measure rural-urban migration (since they are based on separate rural and urban samples with unknown sampling fractions), within both rural and urban areas there was a substantial shift to agriculture. Comparing the December 1983 and December 1984 surveys, we see that the share of the labor force engaged in agriculture increased from 12.5 to 22.6 percent in urban locations and from 65.7 to 72.9 percent in rural areas. This is at least qualitatively consistent with the back-to-agriculture thesis.

Third, the thesis is consistent with the increase in agricultural output that is believed to have occurred. Although estimates of agricultural output in Nigeria are notoriously unreliable, the declining relative price of food noted in chapter 4 is evidence of an increase in output. To check whether this should be attributed to labor supply or ecological change, we fitted a time trend to the yam–guinea corn relative price for the period since mid-1982. If climate is the decisive factor, supplies of guinea corn (a Northern crop) should have increased compared with yams, whereas if labor supply increased, the Southern crop—yams—should have benefited disproportionately. Although the relative price was volatile, there is a negative time trend: yam prices fell relative to guinea corn by about 16 percent a year according to the longer (Lagos) price series (the time trend having a *t*-statistic of 1.8).[5] Falling yam-sorghum prices thus strongly imply a labor-induced supply increase in agriculture. Fourth, the survey evidence on return migration, which we describe below, indicates that many retrenched workers are now working in the agricultural sector.

Table 7.6 Newly Reported Vacancies, 1976–84

Year	Number	Index
1976–80 (average)	1,125	100
1981	660	59
1982	520	46
1983	450	40
1984	310	28

Note: Vacancies were reported to up to 36 employment exchanges; data are average vacancy listings per exchange.

Source: Nigeria, Ministry of Labour, *Quarterly Bulletin of Labour Statistics 1984,* table 2.3.

If retrenchment is not linked closely to the increase in unemployment among the young, what explains the large rise in unemployment rates for this group? Although many firms have retrenched existing workers, both these firms and many others have curtailed recruitment, and young workers, being new entrants to the labor market, are entirely dependent on the rate of recruitment (as opposed to the level of employment) for access to jobs. There are no aggregate time series data on recruitment, but a proxy indicator is the number of vacancies reported to employment exchanges (table 7.6).[6] Evidently, there was a chronic decline in recruitment relative to employment between 1976 and 1984. A similar picture is conveyed from Khan's data on the public sector: a period during which employment increased by 60 percent coincided with a 90 percent decline in recruitment (table 7.7).

Not only did urban recruitment collapse, but the supply of urban secondary school leavers increased substantially. For example, the number of children in Lagos secondary schools increased by 116 percent between 1979/80 and 1983/84 (FOS, *Annual Abstract of Statistics 1985,* table 5.4). There is thus no difficulty in accounting for why a large proportion of urban secondary school leavers failed to gain urban wage employment. However, this does not explain why they are unemployed.

If retrenched workers were able and willing to return to the agricultural sector, why did not the young, educated urban labor force do

Table 7.7 Employment and Net Recruitment in the Public Sector, 1977–84

Year	Employment		Net recruitment	
	Thousands	Index	Thousands	Index
1977–81 (average)	1,108	100	195.9	100
1981–83 (average)	1,611	145	111.9	57
1984	1,774	160	21.3	11

Source: Derived from Khan 1986, table 3.

likewise, rather than tolerate an unemployment rate in excess of 40 percent? There are four possibilities, all likely to have some validity. First, the minimum-wage laws probably constrained entry wages to be above the supply price of new entrants to the labor market, even though average earnings of experienced workers were well above the minimum wage. This distortion of the wage structure may have tempted young job seekers to maintain their search. Second, the urban-born may lack vital agricultural skills and so be unemployable in agriculture. Third, the urban-born may lack access to land. A study by Ross (n.d.) of the land rights of urban residents found that first-generation migrants were able to preserve their rights by visiting or by sending remittances. The same might not be true for offspring, however, and because there is little usable, unowned land, those without land rights can enter agriculture only through the rural labor market. Fourth, the urban-born may develop strong preferences for urban residence and may thus be willing to remain in the cities even if they cannot find jobs.

The three last interpretations all imply that young, urban-born workers were locked into the urban labor market even if it offered significantly lower income than agriculture. Evidence that this indeed occurred is provided in our discussion of rural-urban trends in household income (chapter 6).

Finally, we briefly consider graduate unemployment—a matter the government was particularly conscious of. Graduate unemployment was not especially severe, comprising only 8.7 percent of the labor force in July 1986 (table 7.5). Graduate unemployment, although aggravated by the recession, was the consequence of structural changes in supply rather than transient changes in demand. The output of graduates from Nigerian universities in 1984 was 145 percent above that of 1978.

We have argued that retrenchment did not generate unemployment because retrenched workers returned to agriculture, but that this finding can be juxtaposed against high rates of unemployment for secondary school leavers who, for whatever reason, did not outmigrate in sufficient numbers. We now turn to the agricultural sector to investigate this process from the receiving end.

There are no national surveys of migration or census data from which migration can be inferred. However, a series of sample surveys conducted for the World Bank in August 1985 provide a reasonable basis for the study of migration flows and the rural labor market between 1982 and 1985.

The major survey, the Farm Labour Survey, found between 1982 and 1985 a net flow of return migrants of 0.4 persons per household. According to the FOS *General Household Survey 1982/83,* the average rural household had an adult labor force of 1.67. If all the return migrants had entered the labor force, these figures would imply a 24 percent increase in the rural labor force because of net return migration, as well as a 14 percent increase in the adult population.

Returned migrants made up three groups: those who had returned prior to 1982, those whose post-1982 return was voluntary, and those whose post-1982 return was triggered by an involuntary layoff. The pre-1982 profile of the sectoral origins of return migrants can be compared with the profiles of the post-1982 return migrants to provide some further information on the relative incidence of retrenchments (table 7.8). The table confirms the Shuttle Survey finding that the incidence of re-trenchments in construction was far higher than that in other sectors: the proportion of involuntary return migrants who had previously worked in this sector was more than four times higher than the proportion of those who had worked in construction among the pre-1982 return migrants. Similarly, industry shows an above-average incidence of involuntary layoffs, again consistent with the Shuttle Survey. A final noteworthy feature of the data in table 7.8 is that despite the large increase in unemployment between 1982 and 1985, the proportion of return migrants who were unemployed prior to their return actually declined substantially. This supports our earlier inference that the urban unemployed were composed increasingly of those locked into urban residence.

Return migrants gained relatively swift and easy access to land. Most migrants returned to their original villages. If anything, this was more pronounced during the recession than previously, applying to 84 percent of pre-1982 migrants and 91 percent of post-1982 migrants. Thus the return process did not provide much economically purposive spatial reallocation of labor within the rural areas. The mean age of retrenched migrants was 33 years, well above the age range of the high-unemployment cohorts. Most went into farming on their own account or on their father's farm. The agricultural wage labor market accounted

Table 7.8 Return Migrants during 1982–85 Compared with Pre-1982 Migrants, by Sector

(pre-1982 incidence = 1)

Sector	Voluntary returnees	Involuntary returnees
Army/police	1.42	0.64
Public service	0.89	1.04
Construction	1.00	4.25
Industry	2.00	1.71
Unemployment	0.00	0.50

Source: Horsnell and Collier 1986, table 5.

for, at most, 20 percent of return migrants. This suggests that family land allocation mechanisms were able to accommodate the reentry process, as implied by the study of urban land rights conducted by Ross (n.d.).

The Migration Survey found that there was no tendency for the length of absence from the village to influence the decision to take up farming once back in the village, suggesting that land rights decay only slowly. There was little time lag between return and the commencement of farming: only 14 percent waited for more than one year after return. Further evidence that returning migrants were accommodated within the existing structure of household land rights is that the mean number of fields per household (the best guide to land area) rose by 15 to 18 percent between 1982 and 1985 (depending upon which survey source is taken). Since there was also presumably some intensification of farming (in other words, an increase in the ratio of labor to land), this would suggest an increase in the labor force somewhat above 18 percent.

Although migrants gained easy access to land, their choice of activity was, as of 1985, oriented heavily toward food crops. The Migration Survey found that only 17 percent of those returned migrants who were farming were growing cocoa, oil palm, or rubber (and another survey confirms this figure). However, as a result of reforms after 1986, the relative incentives to cultivate food and nonfood crops changed radically.

We have seen that the return migration process was spatially rather inflexible. However, labor can be reallocated within agriculture even without such flexibility because food crops and nonfood crops are grown in the same locations. The cocoa, oil palm, and rubber belts are all close to the major urban areas (Lagos, Ibadan, Enugu, Port Harcourt, and Benin), so as urban areas shed labor, the return to the home village increases the labor force available for nonfood crops.

The agricultural area with the least to gain from liberalization was the North. Of its two traditionally traded crops, only cotton offered potential; groundnuts had become too risky ecologically in much of the North. The remaining traded crop, maize, was a Southern import and was probably precluded as a Northern export because of high transport costs. Therefore, after the 1986 liberalization the less-urbanized North probably released labor from the cities into nontraded food crop production. This suggests that the South accommodated the resulting increase in Northern food production by further shifting labor out of food into nonfood crops. Northern foods thus replaced Southern foods to some extent.

Although return migration appears to have been substantial, it was probably not the principal way by which labor was reallocated between the rural and urban economies. More important was the effect of the urban recession on the suppression of outmigration from rural areas to the cities. Rural school leavers, who during the oil boom would have migrated to the cities, changed their plans. Some 60 percent of rural house-holds reported having some member of the household who had been discouraged from migration after 1982. Questions on plans and expecta-tions are not easy to handle in surveys, but a correlation with another variable makes the answers appear credible. The dominant channel of information for rural-to-urban migrants in Africa appears to be the fam-ily network (Bevan, Collier, and Gunning 1989). We would therefore ex-pect households with return migrants to have the best information that urban labor market conditions had so deteriorated that migration was not worthwhile. This is indeed what we find: among households with return migrants, 80 percent contained discouraged would-be rural-to-urban migrants, compared with only 47 percent among other households. It appears that much of the rural-to-urban migration that did occur was based on misperceptions of the state of the urban labor market, judging from the 30 percent unemployment rate among recent school-leaver migrants to cities. Those who changed their plans were the better-informed and were right to be discouraged. Thus each urban-to-rural return migrant generated informational externalities that substan-tially geared up the labor reallocation involved. The rural surveys sug-gest that by 1985 the labor reallocation effects of suppressed outmigration were even larger than the direct contribution of return migration.

We now consider how earnings responded during the slump. The most useful source is the NISH General Consumer Expenditure Surveys, which have been running continuously since April 1980. These surveys mea-sure household income and classify households by residence location (rural or urban) and by the principal income source (wages or self-employment). Measuring household income is a difficult undertaking, and such surveys are liable to have large biases. However, as a guide to trends in income as opposed to levels of income, the surveys have some validity.

The data presented in table 7.9 reveal striking changes in living stan-dards and more particularly in income differentials.[7] The real income data reported make no allowance for rural-urban cost of living differ-ences. Most foods and nontradable services are cheaper in rural areas, and most imported and manufactured goods are cheaper in urban ar-eas. Since the former two account for around three-quarters of the con-sumption bundle of the average household, it is highly probable that the rural cost of living is somewhat lower than the urban. Even so, this differential would have needed to be massive to upset the conclusion that as of 1980 the poorest group (which was also the largest) was the rural self-employed. This group experienced the smallest drop in income between 1980 and 1985, though still a substantial 27 percent. The group with the largest drop in income, 54 percent, was the urban self-employed. By 1984/85 their income was below that of the rural self-employed even before any allowance is made for the higher urban cost of living. This suggests that a significant group of the urban population—the young and educated—were locked into urban residence. Unable to gain wage employment because of the collapse in recruitment, they were either unemployed or competing against each other for the limited jobs available. The real living standards of urban wage earners halved during the period, displaying a high degree of real wage flexibility.

The income trends, though powerful, were thus entirely consistent with the product and labor market stories developed above and in previous chapters. The recession squeezed urban income relative to rural income. Retrenched wage earners with access to agriculture would increasingly have been better off to relocate in that sector rather than enter urban self-employment. But many in the urban work force did not have this option, and without access to agriculture, they were confronted with the choice between hopeless unemployment or low and deteriorating incomes in urban self-employment. The sharp growth in the proportion of the urban labor force characterizing their primary activity as agriculture fits in with this account.

Other than the above income data, there are only a few snippets of wage data. Although they do not tell a coherent story distinct from the income data, they do provide a basis for testing that data. This is particularly useful given the limitations of household income surveys.

Table 7.9 Trends in Mean Household Income of Key Groups, 1980–85

Group	1980/81	1981/82	1982/83	1983/84	1984/85
Nominal income (1980/81 = 100)					
Rural self-employed	100	120	124	142	165
Rural wage earners	100	105	108	125	117
Urban self-employed	100	97	93	103	105
Urban wage earners	100	102	106	114	113
All rural	100	119	124	140	161
All urban	100	100	202	109	109
Real income (rural self-employed in 1980/81 = 100)					
Rural self-employed	100	103	95	86	73
Rural wage earners	178	160	147	135	92
Urban self-employed	150	124	106	94	69
Urban wage earners	203	177	164	140	101
All rural	105	107	99	89	74
All urban	166	142	129	109	80

Source: FOS, *General Household Survey* (various years); unpublished FOS data; national, urban, and rural composite CPIs.

Table 7.10 Wages and Earnings of Workers in Lagos, 1982 and 1984
(naira unless otherwise specified)

Item	October 1982	October 1984
Unskilled workers[a]		
Hourly wages	0.71	0.87
Hourly earnings	0.86	1.05
Hours per week	43.2	40.9
Weekly earnings	37.2	42.9
Real weekly earnings	100.0	64.0
Skilled workers[b]		
Hourly wages	0.88	1.01
Hourly earnings	1.10	1.20
Hours per week	43.2	41.0
Weekly earnings	47.5	49.2
Real weekly earnings	100.0	58.0
Urban CPI	100.0	180.0
Skilled-unskilled wage ratio	1.24	1.16

a. Data are for five comparable categories of unskilled laborers.
b. Data are for 25 comparable categories of laborers with manual skills.
Source: Nigeria, Ministry of Labour, *Quarterly Bulletin of Labour Statistics 1982,* table 6.1; Nigeria, Ministry of Labour, *Quarterly Bulletin of Labour Statistics 1984,* table 6.1.

Table 7.10 provides information on wages, earnings, and hours of work for skilled and unskilled workers in Lagos as of October 1982 and October 1984. Most noteworthy is the fall in real income during this two-year period—36 percent for unskilled workers and 42 percent for the skilled.[8] For October 1985 a national snapshot exists of hourly earnings by type of worker (table 7.11). This shows that unskilled plantation workers were earning more both per hour and per month than urban wage laborers: the wide differential in favor of urban employment that had persisted through the oil boom had finally been completely eroded and

Table 7.11 Earnings of Male Urban Laborers as a Percentage of Earnings of Male Plantation Workers, 1985

Worker	Earnings per hour	Earnings per month
Textile laborer	88	94
Publishing laborer	81	85
Manufacturing laborer	68	87

Source: Nigeria, Ministry of Labour, *Quarterly Bulletin of Labour Statistics 1985.*

indeed reversed. As a result, workers had an incentive to leave the cities and take up plantation work.

We have already discussed the scanty evidence on trends in rural wages in our analysis of the urban wage premium. Here we consider the efficiency of operation of the informal rural labor market. The key test of this efficiency is whether ex ante differences in land-labor ratios between farms are equalized by labor transactions, thereby equalizing marginal products across holdings. We begin by surveying evidence on the magnitude of the market.

Nigerian village studies find that of total labor input in peasant agriculture, the proportion supplied through the market is 20 to 60 percent. For the three villages in Matlon's (1977) sample, hired labor constituted 41 percent of total labor input on farms (Crawford 1982, tables III:6 and III:7, p. 47). Another village study found that 50 percent of labor input was hired labor (Longhurst 1980, p. 131). In the cocoa belt of Southern Nigeria, labor hiring is probably even more extensive. In an early survey (1951/52), Galletti, Baldwin, and Dina (1956) found that 40 percent of total farm labor was hired, and Berry found that labor hiring has since become increasingly important—all the farmers in her sample used hired labor (Berry 1975, p. 130).

Labor is hired under a range of contracts. Task rates appear to be markedly higher than casual day rates (Berry 1975, pp. 136–40). Berry suggests that the balance between casual and permanent labor contracts shifts depending upon the strength of the cocoa market and the bargaining position of laborers: when the market is depressed and laborers' bargaining position weak, annual contracts predominate.

The efficiency of the hired labor market is indicated in Longhurst's regression analysis of the production functions of labor hirers and labor sellers. He finds that the value marginal product of labor is not significantly different for net labor sellers and net labor buyers. Nor is it significantly different from the wage rate for the average task. This supports the conclusion of Byerlee and others (1977, p. 107) of "an active and efficiently operated labor market in which the wage rate is a reasonable measure of the opportunity cost of labor."

Longhurst's results suggest that supervision problems and other enforcement costs do not constitute substantial obstacles. However, the evidence indicates that households are cash-constrained. Loan receipts per acre cultivated during the deficit, cash-constrained seasons were not closely related to household cash income. This suggests that credit secured on land was a substantial proportion of total credit receipts. Such a credit market, in which the possession of land is a major determinant of access, has the effect of easing the cash-constraint on land-abundant households relative to land-scarce households. In absolute terms, the former remain more cash-constrained per acre than the latter, but the existence of such a credit market narrows the differential. Therefore land-abundant households could partially rectify their atypical factor proportions by above-average labor hiring per acre, controlling for noncredit means of raising cash. This again suggests that the informal market is fairly efficient.

The Land Market

Table 7.12 summarizes the results of 12 village studies of Northern Nigeria concerning methods of land acquisition. One striking feature is that there is little consensus among the studies, which found that inheritance explains 21 to 78 percent of cultivated land acquisition; purchase, 1 to 36 percent; and tenancy, 3 to 59 percent. This may well reflect actual diversity. However, as Cohen (1980, p. 356) comments on the apparent trend toward the individualization of land rights, "it is tempting to suggest that this is not a shift but a discovery by researchers of underlying reality." In other words, different findings may also reflect different intensities of observation of land rights.

Table 7.12 Method of Acquiring Cultivated Land
(percent)

Study and village	Inherited	Acquired through tenancy			Cleared or received as gift	Other
		Pur- chased	Rented	Pledged		
Ega (in Cohen 1980, p. 389)						
Zaria	21	16	4	2	24	33
Goddard, Fine, and Norman 1971						
Takatuku	74	17	3	0	6	0
Kaura Kimba	49	32	6	0	14	0
Gidan Karma	63	19	11	0	5	3
Longhurst 1980 (table 2.4)						
Day i	38	36	18	2	4	2
Matlon 1977						
Barbeji	74	8	5	2	11	0
Zoza	54	30	12	4	0	0
Roga	45	21	23	10	0	0
Norman 1971						
Dan Mahawagi	57	6	7	5	20	5
Doka	78	1	4	0	13	4
Hanwa	28	3	47	12	0	10
Ross n.d.						
Hurumi	21	31	24	24	0	0

Of the studies cited in table 7.12, the only one that appears to have focused primarily on land rights is that of Ross (n.d.), and his findings are startling. Perhaps the most significant is the substantial dichotomy between ownership and cultivation. Only half of the cultivated land was owned by the cultivator. Only 16 percent of individuals cultivated solely the land they owned, whereas 29 percent cultivated only land they did not own. Fully 90 percent of landowners participated in lending or borrowing plots, which reflected a combination of tenancy and dormant claims. In contrast to Cohen's suggestion that there was a trend toward "a progressive reduction in the number of right holders in a given piece of farmland" (p. 357), Ross found that landownership was being diffused across the population. Per hectare there were 0.84 cultivators, 2.02 adults resident in the village, and 2.57 people with some ownership rights. Of these owners, nearly 70 percent were either absentee principal owners or holders of dormant claims on a share of the land. Furthermore, about 50 percent of those owning claims to land were women. Overall, 78 percent of village residents held some claim to land.

In Nigeria the maintenance of the land rights of an individual—resident or nonresident—rests entirely upon a social consensus of recognition rather than on legal title or on land cultivation. Nonresidents therefore need to maintain social ties with the village community to preserve their land rights.[9] Because land rights are widely (and increasingly) diffused and because many claimants have social obligations to coclaimants who are short of land, they feel sufficiently secure in their claims to leave them dormant. The net effect is a highly flexible system of land allocation in which land usage is more frequently reallocated than is land ownership; the average duration of ownership per plot is 13 years and the average duration of cultivation only 7 years.

Ross (n.d.) found rights of usufruct to be both easily accessible and terminable. "The flexibility of this system derives from the fact that because owners do not necessarily compete for land as cultivators, more land is made available for assignation from a large number of individual sources with greater rapidity and at lower cost to would-be recipients. In combination, these factors enable the redistribution of land that occurs at the beginning of every rainy season" (p. 19). The extent to which this reallocation secures allocative efficiency is suggested by Ross's comparison of the group means for the top 10 percent and the bottom 40 percent of cultivated land holdings. Although Ross (n.d.) does not report labor input per hectare, he does report the number of adult-equivalent units in the cultivating household per hectare. The mean for the bottom 40 percent is only 18 percent greater than that for the top 10 percent, suggesting that even prior to the use of hired labor, land reallocation has substantially eliminated differences in land-labor ratios.

This efficiency of land reallocation has not been caused predominantly by a market in land purchase. Indeed, Ross finds evidence that the amount of land sold has been declining: during the decade 1967–76, 14 percent of the village cultivated land area was sold, compared with 22 percent in the preceding decade. Part of the reason is the self-fulfilling tendency that where a market is thin, there is little expectation that a sale can be made good by a subsequent purchase. However, the result is also consistent with the hypothesis that because of its collateral premium, the land price will be bid up to a level at which purchase for cultivation cannot be financed out of the returns from cultivation.

It should be noted that the efficient reallocation of land on the basis of widely held individual ownership claims has occurred not only in the absence of government registration of land rights but despite government attempts to make such claims invalid. Sale, rental, and pledging are expressly forbidden without central approval, which is rarely granted. Worried by trends in individual tenure outside of Northern Nigeria, where the Land Use Decree was in effect, in 1978 the federal government extended that legislation nationally. Ross's work suggests that such a decree is ineffective and that private rights are consistent with both allocative efficiency and diffusion of ownership. The informal development of rights that has occurred in Northern Nigeria against a background of overt state hostility has avoided all of these drawbacks.

Product Markets

> *Clearly the governments have had their hands on the throat of the goose which is laying the golden eggs. (Lewis 1967, p. 20)*

In the colonial period indirect rule and the British predilection to see and respect ethnic differences, even where they did not exist, meant that the opportunity to introduce and enforce a national legal system was missed. Yet the colonial government also had positive effects. Its main legacy may well have been its contribution, through its infrastructural investments, to a reduction in the cost of marketing, for export crops in particular. In addition to reducing transport costs, the colonial government affected marketing by establishing marketing boards for the main export crops. After independence these boards continued to be the main channel for government intervention. This section is concerned mainly with the marketing boards, but we also consider price controls (which have been fairly unimportant in Nigeria, except in the case of urban retail prices for food) and import controls.

When Sir Arthur Lewis wrote his book on Nigeria in 1967, he feared that agricultural exports, which he considered the engine of growth, would stagnate. Although he was particularly concerned with contemporary distributional changes (the fall in producer prices and the rise in urban wages after 1960), the large gap he noted between world prices and producer prices for export crops dated from well before the 1960s (table 7.13).

The colonial government, in spite of the laissez-faire attitude often ascribed to it, intervened in the marketing of agricultural exports almost as soon as the goose started to lay its golden eggs. For example, the Colonial Office gave the British Cotton Growers Association monopoly buying rights in 1905 and supported (in 1916) the association's campaign against local competition by outlawing the varieties local weavers needed.

In the period after World War I, trade in export crops was conducted by a few British trading companies that purchased from up-country agents. A pattern of oligopolistic competition developed in which intense competition among firms alternated with "pool" agreements under which a cartel of buying firms paid a common price to producers and divided their profits on the basis of market shares. Such pool agreements received the blessing of the colonial government. On two occasions cocoa farmers in the Gold Coast reacted by holding up production. This led to the appointment of a Commission on the Marketing of West African Cocoa (the Nowell Commission). The Nowell Report (1938) recommended the creation of collective marketing agencies, but nothing had been done when World War II broke out. The report paid lip service to the idea that competitive buying was in the interest of peasants, but it managed at the same time to accept the firms' claims that African middlemen were engaged in "undesirable practices"—in other words, competition. Through the Nowell Report the oligopsonists of the 1930s prepared the way for the marketing boards of the 1940s.

World War II brought government control. The private trading companies were now forced to sell all their produce to the British government, which assumed both the risk of acquiring undisposable stocks and the obligation ultimately to return the profits it made to the producers.

Table 7.13 Producer Prices as a Percentage of World Prices, 1948–67

Period	Cocoa	Groundnuts	Palm kernel	Palm oil
1948–52	49.2	35.1	60.9	61.8
1953–57	70.0	47.8	59.2	62.0
1958–62	65.9	62.3	53.3	52.1
1962–67	64.3	67.8	50.2	44.4

Source: Olatunbosun and Onitiri 1974, table 5.

In 1942 the West African Produce Control Board was established, which covered cocoa, groundnuts, and palm produce and had jurisdiction in all four British West African territories. This system was used to tax groundnut and palm produce farmers, while cocoa producers effectively gave the government a forced loan, for the board's profits on cocoa trading (more than £9 million in 1940–47) were invested in British securities.

The machinery for appropriating agricultural surpluses was now set up, but its use was still seen as justified only by the exceptional conditions during (and immediately after) the war. Only much later would the idea that the government acted as trustee for the farmers (and would eventually return any surpluses) be abandoned.

After the war, marketing boards were created with a different objective: price stabilization. A marketing board was set up first for cocoa (in 1947) and then for palm produce, groundnuts, and cotton (all in 1949). These boards acquired enormous surpluses from 1947 to 1954, when Nigeria experienced a commodity boom. By 1954 these boards held £120 million (table 7.14), of which £100 million had been realized as trading profits since 1947. In the Nigerian context this sum was huge; the two main sources of government revenue—import and export duties—generated only £94 million and £57 million, respectively, in the same seven-year period. Farmers lost 20 to 30 percent of their potential income as a result of the pricing policies of the marketing boards (table 7.15). The accumulation of the surpluses was partly accidental— the long commodity boom of 1947–54, when Nigeria's barter terms of trade improved by 75 percent (table 7.16) was not foreseen—and partly deliberate. Price stabilization was, after all, the main function of the boards.

The constitutional changes of 1954 (see chapter 1) were reflected in institutional changes for the marketing boards: they were now organized by region rather than by commodity. In the Northern Region the board continued to be used for stabilization, but in the South the funds inherited from the produce boards quickly came to be seen as convenient sources of government revenue. The regional governments, which had just been given enormous responsibilities for economic development (at the expense of the federal government), could not resist the temptation offered by the huge marketing board reserves. The World Bank was instrumental in the subsequent transformation of the reserves from funds held in trust for farmers to funds used for general development finance. In 1955 the Bank recommended that no further reserves be accumulated and that the bulk of the existing reserves be lent to the government on a long-term basis for development purposes, because they were not necessary for stabilization purposes. The first part of this recommendation was ignored. Once the regional governments saw the potential of the boards as fiscal instruments, they made sure that the

Table 7.14 Accumulation by Nigerian Marketing Boards, 1947–54
(million pounds sterling)

Item	Cocoa	Cotton	Ground-nuts	Palm produce	Total
Initial reserves[a]	8.9	0.3	4.5	11.5	25.1
Trading surplus[b]	33.8	7.0	22.5	21.1	84.3
Excess of other income over expenditure[c]	3.3	1.1	3.6	2.5	10.5
Total	46.0	8.3	30.5	35.0	119.9

a. Reserves accumulated by the West African Produce Control Board before 1947 (cocoa) or in 1947–49 (other products) and turned over to the marketing boards upon their creation.

b. Sales at f.o.b prices minus export duties, value of purchases, total expenses, and decrease in stocks.

c. Largely interest earned on reserves held as British securities.

Source: Helleiner 1966, table 37, based on annual reports of Nigerian marketing boards.

Table 7.15 Taxation of Major Export Crops, 1947–62

Crop and Period	Withdrawals as a percentage of potential producer income		
	Export duties	Produce purchase tax	Trading surplus
Cocoa			
1947/48–1953/54	17.6	0.2	21.6
1954/55–1961/62	17.9	2.0	6.2
Groundnuts			
1947/48–1953/54	11.5	0.4	28.1
1954/55–1960/61	14.0	2.4	-1.4
Palm kernels			
1947–1954	9.4	—	19.9
1955–1961	13.1	3.7	10.3
Palm oil			
1947–1954	9.0	—	8.0
1955–1961	13.3	6.3	5.9

— Not available.

Note: Potential producer income is defined as actual income plus the three withdrawals listed. As Helleiner points out (p. 162, note 17), this underestimates potential producer income if export demand is elastic.

Source: Helleiner 1966, table 38.

Figure 7.1 Terms of Trade, Selected Years, 1913–61
(1953 = 100)

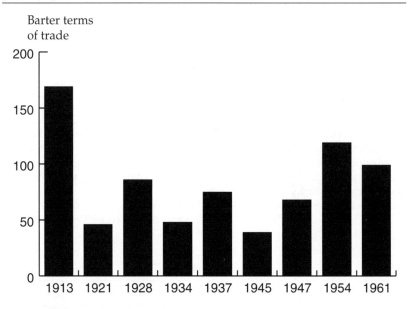

Source: Helleiner 1966, table IV–A–6.

boards continued to earn surpluses (even though world prices peaked in 1954), and they increasingly relied on these funds for their development plans. It was boldly admitted in the Western Region in 1962 that the marketing board was considered the main source of regional government revenue.

With control transferred to politicians, the boards came to be used as a mechanism for appropriating peasant wealth. The taxing of agriculture for the benefit of urban-based industrial development was, of course, in line with mainstream development thought of the 1950s. Helleiner (1966), who was well aware of the taxation implicit in the boards' pricing policies, justified the confiscation of peasants' income on two grounds, neither of which can now be considered credible. First, on the basis of very slender evidence, he was pessimistic about the willingness of peasants to save out of transient income and to invest their savings efficiently.[10] Second, Helleiner argued that the state would make better use of the funds than peasants would in the absence of taxation.

In fact, most of these funds were squandered. Since the boards operated outside the regular legislative budgetary process, political direction, unhampered by treasury control, prevailed. Part of the funds were used for investments in private enterprise at inflated prices; excess payments not only enriched individuals but also financed political activities. The European firms, including the dominant United Africa

Table 7.16 Government Revenue and Public Expenditure in the 1950s
(percentage of GDP at factor cost)

Item	1951/52	1960/61
Government revenue		
Excluding marketing boards	9.0	12.2
Including marketing boards	13.0	12.8
Total public expenditure	5.4	15.1

Source: Helleiner 1966, tables 46 and 47.

Company, moved out of their traditional activities (produce buying and import retailing) in the second half of the 1950s, entering into a partnership with the state for import substitution activities financed from the marketing board funds.

Table 7.16 reveals the fiscal importance of the funds. In the 1950s public expenditure rose rapidly, increasing from 5.4 to 15.1 percent of GDP in nine years. Government revenue (excluding the marketing boards) rose much less; the conventional view of the colonial government's fiscal stance as extremely conservative is, at least for the last decade of the colonial period, wrong (see chapter 8). The marketing boards filled a (rapidly growing) gap; the implicit taxation of agricultural exports became all but irreversible.

The boards also affected constitutional arrangements. At the time of the 1953 conference the South wanted a strong central government, which the Northern Region opposed because it feared Southern dominance under such an arrangement. The Western and Eastern regions were impatient to start "development" and felt, not unreasonably, that they were being held back by the conservative North. The regionalization of the marketing boards held out the promise of realizing these plans without Northern interference; this in turn influenced the Southern regions to give in to the Northern demand for strong regional governments. Although the boards may thus have postponed the constitutional breakdown, they also hastened it to the extent that the board funds were used to finance election campaigns of political parties outside their traditional area—in particular, the activities in the North of the Western-based Action Group in 1959—thereby adding to interregional frictions.

The negative effect of export crop taxation on export volumes was already becoming apparent before the civil war (recall that Lewis's remark about the goose with the golden eggs dates from 1967), but the marketing board regime was not reformed until 1973. Taxes amounting to 20 percent of export prices were first halved by the military government and then abolished, and the power to fix producer prices was transferred from the boards (in other words, from the state government) to the federal government. Producer prices more than doubled in 1973–74 not only because of rising world prices but also because of this reform.

In 1977 the regional boards were abolished, and Nigeria returned to a system of crop-specific boards. In addition to the four traditional crops (cocoa, cotton, groundnuts, and palm produce), rubber and grains were now also brought under the control of marketing boards. Producer prices were announced before the start of the season and were in theory floor prices, with the boards acting as the buyer of last resort. The boards bought crops from farmers through a network of licensed buying agents. Some boards were unable to control the agents, and producers received considerably less than the official produce price. In the case of rubber, for example, the price was fixed for a coagulum with 100 percent dry rubber content; for lower rubber ratios the price paid declined proportionately to a minimum of 50 percent of the fixed price. In fact, smallholders rarely received more than this minimum price, irrespective of the quality of the rubber, whereas the licensed buying agents were paid according to the rules. As another example, a study of the Palm Produce Board found that when the official price was ₦230 per ton, no farmer received more than ₦180 and some were paid as little as ₦135.

The relationship between producer prices and world prices changed dramatically in the late 1970s. After more than three decades in which the boards were agencies through which farmers were taxed, the position was now reversed in a few years' time: in the early 1980s farmers received (except for cocoa) prices well in excess of the world prices (table 7.17). The boards were accumulating losses in the form of debts to the Central Bank.

For food crops, the boards' intervention had little effect on prices. In most years only small quantities were sold at the guaranteed minimum price (GMP), since domestic market prices were far above the GMP. This is consistent with the GMP being above import parity since import controls were in force. The quota fluctuated widely from year to year. As a result of a tightening of import restrictions on rice in 1979/80, for example, the domestic price trebled.

Table 7.17 Ratio of Producer Prices to World Prices, 1978 and 1983

Product	1978	1983
Cocoa	0.48	0.97
Cotton	0.92	1.14
Groundnuts	0.64	1.67
Maize	1.63	2.54
Palm kernel	0.66	1.24
Palm oil	0.82	1.43
Rice	1.40	2.16
Rubber	0.85	1.61

Note: World prices are port parity prices.
Source: Internal World Bank document.

Sudden changes in trade policy made domestic prices unpredictable. For rice the tariff was lowered from 67 to 20 percent in April 1974, reduced to 10 percent in April 1975, raised to 20 percent again in April 1978, and reduced to 10 percent two months later. In October 1978 imports in containers under 50 kilograms were banned; in April 1979 larger consignments were placed under restricted license; in September 1979 all rice imports were banned for six months; and a year later all quantitative restrictions were removed. It appears that for food crops, government interventions affected marketing largely through changes in trade policy rather than through the price offered by the boards.

In food markets there is considerable competition among private traders, and marketing margins do not appear to have been high. A comparison of data on producer prices and retail prices suggests that farmers received 70 to 90 percent of the price at major consuming centers. For maize in 1977 the producer price in Funtua was 95 percent of the retail price in Kaduna; in 1978, 90 percent; and in 1979, 75 percent. For sorghum the percentages were 70, 91, and 63, and for millet, 79, 70, and 87. Table 7.18 shows the differences between domestic and world prices after the imposition (in 1981/82) of import controls on food crops. In 1982/83 all of the crops listed enjoyed considerable protection. The government intervened in agricultural marketing not just through its trade policy and the operations of the boards; it also subsidized inputs including pesticides, improved seeds (50 percent), and, most notably, fertilizer (on which the effective subsidy rate was 75 percent until 1984). The fertilizer subsidy accounted in 1982 for one-third of all agricultural public expenditure. It led to smuggling and, since few farmers had access to fertilizer at the subsidized price, to an active black market in fertilizer.

Import Licensing

The legal basis for Nigerian import control was established in 1950. Wartime regulations then lapsed; the Control of Imports Order (1950) established the director of commerce and industry as the Import Licensing Authority. The authority issued open general licenses and specific licenses, which initially were required for imports from outside the sterling area—a small proportion of Nigerian imports.

Such restrictions were removed in the late 1950s (particularly in 1958, when most imports from Japan and the United States came under open general license); by 1959 most goods could be imported freely from any country except when compliance with international commodity agreements made the retention of licensing necessary. During the first few years of independence, trade policy was extremely liberal, but when civil war broke out, quantitative restrictions were imposed.

Table 7.18 Commodity Board Prices and Border Prices, 1982/83

Product	Producer price	Allowances[a]	Takeover price	Transport fees	Total cost[b]	Border price	Protection rate (percent)[c]
Cocoa	1,300	201	1,501	44	1,545	1,338	16
Cotton	510	224	734	143	591	448	48
Groundnuts	450	147	597	149	448	270	42
Maize	290	35	325	120	205	114	31
Palm kernel	230	96	326	39	365	186	78
Palm oil	495	133	628	39	589	347	49
Rice	596	55	651	50	601	276	54
Rubber	1,200	201	1,401	39	1,440	735	58

a. Allowances cover fees of licensed buying agents, transport costs, and administrative costs of the boards.

b. Transport fees are added to the takeover price for export crops (and subtracted for import crops) to arrive at total cost.

c. Calculated as the excess of total cost over the border price. (This differs from table 7.18, where the producer price is compared directly with the border price, ignoring allowances and transport fees.)

Source: Internal 1984 World Bank report.

The postwar liberalization (in 1970/71) was only partial; it left a large portion of imports subject to specific licensing. Protection of domestic industry now became the main objective. In the administration of the system there were virtually no rules; discretion determined the weighting of such diverse criteria as the location of the applicant, his efficiency, and his nationality. Decisions on distribution of quotas were often highly arbitrary (Fajana 1977). Enforcement of the policy was ineffective: smuggling and black market dealings in licenses were widespread. When the license holder did succeed in obtaining a monopoly, he could maximize rents (given the ineffectiveness of price control) by not importing at all.

Finally, because a single individual was vested with enormous authority as the Import Licensing Authority, the system was unusually open to corruption. Import controls were expanded (and more strictly enforced, partly through preshipment inspections) in 1979. Following the second oil price increase, however, controls were again relaxed in 1980. In 1982 imports were (temporarily) suspended completely, until the Shagari government adopted a new trade policy that included increased reliance on licensing, higher tariffs, and an advance import deposit scheme.

Exchange control was accompanied by an active black market in foreign exchange. From 1974 to 1982 the black market rate was 25 to 50 percent below the controlled floating rate (U.S. dollars). In 1983 the black market rate fell by 70 percent to only 18 percent of the controlled rate. Trade policy was substantially liberalized in 1986, but as chapter 9 notes, much of this was later undone.

8 Government Finance and the Political Economy of Public Policy

This chapter provides extensive data on Nigeria's fiscal performance, considers the motivations behind important policy interventions, and briefly speculates on their effects. In the first section we identify trends in federal and regional revenue and expenditure, discussing in particular the overall size of the public sector, the fiscal balance, the composition of expenditure, and the contribution of the public sector to capital formation.

The next section focuses on political economy. It describes the different sources of rents and rent-seeking generated by the policies of each political period. The periods, and the policies that ensued, are then considered in a discussion of the decisionmakers and the groups that influenced—or failed to influence—them. Agricultural and industrial policies illustrate this discussion.

Most sources of rents arose (and declined) as a result of changes in external (exogenous) circumstances. The oil windfall enabled the government to increase its expenditures and thus provided increased opportunity for kickbacks on contracts. The trade regime became more restrictive as foreign exchange shortages developed, and this gave rise to rents in the import-substitution and importing sectors. One large but impermanent source of rents was, however, endogenous—the wage premium to unskilled workers in the formal sector. This premium followed a path that was determined by the changing influence of different interest groups, and these changes of influence were themselves the outcome of the past history of rents: there was causation in both directions between the power of various groups and the size of the rents they enjoyed.

The third section of the chapter offers a stylized analysis of the trajectory of public sector employment rents.

Trends in Public Sector Revenue and Expenditure

From 1950 to 1969 government revenue averaged around 10 percent of GDP.[1] As Helleiner (1966) pointed out, this was an extraordinarily small share of GDP, even by African standards. Between 1969 and 1973 total revenue rose from 10.7 to 19.5 percent of GDP (1963–73 series), this rise being more than fully accounted for by the rise in oil revenue (royalties plus profit taxes) from around 1 percent to nearly 12 percent (table 8.1).[2]

This dramatic change in fiscal resources predates the first oil shock and reflects the rapidly growing volume of oil production at that time. In a sense, therefore, the Nigerian economy benefited from two favorable oil shocks in rapid succession—a volume shock followed by a price shock. This price shock raised the contribution of oil to revenue from 9.2 percent of GDP in 1973 to 20.4 percent in 1974, the rise again more than accounting for the rise in overall revenue from 15.4 to 24.8 percent.

The overall revenue position then remained relatively trendless at around a quarter of GDP until the end of the 1970s. The second oil price increase raised revenue to a temporary peak of 31.4 percent of GDP in 1980, from which it fell back rapidly to around 20 percent. Nonoil revenue was remarkably passive during this whole history: it was stable at 9 to 10 percent of GDP during the 1950s and 1960s, fell precipitately to 6 percent in the early 1970s, and subsequently stayed at that level. To summarize, overall revenue remained at around 10 percent of GDP during the 1950s and 1960s, tripled during the 1970s to 30 percent, and then fell back in the early 1980s to 20 percent.

With revenue so volatile, expenditure was likely to be volatile also. Although this proved true in Nigeria, more interesting were the large discrepancies between revenue and expenditure, which were not always the simple consequence of expenditure lagging behind revenue changes. The first significant discrepancy was that expenditure grew relatively rapidly during the early period in which revenue was (relatively) stagnant.

Several different expenditure series are reported in the tables. These are difficult to reconcile in detail, but each provides a similar broad picture. Expenditure rose strongly during the 1950s; Helleiner's figures (table 8.2) suggest an astonishing increase from 5.4 percent of GDP in 1951 to 15.1 percent in 1960, with the share of capital formation rising. The figures for current expenditure in table 8.3 suggest a somewhat more modest but still pronounced increase from 6.8 to 11.0 percent over the decade, followed by a plateau until the late 1960s, when the civil war induced a rapid escalation to 15 percent from 1968 to 1973.

Table 8.1 Federal Government Revenue and Expenditure, 1965–84
(percentage of GDP at factor cost)

Item	1965	1966	1967	1968	1969	1970	1971	1972	1973[a]
Revenue									
Federally collected	10.3	9.1	11.9	10.7	10.7	12.0	17.6	19.5	19.5
Statutory allocation to states	4.2	3.5	4.2	5.2	3.9	5.1	5.0	4.6	3.5
Federally retained	6.1	5.5	7.7	5.5	6.8	6.9	12.6	14.9	16.0
From oil	0.8	0.6	2.0	1.2	0.9	3.1	7.7	10.6	11.7
Other	9.5	8.5	9.8	9.5	9.7	8.8	9.9	8.9	7.8
Total expenditure	6.7	7.6	9.4	12.9	10.7	15.9	9.6	13.6	12.6
Current expenditure	5.2	5.3	7.0	10.5	8.1	12.1	7.4	9.5	7.6
Administration and defense	2.1	2.3	3.6	7.0	4.9	8.7	5.1	6.9	5.2
Economic services	1.1	0.8	0.7	0.7	0.6	0.5	0.5	0.6	0.6
Social services	0.6	0.5	0.7	0.5	0.3	0.3	0.3	0.4	0.4
Transfers	0.4	0.4	0.3	0.4	0.2	0.2	0.2	0.2	0.3
Public debt	1.0	1.3	1.6	1.9	2.0	2.5	1.4	1.3	1.1
Internal	0.5	0.5	1.0	1.1	1.3	1.9	0.9	0.9	0.7
External	0.5	0.8	0.6	0.8	0.7	0.6	0.5	0.4	0.4
Loans on-lent	0.8	1.4	0.3	0.9	0.4	0.4	2.2	1.5	1.2
Capital expenditure	2.5	2.3	2.4	2.4	2.6	3.8	2.2	4.1	5.0
Administration and defense	0.7	0.6	0.5	0.3	1.7	2.7	0.9	1.5	1.5
Economic services	1.4	1.3	1.8	1.7	0.8	0.8	0.9	1.9	2.9
Social services	0.3	0.3	0.1	0.1	0.1	0.1	0.2	0.6	0.5
Transfers	0.1	0.1	—	0.3	0.1	0.2	0.2	0.2	0.1
Recurrent surplus	1.9	0.2	0.7	-5.0	-1.4	-5.2	5.2	5.5	8.5
Overall surplus	-0.6	-2.1	-1.7	-7.3	-3.9	-9.0	3.0	1.3	3.4
Financing									
External	—	0.7	0.4	0.7	0.1	0.0	0.6	0.7	0.2
Internal									
Bank	—	0.7	0.8	5.8	4.3	3.2	-2.5	-2.1	0.3
Nonbank	—	0.6	0.5	0.9	-0.6	5.8	-1.1	0.1	-3.9

— Not available.

Note: Any attempt to trace the scope and composition of the public sector over a third of a century is bound to be a hazardous undertaking. New series are started and old series are frequently revised and sometimes discontinued. Furthermore, there are large changes in prices, per capita incomes, and population that render comparison of different years difficult, even when the data are consistent. The most straightforward procedure is to express nominal fiscal magnitudes as a proportion of some nominal measure of national income. The measure adopted here is GDP at factor cost. This measure has been subject to major revision on several occasions, notably in the late 1950s, early 1960s, and early 1970s. In the latter two cases, the estimate of GDP was revised substantially upward. This has two implications for its use as a deflator of public revenues and

1973[b]	1974	1975	1976	1977	1978	1979	1980	1981	1982	1983	1984
15.4	24.8	26.3	25.4	25.7	22.0	26.0	31.4	23.6	21.8	19.7	20.3
2.8	3.5	5.0	4.3	5.0	3.6	4.9	6.4	9.7	7.9	7.9	7.1
12.6	21.3	21.4	21.1	20.7	18.3	21.1	25.0	14.0	13.9	11.8	13.2
9.2	20.4	20.4	20.1	19.4	13.7	21.2	25.5	16.9	14.5	13.6	14.9
6.2	4.4	5.9	5.3	6.3	8.3	4.8	5.9	6.7	7.3	6.1	5.4
9.9	11.5	23.4	25.2	23.2	25.1	17.6	29.1	21.3	23.0	21.6	18.0
6.0	4.8	8.1	10.0	7.2	10.1	7.6	12.4	10.0	9.0	—	—
4.1	3.0	5.0	3.8	3.3	3.7	2.4	3.9	4.2	4.0	6.8	7.4
0.5	0.4	0.6	0.5	0.6	0.6	0.3	1.0	1.0	0.8	5.4	2.9
0.3	0.5	1.4	2.4	1.2	1.6	1.2	1.7	1.9	1.8	2.2	0.9
0.2	0.1	0.2	2.0	1.5	2.1	2.4	4.1	1.3	0.5	4.3	3.5
0.8	0.7	0.9	1.3	0.5	2.1	1.3	1.7	1.6	1.9	2.9	3.2
0.6	0.6	0.7	1.2	0.5	1.7	0.9	1.2	0.7	0.6	—	—
0.3	0.2	0.2	0.1	0.1	0.5	0.4	0.6	0.9	1.3	—	—
1.8	1.5	0.8	1.4	0.3	1.5	0.6	0.0	0.9	3.4	2.2	—
4.0	6.7	15.3	115.2	16.0	15.0	10.1	16.7	11.2	14.0	—	—
1.2	1.5	3.6	3.0	3.2	2.9	1.8	2.7	1.4	1.7	—	—
2.3	2.5	6.3	8.4	10.0	8.7	6.7	11.2	7.2	9.7	—	—
0.4	2.0	4.4	3.4	2.6	3.2	1.5	2.7	2.6	2.4	—	—
0.1	0.7	1.0	0.4	0.1	0.2	0.1	0.1	0.1	0.2	—	—
6.7	16.5	13.3	11.1	13.5	8.2	13.5	12.6	3.9	4.9	—	—
2.7	9.8	-2.0	-4.1	-2.5	-6.7	3.5	-4.1	-7.3	-9.1	-9.8	-4.8
0.1	0.3	0.1	0.1	-0.0	1.9	—	0.5	0.9	0.5	-1.0	2.1
0.3	1.0	1.7	2.3	5.1	3.2	—	1.8	4.7	5.5	10.5	5.2
-3.1	-11.1	0.2	1.7	-2.6	1.6	—	1.7	1.7	3.0	-3.2	-2.6

expenditure. First, there is evidently a discontinuity at the time of the revision; the apparent relative size of the public sector will suffer a downward step. Second, the apparent trends between revisions are rendered suspect. The most plausible interpretation of the revisions is that the semiautomatic procedures often used in preparing the national accounts have failed to capture actual changes since the detailed examination associated with the previous revision. Thus the growth of GDP is biased downward between revisions, and the measured increase in the relative importance of the public sector is biased upward. For the revision of 1958, the converse reasoning applies.

a. Deflated by 1963–73 GDP series.

b. Deflated by 1973–84 GDP series.

Source: CBN, *Economic and Financial Review* (various issues); CBN, *Annual Report and Statement of Accounts* (various years).

Table 8.2 *Government Revenue and Expenditure, 1950–61*
(percentage of GDP at factor cost)

Item	1950	1951	1952	1953	1954	1955	1956	1957	1958	1959	1960	1961
Revenue including marketing boards	10.4	13.0	11.1	9.7	10.0	9.4	9.3	10.0	10.4	12.0	12.8	11.8
Revenue excluding marketing boards	6.6	9.0	8.8	9.2	8.7	8.6	9.3	9.6	10.2	10.6	12.2	11.8
Total expenditure[a]	—	5.4	6.9	7.1	7.0	8.6	8.9	9.3	12.3	14.5	15.1	13.8
Current	—	3.4	3.9	4.1	3.7	5.0	5.0	5.2	6.5	7.6	8.4	8.1
Capital	—	2.0	3.0	3.0	3.3	3.6	3.8	4.1	5.8	6.8	6.7	5.7
General government	—	1.4	1.6	1.9	2.0	2.1	2.2	2.7	4.0	5.2	5.4	4.5
Public corporations	—	0.6	1.4	1.1	1.4	1.5	1.6	1.4	1.7	1.6	1.3	1.3
Federal and regional expenditure[a]	5.0	5.9	6.8	7.6	6.2	7.4	9.5	10.2	12.5	14.8	16.8	15.1
Federal expenditure only	3.1	3.8	3.8	4.4	2.9	3.4	4.4	5.1	7.1	8.0	8.8	7.4
Gross capital formation	—	6.6	8.8	8.8	9.2	10.4	11.6	12.4	16.3	16.4	17.8	18.0

— Not available.
Note: See note to table 8.1.
a. Total expenditure and federal and regional expenditure are computed on slightly different bases.
Source: Helleiner 1966, tables 46, 47, 48, VE7, VE8.

154

Table 8.3 Government Current Expenditure, 1950–74
(percentage of GDP at factor cost)

Year	Admin- istration and defense	Economic services	Social services	Transfers	Public debt	Total
1950	2.9	1.3	0.9	0.4	0.2	5.6
1951	3.9	1.5	0.9	0.3	0.2	6.8
1952	3.4	1.9	1.0	0.4	0.2	6.8
1953	4.5	1.7	1.2	0.4	0.2	8.0
1954	3.2	1.9	1.6	0.8	0.2	7.5
1955	2.7	1.9	1.7	1.3	0.1	7.8
1956	2.1	1.7	2.1	1.1	0.1	7.1
1957	2.2	2.0	2.2	0.7	0.3	7.3
1558	2.4	2.2	2.2	0.5	0.3	7.7
1959	2.9	2.4	3.1	1.2	0.3	9.8
1960	3.1	2.6	3.4	1.1	0.5	11.0
1961	3.2	2.4	3.2	1.3	0.8	10.9
1962	3.1	2.3	3.1	1.4	1.1	10.9
1963	3.1	1.9	2.4	0.7	1.6	9.6
1964	3.4	2.2	2.9	0.9	1.3	10.6
1965	3.3	1.6	2.2	1.0	1.4	9.5
1966	2.8	1.4	2.1	0.7	2.2	5.3
1967	4.0	1.7	2.7	0.7	2.0	11.2
1968	6.5	1.6	7.3	1.0	2.9	14.3
1969	9.6	1.4	2.1	0.8	3.7	17.7
1970	7.7	1.7	2.5	0.4	2.1	14.8
1971	6.7	1.5	2.9	0.4	1.7	13.2
1972	8.1	2.0	3.8	0.5	2.0	16.4
1973[a]	7.3	1.7	3.0	0.8	2.3	15.2
1973[b]	5.8	1.3	2.1	0.7	1.8	12.0
1974	5.1	1.2	2.8	0.6	1.0	10.7

Note: See note to table 8.1.
a. Deflated by 1963–73 GDP series.
b. Deflated by 1973–84 GDP series.
Source: CBN, *Economic and Financial Review,* 17 (2), 1979.

Turning back to table 8.1, federal expenditures rose rapidly in 1965–70, from 6.7 to 15.9 percent of GDP. As already noted, overall revenue rose relatively little over this period; the same was true for the federally retained component, which increased from 6.1 to only 6.9 percent. In consequence, the overall federal deficit increased from 0.6 to 9.0 percent of GDP. It was at this point that the oil volume effect began to appear; coupled with a retrenchment of expenditure after the war, the oil volume increase turned this large deficit into a surplus of 3 percent of GDP in the following year.

The federal budget remained a few points in surplus until the first oil price shock raised the 1974 surplus to 9.8 percent of GDP. Federally retained revenue rose by 8.7 percent of GDP between 1973 and 1974, while federal expenditure increased by only 1.6 percent of GDP. Between 1974 and 1975 federal revenue remained relatively stationary, although expenditure doubled from 11.5 to 23.4 percent of GDP. This dramatic increase was caused largely by an expansion of the capital expenditure component of the budget. The increase was sufficient to drive the federal budget back into overall deficit, where it remained until the end (1984) of the period here considered—with the exception of 1979, when the second oil price shock combined with a temporary expenditure reduction to yield a surplus. From 1975 to 1982 federal expenditure averaged a little more than 23 percent of GDP; thereafter it began to decline. Since federal revenue fell precipitately following 1980, the overall federal deficit increased dramatically during the early 1980s, peaking at nearly 10 percent of GDP in 1983.

This brief description of the path of aggregate public expenditure and its relation to revenue suggests that the budgeting problems experienced by the Nigerian authorities cannot be described accurately as resulting from difficulties in adjusting to shocks. To the contrary, the country showed itself capable of a rapid increase in public spending following revenue gains (1974/75 following gains in 1973/74, and 1979/80 following 1978/79), and also, at least according to the data (table 8.1), capable of a rapid expenditure reduction in the face of a large enough deficit (1970/71 following 1970; 1978/79 following 1978; and 1982/84 following 1982 and 1983).

The underlying budgetary problem in Nigeria has been, rather, that the budget spirals out of control precisely in periods when revenue is relatively stationary and growth in expenditure is excessive. Three such episodes occurred in the period under study. The first was in the decade of the 1950s (table 8.2). The second occurred in the civil war period, 1967–70. The third was the now familiar and spectacular loss of expenditure control during the oil boom years of 1974–80.

One interpretation of these episodes is that they reflect a long-standing predisposition of the Nigerian authorities to lose control of the budget.

However, it is more plausible to regard each of these three episodes as unique. The first involved the run-up to independence under a colonial authority with (initially) an excessively large budget surplus; the second reflected an event that is in no way rooted in budgetary control but inevitably had powerful budgetary consequences; the third involved a familiar phenomenon whereby large windfall budgetary gains generated a loss of budgetary control, partly because the usual disciplines were perceived to be unnecessary and partly because the sudden appearance of large economic rents induced corrupt attempts to appropriate them. Nigeria was protected from this problem during the volume windfall of 1970/72, because the rents had already been preempted by the spending associated with the civil war.

We have so far considered the extent to which the public sector preempted resources but paid little attention to the uses to which these resources were put. The public sector contribution to capital formation is considered next, followed by aspects of the functional distribution of public expenditure and the distribution of revenues and expenditures among different levels of government.

Capital Formation

The figures in table 8.4 suggest that in the late 1950s the public sector's share of total investment was around 40 percent. The flow of funds accounts in table 8.5 give capital formation figures for 1970 to 1978. Total government (federal plus states) capital formation is shown as rising steadily from 3 percent of GDP in 1970 to 5 percent in 1974. It then rose dramatically to 9 percent in 1975, 15 percent in 1976, and 17 percent in 1977 and 1978. This increase was more than fully accounted for by the federal government. During this period the public sector share of capital formation rose from 20 to 55 percent of the total. Private investment as a share of GDP was relatively trendless (though highly volatile), averaging a little more than 14 percent in the period before and during the public investment boom. This evidence does not indicate that the public sector expanded at the expense of private sector investment, and the preponderance of infrastructural investment in public capital formation supports this interpretation. A similar picture emerges from the national accounts data for the shorter period from 1973 to 1978. We do not have public sector capital formation estimates for later years, but assuming a reasonably stable relation between federal capital formation and the federal capital expenditure account, capital formation seems likely to have been sustained at more or less half of total investment until 1982.

From 1973 to 1978 federally retained revenue rose from 12.6 to 18.3 percent of GDP, or by 5.7 percent. Because a surplus of 2.7 percent was transformed into a deficit of 6.7 percent, the federal government's ab-

Table 8.4 *Government Revenue and Expenditure, 1955–65*
(percentage of GDP at factor cost)

Item	1955	1956	1957	1958	1959	1960	1961	1962	1963	1964	1965
Revenue	8.1	9.4	9.0	10.4	11.2	13.6	12.5	11.8	12.1	14.4	15.1
Federal	4.1	4.8	4.5	5.2	5.6	7.6	6.3	5.8	6.3	7.0	7.2
Expenditure	7.7	7.5	7.6	8.5	10.0	10.4	11.1	11.1	11.5	12.8	13.4
Federal	3.5	3.0	3.4	4.0	4.5	4.4	5.2	5.2	6.0	6.1	6.3
Gross fixed capital formation											
Public	—	—	4.2	5.7	7.1	6.6	5.3	4.8	4.5	—	—
Private	—	—	6.7	6.8	7.0	7.2	8.1	7.2	8.1	—	—
Total	—	—	10.9	12.5	14.1	13.8	13.4	11.9	12.7	—	—

— Not available.
Note: See note to table 8.1.
Source: Adedeji 1969, tables 2.8, 2.9, 5.4, 6.2, 6.7.

Table 8.5 Flow of Funds Account, 1970–78
(percentage of GDP at factor cost)

Item	1970	1971	1972	1973[a]	1973[b]	1974	1975	1976	1977	1978
Federal government										
Gross capital formation	1.2	1.7	2.1	3.4	2.7	7.5	7.7	12.6	14.4	14.8
Net surplus	-7.9	2.8	0.0	4.4	3.4	9.5	4.4	-4.6	2.1	8.5
State governments										
Gross capital formation	1.7	2.1	2.4	3.4	2.7	2.2	1.7	2.0	2.3	2.4
Net surplus	-0.3	-0.4	-0.1	-3.2	-2.5	-2.0	-1.4	-1.6	-0.9	-1.3
Recurrent revenue	7.2	8.5	10.4	5.5	4.4	3.7	5.8	7.2	8.2	7.8
Recurrent expenditure	6.4	7.9	9.2	5.8	4.6	3.6	5.5	7.0	7.1	7.0
Operating surplus	0.8	0.6	1.2	-0.3	-0.2	0.1	0.3	0.2	1.2	0.8
Total government										
Gross capital formation	2.9	3.8	4.5	6.7	5.3	4.7	9.2	14.6	16.8	17.3
Net surplus	-8.2	2.4	0.0	1.2	0.9	7.6	3.1	-6.2	1.2	7.1
National gross capital formation	14.6	17.1	19.7	26.9	21.2	16.6	23.5	29.3	30.6	31.4

Note: See note to table 8.1.
a. Deflated by 1963–73 GDP series.
b. Deflated by 1973–84 GDP series.
Source: CBN 1983.

159

sorption of resources rose from 9.9 percent to 25.1 percent of GDP. Of this increase of 15.2 percent, 12.1 percent was accounted for by increased federal capital formation and 3.1 percent by increased public consumption. Private investment contracted (relatively) by 1.8 percent of GDP and state capital formation by 0.3 percent of GDP. Preserving the balance of payments would have required private consumption to contract by a huge 18.3 percent of GDP. However, the actual contraction achieved was only half of this and was accommodated by a massive deterioration in the balance of payments.

The Functional Composition of Expenditure

The data in table 8.3 cover general government current expenditure from 1950 to 1974. The administration and defense category was trendless at around 3 percent of GDP until 1967, when the civil war induced a rapid rise to nearly 10 percent of GDP in 1969; the category subsequently fell back to around 5 percent in 1974. Similarly economic services and transfers (excluding public debt) were relatively trendless. The main changes were the growth of social services (education and health particularly) in the 1950s and the growth of debt service in the 1960s.

Table 8.1 presents data on federal expenditure from 1965 to 1984. The real interest centers on the changes following the first oil price shock. As previously noted, the more pronounced impact was in the capital account, and most particularly in economic and social services. From 1973 to 1978 these two categories increased their shares of GDP by 6.4 and 2.8 percentage points, respectively. Changes in the current account were less dramatic; they accrued mainly in public debt servicing and other transfers and in social services, particularly education.

Revenue and Expenditure by Level of Government

Federal spending constituted roughly half of total expenditure during the 1950s and early 1960s (tables 8.2 and 8.4), and this remained the case in the early 1970s (table 8.1). Both capital formation and current expenditure by the states were similar in magnitude to these categories of federal spending in the early 1970s (table 8.5), but this balance was disrupted by the oil revenues. During the late 1970s, oil revenues were preempted almost entirely by the federal government; state revenues and expenditures stayed at much the same proportion of GDP, while federal expenditure went through the rapid increases already described.

From the fiscal perspective, the central fact of the Nigerian economy is its federal constitution; a large proportion of government activity is conducted at the regional and state levels. This has been a central con-

cern from the inception of the nation, and it placed the problem of revenue allocation at center stage throughout the postwar period. Nigeria's
fiscal system was unified only from 1926 to 1948. Under the 1946 constitution, the three regions were given a large measure of financial responsibility. The principles governing this devolution were enunciated
by Sir Sydney Phillipson, financial secretary to the Nigerian government. The central principle was that of derivation—revenues should
come to the region in which they were generated. This proved problematic in several respects: the rule ran counter to any concept of need,
and it required statistical information that was not available. In consequence, the revenue allocations determined by the Phillipson report
bore little relation to the revenue requirements of the regions or indeed
probably to the real geographic pattern in which revenue was generated.

There were strong feelings in the North that the allocation system was
unfair and that attention should be paid to need, with population being
the appropriate indicator. The Hicks-Phillipson Commission was appointed in response to this sentiment in 1950 and duly enunciated three
additional principles of federal finance. The transfer of specific tax powers to the regional governments was embodied in the principle that these
governments should have independent revenues. The principle of need
was also accepted; however, the population statistics were so poor that
the population of each region had to be proxied by the number of adult
male taxpayers. The third new principle was that of national interest:
the commission suggested that the central government make grants for
specific regional services (education and police) considered to be of national importance.

The central feature of these proposals was a move away from a total
reliance on the principle of derivation toward a system based on multiple criteria. These proposals were embodied, broadly, in the constitution of 1951. Within two years, however, it seemed clear that some further devolution toward a more truly federal system was inevitable in
the face of growing discontent among the regional governments. The
Chick Commission of 1953 was given a restrictive mandate to ensure
that the principle of derivation was followed. The resulting system was
in operation for four years. The disenchantment of the regional governments with the principle of derivation was one factor leading to the 1957
constitutional conference that in turn appointed yet another fiscal commission (the Raisman Commission), this time with much wider terms of
reference.

The recommendations of the Raisman Commission became effective
in fiscal 1959/60 and lasted substantially unchanged until fiscal 1965/
66. The commission attempted to strike a balance between derivation
and the requirement for some regional autonomy on the one hand and

the principle of need on the other hand. It found that the major sources of revenue at the time and in the easily foreseeable future (import and exports taxes, excise duties, and general sales tax) would have to remain within the federal jurisdiction. However, the revenue from export taxes was to be returned in full to the region of origin, which would also have autonomy in fixing the rates of produce sales taxes. Other federally collected taxes, such as import and excise duties on gasoline, diesel oil, and tobacco, were also to be transferred in full to the regional governments.

The fundamental innovation in reallocating revenue was to award the regions complete jurisdiction over the personal income tax. This was a proposal that had been strongly rejected by both the preceding commissions. At the time of the Raisman Commission, income tax jurisdiction over Africans outside Lagos was a regional responsibility, and jurisdiction over non-Africans was federal, with the tax collected and distributed according to the principle of derivation.

The other significant innovation, designed to address the issue of need or equity, was the Distributable Pool Account. Thirty percent of the revenue from mining rents and from (the bulk of) import duties was paid into this account, and funds were to be allocated among the regions after considering four factors: the preservation of continuity in government services, the minimum responsibilities that could properly be laid on a government, the population of the region, and the need for balanced development of the federation.

On the basis of these criteria, 40 percent of the account was to be allocated to the North, 24 percent to the West, 31 percent to the East, and 5 percent to the Southern Cameroons (briefly a separate region). In 1961, when the Southern Cameroons opted out of the federation, the allocations of the other three regions were altered to ratios of 40:95, 24:95, and 31:95, because the regions could not agree on a basis for sharing the 5 percent released. A further modification took place when the Midwestern Region was created from the Western Region. The Western Region's share was divided between itself and the Midwestern Region in the ratio 3:1. Between 1959 and 1966, allocations from the account constituted a sizable share of the regions' recurrent revenue: 21 percent in the North, 24 percent in the Midwest, 14 percent in the East, and 11 percent in the West.

In 1967 the regions were split into 12 states. Because the new state boundaries did not cut across those of the regions, the regional allocations were subdivided. Relative population appears to have been the basis of reallocation among the five new Southern states, but in the North the new states received one-sixth each of the old allocation. There were in any case unacceptable disparities between states, with greatly increased revenues accruing to the two oil-producing states and expenditure burdens falling elsewhere.

The unsatisfactory structure of revenue allocation led to the appointment of a Revenue Allocation Review Committee in 1969. Its report was rejected, but early in 1970 the federal military government made substantial alterations that strengthened the federal government's position, increased the amount of revenue accruing to the Distributable Pool Account, and introduced some fiscal equalization among the states. Later changes included reform of the marketing board system (1973), which deprived the states of one of their independent sources of revenue, and the transfer of all customs and excise duties to the Distributable Pool Account (1975). All these changes further eroded the principle of derivation. The powers of the center were further strengthened by centralization of the power to fix income tax rates and allowances (1975).

The 1981 Allocation of Revenue Act (as subsequently amended) prescribed that all federally collected revenue (with specified exceptions) was to be paid into a federation account for disbursement among the three levels of government, with 55 percent allocated to the federal government, 35 percent to the state governments, and the remainder to local governments, leaving aside minor allocations specific to revenue from mineral production. The states' allocation was distributed according to the following criteria and weights: population (40 percent), minimum responsibility of government (40 percent), social development factor (15 percent), and revenue effort (5 percent). In practice, the attempt to earmark 10 percent of the account for local governments failed, because these funds were routed through the state governments and they routinely neglected to complete the transfer, instead retaining the funds for their own use.

In addition to the statutory allocations, the states also received substantial sums from the federal government on-lent from domestic and foreign borrowing. The states also retained significant revenue sources of their own, including the personal income tax already noted. Thus the revenue allocation system was much studied and much altered, gradually evolving away from the principle of derivation. This evolution was briefly interrupted in the early 1950s but greatly accelerated by the massive growth of oil revenues that made the principle insupportable.

In other respects, fiscal evolution was less satisfactory. The development of a sound federal fiscal structure was impeded by the continued focus on the allocation problem and, in the later part of the period covered by this book, by the easy access to oil revenue.

Rents, Interest Groups, and Policy Decisions

During the whole period since 1950, economic policy initiatives were rare: agents with official responsibility for public objectives seldom used policy instruments to achieve these goals. The major initiatives were industrialization, indigenization, and the structural adjustment of 1986. Yet outcomes were so remarkable that it is unlikely that they would have occurred as the consequence of rational maximizing behavior of private agents unless the agents were grossly ill informed. Thus there is a case for supposing that public agencies bear considerable responsibility for resource misallocation.

The most remarkable outcome is that per capita private consumption was significantly lower at the end of our period than at the start, and the incidence of poverty was probably higher. This is remarkable because for a decade the economy had enjoyed a large terms of trade windfall, much of which had ostensibly been invested, and prior to that decade per capita consumption had been rising. Public action is the apparent culprit for this outcome because the allocation of the windfall was the prerogative of public agencies. In addition to the direct allocation of the oil windfall, a second sphere of public intervention was in the operation of all factor and some product markets. Until the oil slump such interventions tended to accumulate and to inhibit mutually beneficial potential transactions rather than facilitate such transactions.

The major redistributive effects of public interventions in the 1950–70 period were qualitatively different from those in the oil boom era. In the former period they were directly discernable and predictable from partial equilibrium analysis: taxes on export crops accounted for about 95 percent of the funds of development corporations between 1946 and 1962, and these agencies spent their funds on urban activities. Such rural-to-urban redistributions were sufficiently transparent to conclude that they were intended. In the oil boom we have suggested that the major redistributions occurred through general equilibrium effects on relative prices. These effects were probably not intended by those who determined the policies that gave rise to them.

Rents and Rent-Seeking

Public interventions created substantial rents. These are important in explaining why some of the interventions occurred and in assessing their consequences for distribution and growth. Although rents were important throughout most of the years after 1950, their origin differed between periods, and as the sources of rents shifted, the beneficiaries altered. In the 1950s and 1960s the dominant rents were probably in the labor market, in the form of the premium enjoyed by formal sector unskilled workers over their supply price. As shown in chapter 7, during the 1950s and early 1960s unskilled public sector workers acquired a wage premium over their supply price, and this was matched by private employers in the formal sector. Public sector employees were perhaps the only reasonably cohesive occupational interest group to emerge. (We discuss below why others did not.) The magnitude of the rents involved in this wage premium can only be estimated. Kilby (1969, p. 202) estimates formal sector employment at 3.6 percent of the economically active population for 1962. In chapter 7 we estimated the wage premium by the mid-1960s as 56 percent over the supply price. The rents generated by the premium were thus around 2 percent of GDP.[3]

During the second oil boom the primary source of rents shifted to profiteering on government contracts: the wage premium was starting to erode, expenditure on contracts was increasing, and the rental margin on contracts probably also increased with the switch to civilian government. The flow of funds analysis in the first section of this chapter suggests that by the late 1970s gross fixed capital formation in the public sector was 17 to 20 percent of GDP. Even at the Lockheed rate of kickback observed for the early 1970s (8 percent), the rents on the contracts that this expenditure generated would have amounted to around 1.5 percent of GDP, but because by the civilian period the margin was sometimes 100 percent (no services being delivered), this is probably a considerable underestimate.

Another important source of rents came through the control of food imports. Quota regulations on food imports were put in place by the military governments of the 1970s. However, the rents generated by these controls became far more important during the civilian period, 1979 to 1983, because coincidentally food production per capita was declining. As a result, it was possible for both imports and the gap between domestic and world food prices to rise. Estimating the rents involved in food importing is highly approximate. Between 1979 and 1981 expenditure on imported food at domestic prices was approximately ₦5.4 billion, whereas its cost, insurance, and freight (c.i.f.) cost was ₦3.8 billion.[4] Rents per year were thus a maximum of ₦530 million, or 1 percent of GDP, during this period.

During the oil slump the tightening of import restrictions, the decline in public expenditure on contracts, and the rapid erosion of the wage premium all tended to shift the source of rents to the trade regime. However, the recovery of agriculture and the low priority given to food imports meant that the rents from this part of the trade regime probably diminished. In chapter 5 we tentatively estimated the rents accruing from nonfood import controls during this period as 6 percent of GDP, split fairly evenly between importers and import-substitute producers.

When rents are in place for a substantial period it is reasonable to infer that they will attract rent-seeking: real resources will be spent on their acquisition up to the point at which the investment equals the potential return (although there may still be winners and losers, as with any investment). However, when rents are the transient by-product of some unpredictable event, they are less likely to have a counterpart resource cost. The wage premium persisted for so many years that rent-seeking was likely to occur. The increased demand for education and the high urban unemployment rate of the mid-1960s both point to such a phenomenon. Because the erosion in the wage premium rents was unpredictably rapid during the early 1980s, it seems likely that by the mid-1980s the economy was suffering from rent-seeking in excess of the then-current value of the rents.

Rent-seeking on public sector contracts can also be presumed to have developed during the 1970s based on excessive expectations of their future value. For example, the 10 Nigerians who collectively contributed ₦12 million for the construction of the local NPN headquarters in the early 1980s may well have regretted their investment. Note that such expenditures were a use of resources and not a transfer. Rent-seeking on food import quotas was probably modest because the phenomenon was temporary and controlled from the highest reaches of the political hierarchy in order to generate funds both for those regulating the trade and for the NPN. All the trade controls gave rise to smuggling through Benin as well as by air, which incurred avoidable costs. The rent-seeking on nonfood imports during the oil slump occurred predominantly in the import-substitute sector, where it is reasonable to assume that the rents were fully dissipated, because there is no evidence of supranormal profits in the sector during the period.

Agents in Policy Determination

In explaining policy interventions we must first identify the agents who participated in generating them. The cast of direct decisionmakers includes the army, senior civil servants, and politicians. The cast of those who might have influenced the decision process is open-ended; we consider peasants, public sector workers, unions, local communities, and other beneficiaries of rents.

The army, with two brief exceptions, was not sufficiently assertive or cohesive to rule by the continuous and open application of force and preferred to retain power by avoiding actions that would generate strong opposition. In this sense the army excluded other groups from power rather than itself functioning as a power. Bienen and Fitton (1978) demonstrate convincingly that the army provided a buffer by which senior civil servants were able to increase their power. Systematic interviews with a large group of politicians and civil servants active during the first period of military rule established that the civil service had gained most (even more than the military) from the military regime, that civil servants did not want a return to civilian rule, and that they had more power under military than under civilian regimes.

The army had limited direct influence on policy because its interest was confined to military equipment and conditions of service. In an interview with a senior civil servant, Bienen and Fitton record: "When the army wants something for itself it is adamant. It says 'That's it.' But generally they do not come into policy matters" (p. 47). Post-1970 army interests could easily be accommodated, not only because revenue was rising, but because the military budget had been inflated by a civil war that had ended. Thus during the expenditure bonanza of the first oil cycle the share taken by the military decreased. The significance of the army as an interest group was therefore its capacity to shield the civil service from other interest groups.

There have been only two brief phases during which the army asserted itself rather than permitting the civil service to do as it chose. The Mohammed (1975) and Buhari (1984–86) regimes carried out extensive purges against corruption in the civil service. The Buhari regime in particular was characterized by a military ethic of rectitude, but it relied on low-level coercion rather than redesigning the system of decisionmaking.

Senior civil servants thus had a remarkably free hand at running the country between 1966 and 1979, and so their composition and goals are central to the consideration of policy. Recruitment to the senior echelons of the federal civil service required educational qualifications that, in the 1950s and 1960s, were regionally skewed against the North (homeland of the Hausa). During the civil war many Ibo civil servants fled East, leaving promotion opportunities for other groups. By 1970 both the Hausas and the Ibos were underrepresented. However, this was not a pure gift to the Yoruba. The three largest tribes together account for only around half of the Nigerian population, and with two of them thus disqualified, the minority tribes gained some ascendancy. Their interest was to end the contest at the national level between the three largest tribes; that is, their interest was both to strengthen the center and to fragment the regions, thus ending the hegemony of the large tribes over minorities within the regional territories.

To a large extent, the federal civil service succeeded in this long-term transformation from a loose federation with limited central legitimacy, which characterized the 1950s, to a unitary state. The emasculation of the regions was achieved partly by fragmenting the regions into 4, 12, and then 19 states (a process that continued subsequently), partly by establishing parallel federal institutions such as the River Basin Development Authorities, which were better funded than local rivals, and partly by eroding the principle of derivation in revenue allocation and the rights of states to borrow abroad. In 1954 revenue had come overwhelmingly from export crops, and the national, crop-specific marketing boards were replaced by three autonomous regional boards. After the civil war this process was reversed: in 1970 derivation was reduced so that the states received only 60 percent instead of 100 percent of export duties, and 50 percent instead of 100 percent of excise taxes. Oil revenue provided an opportunity for extending this policy: by 1979 the states relied on the federal government for 70 percent of their revenue. This trend was reversed on the return to civilian government, when the ruling NPN was a party of regional baronies without a strong interest in federal control. As already noted, the new revenue-sharing formula implemented in 1981 reduced the revenue share of the federal government to 55 percent.

The emergence of the political case for centralization coincided with support for centrally planned economic intervention. The civil war expanded the role of the state in the wartime economy and demonstrated that Nigeria was vulnerable to outside intervention. The rapid buildup of oil revenue allowed the government to finance interventions without raising taxes or reallocating existing expenditures. However, economic centralism through the public sector had its limits. First, there was never a commitment to socialism (African or Fabian), so the private sector was not viewed with hostility. Second, the public sector projects of the 1960s were manifest and costly failures, and the civil service was aware of its own limitations as a manager of productive activities. Third, there were potentially greater opportunities for rents if public money was used to fund private asset acquisitions than if ownership was retained in the public sector. As a result of these factors, much of the indigenization of industry occurred through the public funding of equity purchases of foreign companies for private Nigerian citizens.

During the two civilian periods, 1960–66 and 1979–83, politicians rather than civil servants were in control. Nigerian politics were remarkably nonideological: politicians did not compete for support on the basis of their beliefs. This left the way open for competition based on either loyalties or interests. Again, remarkably, the former completely dominated the latter: winning politicians did not attract votes primarily by offering rewards but by being the sole feasible candidate of the community. The evidence for this is best seen in the lack of influence of the largest interest group by far—peasant farmers.

Rural interest groups have always been politically weak (Bienen 1984). In 1950 Nigeria was relatively urbanized for Sub-Saharan Africa. In the South, although cash crops had already spread through many areas, nationalist politics were not based on farming interests. The early Nigerian politicians in the period from 1920 to the 1940s were professionals, businessmen, and traders. In the North, politicians were part of a hereditary and religious aristocracy. By independence, each region had a one-party state whose senior echelons completely excluded farmers. In the North, of more than 70 NPC leaders, none was described as a farmer; similarly, in the East, of an executive committee of 70 for the NCNC, only 1 had an agricultural interest (as a plantation owner). In the West, of more than 100 leaders of the Action Group, only 2 had an interest in agricultural production. This pattern continued after independence: in the Western Region's parliament in the early 1960s only 1 of 54 members with identified occupations was a farmer. Similarly, the professions given for heads of state, governors, party chairmen, and parliamentary presidents from 1960 to 1980 show the continued dominance of professionals. Bienen notes that this dominance was unusual by African standards: leaders identified modernity with becoming urban and industrial.

Farmers were not alone in being unable to organize, for no occupational interest groups emerged in Nigeria, nor did any political parties based on occupation. Even the industrial working class failed to generate party or trade union organizations of much substance. Trade unions have been split internally and have not provided a solid organizational base for political leaders. Bienen considers the general strike of 1964 as the high watermark of the trade union movement, and this coincides with the trajectory of the rents (the wage premium) enjoyed by unskilled workers in the formal sector (see chapter 7). Yet studies of organizational participation in Nigeria show that membership in associations is relatively high. The lack of occupational interest groups appears to be the result not of intrinsic free-rider problems of collective action, but of intense linguistic, ethnic, and neighborhood loyalties. These loyalties both motivate organizational participation and preclude occupational associations that would cut across—and thus blunt—these loyalties. The impediment to class formation appears to have been persistent: Bienen (1984, p. 12) judges that "there has been no clear movement from ethnic to class identifications." This is manifested in the type of peasant opposition that the pro-urban redistributive policies generated. Peasants noticed the policy bias and staged violent protests in 1960, 1964, 1966–67, 1968–69, and 1980. However, the revolts were always localized and failed to transcend the communities in which they erupted.

Control of the government has been of overriding importance in Nigeria because status, wealth, and power do not rest primarily on private economic resources or efforts but on the elite positions generated and sustained by state institutions. Those contending for power used communal loyalties rather than occupational interests to build a base of support; constituencies were communally rather than functionally defined. This shaped not only how politicians acquired power but what they did with it. Rimmer (1978) summarizes public decisionmaking in the first civilian period as follows: "Public economic power and patronage were valued mainly as instruments of distribution. . . . [T]he dominant purpose of electoral activity was to control preferment." Bienen endorses this as a description of the second civilian period.

As noted in our discussion of the sources of rents, public sector wage earners were the one exception to the impotence of occupational interest. Yet this group generates a puzzle, for the benefits it enjoyed (the wage premium) peaked prior to the enormous increase in the ability of the public sector to reward its own employees. As Bienen notes, the high watermark of this premium was the mid-1960s, despite the vast increase in the capacity of the public sector to spend during the oil boom. Extra expenditure bought more staff rather than a larger wage premium, and subsequently, with the oil slump, lower expenditure induced cuts in the wage premium rather than cuts in staff. The major exceptions to this were the Udoji pay award of 1974 that increased the public sector pay bill by 50 to 60 percent, but a period of nominal stagnation and rapid real wage erosion followed.[5]

Agricultural Policy

Policymakers operated in almost complete ignorance of agricultural performance. This reflected and also contributed to the low priority attached to the sector until performance became an urgent problem. Agriculture never received a substantial share of government expenditure. In the 1950s agriculture was the prerogative of the regional governments. Despite being the dominant source of revenue for each region, even at the start of our period (1951–55) it received only 8 to 14 percent of government expenditure in the three regions. In the 1960s this declined to 7 percent according to Wells's (1970) estimates. This decline from an already low base is attributed to the planners and politicians, who had other priorities. Planners not only equated industry with modernity, but they also preferred interventions in which the state itself directly used the public resources. This preference tended to exclude agriculture because of the lack of qualified personnel to undertake large-scale agricultural projects. Politicians, as discussed above, were not subject to interest group pressures from farmers and were themselves drawn from nonfarming occupations.

Within the low budgets accorded agriculture, the forms of intervention differed between regions. In the North—which had less export agriculture, a more decentralized Ministry of Agriculture, a stronger colonial legacy, and a more paternalistic elite—expenditure was directed to food-producing peasants through fertilizer subsidies, irrigation investment, and extension projects. In the South peasants were bypassed by large, public export-crop plantations designed to transform the organization of agriculture and to generate more revenue.

In the 1970s the share of agriculture in federal expenditure declined further, to 5 percent (1970–74) and 2.5 percent (1975–79). This occurred although the federal government took over many agricultural responsibilities from the regions—an act probably motivated more by the desire to emasculate the regions than to stimulate agriculture. Bienen suggests that the high priorities afforded to construction and education were in some respects popular, even with rural constituencies, because the rural-urban income gap generated a desire to exit agriculture. We incorporate this effect into a simple dynamic model of competing interests later in the chapter.

Some pro-agriculture policies were nevertheless implemented. Export-crop taxes were phased out and even replaced by subsidies (though these were not sufficient to offset the overvaluation of the exchange rate). There was a substantial fertilizer subsidy, and fertilizer use increased massively. Food prices were guaranteed but at levels so far below market prices that they had no effect. Above all, there was no attempt to implement a cheap food policy by restraining price increases, as happened in several other African economies during this period. The deterioration in domestic food supplies relative to the growth of population, and in particular the resulting increase in food imports, induced policymakers to introduce institutional innovations; improved agricultural performance was sought "through the public sector rather than aimed directly at smallholders. . . . Institutional innovations were an attempt to improve agriculture without altering incentive systems enough and with the same bureaucratic personnel" (Bienen 1984, p. 60).

An interesting policy reversal in the late 1970s permitted foreign companies to acquire large-scale interests in agriculture. The objective of antagonizing foreign investors gave way to the objective of increasing agricultural performance. However, this reversal merely confirmed policymakers' low regard for agriculture. The sector was not sufficiently important for its poor performance to warrant an increased allocation of domestic resources; instead it was reopened to foreign resources.

In addition to institutional innovation, policymakers favored mechanization and large-scale irrigation. Import duties on tractors were abolished and there were subsidies for tractor hiring. The goal was to bypass the traditional small farmer and encourage the emergence of a new class of commercial farmers who would obtain cheap credit from the banks (on which target credit allocations to agriculture were imposed), use imported capital and imported subsidized fertilizer, and farmland acquired from government irrigation schemes. The Land Use Decree of 1978 gave the bureaucracy new powers of land allocation. Koehn and Aliyu (1982), in a detailed study of how this decree was put into operation, conclude that state officials favored public servants and private businessmen. Thus, the new class was to come not from the ranks of peasant farmers but primarily from the military population and the public sector labor force.

By the late 1970s agriculture had risen on the policy agenda because of food imports, but interventions were shaped by the motivations of policymakers; they favored centralization (to weaken the regions), opportunities for patronage and profit, and large-scale, "modern" investment. These priorities coincided in the River Basin Development Authorities. By following rivers, the authorities cut across regional boundaries and so were intrinsically national. They involved large public works and thus the awarding of important contracts on which rents could be taken. Once in place they needed large public staffs, which provided opportunities for patronage. As investments they were massive, visible agricultural transformations, but their rate of return was heavily negative.

Industrial Policy

Industrial policy had two overt objectives: to further "development" and to enable Africans to gain access to the sector of the economy considered most strategic—the "commanding heights." Both of these beliefs were widely shared by Nigerians. During the colonial period both comparative advantage and government intervention had induced the rapid growth of traded agriculture. Yet the colonial power itself was industrial. A natural inference was that Nigeria was not industrialized because of colonial policies that preserved the most lucrative sector for the metropolis. Furthermore, such nonagricultural activities as existed were often owned by Syrians, Lebanese, or multinationals.

The First Development Plan (1962–68) stated the two objectives explicitly and outlined disparate interventions for translating them into policy instruments. The plan listed six initiatives, including a development bank and trade fairs, but at the top of the list was the establishment of a publicly owned, integrated iron and steel complex. By the fourth plan (1981–85) there was a target (of 12 percent) for the share of manufacturing in GDP. The specification of the objective in terms of GDP share is revealing because it suggests that the primary concern was not growth so much as the shape of the economy; agriculture continued to be seen as distasteful. The indigenization objective had been relegated to "consolidation," probably because, as we will see, indigenization had indeed been achieved.

Four new themes were evident in the fourth plan: self-reliance, employment, regional dispersal, and public sector efficiency. Self-reliance meant local sourcing of intermediate inputs. The regional dispersal of industry, antipathetic both to local sourcing and to the pace of industrialization, reflected the fair regional division of patronage that we have suggested characterized the implicit NPN constitution. The concern for public sector efficiency probably reflected the increasingly costly performance of existing public sector industries.

The first industrial policy interventions, in the late 1950s, worked primarily through the tax and trade regimes. Exemptions from income tax and customs duties on inputs were granted on a discretionary basis to "pioneer" industries. In the 1960s increased intervention in the formal credit market (as discussed in chapter 7), motivated originally by the desire for aggregate monetary control, began to be used to direct subsidized credit to the sector. Additionally, some state industries were established. Large-scale public expenditure on industry did not get under way until the first oil cycle. Industrial expenditure included full public ownership (in steel, salt, cement, and paper), the purchase of equity stakes in private ventures (by 1980 the federal government had a stake in 30 large companies, according to Osoba 1987, table 3), start-up grants to private firms, and operating subsidies.

Antagonization received its big push in 1977 when industrial activities were made the exclusive preserve of nationals or limited to firms with a minimum of 60 percent equity participation by nationals. It is not possible to get an accurate breakdown of the ownership of private industry, but a study by Osoba (1987) of 207 industrial companies for which ownership could be determined found that by 1980, 75 percent of them were exclusively Nigerian. However, this percentage may be deceptive because many Syrian and Lebanese businessmen may have retained de facto ownership while handing over de jure ownership to Nigerian nominees. Even with this proviso, antagonization provided a major opportunity for individual Nigerian citizens with good connections to acquire cheap equity, often using public funds.

Industrial protection increased during the civil war as a result of the diversion of foreign exchange to military uses: imports became rationed and prioritized. The trade regime was liberalized with the onset of the first oil boom, but tightened again between 1977 and 1979. Osoba suggests that this was a response to pressure from industrialists, but it might also have reflected a macroeconomic response to foreign exchange shortages as the oil cycle entered its downturn. An estimate of the structure of effective protection for 1977 and 1979 found a marked increase and also found considerable variation in protection across industries, implying resource misallocation among industries. Agro-related activities received negative protection, whereas consumer assembly industries were heavily protected. The same trajectory of liberalization occurred during the second oil cycle. However, the use of trade policy to promote industrialization was constrained in most sectors by the highly porous nature of Nigeria's borders: when champagne imports were banned, Benin became the world's largest champagne importer.

The promotion of industry was thus a constant in Nigerian policy; what changed was the capacity to finance it and the distribution of industrial activity between the public and private sectors and between the regions. The oil boom enabled more to be spent, and the switch from rule by senior civil servants to rule by NPN regional barons probably contributed to the increased emphasis on private ownership and regional dispersion. Like education, industry was a respectable item about which people cared and on which the state could spend money. Yet it had the advantage over public services of providing higher potential rents because ownership of the assets could pass to private agents, the output from these assets could be marketed, and their reliance on imported inputs gave continuing opportunities for overinvoicing.

Outcomes

To what extent were agricultural and industrial policies responsible for agricultural and industrial outcomes? Since for much of the period agricultural policy was modest, it can hardly be considered the cause of poor performance in either the food or traded-crop sectors. As argued in chapter 4, these outcomes were explicable in terms of the general equilibrium effects of Dutch disease and the purchase by the government of labor drawn out of agriculture. Some of the effects of Dutch disease were desirable. Others, though undesirable—with the benefit of the hindsight that enables us to see the oil shocks as partly transient—were reasonable policy errors. However, there were two major and obvious errors that severely accentuated the contraction of the traded agriculture sector through Dutch disease. The first was the accumulation of foreign debts instead of foreign assets during 1977–79 and 1981–84. The debts constituted an additional inflow of foreign exchange. Second, during the 1980s the exchange rate was maintained as an anti-inflation and prestige instrument while becoming increasingly overvalued. Fiscal policy thus harmed the economy directly and damaged the agricultural sector indirectly.

In contrast to agricultural policy, industrial policy was lavish. What is remarkable is that despite the large-scale direction of public resources to industry during the oil boom, the growth of manufacturing was so modest. The sector grew at an annual rate of 3 percent from 1979/80 to 1984, followed by a substantial decline in 1985 and 1986 and widespread bankruptcies after the 1986 exchange rate reform package. This poor performance, of which the steel mills were the prime example, occurred because many of the industries established in the 1970s were not viable without the subsidies provided both directly and indirectly through the cheap imported inputs permitted by an overvalued exchange rate. As foreign exchange and government funding became less available, continued industrial capital formation merely increased the capital-output ratio.

Model of Public Sector Employment Rents

The behavior of the public sector as an employer has entered our analysis at several stages. Two important aspects of that behavior remain unexplained—the expansion in public sector employment (which contributed to the contraction of the rural labor force), and the post-1970 reduction in the rural-urban wage differential, which the government had created in the previous 20 years.

To the extent that public sector decisions do not emanate from a black box, they represent the outcome of a struggle between groups with different interests and different strengths. To accommodate interest groups in the analysis of African public sector labor markets, many economists in the 1960s argued that real wages were "institutionally" rigid. In effect this amounted to claiming that existing wage employees constituted such a powerful interest group that they exerted a veto on proposed wage reductions, whereas opposing interest groups (taxpayers, firms, or beneficiaries of alternative uses of public expenditure) exerted a countervailing veto on wage increases. However this belief arose, it could not be more dramatically contradicted than by reference to the Nigerian public sector. More remarkable even than the long periods of rising or falling trends in real wages are the massive year-to-year fluctuations. For example, in real terms the minimum rate for unskilled government employees jumped by 28 percent between 1963 and 1964 and by 54 percent between 1974 and 1975, while falling by 50 percent between 1983 and 1985 and by 40 percent between 1975 and 1978. Such wild fluctuation in real income is manifestly costly for employees desiring a fairly even consumption path and so could not reflect the outcome of bargaining between two interest groups with different preferences and equal power.

Changes in the magnitude of public sector employment may derive from decisions to provide public services by way of a stable production function. However, as Khan (1985) has commented, it is probably more plausible to interpret a considerable proportion of employment growth as itself constituting the decision objective. For example, from 1971 to 1981 the employment of unskilled workers (messengers, cleaners, porters, gardeners, and so on) in the federal civil service (established plus nonestablished staff) increased as a proportion of total civil service employment from 8 to 18 percent, with an average annual growth rate of 20 percent. This relative expansion in unskilled public employment coincided with a narrowing of skill differentials, so the production process was becoming physically more intensive in the factor whose relative price was increasing. It is thus difficult to characterize unskilled public employment as being merely the outcome of cost-minimizing public production choices.

We regard both wages and employment as being directly chosen through the outcome of a bargaining process between interest groups. The actual configurations of relevant interest groups and the shifts in bargaining power between them may be so complex as to defy economic analysis. Below we suggest a simple model of three interest groups that is broadly consistent with actual experience, without implying any stronger claims.

We distinguish the following groups:

- *Existing public sector employees.* The interest of this group is in exacting a wage premium. Because the Nigerian public sector is more effectively unionized than either private sector wage employees or farmers, we might expect some ability to achieve and maintain a wage differential (controlling for skill). However, except in the period around independence when the influence of the group temporarily increased, in equilibrium this premium is unlikely to be large. The group has neither considerable voting power nor any real power to disrupt.
- *Would-be public sector employees.* This group has an interest in the expansion of public sector employment. The lobbying power of this group is in part a function of the number of those eligible for employment, but it depends primarily on the size of the wage premium. Because education is a criterion for much public sector recruitment, the expansion of education might be expected to increase the size of the lobby for employment creation. Similarly, an increase in the wage premium will make public employment desirable for more people and so increase the size of the lobby. It will also increase the desirability of the public sector for those already in the lobby and hence increase the intensity of their lobbying. Especially in a society in which patronage is traditionally important, senior public employees are

subject to such lobbying pressures from members of client and kin-ship groups to provide jobs. We thus hypothesize that the intensity of this lobbying is functionally related to the magnitude of the pre-mium (or rent) provided by public (unskilled) employment over the supply price of labor: the more desirable public jobs are, the more people will exert pressure to acquire them.

- *Taxpayers and beneficiaries of alternative uses of public expenditure.* This group has an interest in a lower public sector wage bill, achieved by either wage or employment reductions.

Two countervailing pressures therefore determine employment: the interest of the nonpublic-sector labor force in gaining public sector jobs, and the interest of other claimants on public expenditure (for example, taxpayers).

Recent developments in public choice theory (see Olson 1965, Becker 1983, and especially the important applications to Africa pioneered by Bates 1983) have emphasized that lobbies can be expected to have dif-ferent degrees of effectiveness according to their ability to overcome the free-rider problem. We should note, therefore, an important difference between the employment lobby and its competitors. Whereas almost any public provision of goods and services and any tax reduction will benefit a large number of agents, a decision to increase employment can be confined to a single vacancy. The employment lobby can therefore be entirely decentralized, because it is made up of individual job seekers lobbying for the creation of individual vacancies for themselves. By con-trast, because rival lobbying activities confer externalities on those with a common interest, lobbying will be constrained by the free-rider prob-lem. Following Becker's concept of "influence functions," the free-rider problem suggests that the interest of private agents in the expansion of public employment will prevail over an equivalent interest of private agents in alternative uses of public expenditure. This does not, of course, imply an indefinite growth in public employment. As the public sector wage bill rises and increasingly preempts alternative expenditures, it encounters progressively more well-defended rival interests. In equilib-rium all interest groups are able to protect their claims on expenditure against employment lobbying.

This equilibrium is defined formally in the equation

(8.1) $$\dot{E} = \dot{E}\,(w - s, w \cdot E) = 0$$
          $$\pm$$

where E is public employment, w is the public sector wage, and s is the supply price of labor. The first argument $(w - s)$ is the wage premium, which, as discussed, increases the incentive to expand employment, and the second ($w \cdot E$) is the wage bill, which reduces the incentive; hence the signs of the derivatives. For completeness it should be noted that when the wage premium is negative, public employment will contract as a result of voluntary quitting. Formally:

(8.2) $\dot{E}\,(0, w \cdot E) \leq 0$

The second component of the model is a wage function. Public sector employees share a common interest in a high wage premium, and, for a given level of employment, rival lobbies have an interest in a low premium to minimize the public sector wage bill. Because lobbying for a wage increase confers externalities on other public employees, this interest is subject to free-rider problems, which public sector unions attempt to overcome by control of their members. However, because these efforts have generally been unsuccessful, the public sector wage lobby exerts little influence. If unions are sufficiently weak, when employment is in equilibrium the wage will be in equilibrium only at a zero premium. More generally, we posit that when employment is in equilibrium, there is an equilibrium wage premium p over the supply price. The two arguments of the employment function are also arguments of the wage function. The greater the wage premium, the more satisfied the public sector employees and the less hard they lobby for further increases. For a given wage premium, the higher the wage bill, then the greater the pressure from rival lobbies to reduce that premium. These behavioral relationships are stated formally in equations 8.3 and 8.4:

(8.3) $w = w\,(w - s, w \cdot E) = 0$

(8.4) $w\,(p, wE^*) = 0 \, ; p \geq 0$

where E^* is a value of E that satisfies equation 8.1.

   The employment and wage functions are combined in the phase diagram of figure 8.1. The intersection of the schedules determines the equilibrium employment and wage levels, and the four quadrants define regions of disequilibrium behavior as indicated by the arrows.

   Now we consider how this simple dynamic analysis of interest group pressures can be applied to the Nigerian public sector over the past 25 years. We have suggested that there were three sequential exogenous shocks. First, during the period of independence the ability of existing

Figure 8.1 Employment and Wage Functions

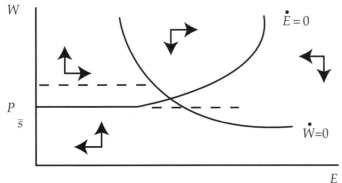

Note: See text for definition of variables.

public sector employees to gain pay increases was temporarily enhanced relative to the ability of taxpayers to stop them. For example, between 1950 and 1965 the real wage for the lowest-paid government workers increased by some 140 percent. Figure 8.2 shows this by a jump in the wage rate at given employment from the initial equilibrium at E_0 to an initial disequilibrium at D_1. Had this shock had the time to work itself out, the system would have returned to equilibrium along a clockwise spiral path. The higher wage premium would initially have increased the incentive to lobby for a public sector job, generating a phase of employment expansion coincident with declining wages.

Figure 8.2 Employment and Wages, 1973–81: Scenario 1

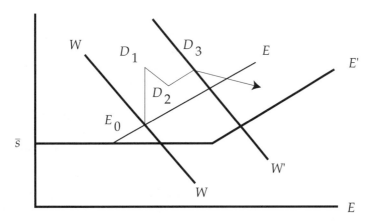

Note: See text for definition of variables.

As the tax burden of the extra employment increased and the wage premium declined (reducing the incentive to get a public sector job), the economy would eventually have entered a phase of declining public employment. In fact from 1965 to 1972 real wages declined but employment expanded continuously. According to our interpretation of events, this was because the Nigerian economy had not reached the phase of declining public sector employment by the time of the second exogenous shock. (Alternatively, independence might, by increasing the efficiency of lobbying for patronage, have produced a permanent shift to the right in the equilibrium employment schedule, so that some of the increase in public sector employment was sustainable.)

The massive increase in the real wages of the unskilled that occurred at independence built up over 15 years, which might seem a long enough period for full adjustment. However, only five of these years were subsequent to independence, and the colonial state had a greater ability and willingness to resist the pressure of job seekers for employment expansion. Thus, to a considerable extent, the determination of wages and employment by the interest groups outlined above only applies postindependence, and this process started from a large disequilibrium in the public sector wage premium over the supply price of labor.

The second shock was, of course, the expansion of oil revenue. This had the effect of reducing the pressure of taxpayers and claimants on public expenditure to resist expansion of the wage bill. In our diagram, both schedules shift to the right (figure 8.2).

Supposing the adjustment in wages and employment from the initial disequilibrium, D_1, to have proceeded as far as D_2 at the time of this new shock, the economy would experience a regime switch into a phase in which wages rise together with employment. However, this phase is temporary, for beyond D_3 the economy reverts to falling wages and rising employment in the public sector.

Our analysis thus predicts that from 1973 to 1981 employment would expand continuously, whereas wages would first rise and then fall. The actual movement of wages was extremely erratic, with some tendency for wages to decline over the period as a whole but with sharp increases occurring in 1974 and 1979. Employment increased rapidly.

The third exogenous shock is the post-1981 contraction in oil revenue, which both reduced government income and deflated the private sector. The former effect increased the pressure to reduce the wage bill from taxpayers and claimants on expenditure. This effect alone shifts both schedules back to the left. However, the contraction in the private sector created considerable labor shedding. Employment in manufacturing and nontraded services declined by around 12 percent, or 1.4 million workers, between 1981 and 1983. The reservation wages of those newly entering the labor market and of those made redundant were thus (temporarily) much lower than they were before 1981. This reduction in s shifts the $w = 0$ schedule farther to the left but shifts the $\dot{E} = 0$ schedule to the right (by increasing pressure for employment expansion). Thus, the net effect on the $\dot{E} = 0$ schedule is ambiguous, with the increased pressure to cut the wage bill being offset by increased pressure to recruit. In figure 8.3 we assume a net shift to the right in the $\dot{E} = 0$ schedule.

If the adjustment in wages and employment from D_3 proceeded as far as D_4 by the time of this new shock, the economy would not switch regimes—that is, employment would continue to rise and wages to fall, but the change in the balance of interests would induce a relative acceleration in the fall in wages. Thus the short-term disequilibrium adjustment impact of the oil contraction would be to accelerate the decline in wage and (depending upon the net effect on the $\dot{E} = 0$ schedule) to accelerate or decelerate the expansion of employment (on the usual assumption that the rate of adjustment is an increasing function of the magnitude of the disequilibrium). In fact, real wages fell considerably between 1981 and 1983, whereas employment continued to expand, although at the reduced rate of 7 percent a year. In the absence of new shocks the economy enters a further adjustment phase beyond D_5, at which point there is a regime switch to falling wages and falling employment. This was probably how the economy could be characterized at the end of our

Figure 8.3 Employment and Wages, 1973–81: Scenario 2

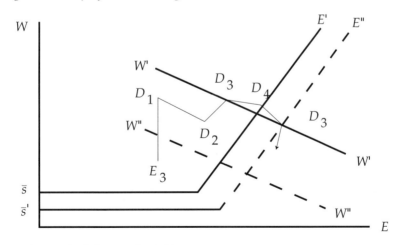

Note: See text for definition of variables.

period. Having increased by only 3 percent in 1983/84, in 1984/85 public sector employment had either stagnated or declined by 1 percent (Khan 1985), while real wages fell by more than 40 percent.

If the economy is not subject to further shocks, then the private sector, having undertaken a once-and-for-all contraction, reverts to normal growth and the reservation wage reverts to its normal level. The public sector union is thus in the long run able to exact the same modest premium over $\bar{s}$ shown by the excess of the wage at E_0 over $\bar{s}$. The equilibrium employment schedule ($E''' - E'''$) reverts to lie between $E - E$ and $E' - E'$ (that is, there is some oil revenue but less than in the 1970s). Similarly, the equilibrium wage schedule ($w''' - w'''$) lies somewhere between $w - w$ and $w' - w'$ (and must also be to the right of $w'' - w''$) (figure 8.4).

Supposing the economy has incompletely adjusted as far as D_6 from the disequilibrium at D_5, then by the time of the recovery of the private sector, the final adjustment phase is marked by employment contraction and wage increases to E_7. This combination has not been experienced in Nigeria during the 35-year period covered by our analysis and thus constitutes an interesting prediction of the model for the late 1980s. The full adjustment path from the initial equilibrium at E_0 to the final equilibrium at E_7 is shown in figure 8.4 and can be summarized as follows:

Figure 8.4 Final Equilibrium Schedule

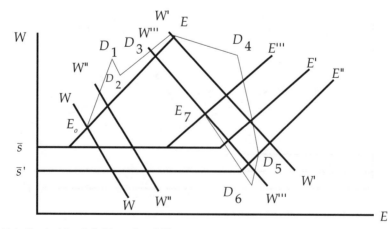

Note: See text for definition of variables.

1950	E_0
1950–65	$E_0 - D_1$ wage increase due to shock
1965–73	$D_1 - D_2$ wage decreases and employment expansion
1973–75	$D_2 - D_3$ wage increases and employment expansion
1975–81	$D_3 - D_4$ wage decreases and employment expansion
1981–83	$D_4 - D_5$ faster wage decreases and possibly faster employment expansion
1983–85	$D_5 - D_6$ wage increases and faster employment contraction.

The evolution of public sector wages and employment in Nigeria during our period is complex and potentially puzzling. Although the model presented in this section is very simple, it can track this evolution closely and provide a plausible explanation for it.

9 *Explaining the Outcomes*

In this final chapter in our analysis of the Nigerian economy from 1950 to 1984 we examine the outcomes of the choices made by decisionmakers and interest groups in Nigeria. Some choices were forced on the actors by outside influences; some evolved because of the decentralized political structure of the country and the competition for power and security between competing groups. We look at growth, distributional outcomes, and the evolution of policy and assess why Nigeria took the path it did.

Growth Outcomes

The national accounts data presented in chapter 6 indicate that total GDP at factor cost was, in constant prices, 3.3 times as large in 1984 as in 1950 (table 6.7). Assuming population growth of 3 percent a year, this implies an increase of 25 percent in per capita GDP over the period, or a growth rate of 0.7 percent a year (table 9.1).

In the 1950s there was little structural change in the economy. Agriculture accounted for approximately two-thirds of GDP in 1950, which means that the agricultural sector accounted for most (60 percent) of the growth in GDP in that decade. Agricultural growth was not due to supportive policies—development policy in this period meant investment in industry and infrastructure, financed to a considerable extent by agricultural taxation—nor was it due to technological change. The growth in agriculture resulted from acreage expansion and, apparently, a commensurate increase in labor input, and it occurred in response to favorable prices (caused partly by the Korean war commodity boom).

Both industry and government grew rapidly during this decade, but from such a small base that they had little effect on total GDP. Thus the 1950s present a simple picture: growth was agricultural, it required no change in technology or factor proportions because land was abundant, and expanding the area under crops (and reducing leisure) was economical because of high prices.

Table 9.1 GDP Growth, 1950–84
(percent)

Period	Real GDP growth over period	Sectoral shares of GDP growth[a]			Annual GDP growth per capita
		Agriculture	Mining	Manufacturing	
1950–60	42	60	0	12	0.6
1960–73	125	11	32	12	3.4
1973–79	23	–18	32	28	0.6
1979–84	–14	16	–83	9	–5.9
1950–84	241	17	18	36	0.7

a. The shares of agriculture, mining, and manufacturing are shown as a percentage of the absolute value of the increase in real GDP over the period. Thus for 1979–84, when both oil revenue and total GDP declined, the share of mining is shown as –83 percent.
Source: Same as for table 6.7.

The next period distinguished in table 9.1 (1960–73) is the only one with rapid growth: GDP increased by 3.4 percent a year. Agricultural growth stagnated in this period (it increased by only 21 percent, which represented a decline of 1.7 percent in per capita terms). This stagnation was the result of falling agricultural prices in the early 1960s. However, starting in the early 1970s agricultural stagnation was associated with *rising* prices. The agricultural GDP deflator increased sharply, by almost 50 percent (relative to import prices), between 1965 and 1973. We argued in chapter 5 that the combination of a decline in food production and an increase in food prices was caused by a shift of labor out of agriculture: as rural labor was drawn increasingly into urban employment, food supply curves shifted to the left.

There is direct evidence on labor allocation from 1970 on, but the shift in labor is likely to have started earlier, in particular because of the phenomenal growth of the public sector in the late 1960s. GDP in the government sector (a good proxy for public employment) was more than four times as high in 1977 as in 1965 (making the subsequent increase during the oil cycle look modest by comparison). On the basis 1973 = 100, government GDP reached 239 in 1981 and then stabilized.

Although agricultural stagnation was related to policies (the expansion of government employment and the wage premium established earlier), the rise of the oil sector was largely an exogenous event that alone accounted for one-third of GDP growth in 1960–73. Most remarkable, however, is that in table 9.1 agriculture, mining, and manufacturing together account for only 55 percent of 1960–73 growth. This is because services (not shown in table 9.1) showed phenomenal growth (5 percent a year).

Because there are no data on the allocation of investment between sectors, it is impossible to say to what extent this growth in 1960–73 was caused by capital formation. However, we do know that capital formation doubled in real terms between 1965 and 1972 and that only 6 percent of investment in this period consisted of land improvement. There is some evidence of increasing capital intensity prior to 1973, but this change appears to have been modest. Since output was growing much faster than population, this suggests that nonagricultural growth in 1960–73 was a result of capital accumulation plus rural-to-urban labor reallocation.

Dutch disease could be an alternative or additional reason for the growth of services in 1960–73. After all, there was a substantial oil boom before 1973: GDP in the mining sector in 1972 was more than 40 times as large as in 1960 and, before the OPEC price increase of 1973, already accounted for 17 percent of GDP. But there is no convincing evidence of a relative price increase of nontradables as a result of this pre-OPEC oil boom. The relative price indexes shown in table 6.8 indicate little change for the government sector and only a modest increase (23 percent) for other services between 1960 and 1972.

For the period of the first oil cycle, four developments deserve to be emphasized. First, agricultural output declined not only in per capita terms but also absolutely (by 14 percent). As in the previous period, this decline was accompanied by a sharp increase (82 percent) in the relative price of agricultural goods. A gap still existed between urban wages and rural income levels, causing labor to shift out of agriculture into urban employment, and this was reinforced by the resource movement effect of Dutch disease: the oil boom drove up the relative price of nontradables, which (even in the absence of a wage gap) induced labor reallocation at the expense of agriculture.

Second, in addition to the price increases, there continued to be considerable volume growth in the oil sector; as in the previous period, oil alone accounted for one-third of total GDP growth. Third, there was substantial growth in services and—a new development—in manufacturing. Industrial output increased by 162 percent between 1973 and 1979. However, when compared with the massive amounts invested in this period (an estimated 85 percent of the windfall income), there was remarkably little growth. National accounts data indicate that the ratio between investment and the increase in nonoil GDP—which had fluctuated between 3.3 and 4.8 since 1950—suddenly jumped to 12.6; the increase would go to 10.0 if agriculture were excluded.

The savings out of the windfall income failed to efficiently transform the boom into a permanent income increase. One reason was that the attempt to raise the domestic level of investment quickly (as opposed to accumulating foreign assets) lowered the efficiency of investment.[1] In addition, much of what appeared as investment in the national accounts in fact represented kickbacks. Also, there was a genuine shift toward more capital-intensive projects (as happened in Indonesia at the same time), the steel industry being a prime example. Finally, it should be noted that the national accounts statistics do not pick up what may well be the boom's most important legacy: the effect of the government's massive investment in education, especially in primary education.

Distributional Outcomes

Many of the outcomes relating to income distribution in Nigeria are unknown because of a lack of data. However, to the extent that distributions are discernible, in rural areas there appears to have been a change toward greater inequality, and in urban areas the distribution was highly unequal at the end of our period. Rural-urban differentials, which were large during the 1950s, were gradually eroded and reversed during the 1980s. Differentials between regions were large and persistent; changes apparently represented fluctuations rather than trends. These outcomes are unlikely to have been the direct consequence of overt income redistribution policies, which were interregional. Redistribution through taxation was significant until the mid-1960s through taxes on export crops, but after the oil boom such redistribution was negligible. Redistribution through expenditure on public services is considered in our discussion of public expenditure policy.

As shown in chapter 6, the most powerful region, the North, failed to achieve any systematic increase in per capita income relative to the other regions. This was partly because the direct effects of transfers were probably swamped by general equilibrium effects. However, additionally, although the North was more cohesive and influential than the other regions, the regional allocation of oil revenue was the outcome not of force but of a compromise embracing many areas outside the North.

Attitudes toward equity differed between the North and the South, with the former having a tradition of paternalism and deference and the latter being more anarchic. These different traditions were reflected in the behavior of the Northern-dominated federal government and the predominantly Southern press, one of the most open and critical in Africa. At the risk of parody, inequalities have been seen in the North as justified by a legitimate hierarchy and in the South as the by-product of legitimate contest. Neither attitude provided a basis for redistributive policies from the rich to the poor. Allegiances were to kinship or linguistic groups. The poor looked to the rich within their group for patronage, rather than to the poor in other groups for collective pressure on the rich.

The political process in Nigeria has therefore been a contest between the elites of each group, who dispense patronage within their groups. An established elite can be undermined most easily by the creation of a subgroup with its own sense of identity and loyalties. The elite of this subgroup then campaigns for separation—that is, for the creation of new states—a process that began in Nigeria soon after the 1973 oil price rise and that the Babangida government resumed. The struggle between group elites did not produce a decisive victory but rather a distributional constitution in which the formula for the sharing of federal revenue was agreed to by a coalition.

We have suggested that the distributional outcomes in Nigeria have been primarily the result either of general equilibrium consequences of the oil boom (and how it was handled) or of rents. During the boom the appreciation of the real exchange rate transferred incomes from the nonoil tradable sector—the nonfood agriculture of the West and East— to the less-tradable food sector located primarily in the North. During the oil slump this movement went partly into reverse, except that until 1986, payments equilibrium was maintained by the intensification of trade restrictions. As a result, relative prices changed within the set of tradable goods, so that the export sector failed to gain while the import-substitute sector gained massively. However, incomes in the nontraded sector, especially in urban areas, fell precipitately, reversing their previous rise.

In addition to the rents arising from trade controls, which occurred primarily after the boom, large rents occurred from the embezzlement of public funds, primarily during the boom. A third form of rents was from public sector wage employment; these rents were at their peak during the 1960s. They emerged not through union power over employers (which might have been sustainable), but because the colonial government and its successor civilian regime were atypically vulnerable to pressure from their own employees, while large private firms needed to emulate the government. This configuration was not sustained, and because the wage premium was not based on direct collective bargaining power over employers, the rents eroded. However, part of the process of erosion was rent-seeking lobbying for jobs. Concessions to the rent-seekers put pressure on the wage bill, which in turn put pressure on the wage premium.

The Evolution of Policy

Two major, related characteristics of Nigeria make it unlikely that any coherent set of economic policies could have evolved during the period of this study. The first characteristic is the failure to achieve a satisfactory constitutional resolution to the problem of welding a nation out of the fragmented geographic and ethnic components inherited from the colonial authorities. The second is the large number of regimes; five different governments—one colonial, two civilian, and two military—held power between 1950 and 1989. In spite of these changes in regime, policy was surprisingly stable.

As is clear from chapter 1, the constitutional problem predated independence. Independence was achieved against a background of extensive constitutional change coupled with threats of secession. Even the impetus to accelerate independence underlined the fragmentary and divisive nature of the Nigerian polity rather than, as in so many other countries, reflecting a cohesive political core. At independence, regional interests were heavily entrenched and the federal superstructure was fragile; dependent on the consent of the regions, the country faced an uncertain future.

A dominant consideration from the start was the problem of designing and maintaining a system of revenue allocation among the regions. If oil had not been discovered, derivation would likely have remained the guiding principle, and the federal government would have remained weak if indeed the federation survived at all. The discovery of oil had several important consequences. It helped to bring the East's threat of secession from imminence to actuality, while making secession even less acceptable to the other regions. It elevated the federal government, in its military manifestation, to its role as the guardian of national unity. It discredited the principle of derivation and, in the absence of acceptable alternative principles of allocation, it ensured a massive centralization as well as augmentation of revenue.

There were further, indirect consequences. The end of the civil war—successfully resolved from the federal government's point of view—took secession off the agenda of Nigerian politics. Also, the creation of central authority set in train a series of constitutional reforms designed to preserve and strengthen the center by dividing the few but powerful regions into progressively larger numbers of smaller and weaker states.

Despite this busy, and in many respects fruitful, sequence of constitutional reforms, the central political problem was still not resolved. There were no political parties with a national constituency until the military imposed a somewhat artificial one on the polity toward the end of the Babangida regime. The lack of national parties was in large measure what led to military rule and sank the attempted return to civilian government. Perceived corruption was doubtless also important, but the extent of corruption and the perception of it are both enhanced in a political system focused on local patronage.

The scale and longevity of this political failure are of central importance in the evolution of Nigerian economic policy. The absence of national parties diverted a great deal of government attention to attempts at constitutional reform, revenue allocation, and other matters relating to regional balance. It ensured that a national policy perspective was only fitfully represented during periods of civilian rule. Also it paved the way for extensive periods of rule by a military with little interest in or aptitude for economic matters.

Had there been an early disaster of economic mismanagement, the government's relatively cavalier attitude would presumably have been modified. However, there was no disaster of this kind. As noted in chapter 8, government expenditure tended to grow rapidly during periods of relatively stationary revenue, and the impending fiscal crises tended to be staved off by sudden growth in revenue. The second oil cycle became the major exception to this pattern. Until then, the apparently inexhaustible buoyancy of revenue permitted successive governments to concentrate on matters other than economic management.

In consequence, the Nigerian authorities were able to maintain, until nearly the end of the period, an unsophisticated economic perspective. They paid relatively little attention to fiscal management or income distribution and virtually none to absolute or relative prices, except for their stubborn insistence on maintaining a grossly overvalued exchange rate. This policy and the associated exchange control are the basis of their extraordinary achievement in inducing a massive black market premium on foreign exchange throughout the two oil price booms.

In short, what might be described as the general equilibrium implications of public policy were almost wholly neglected. Rather, the major focus of policy was on boosting production—by protecting domestic industry through indigenization, by engaging in what was intended to be directly productive capital expenditure, and by providing social and economic infrastructure.

The balance between these items shifted over time. The first two national plans (1962, 1970), for example, stressed increased production as the supreme purpose of development planning. The third plan (1975), drawn up in the light of booming oil revenues, sought to use the revenue to create the infrastructure of self-sustaining growth, including improved educational provision. The policy would have been appropriate in a one-sector world, without adjustment costs, but as it was, the attempt to invest instantly the vast preponderance of the oil income was naive and inevitably wasteful.

This book focuses on the period 1950–84, but we should briefly mention more recent developments. Trade policy was substantially liberalized in 1986, but much of this was undone after 1994.[2] Following the recovery that peaked in 1990 as a result of the Gulf War, the government again lost control over expenditure more egregiously than ever before, with the fiscal deficit approaching 10 percent of GDP during 1991 and 1992. This debt was financed by the inflation tax, the rate of inflation having reached 45 percent by 1992. In response, the government again resorted to overvaluation of the official exchange rate. By 1994 the configuration of macroeconomic policy was back to that of 1984; the liberalization of the late 1980s had proved abortive. The roots of this failure—the political fragmentation, the lack of sound economic advice, and the lack of self-discipline resulting from the oil windfall—help explain the failure of public policy in Nigeria.

II | *Indonesia*

10 *The Colonial Period*

Indonesia was subject to external influences and invasions long before the Dutch appeared on the scene at the very end of the sixteenth century. Links with India go back at least 2,500 years, and Indians were influential from about 200 to 1600. They introduced legal practices, agricultural innovations (including wet rice cultivation), and both Buddhism and Hinduism. Hindu kingdoms were established on Java and southern Sumatra. Around 1300 the Majapahit empire flourished, helping to establish an Indonesian identity and to begin unifying many of the islands that now make up the country.

In the fifteenth century, traders introduced Islam, which quickly replaced Hinduism. European nations arrived in the sixteenth century: first the Portuguese in 1511, then the Dutch in 1596, and subsequently the English. The Europeans introduced new crops (maize, cassava, tobacco, coffee, tea, rubber, and palm oil), but they were mainly attracted by the profitable trade in spices grown on the Moluccas, the islands between Sulawesi and West Irian. For a long time the Moluccas were much more important to the Dutch than Java.

Until 1795 the activities of the Dutch were carried out under the flag of the United East Indian Company (VOC), a private stock company that had been granted monopoly trading rights as well as the right to make treaties, maintain law and order, wage war, build forts, and operate a judicial system. For all practical purposes the VOC was a predatory state. To protect its interests the VOC established fortified trading posts throughout the archipelago (Batavia, the forerunner of Jakarta, was founded in this way in 1619). By enforcing the primacy of trade with Europe, these posts destroyed trade between the islands. The VOC had no territorial ambitions (although it sometimes got involved in Indonesian feuds and then acquired land in return for supporting one prince against another), and it did not try to establish legal and administrative control outside the immediate vicinity of its trading posts. The main exception was the area south of Batavia, Preanger, which was suitable for coffee growing and where traders gradually established plantations and became involved in production.

The VOC was immensely profitable; in the two centuries of its existence its average dividend was 20 percent in spite of the fortunes many VOC employees amassed at the expense of their employer. The difference between the price the company received for spices and what it paid was huge. For example, in the second half of the seventeenth century the VOC paid 3 stuivers (a Dutch coin) for cloves; in Europe they were sold for 75 stuivers (de Jong 1984).

Such profits required a ruthless defense. In the case of cloves, production was allowed on only a few islands. Each year a campaign was conducted to cut down trees on other islands and punish any would-be producers. In protecting its rents the VOC used local rulers. The Sultan of Ternate, for example, received a high salary from the Dutch in return for making clove production illegal in his territory (de Jong 1984, p. 37).

Under the VOC an early form of indirect rule developed. The Dutch offered rulers military protection, gifts, and salaries in return for the delivery of crops or services such as the use of oxen to transport coffee. The demands for such deliveries were passed down the hierarchy, and at each level part of the yield was diverted to private uses. What developed was a system in which the local population was exploited, not directly by a colonial power but indirectly by its own rulers—largely through taxation in kind, including compulsory labor—who now gained in power through Dutch support. The VOC bought the rulers' cooperation by offering them part of the rents it garnered (to a considerable extent indirectly by not objecting when the rulers surrendered only part of what they collected to the Dutch). With the exception of the area around Batavia, where plantations were established, there was no European settlement in the VOC period.[1]

The local rulers were not the only group to benefit under the VOC; the Chinese did also. They had already formed a genuine entrepreneurial class before the arrival of the Dutch, and under the aegis of the VOC they obtained a virtual monopoly over intraisland trade and acted as tax farmers—the rights to impose tariffs, sell salt, and manage other such activities were taken over by the Dutch from local rulers and rented out to the Chinese. Such fiscal monopolies were to remain an important source of government revenue until well into the twentieth century.

The VOC was taken over by the Dutch state in 1795. Governor General Daendels tried to set up a noncorrupt, tightly organized civil service and claimed the ownership of all land for the state, excepting a few independent principalities on Java. In the British interlude during the Napoleonic Wars, Sir Stamford Raffles continued these policies, instructing the civil service to check the abuse of power by the local rulers (the regents) and selling land on a large scale. After the return of the Dutch, the sale of land continued, leading to the emergence of a settler class of European origin. Governor General Van der Capellen forbade further sales of land, much to the annoyance of the regents. This contributed to the revolt led by Prince Diponegoro, the extremely bloody Java War.[2]

In 1830 the Dutch set up a *cultuurstelsel*, or cultivation system. This involved the payment of land rent in kind and amounted to a system of compulsory export-crop production. Coffee production was expanded enormously. Initially 200 million new trees were planted, using forced labor, and subsequently up to 10 million trees were planted annually. Sugar and indigo were planted on land previously used for rice production. In theory the system included a tax rate of 20 percent (half of what had been paid previously in rent): peasants had to give up one-fifth of their land and could be forced to work 66 days per year on it to produce the crops designated by the government. In practice, taxation was much heavier. Occasionally it led to famines on Java, particularly because of the use of forced labor not only for the production of export crops but also for road building, work in sugar factories, and similar tasks. The cooperation of the regents, whose authority had been undermined for more than 30 years (1795–1830) but whose position was now strengthened, and also of the Dutch civil servants who objected to the new system, was bought by giving them a percentage of the sales revenue.[3]

The *cultuurstelsel* differed from exploitation under the VOC not just because a private company had been replaced by the state; the VOC had restricted itself to trade, but the new involvement with production brought Dutch influence to the village level. Under the *cultuurstelsel* private European farming was kept out.

This system was abandoned in 1870, when the compulsory growing of export crops was abolished and the Agrarian Act enabled the government to give out land under long-term leases to non-Indonesians.[4] This was the start of a long period (1870–1914) of phenomenal growth in export agriculture based on Dutch plantations—sugar production, for example, trebled in this period.[5] The traditional export products (coffee, sugar, tea, and tobacco) were overtaken by new commodities: rubber, copra, tin, and oil. In this period the economic dominance of Java started to decline; whereas sugar production remained concentrated on Java, tobacco was grown on Sumatra. Labor for the tobacco plantations on Sumatra was recruited on Java. These workers were ill treated and desertion was high until the tobacco companies succeeded in including clauses in labor contracts that in effect legalized slavery. At the end of the nineteenth century the annual death rate among the Javanese working on Sumatra was 7 percent.

Railway development started in 1870, and oil was discovered in 1880. There is some evidence that this was a period of impoverishment. Rice production on Java, for example, grew by only a third between 1880 and 1920, whereas population increased by 80 percent. This was also the period in which Dutch control was enforced and extended—for example, in the lengthy and bloody Aceh (Atjeh) War.

While plantation agriculture prospered, Dutch liberals became concerned about the effect of the current Dutch policy on the Javanese standard of living. Partly as a result of this concern, the Dutch adopted in 1901 what they termed an "ethical policy." The policy was born out of a sense of shame about nineteenth-century Dutch colonialism, with its emphasis on the extraction of a surplus (the Indonesian contribution to the Dutch government budget) and on indirect rule. Holland was seen as having to repay a "debt of honor" to Indonesia. After 1901 the Dutch saw their role as that of a guardian whose mission it was to ensure justice, improve rural living standards, and protect the Javanese peasants from their own rulers.

This policy included no serious attempt to involve Indonesians in development and was intensely paternalistic. Furnivall (1944, p. 389) described it as coddling: "[T]he villager cannot even scratch his head, unless an expert shows him how to do it and the subdistrict officer gives him permission." The native chiefs were increasingly distrusted and therefore superseded. As a result, the Javanese aristocracy became thoroughly demoralized. At the same time no encouragement was given to nurturing a new elite of future leaders, in part because independence was, until the very last, seen as something in the very distant future (Bousquet 1940; Rice 1983).

The ethical policy brought a new class of colonial civil servants to Indonesia. They "arrived in Indonesia with a special degree in oriental studies, speaking the Indonesian language, and well versed in Indonesian history and culture. Many of these civil servants were genuinely devoted to the cause of raising Indonesian living standards." Nevertheless, development policy was unambitious. "It was limited to a bit of agricultural extension work, a bit of rural credit, an unsuccessful attempt to relieve population pressure on Java by moving people to empty Sumatra, and a very little bit of education" (both quotations from Higgins 1984, p. 58). Most important, the opportunity of realizing significant yield increases in rice production by introducing the new (fertilizer-responsive) varieties successfully being introduced at that time in, among other places, Japan, was missed (Booth 1985). There was investment in irrigation, but not on a big scale: only about $1 million per year was spent in 1900–24.

The ethical policy did not result in economic development. An important reason why the Dutch did not push very hard, despite their noble intention, was their belief (later articulated by the leading Dutch development theorist of the time, J. H. Boeke) in sociological dualism. This included a belief in backward-bending supply curves and a denial of the applicability of economic theory to eastern societies molded by "fatalism and resignation" (Boeke 1953, p. 143, quoted by Higgins 1984, p. 61). Economic growth could not be pursued because the culture of Eastern producers made it impossible for them to follow the Western example. Boeke himself described the government's modest irrigation program as "irrigation fanaticism." This attitude had two consequences. First, to some extent the Indonesians themselves accepted the theory and developed an inferiority complex, which was to affect the conduct of economic policy well into the 1950s (Higgins 1984, p. 64). Second, the last decades of colonial rule showed little growth. When export demand stagnated at the end of the 1920s, Indonesian per capita income, which had increased by 10 percent between 1870 and 1913 and by another 18 percent between 1913 and 1928, stagnated (Maddison 1985, p. 25).

In spite of the emphasis the ethical policy put on education, the Dutch left behind an illiterate population. In 1930 the literacy rate was only 6 percent among those aged 10 years and older. Education did reach the Indonesian elite, but graduates were paid less than Dutch employees with comparable qualifications, and often they did not get a job at all. In any case there were few of them: only 279 Indonesian children graduated from Dutch language schools between 1901 and 1928. In addition, government projects for village improvement were resented and seen as alien interference.

The Emergence of an Independent State

Nationalist movements, forerunners of political parties, date from the beginning of the century. Sarekat Islam was the first one to attract a mass following. The Indies Social Democratic Association, in which the young Achmed Sukarno became active, was founded in 1914. In 1920 it joined the Comintern and became the Communist Party of Indonesia (PKI). Conflicts between the PKI and Sarekat Islam reflected the differences between Java (which was inward-looking, aristocratic, and more affected by Hinduism than by Islam) and the outer islands (which were seafaring, Islamic, and more entrepreneurial).

In the period of competition between Sarekat Islam and the PKI, Sukarno established his reputation. In a famous article titled "Nationalism, Islam and Marxism" (1926) he appealed to both movements to bury their differences and to become aware of the nationalism that united them. The article shows Sukarno as an eclectic unifier but undisciplined in his thought and purposely fuzzy in his eagerness to blur rather than stress differences.

In 1927 Sukarno became chairman of a new, nationalistic party, the PNI. The PNI had no constitutional proposals, economic policy, or social program; achieving independence was its central goal. Although Sukarno did not succeed in bridging the rifts among the parties with his synthesis, he did manage to unify the people. "He reached out . . . beyond the elite and beyond the Javanese, attempting to awaken a sense of identity and an awareness of the evils of colonialism among the masses of the Indies population as a whole" (Legge 1972, p. 105).

Sukarno's stature grew immensely when the Dutch were foolish enough to imprison him (from 1929 to 1931). After his release he became chairman of Partindo, a weak successor to the dissolved PNI, whereas Mohammed Hatta, his future vice president, became one of the leaders of the new PNI. Hatta was one of the group of Indonesians who had studied in Holland and was, unlike Sukarno, Westernized through direct exposure to Western political thought. Hatta, as a student at Rotterdam, became a leader of the Indonesian nationalists in Holland. In 1927 he was arrested and gained considerable publicity for the nationalist cause through the speech he made at his trial.

Sukarno considered Hatta insufficiently uncompromising in his opposition to the Dutch. (Hatta's willingness to consider a candidacy for the Dutch Parliament was one bone of contention.) But their relationship was also strained by differences in personality. Hatta was dry and analytic, and Sukarno described him as "a man totally opposite to me in nature. Hatta is an economist by trade and disposition. Careful, unemotional, pedantic. A graduate of the Rotterdam Faculty of Economics, he was still walking around mentally with those books under his arms, trying to apply inflexible scientific formulas to a revolution" (Sukarno 1965, p. 117).[6] The rationalism of Western-educated leaders such as Hatta and his younger counterparts in the moderate wing of the PNI contrasted with the emotionalism of the revolutionaries whose spirit Sukarno personified, and tensions between the two groups were to become a major political factor in the 1950s.

The colonial government had been fairly tolerant of opposition in the 1920s, but in the 1930s it clamped down. Sukarno was rearrested and sent into exile, as was the PNI leadership. A modest petition adopted in 1936 by the Volksraad (a representative assembly with limited powers) asking for autonomy within 10 years was, after a delay of 2 years, rejected outright.

During the Japanese occupation (1942–45) Sukarno and Hatta buried their differences and collaborated with the Japanese. This affected the postwar struggle for independence, because for a long time the Dutch failed to see the nationalists as anything other than collaborators. But the collaboration was also controversial in Indonesia, and it had a negative effect on popular support for the first cabinet of the republic. The Japanese agreed to the formation of an Indonesian military force (Peta) in 1943 and the People's Loyalty Organization in 1944. Through his positions in these organizations, Sukarno consolidated his leadership. He also obtained military training for groups that the Japanese intended to deploy against the Allies, but which could also be used in the struggle for independence.

In a speech in May 1945 Sukarno outlined his philosophy of Pancasila (at the time usually spelled Pantja Sila), with its five principles of nationalism, internationalism, democracy, social justice, and "belief in one God with mutual respect for one another." Sukarno seems to have given remarkably little thought to the social and economic organization of an independent Indonesia. He summarized the Pancasila speech in his autobiography in the vaguest terms: "Pantja Sila can be unraveled to be 10 parts, 20, 50, 1,000 parts. And if I compress them all into one genuine Indonesian term then I get *gotong royong*. This means toiling hard together, sweating hard together. Acts of service by all for the interest of all. The principle of *gotong royong* is between the rich and poor, the Moslem and the Christian, between Indonesian and non-Indonesian" (Sukarno 1965, p. 199).

On another occasion Sukarno said, "Our Socialism does not include extreme materialistic concepts since Indonesia is primarily a God-fearing, God-loving country. Our Socialism is a mixture. We draw political equality from the American Declaration of Independence, draw spiritual equality from Islam and Christianity. We draw scientific equality from Marx. To this mixture we add the national identity: Marhaenism. Then we sprinkle in *gotong royong*, which is the spirit, the essence of working together, living together and helping one another. Mix it all up and the result is Indonesian Socialism" (Sukarno 1965, p. 75). In spite of this vagueness, the advocates of an Islamic state saw that Pancasila could not be reconciled with their goals. Sukarno did not deny that he did not consider Islam the essence of the Indonesian identity.

Independence was proclaimed on August 17, 1945. The provisional constitution provided for a unitary state and a powerful executive presidency. A committee was set up that, although intended as an advisory body to the president, established itself quickly as a parliament, whose support no government could do without (Legge 1974, p. 209). The situation immediately became chaotic. Sukarno, who saw independence simply as the transfer of power, was confronted by the *pemuda*—young people who had acquired a taste for participation in the Japanese youth organizations and who glorified struggle as a virtue in itself. "Struggle organizations" sprang up everywhere and threatened anarchy. In addition, the government was not fully in control of the armed forces. Three months after the declaration of independence, army commanders elected their own commander in chief and their own minister of defense. The cabinet did not accept the latter appointment but it did accept the commander in chief. At the same time, political appointees to lower army commands "were being replaced by younger men, closer to the *pemuda* they led." Thus by 1945 the army was a force partly independent of the civilian government (Zainu'ddin 1968, p. 230).

Much against the wishes of Sukarno, who wanted a single nationalist organization, new parties were formed: a new PNI, a new PKI, a socialist party, and a Muslim party. The collaboration charge was instrumental in enabling opponents to push Sukarno aside. He became a figurehead president, an important unifier at critical moments but not the leader in charge of the government.

At the time of the independence proclamation, the Japanese had just been defeated but the Allies had not yet arrived in Indonesia. British-Indian and Dutch troops landed in September, and the Allied commander, Lord Louis Mountbatten, made clear that he intended to keep order until the Dutch colonial government resumed control. Fighting between the Indonesians and the Allies broke out. At the end of 1946, after a Dutch military buildup, the British-Indian occupation force withdrew from the country, leaving the republic in control of large parts of Java, Sumatra, and Madura. The Dutch started to negotiate, and the Linggadjati Agreement was concluded in November 1946. This agreement recognized the republic's authority on the three islands and stipulated that a federal state would be founded, the United States of Indonesia (USI), which would, together with the Netherlands, Suriname, and the Netherlands Antilles, form the Dutch Commonwealth. The USI would consist of the republic and separate states for Borneo and East Indonesia (Bali, Celebes, and the Moluccas). The two sides interpreted the agreement differently, however, and negotiations over its implementation broke down.

In July 1947 the Dutch launched a full-scale military action. Under the Linggadjati Agreement the Indonesians had accepted most of the Dutch demands, including the principle of a federal state. The breaking point was the Dutch insistence on a joint Dutch-Indonesian security force, which would have given Dutch troops an official role in the republic's territory. The opposition to the Dutch offensive involved a scorched earth campaign. Roads, bridges, and railroads were demolished and attacks were launched on rubber and tobacco plantations on Sumatra and on the sugar industry on Java. This campaign was directed not only at European properties but also at the properties of the Chinese, who were considered pro-Dutch. Dutch reports indicated that the Indonesians killed as many Chinese residents as Dutch soldiers (Kosut 1967, pp. 18–19).[7]

The Indonesian military position was hopelessly weak. One consequence was that the Dutch were able to set up puppet states (to be incorporated in the USI) on the islands that, under the Linggadjati Agreement, recognized the republic's authority. The military position also affected the stature of the Indonesian government, which, in the eyes of many Indonesians, became tainted by its concessions to the Dutch. The position of weakness from which the government had to negotiate was not well understood. For example, the Renville Agreement of January 1948, which not only left the Dutch in control of much of the republic's territory but also enshrined the Dutch ideas about a Netherlands-Indonesian union, so enraged Indonesian extremist nationalist groups that Prime Minister Sjafruddin was forced to resign.

At the same time, the PKI challenged Sukarno, organizing strikes and urging the seizing of Dutch property. Fighting between progovernment and pro-PKI troops broke out. In September 1948 pro-PKI troops called for an antigovernment revolt. Communist leaders were forced to support the badly organized People's Republic proclaimed in Madiun. The army crushed the revolt, and the "Madiun affair" led to the temporary elimination of the PKI.

The republic was also threatened by extremist Muslim groups. The Darul Islam organization, which favored an Islamic state, waged guerilla warfare in 1948 against both the Dutch and the republic. In December 1948 the Dutch attacked for the second time, in an attempt to crush what was left of the republic. They overran the republican positions, captured Jogjakarta, and arrested Sukarno and Hatta. They did not, however, gain full control; the Indonesians mounted an effective guerilla opposition. The resumption of hostilities lost the Dutch the support of the American government and that of the outer islands, where leaders who had been willing to accept the federal structure because of their fear of Javanese dominance now embraced the ideal of a unitary state.

After many interventions by the United Nations Security Council, fighting stopped in June 1949. In December sovereignty was formally transferred to a federal state consisting of the republic and the 15 states set up by the Dutch. This state was short lived and replaced in August 1950 by the Republic of Indonesia.

Obstacles to National Unity

Sukarno succeeded in achieving national unity—a remarkable feat in view of the many threats to unity. Five possible sources of tension within Indonesia can be identified: differences in ethnic groups, languages, social classes, regions, and religion.

The colonial authorities distinguished, even in law, three ethnic groups: "Europeans" (a group that consisted largely of people of mixed descent and included Japanese), "foreign Orientals" (basically the Chinese), and "natives" (who, with the exception of the population of West Irian, all belonged to the Malay ethnic group). The position of the Chinese was a source of tension. The Chinese had built up a dominant position in internal trade in the period of the VOC. After 1870 they also became heavily involved in moneylending and in the smallholder sector. Chinese middlemen controlled credit, retail trade, and crop procurement. (Sumatra is an important exception; an indigenous trading class did develop there.) The Chinese also had an industrial base, controlling, for example, 40 percent of the textile industry in 1939. Resentment of the Chinese increased during the last decades of the colonial period.

The founding of Sarekat Islam was in part a reaction of indigenous merchants to the Chinese movement into new sectors after residence restrictions on the Chinese were lifted early in the century (Robison 1986, p. 28). The close identification of the Chinese with their relatives in China was a source of distrust immediately after the war, in particular because China considered Indonesian Chinese as Chinese citizens. As in many other countries in Asia (and like the Asians in East Africa), the Chinese formed a middle class in the colonial period whose economic success, organization, and separateness (there was little intermarrying) generated resentment.

Language differences could have become divisive. Dutch education was not unifying since instruction was usually in local languages (except in the Dutch language schools, which, as we have noted, served few students). A crucial step was the adoption of a form of Malay (Bahasa Indonesia, presently the official language) as a national language in 1927. A simple language to learn, it became a unifying force, especially through Sukarno's emphasis on its use as a symbol of national identity.[8] Thus, neither Dutch nor the language of the largest ethnic group, Javanese, but a lingua franca of traders became the national language.

Class differences within the non-Chinese population were not marked. Except on Sumatra there was no substantial indigenous entrepreneurial class (Zainu'ddin 1968, pp. 182–84). Through much of the colonial period the tendency of the Dutch had been to obtain export crops either through taxation and force or by growing them on European-owned plantations, but not by buying them from peasants. To the extent that smallholder agriculture developed, it was in spite of the government's policy.[9] By relying so little on material incentives, the Indonesians' "economic sense grew feebler even than it had been under native rule" (Furnivall 1944, p. 456). In precolonial Indonesia, land was abundant and wealth was accumulated in the form of control over serfs.

Also, the native rulers who might have become an entrepreneurial class were reduced to being colonial tax collectors under the *cultuurstelsel* and then, under the ethical policy, further humiliated and demoralized by the Dutch insistence on protecting the people from them. The Javanese aristocracy became a bureaucracy instead of developing commercial interests, as some of their more independent counterparts on the outer islands did. Thus, at independence Indonesia had no substantial indigenous middle class. Its elite had been, since 1830, oriented toward seeking bureaucratic control, and the functions of the middle class were carried out by the Chinese (Reid 1980, p. 451).

Although the Javanese aristocracy, the *priyayi,* did not use their traditional rights over land and labor to engage in capitalistic agriculture—based on wage labor—or in trade or industry, they did develop something of a landowning class by leasing land to the sugar mills. The growth of this rentier class was, however, dealt a severe blow by the Depression (Robison 1986).

Unlike ethnicity, language, or social class, regional differences were significant. Tensions between Sumatra and Java can be traced to the precolonial rivalry between the empires of Malacca (controlling the trade through the straits) and Majapahit (centered on Java and based on agriculture). Differences in population density were reflected in organizational differences: on Sumatra shifting cultivation was practiced while on Java the population lived in villages. The resulting differences in the development of the state were accentuated by colonialism. Java became the center of the colony and was most tightly controlled, whereas the Dutch initially settled on Sumatra only for strategic reasons.

After 1870, when the plantation economy was developed, Sumatra became more important economically, but Java remained the political center, adding a new element to the tension in Indonesia between a society of traders and loosely organized farmers on the one hand and the combination of feudalism and colonialism on Java on the other hand. Sumatrans dominated the (small) group of indigenous traders. On Sumatra itself they handled trade in smallholder cash crops; on Java they were involved in petty retailing.[10]

The Dutch divide-and-rule policy encouraged regional differences. On the Hindu enclave of Bali, for example, the Dutch preserved the distinct culture and even restored to the conquered rajas their titles and most of their powers as late as 1938 (Forge 1980, p. 221). Even on Java the Dutch encouraged differences. The kingdom of Mataran, for example, after being conquered in the middle of the eighteenth century, was split into two sultanates (Solo and Jogjakarta) and sealed off from the rest of Java.

The failure of Dutch colonialism as a unifying force was only partly a matter of design. It was also the result of the very uneven impact of colonialism. In eastern Indonesia, the area in which the VOC had established and defended its monopoly in cloves, pepper, and nutmeg trade, the traditional way of life was destroyed; on much of Sumatra and Kalimantan there was very little influence, whereas on Java the hands-off policy for Solo and Jogjakarta contrasted sharply with Dutch influence in West Java (Zainu'ddin 1968, pp. 110–14).

Also, the Dutch made no attempt to apply a single system of laws and regulations throughout the archipelago, preferring instead to rule through the regents. As Higgins (1960, pp. 32–33) put it:

> The people of the outlying islands had known the Netherlands East Indies government, if they knew it at all, through their local governor or regent. Many of them were reluctant to acknowledge the right of any government in Djakarta to rule their lives, especially a government which they considered to be dominated by "Javanese Imperialism."

Religious differences, which played a significant role as an obstacle to national unity, coincided in part with regional differences—Islam affected Sumatra more than Java. Islam became a vehicle for nationalism, particularly through the Muhammadiyah movement. This movement, inspired by ideas introduced into Indonesia by pilgrims returning from Mecca and Egypt, attempted to reform Islam. In its modernist approach it clashed with traditional Islamic authorities. It was influential through the "wild schools" movement, establishing schools that offered Western education without undermining (as the government schools were perceived to do) Islamic faith. Sarekat Islam—begun as a cooperative organization of Javanese batik manufacturers aimed against Chinese competition—acquired considerable support among Javanese peasants who saw their official Muslim leaders as compromised by their collaboration with the Dutch. However, even within these unifying and modernizing Islamic movements, factions developed. Once the communists were expelled from Sarekat Islam the main conflict was between reformists and fundamentalists. The latter, organized as Nahdatul Ulama, were to become a divisive force by insisting on the establishment of an Islamic state.

Thus, whereas class distinctions were relatively unimportant, even on Java, and the early adoption of Bahasa Indonesia had preempted the language question, there were substantial regional and religious differences. The Dutch solution of a federal state was attractive for the outer islands since it promised them some protection against Javanese imperialism. This solution might have been implemented if the Dutch had not tried to eliminate the republic militarily. That the country held together after independence in spite of a series of regional revolts was in part the achievement of Sukarno, who repeatedly played a unifying role at critical moments in the 1950s. Also, the sheer size and the dominance of Java, which accounts for two-thirds of the population, meant that it could easily crush an attempt at secession, as it did in the case of the Moluccas.[11]

Economic Conditions

The period of war and revolution from 1940 to 1949 left the country ravaged. Before the war, income had already declined tremendously. Polak's estimates of national income show a decline from a peak of 5.2 billion guilders in 1926 to 2.0 billion guilders in 1934, at the depth of the depression (Polak 1942, table 15.1). There was a sharp recovery in the next four years, but in 1938 national income was still only 2.8 billion guilders. In 1938 per capita income of Indonesians (excluding "Europeans" and "foreign Asiatics") was 60.6 guilders in 1928 prices, still below the 1928 level of 61.4 guilders. It is important to keep the pre-1938 income decline in mind, because data for the 1950s are often compared with data for 1938 as if that year were typical for the prewar period.

Neumark (1954) estimated net national income in 1951 as Rp 2.6 billion in 1938 prices, compared with Polak's Rp 2.7 billion for 1938.[12] Estimating the population at 68.4 million in 1938 and 77.4 million in 1951, Neumark (p. 350) put per capita income at Rp 39 in 1938 and Rp 33.5 in 1951, a decline of 14 percent. The implied population growth rate seems incredibly low. If we assume 2.3 percent annual growth instead, the population would have grown by 35 percent over the period, implying a decline in per capita income of 29 percent. However, even if the lower figure of 14 percent is a reasonable estimate of the income decline between 1938 and 1951, it understates the effect of the war and the revolution for two reasons: because 1938 was an atypically unfavorable year, and because 1951 was an extremely favorable year as a result of the Korean commodity boom, which gave Indonesia a substantial terms of trade gain in the early 1950s. Using Rosendale's (1975) estimates, we find that the barter terms of trade index (1971 = 100) reached a peak of 166.6 in 1951, an improvement of 26 percent compared with 1938 (see table 11.1). There is therefore considerable uncertainty concerning the level of per capita income at the time of independence. However, there can be little doubt that it was substantially below the level reached in the late 1930s.

Economic Interventions

The colonial economy was strongly integrated in the world economy and relied heavily on private enterprise. However, Dutch colonialism involved considerable interventionism and cannot be characterized as economic liberalism, although Indonesians often interpreted and described it this way. For example, Wilopo, the prime minister in 1952–53, explained the background of the famous clause in article 33 of the provisional constitution—that "the national economy shall be organized on a cooperative basis"[13]—by saying:

The pattern of economic development in the past, particularly since 1870, had produced misery and injustice among the great mass of the Indonesian people. This pattern was based on economic liberalism. Article 35 of the Provisional Constitution formulates a new principle and this principle is opposed to liberalism. The antagonism between the concept of liberalism is not only evident from the Government statement at the time of the drawing up of the Provisional Constitution, but is also in conformity with the background of the Indonesian revolution (Wilopo and Widjojo 1959, p. 5).

We have noted the negative effects of interventionism on the development of indigenous entrepreneurship. In addition economic controls were tightened during the 1930s. Indonesia was hard hit by the Depression: the value of exports fell by 75 percent between 1925 and 1935. The government negotiated international agreements for rubber and sugar that involved production restrictions. At this time the government also assumed control over external trade by introducing licensing systems. Thus the colonial government, which had intervened little in external trade until the 1930s, bequeathed an apparatus for detailed quantitative restrictions.

Under the 1950 constitution, Sukarno's position, already weak in actuality but still formally powerful under the 1945 constitution, was reduced to that of a ceremonial president, much like the role of a king in the Dutch constitution. Sukarno's growing dissatisfaction with this situation was to be an important force in the years 1950 to 1957. Thus the initial conditions at the beginning of the 1950s included a legacy of government intervention in the economy, an income level much reduced by the war and the subsequent struggle for independence, and a constitution that made President Sukarno uneasy with his role.

11 Parliamentary Democracy: 1950–57

Confusion and paralysis dominated the period 1950 to 1957. Politically there was agreement on the desirability of a non-Western type of democracy, but what this meant remained unclear. National leaders spent their time in fruitless ideological debate, while economic problems were left unattended. This situation led to disillusion with the parliamentary system and to disappointment with the fruits of independence; it also contributed to discontent on the outer islands, which in turn led to open revolt at the end of the period.

Economic policy was initially controlled by cautious pragmatists who saw little scope for quickly reducing the role of foreign—in particular, Dutch—capital in the economy. In the mid-1950s control shifted to a more radical group. Disillusionment with the continuing foreign dominance led to spontaneous seizure of Dutch properties in 1957. Although cabinets succeeded each other so quickly that many economic policy initiatives were aborted, one policy was common to all: the attempt to create an indigenous entrepreneurial class. By 1957 this attempt was considered a failure, and economic nationalism relied thereafter on state enterprises rather than on private entrepreneurs. Although contemporary commentators seemed most struck by the recurrent budget deficits and the growth of the money supply, in retrospect the lack of ambition of the planners and the small size of the public sector seem more remarkable.

Political Developments

At the beginning of the 1950–57 period an unstable political equilibrium existed among three forces: the PNI, Islam, and the army. Two other actors, Sukarno and the communists, had been reduced to a minor role. By 1957 parliamentary democracy was discredited, the army and the communists had both increased their power, and Sukarno had assumed the role of an executive president.

Immediately upon Indonesia's independence, the government was confronted with serious challenges, first from separatist groups, then from the army, and finally from Muslim groups. Separatist sentiments flared up immediately, in part as a reaction to the government's intention to transform the USI into a unitary state, the Republic of Indonesia. A Dutch officer led a rebellion in West Java in January 1950, and later that year an uprising took place on Celebes involving former Netherlands Indies troops. The most serious challenge was a secession attempt of the Moluccas. An independent Republic of the South Moluccas was declared, and the USI responded in September 1950 by invading Ambon (the most important island in the group) with a force of 20,000. After very heavy fighting the revolt was crushed. Ambonese soldiers had formed the backbone of the colonial army, and there was considerable sympathy in the Netherlands for the Moluccan declaration of independence. All three uprisings therefore contributed to anti-Dutch feelings.

Compared with many other newly independent countries, Indonesia's start was remarkably shaky. The revolts were only the most spectacular signs of instability. The 1950–57 period was marked by increasing disappointment and instability because independence did not bring the expected material improvement, because corruption spread quickly, and because the outer islands were increasingly frustrated by what they perceived as a Javanese-dominated government.[1]

Also contributing to the shaky start was the wide disagreement that existed from the very beginning between and within the political parties on the main policy issues. Within the PNI there was conflict between the party's old guard, the "class of 1927" (the year in which the PNI was founded), and a younger, much less radical group. The party leaders had acquired great authority through their role during the revolution, but after independence they advocated continuing revolution and had difficulty switching to a more constructive role. They also estranged the younger, more moderate wing by their support for the rehabilitation of the PKI (discredited after the Madiun affair) and by their involvement in corruption. Sukarno himself was very much in tune with the class of 1927, always ready to promote national unity by appealing to revolutionary sentiments, if necessary by "discovering" imaginary foreign plots to destroy the Indonesian republic.

The PNI and Masyumi (the Islamic party) were the two main political organizations. Because they cooperated uneasily, a one-party government faced a strong opposition, and a coalition government led to conflicts between opposing wings of the same party. Masyumi favored a pro-American foreign policy and welcomed foreign investments. Various Muslim groups, both within and outside of Masyumi, favored the establishment of a theocratic, Islamic state. The Darul Islam movement pursued this objective through terrorism in West Java and involvement in September 1953 in an open revolt in Aceh (North Sumatra). It took the government two months and some heavy fighting to suppress this revolt.

Sukarno, who always claimed to be a Muslim himself, came to see the demand for an Islamic state as a serious threat to national unity. He openly criticized Muslim extremism in an important speech in 1953, which brought the division between the PNI and Islam (and, implicitly, between Java and the outer islands) into the open. As a counterweight to Masyumi, the PNI welcomed the return of the PKI.

Sukarno's criticism not only exploded the myth of national consensus but also showed him willing to go beyond the role of a ceremonial president. That willingness was clear in 1952. The government had been fairly successful in building a national, professional army out of the guerrilla units and Peta-type organizations involved in the revolution. In the conflict that developed between centralized, professional leadership and local, revolutionary commanders, Sukarno's sympathy was with the locals. And in October 1952 when demonstrators incited by the army leadership asked him to dissolve Parliament (which had been critical of the army reforms), he refused. This "October 17 affair," during which guns were trained on Sukarno's presidential palace and which indirectly caused the downfall of the cabinet, was seen as a serious threat to democracy. Although the army leadership did not succeed in obtaining the dissolution of Parliament (and General Nasution was suspended as chief of staff for his role in the affair), they did establish that they felt "entitled to set limits to what civilian politicians might do," and they made it clear that the army was a political force to be reckoned with (Legge 1972, p. 257).

But the incident also revealed divisions within the army. The reforms pushed by the minister of defense favored a professional, disciplined army under Western-trained officers. This policy strengthened the position of those who had served in the colonial army, thereby enraging their former guerrilla opponents. The conflict was similar to that within the PNI, pitting a moderate Western-oriented group against a group that wished to maintain revolutionary fervor. During the October 17 affair, officers belonging to the latter group removed three of the seven divisional commanders from their posts, and for several years thereafter the two groups openly opposed each other within the army.

The government failed to restore unity. Early in 1955 the officers took the matter into their own hands, holding a conference at which the Charter for the Integrity of the Army was signed. The army could now move independently of the central cabinet. General Nasution was reinstated as chief of staff, and he enhanced central control in the army. At the same time regional differences within the officer corps stood out more clearly. In 1956 regional commanders on Sumatra diverted foreign exchange (through smuggling and barter trade with Singapore) to their own districts, where they took control of local administration. These officers made clear that they recognized Sukarno's authority but not that of the cabinet (Zainu'ddin 1968, p. 255).

Although the chief of staff saw Sukarno and the army as natural allies and as joint custodians of the nation, many regional commanders disagreed. In 1956 there was an attempted coup in West Java and another in North Sumatra, and the Central Sumatran government was taken over by a military commander.

The army was not the only group to gain during the 1950s. The communists staged a remarkable comeback, after having been thoroughly discredited for their role in the Madiun affair (which amounted to an attempted communist coup against the republican government in the middle of the struggle for independence). The leadership of the PKI was taken over by a new generation that could shake off this association. Sukarno, in his role of the great unifier, encouraged the return of the PKI, and the PNI supported this policy because it saw the communists as a potential ally against Masyumi. The new leaders of the PKI were, unlike their predecessors, prepared to support the president in exchange for his protection from the army (which the PKI quickly came to see as their main rival for power).

Because the Sumatran leaders were openly anticommunist, the PKI gained from the failure of the Sumatra revolt. The PKI's stature also grew through the support of the former Soviet Union and several Eastern European countries for the West Irian campaign, not only in the United Nations but also through the sale of arms (which the United States had refused to provide).

Elections for a parliament to replace the provisional parliament of 1945 were held in 1955. The PNI obtained 22 percent of the vote; Masyumi, 21 percent; the Nahdatul Ulama (Muslime Teachers Party), 18 percent; and the PKI, 16 percent. Of these four parties, three (the PNI, NU, and PKI) were revealed to be Javanese parties; of their elected members only 21 percent, 18 percent, and 10 percent, respectively, gained seats representing the outer provinces. In contrast, Masyumi performed strongly in the outer provinces, where it got half its seats.

The election outcome was divisive: regional and religious differences proved unexpectedly deep. Since no clear winner emerged that could play a unifying role, Sukarno's frustration with the constitutional system increased. The Constituent Assembly became deadlocked in a discussion about alternative ideologies—Islam or Sukarno's Pancasila—for the Indonesian state (Zainu'ddin 1968, p. 257). It was against this background that Sukarno became more outspoken in his criticism of parliamentary democracy. He suggested that the parties should be buried and that he had an alternative ideology ready. He also became more partisan—more pro-Java and increasingly anti-Masyumi.

Hatta resigned at the end of 1956 because he no longer agreed with Sukarno's policies. This was a decisive split in the leadership for two reasons. First, those concerned with economic growth could no longer rely on Hatta to warn that political solutions were no answer to economic problems. Second, Hatta had stood for the outer islands, for Islam, and for moderation. His resignation made Sukarno's position controversial. The "lines of division within Indonesia came increasingly to be between those supporting and those opposing the President. Sukarno without Hatta was no longer a unifying force for many groups in society, although he increasingly stressed his own role as leader, as voice of the people, and sought to impose unity where he could no longer, as in earlier days, inspire it" (Zainu'ddin 1968, p. 256). Early in 1957 he proposed an all-party cabinet and a National Council, under his leadership, that would decide on broad lines of national policy. Regional tensions intensified, and there were two further regional coups in support of restoration of the old Sukarno-Hatta leadership—in other words, in support of representation of Islamic, non-Javanese political forces.

Although Sukarno's constitutional proposals were not accepted, he succeeded in establishing the presidential palace as the main center of power. In part to divert attention from the regional problem, he kept the West Irian issue alive. The Dutch had excluded their side of New Guinea from the transfer of sovereignty in 1949, and they refused to negotiate about its status. Indonesia raised the matter several times in the United Nations but failed to get sufficient support. Anti-Dutch demonstrations were backed by the government, and finally, at the end of 1957, Dutch properties were seized and thousands of Dutch people left the country.

The seizures occurred suddenly, "without any prior planning except perhaps in the mind of President Sukarno and a few youth leaders around him. The government seems to have been taken by surprise by what happened and initially divided in its assessment of the appropriate response. Once the deed was done, there was little choice to proceed with nationalization and accept the vast new responsibilities of managing these productive and trading enterprises within the state sector despite the paucity of experienced technicians and managers," (Mackie 1971, p. 50). Handing the enterprises over to private businessmen was no longer considered an option.

The seizures had important consequences. They caused economic disruption, because the departed Dutch were replaced by inexperienced Indonesians. They also increased the power of the army, because officers were put in charge of the seized enterprises, and they encouraged government intervention, because the previous reluctance to discourage foreign investors no longer acted as a brake on "socialism." Finally, there "was also a psychological effect—a sense of daring, confidence and revolutionary fervor after such a big step towards becoming masters in their own house" (Mackie 1971, pp. 50–51).

Economic Policy

Economic policies in the 1950s were influenced in three ways by the colonial legacy. First, the Indonesian government inherited and left largely in place a battery of government interventions installed by the Dutch since the 1930s, including import quotas, minimum price regulations, and legal barriers to entry. The Dutch trade policy, for example, had been a very liberal one until the Great Depression. But in the 1930s the Dutch East Indies participated in several international commodity agreements that were set up to halt the slide of commodity prices. Tin and sugar became subject to production quotas in 1931, tea in 1933, and rubber in 1934. Most of the restrictions were lifted by 1938, but the threat of war led to further interventions.

Exports required permits from the Bureau of Exports under the Crisis Export Ordinance of 1939. Similarly, under the earlier Crisis Import Ordinance (1933), a license from the Bureau of Imports was required for all imports. The machinery for trade control was supplemented in 1940 by the Foreign Exchange Control Ordinance, under which only the government could own gold or foreign exchange. A Foreign Exchange Institute was set up to which exporters had to surrender their foreign exchange and from which importers could acquire foreign exchange. These prewar regulations were taken over by the republic, and many of them remained in effect until after the fall of Sukarno. The 1940 ordinance, for example, survived until December 1964, when private ownership of foreign assets was finally legalized.

A second legacy of Dutch colonization was that some Indonesian leaders had a predilection for interventionism because of their studies in Holland. Although there were enormous differences within the elite between, for example, Hatta (who favored comprehensive planning) and Sumitro (who wanted to limit Chinese competition) on the one hand, and the cautious Sjafruddin (president of the Java Bank) on the other hand, there was no strong intellectual tradition of economic liberalism. "[T]he nationalists, to a man, called themselves 'socialists.' They unanimously rejected capitalism and 'liberalism' which, in its Dutch colonial shape, they held responsible for all the country's ills" (Arndt 1980, p. 432). This socialism was ill defined but it included a contempt for laissez-faire, which was identified (rather improbably) with the colonial experience. At the time of the 1955 elections all major parties claimed to be socialist.

   This uniformity of approach contributed to continuity in economic policy: Indonesian economists favored the sort of regulations the Dutch had introduced. Their interventionism was reflected in two famous clauses in the 1945 constitution: "Branches of production which are important for the state and which control [the supply of] the basic needs of the masses are to be controlled by the state;" and "The national economy shall be organized on a cooperative basis." In practice, according to one of the framers of the constitution, this meant little more than a resolve that "the distribution of the social product should no longer be left to the forces of the market. The organization we have in mind is a planned economy guided by socialist ideals" ("S" 1946, quoted by Arndt 1980) And until 1958 there would, in fact, be very little public ownership.

   A third legacy was that independence left the Dutch firmly entrenched economically. This not only strengthened radical factions that claimed that the revolution had to be completed (culminating in the 1957 seizures), but also undermined the position of liberals: as long as the economy continued to be dominated by the Dutch, liberalism seemed at odds with nationalism. The Dutch owned more than half of nonagricultural capital. The Java Bank, forerunner of the Bank Indonesia, was still largely Dutch owned and controlled by Dutch officers. Private banking was dominated by seven foreign banks, three of them Dutch. Four Dutch firms controlled half of consumer imports (Glassburner 1971a, p. 79).

   The Dutch influence also remained strong in the ministries. About 6,000 former colonial civil servants stayed on in the new Indonesian civil service. They openly used their power and influence to support the Dutch-owned part of the economy. The Dutch codirector of the Foreign Exchange Institute even insisted that foreign exchange should be allocated to foreign firms (especially to the Dutch Big Five), rather than be "wasted" on new, Indonesian entrepreneurs. When Sjafruddin became governor of the Java Bank he still had to operate under a Dutch board of directors.

   The educated elite had been exposed for decades to theories that they were incapable of running a modern economy. Ideas similar to those of Boeke (see chapter 10) continued to be put forth even after independence. D. H. Penny, for example, claimed that in "Indonesia, farmers do not attempt to maximize their incomes nor do they respond strongly to economic incentives" (Penny 1966, p. 27).[2] Although the influence of such theories may have been limited to a small elite, lack of self-confidence extended beyond this group. "There were qualified Indonesians to fill the top level government posts, but insufficient numbers with practical experience in such positions and a serious lack of trained personnel at the middle levels of government. Technologists, technicians, accountants, typists with sufficient training, practical experience and self-confidence to accept responsibility were all in short supply" (Higgins 1984). As a result of the colonial education and employment policies, at all levels of government people were doing jobs for which they did not have adequate training or experience.

Indonesia's first four cabinets were dominated by pragmatic conservatives who accepted the dominant position of foreign capital. Economic nationalism had to operate within the constraint that foreign investors were not to be antagonized. The first cabinet, led by Hatta, took drastic stabilization measures. Currency reform involved the 50 percent reduction of all bank deposits larger than 400 guilders, with compensation in government bonds. As part of the monetary reform program, the unified exchange rate system was abandoned and foreign exchange certificates were introduced. Exporters were paid in certificates for 50 percent of the foreign exchange they surrendered; they could use the certificates either to import (at the official rate, which was maintained at Rp 3.8 per dollar) or to sell (at a price that government intervention kept at 200 percent of the official exchange rate).

Because the certificate represented the right to buy foreign exchange at the official rate, this system, called Bukti Expor (BE), meant that the cost of dollars trebled for importers, from Rp 3.8 to Rp 11.4, whereas it doubled for exporters, from Rp 3.8 to Rp 7.6. The difference between the two rates represented a rent accruing to the government: the BE system amounted to a 33-1/3 percent export tax. In operation from March 1950 to February 1952, it produced enormous revenue because of the Korean commodity boom. However, in marked contrast to what happened at the time in Nigeria, the system was abolished when the government realized that it had a negative effect on exports. This reform implied a greater reliance on price signals in the allocation of imports.

Importers were quick to complain about the effects of the de facto devaluation caused by the BE system and, by stressing nationalism, succeeded in securing privileged treatment. Less than two weeks after the devaluation in March 1950 the government announced that it would aid indigenous importers (later to be known as the Benteng group) by arranging bank credit for them and by excluding all others from certain lines of imports. The goal of the Benteng program was to replace the Dutch and Chinese with an Indonesian entrepreneurial class. It failed at this: the program did not create entrepreneurship but rent-seeking. Import licenses tended to be allocated to friends of politicians and to friends of the bureaucrats controlling the allocation, and most Benteng firms did not use the licenses for importing but sold them to genuine importers (who tended to be Chinese). "What was being consolidated was not an indigenous merchant bourgeoisie but a group of license brokers and political fixers" (Robison 1986, p. 45). Only the already well-established Sumatran trading groups seemed to be able to use the Benteng privileges effectively (Robison 1986, pp. 52–53).

Although the failures of the Benteng program were widely known, the government maintained it for seven years. Opposition to the program from groups favoring competition, like Masyumi, the Socialist Party (the PSI), and the moderate wing of the PNI, and from economic nationalists like Sukarno, the PKI, and the radical wing of the PNI led to its demise in 1957. By then the economic nationalists were convinced by the Benteng experience that state enterprises—not indigenous capitalists— should form the backbone of the national economy.

Following on the heels of the 1950 economic reform came the Korean commodity boom. Rubber prices quadrupled in a single year (March 1950 to March 1951). The effect of the price increases on export values was reinforced by strong supply responses (copra exports, for example, rose from 291,000 tons in 1950 to 542,000 tons in 1951). The value of nonoil exports rose from $631 million (1950) to $1,091 million (1951). The boom led to an enormous buildup of reserves, from $145 million in March 1950 to $352 million at the end of 1951, because the process of extending credit and granting import licenses failed to adjust quickly to the rise in export revenues. The combination of import controls and the prohibition of foreign asset acquisition by private citizens led to a rise in government-owned foreign assets and to unusually high increases in the prices of nontradables. This happened because less was saved and more was spent on domestic (rather than imported) consumption goods than would have been the case otherwise.[3] Wages for farming perennial crops, for example, increased in one year by 47 percent on Sumatra and by 30 percent on Java, while rural food prices trebled.

The boom was short-lived. Export prices fell sharply in 1952 (table 11.1). At the same time import controls were relaxed and the government ran a huge deficit. As a result, the foreign exchange reserves were depleted, and the benefits of the boom were transferred to the beneficiaries of public expenditure—largely to urban dwellers and in particular to civil servants. Adjustment to the end of the boom involved more than just the use of reserves, which did fall dramatically: from Rp 6.2 billion at the end of 1951 to Rp 2.0 billion two years later (table 11.2). The Wilopo cabinet (1952–53) reintroduced tight import restrictions and succeeded in cutting public expenditure, although not by as much as the 25 percent cut that Sumitro, then minister of finance, had aimed at.

The government's labor policy led to sharp increases in labor costs and to a huge increase in public employment. The Labor Law of 1948 established a 40-hour work week (almost unique in the world at that time), and although this law was not rigorously enforced, working hours were reduced substantially. Government employment grew rapidly— government jobs were used to reward those who served in the independence struggle—and had already reached five times the prewar level by

Table 11.1 Volume and Price Indexes for Exports and Imports, Selected Years, 1938–57
(1971 = 100)

Year	Exports		Imports		Barter terms of trade
	Volume	Price	Volume	Price	
1938	39.3	61.9	45.5	46.7	132.5
1939	42.0	61.5	41.9	44.6	137.9
1940	42.3	69.1	35.2	48.6	142.2
1950	46.0	140.6	43.4	85.9	163.7
1951	53.8	185.3	59.4	111.2	166.6
1952	51.7	141.3	71.1	115.3	122.5
1953	51.5	120.7	60.0	113.9	106.0
1954	55.3	114.3	63.5	98.8	115.7
1955	50.0	137.5	57.3	95.9	143.4
1956	52.4	126.1	77.1	91.4	138.0
1957	54.9	120.6	74.3	94.7	127.3

Source: Rosendale 1975.

1951. Trade union activity, which was influenced by nationalist sentiments, was directed particularly at Western firms. Labor relations became so problematic that some entrepreneurs dropped industrial activities and switched to other sectors.

Import restrictions were particularly severe for consumer goods. For example, the price of powdered milk doubled between August 1952 and April 1953. Since this item was not subject to an import surcharge, the difference must have accrued largely as a rent. And although only luxuries were subject to surcharges in 1952, 30 percent of the value of imports became subject to a 33-1/3 percent surcharge and another 20 percent to surcharges of 100 percent in 1953.

Table 11.2 Government Finance and Foreign Exchange Reserves, 1951–56
(billions of rupiah)

Year	Revenue	Expenditure	Foreign exchange reserves (end of year)
1951	11.8	10.6	6.2
1952	12.3	15.0	3.6
1953	13.6	15.7	2.0
1954	11.5	15.1	1.7
1955	14.2	16.3	2.7
1956	19.2	20.8	1.6

Source: Paauw 1960.

The Wilopo cabinet succeeded in controlling public expenditure, but when this cabinet fell in June 1953, fiscal prudence was again abandoned. Government debt trebled (albeit from a small base) in the following nine months. In fact, the government's scope for running a deficit was legally limited. When the Bank Indonesia was established in 1953, a law stipulated that it could not lend the government more than 30 percent of the treasury revenue in the preceding budget year. What could be counted as revenue was not clear, but even under the broadest interpretation the limit would already have been exceeded in 1955. That year the government had to ask Parliament for an increase in the limit—a matter taken very seriously. Although the budget was submitted too late to enforce much discipline—the budget for 1954 did not reach Parliament until September of that year—the legal limit did have an effect. In the stern words of the president of Bank Indonesia in the bank's annual report:

> It may be recalled to memory that legislators incorporated the article in question in the Bank's charter because of the non-existence of sufficient safeguards against arbitrary actions on the part of the Government in the sphere of public expenditure. Though it must be stated that the incorporation of this regulation has been of no avail to prevent the Government appeals to the Central Bank from going on unabatingly, yet this fact must not lead to the conclusion that it should thus have lost its value. For by (yearly) fixing a set limit, Parliament can, despite the too late arrival of the budget, exercise control on public expenditure.

Quantitative restrictions on imports were extended and intensified dramatically in May 1954. This break with past policy, which had relied more on surcharges and prepayment schemes to reduce imports, was motivated not just by the seriousness of the situation (reserves were falling dangerously low) but also by nationalism. Direct control over foreign exchange allocation was seen as a convenient instrument for increasing the Indonesian share of import trade. Many "new businessmen" acquired rents by selling their licenses to established importers, allegedly at profits of 50 to 100 percent. Even the deputy prime minister admitted that 80 percent of licenses issued to national importers were later sold to nonindigenous firms. Transaction costs went up as the marketing chain became longer. Corruption in the Central Import Office became a target of public criticism, but a parliamentary inquiry came to nothing.

The Benteng program, originally intended as a way of displacing foreign enterprise by supporting indigenous entrepreneurs, now became the channel through which the minister of economic affairs bought financial support for his party with import licenses. This led to a crisis in

Parliament and the minister's resignation in November 1954. The Harahap cabinet (August 1955–March 1956) benefited from a short-lived rubber boom in the second half of 1955. These events were the background of the Sumitro reform of September 1955. Quantitative restrictions were abolished, the discredited Central Import Office was replaced by a new institution that could issue a joint import–foreign exchange license, and fraudulent importers were identified in a reregistration procedure. Although surcharges were raised and prepayment requirements were tightened, the effect on the relative price of imports appears to have been offset by a policy of easy credit for importers. Sumitro's objective was not to reduce the volume of imports but, on the contrary, to expand both imports and exports.

Rubber prices peaked at the end of 1955 and fell sharply thereafter. The liberal import policy, however, was continued for some time, leading to a loss of reserves. The cabinet reintroduced fiscal discipline, eliminated corruption in the import licensing system, and required 100 percent prepayment of imports. It discouraged private foreign investment by unilaterally abrogating the 1949 Round Table Agreement, which included safeguards for compensation in the case of expropriation. The next government was headed by Ali Sastroamidjojo, who had been prime minister of the cabinet before the Harahap government. He immediately ran a large budget deficit again. Shortly after Sukarno introduced the concept of guided democracy (see chapter 12), the government fell. The Djuanda cabinet that succeeded it reintroduced the BE system under which an exporter was paid in certificates (which could be sold freely) for the foreign exchange he surrendered. This large de facto devaluation was intended to placate the exporting outer islands: in April 1958 the market price of the certificates was more than 300 percent of the par value.

Economic policy in the 1950–57 period was confused. Cabinets changed so quickly that plans could not be formulated or executed. There was a bewildering succession of governments. Brief episodes of extremely strict fiscal and monetary policies alternated with periods of laxity. Three changes are worth singling out in this period: the transformation of trade and exchange rate policy, the change in the government's attitude toward foreign capital, and the failed attempt to establish an indigenous capitalist class.

By 1957 complicated dual exchange rate systems and quantitative restrictions on imports were well established. Trade policy increased outer island resentment of Java. Huge rents were created for those with access to import licenses at the expense of exporters. "Combined with fixed exchange rates, domestic inflation threatened the incomes of indigenous exporters in the Outer Regions, where the bulk of exports originate. Dwindling real incomes there caused increased resentment towards populous Java, where most of the nation's imports were being absorbed" (Schmitt 1962, quoted by Robison 1986, p. 59).

The change in attitude toward foreign capital was the outcome of what Glassburner (1971a, p. 71) has described as "a hopeless losing battle on the part of a very small group of pragmatically conservative political leaders against an increasingly powerful political opposition of generally radical orientation," with the turning point occurring in 1953 with the fall of the Wilopo cabinet. The early cabinets were dominated by men who, though nominally socialists, were essentially pragmatic. They all wanted to weaken the position of the foreign enterprises, particularly Sumitro, but were convinced that foreign capital could not be replaced quickly. At most there could be "tinkering around the edges" (p. 77). There were no nationalizations except for the railways and the Java Bank. The position of these intellectuals was eroded by Indonesia's disappointing economic performance, and control passed to the "mass leaders" (p. 82). However, apart from the abrogation of the Round Table Agreement, little concrete progress was made in reducing Dutch (and other foreign) influence until the 1957 seizures.

In 1950 there was no consensus as to what should replace foreign capital. Hatta stood alone in taking the constitutional clauses about cooperatives literally. The PKI favored state enterprises but was not in power. The other parties wanted to use the state to encourage indigenous (and non-Chinese) entrepreneurs.

The Benteng program was only one of several unsuccessful attempts to create an indigenous entrepreneurial class. Under the 1951 Economic Urgency Programme, the industrial bank (Bank Industri Negara) was to finance industrial projects that would eventually become partly or wholly privately owned. In most cases, however, indigenous capitalists were unable or unwilling to enter into partnerships, and the state had to retain ownership. In banking, national banks accounted for only 11 percent of outstanding domestic credit in 1956 in spite of strong government support. The Bank Industri Negara was forced to operate some large agricultural estates as state subsidiaries because it could not find private capitalists. In rice milling and copra, export trade attempts to break Chinese monopolies were abandoned. Increasingly it became clear that protection of Indonesian businessmen against foreign and Chinese competition had the effect of consolidating the position of the Chinese.[4]

None of the programs to develop indigenous entrepreneurs succeeded. Either the Indonesian businessmen became capitalists in name only, dealing through the Chinese, or—as happened in the case of copra—the performance of a sector deteriorated when Chinese traders were replaced (Robison 1986). It was probably unrealistic to expect that these policy initiatives would create entrepreneurs. Where the Chinese had the experience, the trading network, and the access to informal credit, it was rational for the recipient of an import license to import through the Chinese (and to share the rent associated with the license with them), rather than compete with them. However, the disappointing result of the various experiments, in particular the Benteng program, was interpreted as showing that an economic policy relying on private capitalists was not viable. As a result opinion had already shifted in favor of state ownership when, in 1957, the opportunity to convert foreign enterprises into state enterprises presented itself—and was taken.

Although after the seizures private businessmen lobbied for the transfer of the Dutch enterprises to the private sector, disillusionment with the performance of the private sector was by then widespread. At a conference held at the end of 1957 Hatta discussed the roles of government and the private individual in furthering economic development. He sympathized with those who wanted the private entrepreneur to play the leading part, but he argued that the opportunity for the Indonesian capitalist had come too late. "Freed from the shackles of colonialism, newcomers came forward in droves . . . but bitter experiences over the last eight years had entirely shattered those sentiments favorable to the private entrepreneur" (Thomas and Panglaykim 1973, pp. 56–59, quoted by Robison 1986, p. 73). Hatta had been an ardent opponent of the Benteng system, and it was the "bitter experiences" of that program to which he was referring.

Independence did not bring an expansion of the government sector. On the contrary, government expenditure, which had amounted to 13 percent of GNP in 1939, was 12 percent of GDP in 1951, peaked at 15 percent in the following year, and then declined to only 9 percent in 1955. An important reason for this contraction was the combination of a tax system that relied heavily on trade taxes—so that when the terms of trade deteriorated, government revenue fell from 14 percent of GDP in 1951 to only 8 percent in 1955—and legal limitations on deficit financing.

The Five-Year Development Plan for the period 1956–60 is interesting not for its effect on actual events but for what it reveals about the modesty of the planners' ambitions. In the first half of the 1950s per capita income had probably increased by only 1.3 percent per year, which implied that income levels had still not attained prewar levels. Investment was only 6 percent of GDP. Nevertheless the plan foresaw only very small increases in the rate of investment: to 8 percent in 1960 and 12 percent in 1965. About 25 percent was allocated for transport and communication, 25 percent for industry and mining, 25 percent for power and irrigation (9 percent for irrigation alone), 13 percent for agriculture, and 12 percent for education and welfare (8.4 percent for education alone). The irrigation plans aimed at raising the production of rice from 241 grams to 250 grams per person per day and of maize from 60 grams to 70 grams.

Table 11.3 Structure of Production, 1952

Sector	Billions of rupiah	Percent
Agriculture	46.1	56.5
Mining	1.8	2.2
Industry	6.7	8.2
Transport and communications	2.5	3.1
Trade, banking, insurance	10.9	13.4
Government	5.9	7.2
Other	7.7	9.4
Net domestic product (factor cost)	81.6	100.0

Source: Neumark 1954.

These figures too are remarkably modest, at least compared with the rapid economic growth targets in the development plans of other developing countries (including Nigeria) at the time.

Information on the structure of national income is available from Neumark (1954). His estimates for 1952 (table 11.3) indicate agriculture's share in net domestic product to be 56.5 percent. A comparison with Polak's (1942) estimates suggests that the prewar share was higher. Planning Bureau estimates indicate that the increase in the share of agricul-

Table 11.4 Agricultural Production, Selected Years
(thousands of metric tons)

Crop	Average, 1935–39	1951	1954
Food crops			
Cassava	7,637	7,900	9,569
Rice	6,229	5,805	7,529
Maize	2,235	2,350	2,721
Potatoes	1,183	1,030	2,112
Export crops			
Sugar	1,095	436	650
Rubber	353	805	775
Coffee	118	60	42
Tea	86	37	47
Palm oil products	241	151	212

Source: Muljatno 1960.

Table 11.5 Net Domestic Product, 1951–55
(at factor cost, billions of rupiah at 1952 prices)

Sector	1951	1952	1953	1954	1955
Total agriculture	43.2	47.1	51.5	55.1	54.5
Peasant food crops	25.6	27.9	30.9	33.7	32.5
Peasant export crops	7.4	8.0	7.4	8.0	8.1
Estate crops	3.3	3.9	4.6	4.2	4.4
Livestock, forestry, and fishing	6.9	7.3	8.6	9.2	9.5
Net of export duties and "statistical tax"	41.9	45.6	50.5	54.6	53.5
Nonagriculture	36.7	33.6	39.3	41.5	43.9
Net domestic product	78.7	79.2	89.8	96.1	97.4

Source: Muljatno 1960, table IV.

ture in the 1940s continued in the 1950s, rising from 53 percent in 1951 to 58 percent in 1958. This is consistent with Paauw's (1960) thesis that postwar development activity was effective in raising output in the labor-intensive (largely agricultural) part of the economy, but much less effective in the capital-intensive part.

For agricultural production, output levels in the 1950s are compared with prewar averages in table 11.4. Most export crops remained far below prewar output levels. The notable exception is rubber production, which more than doubled (an output increase that occurred largely in the smallholder sector).

Food output in 1954 was higher than before the war but did not keep pace with population growth. Rice output, for example, increased by only 21 percent in 17 years when population growth was 1.7 percent a year. The fall in per capita rice production was reflected in an increase in rice imports. The colonial government had achieved its objective of eliminating rice imports just before the outbreak of war. In 1941 there was a

Table 11.6 Net Domestic Product, 1953–58
(at factor cost, billions of rupiah at 1955 prices)

Item	1953	1954	1955	1956	1957	1958
Agriculture	62.0	67.7	67.6	68.5	70.7	77.9
Nonagriculture	47.0	49.1	53.9	56.0	63.8	52.1
Net domestic product	109.0	116.8	121.5	124.5	134.5	130.0
In current prices	84.1	91.9	121.5	141.0	166.0	175.0

Source: United Nations 1960, p. 114.

Table 11.7 Per Capita Net Domestic Product, 1952–58
(at factor cost, in 1952 prices, 1951 = 100)

Year	Agriculture	Nonagriculture	Total
1952	106.4	89.5	98.4
1953	115.2	102.3	109.0
1954	121.7	105.6	114.1
1955	116.6	109.2	113.0
1956	115.5	110.9	113.2
1957	116.5	123.5	119.5
1958	113.0	113.2	112.9

Note: Data assume 2.3 percent annual population growth.
Source: Tables 11.5 and 11.6.

small export surplus (41,000 tons). Rice imports in the 1950s were 332,000 tons in 1950, 409,000 tons in 1951, 650,000 tons in 1952, 311,000 tons in 1953, 253,000 tons in 1954, and 125,000 tons in 1955.

National accounts statistics for the 1950s are notoriously shaky. The two series shown in tables 11.5 and 11.6 must therefore be treated with great caution. If we link the two series at 1955, the last year they have in common, and assume 2.3 percent a year population growth, then the data imply rapid growth in per capita income between 1951 and 1954, particularly for agriculture (consistent with the crop data of table 11.4). After 1954, however, there is stagnation (table 11.7). In 1958 per capita income is virtually the same as at its peak in 1954.[5] Thus, although there was considerable scope for income growth given the levels reached before the war, the rehabilitation potential was realized only to a very limited extent—a few years of rapid recovery were followed by stagnation. The full potential was not realized until after 1965.

12 *Guided Democracy: 1957–66*

During the late 1950s the apparatus of "liberal" or parliamentary democracy was dismantled. In the authoritarian regime that took its place, the president and the army shared power. Control was exercised through several appointed bodies such as the Cabinet and the Supreme Advisory Council. With the exception of the Communist Party (PKI), the role of political parties was greatly diminished; they were regarded with suspicion by the military, had little say in the membership of the appointed bodies, and their political raison d'être was undercut by the emergence of the concept of guided democracy, described by President Sukarno as a mixture of nationalism, Islam, and Marxism. According to this concept, democratic representation was more appropriately vested in functional social groups such as the army, peasants, trade unions, women, and youth than in political parties.

In the parliament of 1960, more members were appointed to represent functional groups than parties (Feith 1963). In the words of Robison (1986, p. 70), "While power became authoritarian, its ideological expression became a kind of populist corporatism in which the social and political conflict embodied in the party system was to be replaced by a consensual system of mutual co-operation presided over by the President."

These developments are discussed in more detail in chapters 18 and 19. Here we note only that Indonesia faced a genuine problem in trying to set up a system of representative government without splitting along ethnic or regional lines. In these circumstances a rejection of the simple majority-vote version of democracy is understandable and may have been necessary for Indonesia to develop as a reasonably cohesive entity. In this sense, guided democracy can be seen as an attempt to construct a de facto constitution, with functional groups being the major constitutional innovation. It was also one way to ensure a more substantial institutional continuity in Indonesian history than first appearances suggest. The New Order regime—the government led by Suharto that came to power in 1966—in some measure echoes these aspects of guided democracy.

These changes in the political arena in the late 1950s were the culmination of trends apparent throughout the 1950s, but they were triggered by widespread revolts in the outer islands in 1957. Their formal constitutional embodiment was the reintroduction in 1959 of the constitution of 1945, which had bestowed wide powers on the president. Accompanying this redefinition of the president's role were several changes that greatly strengthened the political power of the army. The direct response to the revolts was the declaration of martial law in March 1957. Supervision was vested in the Supreme War Authority: the military was also able to secure strategic positions in the Cabinet and the Supreme Advisory Council as well as in regional and local administration. Under martial law the military was able to promulgate the most potent regulations, including those expropriating Dutch property at the end of 1957. In the absence of other managerial cadres, these expropriations gave the military a direct stake in the emergent state capitalism, with authority over trading houses, estates, and oil companies.

The years 1958 and 1959 saw additional regional rebellions. These also failed and led to more consolidation and centralization of power. Several leaders of the Socialist Party (PSI) and of Masyumi (which drew much of its support from the Muslim merchant bourgeoisie) had associated themselves with the rebel cause. These were the parties most strongly opposed to guided democracy and the related concept of a guided economy. Their association with the failed rebellion provided Sukarno with the grounds to ban them and thus to emasculate the most articulate opposition to his program.

The third element in the political triangle of these years was the PKI. The relationship was commonly pictured as a seesaw with the PKI and army leadership at opposite ends and the president using his position at the fulcrum to maintain balance between them. Mackie (1967) argues that this picture was misleading and that the relationship was far less static. During 1959–61 the role of the PKI was one of the issues in dispute between Sukarno and the army, with the party itself exercising relatively little direct power. By the end of 1961, however, it had gained a good deal of influence, just at the time that the army was losing some of its leverage with the president. The PKI's position was further strengthened in the two years following Indonesia's break with Malaysia in September 1963, and the army seemed powerless to oppose the general shift to the left (the period of martial law ended in May 1963).

The shift in the political complexion of the coalition during these years raises the question of how robust the coalition was. Many commentators have stressed that, appearances to the contrary, the regime was inherently weak. It is worth quoting two of them at some length. Mackie (1967, pp. 19–20) wrote:

We must start with the paradox that this highly authoritarian and apparently broadly-based government which did not have to worry unduly about an electorate or public opinion polls or the reactions of its opponents, was not at all strong when it came to applying policies which hurt its supporters. While it was able to put through some extraordinarily radical, controversial, and harshly disruptive measures from time to time (e.g. the B.E. system of 1957, the take-overs of Dutch enterprises, the "monetary purge" of August 1959, the 1963 trade break with Singapore-Malaysia), these have all been sudden and irreversible decisions, made without prior debate. Their immediate political impact was indiscriminate or uncertain. . . . Always, too, government statements explained these desperate leaps into the unknown in an apocalyptic vein, as if they signified the beginning of a new era of economic life. . . . By contrast, attempts to restrain the inflation firmly and persistently at its source, by holding the budget in approximate balance over a long period, failed on almost every occasion they were tried. . . . The loose coalition of political groups supporting President Sukarno was never stable or united enough for the Finance Minister to be allowed to take any risks of causing dissension among them by slashing expenditures.

Somewhat earlier, Feith (1963, p. 408) summarized his view of government during the guided democracy period:

This is not a government which can easily exert much weight of power. Many of its decrees are effectively ignored by those who are charged with their implementation. This is sometimes attributed to the ineffectiveness of its administrative machinery. But it is more accurately described in terms of the weakness of the political elite's cohesion, the heavy dependence of this elite on the bureaucracy as a social class, and the great importance of intra-bureaucratic politics as a force for immobilisation of the government.

In addition to this underlying weakness in execution, two other features of the coalition appear to be central to any explanation of the collapse of coherent economic policy in the period. One was the "utter unrealism and apparent unconcern in economic matters" for which Sukarno was famous (Mackie 1967, p. 19). The other was the apparent lack of any important group with a powerful interest in stabilization or in economic rectitude.

The 1957–58 Expropriations and the Move to State Ownership

The initial impetus for the 1957–58 expropriations appears to have been a spontaneous, syndicalist takeover of some Dutch firms by workers and unions in December 1957. However, General Nasution intervened rapidly and in the same month ordered military supervision of all Dutch assets. Formal endorsement of the expropriations by Parliament followed a year later. Given the preeminence of Dutch concerns in plantations, foreign trade, banking, and shipping, as well as in a host of other enterprises, the seizures transformed the structure of the economy. There was a gap of several months between expropriation and nationalization. During this period "private businessmen made a bid to persuade the Government to transfer certain of the ex-Dutch companies to the private sector. This was a rather forlorn hope because leaders of several political groupings had launched a strong attack on the performances of private enterprise at a National Economic Conference in November–December, 1957" (Thomas and Panglaykim 1973, quoted by Robison 1986, p. 73).

Indigenous private capitalists were not regarded as competent to take over even a portion of the assets because of their dismal record through the 1950s—consuming state credit and concessions at a rapid rate while showing few signs of entrepreneurial or managerial ability. The Benteng program, terminated in 1957, was widely held to demonstrate that indigenous capitalists could not be used as the vehicle for a nationalist economic revolution of the sort desired by Sukarno and his confederates. Nor was it politically feasible, even if it had been desired, to entrust the assets to Indonesian Chinese capitalists.

The alternative was state ownership. In April 1958 the confiscated Dutch trading houses were incorporated into six new state trading corporations, bringing the total to eight. These were granted monopolies, giving them effective control of 70 percent of imports. The state trading corporations (STCs) were allocated a central role in the management of the economy; they were to control prices and the supply of basic necessities and to act as a major source of revenue for development.

Although some state corporations proved reasonably efficient and profitable, overall they were a failure. The capital stock declined sharply and the dollar value of exports fell, particularly that of estate crops. For example, the dollar value of exports of estate rubber was halved between 1958 and 1966. By 1963, with a deepening balance of payments crisis, the government took several steps that weakened the position of the STCs, forcing the banks to cut credit extended to them, requiring them to slow sales of imported goods, and even removing their monopoly on essential imports.

The STCs were plagued not only by managerial inefficiency but also by theft. Their failure to make contributions to state revenue at the expected levels was in large part a consequence of the common practice in which officials, often military men, sold goods at market prices, declared profits based on sales at official prices, and expropriated the difference. The STCs also created a class of conspicuously wealthy individuals and groups with experience and skill in rent-seeking and an established interest in the continuation and extension of opportunities for this activity. Finally, the system institutionalized mechanisms for diverting the flow of revenue from the state to private individuals; this was to play an important part in the fiscal collapse that followed.

Macroeconomic Policies

The universal and incontrovertible characterization of macroeconomic policies in this period is one of large budgetary deficits leading inexorably to runaway inflation. A loss of expenditure control is sometimes treated as the primary cause, but although control was lax and ineffective in many ways, the fiscal crisis was induced overwhelmingly by a catastrophic collapse of revenue. This alone is enough to make the Indonesian budgetary crisis highly atypical, and, as argued later, it makes it difficult to draw clear-cut lessons from the successful stabilization that followed during 1966–70.

Until the end of 1956, budgetary policy was subject to significant legal and political limitations. The Bank Indonesia Act of 1953 imposed a statutory requirement that the bank retain gold and foreign exchange reserves to the value of 20 percent of its advances, unless emergency provisions were invoked with the approval of Parliament. Although this approval had been sought and obtained on several occasions, the government incurred severe criticism in Parliament on each occasion. Thus, although the statutory limit was breached from time to time, it nonetheless imposed an effective budgetary brake on government. The budget was in deficit throughout the 1950s (with the exception of 1951, when revenues benefited from the Korean commodity boom), and the government had accordingly been the subject of repeated strictures from the IMF and other agencies and commentators. However, the deficits had been relatively modest in scale, averaging 15 percent of revenue until 1957. From 1957 to 1959 the average deficit rose to 40 percent of revenue.

Since the deficits of 1957 and 1958 were financed by borrowing from the Central Bank, it was inevitable that inflationary pressures would be strengthened. Another significant turn of the inflationary screw was the sharp (though temporary) reduction in agricultural production and exports following expropriation in 1958. These pressures were more easily expressed in outright price rises after the government's first major reform—the introduction of the BE certificate system in June 1957, which was in effect a devaluation to a floating exchange rate.[1] Faced with the apparently inexorable (and hardly surprising) continued decline in the rate, the experiment was abandoned in April 1958, and the rate was pegged once more.

The years 1958 to 1959 saw rapid growth of price controls and direct intervention in markets, but these measures were broadly unsuccessful in stemming the rise in prices and liquidity. August 1959 saw the first of several attempts to bring the situation under control, with a monetary purge. All bank notes in denominations of Rp 500 and Rp 1,000 were reduced to 10 percent of their face value, and 90 percent of bank deposits of more than Rp 25,000 were frozen by forced conversion into government bonds. The government also devalued the currency from Rp 11.4 per U.S. dollar to Rp 45, drastically revised the foreign exchange regulations, reformed the direct tax structure, and imposed budgetary restraint that reduced the deficit from Rp 133 billion in 1959 to Rp 8 billion—or about 15 percent of revenue—in 1960.

During 1960–61 these measures appeared to be working well. Inflation slowed and foreign exchange reserves rose, enabling the government to liberalize import restrictions in August 1960. This in turn had favorable consequences for revenue and prices. By the beginning of 1961 it would have been easy to believe that the worst was over, with the political turmoil of 1957–60 ending, the new public sector beginning to emerge from its teething troubles, and some return to fiscal prudence under way.

Within a year it became clear that this rosy picture was far from the case. Inflation was accelerating, and 1962 was to prove an economic disaster, the beginning of the true fiscal crisis. There are many reasons for this renewed and rapid deterioration, mostly noneconomic in origin. The loss of expenditure control in the late 1950s was not something that could easily be reversed. The budgetary improvement, in any event, was achieved more by revenue increases than by expenditure restraint—1960 expenditure was actually 30 percent higher than in 1959. The improvement in exports was largely due to high world prices during 1959 and 1960 rather than to any recovery in export volume. The monetary purge itself (which reduced currency in circulation from Rp 34 billion to Rp 21 billion overnight) created an intense liquidity crisis that had to be relieved by extensive bank credits; within six months the volume of money was back to its original level.

Furthermore, in spite of all these signals that caution was in order, the government embarked on a wildly ambitious program including the

Eight-Year Overall Development Plan, described by Sukarno with unintentional irony as being "rich in fantasy" (Mackie 1967, p. 27). The plan had little basis in economic realities and was soon abandoned, but it did have the important consequence of ensuring a commitment to heavy development expenditures in 1961 and thus contributing to the next inflationary bout.

More important in the longer run was the intensification of the government's dependence on foreign trade for revenue. Direct taxes failed to rise automatically in line with prices, and discretionary changes were limited to 1959, whereas taxes on imports and foreign exchange (and hence on exports) were changed at least annually and with each change increased more drastically. In 1960 the government began to sell a fraction of the foreign exchange available for "free-list" imports at a very high premium (Rp 200 per U.S. dollar, when the main effective rates ranged from Rp 45 to Rp 82). Subsequently the government "became so dependent on this source of revenue that it lost effective power to regulate the use of a large fraction of its shrinking foreign exchange" (Mackie 1967, p. 26).

With these factors in the background, the partial improvement in 1960–61 was a fragile affair, and the government's control of the economy and of its own budget was tenuous. In the autumn of 1961 rice prices jumped dramatically following a drought: between September 1961 and March 1962 the Jakarta retail price index for rice rose by a factor of five, and the food price index doubled. The government's program of purchasing rice in rural areas was functioning badly, since peasants were unwilling to sell at prices that consistently lagged behind the rising free market price. Despite a record harvest in 1962, heavy rice imports became necessary.

This shock was soon accompanied by another of the government's own making, when the decision was made to turn the West Irian campaign into an overt military conflict in December 1961. The decision had dramatic consequences for the budget deficit, which had already reached more than 40 percent of revenue and which topped 65 percent in 1962.

By the end of 1962 it was clear that the government was contemplating some stabilization scheme with the assistance of the IMF. Action was delayed well into 1963, when the May 26 regulations were introduced. These constituted a standard stabilization package: relaxation of price controls, increases of 400 to 600 percent in public utility charges, budgetary austerity (the deficit was to be halved in 1963 and eliminated in 1964), and a release of foreign exchange for intermediate inputs and raw materials backed by foreign credits and loans. At the same time there was an implicit devaluation, and salaries and allowances of civil servants were roughly doubled to compensate for inflation.

The package was deeply resented, but in the few months during which it was actually pursued, there were signs of improvement in the economic situation, with the price index decelerating between June and August. Despite a chorus of protests, the government was still expressing a determination to continue with the program in early September. At this point the simmering conflict with Malaysia flared up, mobs assaulted the British and Malaysian embassies, and all commercial relations with Singapore and Malaysia were broken off.

These events made the program infeasible. Foreign aid from the IMF, the United States, and other countries of the Organization for Economic Cooperation and Development (OECD) was terminated; export earnings plummeted with the attempted diversion of almost half of Indonesia's export trade; and any prospect of bringing the budget under control vanished. In both 1963 and 1964 the deficit exceeded revenue.

In some respects the main puzzle of the period 1964–65 is that the economic situation did not deteriorate faster than it did. Part of the explanation lies in the recovery of illegal exports to Singapore to something like preconfrontation levels by mid-1964, and a good harvest in 1965. In any event, by the end of 1965, prices were rising at an unprecedented rate, despite a further drastic devaluation, currency reform, and related measures.

Overall this period was a dismal one in terms of economic management and of outcomes. As is clearly shown in tables 16.1 and 16.2, per capita consumption fell and real wages plummeted by around one half. This poses a conundrum: wage earners were a favored group, yet wages fell rapidly relative to average incomes. The apparent incompetence of the government in controlling wages presumably reflects its revenue difficulties. Because of these difficulties the government was not in a position to protect its own employees (see the following section), and it would have been politically impossible, even if desired, to protect employees in the private sector with effective minimum wage policies.

Although much of the poor performance was directly attributable to poor economic management, it should be stressed that this period would in any case have been difficult for Indonesia.[2] The terms of trade declined by more than 40 percent during 1960–66. Such a drop would have proved a severe test for the best of managers; as it was, it probably accelerated the crisis.

The Squeeze on Civil Service Incomes

The continual price rises during 1957–66 evidently put severe pressure on fixed-income employees, particularly the civil servants, whose cash incomes were raised by infrequent and inadequate jumps so that they lagged further and further behind prices. The salary of a middle-level official rose by a factor of around 12 between 1957 and 1964, while prices rose by a factor of 30. (Industrial workers were less severely squeezed:

their real wages were halved during these years.) Early in 1963 General Nasution himself acknowledged that it had become impossible for civil servants to live unless they had more than one job. Apart from job duplication, there were several devices of varying legality to supplement family income. These included the use of pervasive travel allowances (particularly for those fortunate to travel abroad) and a whole variety of acts of corruption and malfeasance, ranging from theft and resale of textbooks by school teachers to the large-scale sale of licenses.

Given the highly regulated nature of the economy, opportunities for corruption were widespread. The squeeze on incomes meant that corruption shifted from being simply a matter of personal dishonesty to one of risks becoming institutionalized. In many respects, this appears to have happened less in Indonesia than might reasonably have been expected.

The Overthrow of Sukarno

The collapse of the economy divested the Sukarno regime of most of its popular support, particularly among the middle classes. The political atmosphere became exceedingly tense as the future of the coalition became more uncertain. Fighting broke out at the end of September 1965. What exactly happened is still controversial. According to one version, the PKI mounted an attempted coup that failed and that was rapidly followed by a successful countercoup by the army. Sukarno's ambivalent attitude toward the original coup cost him further support, and in March 1966 he was in effect replaced by General Suharto, Adam Malik, and the Sultan of Jogjakarta. During the intervening period the army and anticommunist civilian groups took bloody revenge, killing up to 500,000 alleged members and sympathizers of the PKI—eliminating it as a political force—and a very large number of Chinese.

The countercoup can be interpreted either as the eventual triumph of the military over its original partners and rivals in the coalition or as the victory of the middle classes over the communist threat. But Robison (1986, p. 95) urges caution in these interpretations:

> It is possible to view the New Order as a counter revolution against "socialist" forces, and to the extent that the PKI was seen as a threat to the propertied classes, it was. But upon close inspection there is little that was genuinely socialist about Guided Economy; rather, it was a ramshackle, underpowered form of state capitalism operated by, and largely for, the benefit of the politico-bureaucrats who dominated the state apparatus, notably the military themselves.

13 Stabilization and the New Order: 1966–73

The new regime faced a daunting task in early 1966. Any realistic policy to check inflation required a huge turnaround in the fiscal situation and probably a sizable inflow of foreign aid. The rapidity with which these objectives were achieved is a considerable achievement, and this period is often regarded as a classic example of successful stabilization policy in the IMF tradition. Indonesia had in fact withdrawn from the IMF (and the World Bank) in August 1965 in protest at Malaysia's admission to U.N. membership. Nevertheless, the IMF was active in helping prepare the stabilization program before Indonesia formally rejoined the Bretton Woods organizations in February 1967.

The Indonesian government unveiled its program of rehabilitation and stabilization in April 1966. The objectives included a more central role for market forces and for domestic and foreign capital, the achievement of a balanced budget, and the pursuit of appropriate credit and exchange rate policies. Considerable attention was also to be paid to the supply side, in particular to the restoration of production in a number of key sectors—food, infrastructure, clothing, and exports.

Fiscal Policy

The objective of a balanced budget had been taken very seriously since the late 1960s, at least for presentational purposes:

> Since the late sixties the Indonesian budget as presented at the beginning of the financial year has always been in balance, and the realized budget balance has also been close to zero. The explanation for this feat of apparent fiscal discipline is almost entirely definitional; it lies in the fact that items which in most countries are classified as *means of financing* the deficit are classified as *revenues* in Indonesia. (Booth and McCawley 1981, p. 143; emphasis in original)

However, only some financing items were misclassified as revenue, notably foreign assistance. Thus the balanced budget policy, although permitting the government to run substantial deficits in the conventional sense, had the important consequence of curtailing domestic borrowing. From 1968 to 1975 the budget had, on average, negligible monetary impact.

Of course, the balanced budget policy did not eliminate money creation. With the government no longer preempting the economy's credit, there was a revival of lending to the enterprise sector (private and public). Indeed, in the absence of an adequate financial market and with business income low, the recovery of enterprise investment depended on the banking sector and money creation.

In line with the new approach, the budget adopted for 1967 showed revenue and expenditure exactly balanced, whereas the outturn was reported as a deficit equivalent to 3 percent of revenue. At face value this was an astonishingly rapid turnaround from the 1966 position, in which the deficit reached 128 percent of revenue. However, this conclusion must be treated with some caution. If foreign assistance is stripped from the budgetary figures, the 1967 deficit rises to 45 percent of revenue. If certain expenditure items recorded as extrabudgetary are added back in (a salary increase for December 1967 and advances to the official rice procurement agency for imports), the deficit rises to 60 percent of revenue.

These figures make it clear that the rectification of the budget was not a domestic conjuring trick but was heavily dependent on the resumption (and enhancement) of the aid flows that had been suspended following the adoption of a policy of confrontation toward Malaysia. Viewed from this perspective, the suspension of aid had played no small part in the revenue collapse of 1964–65, just as it constituted a substantial part of the revenue recovery, from around 4 percent of GDP in 1966 to the more normal level (by historical Indonesian standards) of 10 percent in 1967.

This is not the whole story, however. There was indeed an austerity program for expenditure after 1966: the bulk of Sukarno's "special projects" were abandoned, confrontation was ended, and normal budgetary procedures were reimposed. More interestingly, there was also a marked improvement in domestically generated revenue. Partly this reflected a considerable recovery in the efficiency of tax collection—realized income tax receipts were more than twice the budgeted level, and those for corporation tax were up 50 percent. Partly the improved revenue picture reflected an arrangement whereby the government in effect charged a commission to users of foreign exchange made available by aid donors. The Inter-governmental Group on Indonesia, which acted as a coordinating body for Indonesia's Western donors, initially resisted this arrangement, but, given support from both the IMF and the Netherlands, it was eventually accepted (Posthumus 1972).

The rate of inflation slowed dramatically between 1966 and 1967 by a factor of six, from 635 to 112 percent. It originally appeared likely to fall even faster, but the final quarter of 1967 saw a temporary recrudescence of inflation associated with the rice crisis. This reconfirmed the importance of ensuring adequate supplies of rice, which became a major component of policy in the period.

A similar fiscal pattern was pursued in the next few years. Revenue inclusive of aid receipts ran at around 10 percent of GDP, sufficient to cover expenditures, but the deficit, conventionally defined, ran 30 to 40 percent of conventionally defined revenue.

Financial Reform

The rectification of the budget made it feasible to place the financial system on a sounder footing. The banking conglomerate formed in the previous period (whose function had been merely to finance the deficit) was dismantled in 1967, and a degree of independence was restored to the state banks as the dominant credit-providing institutions. In 1968 Bank Indonesia discontinued its commercial banking role and concentrated on the more usual functions of a central bank.

Even prior to these institutional changes several steps were taken to enforce a change in financial direction. A legal minimum reserve requirement of 30 percent was enforced on all banks, various credit restrictions were introduced, and interest rates on loans from state banks were raised more than threefold to 6 to 9 percent per month. Most important, deposit rates were increased: after October 1968 12-month deposits were 6 percent a month; 6-month deposits, 5 percent; and 3-month deposits, 4 percent. These high rates were initiated by Bank Indonesia to encourage private savings within the official banking system. (Private banks no longer subject to rate restrictions had already been attracting a growing volume of time and savings deposits.) Since the average time deposit rate was higher than the average lending rate of the state commercial banks, Bank Indonesia stepped in to subsidize the operation. In addition to the high rate of interest offered to depositors, the interest earned on time deposits was made tax-free, and the government guaranteed repayment of deposits and agreed that no questions would be asked about their origin.

With inflation decelerating rapidly, these high nominal rates had to be cut back frequently: by September 1969, for example, the three rates had been reduced to 2.5 percent, 2.0 percent, and 1.5 percent, respectively. Nevertheless, the principle that these deposits should pay appropriate real rates of return was established. In consequence there was a remarkable growth in broad money measures during the period. Broad money as a percentage of income rose during the period from a historic low of 5 percent to a level of 25 percent (where it stabilized), with a substantial part of the expansion resulting from the growth of time deposits, which were negligible in 1966–67.

It was also true that nominal balances of narrow money grew considerably faster than prices during these years. It is difficult to disentangle how much of this growth in real balances was simply a reversal of the contraction induced before 1966 by the accelerating inflation and how much represented real growth and financial deepening in the economy (see Sundrum 1973). Whatever the cause, this growth permitted the authorities to expand the money supply relatively rapidly without necessarily incurring any inflationary consequences. Despite this generous cushion, and despite the fact that price stability was now a primary goal of economic policy, the increase in money supply rose after 1971 to a level that was inconsistent with stability (table 13.1).

Grenville (1981) argues that although the instruments of control were blunt, the authorities were technically capable of regulating money creation and that incompatible goals led to excessive increases. Indonesia's relatively high dependence on foreign trade coupled with its low degree of monetization made its money supply particularly susceptible to instability generated by foreign reserve movements.

Until 1972, foreign reserves were negligible and often negative, so this channel was inoperative. Before 1966 this was because direct controls were used to allocate foreign exchange; afterward the exchange rate was adjusted to clear the market in foreign exchange so that reserves did not rise. After a devaluation in August 1971, however, the exchange rate was pegged until November 1978, and reserves began to rise. Fiscal policy was not used to neutralize this expansion: the balanced budget policy

Table 13.1 Increase in Money and Prices, 1966–73
(percent)

Year	Increase in narrow money	Increase in prices[a]
1966	763	635
1967	132	112
1968	120	85
1969	61	10
1970	36	9
1971	28	2
1972	48	26
1973	41	27

a. Jakarta cost of living index, December to December.
Source: Bank Indonesia, *Annual Report,* various years.

was maintained. It appears that the return to moderate inflation in the early 1970s was a policy accident.

Trade and Exchange Liberalization

By 1966 Indonesia had acquired a bewilderingly complex multiple exchange rate system and associated trade controls. A central objective of the early program of the New Order was to dismantle this system, albeit gradually. The rupiah was allowed to float from late 1966 to the end of 1968, during which time it depreciated from Rp 85 per U.S. dollar to Rp 326. At the same time the proportion of foreign exchange earnings that exporters had to sell to the authorities at unfavorable terms was progressively reduced, import regulations were liberalized, and the 200 percent surtax on imports was lifted. Although the rate was stabilized from the beginning of 1969, it was adjusted by substantial amounts in 1970 and 1971 in line with foreign exchange market pressures.

This policy had three clear effects (Rosendale 1981). First, it led to a substantial reduction in export smuggling and consequently a marked increase in export receipts covered in the official statistics. Second, the relative price of imports rose dramatically relative to domestic prices. Finally, it boosted the confidence of potential aid donors and of foreign investors and residents, who repatriated capital that had previously been in flight. This policy was held in place as long as downward adjustments in the exchange rate were required, to prevent the emergence of serious foreign exchange shortages. From the early 1970s symmetric logic would have entailed revaluation in the face of a tendency to accumulate foreign reserves. Despite the success of the experiment with floating, this logic was not pursued, and more weight was given to the case for management of the exchange rate as a protective device.

It was also during these years that a commitment to currency convertibility emerged that became, like the commitment to budgetary balance, one of the central planks of the extremely durable de facto "economic constitution" of Indonesia. These two commitments, originally induced by a determination not to repeat the errors of 1965, have undoubtedly played an important role in the success of subsequent macroeconomic management.

Stabilization, Growth, and Income Distribution

Stabilization policies are often held to have deeply adverse consequences for both growth and income distribution. These aspects are considered in detail in chapter 16; the discussion here is correspondingly brief. The Indonesian program appears to have been a clear case of stabilization with growth; somewhat less certainly it also appears to have been achieved without deterioration in income distribution.

GDP growth in the early 1960s was only 2 percent at constant prices, whereas that over the 1965–71 period was three times as high. The switch was particularly dramatic in construction (–1.3 percent to 17 percent) and mining (2.1 percent to 13.4 percent), but it occurred across the board, not least in agriculture (1.4 percent to 3.8 percent). This recovery was not immediate: GDP grew only 2 percent in 1966 and 1967 before jumping 11 percent in 1968 and then settling down to grow at around 7 to 8 percent for the next four years. A part of this performance should be attributed to rehabilitation and to the return into use of spare capacity— in the years before stabilization, capacity utilization had declined to 30 percent as a result of the shortage of foreign exchange and thus of spare parts, intermediate inputs, and raw materials. However, the period also saw an investment boom encouraged by the new Foreign and Domestic Investment Laws, and productive potential increased markedly.

As far as income distribution is concerned, the picture is a "blurred and confused" one, but some work suggests that what were often deteriorating trends before 1966 or after 1970 were halted or even reversed during the stabilization episode (Booth and Sundrum 1981). Snapshots of the distribution of expenditure for 1964, 1967, and 1970, shown in table 16.5, indicate that the poorest 40 percent of the population gained substantially at the expense of the top quintile. Similarly, Papanek (1980) found strong growth in real wages in industry and estate agriculture from the mid-1960s, reversing the downward trend noted earlier.

Rice Policy

Rice policy was far from neglected during the guided democracy era, and in many respects the main components of policy from 1966 had already been assembled under Sukarno. However, the rice economy inherited by the New Order government was in a sorry state: rice production in Java had risen only 2 percent above the level of 1954, which had itself represented a recovery only to prewar output. Yields throughout Indonesia had been stagnant for a decade, and production increases were obtained only from expanded acreage in the outer islands.

The main vehicle for the attempt to place rice production on a satisfactory footing was the Bimas (mass guidance) program, which originated as an extension service in 1963. As well as advice, the program was to provide loans and handle the distribution of essential inputs, notably fertilizer. Any doubts about the importance of the program would have been settled by the "rice crisis" of late 1967, already mentioned. In any event, the intensification program was a great success. Over the period 1968/69 to 1973/74 rice production rose at an average annual rate of 4.5 percent with the spread of fertilizer-responsive seed technology. At that time the long-cherished but elusive goal of rice self-sufficiency had to be given more favorable treatment precisely because they needed to be lured into Indonesia, unlike their domestic counterparts (Sadli 1970). However, there were powerful countervailing forces who wanted to encourage domestic investment. By the late 1960s the bureaucratic capitalists whose emergence was discussed in the previous chapter were using their powers of administration to allocate licenses, credit, and contracts to build large corporate empires, usually with Indonesian Chinese partners. They were also able to organize lucrative joint venture partnerships with foreign companies. To underpin this strategy, they required organized protection and the adoption of an import-substituting approach to industrialization.

Contrary to expectations, foreign capital, predominantly Japanese, concentrated in the heavily protected industrial sector and became the principal beneficiary of the protections it enjoyed. There was increasing unrest over this issue and a reemergence of economic nationalism. In 1970 the government legislated to exclude new foreign investment from 30 areas of light industry. Further restrictions involving trade and forestry followed, but these were not sufficient to satisfy the critics of the Bappenas strategy.

The main thrust of the economic nationalist position was a return to and refinement of the concepts that underlay the establishment of the state corporate structure of the guided economy period. A crucial difference at this time was that a leading adherent of economic nationalism was Ibnu Sutowo, the president-director of the state oil company, Pertamina, which "represented the only source of finance, or means of raising loans, which was both significant and outside the control of the Bappenas technocrats" (Robison 1986, p. 152). In the next few years vast loans were raised, principally from the Japanese and with Suharto's enthusiastic support.

Despite the prominence of the Bappenas technocrats during this period, their fortunes were mixed following their early successes in devising and managing the stabilization program. In particular, the reemergence of state corporatism, protectionism, and the shift to import-substituting industrialization must all be regarded as major setbacks for their agenda.

Since the New Order's microeconomic policies were so often flawed, it is interesting that the economy performed so well in this period. Partly this reflects the great scope for recovery that the government inherited; partly it reflects good fortune. It has already been noted that the early 1960s saw a dramatic deterioration in Indonesia's terms of trade. In contrast, the period 1967–71 saw a partial recovery of 20 percent. Later the commodity boom of 1972/73 and the two oil price booms occurred. Another piece of good fortune was the green revolution, already noted.

appeared to be within reach. Thus although the green revoluti
exogenous event, the Indonesian authorities were receptive
chapter 16 for more detail).

Economic Policy and the Technocrats

The early years of the New Order saw the rise to prominer
Bappenas (the National Development Planning Board) tec
sometimes called the Berkeley mafia, who negotiated the main
of the stabilization program with the IMF. They were comm
relatively free market prescription for the economy and to a
open-door approach to foreign capital. However, as Robison (19
cautions, not too much should be read into the expressed ideo
tachments of the technocrats in explaining Indonesian economi

> Free-market, open-door ideologies were able to flourish ir
> years of the New Order because, given the political opti
> to a counter-revolutionary regime presiding over a de
> economy in a state of chaos and collapse and desperatel
> to renegotiate debts and attract foreign investment, there
> choice but to accept the IMF/IBRD/IGGI policy prescriptio

Following this reasoning, dependency theorists are inclined to
the period as one of subservience to the IMF, with the econom
tured to suit the needs of international capital. Others,
Glassburner (1979), stress the extent of continuity with th
economy period—with economic nationalism, state interven
protectionism remaining as important themes of policy. From
spective the Bappenas policy can be seen as providing a fr
within which domestic capital could be nurtured, in the forr
corporations and also companies owned by coalitions of the
and Chinese entrepreneurs.

The two most important pieces of legislation in the period 1
capital accumulation were the Foreign Capital Investment Lav
ary 1967 (PMA) and its domestic analogue of July 1968 (PMDN).
law provided guarantees that the government had no intenti
tionalizing foreign assets, and it guaranteed compensation if
ization did occur. There were also guarantees of the duration
tion (30 years, with the possibility of extension), of the right
and recruit foreign management and technicians, and of the ri
patriate profits, depreciation funds, and the proceeds from tl
shares to Indonesian nationals. The law also set forth a range o
day provisions for import duties and corporation and divider

The following year similar tax and duty concessions were ex
domestic investors. The Bappenas position was that foreign

As regards recovery, the essential step was to achieve and maintain financial stabilization, the arena within which the New Order was cohesive and at its best. Once this had been achieved, and with it some flow of foreign and domestic savings, a huge number and wide range of high-payoff projects resulted. With so much to rehabilitate, even an imperfect choice of project or of phasing would still produce high returns. At the start of the period the incremental capital-output ratio was as low as 1.2, and rehabilitation of infrastructure continued up to 1973. At this time there were also possibilities for easy import substitution. A tentative conclusion is that this period was one in which it was vital to get macro-economic policies right, but one that was relatively forgiving of poor microeconomic policies.

14 The First Oil Boom: 1973–79

Following the sharp increase in the posted prices of the Arab oil-producing countries in October 1973, Indonesia doubled its oil export price early in 1974. Although this price increase is the single most important event of the period covered in this chapter, the export boom that Indonesia enjoyed was only partly an oil boom. And even for oil, export prices had already been raised three times in 1973 (table 14.1). Those adjustments had doubled the 1972 price, so there would have been a substantial oil boom even in the absence of the 1974 price changes.

In addition, Indonesia benefited not only from oil price increases but also from substantial volume increases because of earlier exploration efforts. The volume of crude oil exports rose by 55 percent between 1972 and its peak in 1977 (table 14.2). Taking these volume increases as given, we calculated the extra revenue generated by the price increases under the assumption that in the counterfactual case the price of oil exports relative to import prices would have remained constant at the 1972 level. Under this assumption, income rose from $620 million in 1973 to $7.1 billion in 1979 and totaled $29.3 billion for the period, or 266 percent of 1972 GDP.

This huge windfall still does not take into account favorable developments for nonoil exports. Timber and coffee exports increased in volume, and world prices for rubber, palm oil, and tin rose substantially in 1973 and 1974 and for coffee in 1977. The barter terms of trade improved substantially, even when oil exports are excluded: by 26 percent in 1974 and by almost 60 percent in 1979, compared with 1972 (table 14.3).

Unlike the 1979–83 period, no pronounced boom-slump cycle occurred from 1973 to 1979 (table 14.2). Oil production fell in 1975, but only marginally. Between 1977 and 1979 there was a large fall (16 percent), but dollar revenue continued to rise. The relative price of oil rose enormously in 1974 and stayed high for the remainder of the period.

These favorable developments came at a most convenient time for the government, since its position was shaken, first in 1972 by rice short-

244

Table 14.1 Oil Export Prices, 1972–74
(f.o.b. prices of Minas crude oil)

Date	Price (dollars per barrel)
April 1, 1972	2.93
April 1, 1973	3.70
October 1, 1973	4.75
November 1, 1973	6.00
January 1, 1974	10.80
April 1, 1974	11.70

Source: Grenville 1974, p. 2; Arndt 1974, p. 2.

ages and then in 1973 by a rise in economic nationalism. After four years of stable rice prices, a disappointing harvest led to enormous price increases (the Jakarta food component of the CPI rose from 626 in December 1971 to 925 a year later), because Bulog (the National Logistics Board, responsible for stabilizing the price of basic commodities such as rice) had inadequate stocks and prices of imported rice were rising at the same time. The government reacted in three ways to this new rice crisis. It first introduced institutional reforms to improve rice marketing. Village cooperatives (the BUUDs) were charged with procurement tasks for Bulog. When it turned out that physical targets were not met because

Table 14.2 Oil Exports and the Magnitude of the Boom, 1972–79

Year	Volume (millions of barrels)[a] (1)	Value (billions of dollars) (2)	Relative price[b] (3)	Extra revenue[c] (4)
1972	345	0.9	1.85	n.a.
1973	426	1.4	2.67	0.62
1974	424	4.6	6.71	3.33
1975	400	5.1	6.98	3.75
1976	485	6.1	5.86	4.17
1977	535	7.3	6.27	5.15
1978	502	7.4	6.22	5.20
1979	448	10.3	5.96	7.10

n.a. Not applicable.
a. Crude plus products.
b. Relative to general import price index (1971 = 1).
c. Column 2 (column 3 − 1.85)/column 3.
Source: Warr 1986, table 9.7, based on Bank Indonesia, *Indonesia Financial Statistics*, various issues, for column 1; and Central Statistical Bureau, *Indicator Economics*, various issues, for columns 2 and 3.

Table 14.3 Relative Prices and Quantities, 1972–79
(1972 = 100)

Year	Relative prices[a] P_e/P_n	P^*_e/P_n	P_m/P_n	Agriculture	Mining	GDP indexes[b] Manufacturing	Government	Services[c]	Total
1972	100	100	100	100	100	100	100	100	100
1973	132	142	113	109	123	115	103	110	111
1974	231	154	122	113	127	134	113	123	120
1975	181	102	106	113	123	150	144	132	126
1976	154	102	91	119	141	165	152	139	134
1977	150	111	80	121	159	179	178	153	144
1978	149	115	82	126	156	219	195	172	158
1979	233	143	90	131	155	247	205	187	168

a. Prices of exports (P_e), nonoil exports (P^*_e), and imports (P_m) relative to prices of nontradables (P_n). Housing is used here as a proxy for nontradables.
b. GDP in 1973 prices.
c. Services is defined residually; it includes electricity and water supply.
Source: Warr 1986, tables 9.3 and 9.4.

many BUUDs could not compete successfully with private traders, farmers were forced, sometimes by soldiers, to sell to the BUUDs. This procedure was quickly abandoned, but it is revealing in showing that a distrust of markets had not disappeared with the guided economy.

A second step was to intensify the rice extension programs. Third, the oil money was used to subsidize rice consumption. The rice production programs (Bimas and Inmas) were expanded, which involved increased provision of improved seeds, fertilizer, credit, and extension services. Rice support prices were raised substantially (from Rp 13.2 per kilogram in October 1972 to Rp 17.5 in March 1973), and large quantities of rice were imported to bring down domestic prices. However, as world prices of rice began to increase sharply, domestic prices were kept stable, and the resulting subsidy quickly became one of the largest items of public expenditure, already accounting in 1973/74 for Rp 127 billion out of a total of Rp 713 billion for "routine" (nondevelopment) expenditure. In the short run, subsidies on imported food and fertilizer (which together cost $1 billion in 1974/75) were to be a major use of the windfall income.

Bappenas versus Economic Nationalism

The foreign and domestic investment laws of 1967 and 1968 had swept away the rigid investment controls of the Sukarno era, and in the early 1970s new investments began to bear fruit. There was rapid industrial growth, especially in the textile sector, where output increased by 36 percent in two years (1970–72). Much of the new investment was foreign, particularly Japanese, and much of the domestic investment was Chinese.[1] Resentment of this development led to a revival of concerns about the interests of indigenous entrepreneurs—the *pribumi*—and became part of a wide-ranging critique of the regime and of the development policy identified with the Bappenas technocrats. Eventually the proponents of economic liberalism lost, but although measures were taken to placate the *pribumi*, the revival of economic nationalism led not to private indigenous entrepreneurs replacing foreign and Chinese capitalists but to state-led capitalism dominated by military and political factions.

Bappenas policy was identified with the policy advice of the IMF, the World Bank, and the bilateral aid donors united in the Inter-governmental Group on Indonesia. The extent of the intellectual commitment to economic liberalism by the technocrats is uncertain, but in any case there was no choice. Free market, open-door ideologies were able to flourish in the early years of the New Order, because for a counterrevolutionary regime presiding over a debt-ridden economy in a state of chaos and collapse and desperately seeking to renegotiate debts and attract foreign investment, there was little choice but to accept the policy prescriptions of the IMF, the World Bank, and the Inter-governmental Group on Indonesia.

Opposition to Bappenas came from four very different groups. One consisted of indigenous, small-scale entrepreneurs, who were adversely affected by foreign competition. In the textile sector (where almost half of foreign industrial investments occurred), resentment built up as hand looms were replaced by large, mechanized, foreign-owned factories (Healey 1981, table 13).[2] This fueled a demand for protection, at odds with the Bappenas open-door policy. The second group was made up of intellectuals (including two famous politicians of the 1950s: Hatta and Sjafruddin) concerned with the increase in income inequality. A third group included generals, politicians, and bureaucrats who were involved in business, both in state enterprises (most notably the state oil company, Pertamina) and in private corporations. This group wanted state intervention in the allocation of licenses, credit, and government contracts in support of the large corporate conglomerates they were building. Although this group used the revival of economic nationalism to its advantage, it made extensive use of foreign capital and Chinese entrepreneurship. Finally, a group of intellectuals objected to an industrial strategy in which comparative advantage would limit Indonesia's production to labor-intensive consumer goods. This group favored protection of intermediate and capital goods production and a subordination of foreign investment to national priorities.

The first two groups formed an unlikely coalition that attacked Bappenas "for providing a policy framework which had the effect of increasing inequality and concentrating economic and political power in the hands of a coalition of foreign capitalists, Indonesian generals and their Chinese business associates" (Robison 1986, p. 146). Quite different from this reformist-nationalist critique was the bureaucratic-nationalist position of the third and fourth groups, which "envisaged a state-led corporatist society in which the economy was driven by large-scale state investment in industry with economic power vested in the hands of a domestic corporate bourgeoisie" (p. 146). In this vision the state would determine investment priorities and act as leader by setting up vertically integrated conglomerates, protected against domination by foreign capital and eventually to be privatized. As "the private domestic bourgeoisie began to accumulate capital, it would be expected to repay loans and purchase state-held equity, a process which would sort out the opportunists from the accumulators" (p. 150). Sutowo, the president of Pertamina, and two generals, Murtopo and Soejono, pushed this concept of state capitalism. Influenced by the bureaucratic-nationalists, industrial policy changed dramatically after 1973, although corporatism was to receive a severe setback in the Pertamina crisis.

The *pribumi* issue had already been debated in 1972 in the press and in Parliament. It was reported that only 10 percent of importers were indigenous, that of the textile companies investing under the domestic investment law only one in seven was indigenous, and that most bank credit went to the Chinese. The government quickly indicated that it was willing to protect the *pribumi*. President Suharto, in his 1972 Independence Day address, said:

> The policy measures being prepared are designed to enlarge the ability of the economically weak group to participate in the process of development. This does not mean that we are to wipe out or kill the economically strong group. It would be very detrimental if we neglect domestic capital, skills and economic potential only because they belong to a non-indigenous group.

Sumitro explained in an interview the need for protection: "If a person has children and one of them is ill, it is right if he is given vitamins and additional attention" (Grenville 1973, pp. 22–23).

At the end of 1973 criticisms of the dominant position of Japanese and Chinese investors widened into attacks on the misuse of foreign aid, the luxurious lifestyles of government officials, foreign influence on the technocrats, and the alleged political influence Japan obtained with its development aid. In January 1974 the visit of the Japanese prime minister, Tanaka, led to large-scale demonstrations and the burning of shops and cars.

The government was quick to react. New regulations introduced in January 1974 specified that new foreign investment should take the form of joint ventures with *pribumi* businessmen and that in all enterprises financed by foreign investment the *pribumi* should gradually be given a controlling interest. Also, banking regulations were changed in favor of the *pribumi;* for example, medium-term investment loans were restricted to *pribumi* borrowers.

In the years 1973 to 1975 restrictions were introduced on investment that went well beyond favoring the *pribumi* and eroded the liberalism of the 1967 and 1968 laws. Tax advantages for foreign investors were tightened and stricter local employment requirements were imposed, but the measures quickly went further. The direction of foreign investment became an object of government policy.

Some sectors were declared closed to foreign investment, and eventually investment bans were also applied to domestic investors. In 1976 investment priorities were announced; whereas some sectors were closed to foreign (but not to domestic) investment, others were closed to all investment. The list of investment priorities was used to direct investment toward the production of intermediate and capital goods. But the list was also used to reserve some sectors for the *pribumi.* In 1974 investments in low-quality textile manufacturing were banned on Java and were restricted to *pribumi* investors on the outer islands (Robison 1986, p. 185).

The reformist-nationalist critique received considerable press coverage and was popular with students. It emphasized the decline of the indigenous bourgeoisie, increasing inequalities of income and wealth, foreign influence through the IMF, but also corruption. It is interesting that these criticisms affected economic policy significantly, in spite of the fact that their proponents had no real basis of political power. One reason was that the press was largely owned by the proponents of this view; another was the success of demonstrating students (and others) in conveying "their interpretation of the regime as bloated, corrupt and extravagant and of foreign capital[ists] as exploitative 'economic animals'" (Robison 1986, p. 164). But in addition the proponents could make common cause with popular resentment of the Chinese and foreign investors.

The Malari riots (January 1974) showed the danger of such an alliance to the government, which saw its legitimacy undermined by charges of being as corrupt as its predecessors. The opposition of the liberal intellectuals was quickly silenced. Some of the student leaders were imprisoned, the most critical newspapers were closed down, and by 1979 the government had developed effective control over the press, the universities, and the civil service. Thus 1974 marked a turn toward authoritarianism.

The protection of the *pribumi* in the 1974 regulations may be seen as a necessary concession of the regime. It should also be seen in the context of one of the early legislative initiatives of the New Order government (1967), which guaranteed Chinese commercial and individual rights for 30 years. There was thus an element of tokenism in the restrictions now put on foreign and Chinese capitalists, because, first, (as in the 1950s) there was no real alternative available, and, second, the regime was heavily involved in the conglomerates, which used both Chinese and (as Pertamina did) foreign capital.

In 1974 the great expansion in government revenue called the liberal Bappenas strategy into question. Although economic nationalism was the main reason for the policy change, the new industrial policy was not based solely on the *pribumi*. The change was an increased role for the state and an emphasis on divorcing investment planning from market forces.

The combination of the January 1974 oil price increase and the decision to raise the government take to 85 percent of the foreign oil companies' net operating income led to a huge increase in revenue. In the 1974/75 budget (as revised in March 1974) receipts in the routine budget were estimated as Rp 1.969 trillion—3.4 times the actuals for 1972/73 and more than double the revised estimates for 1973/74. Expenditures were quickly adjusted upward (by 63 percent in the revised 1974/75 budget, compared with the earlier estimates), but the government was remarkably cautious. For the first time the balanced budget policy was abandoned and a substantial budget surplus was planned (11 percent of total receipts), which the government intended to keep with the Central Bank for the time being while it considered possible uses for the funds, such as paying off the external debt or increasing the program of stockpiling of essential commodities (particularly rice).

The boom was quickly reflected in imports (table 14.4), especially of rice, fertilizer, and capital goods. Public expenditures also were quickly adjusted to the increase in oil revenue. Government salaries had already been raised substantially; the 1974/75 budget included large additional increases, including a 200 percent increase in basic salaries. However, at the end of our period, total personnel cost as a percentage of GDP had returned to the initial level; after rising from 3.9 percent in 1972/73 to 4.5 percent in 1975/76, it fell back to 4.0 percent in 1979/80.

Although the increase in the share of routine expenditures in GDP was modest (from 8.6 percent in 1972/73 to 11.5 percent in 1979/80), development expenditures rose much more substantially (from 5.8 percent to 11.4 percent). The initial adjustment (between 1973/74 and 1974/75) included large increases for agriculture and irrigation (from Rp 41.3 billion to Rp 96.1 billion) and for education (from Rp 18.8 billion to Rp 48.6 billion). The combination of public criticism of the government's development policy and the sudden increase in oil revenue led to a large increase in social expenditure, largely for irrigation, rural water supply,

Table 14.4 Imports, 1972–74
(millions of dollars)

Item	1972	1973	1974
Rice	198	438	483
Fertilizer	66	153	834
Machinery	265	458	526
All imports	1,453	2,602	3,906

Source: Indonesia Ministry of Finance, BPS, *Statistical Pocket Book of Indonesia*, various years.

and schools (Arndt 1974, p. 16). A crash program resulted in the building of more than 5,000 schools in less than half a year.

The conservatism of the March 1974 revision of the 1974/75 budget was matched by changes in monetary policy. The memory of hyperinflation was still fresh. The sudden jump in the rate of inflation, from 2 percent in 1971 to more than 25 percent in 1972 and 1973, had already triggered restrictive monetary measures. The domestic spending of the oil money raised the possibility of a further acceleration of inflation, and policy now changed from moral suasion to direct control. Credit ceilings were imposed, reserve ratio requirements were tightened, and interest rates were raised.

The Second Five Year Plan (Repelita II) started in April 1974. It was quickly revised to take the oil revenues into account. The production capacity of the Krakatau steel project, for example, was raised from 0.5 million tons to 2 million tons per year. Many of the new projects were already being implemented when, at the end of 1974, the Pertamina crisis forced severe pruning of the plan (the Krakatau project was again reduced to 0.5 million tons). Although the commitment to a balanced budget was such an important element of the economic constitution that a loss of fiscal control as a result of the oil boom was already unlikely, the Pertamina crisis had the effect of strengthening fiscal discipline.

Pertamina

Established as the state oil company, Pertamina had diversified into an extremely wide range of economic activities, including shipping, petrochemicals, hotels, fertilizer, and steel. It was a spectacular example of the sort of conglomerate favored by the bureaucratic-nationalist group (of which its president was a prominent member). Pertamina had become a state within the state. Its independence in contracting external debt was seen as a serious problem as early as 1972. Pertamina was reported as borrowing, especially in Japan, without government approval and in breach of restrictions on short-term borrowing agreed to with the IMF. In May 1972 a law put Pertamina under the ultimate control of a committee consisting of the chairman of Bappenas and the ministers of mining and finance; henceforth all loans to public corporations such as Pertamina required Ministry of Finance approval.

The kind of activity that Pertamina engaged in is exemplified in the story of the Krakatau steel mill (Arndt 1975). In the 1950s the Soviet Union was asked to establish a steel mill at Cilegon (northwest Java) that would make use of iron ore deposits in Lampung (just across the Sunda Strait). Later, after it was discovered that there was no iron ore at Lampung, the plan was to use scrap iron, but the Soviets departed in 1966, leaving behind a considerable amount of equipment. In 1970 Krakatau Steel was formed as a joint venture by Pertamina and the government to revive the plan. In 1972 a German feasibility study was completed for a huge integrated steel complex, including a 500,000-ton-per-year steel mill (using the direct reduction method) and three processing plants: for steel sheets and bars (1 million tons), a strip mill (350,000 tons), and a wire rod mill (250,000 tons).

The necessary infrastructure for the German plan included an enormous power station (400 megawatts) to be fueled by natural gas from a Pertamina field 200 kilometers away; a large port (to receive iron ore bulk carriers); and an internal railway. In 1973 PT Krakatau decided, apparently without consulting the government, to increase the capacity of the smelter from 500,000 tons to 2 million tons. Construction started in 1974, and much of the 1974 short-term external borrowing that led to the Pertamina crisis seems to have been for payments to the German contractors. Work was evidently overinvoiced and funds misspent on extravagant houses for the firm's staff (including a $1 million house for the managing director). In addition, the direct reduction method to be used had apparently not been tested adequately, and the mill was not sited where a cheap energy supply was ensured.

To finance its highly ambitious investment program, Pertamina borrowed abroad at short maturities. When it could no longer service its debts, it withheld Rp 350 billion in taxes that it had collected on behalf of the government from the foreign oil companies (which alone wiped out the budget surplus planned for 1974/75). The government then bailed out the company, cutting its investment program severely and stripping it of the autonomy that had made it a state within a state. From then on, government revenues from the foreign oil companies were to be surrendered directly to the treasury (rather than via Pertamina), Pertamina could not borrow abroad without Bank Indonesia's consent, and government approval was required for its investments. Ibnu Sutowo was replaced in March 1976 as president of Pertamina by General Haijono, who proceeded to sack a large number of corrupt executives. Unfavorable contracts were renegotiated by the government when possible, and a substantial part ($1.5 billion) was canceled (Rice and Lim 1976, p. 6).

The Pertamina crisis had two important consequences. First, it stopped the development toward semiautonomous state enterprises. Bappenas, the Treasury, and the Central Bank reestablished control. Sutowo's free-wheeling approach (he claimed to have signed 1,400 promissory notes totaling $364 million without paying attention to their value) and the unusual and untested technologies he preferred (such as a floating fertilizer factory) were thoroughly discredited (Grenville 1977, p. 5). Second, the crisis led to fiscal strictness at a time when, because of the oil revenue, one might have expected public expenditure to go out of control. In 1975 it became clear not only that Pertamina had an outstanding debt of more than $10 billion, but also that a substantial part of this debt would have to be serviced by the government. Adding to the increases in external borrowing by other public enterprises and by the government itself, commentators estimated in 1976 "that from 1976 through 1979 public sector debt servicing obligations will be $2^1/_2$ to 4 times greater than they were estimated to be at the end of 1973" (Rice and Lim 1976, p. 7). This awareness led to cuts in the public investment program.

The share of investment going to agriculture increased rapidly between 1974 and 1978 (table 14.5), and was high compared with that in Nigeria, for example, which was only 2 percent in the same period. Much of the agricultural investment was used to develop and rehabilitate irrigation networks and to extend the area devoted to rain-fed paddy by reclaiming swampland. Industrial investment was huge, absorbing as large a share of the development budget as agriculture, at least in the early years of Repelita II.

Industrial Policy: Rising Protectionism

In the early years of the Suharto period the industrial sector grew rapidly, because of several factors: the encouragement given to both Indonesian and foreign investors by the investment laws of 1967 and 1968; the drastic removal of trade, foreign exchange, and investment controls;

Table 14.5 Shares of Selected Categories in Development Expenditure, 1974–78 (percent)

Category	1974/75	1975/76	1976/77	1977/78
Agriculture and irrigation	31.0	19.0	17.8	17.6
Excluding fertilizer subsidy	7.7	9.6	12.7	14.6
Industry and mining	7.3	8.4	9.5	6.4
Electric power	8.1	8.6	11.0	10.3
Transportation and tourism	12.9	22.9	20.0	16.5
Education	5.3	8.0	6.7	9.5

Source: World Bank 1983, annex III, table 5.5.

and the large potential for import-substitution that remained. By the early 1970s the sector was dominated by consumer goods, which accounted for 80 percent of industrial value added (table 14.6); food, beverages, tobacco, and textiles alone accounted for 77 percent in 1971. Production of items such as textiles, cigarettes, paper, and tires had increased enormously since the late 1960s (table 14.7). As the opportunities for easy import substitution projects were gradually exhausted, industrial growth slowed down, which was one of the reasons for demands for protection.

There were several other reasons (other than the economic nationalism discussed above) to ask for protection. First, the maintenance (from August 1971 to November 1978) of a fixed exchange rate (with respect to the dollar) made competing imports more attractive. In addition, there was evidence of a "hog-cycle" problem. Investments made in response to excess demand in the early 1970s were contributing to excess capacity when coming onstream in the mid-1970s. Grenville gives the example of gunnysacks, for which capacity was 65 million bags per year although demand was 35 million. Other examples were reinforcing rods (700,000 ton capacity and 400,000 in demand), and polyvinyl chloride (PVC) pipes (31,000 ton capacity and 11,000 in demand). At the end of 1976 producers of these three goods and also of textiles, wire, nails, and synthetic yarn all lobbied for protection. This was quickly granted: importing was made more difficult by prohibiting bank credit for importing and by imposing more stringent prepayment requirements for imports of specific goods, which included textiles, reinforcing rod, synthetic yarn, and gunnysacks (Grenville 1977, p. 24).

Domestic producers were favored not only by trade policy in this period but also by the decline in foreign investment. There were several reasons for this: the recession in OECD countries, the Pertamina problem, the 1974 disturbances, and the exhaustion (particularly in the case of

Table 14.6 Composition of Industrial Value Added, 1971 and 1980

	1971		1980	
Item	*Percent*	*Billions of rupiah*[a]	*Percent*	*Billions of rupiah*[a]
Consumer goods	80.8	110	47.6	1,014
Intermediate goods	13.1	18	35.5	756
Capital goods	6.1	8	16.9	360
Total	100.0	136	100.0	2,130

a. Current prices.

Source: Roepstorff 1985, table 4, based on data from the United Nations Industrial Development Organization.

Table 14.7 Industrial Production of Selected Items, 1969/70 and 1977/78

Item	Unit of measure	1969/70	1977/78
Textiles	Million meters	400	1,332
Cigarettes	Billions	30	64
Glass bottles	Thousand tons	17	60
Car tires	Thousands	366	1,883[a]
Paper	Thousand tons	17	83

a. Figure is for 1976/77.
Source: World Bank 1983, annex III, table 5.1, for 1969/70; McCawley 1981, table 3.2, for 1977/78.

textiles) of the most profitable opportunities. But the decline in foreign investment also reflected policy. Partly as a result of the Pertamina experience, conditions for foreign investors were made stricter, and at the end of 1977 the trading activities of 19 foreign companies, including IBM, had to stop because the transitional period defined in the 1968 investment law was coming to an end (Arndt 1978, p. 9).

By this time the subsidies that had loomed large in the beginning of the period had declined in the case of fertilizer because domestic production had been substituted for imports, and in the case of cereals because world prices declined after 1974. In 1977 a new subsidy appeared when the government decided to keep domestic fuel prices constant at their 1976 level. This subsidy, which in 1977/78 still amounted to only Rp 65 billion, would grow to Rp 1.316 trillion five years later.

The first oil boom in Indonesia is a case of the dog that did not bark—the potential for trouble did not materialize. First, the boom did not result in a loss of fiscal control and an enormous increase in public expenditure. Although the Pertamina crisis was a spectacular example of such a loss of control, heavier spending was well under way before the oil price increases, and by the end of 1975 it was under control. Although the government sector grew relative to the private sector, public consumption increased only modestly as a percentage of GDP: from 9.1 percent in 1972 to 10.7 percent in 1978. Second, in that same period, outstanding debt fell relative to GNP from 37 to 27 percent, and reserves rose from 2.2 months of imports to 2.5 months (Warr 1986, table 9.2). Thus, Indonesia managed to avoid the problems that plagued many other oil producers.

What the boom did not do was to raise the rate of investment appreciably. Although oil income was recognized as temporary and depletion was a concern (the possibility that oil exports would cease in 20 years was one of the considerations leading to the 1978 devaluation), investment rose little, from 18.8 percent of GDP in 1972 to 20.3 percent in 1978. The use of the windfall has been estimated by Booth (1992, table 1.3).

Taking the windfall period 1974–81, she assigns the increment in gross domestic income to private consumption (65 percent), public consumption (13 percent), and investment (24 percent), with the 3 percent discrepancy financed by extra foreign borrowing. This is in marked contrast with the use of the windfall in Nigeria, where most of it was absorbed by public investment.

Public investment was concentrated in sectors producing tradables. Within agriculture there was substantial expenditure on irrigation, and within industry on petroleum fertilizer and cement production. The sharp fall in the price of importables relative to nontradables represents the boom's Dutch disease effect. Public investment, particularly in manufacturing, partly offset the adverse effect of the relative price changes on the output of tradables. Although agriculture declined relatively (growing at less than 4 percent a year from 1972 to 1979), manufacturing grew extremely rapidly (by almost 14 percent a year in real terms). However, public investment was concentrated on a small number of large, extremely capital-intensive projects. These projects contributed little to the Repelita II objective of employment generation.

Traditional, nonoil agricultural exports continued to grow (especially coffee and palm oil), but at much too slow a rate (3.6 percent a year between 1972 and 1977) to finance the imports of a rapidly growing economy. Thus, the inward-looking, capital-intensive nature of industrialization became an important issue in the late 1970s.

The 1978 Devaluation

In 1978 foreign exchange reserves were still rising, but it was clear that the boom in oil, coffee, and timber was coming to an end. There was an active debate in the press on the merits of a devaluation to support a strategy based on labor-intensive nonoil exports. The rupiah, although fixed in terms of the dollar since August 1971, had by August 1978 depreciated 45 percent relative to import-weighted exchange rates of seven currencies, with most of the depreciation occurring after 1976 (Arndt 1978, table 1). In November 1978 the tie with the dollar was broken and a managed float against an (unspecified) basket of currencies was instituted, implying a devaluation from $1 = Rp 415 to $1 = Rp 625.

The devaluation was unexpected, unusual, and courageous. There had been public discussion of a devaluation for a year, but the decision itself came as a complete surprise. It was unusual in that the aim was structural change rather than solving a balance of payments problem (foreign exchange reserves amounted to $2.5 billion). The objective was to make the economy more export oriented and to increase employment through the stimulus given to the production of tradables. The devaluation was also courageous since it redistributed income from politically powerful groups (notably urban consumers) to politically weaker groups (notably farmers producing export crops on the outer islands).

Three aspects of the devaluation deserve to be emphasized: the reason for it, the policy measures taken in its wake, and, finally, its effect on relative prices. The motivation for the devaluation appears to have been mainly protectionist. The director of the Central Bank declared that the devaluation "was carried out with a view to improve Indonesia's international competitive position and thus to stimulate the development of export- and import-substitution industries, which had been under increasing cost pressure because of a faster rate of inflation in Indonesia in the recent years than the rate abroad" (Ismael 1980, p. 103, quoted in Warr 1986, p. 298).

Warr (p. 299) interprets this as "the policy objective of shielding Indonesia's non-oil traded goods producing sectors from the general equilibrium effects of the oil boom." The plausibility of exchange rate protection to prevent Dutch disease effects depends on whether the oil boom is seen as a price or volume increase. In the former case, if the government foresaw that the oil price would be high only temporarily (for a period that was short compared with the period in which the relative price effects of a devaluation could be expected to wear off), exchange rate protection could be a sensible way of avoiding a costly contraction of the nonoil traded goods sector, which would have to be reversed later. However, in this case the decision should have been made when the price increases occurred, at the end of 1973, rather than five years later when most of the damage would already have been done. Indonesian commentators, however, seem to have been concerned about a volume effect. Extrapolations of recent trends in production and domestic consumption suggested that oil exports might disappear within 20 years. "It was contended that, if oil exports were to run out so quickly, it was both economically wasteful and politically dangerous to allow the nonoil traded goods sector to contract in the short run only to be required to expand again a decade or two later (Warr 1986, p. 299).

In this case, too, it is not clear why the decision came so late or why the devaluation was small relative to the change in relative prices that had occurred since 1973. Just before the devaluation, Warr's tradable/ nontradable relative price index (column 4 in table 14.8), had reached a level of 70 (1974 = 100). It then rose to 87 and fell back to 82 in a few months. At that point only one-quarter of the fall in the relative price of tradables had been offset.[3] Thus, if this was indeed the motivation, it seems a matter of too little, too late.

The devaluation also had its bizarre side. When prices rose and there was evidence of hoarding and capital flight, the government ordered prices to be returned to predevaluation levels for a transitional period. This period ended after six weeks, but then it was announced that for some essential commodities (in January 1979 more than 200 were so classified), price increases would be limited. Price control was imposed at the wholesale level. As a result, retailers made large profits. This in turn led to tensions between the government, which accused traders of antisocial practices, and the business community. The government apparently failed to realize that the devaluation could not have its intended effects if prices were frozen.

Trade policy was also adjusted in a counterproductive way. Tariffs on imported inputs were cut by 50 percent (apparently to offset the devaluation's effect on their cost in domestic currency), whereas tariffs on final goods were kept unchanged. Thus there was a substantial increase in effective protection for import-competing industries. Also, a range of exportables (including agricultural commodities but also cement, fertilizer, paper, and car tires) were subjected to export quotas. Thus the desire to protect domestic consumers frequently interfered with the intention to stimulate exports.

One reason for this convoluted trade policy was that vestiges of the guided economy mentality remained. Admiral Sudomo's attempts to contain price increases by administrative measures, by inspection of the market place, and by not-so-gentle persuasion of Unilever (which was selected as a convenient scapegoat) revealed the government's suspicion of the working of the market. But the strange sequel to the devaluation can also be seen as a buying of political support through compensation for the groups who stood to lose from a devaluation. Under that interpretation there was less scope for large relative price changes than the magnitude of the devaluation itself suggested, and regulations had to become more restrictive (Dick 1979, p. 43).

Table 14.8 Price Indices for Tradables (T) and Nontradables (N), 1972–79
(1974 = 100)

Year	T (1)	N1 (2)	N2 (3)	T/N2 (4)
1972	60	73	53	113
1973	76	83	64	118
1974	100	100	100	100
1975	109	125	121	90
1976	117	157	139	85
1977	122	184	163	75
1978	130	199	181	72
1979	188	255	229	82

Note: T, wholesale price of imported commodities. N1, Jarkarta consumer price index (CPI)(housing). N2, Warr's index for nontradables based on unpublished BPS data for eight CPI components, Jakarta only. Original series lost; column 3 is derived from the ratio of columns 1 and 4. Column 4, Warr's tradable/nontradable relative price index, from figure 9.1 in Warr 1986.

15 *The Second Oil Cycle: 1979–88*

By the late 1970s the New Order regime had been in power for sufficiently long that the nature of politics was changing from survival to specific policies. Elite politics became an exercise in pressure by groups and leaders who increasingly took the regime for granted. At the onset of the second oil cycle, four distinct factions, each with its own priorities, cohabited within the bureaucracy. None had dominance, and key decisions were made by the president, who explicitly aimed to preserve a broad balance of interests.

One group, including engineers, believed in national economic self-sufficiency and high-technology enterprises, such as the aircraft industry. Habibie, the minister for research and technology, was the leading force in this camp. The president enthusiastically supported glamorous schemes, and the State Secretariat, which controlled procurement, was committed to a preference for domestic goods. A second group, the technocrats, was concerned with employment and macroeconomic consistency. Widjojo and the rest of the Berkeley mafia who made up this group were supported by the World Bank. Their influence was to wane with the boom, only to increase with the onset of the oil slump. A third group favored indigenous entrepreneurs and villages as opposed to foreign and Chinese investors and urban areas. A fourth group was that component of the bureaucratic and military elite who had commercial transactions with foreign or Chinese investors, exchanging political favors and an ability to work the system for a share of the assets.

Although by the end of the 1970s a substantial domestic capitalist class had arisen, it had not established political authority over the state apparatus (Robison 1986, p. 373). Regionalism, perhaps the most potent cleavage of the 1950s, by now found no expression in elite interest groups. Favorite-son appointments had been completely overcome: by 1979 none of the outer island territorial commands within the army was headed by a native—virtually all were Javanese. The state political party, Golkar, was an effective mass organization, and active and retired military officers were ubiquitous, ensuring that the state was well represented at the local level. The state's control of the media and primary school education facilitated the imposition of the Pancasila state ideology on all youth groups and political parties. Ultimate power resided with the senior officers of the Java-based divisions of the army and the general staff.

We turn now to consider four phases in the second oil cycle—the boom of 1979–81, the slump of 1981–83, the 1983 crisis and its short-term consequences, and the postcrisis reforms of 1984–88.

The Boom Phase: 1979–81

As with the first oil cycle, the increase in the oil price occurred in this cycle just after the launch of a five-year plan. These plans were not so much detailed agendas for action as expressions of the balance of aspirations among the different groups. The third plan aimed to achieve a more even distribution of benefits and set a target growth rate of 6.5 percent a year. Because the implicit incremental capital-output ratio (ICOR), at 3.6, was somewhat higher than the 2.8 ratio of the first oil cycle, the rehabilitation phase of the economy was perceived as clearly over. The plan envisaged a temporary boom in government development expenditure without a significant alteration in government savings rates (table 15.1). The composition of the development budget was shifted away from agriculture and government capital participation in business toward defense and transmigration—the mass relocation of the agricultural population.

Table 15.1 Planned Savings and Development Expenditures before the Second Boom, 1978–84
(percentage of GDP)

	Savings	Development budget
Realized		
1978/79	6.9	10.6
Planned under the third development plan		
1979/80	7.4	13.0
1980/81	7.3	12.7
1981/82	7.2	12.4
1982/83	6.9	12.0
1983/84	6.9	11.8

Source: Booth and Tyabji 1979, p. 32.

The basic assumptions of this third five-year plan were immediately invalidated by the 1979 increase in the world price of oil: the second boom increased government revenue and foreign exchange by as much as the first boom. Between 1978/79 and 1981/82, oil and gas taxes as a proportion of government revenue increased from 53 to 70 percent. Foreign exchange from oil and gas rose from $7.4 billion to $19 billion, increasing as a proportion of total foreign exchange earnings from 65 to 82 percent.

In addition to the balance of power of interest groups, the policy initiatives of the first oil slump became an important influence on the reaction to this second boom. Immediately prior to the boom the government had devalued to improve the competitiveness of nonoil exports, and it had increased tariff protection (Dick 1979). As a result, the government was concerned about the inflationary pressures generated by the devaluation, and these fears possibly made it more cautious in its reaction to the second oil windfall. The government disliked inflation not just because of its unpopularity among those on fixed incomes but because it served as a rallying point for other complaints against the government, notably of corruption, inequity, and foreign borrowing (Garnaut 1979). Furthermore, the 1978 devaluation had been combined with export taxes. These plus the resulting inflation caused the real incomes of many groups to fall in 1979, despite the terms of trade gain.

Unlike at the start of the first cycle, the government was slow to formulate a response to the extra resources. Spending and especially borrowing levels were held down, and reserves were accumulated. Current account surpluses of $2.2 billion and $2.1 billion were generated in 1979/80 and 1980/81. Between April 1978 and April 1980 outstanding public sector foreign debt increased from $9.5 billion to $14.9 billion, whereas reserves plus assets in the banking system grew by $12.7 billion, resulting in net reserve accumulation. In 1980 the Central Bank bought an additional $1 billion of gold, one of the largest gold purchases ever made by a central bank. With debt service payments on foreign borrowings of $2.1 billion and world interest rates of 15 to 20 percent, Indonesia was about to become a net receiver of investment income. There was also a projected payments surplus for 1981/82 of $2.7 billion. Nevertheless, the main activity of the government was to arrange off–balance sheet foreign borrowing for large projects—a continuing response to worries about the public debt service ratio.

The 1979/80 budget did not react to the oil price increase, and pressures to revise it during the year were to some extent contained: expenditure outturns were 16 percent above plans. In real terms government expenditure increased by around 25 percent yearly. Even this degree of slippage did not persist. The 1980/81 budget outturn showed that actual revenue exceeded planned by 13 percent, whereas expenditure was under budget on all items except subsidies. There was also a large hidden surplus: the government counted as expenditure money that was transferred to the bank accounts of the regions, even though the regions considerably underspent and the central government reclaimed funds after three years. Most provincial governments had unused funds amounting to 12 to 18 months of current-year grants. The contrast with Nigeria is clearly enormous.

Expenditure decisions pointed in different directions: the Bulog intervention price for rice was raised after the harvest to reduce the rice subsidy to consumers, whereas the 1980/81 budget increased the wages of government employees by 50 percent.

During 1980, protest increased significantly. There was a marked upturn in labor unrest, perhaps because although civil service salaries increased, the official minimum wage rose much less than prices during both 1979 and 1980. However, the minimum wage was not enforced, and a more significant officially determined wage rate, the floor wage paid by the government for rural public works, rose rapidly: on Java it was Rp 350 per day in 1979/80 and Rp 525 in 1980/81 and 1981/82.

Another source of discontent was emerging evidence that the government had paid commissions of 5 and 7 percent, respectively, on arms deals with Israel and the Federal Republic of Germany. A group within the elite, including retired generals, released a Petition of Fifty that criticized the government. This opposition was channeled through a constitutional forum, however—an indication of how secure the regime was. Suharto's response was to cut these retired generals off from state credit and contracts—perhaps a reminder to the generals currently in business.

Anti-Chinese riots were also widespread. The antipathy of the *pribumi* toward the Chinese business community was not only an indirect protest against an Indonesian elite that was heavily embroiled financially with the Chinese, but also a constraint on the evolution of economic policy.

The oil windfall started to be spent in the 1980 budget chiefly through subsidies and contracts. Commodity subsidies rose fivefold from 1978/79 to 1981/82 and were directed primarily at fuel oil, rice, and fertilizer. The fuel oil and rice subsidies, however, were driven by exceptional short-term increases in world prices that were not matched by domestic prices. Thus, temporarily, both rice and oil prices were subsidized at well below these exceptional world prices. Domestic fuel prices gradually edged up toward world prices, with domestic oil prices raised in both 1979 and 1980 by 50–70 percent. Even this was not enough to compensate for the increase in the world price, so the fuel subsidy increased.

The major argument for a fuel subsidy was the spurious one that kerosene was consumed disproportionately by the poor. In reality, the income elasticity of kerosene was around unity (from household survey data), and overall fuel oil was consumed disproportionately by the rich. By 1980 the true fuel subsidy was running at $2.9 billion (Rp 1.8 trillion)—some 15 times the fertilizer subsidy. Most of this was not shown in the budget, which did not include the foregone revenue from oil paid in kind by the oil companies. In 1979/80 net foreign exchange earnings from oil and gas were $7 billion. Thus the fuel subsidy alone was equivalent to 40 percent of the oil windfall. Not only was the fuel subsidy distributionally regressive, it also affected industrialization. Fertilizer, steel, and cement plants were all gaining access to gas at an oil equivalent of between $2 and $7.6 per barrel when the world price was $37.

The third subsidy, that on fertilizer, was substantially responsible for a remarkable growth in rice production. The government set a goal of rice self-sufficiency by 1985, which informed commentators at the time, such as L. A. Mears, considered highly unlikely to be met. Between 1979 and 1981 the rice harvest increased by 22 percent. The 1980 rice harvest not only was a record but also suggested an acceleration in the trend growth of production. A major stimulus to this growth was the rapid increase in the use of fertilizer. Fertilizer application in food production, which had grown at 11.6 percent a year in 1969–76, grew at 24.4 percent in 1977–81. This accounted for around half of the increase in the 1980 crop. The increased use of fertilizer, in turn, was stimulated by government subsidies of fertilizer. Policymakers always set the fertilizer price relative to the rice price: for a long period parity had been the norm. However, starting in 1976 the government systematically lowered the price of fertilizer from 1.17 times that of rice to 0.93 in 1978, 0.67 in 1980, 0.58 in 1981, and 0.52 in 1982 (Warr 1980, p. 13; Daroesman 1981, p. 20; Dick 1982, p. 31). The rate of fertilizer subsidy by 1980/81 was 58 percent of the production cost of domestic fertilizer and 80 percent of the cost of imported fertilizer. The fertilizer subsidy was costing around 10 percent of the wholesale cost of rice, a total cost of $191 million (Rp 119 billion).

The success of fertilizer take-up was also related to the introduction of the rice variety IR36, which, because it was short stemmed, could absorb much more fertilizer without lodging ill effects. By 1980, 85 percent of Javanese rice was IR36. Adoption was stimulated by attacks of wereng on other varieties in 1977; IR36 was relatively immune. The shorter, 90-day growing season of IR36 permitted triple cropping in many areas, which became an important development in 1980. Additional stimuli to rice production were the public programs of extension, Bimas and Inmas, and irrigation. The New Order promoted irrigation, but mainly small schemes and rehabilitation efforts. The first plan (1969–74) concentrated on rehabilitation of Dutch canal systems. The main focus of the second plan (1974–78) became expansion of existing systems and creation of new ones—mainly small-scale systems of under 2,000 hectares—off Java. The third plan further de-emphasized major water storage projects and concentrated on tertiary and quaternary canals within existing systems. As a result there was a significant improvement in efficiency.

As government expenditure on contracts increased, considerable attention was paid to the process of contract allocation. Initiatives were taken to alter the agencies awarding contracts, the companies eligible for them, and the magnitude of the rents involved. Responsibility for awarding contracts was shifted substantially away from central ministries to local government. Decentralization of the development budget was considered one of the government's most important tools in a new emphasis on equity. Decentralization was an extension of the Inpres program begun in 1970, whereby funds were allocated to local governments instead of through the central ministries. Inpres allocations took into account population and poor infrastructure through proportionately larger grants outside Java. Decentralization of expenditure was pursued so vigorously that already during 1980 there was concern that provincial governments were reaching the saturation point in numbers of projects.

The eligibility of firms for contracts and the rents involved were addressed by Presidential Decree 14A of 1980, which reemphasized preferential treatment of *pribumi* firms. All contractors using government funds were required to use domestic goods as far as possible. Contracts under Rp 20 million were reserved for the "weak economic group," which was defined as firms in which *pribumi* own at least 50 percent of the capital and comprise more than half the directors. Contracts of Rp 20 million to Rp 50 million were reserved for local firms; the weak economic group was to be given preference when its tenders were up to 10 percent higher than those of others. The local chamber of commerce would grant contractor status to firms. No special facilities were provided for determining whether weak economic group requirements were met, and there was grumbling that the old boy network was the main selection process. A further presidential decree extended the ban on foreign companies on all construction contracts valued at less than Rp 200 million. Since around half of the development budget was spent on construction projects, this was a major extension; however, it was a natural continuation of previous exclusions—the indigenous population was to be given preference.

Offsetting the concern about the allocation of rents on contracts was a concern about the control and limitation of rents. In 1980 a high-level team cutting across ministries reviewed all contracts of more than Rp 500 million to check on value for money. Despite this scrutiny, the World Bank estimated in 1981 that 25 to 33 percent of government expenditure on development projects was lost to contract inefficiencies.

Expenditure of oil revenue accelerated during 1981. The 1981/82 budget planned for a 32 percent increase in expenditure in nominal terms (14 percent in real terms). The fuel and food subsidies were the fastest-growing part of the budget; both were planned to rise by 82 percent. Of the two, fuel was dominant, with an estimated increase from 7.8 to 10.9 percent of the budget. The fertilizer subsidy was also increased by 48 percent. The fuel and food subsidies grew so rapidly only because of the unusual behavior of the world prices of oil and rice.

The expansion of the development budget was dramatic. At its peak in the early 1980s, about 23 percent of GDP and 55 percent of domestic demand were being generated by government development expenditure. As public expenditure caught up with revenue and the latter started to falter, the reserves passed their peak. Between April 1981 and April 1982 debt rose by $2.1 billion and reserves fell by $1 billion. However, at the onset of the oil slump the ratio of debt service to net exports (in other words, net of oil companies' take) was only 13.2 percent. Nor was expenditure out of control. For example, the government was able to assign a much higher priority to the expansion of the equity-focused Inpres projects, on which expenditure was budgeted to increase by 40 percent, than to the civil service salary bill, which was allocated an extra 17 percent.

The expansion of the development budget enabled the government to promote industrialization, which all interest groups wanted. One strand of policy was to move "upstream" to the processing of primary products, and to do this by decree. In 1980, log exports were limited to 32 percent of total output, and in 1981 they were banned unless companies had investments in processing. As a result, plywood manufacturing investment increased substantially under joint ventures with the Japanese, although U.S. and European firms dropped out. Foreign companies were similarly restricted in the milk industry as of 1981, with the result that the largest company withdrew from the market. A second strand of policy was indigenization. Under the 10-Year Indonesianization Rule, during the subsequent decade all existing joint ventures had to become majority Indonesian owned.

There were limits, however, on manufacturing fetishism. Major emphasis was given to export crops, especially rubber, palm oil, and timber. The smallholder rubber industry was the object of ambitious development plans: an investment of Rp 44.5 billion of replanting and rehabilitation aimed at raising output by 1990 from 1 million tons to 1.9 million tons and increasing world market share from 25 to 33 percent. Much of the concern for nonoil exports dated back to the first oil slump. At the same time policies were maintained even if they were liable to be unpopular. For example, in 1978 the government had decided on a policy of switching palm oil from export to home use, thereby releasing the higher-priced coconut oil for export. By 1980 when the policy was due to be implemented, the need for foreign exchange was greatly reduced; nevertheless the policy was implemented.

Manufacturing growth between 1979 and 1981 was strongly influenced by industrial policies. At domestic prices manufacturing accounted for a quarter of incremental GDP during the two years. Mostly, it was on a large scale, much of it was public, and it all received subsidized capital and energy; thus it was likely to be inappropriate. The World Bank pointed out these criticisms in a 1981 industrial survey. This triggered a debate on the direction of policy, which provided further evidence that the economic decisions of Indonesian policymakers were constrained by adherence to the de facto economic constitution, which has existed since the late 1960s. Many government officials felt that the Bank's emphasis on the role of private entrepreneurs was counter to section 33 of the 1945 constitution, which was commonly interpreted to mean that private enterprise may operate only in those areas not connected with the basic needs of the people. The attitude toward enterprise was, however, ambivalent, for there was a desire to develop entrepreneurship: since 1976 this had been a requirement of school curricula.

Despite the emphasis on industry, growth during the second oil boom was spread widely across sectors. As we have seen, the most remarkable success was the growth of food production, and much of this was attributable to policy. There were also indications that, especially as a result of decentralized expenditure, the consequences for income distribution were favorable. By early 1982 seasonal labor shortages were emerging in rural Java. The household surveys reported in chapter 16 show that the income share of the poorest 40 percent of the population rose between 1978 and 1981 from 18.1 to 20.5 percent. In the elections of May 1982 opposition campaigning was concentrated on such noneconomic issues as Muslim solidarity and Sukarno's memory. The economic criticisms were only that Golkar was the bosses' party and that reliance on foreign loans threatened sovereignty. Thus the key management policies of the windfall were not really challenged.

The Oil Slump: 1981–83

Average oil production in 1981 was 1.60 million barrels per day. By mid-1982 production was down to 1.25 million. This downturn marked the beginning of the oil slump, which was to become far more accentuated. The oil slump posed three policy problems. First was a loss of foreign exchange that, with the existing exchange rate and trade regime, would lead to a rapid reserve loss. Second was a loss of government revenue that, at existing levels of expenditure, would lead to a budget deficit. Third, the security of the government appeared to be pinned to its continuing delivery of growth, and this could no longer be realized by investment of oil revenues.

Thus, with the onset of the oil slump, pressure for change surfaced. The economic constitution, guaranteeing a balanced budget and convertibility, meant that if the constitution was adhered to, the scope for policy response was limited: either nonoil revenue would have to be increased dramatically or expenditure would have to be curtailed, and either the exchange rate would have to be depreciated or trade restrictions imposed. Robison (1986, pp. 375, 391) identifies three pressures for change. The first was the pressure to open the economy to international investment in the pursuit of allocative efficiency. This involved inflicting losses upon domestic capitalists who had benefited most from protection. A second source of pressure arose because the decline in the state's capacity to finance contracts diminished the role of the state in capital formation and its ability to favor indigenous entrepreneurs. Restraints on the Chinese were therefore likely to slacken. Third, the greater need for a nonoil revenue base encouraged a regularization of the state apparatus, making the tax and customs services less discretionary and thereby reducing the autonomy of the politico-bureaucrats. The obstacle to such regularization was that the absence of class-based political power permitted the officials of the state, in particular the military, to appropriate the apparatus of the state. The business elite was dominated by the Chinese and foreign companies, neither of whom could wield overt public power.

The first warning that oil prices were about to begin falling came through the head of the IMF mission in July 1981. By September the government was preparing a policy response to a prospective decline in revenue. The maintenance of growth had always been viewed by the New Order regime as something to be achieved by focusing on supply at the sectoral level rather than demand at the aggregate level. But different parts of the bureaucracy promoted expansion of different sectors. At the onset of the oil slump, nonoil export industries came back into favor. The devaluation in 1978 had to some extent been a response to this objective, and by 1981 the real exchange rate improvement that devaluation afforded had been eroded. However, in 1982 the government entered a brief phase of dirigisme. The move into export industries was intended to be achieved through the planning of linkages, a good example being the timber industry (see above). Initially, a major devaluation was considered (Dick 1982, p. 1). Instead, it was decided that there was no immediate need; nonoil exports were to be stimulated through the New Trade Policy, of which counterpurchase was the most controversial component. In return for government contracts, foreign tenderers were required to provide extra nonoil exports equivalent in value to the import content of the contract. The scheme was hastily announced soon after the minister of trade's visit to Eastern Europe and before the department had been able to work it out. Other elements of the New Trade Policy were concessionary interest rates to exporters and free disposal of their foreign exchange for exporters.

The countertrading element of the new policy, vigorously criticized within Indonesia as a reversion to the economics of Sukarno, was nonetheless accepted. One interpretation (Scherer 1982, p. 14) is that by introducing long and complex negotiations, bureaucrats opposed to the new industrial projects were able to kill them despite their political popularity. There was certainly scope for such a Machiavellian role. Policy statements continued to reflect a structuralist approach to industrial development: public investment was to be channeled into "key," "basic," and "upstream" activities with little if any concern for efficiency or border prices. Establishment of nearly all new industries as state enterprises was taken for granted.

In many respects such instincts were more pronounced during the onset of the slump. In August 1982 the president signaled a shift toward basic or key industries: steel, aluminum, cement, fertilizer, artificial fibers, rubber, and chemicals. The Ministry of Industry stated that an important by-product would be that many of the natural resource-based heavy industries would be on the outer islands. Fifty-two key industry projects were in preparation as of August 1982 at a combined cost of $12 billion. The ministry was also pressing hard during 1982 for greater resort to quantitative restrictions, including absolute prohibitions on a wide range of items. This was adopted in the 1983 budget, which tightened import restrictions on a range of "nonessential" items. Not only the Ministry of Industry but also Bappenas echoed the heavy industry line without reference to efficiency. According to the 1981 Long Range Industrial Development Plan, "due to the large capital and the high risks involved [and] taking into account the significance of these basic/key industries," the private sector was unlikely to be interested in investing in them, so they were to be state owned.

> The anti-market philosophy which is widely held within the Indonesian bureaucracy has had a pervasive effect upon policy. There is a tendency for bureaucracy to intervene at sectoral levels with the aim of fine tuning both prices and the quantities of inputs and outputs. Schedules of state controlled prices and taxes are often extraordinarily complicated, and licensing requirements in many sectors are time consuming. . . . One cannot ignore the influence that is inevitably being exerted on industrial development policy by the military/bureaucratic network whose economic fortunes are being advanced by the establishment and operation of large state enterprises (Gray 1982, p. 49).

The direction industrial and trade policy took in lieu of devaluation suggests that the dirigistes had increased their influence relative to the liberal economists since the first oil downturn. This is a credible hypothesis. The first oil downturn occurred shortly after the Pertamina crisis, which shocked the president out of support for dirigisme. As this event receded and oil revenues increased, the underlying sympathy with public ownership (as enshrined in the 1945 constitution) and with glamorous import-substituting industry regained influence. The oil downturn was not yet seen as a potential crisis. The public statements of the president and others insisted on maintaining "momentum" and rejected any cancellation or stretching of project expenditures. "As of October 1982 one sensed that the President had not yet been fully apprised of the magnitude of the burgeoning resource constraint, nor had the struggle for constant slices of a reduced cake yet been joined in earnest" (Gray 1982, p. 51).

There were countervailing pressures to deregulate as a means to encourage growth. Whereas one part of the bureaucracy was busily generating the incremental controls discussed above, another was dismantling other controls and attempting to regularize procedures. In late 1981 the government replaced the directors-general of both customs and taxation in an effort to improve the honesty of collection and generate more revenue. In January 1982 export procedures were changed significantly, simplifying customs. There was also much discussion of the establishment of trading houses to overcome the fragmentation of the nonoil export sector. The Ministry of Industry was an advocate of trading houses to promote manufactured exports. However, this potential initiative ran afoul of the dilemma of ownership. Only the state and the Chinese had the capital to do this. The experience in the 1960s with state trading houses was most unhappy and the Pertamina crisis confirmed this. Yet the extension of Chinese ownership was unpalatable and dangerous in view of the open hostility of the mass of the *pribumi* population.

Although the initial attempt to maintain the growth of favored sectors by supply-side interventions was somewhat confused and, on balance, dirigiste, there was a swift response to the impending budgetary problem. By mid-1982 the budget was heading for its first serious deficit because of a downturn in oil revenue and lower nonoil receipts than expected. The projected deficit was around 20 percent of expenditure. The immediate budget problem was solved by raising domestic fuel prices by 60 percent and measures to raise nonoil revenue. By early 1983 the domestic price of fuel had been raised to 97 percent of the world price. The extra funds were spent on the development budget, notably a two-thirds increase in the allocation to education. This was all done four months before an election, despite unpopularity and despite a previous presidential commitment not to raise fuel prices during 1982. Similarly, the growth of only 3 percent in civil service outlays was a courageous decision in view of the power of this pressure group. Another segment of the elite—property owners—began to be affected by nonoil taxation when the property tax was doubled to 1 percent of the value of property in excess of Rp 15 million.

The 1983 budget planned for little or no growth in expenditure in real terms, the basic plan being a switch from fuel and food subsidies to development spending instead. The food interventions—fertilizer subsidy, producer support price, and consumer ceiling price—were becoming very expensive because of the growth of output. The consumer price could be raised rapidly only at the cost of inflation, and the government could not renege on its producer support price. Nevertheless, the government gave top priority within the set of food interventions to the fertilizer subsidy, which we have seen was highly successful in raising output. In a budget in which other subsidies were pruned, the fertilizer subsidy was budgeted to rise by 50 percent to Rp 461 billion. However, even this exception began to be unwound later in the year. The fertilizer price, which had stayed constant in nominal terms from 1976 to 1982, was raised by 30 percent in November. Oil revenue continued to decline.

In the January 1983 budget the president told the nation to "pull in the belt." For the first time since the 1960s the public sector was required to produce strict economies. Faced with a downturn in forecast revenue from 22 to 18 percent of GDP, the budget proposed to reduce expenditure as a percentage of GDP from 25 to 22 percent. There was a provision of only a 4 percent nominal increase for the civil service salary bill (McCawley 1983, p. 16). The construction of new buildings for government departments was halted, many official cars were sold, and the departure tax for Indonesian nationals was hiked significantly, to $215 per trip.

Another problem posed by the oil slump was the balance of payments. The easiest option was to avoid adjustment by using the reserves and by borrowing abroad. There was modest borrowing from the IMF commodity buffer stocks scheme and a $1 billion loan from Morgan Guaranty. However, by mid-1982 a current account deficit of $7 billion was being forecast—$4.6 billion above 1981/82 and $2.4 billion above the budget estimate. In the second and third quarters of 1982 the Central Bank lost nearly 30 percent of its reserves. Some action became essential. During 1982 total foreign exchange reserves were depleted by $2 billion, from $10 billion to $8 billion (including those held by commercial banks). By 1983 the ratio of public debt service to net exports had risen to 25 percent. There was additionally some $4 billion of private debt (Arndt 1983b, p. 17).

Rumors of another sharp devaluation were rife during the 1982 election campaign. In August the president's Independence Day address ruled out a discrete devaluation in favor of a crawling peg. However, this proved inadequate: during the course of 1982 the real exchange rate rose above its pre-1978 devaluation level as the slow crawl down against the dollar was more than offset by the dollar's rise and by faster inflation.

The 1983 Crisis

The government's handling of the early phase of the oil slump was thus a combination of conservatism at the level of aggregate demand, procrastination on the exchange rate, and dirigiste sectoral supply interventions. Although the gradual extension of nontariff barriers began to push up costs, the policy stance could have been maintained but for unfavorable exogenous shocks early in 1983, which led to a crisis. Bad weather hit the rice harvest, and then the oil price slipped from $37 to $30. Although there was a change of key policymakers, Professor Widjojo being replaced by Professor Wardhana as coordinating minister for economic affairs, Widjojo retained considerable power, and the change did not constitute an alteration in the policy advice given by the ministry.

The combination of exogenous shocks created an atmosphere of crisis for the first time in many years. This appears to have strengthened the hand of the liberal economists, who were well prepared by informed analysis and contingency planning. For example, during 1982 the *Bulletin of Indonesian Economic Studies* had published an analysis of the budgetary implications of a $20 oil price for the mid-1980s, calculating that a 29 percent devaluation was required to eliminate the projected budget deficit (Gray 1982, p. 31). The government reacted swiftly to the crisis. It devalued by 27.6 percent at the end of March, motivated by the pressure of a speculative capital outflow of crisis proportions. This indicated a discipline imposed by the economic constitution: convertibility ensured that the exchange rate could not be preserved at a level incompatible with other policies.

A second reaction was to shelve 47 major capital projects worth $14 billion. In October routine expenditures by the armed forces were cut by 50 percent and other categories of military expenditure by 10 to 30 percent. The government also made an important start on deregulation. In June a major banking reform removed interest rate controls and required the state banks to become competitive. The objective was to mobilize private savings now that public savings were being reduced. This reform provoked a debate on how and whether subsidized credit—provided chiefly through the Bimas, KIK, and KUD credit schemes—should be continued. The decision was to continue these schemes despite deteriorating repayment rates, given widespread agreement that the "truly" economically weak must still be supported with subsidized credit.

In another step the government announced a start to tax reform: there was to be a movement away from negotiation to enforcement, as well as a higher overall level of taxation. Finally, there was some movement on the policy of state ownership. Privatization of and private participation in state agricultural projects and cement were initiated. Since the only domestic entrepreneurs with the financial scale and corporate structures to deal with the state at this scale of participation were the Chinese, the government tried to increase the commitment of the Chinese to keeping capital in the country. For example, in 1984 General Murdani appealed for an end to the categories of *pribumi* and non-*pribumi*—an idea endorsed by the chamber of commerce. The official language of ethnic intervention was changed: the term *weak group* was redefined to include small-scale Chinese entrepreneurs with Indonesian citizenship.

This rapid sequence of policy initiatives suggested that in a time of economic crisis the president turned to the economic technocrats, who thereby regained influence. The virtue of the so-called economic constitution was that in the spheres of fiscal and exchange rate policy the balanced budget and convertibility rules compelled rapid responses to an exogenous downturn: the consequences of the oil slump could not be disguised by printing money and rationing foreign exchange. By creating a crisis the constitution shifted the balance of power to those trusted in crisis management: "In some respects the atmosphere with respect to economic policy is reminiscent of that of the late 1960s when the need for major policy change was so obvious to all concerned that such a radical change as exchange rate unification could be accomplished without major objection from either the business community or within the government" (Glassburner and Poffenberger 1983, p. 14). These changes aroused surprisingly little opposition:

> One reason is that the news about Mexico and Nigeria is known and serves as a warning of what can happen, if indeed any were needed after the 1960s. Another is there is real respect within the elite towards the technocrats, most especially when a crisis threatens. A third reason is rather clever tying of unpopular with popular steps—a fuel price increase was announced with the earmarking of the unused portion of the subsidy for politically popular education programs. A fourth is the government controls a few major prices such as rice, cooking oil, and sugar with great care. The basic cost of living does not fluctuate wildly. Finally, most people are much better off than a decade ago (Dapice 1983, p. 15).

The growth rate in 1983 plummeted to 2 percent, and employment became a serious concern. Again this was couched in constitutional terms: the minister for manpower pointed out that full employment was required by article 27 of the 1945 constitution. In May he announced that importing firms wishing to dismiss workers must wait six months. The concern about employment led the government to reallocate the domestic currency component of expenditure on four large projects canceled in the 1983 budget to other projects with higher labor intensity.

Whereas Indonesians resisted devaluation for only a year, until capital flight became overwhelming, and similarly conceded to the rephasing of government projects relatively quickly, no overwhelming conditions forced bureaucratic and trade policy reforms. Trade policy therefore evolved more slowly and piecemeal: "negative lists" grew progressively longer, decided by the Investment Coordinating Board (BKPM). The minister for industry, Habibie, pushed high-technology import substitution such as aircraft, whereas the junior minister for domestic production pushed an infant industry line. Local sourcing rules continued to proliferate; for example, commercial vehicles were required to have full local content between 1983 and 1986. The local production of engines was estimated to raise their costs by more than 30 percent. Following the Krakatau steel plant, a cold rolling mill jointly owned by the government and a Chinese group was scheduled for production in 1989. In the meantime the group was given an import monopoly on rolled steel and in early 1984 was selling it at $550 per ton against a world price of $380.

However, nonindustrial sectors continued to have their advocates and to be promoted in language inconceivable in Nigeria. For example, in the drive to expand nonoil exports, the minister of agriculture described oil palm as the "prima donna," and massive production increases were planned. Yet export-crop policy was subject to numerous conflicts. First, palm oil exports were restricted in an attempt to hold down the domestic price of cooking oil, one of the nine basic commodities.

Second, oil palm was an estate crop, yet policy in the estate crop sector was still handicapped by the colonial stigma attached to large private landholdings: new estate owners were required to sell 80 percent of their plantings to smallholders as the trees reached maturity, and they were awarded leases for only 35 years (versus 99 years in Malaysia). Private investors were reluctant to invest under these rules. By 1983, 86 percent of land under cash crops was cultivated by smallholders, 8 percent by government-owned estates, and 6 percent by private estates. The estates had value added per hectare nearly five times that of smallholders, up from 2.7 times the value added of smallholdings in 1979. There had been rapid technical progress on the oil palm estates, but virtually none on smallholdings for many years. The main reason for this dualism was the substantial development assistance accorded to estates by the government. The government estates on Sumatra (rubber and oil palm) had yields comparable to those in Malaysia. Not until the third development plan had attention been directed to smallholder cash crops, which became a major focus of the fourth plan launched in late 1983. The chosen interventions were the nucleus estate scheme for resettlement and a mass program, UPP, which was like Bimas for cash crops: credit plus extension.

A third weakness of export-crop policy was that it was influenced by the same structuralist planning objectives as industrialization. In the urge to create upstream sectors and a fully integrated economy regardless of efficiency, the government embarked on the creation of a cotton belt to supply the cotton industry. However, since cotton is pest susceptible and prefers a dry climate, Indonesia probably was an inappropriate producer.

During the first two phases of the oil slump, from mid-1981 to end-1983, the totality of government actions were rather successful. Financial confidence was restored by the response to the March 1983 crisis. Between mid-1983 and mid-1984 reserves grew strongly partly because of a reversal of capital flight. International banks oversubscribed to a syndicated loan of $750 million. Donors were also supportive: during 1983/84 there was such a marked increase in government receipts of aid and borrowing that total receipts were roughly the same percentage of GDP as at the height of the second oil boom. This accounted for the switch toward development expenditure in the 1983 budget.

The policy response yielded other effects besides international financial support. Recall that during the second oil boom (1979–81) manufacturing accounted for a quarter of incremental GDP, whereas agriculture accounted for 18 percent. During 1981–83 this ranking was reversed to 8 percent for manufacturing and 34 percent for agriculture. Furthermore, the balanced budget rule produced a swift curtailment of the government sector: government services accounted for 14.3 percent of incremental GDP between 1979 and 1981 but only 11.9 percent between 1981 and 1983. By 1984 in several respects the economy had already adjusted: a record rice harvest made the country a net exporter for the first time in a century, and both nonoil exports and GNP grew rapidly. Furthermore, this adjustment was achieved without a worsening in the distribution of income. The household survey data discussed in chapter 16 show that between 1981 and 1984 the share of the poorest 40 percent of the population continued to rise slightly.

Postcrisis Reforms: 1984–88

We now consider the final phase of the second oil cycle, the years 1984 to 1988, when the oil price collapsed. As previously, such a negative shock and its consequences for the budget and payments deficits immediately tested adherence to the economic constitution. The key element to be tested by the continuation of the oil slump was the necessity to balance the budget. Because the devaluation and fuel price increases had squared the budget, there was no problem in 1984, and the budget of that year was relatively relaxed. There was a 15 percent increase in government pay rates and a 17 percent increase in the salary bill. The fertilizer subsidy was retained, although the food subsidy was discontinued and the oil subsidy cut back. However, in the following November the fertilizer price was raised by 11 percent, compared with only a 6 percent increase in the floor price of paddy rice. By 1985 the demands of recurrent expenditure began to squeeze out development spending—the reverse of 1983. The civil service salary bill increased by 29 percent against only 2 percent for development expenditure.

The critical test of the principle of balance came in 1986. The government adhered firmly to the constitution, apparently influenced by fears of becoming another Mexico. There was a 7 percent reduction in expenditure, with the development budget cut by 22 percent in nominal terms. The development spending of the central government ministries was cut by 48 percent, and the salary bill increased only 2.3 percent. A retrenchment of this magnitude convinced some economists of the need to abandon a balanced budget. "The costs of a hyperconservative policy may well turn out to be very high" (Glassburner 1971a, p. 22).

At the time the budget was announced in January 1986, the revenue from oil and gas was expected to be down by 13 percent based on a $25 oil price, which indeed applied in January. However, it was clear by March that this revenue estimte was far too optimistic. The outcome of the 1986/87 budget was that revenue undershot by 6.5 percent and expenditures overshot by 8.2 percent. The latter was entirely accounted for by the increase in debt servicing following the devaluation of September. The 1987 budget continued the task of achieving balance. Development expenditures were again reduced in nominal terms. The civil service salary bill was budgeted to rise by only 2 percent and total expenditure by 6.4 percent, much of this debt service. There was at last a basis for a substantial tax effort because of the reforms described below; nonoil revenue was budgeted to increase by 27 percent.

The second key element of the economic constitution to be tested was convertibility. Following the 1983 devaluation the currency had been allowed to float down with the dollar so that by mid-1985 the real effective exchange rate was the same as just after the devaluation; by March 1986 it was some 10 percent below that level. By then total reserves stood at $10 billion with undrawn commercial borrowings of $2.5 billion. Thus despite the collapse in the oil price, the Central Bank was in a strong position to defend the currency should it have chosen to do so. There was no market pressure for a devaluation. Taking the markets completely by surprise, in September there was a devaluation of 31 percent. The decision also astounded most Indonesians; only the president and two or three of the technocrats appear to have been parties to the decision. The devaluation was a farsighted, unforced, and speedy reaction to an exogenous deterioration. It perhaps indicated that after several years of economic difficulties the technocrats had decisively regained the influence that had receded during the second oil boom.

If the economic constitution served Indonesia well as far as budgetary and exchange rate policies were concerned, it appeared to be unhelpful at the sectoral level. It could be (and was) interpreted as hostile to the private sector and in favor of self-sufficiency rather than trade. The full employment commitment could be used to justify any exotic scheme that directly employed people. Deregulation had repeatedly run afoul of these tenets. For example, the banking reform had raised the question of how *pribumi* firms were to be helped if credit was determined in the market rather than preferentially allocated.

The technocrats were never in a position to challenge the economic constitution directly. But the continuing economic crisis strengthened their hand, and they were gradually able to introduce reforms in areas of policy, trade, and taxation, and in sectors over which the economic constitution was either neutral or had been an obstacle to reform. By 1985 the technocrats were on sufficiently high ground to interpret the constitution as favoring rather than opposing reform in these areas. In a major debate on the "high-cost economy" the economics profession came out squarely against controls and linked them to oligopoly. The control regime was accused of raising costs in manufacturing, thereby reducing competitiveness and employment. Professor Sumitro used his authority to emphasize that controls were inconsistent with the original economic philosophy of the New Order, whereas efficiency of resource allocation was consistent with Pancasila.

The constitutional case against controls went back to the wave of deregulation that had taken place in 1967. But by linking controls to oligopoly and high costs, the constitutional case against them was made much more robust. Bigness and abuse of market power had been regarded with hostility since independence. For example, in parliament at much the same time, there was enthusiastic support for an antimonopoly bill. However, in the parliamentary debate no link had been made with either trade or licensing policies. Similarly, the negative employment implications of the high-cost economy were emphasized, thereby appealing to the full employment clause of the 1945 constitution. Thus by emphasizing such links the technocrats were able to create an environment in which for the first time the authority of the constitution could support rather than hinder deregulation.

The reform program that had been initiated in 1983 with banking deregulation and the design of tax reform was extended to trade—an area where control was more entrenched through procedural regulations and quantitative restrictions. In April 1985 the customs inspection procedure was significantly reformed, with inspection transferred to the Swiss company SGS and half of the customs staff sacked. Only 1 signature became needed instead of 20, clearance costs fell to about 20 percent of their previous level, and the use of export and import check prices was abandoned. In 1986 the trade reforms were extended to the quantitative restrictions themselves. In May complete exemption from duties and controls and the right to import directly were given to firms exporting more than 85 percent of production, with a drawback system for those below 85 percent. In October 165 import monopolies were abolished and replaced by tariffs. This was a significant establishment of a principle, but many of the most important monopolies were preserved because Suharto's family had personal stakes in many of them. Only 3 to 4 percent of nonoil imports were affected by the liberalization, the major continuing restrictions being on steel, plastics, tin plate, cotton, and industrial machinery (*Asian Wall Street Journal*, November 24–25, 1986).

In a second area of regularization, the tax reform initiated in 1983 bore fruit in 1985. Short-term efficiency and equity rather than revenue provided the rationale for a new income tax that, since only 10 to 15 percent of the population was to pay, would be more equitable. For the first time government employees became subject to income tax. After implementation difficulties, a value added tax (VAT) was introduced in April 1985 in place of a sales tax, with revenue more than doubling as a result. A third deregulation addressed foreign investment. In May 1986 the number of areas in which foreign companies were allowed to invest was doubled. Before this more than 1,000 products were subject to import regulation and license. In September 1986 these deregulations were complemented with a further devaluation. The trade reform was extended to steel and textiles in January 1987; around 40 percent of manufacturing sector import restrictions were removed. There was a further trade liberalization in 1988. In 1989 the attention of the liberalizers turned to the financial sector with far-reaching reforms.

Thus the second oil slump increasingly became an opportunity for liberalization rather than for intensification of controls: after setbacks during 1982–84 the technocrats began to gain ascendancy over the dirigistes. One factor strengthening the technocrats was the old story of actual or potential crisis. During the mid-1980s not only did the oil price collapse but debt accumulated rapidly, with the potential for a Mexico-type loss of confidence. During the first half of the 1980s this occurred incrementally, since the strictures of the economic constitution on the budget deficit applied only to domestic money creation: total debt doubled between 1980 and 1986. However, beginning in 1986 the situation was aggravated by a debt shock caused by the appreciation of the yen relative to the dollar. Since around 40 percent of debt was yen denominated, this added more than $1 billion to the cost of debt service. The potential loss of confidence of debt holders was accentuated by the open capital account, and there were speculative runs on the currency in 1984 and 1987. Although in each case these were arrested when the government sharply increased interest rates, they may have made the government sufficiently wary of capital flight that it was able to take early action to avoid a loss of confidence.

A second factor strengthening the technocrats was that they were able to formulate their arguments with the help of the universities, using language that commanded a wider audience but that focused on genuinely important issues. For example, the debate on the high-cost economy was a good preparation for trade and exchange rate liberalization.

It is noteworthy that the Indonesian intelligentsia was promoting the policies needed for international competitiveness at the same time as the Nigerian intelligentsia was united in denigrating them. A symptom of this difference in intellectual position, which itself had direct economic consequences, was Indonesia's radically better relations with the IMF and the World Bank. As one Indonesian insider noted, "The relationship with the IMF and the World Bank had been friendly from the beginning in 1967 . . . based on a sympathetic understanding and trust between the Widjojo group at the Indonesian end and personalities such as Bernie Bell (World Bank) at the other. . . . These remarkable relations with the Bank and the Fund remain even today" (Sadli, cited in Hill 1992, p. 55).

Another factor leading to successful reform was that some interventions had time to succeed without the disturbance of further shocks. For example, unlike the 1978 devaluation, which had been overtaken by the second oil boom, that of 1986 produced relative price effects that persisted for several quarters, and it was followed by a 50 percent increase in manufacturing exports in 1987. By 1990 manufactures constituted one-third of exports as against 6 percent in 1983. Not only did this success strengthen those advisers who had promoted liberalization, but a manufacturing export sector of this scale itself became a political lobby preventing policy retrogression. A fourth factor leading to success was that reactions to economic policy were normally muted. In October 1984, prior to the reforms, there were bombs and riots apparently directed against the Chinese. Following the May 1986 trade reforms, a few upstream industries publicly complained about the reduction in their protection. But no significant opposition developed.

Not all the reforms worked smoothly, however. The first banking deregulation was followed by a financial crisis in September 1984, with a rush into dollars and a sudden rise in the Jakarta interbank rate. This was seen as demonstrating the difficulties of policymaking in a partially liberalized economy, and there was a reversion to some quantitative restrictions on the banks. The May 1986 trade reforms depended on the cooperation of the bureaucracy and upstream firms for their success. In other words, there were continuing opportunities for rents. Finally, the foreign investment reforms failed in the short term to attract a significant increase in foreign capital.

On the positive side both the tax reforms and financial deregulation generated large cuts in the implicit subsidy for capital-intensive projects. In the longer term this could be expected to change the composition of industry away from high-capital use and energy-intensive production toward labor-intensive export goods. Many of the latter, such as labor-intensive electronics, were barely established because of the past difficulties of moving goods through the ports.

The pattern of growth involved a substantial shift from capital formation to consumption, which was reasonable either as an adjustment measure or if the downturn was temporary. In 1984 and 1985 GDP growth averaged 4 percent, capital formation declined at an average rate of 4.8 percent, and private and public consumption grew at 3.6 percent and 7.0 percent, respectively. In part, the lower rate of growth reflected a final end to the easy growth generated by reconstruction. For example, in the fourth plan (1983/84–1988/89), the composition of public investment shifted toward education because the scope for quick payoffs in other sectors was believed to be more limited than in the past. The opportunities for reconstruction, which had contributed to the high growth rates in all previous phases of the New Order, were finally exhausted.

The major publicized achievement of the period was the attainment of rice self-sufficiency in 1984. During 1979–84 rice production grew at an annual average rate of 6 percent. By 1984 the rice problem was that too much rice was being produced for the country's needs and Bulog, the parastatal with monopoly distribution rights, was incurring huge storage costs on 2.5 million tons.

Conclusion

To conclude, the second oil cycle was a significant period for both outcomes and policies. The distribution of income appears unambiguously to have improved during both the boom and slump phases, seriously undermining previous claims by researchers critical of the New Order regime that distribution was worsening. Economic growth was rapid in the boom phase and ahead of population growth even in the slump phase. Combined, these trends meant substantial progress in both poverty alleviation and the typical standard of living.

The responses of the government demonstrated the utility of the economic constitution. Partly an inheritance from 1945, it enhanced the legitimacy of the government both by the sense of continuity it afforded and by the association with the heroic era of liberation: this constitution was forged on the battlefield rather than in The Hague. There had, of course, been important additions in 1967. Some parts of the constitution were explicit, such as convertibility. Some were fuzzy but still had bite, such as the balanced budget requirement, and others were deeply obscure but could nevertheless be invoked to advance or retard a cause. Because the president ruled by maintaining a balance of power among interests, the defense of the economic constitution, with its obvious associations with political legitimacy, remained a potent influence on policy.

The economic technocrats were skillful in invoking the constitution as a means of strengthening their position. However, a boom weakened and a slump strengthened the technocrats relative to the dirigistes. In the boom the convertibility rule did not constrain actions, and budget balance assisted the dirigistes in their wish to spend resources on industrial projects. In the slump both rules rapidly triggered crises. The crises not only demanded policy initiatives but also created an atmosphere in which dirigisme appeared risky and the technocrats were viewed as the custodians of economic security. Because of this shift in the balance of influence on the president, the amorphous parts of the constitution could be reinterpreted to enable an assault on the accumulated dirigiste interventions. These interactions of the economic constitution and the technocrats more than offset what would otherwise have been (and in Nigeria was) the automatic tendency of the oil slump to favor dirigisme, with a mounting shortage of foreign exchange giving rise to quantitative restrictions on trade. This process, which became acute in Nigeria, was thwarted first by the convertibility-induced devaluations and second by the growing influence of those opposed to controls.

16 *Long-Term Trends in Poverty and Equity*

In this chapter we begin by considering the evidence on long-term changes in mean living standards. In principle four methods can be used to measure such changes: national accounts data on consumption can be combined with population census data to yield series of per capita private consumption at constant prices; household level survey snapshots can be compared with yield per capita expenditures; firm-level data on wage series can be used to show earnings for a significant group of the population; and, finally, agricultural data can be used to measure per capita food availability. Unfortunately, it is not possible to construct all four of these approaches for the entire period in Indonesia. In particular, virtually no household surveys exist prior to 1963/64.

Evidence on Mean Living Standards

There is one fascinating exception to the lack of household survey data prior to the mid-1960s. Keyfitz (1985) undertook fieldwork in the same East Javanese village in 1953 and 1985, thus spanning our period. He estimates that per capita income in real terms increased by a factor of around 2.5. Although this is a soft number, he supports it with a precise calculation of the wage per day worked in the fields by an adult male in units of rice. This rose from 2.2 kilos to 3.6 kilos, an increase of around 60 percent. Keyfitz also notes dramatic improvements in the standard of housing (for example, the elimination of bamboo and thatch, the most common roofing materials in 1953) and in clothing (children dressed in uniforms instead of rags). Finally, he notes an important social change. In 1953 social prestige was unidimensional: the owner of irrigated rice land was more important than a nonowner, irrespective of how the owner lived, because ownership created patron-client relationships. By 1985 there were multiple sources of prestige: housing, consumer durables such as motor scooters, and income from trading, all providing status alternatives to land.

The changes in one village of course do not provide a statistical basis for inferences about the long-term change in Indonesian living standards. Nevertheless, the Keyfitz study provides a unique additional viewpoint to our inevitably murky statistical story. For the period prior to the mid-1960s the other data routes to trends in living standards are some fragile estimates of national accounts, doubtful data on food availability, some wage series, and a variety of possible deflators.

The cost of living for 1950–73 has been carefully analyzed by Papanek and Dowsett (1975). The choice of deflator is important because of several factors: a phase of hyperinflation, price trends that varied by region over a geographically dispersed economy, and substantial relative price changes with indexes sensitive to their weightings. Unfortunately, none of the indexes proposed by Papanek and Dowsett is very satisfactory; the ones they prefer are composed almost exclusively of food and are specific to rural or urban areas.

Table 16.1 shows per capita private consumption as estimated from the national accounts, together with some wage series. The real wages of household servants and plantation laborers move together quite closely, suggesting that the unskilled labor market was relatively integrated. Between 1950 and the early 1960s both groups show a drastic reduction in real wages of 60 percent, most of this fall occurring post-1957. Papanek (1980) uses his own food price deflator for 13 wage series and reaches a similar conclusion that the labor market was integrated and that real wages fell massively. Table 16.2 shows his main real wage series covering 1951–78.

There is little correspondence between the national accounts and real wage series. By the original Neumark (1954) estimate, private consumption per capita fell by around 15 percent during the 1950s. According to the revised series by Muljatno (1960), consumption started from a lower base in 1951 but grew rapidly until 1955. By 1960 it had fallen by around a tenth. In conjunction the two estimates imply a substantial fall in private consumption during the late 1950s, though far less than the decline in real wages. Thereafter, consumption was in effect constant through the 1960s. Either the national accounts are seriously deficient or powerful redistributions against wage earners were occurring. According to the latter interpretation, the effects of accelerating inflation on the group whose incomes were determined by nominally specified contracts more than outweighed the increasing political power of organized labor under Sukarno.

Table 16.1 also provides limited data on per capita rice consumption. Consumption deteriorated during the 1960s. The annual estimates of rice availability show rapid rises in the early 1950s. The peak attained in 1958 is not restored until 1973. In between there is a substantial deterioration, with the trough in 1967. The juxtaposition of rising rice consumption with falling wages suggests that the nonpeasant wage rate was not closely related to mean consumption levels in the rest of the economy, at least in the short term.

From the mid-1960s, survey snapshots become available. One of the most readily comparable numbers across surveys is per capita rice consumption, since this is generally observed as a quantity, not merely an expenditure. Seven urban surveys spanning 1963–78 provide this information. Five of these cover the major urban areas of Java and Madura; the other two are confined to Jakarta. These surveys reveal remarkable stability in rice consumption. There is a significant discrepancy between the stagnation implied by these figures and the rising real wages during the period noted by Papanek (1980) and King and Weldon (1977).

For the period after 1970 there is again a substantial discrepancy in the two key data sources—the household surveys and the national accounts. Four survey snapshots of 1970, 1976, 1978, and 1980 show a growing underreporting of private consumption relative to the national accounts, from 71.3 percent in 1970 down to 58.6 percent in 1980. This persists during 1981–87. In consequence, rather different growth rates are implied (as shown in table 16.3). However, both sources agree that there was sustained growth in mean per capita consumption.

The household surveys have large sample sizes, ranging from 18,000 households to 56,000 households. One reason for the divergence from the national accounts may be underreporting of high income consumption, especially of durables, housing rental, and luxury services. A second reason is that the national accounts probably overestimate private consumption since it is arrived at as a residual. For example, the omission of private inventory accumulation leads to an overstatement of consumption.

Poverty

Table 16.4 provides an estimate of the incidence of absolute poverty for 1963–84. Prior to 1963 there are no data with which to estimate trends in poverty, other than those reported in the first two tables. Survey snapshots of Java and Madura for 1963, 1967, and 1970 provide the first basis for comparison of the incidence of absolute poverty. Unfortunately, during this period the CPI rose so rapidly—officially by 541 times its starting level—that it cannot be presumed to be accurate. An alternative is to compare the quantities of the major good—rice—consumed in each period. Mean per capita rice consumption was virtually identical in the 1963 and 1970 surveys: in rural areas it was 2 percent higher in the later survey and 1 percent lower in urban areas. Our procedure is therefore to assume that mean consumption was constant in both rural and urban areas, so the incidence of poverty might change over the period only

Table 16.1 Per Capita Private Consumption, Real Wages, and Rice Consumption, 1950–85

Year	Real per capita private consumption (1950 = 100)	CPI Series 1	CPI Series 2	Wage of servant in Jakarta (1950 = 100) Nominal	Wage of servant in Jakarta (1950 = 100) Real	Wage of plantation laborer (1950 = 100) Nominal	Wage of plantation laborer (1950 = 100) Real[a]	Wage for hoeing (1950 = 100)[b]	Per capita rice consumption Urban (kilograms per week)	Per capita rice consumption Overall (kilograms per year)
1950	100.0[c]	60	—	—	100	2,030	100	—	—	80[d]
1951	100.0 (118.3)[e]	85	—	—	79	2,615	97	—	—	80[d]
1952	109.2 (121.2)[e]	92	—	—	95	2,890	93	—	—	80[d]
1953	104.7	100	—	100	115	3,003	89	—	—	—
1954	109.8	103	—	—	117	3,196	92	—	—	87[f]
1955	114.3	127	—	—	106	2,879	88	—	—	87[f]
1956	—	143	—	—	100	3,439	93	—	—	87[f]
1957	—	159	—	130	94	3,534	86	—	—	87[f]
1958	—	225	—	166	85	4,334	75	—	—	91[g]
1959	—	280	—	200	82	4,757	66	—	—	91[g]
1960	101.3	367	—	233	72	4,698	50	—	—	107
1961	106.8	487	—	277	66	6,400	51	—	—	101
1962	111.7	1,324	—	458	40	13,525	40	—	—	106
1963	104.9	2,927	—	1,038	40	30,452	40	—	2.111[h]	93
1964	103.2	6,106	—	1,762	33	—	—	—	1.853	96
1965	103.2	24,715	—	5,718	26	—	—	—	—	92
1966	99.3	318,299	76	50,563	18	—	—	—	—	93
1967	105.5	924,761	206	606,396	76	—	—	—	2.194[h]	91
1968	106.8	2,058,666	464	769,213	43	—	—	100[i]	1.086[k]	98
1969	110.5	—	545	—	—	—	—	—	2.100[h]	107
1970	111.2	—	612	—	—	—	—	97	2.119[h]	109
1971	113.4	—	639	—	—	—	—	111	—	110

Year										
1972	118.2	—	—	—	—	680	—	—	—	108
1973	118.5	—	—	—	—	891	—	112	—	118
1974	133.4	—	—	—	—	1,253	—	—	—	116
1975	135.8	—	—	—	—	1,492	—	136	—	113
1976	140.8	—	—	—	—	1,788	—	—	—	119
1977	146.8	—	—	—	—	1,985	—	132[i,j]	1.985[k]	122
1978	153.6	—	—	—	—	2,146	—	—	—	123
1979	171.6	—	—	—	—	132.3[l]	—	—	—	134[m]
1980	189.2	—	—	—	—	156.3	—	—	—	134[m]
1981	215.8	—	—	—	—	175.5	—	—	—	—
1982	218.2	—	—	—	—	192.1	—	—	—	—
1983	205.1	—	—	—	—	214.7	—	147[l]	—	—
1984	210.3	—	—	—	—	237.2	—	—	—	—
1985	—	—	—	—	—	248.4	—	—	—	—

— Not available.

a. Pre-1955 data are for permanent laborers only; later data are for permanent plus temporary laborers.

b. Data are for male laborers on small farms at peak of season.

c. 1950 is assumed to equal 1951.

d. Period average for 1950–52.

e. Figures in parentheses are from Neumark 1954; other figures are from Muljatno 1960.

f. Period average for 1954–57.

g. Period average for 1958–59.

h. For Java and Madura.

i. Coverage is for six villages in West Java. The deflator is the local rice price.

j. Coverage is for seven villages in West Java. The deflator is the CPI (nine basic commodities, with rural consumption weights). This is chain-indexed to the 1970–77 series.

k. For Jakarta.

l. CPI for 17 cities.

m. Period average for 1979–80.

Source: Indonesia Ministry of Finance Bureau of Statistics (BPS), *Statistical Pocket Book of Indonesia,* various years; Bureau of Statistics (BPS) surveys; Muljatno 1960; Neumark 1954; Booth 1983; Mears and Moeljono 1981; Manning 1986; Mazumdar and Husein 1985.

Table 16.2 Real Wages, 1951–83
(1955=100)

Year	Weekly					Plantations			
						All Indonesia		Java,	Sumatra,
	Medium firms	Large and medium firms	Foreign firms	Unskilled workers	Yearly wages, large firms	Temporary and permanent workers	Permanent workers	temporary and permanent workers	temporary and permanent workers
1951	—	—	—	85.3	—	—	112.6	—	—
1952	—	—	—	116.8	—	—	142.8	—	—
1953	—	—	—	—	—	160.5	148.5	255.2	141.3
1954	—	—	—	—	107.5	161.2	117.4	249.5	145.2
1955	100.0	100.0	100.0	100.0	100.0	100.0	100.0	100.0	100.0
1956	—	—	—	—	97.9	107.4	104.6	165.2	102.3
1957	—	—	—	118.3	95.1	108.1	107.3	165.0	106.3
1958	—	—	—	118.5	78.5	87.3	93.7	141.3	76.4
1959	77.8	77.6	83.3	179.1	76.4	71.8	84.2	101.6	81.4
1960	91.1	93.7	95.6	183.6	69.8	64.5	85.5	87.3	77.1
1961	—	—	—	166.7	67.7	62.0	75.7	77.3	79.3
1962	52.2	46.3	48.4	111.3	44.8	—	—	—	—
1963	42.3	31.0	40.7	91.2	49.1	48.1	55.1	64.7	55.9
1964	—	—	—	86.5	45.6	—	—	—	—
1965	—	—	—	70.9	50.1	—	—	—	—
1966	—	—	—	106.7	53.8	56.5	73.0	77.2	89.4
1967	—	—	—	96.6	66.1	38.8	74.9	45.9	78.4

Year									
1968	—	—	—	70.3	—	51.5	64.8	66.3	72.0
1969	—	—	—	84.2	—	82.5	79.3	111.5	96.9
1970	116.0	96.7	78.5	93.7	—	96.9	94.8	134.8	116.5
1971	—	—	—	100.2	72.2	93.9	94.8	130.4	113.3
1972	—	—	129.9	116.2	81.6	94.1	96.2	136.2	115.2
1973	—	—	—	158.9	82.3	80.9	87.7	113.2	92.0
1974	—	—	—	—	—	79.6	80.9	119.5	85.9
1975	111.5	—	124.1	—	—	87.5	88.8	127.3	106.4
1976	113.0	—	128.7	—	—	92.9	89.5	125.0	126.3
1977	116.1	—	132.1	—	—	93.8	90.6	135.2	117.5
1978	—	—	—	—	—	93.7	92.4	125.8	118.7
1979	—	—	—	—	—	100.0	—	—	—
1980	—	—	—	—	—	128.8	—	—	—
1981	—	—	—	—	—	141.0	—	—	—
1982	—	—	—	—	—	150.3	—	—	—
1983	—	—	—	—	—	152.2	—	—	—

— Not available.

Note: Papanek reports the rice price as the deflator; for 1979–83 we use the CPI deflator given in table 16.1.

Source: Papanek 1980, tables 4.3 and 4.5.

Table 16.3 Annual Growth of Real Per Capita Private Consumption, 1970–80
(percent)

Year	National accounts	Household survey data
1970–76	5.6	1.8
1976–78	5.1	5.2
1978–80	4.8	4.5

Source: Rao 1984, table A4.

because of a change in the distribution of expenditure over the population. We have adopted a poverty line consistent with Rao (1984) for 1970–80; that is, our poverty line generates the same incidence of poverty in 1970 as found by Rao for that year. The results show a marked increase in poverty between 1963 and 1967 in rural areas but a marked reduction in urban areas. Between 1967 and 1970 these changes were partially reversed, and the overall incidence of poverty declined.

Surveys for all rural and urban Indonesia provide snapshots for 1970, 1976, 1978, 1980, 1984, and 1987. Rao measured the incidence of poverty across the first four of these surveys using a common poverty line. This shows a rapid decline in the incidence of poverty, especially in urban areas, where it declined from 50 to 20 percent of the population. This can be checked by the comparison of two surveys conducted in Jakarta in 1968/69 and 1977/78. From published tables on the distribution of households over expenditure groups broken down by household size, we computed a per capita frequency distribution of expenditures. The CPI was then used to deflate 1977/78 to 1968/69 prices (the deflator being 4.094). Two poverty lines were then imposed—those that cut off each of the two lowest quintiles in 1968/69. The comparison reveals a dramatic reduction in the incidence of poverty in Jakarta over this decade. By 1977/78 only 3.7 percent of the population fell below the lower poverty line, compared with 20 percent in 1968. The higher poverty line,

Table 16.4 Percentage of Population in Poverty, Selected Years, 1963–84

Population	1963	1967	1970	1976	1978	1980	1984
Urban	56.7	50.2	50.7	31.5	25.2	19.7	5.7
Rural	47.9	60.4	58.5	54.5	54.0	44.6	26.9
All	51.8	58.5	57.1	50.1	48.5	39.8	22.7

Source: For 1970–80, Rao 1984, table C. For 1980–84, household survey data and authors' computations using CPI deflator of 1.5173. For 1963–70, authors' computations assuming constant mean; see text.

which had cut off 40 percent of the population, by 1978 cut off only 11.5 percent.[1]

A nutritional poverty line has also been used to compare the incidence of poverty in 1970 and 1976 (Rao 1984, p. 33). Three cutoff points were adopted: expenditure consistent with 100, 90, and 80 percent of the World Health Organization (WHO) norm of 2,150 calories per day. The lowest of these poverty lines is probably of most interest since the other two cut off a high proportion of the population and the WHO norms have subsequently been revised downward. This exercise supports the hypothesis of a reduced incidence of poverty in urban Java but suggests that rural poverty on Java increased, contrary to the previous results. This probably reflects the change in relative prices, and in particular the rise in food prices relative to the general index. The nutritional poverty line is, in effect, deflating by the most rapidly rising price in the consumption basket and so will produce an upper bound to the increase in poverty.

For the period 1980–84 we compared national snapshot surveys for 1980, 1981, and 1984. The poverty line was that of Rao—the level that produced the same incidence of poverty in 1980. The results suggest a continued rapid decline in the incidence of poverty.

Finally, and most comprehensively, Booth (1992) has collated poverty measures for the period 1964/65 to 1987 using three different poverty lines for rural and urban areas. On the official poverty line, poverty has fallen steadily: in urban areas from 38.8 percent in 1976 to 20.1 percent by 1987, and in rural areas even more substantially, from 40.4 percent in 1976 to 16.4 percent in 1987. The other two indexes, those of Sajogyo and Esmara (in Booth 1992), are chiefly of interest in that they cover the period 1964/65–1976. Both of them show a steady decline in rural and urban poverty during this period. To summarize, there is no basis for estimating poverty during the 1950s, but in the 1960s prior to the New Order it was increasing. From 1967 onward there is evidence of falling poverty, initially hesitant but then becoming rapid and sustained.

Inequality

After a review of the evidence on the overall distribution of expenditure by population quintiles, we focus on the important political and social cleavages: regional, rural versus urban, intraurban, and finally intrarural.

Overall Trends in Inequality

For the period 1950–63 inferences about trends in inequality can only be drawn from the divergences between the various series set out in the first section of this chapter. Real wages evidently fell far more rapidly than mean per capita private consumption, and food grain supplies actually rose. Thus it seems safe to conclude that there was a powerful redistribution away from wage earners.

One long-term series with data back to 1950 is the relative incidence of infant mortality. McDonald (1980) uses the World Fertility Survey to identify 39 ranked social groups according to the education, occupation, and residence of the parents, and he compares infant mortality rates for the three periods 1950–60, 1961–66, and 1966–71. The infant mortality rate declined from 23 in the first period to 19 in the second and 15 in the third. Taking the length of time between the midpoints of the two surveys, we calculate from McDonald's data that the annual rate of decline in infant mortality was 2.2 percent between the first and second periods and 4.6 percent between the second and third periods. This suggests that living standards were rising more rapidly in the late 1960s than in the early 1960s, and social groups were slightly farther apart during the late 1960s. Taking the mean mortality rate for the 16 groups above the overall mean, between the first two periods mortality declined by 18 percent against 17 percent for all groups, whereas between the two later periods it declined by 20 percent against 21 percent for all groups.[2]

For the period 1963–90, 11 snapshot surveys can be compared to show changes in the distribution of per capita expenditure by population quintile (table 16.5). As with all such exercises the results are subject to qualification. To quote Hughes and Islam (1981, p. 50), "We would not wish to dismiss the possibility that the [household] data are sufficiently biased to invalidate any conclusion about inequality which we have obtained but in the absence of more concrete evidence about the nature of these alleged biases we feel that there is no justification for eschewing the use of these data." The specific criticisms of the household surveys are discussed below.

Since the time periods between these snapshots differ, to the extent that they identify genuine processes of change it is helpful to discuss the data in terms of annual rates of change. A simple concept deployed below is the annual rate of change of the share of a particular group relative to the mean. Were the mean living standard constant throughout, this would fully describe the rate of change in the living standard of the group. Since over most of the period the mean wage itself is changing, our measure shows the contribution to the change in living standard caused purely by distributional changes. We focus on the poorest 40 percent and the richest 20 percent of the population.

The most striking feature of table 16.5 is that the distribution is rather stable over this long period. Taking the opening and closing surveys, the poorest 40 percent gained relative to the mean at an annual rate of 0.3 percent. Since the national accounts data on per capita private consumption (table 16.1) show that mean to have been rising over the same period by 3.4 percent a year, this distributional change in favor of the poor was trivial relative to the growth effect. Similarly, the top quintile gained relative to the mean at 0.2 percent a year. However, the latter result is misleading since more than the entire gain in the share of the top quintile occurred between 1963 and 1964. Furthermore, the 1963 snapshot can be based only on computations from published frequency distributions, whereas the other observations are direct. Between 1964 and 1984 the top quintile lost relative to the mean at 0.2 percent a year— a rate that still permitted substantial absolute growth.

The attempt to discern phases within this 27-year period appears unpromising: shares fluctuate in a way that may well reflect either statistical noise or transient economic phenomena. However, between 1963 and 1967 the poorest 40 percent lost relative to the mean at the fast rate of 1.5 percent a year, while the top quintile gained, so there is some basis for concluding that during this period the distribution of expenditure (and hence of expected permanent income) was becoming less equal. Between 1967 and 1976 there appear to have been no powerful changes in distribution at the aggregate level, although we will see that this is the result of offsetting changes at a more disaggregated level. Since 1976 the distribution of expenditure appears to have become modestly more equal: the poorest 40 percent of the population gained relative to the mean at an average annual rate of 0.7 percent. During the oil slump and economic liberalization, the share of the poorest 40 percent scarcely changed: massive macroeconomic events occurred without distributional consequences when the distribution is measured not across socioeconomic groups but in terms of a poverty ranking.

Although a look back at such a long sweep of surveys suggests a stable distribution with a modest trend toward greater equity, researchers during the period had to contend with a gradual buildup of data, the signals from which appeared confused. Most analyses were based only on a comparison of adjoining surveys. This inevitably incorporated statistical noise and temporary deviations. For example, with the benefit of three subsequent surveys, we can conclude that the distribution found in 1978 was atypical: either the year or the sample was peculiar. Yet at the time of its publication, the 1978 results appeared to confirm the perceptions of those who had interpreted the 1967–76 data as showing a trend toward increased inequality. Furthermore, as discussed below, analyses tended to be based on the distribution of current income as opposed to expenditure. Yet the latter, which is both a better guide to permanent income and probably more accurately measured in surveys, tells a different story from the former. The rise in inequality during the New Order was readily accepted as a stylized fact, perhaps because it coincided with the political stylized fact that the change to the New Order had been a shift to the right. With the benefit of a longer data series it appears to have been a stylized fiction.

Table 16.5 Distribution of Per Capita Expenditure by Population Quintile, Selected Years, 1963–90
(percent)

Quintile[a]	1963	1964	1967	1970	1976	1978	1980	1981	1984	1987	1990
Q1	6.9	7.2	6.6	7.6	8.0	7.3	7.7	8.3	8.1	8.8	8.7
Q2	12.5	11.4	11.8	12.3	11.5	10.8	11.8	12.2	12.3	12.4	12.1
Q3	17.0	15.8	16.9	16.6	16.0	14.8	16.0	15.6	16.2	16.1	15.9
Q4	23.4	22.1	22.5	22.7	22.0	21.8	22.2	21.8	21.8	21.5	21.1
Q5	40.2	43.4	42.3	40.8	42.5	45.3	42.3	42.1	41.6	41.2	42.3

a. Ranked from poorest to richest.
Source: For 1976–81, Indonesia, Ministry of Finance, Bureau of Statistics (BPS), Statistical Abstract 1985, table 10.2.14. For 1963 and 1967, authors' computations from published frequency distributions over class intervals for Java and Madura only. For 1964 and 1970, Indonesia, Ministry of Finance, Bureau of Statistics (BPS), Statistical Pocket Book of Indonesia 1979/80, T.IX.7. For 1984–87, World Bank 1990, table 1.3. For 1990, World Bank 1995, table 30.

Regional Inequality

Two levels of regionalism are important in Indonesia. Two-thirds of the entire population lives on Java, which is therefore both culturally and politically dominant. Thus, the distribution of wealth between Java and the outer islands is inevitably sensitive. Additionally, Indonesia is divided into 27 provinces, and interprovincial distribution is also significant.

Table 16.6 sets out time series for 1964–84 on inequality between Java and the outer islands. Uncorrected for differences in the cost of living, per capita expenditure was lower on Java throughout the period. However, for 1976 Hughes and Islam (1981) provide a price level-corrected spatial decomposition of inequality. They found that in real terms per capita expenditure was identical on Java (63 percent of the population) and the outer islands (37 percent). Thus, there was no between-group inequality. Over time there was a substantial change in favor of Java, which gained at an average annual rate of 1.9 percent relative to the outer islands. Taking into account the Hughes and Islam result of equality in 1976, this suggests that during the 20 years, the original differential in favor of the outer islands was reversed. This is all the more remarkable since the rapid growth of oil income within this period occurred largely on the outer islands: thus we may infer substantial redistribution of income.

We investigate this redistribution at the provincial level. Data for 1976 provide rather full information on provincial inequalities in that year (Islam and Khan 1986). For 25 regions information is available on per

Table 16.6 Java–Outer Islands Inequality, Selected Years, 1964–84

Item	1964	1969/70	1976	1978	1984
Per capita expenditure (rupiah)					
Java	4,832	1,214	4,113	5,113	16,105
Indonesia	5,704	1,412	4,489	5,568	16,316
Ratio					
Java/Indonesia	0.85	0.86	0.92	0.92	0.99
Java/outer islands[a]	0.67	0.69	0.80	0.81	0.97
Java/outer islands, price corrected[a]	—	—	1.00	—	—

— Not available.

a. Derived from the Java/Indonesia series assuming a constant population split of 63:37.

Source: Authors' computations from published frequency distributions or direct from published household survey results.

Table 16.7 Provincial Inequality before and after Redistributions, 1976

Province	(1) *Ex ante per capita expenditure*	(2) *Ex post per capita expenditure*	(3) *Ratio of col. 2 /col. 1*
Bali	69.332	74.947	1.081
Bengkulu	54.099	85.796	1.586
DKI Jakarta	196.423	153.534	0.782
Daerah Istimewa Jogjakarta	52.436	84.412	1.610
Daerah Istimewa Aceh	81.152	107.458	1.324
Jambi	70.846	93.808	1.324
Jawa Barat	67.303	85.966	1.277
Jawa Tengh	54.188	85.608	1.580
Jawa Timur	152.436	71.326	1.360
Kalimantan Barat	75.645	92.305	1.220
Kalimantan Selatan	73.574	94.594	1.286
Kalimantan Tengah	82.079	97.652	1.190
Kalimantan Timur	622.126	92.458	0.149
Lampung	72.045	61.502	0.854
Maluku	89.784	67.362	0.750
Nusa Tenggara Barat	43.594	72.556	1.664
Nusa Tanggara Timur	38.209	62.271	1.630
Riau	777.665	85.505	0.110
Sulawesi Selatan	60.586	80.021	1.321
Sulawesi Tengah	58.687	74.982	1.278
Sulawesi Tenggara	68.060	56.890	0.836
Sulawesi Utara	69.589	71.189	1.023
Sumatera Selatan	124.750	85.300	0.684
Sumatera Utara	89.398	84.292	0.943

Note: Nationally, private expenditure in 1976 was 0.7845 of GDP. Ex ante private expenditure in each region is calculated by applying this to the GDP of each region. The national accounts data must then be reconciled with the household survey data, which underrecords expenditure. To make the two compatible in aggregate for the 24 provinces for which there is both GDP and survey data, the latter are rescaled by 1.42. The national accounts data, described as ex ante expenditure, are shown in column 1. Column 2 is the price level-corrected household survey data from Hughes and Islam 1981. Regional transfers are calculated as half the sum of the moduli of the differences between ex ante and ex post private expenditures in each region.

Source: National accounts; Hughes and Islam 1981.

capita expenditure adjusted for differences in regional price levels, for the incidence of poverty, and for the dimensions of regional inequality. The latter two have been computed for all the major indexes: head count, poverty gap, Sen, Anand, Atkinson, and Theil. As it happens, the rankings of regions by these measures are highly correlated. Regional differences are fairly small: abstracting from Jakarta, the differential between the regions with the lowest and highest real per capita expenditure is less than 1:2. For 24 of these regions there are also data for GDP per capita for the same year. From this we calculate ex ante per capita expenditure—that is, the expenditure that would have been observed had each region spent a common fraction of its income (table 16.7). The per capita expenditures observed in the household surveys are ex post of government and other transfers. To quantify the magnitude of transfers requires a reconciliation of the household data and national accounts estimates of private expenditure, which is described in the notes to the table.

The results reveal significant transfers between regions, amounting to 21.1 percent of private expenditure. The final column of table 16.7 shows the ratio of ex ante to ex post expenditure for each region. The note to the table explains how the transfers are calculated. It can be seen that the direction of transfers is highly progressive. The high-income regions of Riau, Kalimantan, Jakarta, and Sumatera Selatan all make large transfers; the low-income regions of Nusa Tenggara, Yogyakarta, and Bengkulu all receive large transfers. The Spearman rank correlation of columns 1 and 3 is -0.84. Finally, we computed the marginal incidence of transfers by regressing the transfer as a percentage of ex ante expenditure, on ex ante expenditure as a percentage of the mean:

$$Y = 0.35 - 0.15X$$
$$(0.07) \quad (0.03)$$

$$r^2 = 0.61$$

where parentheses indicate standard error, Y = column 2 – 1, and X = column 1 ÷ national mean. The incidence of transfers is well explained by per capita real GDP, the rate of transfer being 15 percent of the difference between that and the national mean. Thus interprovincial redistributions appear to be both large and coherent.

Rural-Urban Inequality

The earliest survey evidence, for 1963, suggests that in real terms rural-urban differences in per capita expenditures were around 2:1. However, these differences are unlikely ever to have accounted for a substantial component of overall inequality. Hughes and Islam (1981) provide a price level-adjusted decomposition of inequality for 1976. Allowances are made for both regional and rural-urban differences in the cost of living, and inequality is measured in terms of real per capita expenditure. For Indonesia as a whole, rural-urban inequality accounts for only 9.6 percent of overall inequality using a Theil Index (and between 6.8 and 11 percent using other decomposable indexes).

Urban Inequality

The decomposition analysis of Hughes and Islam finds inequality within urban areas to be more important than rural-urban inequality, although the extent depends on the index. (Recall that the decomposition is for 1976 and corrects for differences in the cost of living between locations.) Inequalities within urban Java accounted for 24 percent of national inequality, and inequalities with urban areas in the outer islands accounted for a further 8 percent on a Theil Index. Since urban incomes are above the national average, other indexes more sensitive to inequalities among lower-income groups find the share accounted for by urban areas to be considerably lower: on the Atkinson Index with $E = 3$, the two urban groups account for only 12 percent of inequality.

   Trends in urban inequality can be studied only for the post-1963 period. We divide this into three phases: 1963–70, 1970–76, and 1976–84. The distribution of income during the first phase, which spans surveys conducted in 1963/64, 1964/65, 1967, and 1969/70, has been analyzed by King and Weldon (1977); the key data are shown in table 16.8.

   In terms of income, the share of the poorest 40 percent declined markedly from 22.1 percent in 1963 to 20 percent in 1970, implying an annual rate of income decline for the poor of 1.7 percent if mean income were constant. Recall from the first section that the constancy of mean income for 1963–70 is a reasonable first approximation: the national accounts imply only a modest increase in per capita private consumption, and the

Table 16.8 Distribution of Urban Income by Population Quintile, Selected Years, 1963–70
(percent)

Quintile[a]	1963	1964	1967	1970
Q1	9.5	8.5	9.0	7.8
Q2	12.6	12.8	13.1	12.2
Q3	17.5	16.6	16.5	15.9
Q4	23.8	22.7	21.5	22.6
Q5	36.7	39.5	39.8	41.5

   a. Ranked from poorest to richest.
Source: King and Weldon 1977, table 1.

Table 16.9 Distribution of Urban Expenditure by Population Quintile, Selected Years, 1963–87

(percent)

Quintile[a]	1963	1964	1967	1970	1976	1978	1980	1981	1984	1987
Q1	7.3	7.5	7.3	7.5	7.8	6.7	7.3	8.0	8.3	8.1
Q2	12.7	11.4	12.4	11.9	11.7	10.7	11.4	12.8	12.3	12.4
Q3	17.3	15.6	16.4	16.7	15.7	14.7	16.4	15.2	17.1	16.2
Q4	24.4	21.4	24.4	21.8	21.8	21.7	21.4	22.1	21.2	22.0
Q5	38.3	43.9	41.5	42.0	43.0	46.2	43.6	42.0	41.1	41.3

a. Ranked from poorest to richest.

Source: For 1963 and 1967, authors' computations from published frequency distributions over class intervals for Java and Madura only. For 1964 and 1967, Indonesia, Ministry of Finance, Bureau of Statistics (BPS), *Statistical Pocket Book of Indonesia, 1980,* table IX.7. For 1976–84, Indonesia, Ministry of Finance, Bureau of Statistics (BPS), *Statistical Abstract 1985,* table 10.1. For 1987, World Bank 1990, table 1.3.

surveys show urban per capita food consumption as virtually constant. The top quintile increased its share, raising income relative to the mean by 2.1 percent a year. However, most of this occurred between 1963/64 and 1964/65, before the change in political control. On the basis of these results, King and Weldon concluded that income distribution worsened significantly during the period. However, the results are contradicted by the expenditure data. The latter are possibly a more certain measure of income and probably a better reflection of permanent income than survey attempts to solicit information directly on current income.

Our computations on the distribution of per capita expenditure are shown in table 16.9. There are large changes between 1963 and 1964, which may reflect the inferior method that must be relied on for the former data or the genuine but temporary effects of very rapid inflation. Between 1964 and 1970 there is an unambiguous reduction in inequality as the bottom 40 percent gain relative to the mean at 0.4 percent a year and the top quintile loses at 0.7 percent a year, both trends being contrary to the income data.

The distribution of income during the period 1970–76 has been analyzed by Sundrum (1979) and Dapice (1980), who disagree on the interpretation of the data. Both agree, however, that there was a continuation of a marked increase in inequality, chiefly by way of gains by the top quintile. Recall that the thesis of a continuation is highly questionable since it is contradicted by the expenditure data: Dapice and Sundrum reached a consensus about the 1960s that was unsustainable. Despite their disagreement on detail, they then came to another consensus about the 1970s (up to 1976). To test the robustness of their interpretation we again turn to the distribution of expenditure. Again this fails to confirm either the Sundrum or the Dapice accounts, since the share of the poorest 40 percent rose slightly. Specifically, the poorest 40 percent increased its share from 19.5 to 19.6 percent, an annual gain of 0.1 percent, and the top quintile increased share from 42 to 43 percent, an annual gain of 0.4 percent.

Much of the antipathy to such results has been aroused by the conspicuous consumption of the Jakarta elite. To test whether this elite was indeed capturing a larger share of expenditure, we computed from the two Jakarta surveys expenditure shares in 1968/69 and 1977/78, on the same basis as for our poverty lines. This indeed reveals some concentration. The poorest 40 percent lost relative to the mean at an annual rate of 0.6 percent, while the top quintile gained at the rate of 0.5 percent. The Jakarta elite did not, therefore, gain significantly more than the elite in other urban areas, although the Jakarta poor appear to have fared worse relative to the mean than the other urban poor. Of course, focusing upon the top quintile defines the "elite" rather broadly. The offending conspicuous consumption is perhaps confined to something more like the top 0.1 percent, and the position of such a group is not measurable from budget surveys. It would be convenient to be able to dismiss the aggregate consumption of such a small group as statistically trivial. Although this may be the case, recent data on the consumption pattern of former Philippine President Marcos suggest that no such assumption can be made.

For the period 1976–87 we compare the distribution of per capita expenditure. The share of the bottom 40 percent increased from 19.6 to 20.5 percent, implying an annual increase of 0.5 percent relative to mean expenditure. These gains by the poor were at the expense of the top quintile, whose share declined from 43.0 to 41.3 percent, an annual decline of 0.4 percent relative to the mean.

To summarize, during the 1960s the inequality of income possibly increased. Thereafter, it was modestly reduced: the poor gained, but by only 0.4 percent a year relative to the mean, and the top quintile lost even more modestly, at 0.2 percent a year, made up of a small gain in the first half of the 1970s that was subsequently reversed. Taking the probably more reliable expenditure data, the share of the poor was static between 1963 and 1976 but thereafter rose modestly, whereas the rich slightly increased their share between 1963 and 1976, thereafter losing part of these gains.

These national survey data are at odds with the impressions of a vocal group of researchers (V. White, G. Hart, W. Collier, and D. Dapice). First, they question the deflator: Dapice (1980) argues that prices for the goods consumed by the poor rose substantially more than for other groups. Second, they argue that the consumption of the urban elite is underrecorded in the household surveys and that it grew rapidly.

There is some substance in the claim that relative prices moved against the poor in the 1970s. With 1971 as a base, food prices had risen 15 percent relative to the general index by 1978 in Jakarta. However, this was subsequently largely reversed. The 17-city CPI, based on 1977/78, showed food prices to have fallen 8 percent relative to the general index by 1985. Thus, over the whole period 1971–85, food prices rose relatively by only 5 percent. Of course, food/nonfood is not the only dimension in which prices may have turned against the poor, but it is likely to be the most significant.

There is also likely to have been some systematic underreporting of the expenditure of high-income groups on durables. But again the 1970–76 period may have been peculiar. We noted above (table 16.3) that it was only in this period that there was a substantial divergence between the household data and the national accounts.

Rural Inequality

Inequality within rural areas accounts for the majority of Indonesian inequality. Hughes and Islam (1981) find that the sum of intra-Javan inequality and inequality within the outer islands ranges from 58 percent of the total (using a Theil Index) to 80 percent (using an Atkinson Index, with $E = 3$). Our discussion of trends in intrarural inequality retains the three phases 1963–70, 1970–76, and 1976–84.

King and Weldon (1977) again provide an analysis of the distribution of rural income during the first period, reproduced in table 16.10. There is little systematic change in the distribution of income during these seven years. The poorest 40 percent of the population had a slightly reduced share, declining from 22.0 to 21.3 percent. Had mean incomes been constant, this loss of share would represent an annual rate of income decline of 0.5 percent. The top quintile increased its share relative to the mean by 0.7 percent a year. However, as in urban areas, most of this gain occurred between 1963/64 and 1964/65, before the change in political control. Again these conclusions are at variance with the expenditure data in table 16.11, which shows that the share of the poorest 40 percent actually rose slightly. Although this was also true of the top quintile, more than the entire increase took place between 1963 and 1964—a result that, as previously discussed, might be expected to be either transient or bogus.

The distribution of rural income during the period 1970–76 has been analyzed by Sundrum (1979) and Dapice (1980). According to Sundrum there was some reduction in inequality. The expenditure data support Sundrum's conclusion: the share of the poorest 40 percent rose, whereas that of the top quintile fell markedly. Specifically, the poorest 40 percent increased its share at an annual rate of 1.3 percent, whereas the top quintile lost at an annual rate of 0.8 percent.

Table 16.10 Distribution of Rural Income by Population Quintile, Selected Years, 1963–70

Quintile[a]	1963	1964	1967	1970
Q1	7.6	7.7	10.8	8.7
Q2	14.4	12.4	11.6	12.6
Q3	16.8	16.5	19.5	16.6
Q4	23.0	22.9	21.3	22.3
Q5	38.2	40.5	36.8	39.8

a. Ranked from poorest to richest.
Source: King and Weldon 1977.

For 1976–87 we compare only the distribution of per capita expenditure. There was a continued decline in inequality, with the share of the poorest 40 percent rising at an annual rate of 0.7 percent relative to the mean. These gains by the poor were at the expense of the top quintile, whose share declined at an annual rate of 0.7 percent.

For this final period there is at last corroborative evidence from comparable surveys. The Agro-Economic Survey for Bogor collected panel data in 1976 and 1983 for six villages in West Java regarded as representative. Such data sets have strengths and weaknesses, but they are far more reliable than those available to researchers during the 1970s. Since the same households were covered in both surveys, the data are particularly valuable on the relative fortunes of different socioeconomic classes. However, the same feature makes the data unsuitable for comparisons of the overall distribution of income, since there is a systematic bias in the exclusion of newly formed households.[3]

Table 16.11 Distribution of Rural Expenditure by Population Quintile, Selected Years, 1963–87

Quintile[a]	1963	1964	1967	1970	1976	1978	1980	1981	1984	1987
Q1	6.9	7.3	6.9	7.7	8.4	8.2	8.4	9.2	9.2	9.8
Q2	12.5	11.6	12.0	11.8	12.8	11.7	12.7	13.6	13.2	13.6
Q3	17.0	15.7	17.2	15.8	16.6	16.0	17.1	16.7	18.4	17.0
Q4	23.3	22.4	22.9	22.9	22.2	22.2	21.9	22.7	21.4	21.8
Q5	40.3	43.0	41.0	41.8	40.0	41.9	39.8	37.8	37.8	37.7

a. Ranked from poorest to richest.
Source: For 1963 and 1967, authors' computations from published frequency distributions over class intervals for Java and Madura only. For 1964 and 1967, Ministry of Finance, Bureau of Statistics (BPS), *Statistical Pocket Book of Indonesia, 1980,* table IX.7. For 1976–84, Ministry of Finance, Bureau of Statistics (BPS), *Statistical Abstract 1985,* table 10.1. For 1987, World Bank 1990, table 1.3.

The data can be used to investigate two common hypotheses about the fortunes of particular socioeconomic classes. The first is the relative impoverishment of landless agricultural laborers, allegedly caused by the switch from knives to sickles for harvesting, and the increased power of large farmers to use contract labor.[4] The second hypothesis is that the chief beneficiaries of agricultural growth have been the larger farmers, who were allegedly in a better position to intensify cultivation. Both hypotheses are at variance with the results of these village surveys. Relative to the mean, in households whose major source of income was farm labor, income increased by 0.9 percent a year. Conversely, the income of large farmers declined relative to the mean by 0.6 percent a year. These results by socioeconomic class are consistent both qualitatively and quantitatively with the household data on the distribution of expenditure considered above. They suggest that from the mid-1970s the rural poor were benefiting from both rapid overall growth and redistribution in their favor.

To summarize, during the 1960s inequality increased if measured by income but decreased if measured by expenditure. Thereafter, it was significantly and fairly continuously reduced. The increase in the share of the poorest 40 percent raised their living standards by 1 percent per year relative to the mean over 14 years. The top quintile lost more than the bottom 40 percent gained, losing relative to the mean at 0.7 percent a year.

Again these national survey data are at odds with the impressions of the group of researchers cited above. Two counterclaims are made. First, as with the urban results, the researchers question the deflator: Dapice (1980) claims that prices for the goods consumed by the poor rose substantially more than for other groups. Second, the researchers argue that the evidence from village labor market studies shows that inequalities have widened and that the poorest groups have suffered from economic change as their traditional employment opportunities have been eroded.

There is considerable truth to the claim that relative prices moved against the rural poor. Recall that within urban areas food prices rose relative to nonfood prices during the 1970s. Furthermore, prices in rural Java rose considerably more rapidly than in urban areas, not only in the 1970s but until 1984. During 1970–84, rural prices rose by 28.9 percent relative to the urban price index we have adopted as our deflator. Thus it may indeed be the case that although the poor increased their share of expenditure, their living standards failed to rise relative to other groups. However, this is not the principal thrust of the village-based studies.

The village-level studies tend to focus on processes rather than time series data on income, expenditure, or wages. They tend to argue that because the labor market is rationed, wages are not a guide to opportunities, which have deteriorated for the really poor. Not all the village studies point in this direction. Keyfitz's (1985) study was entirely consistent with the national accounts data on rising mean living standards and with the household data implying a redistribution toward the poor. The former suggest a doubling in mean private consumption from 1953 to 1985, and the latter imply that the rural poor gained around 15 percent relative to the mean during 1969–84. If there had been no net distributional changes in earlier periods, this would imply an increase in living standards from 100 in 1953 to 231 in 1985 for the rural poor. Keyfitz infers from his village revisit an increase to around 250.

GDP Growth

National income accounting for Indonesia goes back to the estimates for the years 1921 to 1939 prepared by Polak (1942). In 1954 Neumark, a U.N. adviser, published estimates for 1951 and 1952. These implied that per capita income (in 1938 prices) had fallen from Rp 39.0 in 1938 to Rp 33.5 in 1951 and Rp 34.4 in 1952 (Neumark 1954, p. 350). Unlike Polak, Neumark had no reliable primary data on which to base his estimates. In the *Yearbook of National Accounts Statistics* (United Nations 1960, p. 114) a series appears for 1953–59 that is described as "calculated by using rough estimations and extrapolations" based on the Neumark estimates. These extrapolations should not be trusted, since Neumark used unpublished information and did not leave his worksheets behind or the statistical material he had collected himself. In his report he describes procedures that sometimes simply amount to guesswork (for example, without further explanation, profits in industry are taken to amount to 10 percent of the value of gross output) or that are wrong.[5]

A program of data collection was started in 1962 with U.N. help. Agricultural and industrial censuses were held in 1963, but the program faltered when the U.N. team left after Indonesia's break with the United Nations. Although the BPS released estimates for 1958–62 and for 1960–64, these were based on "exceedingly crude guesswork," since of the industrial census only 1 percent was processed, only part of the agricultural census became available, and only one national sample survey was conducted. Even as late as 1970 it could be written that:

> [It] is still very much easier in Indonesia to find out what is happening in the fields of policy, finance and trade than in real economic activity, production and capital formation. Output estimates for rice and other staple foodstuffs and even for estate and smallholder export products are still very poor. Estimates of the 1969 rice harvest vary within a wide margin. Volume indices for export commodities during 1969 published by the Central Statistical Office are based on incomplete data (without any indication to the reader that this is so). While oil and mining output data are considered fairly complete and reliable, there is no index of industrial

production or even reasonably up-to-date or comprehensive information on the output of individual manufacturing industries. Nothing quantitative is known about the building and construction sector in which output and employment appear to have expanded very considerably in the past year. The whole service sector, including shipping and other transport, distribution, etc. is an almost complete statistical void. (Arndt 1970, pp. 26–27)

In 1970 the BPS published national accounts series starting in 1960. Although these are not without problems either, they represent a great improvement (Arndt and Ross 1970).

Table 16.12 shows growth in sectoral value added in five periods from 1953 to 1988. GDP grew at slightly more than 3 percent a year from 1953 to 1959; GDP per capita grew until 1957 and then stagnated. This trend continued from 1960 to 1966, when GDP grew at only 2.1 percent a year. With two exceptions (electricity and water supply; public administration and defense), all sectors of the economy showed little growth. The table illustrates the dramatic turnaround in the New Order period, with growth rates of 6 percent (1966–68), 8.2 percent (1968–73), 7 percent (1973–79), and 6 percent (1979–84).

Table 16.12 Average Annual GDP Growth by Sector, 1953–84
(percent)

Sector	1953–59	1960–66	1966–68	1968–73	1973–79	1979–84
Agriculture	3.0	1.9	4.0	4.1	3.1	4.6
Mining	5.3	1.2	21.7	17.6	3.9	–0.9
Manufacturing	1.9	1.8	6.0	12.9	13.6	10.3
Construction	1.0	4.7	23.3	13.6	7.1	—
Public utilities	7.5	16.3	11.8	14.5	13.1	—
Transport and communication	3.9	0.8	2.3	8.9	13.9	7.9
Trade	2.4	10.5	10.7	7.0	6.1	—
Public administration and defense	—	5.5	8.9	6.5	12.1	9.2
Other services	—	1.8	3.8	8.9	8.3	6.2
Total	3.2	2.1	6.0	8.2	7.0	6.0

— Not available.

Note: The growth rates for the 1953–59 period are for net domestic product. Constant prices are those of 1955 for 1953–59, of 1960 for 1960–70, of 1973 for 1971–82, and of 1983 for 1983–84. The series are spliced in 1971 and 1983 so that, for example, growth during 1968–73 is measured in terms of 1960 prices for 1968–71 and in terms of 1973 prices for 1971–73. For 1956–59 no breakdown of services is available.

Source: For 1953–59, United Nations 1960. For later periods, Booth 1992, table 1.1.

Table 16.13 Composition of GDP *at Factor Cost, Selected Years, 1953–88*
(percent)

Sector	1953	1960	1966	1968	1973	1979	1984	1988
Agriculture	56.9	53.9	53.4	51.4	40.1	32.0	24.0	24.1
Mining	2.3	3.7	3.5	4.6	12.3	10.3	18.7	11.6
Manufacturing	8.5	8.3	8.2	8.2	9.6	13.7	12.3	18.5
Construction	2.0	1.9	1.9	3.9	5.5	5.8	—	5.0
Public utilities	0.3	0.4	0.5	0.5	0.7	0.8	—	0.6
Transport and communication	2.3	3.7	3.4	3.2	3.8	5.5	5.5	5.8
Trade	14.3	14.6	15.9	16.6	16.5	15.5	—	17.3
Public administration and defense	4.5	5.5	5.8	6.0	7.9	7.8	—	6.8
Other services	9.2	9.1	8.7	7.3	7.8	9.5	—	10.3

— Not available.
Note: Factor cost calculated in 1975 prices for 1953; in 1960 prices for 1960, 1966, and 1980; in 1973 prices for 1973 and 1979; in 1983 prices for 1984; in 1988 prices for 1988.
Source: For 1953, United Nations 1960. For later years, Booth 1992, table 1.1.

Four points of sectoral detail may be noted: agricultural growth was respectable for each of the post-1966 periods shown; there were large volume increases in mining (the oil sector) before the first oil boom; after 1968 the industrial (manufacturing) sector grew at more than 10 percent per year; and, finally, except during the first oil boom, the public sector did not grow appreciably compared with the rest of the economy.

Sectoral change is shown in table 16.13. The initial situation was one in which agriculture accounted for 57 percent of GDP and manufacturing for less than 9 percent. In the 1970s and 1980s the share of agriculture declined and that of mining increased, but otherwise the only substantial change occurred late in the period: industry grew to more than 18 percent of GDP. The public sector, which, as we just saw, grew rapidly during the first oil cycle, still accounted for less than 7 percent of GDP in 1988.

There is no prima facie evidence of Dutch disease. Agriculture continued to grow right through the oil boom, unlike in Nigeria. Manufacturing grew extremely rapidly before, during, and after the oil boom. If services are considered as nontradable, then during the oil boom nontradables were not growing notably more rapidly than tradables.

Data on the level and the efficiency of investment are shown in tables 16.14 and 16.15. The rate of investment was already low in 1950 and fell to a dismal 4.5 percent in 1966 (a year in which foreign savings, as measured by the difference between imports and exports, amounted to 10.7 percent of GDP, so that domestic savings were negative). Only during

Table 16.14 Expenditure on GDP at Market Prices, Selected Years, 1951–84
(percentage shares, current prices)

Expenditure	1951	1960	1966	1968	1973	1979	1984
Private consumption	78.1	79.8	96.0	88.8	71.1	60.9	59.8
Public consumption	11.8	11.6	8.8	7.2	10.6	11.7	10.4
Investment	8.6	7.9	4.5	8.9	17.9	20.9	26.3
Exports	13.3	12.8	11.4	20.1	30.1	27.2	—
Imports	11.5	12.6	22.1	16.4	19.7	23.5	23.7

— Not available.

Source: For 1951, Muljatno 1960. For 1963 and 1967, authors' computations from published frequency distributions over class intervals for Java and Madura only. For 1964 and 1967, Ministry of Finance, Bureau of Statistics (BPS), *Statistical Pocket Book of Indonesia, 1980,* table IX.7. For 1976–84, Ministry of Finance, Bureau of Statistics (BPS),*Statistical Abstract 1985*, table 10.1.

the oil cycles were substantial savings rates realized. The crude ICOR calculation of table 16.15 reveals that the periods 1966–73 and 1973–79 had atypically low ICORs. The high return to investment in these periods reflected rehabilitation.

To conclude, the New Order government turned around a previously slow-growing economy without a dramatically large investment effort like that made in Nigeria. Growth, already rapid prior to the oil boom, was sustained during the boom and broadly based across agriculture and manufacturing. Most remarkably, manufacturing growth was sustained after the boom, whereas in Nigeria manufacturing output collapsed by around 40 percent.

Table 16.15 Investment and Growth, 1960–84
(billions of rupiah, 1960 prices)

Item	1960–66	1966–73	1973–79	1979–84
Total investment	216.5	412.7	967.3	1,497.1
Increase in GDP				
(factor cost)	51.7	296.1	504.9	374.4
Ratio	4.2	1.4	1.9	4.0

Note: A one-year lag is assumed (for example, for the period 1966–73, the difference between GDP in 1974 and in 1963 is related to investment in the years 1966, . . , 1972).

Source: Booth 1992, table 1.1.

17 *Factor and Product Markets*

In this chapter we consider the labor market, formal financial markets, the markets for land and rural credit, product markets, and food policy. Because of its importance in explaining growth and distribution outcomes, we devote the most space to the labor market.

The Labor Market

The purpose of this section is to identify, first, whether the extent of allocative efficiency in the labor market changed from 1950 to 1986, thus affecting growth, and, second, whether at times particular groups acquired rents, thus influencing income distribution. We suggest that there has been a long-term trend toward reduced labor market segmentation and greater allocative efficiency. Rents changed substantially over the period, but from the early 1970s they have been negligible. The public sector appears neither to have developed a wage premium nor to have expanded rapidly relative to the economy. The pattern of rents falls sharply into three phases, which we consider in turn.

Impotent Institutions: 1950–60

During the 1950s the labor market was highly politicized. There were some 1,500 unions with 2 million members—a quarter of the wage labor force—and membership was on the rise. These unions were organized into no less than 12 federations, of which the important groups were the communists, nationalists, and Muslims (in that order). The unions played a large part in the independence and nationalist movements, and they were well integrated into the political parties; their leaders were often politicians. Strikes were frequent, and in some cases unions seized plantations from the Dutch.

The other major actor of the 1950s was the government. Because of its intimate connection with the labor movement and because the employers were predominantly foreign, the government was prolabor. Although there were no minimum wage laws, the rate paid by the government to its own unskilled workers tended to set wages more widely. There was considerable regulation of employment. Despite the prolabor stance, strikes were prohibited in key industries and an elaborate system of arbitration was institutionalized, both responses to the exercise of union power. The government was a substantial employer, but less so than in most developing countries: as of 1953 only some 5 percent of the work force was in government employment.

With these powerful institutions (government and unions) being pro–wage labor, we might expect to observe growing rents for this group through rising real wages and rapidly expanding public employment. Neither of these phenomena appear to have occurred. Whereas this can be established with reasonable confidence, the data base on both employment and income differentials is fragmentary for the 1950–60 period, so some issues must remain open. In particular, it is possible that wage earners in public and large private enterprises were receiving rents at the start of the period (though these diminished rather than grew). One symptom of public sector rents, at least for some workers, was that earnings were quite powerfully related to needs rather than to function. There were substantial allowances for wives and children, plus payments in kind in subsidized rice. This pay structure perhaps reflected a preference for equity, itself part of a deeper preference for "balance," which has been a fundamental aspect of Indonesian culture.

In the absence of data on wages and incomes, the best available diagnostic of both rents and allocative efficiency is the rate and composition of unemployment. The earliest data on this are from the Labor Force Survey of 1958, which covered Java and Madura (which include two-thirds of the Indonesian population) and probably provides a reasonable picture of the labor market during the period.

Unemployment was found to be almost entirely an urban phenomenon, with the male urban unemployment rate at 8.0 percent (table 17.1).[1] Another 1958 estimate—for the city of Medan, Sumatra—put male unemployment at 10.7 percent (Blake 1962, table II). A national survey of 1961 supported these figures, finding 7.2 percent for urban Java and a higher rate for urban areas of the outer islands. Such a rate, though higher than in later periods, was not so high as to suggest a substantial wage premium. Since the composition of the unemployed was skewed toward older workers, some of the unemployment may have been accounted for by retrenchments following economic disruption. This hypothesis of only modest rents in favor of urban wage earners is indirectly

Table 17.1 Male Unemployment Rate, Selected Years, 1958–82
(percent)

Year	Urban		All	
	Java	Indonesia	Java	Indonesia
1958	8.0[a]	—	1.0[a]	—
1961	7.2[b]	7.4[b]	5.0[b]	4.8[b]
1971	5.2[b]	5.0[b]	2.5[b]	2.4[b]
1973	3.8[c]	—	—	—
1976	6.7[b]	6.4[b]	2.4[b]	2.7[b]
1978	—	7.0[d]	—	—
1980	3.0[e]	2.9[e]	1.6[e]	1.5[e]
1982	—	5.6[f]	3.4[g]	3.0[g]

— Not available.
a. 1958 Labor Force Survey.
b. Leiserson and others 1980.
c. Unpublished 1982 household survey data, cited in Manning and Mazumdar 1985, table A.X.
d. Sakernas Survey, Government of Indonesia.
e. 1980 population census.
f. Migrants only; source, Aklilu and Harris 1980.
g. Male and female.

supported by a wage survey of Jakarta in 1953 that found wide differentials between skilled and unskilled wage earners.[2] Such differentials would have been unlikely had the rate for the unskilled wage earners been pushed up well above its supply price, since a normal response by firms is to reduce differentials (Collier and Lal 1986).

Outside the urban economy the principal group of wage earners potentially in receipt of rents was the unionized plantation workers. By the late 1950s the plantations were largely government owned. Despite this conjunction of union power and a prounion government employer, no rents were generated. In wage rate determination, union power appears to have been slack, for wage rates were above those set in collective agreements. Also, a conclusive symptom of the absence of rents was that there was a labor shortage on the estates outside Java (Blake 1962).

Whether or not wage earners had rents at the start of the 1950s, their relative position was clearly eroded during the 1950s. Despite the increasing industrial power of unions relative to management and despite the prolabor stance of the government, real wages declined (table 16.2). This was the more remarkable because wages had already fallen by around one-third during the 1940s (Papanek 1980, p. 84). Between 1950 and 1960 the plantation wage halved relative to mean consumption (table 16.1).[3]

On the other dimension of labor market rents, overstaffing, rents were probably increasing but only modestly. In the private sector, the unions and government were able to force plantations and some industrial firms to add new people to the payroll. However, in the public sector there is little to suggest a similar trend. There are three indicators of trends in public employment: the government wage bill annually from 1953, snapshots of public service employment in 1930 and 1961, and snapshots of government employment in 1953 and 1958. Between 1953 and 1960 the government wage bill rose in real terms by only around 1 percent a year. Since real wages probably declined, with an acceleration starting in the late 1950s, there was probably some expansion in public employment, but not a dramatic one. This corresponds with the trend that can be derived from labor force snapshots in 1930 and 1961; between these dates public service employment expanded at 0.7 percent a year, from 2.7 million workers to 3.4 million. Similarly, snapshots of government employment in 1953 and 1958 show an annual growth rate of 3.3 percent.

Hyperinflation and Eroding Rents: 1960–68

During the hyperinflation period of the early 1960s there was a severe decline in real wages, which was reversed in the late 1960s. Despite the supposedly powerful prolabor institutions, wages collapsed both absolutely and relative to other groups.[4] There seem to be four explanations for this. First, since inflation was rapidly accelerating (table 17.2), there might well have been systematic downward errors in the inflation expectations of both employees and employers, so that contracts were inadvertently low in real terms. Papanek (1980, p. 100) regressed plantation wages on current and lagged inflation. He found that there was only a 0.71 adjustment to current inflation, so in periods when inflation accelerated, real wages generally declined.

A second reason for the wage collapse was that the government as the major employer had a declining capacity to pay because of its progres-

Table 17.2 Inflation Rate, 1958–70

Year	Rate (percent)	Year	Rate (percent)
1958/59	24	1964/65	305
1959/60	31	1965/66	1,188
1960/61	33	1966/67	191
1961/62	172	1968/69	123
1962/63	121	1969/70	17
1963/64	109		

Source: Calculated from table 16.1.

sive loss of revenue relative to GDP. Between 1960 and 1965 government recurrent expenditure deflated by the CPI, which is our nearest proxy for the government real wage bill in this period, declined by 56 percent. Civil servants lost even relative to other wage earners. Third, the plantations suffered a loss of income because of the decline in the terms of trade and the increased taxation of exports resulting from exchange rate policy. Fourth, manufacturing firms were dependent on imported inputs, the availability of which declined from the late 1950s, causing excess capacity. Thus by the mid-1960s real wages had fallen relative to their level in the 1930s in two periods: during wartime destruction and hyperinflation.

The political changes of the mid-1960s had an impact on the institutions of the labor market. The very proximity of the unions to political parties, particularly to the communists, meant that they became suspect organizations, and many were banned. Strikes became illegal and when union organization was permitted, it was at the enterprise level rather than the industry level. Furthermore, the new regime was more favorably disposed toward foreign employers. Thus the institutional changes implied a further reduction in the power of organized labor. However, offsetting this, between 1965 and 1968 there were changes in all four of the factors that accounted for the previous decline in real wages. Inflation swiftly decelerated, government revenue rose absolutely and relative to GDP, prices for plantation crops improved, and imported inputs ceased to be rationed. The decline in real wages was swiftly reversed (table 16.2), suggesting that the direct consequences of labor market institutions were modest compared with changes in the macroeconomic environment.

Although the U-shaped trend in the wage earner–peasant differential is clear enough, the level of rents, as opposed to their trend, is hard to determine. One possibility is that by the mid-1960s wage earners received substantially less than peasants. A second possibility is that in the early 1950s they received substantially more. Third, they may have received somewhat less by the mid-1960s, having received somewhat more in the early 1950s. Unfortunately, there is little basis for deciding among these possibilities.

The other dimension of rents, overstaffing, is again hard to measure. During the economic collapse of the early 1960s the government and unions forced firms to maintain employment above that required by feasible production. This pressure culminated in Act 12 of 1964, under which private firms could not discharge employees without the prior consent of a government-appointed committee. This was clearly a response to employment contraction: the collapse in the private sector must have increased pressure for the expansion of public employment. However, between 1961 and 1971 the share of the labor force in public service employment increased only slightly (table 17.3). By contrast, the civil service (a more narrowly defined component of public services) may have grown quite rapidly: Brand (1968, p. 58) suggests an annual growth rate of 11 percent from 1963 to 1968, although the basis for this estimate is fragile. He also suggests considerable overstaffing by 1968.

Growth without Rents: 1968–86

During the 1970s the labor force grew markedly more rapidly than it had in the 1960s (2.8 percent as against 1.7 percent). This was a result of low fertility and high mortality during the 1940s with a consequent change in the dependency ratio, which rose from 80 in 1961 to 87 in 1971, falling back to 79 by 1980.[5] This should have slackened the labor market in the 1970s relative to the 1960s.

Throughout the period the government prevented the reemergence of powerful trade unions. The 1964 law on dismissals, although not repealed, was executed in such a way that permission for firms to dismiss labor was generally automatic and rapid. In the mid-1970s pressures developed within the Department of Manpower for wage regulation. In 1976 the department conducted a survey that purported to find that the vast majority of workers received less pay than required to meet their minimum physical needs. From 1977 onward a plethora of minimum wage regulations were issued, all being either locality or sector specific. Manning and Mazumdar (1985, p. 20) note, "The rationale for having regulations with different levels of coverage, or for the selection of particular regions and sectors for attention and the timing of revisions to existing minima, is not entirely clear. Sporadic revisions seem to be largely

Table 17.3 Labor Distribution by Sector, Selected Years, 1930–82 (percent)

Sector	1930	1958[a]	1961	1971	1976	1982
Agriculture and mining	68.8	70.4	73.6	66.2	62.0	55.3
Manufacturing, construction, and utilities	10.6	9.5	7.8	9.9	10.1	14.2
Trade and transport	7.7	12.4	8.9	13.5	17.3	28.1
Public services	12.9	7.8	9.7	10.4	10.6	12.3
Total	100.0	100.0	100.0	100.0	100.0	100.0
Labor force (millions)	20.9	—	34.8	44.1	51.0	59.6

— Not available.

a. Data are for Java only.

Source: Papanek 1980, table 1.2; *Statistical Yearbook, 1985,* tables 3.2.4 and 3.2.8; 1958 Labor Force Survey, table 9.

in response to occasional press or public attention to the issue in certain regions." Both the levels and the rates of change varied considerably.[6]

However, not only was the enforcement procedure weak but the rates appear to have been at or below market levels. One reason why enforcement was limited was that the promulgation process was confused: it was not clear whether the rates were advisory or mandatory, nor to which enterprises they applied. Manning and Mazumdar show that the Jakarta minimum was closely related to the actual wages paid at the lower end of the market. Since the male unemployment rate in Jakarta was only 3.7 percent (according to the 1980 population census, table 32.1), this suggests that the minimum wage was determined by actual wages. In other areas the official minimum was well below market rates. Thus we may conclude that despite the introduction of minimum wages, labor market regulation was limited in this period.

From the late 1960s the data sources are sufficiently improved for the level of wage earner rents to be estimated. There is solid evidence that such rents were negligible. Growth in both real wages and employment was rapid, although not especially so in the public sector. The period can thus be characterized as one of growth without rents in the labor market.

The first evidence we examine on wage earnings comes from a series of urban surveys conducted in 1968. Households headed by a government employee had an income 22 percent above the mean for all households, which at first view might suggest a premium in favor of the public sector. Furthermore, government employees earned 38 percent more than the average for all wage employees. However, using the Jakarta survey, we can show that this premium is fully accounted for by the different educational, age, and gender composition of government employment. If we disaggregate education into eight levels and suppose that government employees at each level received the mean wage for all employees with that level, then, because government employment was skewed toward the more educated, the average government employee would have earned 33 percent more than the average employee. Government employees also tended to be older: only 12 percent were below the age of 25, versus 16 percent in the labor force as a whole. Applying age-specific urban wage rates for 1968 (Sundrum 1979, table 8), this accounts for a further 1 percent of the premium. Finally, males tended to earn more than females and 86 percent of government employees were males, compared with only 81 percent among all employees. Although it is not possible to quantify this last effect on the mean wage of government employees, it is clear that the 38 percent apparent wage premium is fully accounted for. As of 1968 there was no premium for government employees over other urban wage earners.[7]

This finding fits conveniently with our second source of evidence, which is from a survey of urban migrants in Jakarta conducted in 1973

(Aklilu and Harris 1980). Although this survey failed to distinguish government from other wage employment, it can be used to measure whether there was a premium for wage earners as a group. The results of the survey provide powerful evidence that in 1973 there was no significant labor market segmentation. As the survey authors note, "It is doubtful whether the distinction between formal and informal sectors serves any purpose in the Indonesian context. Systematic institutional differentiation between the sectors as a result of legislation, organized union activity, and labor practices of government and parastatal organizations has not been far reaching, as is the case in many countries, particularly in Africa" (p. 134). The overall unemployment rate among those rural migrants to urban areas who had migrated during the preceding five years was very low at only 3.8 percent: "Rural-urban migrants manage to find some sort of urban employment rather quickly" (p. 137).

Furthermore, within urban areas migrants' earnings, though sensitive to workers' personal characteristics such as education, were not sensitive to the type of employer or employment. For males, earnings in small-scale self-employment such as peddling were not significantly different from wage employment outside the large private firm and government sectors. Earnings in the latter two sectors were only around 10 percent higher than in self-employment. Finally, the inclusion of 13 dummy variables for different cities of Java revealed negligible spatial earning differentials.

This evidence is important in establishing two key results: there was only a very small premium for large-scale or government employment over other urban work, and there was no significant premium of urban over rural work, controlling for personal characteristics. The first result is established directly by the small size of the regression coefficient on this type of work. The second follows from the conjunction of the first and the observation of negligible unemployment. Were there a significant urban income premium, rural migrants would enter the urban labor market and either search for a job while unemployed or crowd into the free-entry self-employment activities, depressing earnings in those activities to the level of the rural supply price and opening up an intraurban differential.

Further evidence exists for the proposition that rents were negligible. Leiserson (1979, p. 53), analyzing data for 1974/75, found "no evidence of a substantial gap between urban and rural wage levels for similar occupational categories. The absence of such a gap is consistent with a high degree of mobility, seasonal and otherwise, between rural and urban areas and the relative unimportance of institutional influences." Similarly, within the urban labor market Leiserson found that government employees were not paid more than those in large firms (as of 1977), and that daily wage rates in the informal sector were close to the levels of unskilled earnings observed in large enterprises. Manning (1979), using manufacturing wage data for the period 1974–76, found rural-urban location to be insignificant in his wage regressions. However, he did find that foreign and capital-intensive firms paid considerably more than other firms.

Lluch and Mazumdar (1985), who make much of the insignificance of location, agree that because of circular migration the rural-urban gap is negligible. They do, however, claim that there is segmentation within both the urban and rural labor markets. In the urban market they identify the restricted-entry elite sector as being composed of large, private foreign firms. The evidence on this appears to be mixed; however, even if wages were higher in this sector (which was small), this was probably not the result of institutional pressures by unions or the government on the parties to the contract.

By the late 1970s some modest pay premium had emerged for unskilled workers in the public sector, matching that in large firms. (At the higher levels the public sector paid far less than the private sector.) Between 1969 and 1975 the real wage of the bottom grade of civil servant increased by 23 percent a year, though much of this was belated recovery from the previous collapse (Booth and Glassburner 1975, p. 19). By 1975, Booth and Glassburner estimate, such a civil servant would have had an income equivalent to that of a rice farmer with half a hectare (which, as the 1973 agricultural census shows, was about the median holding in Indonesia).

In 1976/77 there was a large pay award to civil servants, skewed toward the lower-paid workers, and real wages for the lowest grade nearly doubled. Household surveys for Jakarta reveal that although households headed by government employees had an income only 18 percent above mean household income in 1968, by 1978 this had widened to 34 percent. Recall that for 1968 we have already established that there was no premium for government workers, provided allowance is made for their better education. Although the increase in relative earnings may reflect a pure compositional effect, it is at least suggestive of a modest premium. Since the 1977 award, however, the wage premium has been reduced; real civil service salaries rose at an annual rate of 2.3 percent (to 1984) against a growth rate of mean private consumption of 5.3 percent (derived from table 16.1).

A snapshot of wage differentials in 1980 is provided by Manning and Mazumdar (1985, table 5). Normalized on the hourly male hoeing wage in rice cultivation in Java other than in Jakarta, the rate in light manufacturing was 118, in harvesting work on the estates 134, and in rural construction work 152. Such differentials, though not small, probably reflect differences in the effort required, the discipline imposed, and the transport costs incurred. It is hard to imagine an institutional explanation for such a hierarchy. On the outer islands nominal wage rates were typically 40 to 80 percent higher. However, a substantial part of this is probably explained by cost of living differences rather than spatial segmentation.

By the time of the Aklilu and Harris survey of 1973 there were evidently no significant rents in the formal sector, if indeed such a sector could be identified. If it is true that rents were negligible in 1973, then there were definitely negative rents during the period of hyperinflation. At their trough in 1965, real wages were around half their level in 1973, whereas mean per capita consumption was 87 percent of its 1973 level.[8] Thus unskilled wage earners must have been earning substantially less than peasants in 1965 and were thus "involuntarily employed" in the sense of temporarily working for wages that ex ante would not have been acceptable on a permanent basis.

Comparing 1973 with 1955, mean per capita consumption (our proxy for peasant living standards) was almost the same (table 16.1). Thus, if real wages were higher in 1955 than in 1973, this would be evidence for positive rents in that period. Unfortunately, the wage series are ambiguous: the plantation series tend to show wages higher in 1955, and the industry series tend to show them lower. Any inference from such a confused picture must be highly tentative, but perhaps the most plausible interpretation is that any rents were modest.

The other dimension of labor market rents, overstaffing, was probably reduced compared with the 1960s. In the private sector, unions were weakened, governments ceased to be antiemployer, and fewer firms wished to contract employment, so the overstaffing that had been forced on firms during the hyperinflation phase was presumably reversed. In 1968 the government temporarily halted civil service recruitment, and in the following decade employment grew slowly. Between 1969 and 1978 it increased at an annual average rate of only 1.3 percent. Growth accelerated to 7.5 percent a year from 1978 to 1984. Public sector employment more widely defined grew more rapidly than in any previous period. Whereas in 1961–71 public service employment increased at an annual rate of 3.1 percent, in 1971–82 it increased at 4.3 percent. However, this was fully accounted for by the faster growth of GDP . As a share of GDP the civil service salary bill was trendless. We should note that this disagrees radically with a World Bank analysis that suggests large increases in both employment and real wages for the civil service in 1969–84 (World Bank 1985b, appendix 1, tables 14 and 16). However, the product of the wage and employment growth claimed by the Bank implies a 24-fold increase in the real wage bill over this period against a 4-fold increase according to budget data. The latter appears more reliable, especially since the Bank figures are described as "staff estimates."

Perhaps because it was evident that there was no significant rural-urban or intraurban segmentation, during the 1970s academic attention turned to the rural labor market. Lluch and Mazumdar (1985) characterized this market as segmented, with wage labor for rice cultivation at the top of the hierarchy and rents preserved by entry barriers in the form of social class. In emphasizing segmentation within the agricultural labor market, Lluch and Mazumdar relied upon analyses developed by Collier and others (1982), White (1976), and Hart (1986). A theme of their work is that changes in rice harvesting technology together with the breakdown of rural community obligations have undermined the access of the rural poor to harvest time employment. The change from small knives to sickles enormously increased the productivity of harvest labor.

Also, during the 1970s the tradition that anyone could work on the harvest and claim a share of the crop appears to have become less common. Landlords started to exclude would-be workers, selling the crop in advance to contractors who used teams of nonlocal hired labor. In turn, it is argued, this closure of opportunities for the poor depressed earnings in those occupations still open to them. Collier and others argued that although technically the switch from knife to sickle became possible as a result of the new varieties (which were short stalked), this change, together with the shift to contractors, was made possible only by the decline in the bargaining position of the landless because of population pressure and the revolution of 1965.

Hayami and Hafid (1979) reexamined the Collier hypothesis through a survey of 48 Javanese villages. They found that the switch to contractor harvesting had in all cases preceded the adoption of the sickle, which was used equally by contractor and communal harvesting. As a result, the switch to contract labor did not significantly reduce total labor input. They did find that the switch to contractors reduced the total number of people working on the harvest per hectare. When access was unrestricted, diseconomies of scale were encountered in the trampling of rice. However, presumably because of this, the communal system had seldom been open access. Restrictions were usually imposed even in the 1960s. The switch to contractors reduced the share of output going to harvest labor. In villages without contractors this share was 13.6 percent; in villages with contractors on those holdings still harvested communally, the share was 10 percent; and on those harvested by contractors it was only 8.2 percent. This erosion of share is certainly consistent with Collier's hypothesis of a decline in the bargaining power of labor. However, Hayami and Hafid suggest an alternative explanation: that the enormous increase in the use of fertilizer reduced the ratio of value added to price and so required a reduction in labor's share to generate a return on the extra inputs.

We are left with three technical changes—the introduction of high-yielding varieties, the switch to sickles, and the use of fertilizer, the first and the third of which are labor using whereas the second is labor saving. However, since the second enhances income, it generates a derived demand for labor in other activities. Much was made of this reduction in the demand for harvesting labor because during most of the 1970s the data on rural wages were so thin that they permitted several different interpretations, one of which was that wages were falling and that the poor were being impoverished. By the mid-1980s the evidence for greater rural equity (see chapter 16) made this position scarcely tenable.[9]

Rural wage rates clearly rose substantially during the New Order period, although time series remain inadequate. Tables 16.1 and 16.2 provide two such series—one for hoeing work by males on small farms at the seasonal peak; the other for plantations. The hoeing wage rose by around 50 percent between 1968 and 1983. The plantation wage, after being trendless during most of the 1970s, rose by around 60 percent between 1978 and 1983. Whether or not access to wage labor on rice was rationed, it seems unlikely that access became more difficult. A striking feature of employment in rural Java is that its structure has altered so little. The Labor Force Survey of 1958 and the population census of 1980 provide comparable snapshots of male employment. As shown in table 17.4, the proportion of wage labor remained constant at about 28 percent.[10] It does not appear that this was the result of compensating growth in the nonagricultural sector. The occupational structure of the rural male labor force was similar in the two snapshots; the proportion whose occupation was either farmer or agricultural worker was 71 percent in 1958 and 64 percent in 1980.

A final refutation of the thesis that the rural poor were being marginalized comes from surveys of six villages in West Java for 1976 and 1983 (Rural Labor Market Surveys and Agro-Economic Survey for Bogor). The same households were covered in the two surveys, and the villages are regarded as typical. Total agricultural employment in hours worked actually increased by nearly 20 percent. There was a sharp reduction in hours worked in household industry, the activity with the lowest return and the one that would have expanded if the poor were being marginalized. Finally, landless farm laborers increased their incomes not only absolutely but relative to both the average household and to large farmers.

In the decade after the mid-1970s the Javanese labor market became spatially more integrated with the growth of very cheap rural transport by means of minibuses, which increased the feasibility of commuting. Manning and Mazumdar (1985, p. 15) suggest that "the dichotomy between better paid permanent employees in the private sector consisting of permanent rural-urban migrants and temporary migrants in the

Table 17.4 Characteristics of the Javanese Rural Male Labor Force, 1958 and 1980

(percent)

Characteristic	1958	1980
Employment category[a]		
Employer	13.0	1.7
Self-employed	51.2	56.4
Wage employee	28.8	28.2
Family worker	7.1	13.7
Total	100.0	100.0
Professional and administrative	1.6	2.4
Clerical	1.0	2.8
Sales	9.4	8.9
Agricultural	71.3	63.6
Services	4.3	2.3
Other	12.4	20.0
Total	100.0	100.0

a. The definition governing the split between "employer" and "self-employed" is not the same in the two surveys.

Source: 1958 Labor Force Survey, tables IXA and XIIIA; 1980 population census, tables 36.4 and 38.

casual urban labor market is probably much less marked than in the early and mid-1970s." Interprovincial mobility has also increased. Booth and Sundrum (1981) show that for rural unskilled workers on local public works, the coefficient of variation of provincial wage rates declined from 44 to 27 percent between 1971/72 and 1976/77. Since then the transmigration program has expanded to make a significant contribution. During the period 1980–85, when the program was at its peak, some 6 percent of the increment to the rural Javanese labor force was relocated outside Java. Manning and Mazumdar (1985, p. 31) conclude that "the overall impact of transmigration on the geographic distribution of large unskilled labor supply has been substantial since the mid-1970s."

The labor market has also probably become temporally more integrated. The 1958 Labor Force Survey found a large variation in hours of work in rural areas between the peak and slack seasons (6.2 hours versus 3.2 hours per day). The introduction of a more rapidly maturing variety of rice permitted both an extra crop and the use of the sickle during harvest, the former raising off-peak demand for labor and the latter lowering peak demand. Spatial integration has also increased temporal integration as the rural-urban commuting flow varies through the year.

In both urban and rural areas unemployment was lower in the 1970s and early 1980s than it had been at the time of the earlier snapshots in 1958 and 1961. Compared with the earliest snapshot in 1958, by 1980 the composition of unemployment had skewed markedly toward the young; the age group 15–24 constituted 64 percent of the total compared with only 37 percent in 1958 (table 17.5). However, this did not indicate a growing problem of youth unemployment: the unemployment rate for this age group fell from 15 to 8 percent. Rather, it suggests that the labor market was functioning so efficiently in 1980 that, other than the initial entry process, unemployment was negligible.

Conclusion

We have suggested that the labor market went through three phases. In the first, 1950–60, institutions favoring organized labor were ostensibly powerful, but this had no discernible impact on income differentials between wage earners and peasants. In the second phase, 1960–68, there was a temporary but massive erosion of the incomes of wage earners caused by a conjunction of macroeconomic events. Organized labor experienced negative rents precisely at a time when it was politically most powerful and recovered when it was politically weak. In the third phase, 1968–86, segmentation was negligible, the labor market became increasingly integrated, and real wages rose rapidly, with some tendency for wage premiums to emerge in the late 1970s in the public sector and large firms.

Thus, on the first dimension of labor market rents—wage premiums— the whole period was characterized by a U-shaped path in which the premium for organized formal sector labor was initially probably

Table 17.5 Unemployment by Age Group, 1958 and 1980
(percent)

Age group	Urban Java, 1958			Urban Indonesia, 1980		
	Distribution of labor force	*Composition of unemployment*	*Unemployment rate*	*Distribution of labor force*	*Composition of unemployment*	*Unemployment rate*
12–14	0.5	0.0	0.0	0.9	1.9	6.1
15–24	20.6	37.5	14.6	23.9	64.1	7.8
25–44	54.3	43.8	6.5	52.9	25.8	1.4
45+	24.6	18.8	5.9	22.3	8.2	1.2
All	100.0	100.0	8.0	100.0	100.0	2.9

Source: 1958 Labor Force Survey (Java); 1980 population census, table 31.1 (Indonesia).

modest, then became heavily negative, then hovered at zero for around a decade, and finally reemerged to a modest extent. On the second dimension—overstaffing—apart from a brief phase in the private sector during the collapse of the economy in the early 1960s, there was for most of our period not much evidence that such rents were significant. Until the 1970s public sector employment grew only slowly, and in the remainder of the period the public payroll did not expand relative to GDP. However, by the late 1980s there appears to have been significant overstaffing in government departments (see the August 1988 survey in the *Bulletin of Indonesian Economic Studies*).

Financial Markets

Several aspects of financial markets in Indonesia are relatively undeveloped. Three factors in particular have militated against the development of fully integrated markets. First, there has never been a bond market.[11] Second, domestic credit has been highly controlled and segmented since independence, with allocations affecting both the sectoral availability of credit and the terms on which credit was available to a sector. Third, foreign direct investment has been subject to detailed controls. The first and third points taken together mean that even the removal of exchange controls early in the New Order period had limited integrating effect. Foreign currency deposits held in Indonesia paid markedly lower rates than domestic assets (Arndt and Suwidjana 1982). Foreign-denominated assets could play only a very limited integrating role.

Since the early 1960s there have been four principal phases in the regulation of the financial system. During the first phase, the period up to 1966, the banking system was reduced to a "mere secondary channel. . . . The state banks, even before their merger with Bank Indonesia [in 1965] were under the most direct central bank control. . . . The distribution of credit came under direct central bank control" (Arndt 1979, p. 107). "The distribution of credit came to be determined by more or less illegal market processes, which tended to channel most of it to speculative trading, and by more or less arbitrary exercise of official authority and political or personal influence" (Arndt 1971, p. 375). In the last two years of the Sukarno regime, as inflation accelerated and the banks found it increasingly difficult to attract and retain deposits, they became directly dependent on Central Bank finance.

The second phase of financial regulation ran from 1966 to 1974 and constituted a liberal episode. The first steps were necessarily drastic, involving a complete shutdown of overdrafts and new investment credits, followed by severely restrictive qualitative controls on bank credit and higher official interest rates of 6 to 9 percent per month. From 1967 to 1969 a systematic effort was made to create a banking system that could play an active role in development as the principal financial intermediary, subject only to indirect control by the Central Bank.

In 1968 the central banking bill reconstituted the Bank Indonesia as a pure central bank divested of commercial banking functions; the six state banks (subsequently eight) were given specialized but overlapping functions. Foreign banks were also encouraged to return to Indonesia.

The money supply continued to rise rapidly, but the rapid growth in the public's demand for real balances (particularly for time deposits, reflecting the high nominal rates being offered) made it possible to accommodate the expansion of the money supply with a remarkably rapid and steady decline in the inflation rate. During this period the banks were controlled primarily through a 30 percent minimum liquid asset ratio, supplemented by some degree of qualitative control through central bank refinancing facilities. This control was used, for example, to foster the rice intensification (Bimas) program.

The third phase ran from 1974 to 1983. The liberalized system came under strain during the 1972/1973 world commodity boom, given the convertibility of the rupiah. The following year the system was "overwhelmed by the avalanche of liquidity that followed the increase in the price of crude oil" (Arndt 1979, p. 110). The government's commitment to the balanced budget, which had been immensely helpful in the fight to control inflation, now became an obstacle, with domestic monetary effects similar to deficit financing.

The 30 percent reserve requirement was inadequate to prevent excessive expansion; in April 1974 the Central Bank abandoned the policy of indirect control and reverted to a system of direct control via credit ceilings. This policy was remarkably successful in keeping the inflationary effects of the oil boom under control, but it was achieved "at the price of almost complete subordination of the commercial banks to discretionary central bank control which deprived [them] of any incentive to compete with one another for business and limited their opportunities to exercise skills and initiative in the allocation of bank credit. It was a system inconsistent with the proclaimed objective of the authorities to develop a dynamic capital market for development" (Arndt 1979, p. 115).

In place of such a market solution, the government was active in developing a wide range of subsidized credit initiatives during this period. The Bimas scheme has already been noted; by 1980 it had more than 4.5 million loan accounts outstanding, averaging $50 each (Bolnick 1982). Although this was the largest program in number of customers, the schemes for concessional credit to indigenous small-scale enterprise begun in 1974 (KIK and KMKP) were the largest in amount loaned: Rp 831 billion in mid-1981, or nearly 13 percent of the total rupiah credit of the banking system, excluding direct lending by Bank Indonesia. These schemes had 600,000 accounts outstanding at that time, distributed over all sectors of the economy, with around one-third in agriculture and one-tenth in industry.

These and the many other concessional schemes introduced in the period had their share of problems, not least that of recovery (collection rates are difficult to establish but may have been as low as 50 percent on some categories of loans). The usual caveats also apply concerning allocation and subsidization of credit, though Bolnick (1982) makes a spirited defense of the schemes, principally on the ground that there are so many market imperfections—many government induced—that a market-clearing solution is unlikely to be adequate.

The fourth phase started in 1983 with an attempt to deregulate the banking system and end the period of financial repression. The reform involved a partial deregulation of interest rates, elimination of credit ceilings, reduction in the scope of Bank Indonesia subsidized credits to state-owned banks, as well as a catalog of piecemeal measures (Nasution 1986). There was a further bank reform in October 1988.

The principal objective of deregulation was to increase competition in the financial market and increase savings mobilization through the banking system. In many respects the response of the system was very positive: deposit rates were bid up and time deposits nearly doubled in the year following the reforms. However, the system had been heavily repressed for a decade, the capital base was weak, and neither the market nor the securities existed for open market operations. It is not surprising that deregulation was followed by a banking crisis in late 1984, primarily because of lack of liquidity and exacerbated by the ease of substituting into foreign currency while controls in the real economy were becoming more severe.

The Market in Land and Rural Credit

Indonesia is a prime example of interlinked rural markets. Geertz's (1963) characterization of these cannot be bettered as :

> a dense web of finely spun work rights and work responsibilities spread, like the reticulate veins of the hand, throughout the whole body of the village lands. A man will let out part of his one hectare to a tenant—or to two or three—while at the same time seeking tenancies on the lands of other men thus balancing his obligations to give work . . . against his own subsistence requirements. A man will rent or pawn his land to another for a money payment and then serve as a tenant on that land himself. . . . The structure of land ownership is thus only an indifferent guide to the social pattern of agricultural exploitation, the specific form of which emerges

only in the intricate institutional fretwork through which land and labor are actually brought together. (Cited in Sturgess amd Wijaya 1979, pp. 99–100)

A bewildering variety of contractual forms of ownership, sharecropping, and cash leasing exist. There are, for example, three categories of village landownership: land owned by the village and used to finance collective activities; land given to village officials, past and present, in lieu of salary or pensions; and owner-occupied land.[12] There are also three distinct forms of sharecropping, depending on the shares, which in turn depend on the relationship between the owner and the sharecroppers (Utami and Ihalauw 1973). Under one arrangement the tenant bears all inputs other than taxes and gets half the yield; in practice, this is restricted to brothers, father and son, or officials on village land, or to arrangements whereby the tenant pays a cash sum in advance. More commonly the tenant gets only one-third of the yield. An arrangement that is becoming even more common is one in which the tenant provides only labor and receives one-fourth of the yield.

There are also a variety of cash leasing contracts, in which some set of rights to land and its produce are traded for cash. Wijaya and Sturgess (1979) analyze four of these in the light of survey data and conclude that they offer a flexible credit system with distinctive risk-spreading characteristics. Some contracts function as substitutes for farm mortgages, some for non-real estate credit, and some for trade credit. The lender assumes entrepreneurial and price risks to varying degrees, but other lending risks are usually reduced. There is little information on the profitability of these types of lending. The apparently high costs to the borrower reflect a combination of factors: the lack of availability and high effective cost of formal sector credit, and the fact that the lender is bearing risk and assuming an entrepreneurial function.

Organized rural credit, a government priority for many years, is provided by a plethora of different agencies. Partadireja (1974) surveyed 11 Javanese villages in the early 1970s and found 20 formal credit facilities of nine distinct types, including banks, pawnshops, and cooperatives. He concluded "that the number of agencies is so large that one wonders about the cost of administering them, especially when one considers how small the loans to farmers usually are (p. 56)." Even so, a small fraction of rural credit was derived from these agencies. Even when credit generated by cash leasing is excluded, one study found that in the 1960s only 2.2 percent came from institutional sources, with the overwhelming bulk being provided in roughly equal shares by relatives, friends, and traders (Ronohadiwirjo 1969, p. 181, quoted by Partadireja 1974). This position had altered radically by the 1980s, as noted above.

Apart from the positive effort to supply rural credit, the other main activity of government in these interlinked markets was an attempt to outlaw a number of the existing contract arrangements. Several laws were enacted in 1960 that, if fully implemented, would have placed strict controls on share contracts (for example, restricting shares to 50 percent) and at some unspecified later date prohibited all leasing of agricultural land. The laws were enacted and partly implemented during the period of guided economy with the intention of freeing cultivators from the exploitation of landlords. The laws also stipulated maximum hectarage not only to ownership but also to land at the cultivator's disposal through pledging or lease. This was a response to the fact that large worked farms were typically built up using the land of peasants too poor to work it themselves.

The early implementation of land reform caused much bitterness. Following the abortive coup of late 1965, implementation was stopped and partly reversed; land reform was stigmatized as a product of the Communist Party. Although land redistribution did continue under the New Order, the issue ceased to be a live one, as did the attempts to outlaw devices to link rural markets. Through benign neglect, traditional contracts and the linking of rural markets continued. Many authors have stressed how difficult it would be for formal credit arrangements to substitute for the traditional sharing and leasing contracts, and expressed the hope that this neglect of the agrarian laws of 1960 would long continue.

Product Markets: Institutions and Interventions

Although it is our thesis that there was considerable continuity in government policy in product markets before and after Sukarno's fall, it is useful to consider these two periods separately.

The 1950–65 Period

After the abolition of the *cultuurstelsel* in 1870, the colonial government intervened rather little in product markets until the Great Depression. Import licenses were introduced in 1933 and export licenses in 1939. Foreign exchange control was introduced in 1940. During the next decade other controls were added, first by the Dutch, then by the Japanese, and finally by the government of the republic.

As noted in chapter 11, soon after independence, in March 1950, the Hatta cabinet initiated a far-reaching trade liberalization. An important element of this was the introduction of the foreign exchange certificate, the first of a long series of policy initiatives concerned with exporters' right to retain foreign exchange earnings. This effectively established a dual exchange rate system. Exporters received, in exchange for the foreign exchange they surrendered, both rupiah and certificates. The latter were negotiable; importers had to surrender certificates for the amount of value of their imports. Although this system in itself amounted to an export tax rather than liberalization, tradability of the certificates implied a relaxation of foreign exchange control.

In addition, the Hatta cabinet introduced a system of imports that was not subject to quotas. A large number of commodities were placed on the free list, in part as a deliberate attempt to undermine the dominant position of the Dutch trading houses. In 1951 the system was changed so that imports were completely free from quantitative restrictions (QRs): certificates could be used to import goods subject to quotas or even import bans. The system of certificates was equivalent to a $33^1/_3$ percent export tax. It produced enormous revenue during the Korean commodity boom but was removed in 1952 when the government became aware of its adverse effect on export volumes.

Already in 1950, trade policy was used to promote Indonesianization. Under the Benteng system (as discussed in chapter 11), licenses for certain categories of imports were reserved for native Indonesian businessmen in an attempt to shift import trade from the Dutch and the Chinese to indigenous entrepreneurs. In this it failed; the Benteng system became a source of corruption, and few of those holding licenses were actually involved in trading.

The 1950/51 liberalization was short lived. Import restrictions were tightened again at the end of 1951 when export receipts started to fall. The next year saw the creation of the Jajasans, the import monopolies, which, although private, were indirectly controlled by the government. The Jajasans marked the beginning of massive interventions. In 1954, for example, when reserves were falling desperately low, all textile imports were to be channeled through one Jajasan responsible for allocation to wholesalers. At the same time, traders' markups were fixed.

The period in which imports became increasingly rigidly controlled was also the one in which trade policy became politicized. The granting of import licenses became an important source of revenue for the PNI. In the first few years of independence surcharges were relatively unimportant, applied only to imports of luxuries. They became important in 1953 when 50 percent of imports came under surcharges (at a rate of $33^1/_3$ percent for 30 percent of imports and a rate of 100 percent for another 20 percent of imports).

Quantitative restrictions were introduced in 1954 at a time when reserves were falling dangerously low and when direct control over imports promised to be a convenient instrument for favoring Indonesian businessmen. Industries producing consumer goods were heavily protected by both quotas and tariffs. Firms producing "essential" commodities were favored in the allocation of foreign exchange and thus could operate at 60 percent of capacity, whereas for other firms capacity utilization in 1950–57 was as low as 20 percent. In the early 1950s import prepayment requirements, import surcharges, and import entitlement schemes (linked to export receipts via foreign exchange certificates) were introduced; in a bewildering succession of changes and amendments they dominated trade policy until the 1966 reform. Throughout this period the rupiah was overvalued. The wide gap between official and black market exchange rates made smuggling of rubber and copra attractive and contributed to the anti-Java revolts on the outer islands in 1957 and 1958.

For a short period (June 1957 to April 1958) Indonesia had what amounted to a floating rate system. Exporters received export certificates or BEs at the official rate ($1 = Rp 11.4) that they could sell to importers. In April 1958 the government intervened, pegging the BE at 332 percent of its face value.

From 1950 to 1957 several other attempts were made to liberalize. The most important one was the Sumitro reform of 1955. Sumitro abolished the QRs and reduced the room for bureaucratic discretion by introducing a joint import/foreign exchange license. However, this reform was short-lived: when rubber prices fell, import controls were tightened again, and when Sukarno introduced his concept of the guided economy, the temporary liberalization of the BE system ended.

When in 1957 Sumatra and Sulawesi refused to surrender foreign exchange, another short-lived liberalization occurred. Most quotas were abolished, and an export certificate system was introduced equivalent to a floating exchange rate. The system succeeded in raising official exports but failed in its objective of preventing the secessionist rebellions by buying off the export regions.

An elaborate system of bureaucratic foreign exchange allocation was then set up. Government enterprises could import enough to operate at full capacity, at least in theory; in practice, rationing applied to even this most favored group of applicants. After 1957 a very large fraction of imports (80 percent in 1959) was controlled by the state, largely through the Bhaktis, the big former Dutch trading companies that had been nationalized and converted into state trading corporations, and partly through the state import monopolies, the Jajasans.

The state trading corporations were given a monopoly over the imports of rice, textiles, and 11 other basic commodities. The number of private importers was reduced to 400.[13] Since the Benteng program was considered a failure, the economy was now to be based on state enterprises whose policies were controlled by bureaucratic supervisory boards. The military who controlled the state enterprises regarded them as useful vehicles for personal enrichment, selling at market prices and appropriating the difference from official prices. Price, trade, and exchange controls were widely evaded. When, for example, imports of raw cotton were so severely rationed that West Java mills could on average operate at only 11 percent of capacity, there was an active market in cotton quotas. Overinvoicing was used to accumulate assets abroad, apparently on such a large scale that this capital, "brought back into Indonesia after 1965, largely by the Chinese, provided much of the finance for investment in the early New Order period." Smuggling took place, with active participation of the military, on a large scale (Robison 1986, pp. 73, 78, 82, 84, 97).

The period until 1965 was marked by heavy reliance on QRs and price controls and by the growth of smuggling and black market activities. There were again two short liberalization episodes (March 1962–May 1963 and April 1964–December 1965), which, as before, involved the use of foreign exchange certificates. At the end of 1965 these certificates were trading at a rate almost 250 times the official exchange rate. Smuggling in this period was widespread. The huge difference between the official and the black market exchange rate was partly bridged by a curious system of legal underinvoicing: what exporters had to surrender was calculated on the basis of a check price that could be well below the price actually received.

Thus there was a series of short-lived liberalizations. In 1963 Sukarno decided to liberalize in a more substantial way. An American economic team had visited Indonesia, and the liberalization measures they proposed appeared to be the price Sukarno would have to pay for access to Western aid. The government announced the DEKON program—a structural adjustment program—before such programs were formally initiated by the international agencies. It involved the abolition of price controls, the intention to balance the budget within a year, and a simplification of the multiple exchange rate system, which led to very large price increases for basic consumer goods such as textiles. The program met with strong opposition (partly on ideological grounds, partly as a result of the price increases) and eventually became the victim of *Konfrontasi*, which removed any wish to please the Americans.

In the oil market the government intervened in two ways: it controlled prices of oil products, which remained constant throughout the 1950–65 period, and it restricted the foreign oil companies to their prewar concessions. This stop to exploration in new areas may have halved Indonesian oil output in the period. Exports fell as domestic demand increased. Price control led to a huge black market in petroleum products, with prices as high as 20 times the official price.

The Suharto Period

Shortly after coming to power the Suharto regime initiated a sweeping reform. Import license requirements were almost entirely removed, and at the same time price control and consumer subsidies were, with few exceptions, abolished. Gasoline prices were raised from Rp 4 to Rp 1,000 per liter.

Although the reform was sweeping it did not involve full-scale liberalization. Exchange rate policy, for example, remained complicated and highly regulated until 1970. In addition to the official exchange rate, there were distortions because of BE certificates and DP exchange—the foreign exchange that exporters earned in excess of an official check price. Like BE certificates, this DP exchange, the result of officially sanctioned underinvoicing, could be used to import, but under different rules.[14] Thus, the two implicit exchange rates differed not only from the official one but also from each other. Such effective exchange rates depended not only on the prices of BE certificates and of DP exchange but also on the percentage of the export proceeds that was converted into BE certificates and on the difference between the check price and the world price. Both changed continually, making effective exchange rates unstable.

All of this applies, of course, only to legal trade. However, large-scale smuggling took place in rubber and other exports. There is indirect evidence of this in the difference between the wholesale and the f.o.b. price of rubber. This difference was (until the 1966 reform) large and positive. This paradoxical result arises because legal trade may—through underinvoicing, misgrading, or other means—be a good channel for illegal trade and because the apparent loss on the legal side of the transaction may be offset by the profit on the illegal part. Only in April 1970 was the check-price/over-price system abolished and a single exchange rate ($1 = Rp 378) introduced.

When import controls were removed, capacity utilization in industry (especially textiles), already very low because of controls on imported intermediate inputs, fell even further. The government came under pressure to protect industry. It gave in with a combination of surcharges, prepayment requirements, and increases in the exchange rate used in customs duty valuations. Before long there was again a bewildering variety of effective rates of protection. However, the government did not go back on the abolition of the license and quota system.

Trade policies started to become less liberal early in the 1970s. Initially the concern was that imported inflation would mean a return to hyperinflation (in 1971 inflation was only 2 percent, but in 1972 more than 20 percent). Although the Suharto regime stuck to its liberalization of the exchange regime, industrial protection, which diminished in the initial wave of reforms, came back, particularly in the 1970s, when industrialists started to complain about the Dutch disease effects of the oil price increases.

Industrial policy in the Suharto period involved a complicated and changing mixture of interventions in product markets, consisting of both trade policy measures and investment controls. Initially, the import controls of the Sukarno regime were replaced by tariffs. The level of protection seems to have declined at the same time, leading to a fall in industrial capacity utilization in 1967 and 1968. However, direct controls quickly reappeared. In 1969, for example, imports of commercial vehicles were banned and competition in the imports of cars was restricted by designating firms as sole importers for particular types of cars. Textile production was encouraged by the introduction in 1973 of a preferential rate of exchange for cotton imports. The revival of protectionism after 1982 (some of which was later reversed) led to further restrictions on industrial imports, including a ban on the import of ships and quotas for assembled engineering products.

Direct controls were also applied to exports. In 1969 the export of low-quality rubber was banned to encourage the manufacturing of crumb rubber. In the aftermath of the 1978 devaluation, export quotas were used (for such products as coffee, pepper, and palm oil) in a curious attempt to offset the devaluation's effect on the relative price of tradables. In the 1980s the wood industry was protected through export bans. In 1978 Indonesia still accounted for half of the world's supply of tropical hardwood. Two years later exports of unsawn logs were restricted in an attempt to shift plywood production from Japan to Indonesia. When in 1982 plywood firms were operating at only 50 percent of capacity and log exports still amounted to 4 million cubic meters, log exports were completely banned, effective in 1983.

Investment controls were reintroduced in the mid-1970s. Initially the use of this instrument was linked to the reemergence of economic nationalism (see chapter 13). In a reversal of the liberal investment policy established in 1967 and 1968, some sectors were declared closed to foreign investment. Increasingly, however, investment bans were also used to keep out new Indonesian entrants to a sector. In 1976 a list of investment priorities was announced. Some sectors (such as rice milling on Java and the production of *kretek* cigarettes) were closed to all investment, whereas in other sectors (fertilizer and alcoholic beverages) domestic investment was possible but foreign investment was banned.

In the mid-1980s the system was based on a combination of trade policy and investment controls. Typically, an industrialist would first establish himself in a particular line of production and then appeal for tariff protection. If his product was labor intensive, protection was likely to be granted. Protection would attract new entrants, which would lead to a process of tariff escalation. In older industries the tariff often became prohibitive. The government (which considered the entry of new firms as wasteful when existing capacity was underutilized) supported protected firms in their attempts to limit competition by, for example, declaring industry closed to investment. Collusion was common, and where there were no QRs, the end result might be the same. In the aluminum sector, for example, there was a single producer of wide sheets who supplied firms that had agreed not to import (in return for the monopolist's withdrawal from the downstream industry), an agreement supported by the Department of Industry (in return for a promise by the monopolist not to raise the domestic price). The effect of this system was that protection increased with labor intensity and also (contrary to the infant-industry argument) with age. Again taking the example of the aluminum sector, the older (and least capital-intensive) parts of the industry (producing utensils, extrusions, and sheets) enjoyed nominal protection of 35 to 60 percent and effective protection from 50 to almost 200 percent. Foil, rod, and ingot production, established in the early 1980s, however, enjoyed effective protection of 5 to 25 percent.

It might seem that this process would tend to a long-run equilibrium in which a monopolist would be protected from import competition by prohibitive tariffs and shielded from domestic competition by barriers to entry. However, the central government's restrictions on investment could sometimes be evaded: lower authorities were often willing to grant investment permits.

The incentives resulting from the government's industrial policy varied widely over time. A case in point is the monosodium glutamate industry. In this sector a combination of tariff protection and tax breaks had led to a production capacity of almost 27,000 tons in 1971, when domestic demand was less than 5,000 tons. Competition then drove down prices, but in 1973 the sector was closed to investment and in 1975 existing producers were protected from "the rigors of competition" by the imposition of a minimum price. Effectively, the government imposed a cartel, rationing the existing plants to produce at 30 percent of their capacity. A few years later, however, both the investment ban and the minimum price regulation were lifted. "Although production capacity was still more than twice domestic consumption of 12,000 tons, the Government agreed to subsidize investment in two new plants with a combined capacity of 6,900 tons. There is no reason to believe that this is an atypical example of industrial policy in Indonesia, which seems to consist basically of trying to maximize the rate of growth of capacity by tariffs (or import bans), taxation incentives and concessional interest rates" (Dick 1979, pp. 26–27).

Industrial policy varied not only over time but from sector to sector. Instead of setting tariffs to protect the sector producing tires and tubes, for example, the government granted an import ban once a producer proved itself capable of meeting all domestic demand for a particular type of product.[15] Also, the government did not encourage monopoly in this sector but, on the contrary, encouraged domestic competition by a liberal licensing policy. It was, however, not successful in preventing collusion in the sector.

In the industrial sector the government also intervened in product markets by imposing local content requirements. These requirements, usually called deletion programs in Indonesia, date from the mid-1970s, when the easy phase of import substitution was coming to an end. In the automobile industry, for example, the Ministry of Industry started a deletion program in 1976 that involved the gradual elimination of the use of imported components by assemblers. A 1983 directive (Ministerial Decree 371) stipulated that by 1986/87 all four-wheeled commercial vehicles should be "manufactured fully" in Indonesia, meaning that all main components (including the engine, transmission, steering and brake systems, and so forth) should be made in Indonesia. Deletion programs involved detailed import-substitution timetables. For motorcycles and scooters, for example, the schedule listed 25 components (including the battery, exhaust pipe, and brake cable) that had to be manufactured domestically by 1979, and there was a similar level of detail for each of the following six years (for example, spark plugs in 1980, the air filter in 1981, the head lamp in 1982, and the piston in 1983).

The deletion programs led to two other interventions. First, while assemblers of imported CKD (completely knocked down) kits used to cater to the demand for a wide range of models, the government limited the number of models a firm could assemble. For motorcycles, for example, the maximum was put at five models for every make of which it had the agency (Wie 1984, p. 18). Second, in an attempt to stimulate the development of backward linkages from assemblers to small-scale domestic suppliers, the government limited the extent to which firms could satisfy the local content requirements by in-house production. The resulting subcontracting arrangements seemed, however, to have benefited mainly the large subsidiaries of multinational corporations. Wie concluded for the engineering goods subsector that "deletion programs have been quite successful in raising the local content of various engineering goods, but quite unsuccessful in promoting subcontracting with small and medium supplier firms" (p. 43).

In the mid-1970s important changes occurred in industrial policy, including the government's attitude toward foreign direct investment in manufacturing. The relatively easy early phase of import substitution, based on simple consumer goods and consumer durables, had been completed, and it was decided to concentrate industrialization efforts on resource processing and on technology and capital-intensive basic industries. Local content requirements were used to force the development of backward linkages. At the same time the role of foreign investment was redefined. In retrospect the open-door policy of the 1967–73 period, inaugurated with the very liberal Foreign Investment Act of 1967, may be seen as an aberration (Wie 1986a, p. 1). After 1973 some sectors—in particular, consumer goods industries—were even completely closed to foreign investment.

The ideas behind the new emphasis on basic industries had little to do with economics. They reflected a structuralist fascination with linkages and a revival of economic nationalism, this time directed against Japan. In 1980 the minister of industry expressed the hope that "through these linkages new 'upstream' and downstream manufacturing industries would be established which would not only lessen Indonesia's large external dependence, but would also ensure simultaneously that the manufacturing sector would be 'more deeply rooted' in the Indonesian economy" (Soehoed 1980, pp. 5–7).

Restrictions on foreign direct investment took several forms. Increasingly, as noted above, industrial activities were declared closed to new foreign investment. In addition, after 1974 there were "dilution requirements." These stipulated that foreign investment had to take the form of a joint venture, that the Indonesian equity participation had to be at least 20 percent, that this share should exceed 50 percent within 10 years, and that half of the Indonesian equity participation should be in the hands of *pribumi* enterprises. This latter requirement indicates that the measures were aimed at reducing the influence not only of foreign (particularly Japanese) businessmen but also of Chinese-Indonesians (Arndt 1974; Wie 1986b).

The emphasis in industrial policy since the early 1970s on production of intermediate and capital goods was accompanied by a revival in the role of state enterprises, leading to a combination that has been called "upstream socialism, downstream capitalism" (Wie and Yoshihara 1986, p. 29). Only state enterprises were involved in petroleum refining, aluminum smelting, and the fertilizer sector; state enterprises also played a dominant role in steel and shipbuilding (Wie and Yoshihara 1986, table 1). An important reason for maintaining state enterprises seems to have been that in their absence, industry would have been dominated by Chinese entrepreneurs.

Food Policy

The colonial government until the 1930s had an interest in keeping retail prices of food—especially rice—low, not so much to protect the living standards of urban consumers as to ensure that the plantations could acquire cheap labor.[16] When this objective was threatened by rice harvest failures, the government intervened in an ad hoc fashion in the market by canceling import duties, prohibiting exports, or reducing land taxes. During the Depression the government's involvement grew: price controls and import licensing were introduced, and the government became involved in intraregional and interregional rice trade. In 1939 a special government agency for rice marketing (the *Voedingmiddelenfonds,* or VMF) was founded.

Under Sukarno the controls were kept in place, but the objective changed to protecting the real income of civil servants and the military. These groups received part of their income in kind, as rice. The government's role in procuring rice for its own employees made rice marketing a political issue, since aggregate rice availability was declining alarmingly. Yields were virtually stagnant: in 1954 the national average was 1.18 tons of milled rice per hectare; in 1965, 1.20 tons (Mears and Moeljono 1981, table 2.1).[17] The harvested area increased but only on the outer islands; the net result was a production increase of only 12 percent, from 7.84 million tons in 1954 (in itself a decline in per capita terms from prewar levels) to 8.80 million tons in 1965.[18] Since the population was growing at 2.3 percent a year, this meant a decline of almost 13 percent in per capita production. The decline had an especially severe effect, which was not mitigated by massive imports (about 1 million tons per year) in the early 1960s: per capita availability declined from 107 kilograms in 1960 to 92 kilograms in 1965 (new series estimates, Mears and Moeljono 1981, table 2.2).

A program launched in 1959 to achieve food self-sufficiency in 1962 was unsuccessful, as was an attempt (in 1963) to substitute corn for rice in the rations of the military and the civil servants. The Bimas extension program (which relied on students who lived and worked as extension officers in villages) was developed in 1964. It laid the groundwork for the production increases realized in the Suharto period. In 1967 Bulog, the agency that was to develop into a parastatal with monopoly control over the distribution of basic commodities, including rice and sugar, was established. Initially Bulog exercised the old function of procuring rice supplies for the military and for the civil service, importing when needed. After the rice crisis of 1967/68, the objective became to keep retail prices low through a combination of imports and buffer stock operations.

Concerns quickly developed about the effect of this low-price policy on domestic rice production. It became clear that the Bimas and Inmas extension programs would have to be supported by a price policy. Protecting the incentives of rice farmers became a second, and conflicting, objective, and policy was confused as a result. Lip service was paid to supporting prices to growers (and a target relative price—of rice relative to fertilizer—was announced), but initially the command nature of the Bimas program was maintained. In 1970 ceiling retail prices and floor producer prices for rice were announced for the first time, to be defended by Bulog's buffer stock operations.

After 1973 the inherent conflict could be resolved: oil revenue was used to finance the subsidy needed to reconcile farmers' incentives with low retail prices. In the meantime, the 1972 rice crisis (when Bulog could not prevent a doubling of the price) led to institutional change. Cooperatives (BUUDs and KUDs) were set up at the village level and charged with procurement tasks for Bulog. Bulog's ability to defend a minimum price for farmers by acting as buyer of last resort was limited in two ways. BUUD/KUD officials sometimes abused their power as procurement officers by turning away farmers willing to sell at the Bulog price, buying on their own account in the free market and selling to themselves at the higher Bulog price. Sellers also had to be refused because of Bulog's limited storage capacity. However, Bulog embarked on a program of warehouse construction and by 1979 had built a storage capacity of 1 million tons.

In addition there was initial confusion about the objective of the BUUD/KUD operations. Financial targets were often interpreted as procurement targets. When cooperatives stopped buying because market prices rose above the controlled price, these physical targets were not realized. The reaction in some areas of Java was to order farmers to sell to the BUUDs at the controlled price. Village headmen were used to force farmers unwilling to sell at the lower price. However, in July 1973 the government announced the abandonment of rice procurement targets (Mears and Moeljono 1981, p. 39). The BUUDs borrowed to finance their rice procurement, but many of them were denied access to new loans because of arrears. Because of this credit constraint, half of the cooperatives could not buy paddy, and in some cases rice prices fell below the floor price.

The policy toward private trading in rice was ambiguous. Credit for private traders was curtailed in an attempt to support the BUUD/KUDs, but when cooperatives in arrears could not buy crops, the reaction was to channel more credit to private traders rather than the cooperatives. Until 1973, price support levels were similar throughout the country, so there was no incentive for private traders to transport rice from surplus to deficit areas. In 1973, however, price differentials were introduced to cover transport cost. Although these two examples show an undogmatic willingness to reverse a policy with a negative effect on private traders, the effect of pricing policies on private storage was permanent. The policy of raising producer prices and lowering retail rice prices was reflected in a dramatic narrowing of marketing margins (the retail price on Java was 123 percent above the floor price in 1973, but only 11 percent higher in 1979), deterring private storage. Increasingly, the rise of Bulog stocks compensated for a fall in private stocks. Data for the city of Bandung suggest that margins not only fell but actually became negative for some periods of the year (Mears and Moeljono 1981, table 2.10).

The policy succeeded in reducing the price of rice to urban consumers: with the notable exception of 1973, prices after 1966–68 remained well below the levels reached in those years. Conversely, the incentive to farm paddy, as measured by the rice/fertilizer price, increased by about 50 percent between 1969 and 1979. The number of kilograms of rice needed to buy a kilogram of fertilizer fell from 0.72 to 0.50 in this period, which suggests that a rupiah spent on fertilizer increased the value of the extra rice from (an already high) level of Rp 5.6 to Rp 8.0 over this decade. Hence the rice policy not only succeeded in stabilizing rice prices through imports and buffer stock operations; it also, through subsidies, yielded output growth through the encouragement given to increasing fertilizer use.

Table 17.6 Agricultural Output and Prices, Selected Years, 1930–84

Sector	Value added (billions of rupiah)[a]			Growth rate, 1950–84 (percent)	Price in 1984[b]
	1930	1950	1984		
Food crops, Java	34.7	34.5	124.2	3.8	100.0
Food crops, other islands	16.6	18.4	77.0	4.3	98.2
Livestock	5.5	5.1	11.3	2.4	104.1
Export crops, smallholders	9.1[c]	21.5	63.6	3.2	55.3
Export crops, estates	31.4	12.1	41.6	3.7	58.7
Total	95.9	91.6	317.1	3.7	n.a.

n.a. Not applicable.
a. 1960 prices.
b. The price is an index (1960 = 100) relative to the index for food crops (Java).
c. This figure is atypically low; it was 11.8 in 1925, 12.3 in 1930, and 17.1 in 1940.
Source: Based on tables A.1.1–A.1.5 in the 1987 draft of Van der Eng 1993.

Growth was not limited to rice or even to food crops. Smallholder export crop production grew at 3.2 percent a year (1950–84), compared with approximately 4 percent for food crops (table 17.6). The data indicate that factor use increased substantially over this period (both agricultural employment and land use increased by approximately 45 percent). However, most of the production increase is not explained by increased land and labor use but by productivity increases at virtually constant factor proportions; there is very little change in the land/labor ratio (table 17.7). The output increase in the early 1950s was probably caused largely by rehabilitation. Three factors accounted for the productivity increases realized in the 1970s. One involved capital accumulation (or rather reparation)—for example, the investment in irrigation starting (during Repelita I) with the rehabilitation of the colonial canal system. The second factor was an exogenous event—the availability of the new high-yielding rice varieties. Finally, agricultural growth was related to the deliberate use of price incentives.

Table 17.7 Productivity and Factor Proportions in Agriculture, Selected Years, 1950–84

(1930 = 100)

Year	Agricultural employment	Available land	Land/labor ratio	Labor productivity	Land productivity	Per capita output
1950	132.4	105.7	79.8	72.1	90.3	73.9
1963	150.6	117.4	77.9	89.8	115.2	80.8
1973	169.6	132.6	78.2	111.3	142.3	91.3
1984	180.0	145.5	80.8	178.6	221.0	120.4

Note: 1963 and 1973 are years in which agricultural censuses were conducted.
Source: Based on table A.4 in the 1987 draft of Van der Eng 1993.

18 Government Finance and Public Policy

In this chapter we look at fiscal policy—revenue, budgets in the New Order, measurement of budgetary impact, and use of oil revenue—and then examine the political economy of Indonesia.

Fiscal Policy

Most accounts of Indonesian economic development agree in according a central role to fiscal policy. In a limited sense this must be true for any economy, since the potential for budgetary mismanagement always exists, and even if economic developments are relatively insensitive to the specific pattern of government activities when these are competently budgeted, they will not be insensitive to gross budgetary mismanagement. According to this interpretation, fiscal policy is likely to be most important precisely when it is badly designed or executed or when some correction is required for previous mismanagement or external shocks.

In this connection, what makes the Indonesian fiscal experience particularly interesting is the apparent juxtaposition of a spectacularly incompetent period (prior to 1966) with a spectacularly competent one (subsequent to 1966). The 1950s were marked by consistent deficit financing, with a brief exception during the Korean commodity boom. During the early 1960s the scale of deficits increased rapidly, as did the associated inflation. When the New Order was instituted in 1966, it took over an economy suffering from hyperinflation as well as from massive disequilibrium in the balance of payments and in the budget. The program adopted then is cited frequently as a classic stabilization exercise and a vindication of the effectiveness of the macroeconomic strategy favored by the IMF.

After 1966 the economy was subjected to a sequence of oil shocks, posing fresh problems of economic and particularly of fiscal management, since oil revenues are largely channeled into the budget. Broad comparisons with other countries experiencing large trade shocks suggest that the Indonesian authorities were relatively successful in meeting this challenge.

Indonesia thus appears to provide useful lessons in economic management in at least three respects. The early period provides a case study of progressive loss of fiscal control with increasing deficits; the middle period is a case study of how a country may rapidly regain fiscal control even after it has been decisively lost; and the later period is a case study of how a trade shock may be efficiently managed without destabilizing the economy.

It is relevant to inquire whether, on closer examination of the fiscal record, the conventional story needs to be qualified in any way, and how that might affect any general lessons that might be drawn from the particular Indonesian experience. Several qualifications must in fact be made. First, the really dramatic loss of control that occurred in the early 1960s was a revenue crisis rather than a loss of expenditure control. This feature was not apparent to most contemporary observers because inflation was accelerating rapidly and price indexes were inadequate.[1] Both revenue and expenditure were rising in nominal terms, the latter somewhat faster. Given a propensity to underestimate the rate of price change, it was easy to perceive the situation as one in which real revenue was holding up satisfactorily but real expenditure was rising, rather than one in which real revenue was collapsing while real expenditure was broadly stationary or even falling.

This feature of the fiscal debacle of the early 1960s makes it far less useful as a representative case study of loss of fiscal control. Such loss of control far more frequently involves an expansion of government spending ahead of stationary or even rising real revenue. Cases of real revenue collapse are much less common, though they do still occur, as in Uganda and Ghana in the late 1970s and early 1980s.

More important, the specific nature of the Indonesian crisis means that the potentially representative nature of the subsequent stabilization exercise is also compromised. If a deficit is caused primarily by reduction of revenue, eliminating it simply requires that the old sources of revenue be retapped or new sources found to replace them—for example, by raising the tax burden (and possibly nontax revenue) back to its old level. How difficult this is to achieve depends, among other things, on the reasons for the collapse and on how long it is allowed to persist. If, instead, a deficit results from expenditure increases, its elimination requires that the spending increases be reversed (which experience shows to be an arduous and uncertain undertaking), or that revenue be raised to hitherto unfamiliar levels, or that some combination of both be tried. Stabilization in these circumstances is likely to be a different and more difficult exercise.

The second notable feature of the Indonesian fiscal structure is the relatively small size of the government sector prior to the oil boom. This reinforces the previous point. Suppose that it is necessary to close a fiscal deficit equal to 5 percent of GDP, and that this involves raising total revenue from 5 percent of GDP to 10 percent, as was done (roughly) in the Indonesian stabilization of 1966. With base revenue so low, it is apparent that there must be some combination of unutilized tax bases and either low nominal tax rates or widespread evasion or misappropriation. Thus there must be a set of obvious avenues along which the search for additional revenue can be pursued. Conversely, any attempt to cut expenditure from its relatively modest level may prove extraordinarily difficult, and an attempt to make the full adjustment on the expenditure side may not be feasible.

Now consider the case of a more typical developing country, in which total revenue needs to be raised from 20 to 25 percent of GDP or expenditure cut by similar amounts. The relative feasibility of achieving either of these courses of action is likely to be quite different from the case just discussed. Taxes are already being levied at relatively high effective rates on broad tax bases. It may be extremely difficult to identify new tax handles or to push rates much higher without encountering serious problems of evasion and disincentives. Conversely, the level of expenditure is high, and the proportional reduction required is relatively modest. This suggests that although a stabilization exercise that involves doubling revenue—albeit from a low base—looks ambitious, it may be far simpler than raising revenue from a more typical base by, say, a quarter.

The third feature to be noted is the relatively low ratio of money supply to national income that characterized Indonesia throughout the period. Of course, the ratio fell to very low levels during and immediately after the inflationary surge of the mid-1960s, but it was low compared with other developing countries both before and after this surge. One consequence of this low monetization of the economy, coupled with the absence of a bond market, is that even small budget deficits may have powerful inflationary consequences. The much-criticized deficits of the 1950s, which were repeatedly condemned for their size and irresponsibility, look relatively modest by present-day standards.

To set these remarks in perspective, it is necessary to consider the magnitudes of revenue and expenditure and the overall deficit over the period. This presents certain difficulties. The nominal series are hard to interpret because the rate of inflation is so variable and, in the middle of the period, so high. The usual procedure of deflating the nominal series to obtain constant price series is not a satisfactory solution: as noted previously, the price indexes for the earlier years are deficient, and the poor quality of national income estimates means that adequate implicit price deflators do not exist. In view of these data shortcomings, the best procedure appears to be to present nominal fiscal magnitudes as a percentage of nominal GDP.[2] Although there are significant difficulties in constructing such a series, particularly for the years 1953–57,[3] these are not likely to distort the broad qualitative conclusions overall.

Revenue Problems

The foregoing discussion is not intended to absolve the Indonesian authorities from responsibility for the budgetary crisis in the early 1960s, but it does locate the problem rather differently. The question is not how they managed to lose control of expenditure, but how they managed to cause or permit revenue to erode so rapidly. Table 18.1 presents summary data for 1960–72; the figures demonstrate the magnitude and speed of the phenomenon.

Although there may be some doubt about the actual figures, there is no doubt at all that revenue declined calamitously during these years. Broadly speaking, this was not because tax rates were lowered or exemptions increased—in fact the contrary occurred—but because compliance fell precipitately in the face of an unrealistic tax structure.

The transition to a progressively less realistic tax structure was partly a consequence of inertia in the face of inflation, and partly a consequence of desperate attempts to shore up the flow of revenue as it fell. As an example of the first phenomenon, income tax was levied in 1959 on those with incomes of more than Rp 3,000 who had some claim to being considered wealthy at that time. No change was made in the exemptions

Table 18.1 Revenue, Expenditure, and Deficits as a Percentage of GDP, 1960–72

Year	Revenue	Expenditure	Deficit
1960	12.9	15.5	2.6
1961	13.2	18.8	5.6
1962	5.6	9.1	3.5
1963	5.1	10.3	5.2
1964	4.0	9.6	5.6
1965	3.9	10.7	6.8
1966	4.2	9.5	5.3
1967	10.0	10.3	3.2
1968	8.8	8.8	1.7
1969/70	11.7	11.7	3.2
1970/71	13.6	13.4	3.3
1971/72	14.5	14.0	3.0

Source: Tables 18A.1, 18A.2, and 18A.3.

for several years despite the high inflation, so by 1964 even the lowest-paid workers were technically liable for income tax. In practice the authorities were unable or unwilling to levy the tax on any but an infinitesimal proportion of the eligible population.

However, lax enforcement of formal tax liabilities could not be confined to those below some notional threshold, but was bound to spread throughout the entire income tax apparatus. The consequence was a large discrepancy between high rates and low yield, with only a portion of registered tax payers actually paying tax, and many of those paying only part of what was legally due. The mechanisms permitting this low taxpayer compliance were two central features of the Indonesian tax administration—tax compromise and tax targeting. Lerche (1974, p. 2) describes tax compromise in the following terms:

> Tax compromise—the Indonesians also call it "tawar-menawar" (push and pull) or "main-main" (to play games)—is based on the Javanese philosophy of consensus and avoidance of conflict or clear-cut decision. A compromise is preferred to an unequivocal enforcement: to leave a situation with open dissent is considered very crude and unthinkable behaviour. The compromise attitude is encouraged by the lack of tax data, often leaving assessments to pure guesswork of the tax collector. Even if the tax administrator has not made a good "bargain" he is not willing or able to apply legal sanctions provided by the law. This is because the tax collector, being part of the traditional society, does not want to become unpopular or lose face. During the past 25 years, despite obvious acts of tax evasion, not one tax violator has been prosecuted and property foreclosures to enforce payments are very rarely done. . . . Even a bonafide taxpayer has little choice but to bargain for a reasonable settlement in order to stay in business. Usually the tax collector who considers all taxpayers dishonest adds 50–200 percent to the figures given by the books or the taxpayer. Outside the tax administration there are practically no ways to direct or appeal on tax decisions.

Arguably, this capacity to compromise provided an important safety valve for the tax system when the authorities had raised rates to truly unreasonable levels. For example, the heavy reliance on trade and exchange taxes in the mid-1960s meant that importers and exporters who chose not to—or were unable to—evade the regulations altogether would have been unable to compete with those who could, if tax officials had not taken a "reasonable" view.

Tax targeting had an equally insidious effect. Targeting involved the fixing of more or less binding quotas and norms within the hierarchy of the tax apparatus, with the norms based on relative power and bargaining talents and on history rather than on any analysis of sectoral or regional taxable capacity. The targets served not only as rough guidelines but also as measures of administrative efficiency.

Since actual tax collections were related to the true tax base and formal tax structure only in this extremely indirect way, apparently paradoxical responses could easily arise. Not only could real collections fall when tax rates rose, but the reverse was also true. Domestic tax revenues recovered rapidly in the early years of the New Order, but the revenue increase continued in the early 1970s when tax rates were cut.

Lerche (1974) calculated that even after the recovery of the late 1960s only about 20 percent of assessed income taxes and 60 percent of the sales tax were collected in 1971, and that in Jakarta only 20 percent of industrial properties fully met their real estate tax liability. Between 1969 and 1974 the income tax exemption level was raised from about half of average national household income to about 130 percent of it; at the same time progression was reduced. Corporate tax rates were also lowered. According to Lerche's (1983) computations, the share of taxable income to national income correspondingly fell from 11.5 percent in 1969 to 6.5 percent in 1972 and to 4.3 percent in 1974. In absolute terms, Lerche estimated that legal liabilities fell by 35 percent between 1970 and 1973/74. Meanwhile—another anomaly—actual income tax revenues rose by 100 percent. Between 1968 and 1972/73 the percentage of actual revenues to legal liabilities rose from 7 to 13 percent.

A similar set of calculations holds for the sales tax. Taking direct taxes, the sales tax, and the land tax (Ipeda) together, it appears that the change in tax bases explains only one-third of the growth in revenue during 1969–73. Since there is no reason to believe that the built-in elasticity of this combination of taxes would exceed unity, and since rates were lowered, there appears to be no alternative to the conclusion that the revenue gains were caused primarily by improved compliance, but that compliance remained very poor even so.

Historically, Indonesia had a small public sector and a correspondingly low share of GDP raised in taxation. Table 18.2 shows that the revenue recovery of the late 1960s and early 1970s still left domestic taxation as a low proportion of GDP; what enabled the public sector to grow was the explosion of oil revenue.

Several attempts were made to improve domestic tax performance during the decade following the first oil shock, 1973–82, but the ready availability of oil revenue weakened these efforts. As table 18.2 shows, by 1982/83 the domestic tax effort fell back to 6.7 percent of GDP from the fairly steady level of 7 to 8 percent. With the fall in oil prices after late 1982, this relaxed attitude toward domestic revenue was bound to change, triggering three major reforms.

Table 18.2 Revenue as a Percentage of GDP, 1966–74 and 1982/83

Year	Overall revenue (including foreign aid)	Nonoil domestic revenue (excluding foreign aid and oil revenue)
1966	4.2	4.2
1967	10.0	6.2
1968	8.8	5.6
1969/70	11.7	6.2
1970/71	13.6	7.2
1971/72	14.5	7.4
1972/73	14.6	7.1
1973/74	15.1	7.6
1982/83	22.7	6.7

Source: Tables 18A.1, 18A.2, and 18A.3.

The most significant reform was the replacement of the multirated sales tax with a value added tax at the flat rate of 10 percent. A major advantage in the Indonesian context was that a value added tax eliminated the problem of underinvoicing that plagued the turnover tax; it also avoided the bias toward vertical integration induced by the turnover tax. The second reform was to replace the system of official assessment with one of self-assessment with selective audit. The third was a unification and reform of the direct tax arrangements. These reforms had a variety of objectives, such as improving the efficiency and equity of the system, but perhaps the central intention was to improve revenue performance and to raise the contribution of nonoil revenue as the contribution of oil revenue declined.

The reform of direct taxes was not expected to generate much revenue gain, at least in the short term; the gain was to be achieved through the value added tax. The new taxes were introduced during 1983–86, with the value added tax coming on line in April 1985. The ratio of nonoil revenue to GDP rose sharply (by 2 percent) in 1985/86 and 1986/87 over the preceding low level. Even so, nonoil revenue remained well below 10 percent of GDP—a very modest value by the standards of nonmineral economies. Although the reforms were generally regarded as a success, it remained to be seen whether they raised tax buoyancy—as intended— rather than simply having a beneficial effect on revenue.

Budgets in the New Order

As a response to the excesses of the guided economy period, the New Order elevated the concept of a balanced budget to become a major symbol of good government. According to the official presentation, the budget had been more or less balanced (usually with a very small overall surplus) since 1967. However, this presentation was misleading (Glassburner 1979). The appearance of balance was achieved by two devices. The first, as discussed in chapter 13, was the inclusion of official foreign capital flows as a revenue item rather than an item financing the deficit. As already noted, the resumption of aid played a large part in the recovery of government finances in the late 1960s. Using the more conventional definition of aid as a means of deficit financing, the overall deficit was reduced to around 3 percent of GDP in the late 1960s (table 18A.3 in the appendix to this chapter). This level remained fairly stable for the next decade. This is not very different from the average level experienced in the 1950s, but it does represent a significant improvement on the 5 percent averaged during 1960–66.[4]

The second device was to classify increases in government funds held with the banking system as expenditure. For much of the period following 1975 a substantial hidden surplus existed, much of it in the form of unspent development funds. In some cases projects had not drawn their funds because of implementation delays. In other cases the central government "spent" the funds by transferring them to a provincial or *kabupaten* account, where they could remain for up to three years before they had to be returned as "unspent" (Daroesman 1981). This explains the otherwise incomprehensible skill of the government at spending unanticipated revenue. Scherer (1982) has shown that increases in the governments' holdings with the banking system corresponded closely to the excess of realized over anticipated revenue. This hidden surplus was substantial during 1976–81, averaging 2.4 percent of GDP and peaking at 3.7 percent in 1980/81 (table 18A.4).[5] For that year this correction outweighed the correction for aid, and for the first and probably last time the government actually ran a true surplus. Subsequently the hidden surplus fell rapidly and became a deficit in 1982/83.

These two accounting devices make nonsense of the balanced budget but have the advantage, particularly the second, of permitting some budgetary flexibility behind this politically important facade. However, they make it difficult to disentangle the likely impact of the government's activities on the economy, particularly if, as has been suggested, government holdings are underreported. Three further complications exacerbate this difficulty. The first, considered in the following section, is the distinction between domestic and foreign components of the budget. The other two are off-budget items such as parastatal activities and the nonbudget component in the fuel subsidies.

Some idea of the importance of off-budget items can be obtained by looking at the "assets of official entities" row in table 18A.5. This is typically a substantial positive item, often similar in magnitude to the entire increase in the money supply. There is a particularly huge entry in 1975/

76, nearly 7 percent of GDP. This reflects the financial crisis at Pertamina that was brought on by the oil company's overborrowing at very short terms (Glassburner 1979). Bank Indonesia was obliged to draw reserves down sharply, so the overall expansion of the money supply was relatively modest, at 3 percent of GDP.

Fuel subsidies appear as budget items and became important in the years following the second oil price boom. They amounted to 1.5 percent of GDP in 1979/80, 2 percent of GDP in 1980/81, and 3.7 percent of GDP in 1981/82. This was sufficient to make them one of the largest items of government expenditure, accounting in 1981/82 for more than 20 percent of the routine budget. However, this was only the tip of the iceberg, since the government's arrangements with the oil companies involved the transfer of a high proportion of oil to the government at cost. If this oil is revalued at opportunity cost—in other words, at world prices—the true subsidy is much larger. Warr's (1980) calculation for 1979/80 suggests that the true subsidy was more than three times the reported amount—around 5 percent of GDP, or the equivalent of 40 percent of the net foreign exchange revenue obtained from oil. Arndt's (1981) figures imply a true subsidy in the following two years that was still higher—possibly 7 percent of GDP.

Domestic and Foreign Budgets

For Indonesia as for other oil exporting countries, the oil boom had the effect of massively increasing the foreign exchange component of government revenue. Unless the government elected to increase its imports to an equivalent extent, a balanced budget overall meant a surplus in the foreign budget balance, offset by a deficit in the domestic budget balance. This raises the question of what is the appropriate measure of budgetary impact. The analysis of trade shocks has increasingly relied on the distinction between tradable and nontradable goods, and budgetary policy during a trade shock could also be conveniently analyzed in these terms. However, budget data are usually not available in this disaggregation, and certainly not for Indonesia.

The question is whether the domestic-foreign distinction is a useful approximation of the nontradable-tradable distinction. This appears unlikely to be the case. In particular, a large but stable domestic deficit does not necessarily signal a powerful reflationary impact of budgetary policy on the domestic economy. However, it remains true that a sudden change in the domestic deficit will imply a domestic impact, even if accompanied by an offsetting change in the foreign budget, unless steps are taken to redirect private expenditure.

According to this analysis, changes in the domestic deficit are likely to prove more interesting than the actual level. Booth and McCawley's (1981) calculations for the 1970s (table 18.3) suggest that the domestic deficit was less stable than the overall deficit, though not dramatically so; in particular the budget became much more expansionary domestically after 1975/76.[6] These calculations make no allowance for the hidden surplus items previously discussed. Those items could be regarded as reductions in foreign expenditure; they would increase the recorded foreign surplus but leave the domestic deficit unaltered. However, it seems equally or more plausible to consider the hidden surplus as reflecting unspent domestic expenditure. On that basis the expansionary impact of the oil boom was much reduced until 1981/82; the exception is 1975/76, again reflecting the domestic impact of the Pertamina crisis.

The Use of Oil Revenue

As in many developing countries, the expenditure side of the budget is split between a routine or recurrent category and a development category, although these categories are of dubious analytic utility and imperfectly represent the distinction between current and capital expenditure. Nevertheless, it is of interest that the development category showed far more rapid growth during the 1970s. Booth and McCawley (1981) calculated the elasticity of expenditure with respect to GDP from 1969/70 to 1977/78 as 1.13 for routine expenditure (and only 1.05 for wages and salaries), whereas that for development expenditure excluding aid was 1.44 and that for project aid, 1.78. Within the development category

Table 18.3 Budget Deficit as a Percentage of GDP, 1972/73–1982/83

Year	Overall deficit[a]	Domestic deficit[b]	Domestic deficit[c]
1972/73	2.6	2.7	2.5
1973/74	2.4	0.5	0.3
1974/75	2.4	2.7	3.1
1975/76	3.8	4.8	4.9
1976/77	2.6	4.2	2.0
1977/78	2.6	4.8	3.5
1978/79	2.6	3.5	1.9
1979/80	0.5	6.8	3.4
1980/81	(0.6)	5.8	2.1
1981/82	2.7	6.3	5.9
1982/83	4.3	6.0	7.2

Note: Parentheses indicate a surplus.
a. Official deficit plus aid minus increase in holdings with monetary sector.
b. Domestic deficit as computed by Booth and McCawley 1981.
c. Column b minus the increase in holdings with the monetary sector.
Source: Derived from Scherer 1982.

two disaggregations are of potential interest. Disaggregation by functional category shows relatively little variation, with expenditure on agriculture, irrigation, and transport lagging slightly, and expenditure on health, education, industry, and power growing slightly faster. Disaggregation by institutional form of spending shows much greater variation. The elasticities here were 1.11 for government departments, 1.73 for development grants to the regions, and 2.21 for the residue (chiefly capital participation in state enterprises and the fertilizer subsidy).

One effect of the tremendous concentration of revenue in the hands of the central government was the establishment of transfers from the center as the principal component (about 75 percent) of total regional revenue. These transfers were also an important component of the central budget, averaging around 17 percent. In a cross-country comparison carried out by the World Bank, regional dependence on the center was typically only half the Indonesian figure; interestingly, only Nigeria matched the Indonesian rate.

It would be wrong to conclude, however, that the centralization of revenue in Indonesia was a consequence, as it was in Nigeria, of the oil boom. It had a far longer pedigree and reflected a long tradition of fiscal centralization. Shaw (1980) noted that the provincial and subprovincial levels in the early 1970s were starved of resources, that what resources they had came almost entirely from the center, and that grant allocations were not linked in any obvious way with local revenue effort or with need. Booth's (1985b) assessment was that the first of these criticisms was no longer valid by the end of the decade, but that the other observations stood. However, allocation by need is a problematic concept for Indonesian regions, since regions with low per capita income sometimes have relatively good infrastructural endowments and vice versa. For example, several poor provinces in the outer islands have elevated school enrollment ratios and high per capita provision of health facilities as a result of missionary activity. Similarly, Java is well endowed with roads and irrigation infrastructure but has relatively low income. Booth's analysis (1977, 1985b) suggests that because grants were allocated as a function of existing infrastructure, they tended to widen asset disparities, but since assets correlated so little with income, no presumption should be made that the transfers were disequalizing (or indeed, the converse).

The Political Economy

The evolution of the polity in any recently independent country will be responsive to the detailed sequence of events following independence. The polity's nature and capacity for change will also be shaped by, among other influences, the political, social, and economic structures of the precolonial period and the nature of the colonial regime. Commentators have differed widely on the relative importance of these influences in determining the subsequent complexion of Indonesian society in general and of its political economy in particular. Writers of very different persuasions nevertheless agree on one central feature of the Indonesian story—the failure of Dutch colonialism to generate an indigenous capitalist economy or an indigenous bourgeoisie. Geertz (1963), for example, argued that the development of state plantations in the nineteenth century entrenched precapitalist social structures in Javanese villages and retarded the development of private landownership and indigenous entrepreneurship. He also argued that the latter was greatly set back by the heavy drain of economic surplus from Indonesia to Holland.[7]

Despite a limited amount of import-substituting investment in the 1930s, the Dutch left an economy that specialized in the export of primary products and the import of manufactures. Thus the two potential avenues for the development of an indigenous capitalist class were land ownership and trade. Robison (1986, pp. 11–12) argues that "one of the most crucial developments in the colonial period was the failure of the Javanese *priyayi* [the nobility and administrative literati of the agrarian kingdoms of Java] to transform their traditional rights of appropriation over land, labor and produce into rights of private ownership on a large scale." A possible reason for this failure to develop rights of private ownership is that relatively abundant land had traditionally forced the *priyayi* to concentrate on the control of labor rather than land. In addition, the Dutch East India Company reinforced this mode of accumulation by exercising political power to shore up the authority of the *priyayi.* By the end of the colonial period the *priyayi* were essentially officials in the service of the Dutch colonial administration.

Robison (1986, p. 11) identifies three major factors to explain the failure of an agrarian landowning bourgeoisie to develop. The first is the "weakness of the institution of private property in precolonial society and the dominance of politically secured but alienable rights to use land or to appropriate produce and labor." Second, he cites the "continuing importance, under colonial rule, of the state in economic activity and the persistence of political appropriation as the basis for accumulation." A third factor is the "use of state power to establish foreign corporate capital as the dominant element in the agrarian commercial economy from the late nineteenth century onward." In any event, there has been no tradition in Indonesia, as in some other Southeast Asian countries, of large landowning families emerging from the countryside to dominate politics or business.

In contrast, the nineteenth century saw the rapid development of a class of traders collecting agricultural produce, distributing goods, and providing credit. Until the seventeenth century both Javanese and Chinese were active in trade. When the Dutch East India Company established its hegemony over Java, the Javanese traders were eclipsed by the Chinese. This was partly because the leading Javanese traders had relied heavily on the exercise of political power to support their activities, and partly because it suited the Dutch to use nonindigenous people as tax collectors and as operators of monopolies. When tax farming (privatized tax collection) and monopolies ceased to be available to the Chinese, they moved to operating pawnshops, running gambling dens, and dealing in opium, and then into credit and retail trade.

Small-scale Javanese traders received a further setback in the early years of this century when the removal of travel and residence restrictions on the Chinese enabled them to extend their dominance to the villages and smaller towns. It was the Sumatrans who were to become dominant among indigenous traders. They spread to Java, generally as peddlers and small retailers; a few were able to expand beyond the petty trade sector into import and export activities in the 1920s and 1930s and then into manufacture in the 1950s.

There was also a small indigenous manufacturing base, consisting mainly of workshops or cottage industries focused primarily on weaving, spinning, batik work, and *kretek* cigarette making. Production was controlled by the merchants, who imported and supplied the raw materials and paid a commission on work done. In the 1930s this system of production was bypassed by a more mechanized mode of small- and medium-scale factory production, financed largely by the Chinese.

By the time that independence was formally achieved in 1949, all the major political parties had committed themselves to broad programs of economic nationalism. Although the chosen vehicles differed (state ownership for the PKI, indigenous private capital for Masyumi), there was consensus on two objectives: the transfer of economic power to Indonesian nationals and the replacement of a colonial, export-crop economy by a more industrialized and self-sufficient economy. Even so, the various coalition governments made no move toward wholesale expropriation of the Dutch assets that dominated the economy. The indigenous entrepreneurial class had experience in trading and manufacturing operations at only the smallest scale, and the state did not possess the administrative machinery to manage a potentially vast public sector.

The early coalition cabinets inclined to what became known later as the technocratic view, favoring market mechanisms and the role of foreign capital. The primary role of the state was to provide infrastructure and finance and to create the conditions for the development of domestic private capital, possibly by initiating and operating enterprises preparatory to handing them over to cooperatives, private owners, or joint state-private ownership. During 1949–57, accordingly, the Java Bank was taken over and reconstituted as the Bank Indonesia; two state finance banks were set up (one to finance industry and the other to finance imports); and several state corporations were established.

In addition, the Benteng program was created in 1950 to secure a greatly enhanced indigenous role in the import sector. This effort appeared particularly promising because of the apparatus of state control of import licenses and the limited capital and organizational demands of importing. Successive governments persevered with the scheme until 1957, despite early and eventually overwhelming evidence that it was being grossly abused. Benteng firms were typically not using the licenses for importing but were selling them to genuine importers, mostly Chinese, for up to 250 percent of their nominal value. In Robison's view (1986, pp. 46–47) this episode had three social and political consequences:

> First, it became clear that Chinese-owned capital was so integral to the structure of Indonesian capitalism that, short of a radical, socialist transformation of the economy, it would continue to constitute the dominant element of domestic investment. Second, indigenous capitalists proved generally unable to expand beyond petty trade and petty commodity production. Third, the resources of private domestic capital, including Chinese, were insufficient to replace foreign capital.

According to this argument, by the mid-1950s a choice had to be made between two alternatives. Either the program of economic nationalism would have to be postponed for the foreseeable future, while foreign and Chinese capital acted as the engine for economic development, or this whole program would have to be accelerated by giving a more central role to the state, possibly coupled with wholesale expropriation of the remaining Dutch enterprises.

The first alternative of partial retreat and gradualism was advocated by the parties who had formed the early coalition governments (PSI, Masyumi, and the moderate wing of PNI). Sukarno's preference went the other way. Given the circumstances surrounding the expropriation, the military acquired control of most of the new state corporations and thus a vested interest in a state capitalistic system.

In one important respect, however, there was no discontinuity of kind between the liberal democratic period and that of guided democracy, although there was a change of degree. This was the patrimonial aspect of state power. Already in the 1950s the political parties had taken steps to establish control over strategic government offices that allocated credit, concessions, and licenses. These were then granted to companies owned by the party, relatives, or business groups with which partnerships could be arranged. This practice, whereby individuals and political factions appropriated the apparatus and authority of the state for their personal benefit, became still more widespread in the congenial circumstances of guided democracy, when the practice became known as "bureaucratic capitalism."

The pervasive nature and large rewards associated with bureaucratic capitalism played a major distorting role in the development of the economy. For indigenous individuals of energy and ambition, the obvious way forward lay in achieving seniority in one of the political-bureaucratic alignments rather than in pursuing an entrepreneurial route. Even for those who chose business, the way to succeed lay in preferential access to licenses and other concessions rather than in investment and cultivation of a market. Access was not simply obtained by bidding on a one-off basis but often by forming a long-term politico-business alliance. In any event, licenses and other concessions were very expensive. Some might argue that this element of business cost simply substituted for the taxes the government was unable or unwilling to collect, but this interpretation makes no allowance for the greater uncertainty and unpredictability involved and thus for the forces inhibiting businessmen from taking a long view.

After the expropriation of Dutch property in 1957, the military acquired direct control of a large sector of the economy and became major participants in and beneficiaries of bureaucratic capitalism. Following the coup of 1966 their position was further strengthened; the New Order was a military regime and its earliest actions amounted to the political (and largely physical) elimination of the left from Indonesian public life. In this it was abetted by powerful and widespread anticommunist sentiment in the population.

Emmerson (1983) argues, however, that the longevity of the New Order regime was due not to civilian anticommunism but to military unity; that this unity was achieved by a decisive eradication of alternatives not only outside the armed forces, but also, and more important, within; and that this accounts for the otherwise anomalous restraint on military spending. It is certainly true that far from participating in a spending bonanza, the military cut back its personnel and received a smaller share of the budget. During the 1970s the combination of rapidly expanding government revenue and the campaign in East Timor might have presented the military with both the capacity and the justification for a rapid expansion. However, whereas the military forces of three other members of the Association of Southeast Asian Nations (ASEAN)—Malaysia, Singapore, and Thailand—increased their personnel by around 30 percent during the 1970s and the Philippine military expanded by 169 percent, Indonesia's fell by 30 percent. As a proportion of central government expenditure, Indonesia's military funding declined from the second highest to the second lowest among the five: from 25 percent in 1971 to 10 percent in 1980.

This relative parsimony requires some explanation. One argument is that Indonesia faced no credible external military threat and so had no need of large forces. Although this may have been objectively true, Southeast Asia in the 1970s was in such turmoil that it is far from clear that this lack of an external threat would have been self-evident from Jakarta. The other argument is that the military apparatus had to be purged. Prior to 1966, as the military became bigger, it became riven with internal divisions and was faced with the emergence of regional warlords, the rebellions of the late 1950s, and political conspiracy. The New Order regime had therefore to put its own house in order.

The successful containment of the growth of public sector employment offers a particularly striking contrast with Nigeria. During the later Sukarno period, for example, the political process took on many of the aspects of a contest for patronage, and organized labor was politically better-connected with the government than at any time in Nigeria. Both of these factors might have led to the expansion of public employment. A second period when public sector employment might have been expected to expand rapidly was the later Suharto period, because of the increase in public revenue. However, not only did public employment fail to become inflated as part of an expanding patronage system, but there was at no stage a significant wage premium in favor of the public sector. We have even identified one phase—the hyperinflation period of the 1960s—when public sector workers, along with other wage earners, must have suffered negative rents: they were involuntarily employed in the sense of working for incomes below those that would have attracted recruitment.

In Nigeria, where there was both a wage premium and patronage-based employment expansion, we developed a model that sought to explain the employment expansion in terms of the wage premium. The exogenous emergence of a wage premium during the 1950s (because of colonial policies) induced rent-seeking behavior by would-be public sector employees. This lobbying for jobs in turn induced patronage-based employment expansion.

Indonesian experience is consistent with this political-economy model. In the 1950s there was either no premium or only a small one in favor of the public sector, and so little pressure for employment expansion. In the 1960s the political power of unions and the prolabor stance of government meant that conditions were ripe for the emergence of a wage premium. However, because of the impact of inflation on revenue, the government's budget constraint tightened severely. With a drastically reduced command over resources, the real wage bill of the public sector was unavoidably reduced. The attempt by the government to protect the real value of wages by deficit-financed increases in nominal wages merely raised the price level. Not surprisingly, the reduced wage bill was achieved by reductions in real wages rather than in employment. As government revenue was restored, these wage cuts were reversed.

Our thesis is that this phase of negative public sector rents tended to immunize the Indonesian government from lobbying pressure. During much of the 1960s public sector employment was sufficiently unattractive that would-be public employees must have formed a relatively small group, and the intensity of their lobbying for jobs must have been relatively weak. Because on the eve of the first oil boom this lobby was unimportant (in marked contrast to Nigeria, where it was at its peak), it was that much easier for the government to contain the payroll at a constant share of GDP.

The oil boom did, of course, relax the budget constraint and thereby provided a second opportunity for existing public sector employees to achieve a wage premium, although in politically less favorable circumstances. Some signs of this were, for example, the 66 percent real pay increase for civil servants in 1976/77 (similar in both magnitude and timing to the Udoji award in Nigeria). Such an increase must have strengthened the incentive to lobby for public employment, and some elements of patronage-induced recruitment might well have developed after that. The essential difference with Nigeria, however, is the weakness of the lobby for public sector employment expansion *just before* the boom.

The diagrammatic representation of the model as applied to Indonesia is shown in figure 18.1. The 1950s are characterized by a zero rent equilibrium E_0. The model predicts no pressure to expand employment, and our best estimate was that during the 1950s employment in the public

Figure 18.1   Relation of Public Sector Pay and Employment

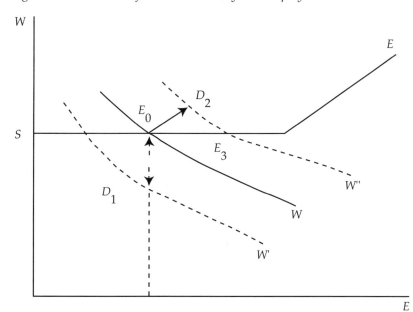

Note: W–W", wage equilibrium locus; S–E, labor supply locus.

sector expanded only slowly (between 0.7 and 3.3 percent a year). During the early 1960s the government budget constraint tightened, shifting the wage equilibrium locus, $W–W$ to $W'–W'$, and changing the outcome to the temporary disequilibrium D_1. Recall from chapter 17 that real wages were halved in this phase. During the late 1960s this was reversed, returning the economy to E_0. The oil boom relaxed the budget constraint to $W''–W''$, turning E_0 into a disequilibrium. According to the model, the disequilibrium response raises both wages and employment until D_2 is reached. Beyond this level of employment and wage premium there is continued pressure for employment expansion, but at the price of reductions in the wage premium, until the economy reaches the new equilibrium E_3.

Public sector employment indeed grew more rapidly during the oil boom than earlier (at 4.3 percent a year during 1971–82, against 3.1 percent during 1961–71). Public sector pay initially rose relative to mean income as a result of the 1976/77 wage awards, but thereafter it declined. Between 1977 and 1984 per capita consumption in the economy grew at 5.3 percent a year (table 16.1), whereas civil service salaries rose by only 2.3 percent a year; thus any rents were being eroded. The oil slump (not shown in figure 18.1) shifts the $W–W$ locus back inward, leading to a phase of falling wage premiums and employment. The real wage bill for the civil service peaked in 1981, suggesting that both real wages and employment were being squeezed. Although we do not wish to claim too much for such a simple model, the broad pattern of public sector pay and employment over the period does appear to be consistent with its predictions.

Another puzzling question is why the economic policies of the technocrats were generally followed (with many lapses), even though this sometime required the government to apply very unpopular policies. The reliance on the technocrats during the stabilization program was rational enough: the economy was in a sharp Lies, and there appeared to be no prospect of returning it to an even keel without abandoning the previous, discredited economic stance (and replacing it with a more coherent market-oriented strategy) and without massive foreign assistance. The technocrats were the obvious and indeed the only group who could manage this changeover. The continued reliance on the technocrats thereafter is a less straightforward tale.

In the early years of the New Order, the Suharto government was supported by a broad coalition of anticommunist activists made up of student groups, urban intellectuals, Muslim organizations, and the more strongly anti-Sukarno elements in the army. However, this power base, institutionalized in Golkar—the government-backed state party—was steadily narrowed throughout the 1970s. The Muslim organizations in particular became increasingly alienated from the government and by the late 1970s represented the principal articulate opposition.

The relationship of the government with business was also somewhat tangled. The wealthier Chinese business owners came to depend heavily on the opportunities created by the New Order's economic strategy, despite their initial reservations. Meanwhile, the indigenous business leaders were far less successful in seizing these opportunities and thus far less committed to the underlying policies.

In many respects the economic record of the New Order regime in this period was one of relatively high macroeconomic competence coupled with microeconomic performance ranging from lackluster to incompetent. With the partial exception of agriculture, the sectoral management of the economy was not impressive. Most of the enterprises taken over in 1957 remained in the government's hands. At best these organizations were kept ticking without serious disaster or significant advance; at worst they were involved in extensive corruption and massive waste of resources, a leading example being the Pertamina debacle.

Mackie (1983) argues that a deep-seated ideological ambivalence toward capitalism made it difficult for the technocrats to prevent the growth of bureaucratic controls. The damage caused by these pervasive microeconomic distortions and, in particular, by the import monopolies could be absorbed without causing undue political tension during the period of high oil revenues. During the 1980s, with this cushion progressively deflated by falling oil prices, matters became more difficult. The whole web of state-supported privileges came under greater pressure than before. In late 1986 the government announced the abolition of 165 trade monopolies as part of the policy change in response to these difficulties, but it left the most important monopolies in place. There was an acceptance that some ground had to be yielded, but the amount was still unresolved.

The appendix (tables 18A.1–18A.6) begins on the next page.

Table 18A.1 Budget Items as a Percentage of GDP, 1951–59

Item	1951	1952	1953	1954	1955	1956	1957	1958	1959
Direct taxes	2.10	2.05	2.20	2.43	2.42	1.76	1.70	1.95	1.87
Transition	0.71	0.73	0.71	0.80	0.73	0.66	0.70	0.77	0.66
Income	0.20	0.21	0.25	0.24	0.23	0.19	0.17	0.17	0.12
Company	0.88	1.01	1.18	1.33	1.40	0.89	0.76	0.89	0.99
Free sales	0.27	0.07	0.02	0.01	0.01	0.00	0.00	0.09	0.06
Other	0.05	0.03	0.04	0.05	0.06	0.03	0.07	0.04	0.03
Indirect taxes	5.72	5.76	4.86	3.95	3.43	3.03	2.75	3.11	2.55
Sales	0.88	0.70	0.69	0.61	0.43	0.53	0.40	0.52	0.38
Import duty	1.88	1.57	1.39	0.99	0.85	1.06	0.86	0.75	0.63
Export duty	1.75	2.04	1.10	0.54	0.58	0.24	0.10	0.13	0.14
Excise	1.00	1.32	1.47	1.59	1.42	1.06	1.25	1.61	1.31
Other	0.21	0.12	0.21	0.21	0.15	0.13	0.15	0.10	0.09
Total taxes	7.83	7.81	7.07	6.38	5.85	4.80	4.45	5.06	4.41
Government enterprise profits	0.18	0.33	0.22	0.06	0.08	0.27	0.17	0.06	0.13
Other profits	5.79	2.73	3.26	1.99	2.04	3.85	3.51	3.85	4.54
From foreign exchange certificates	5.52	2.34	2.08	1.18	1.43	2.82	2.12	3.03	3.71
Total revenue	13.79	10.87	10.55	8.43	7.97	8.91	8.12	8.98	9.09
Deficit	—	6.02	3.31	3.52	1.36	1.28	2.81	4.35	4.52

— Not available.

Source: Bank Indonesia annual reports; national accounts; authors' computations.

Table 18A.2 Budget Items as a Percentage of GDP, 1960–65

Item	1960	1961	1962	1963	1964	1965
Routine revenue	12.72	11.06	5.42	4.99	3.92	3.87
Direct taxes	2.24	2.53	1.33	1.04	0.99	1.12
Income	0.67	0.62	0.45	0.40	0.40	0.18
Wage	0.13	0.06	0.01	—	—	—
Corporate	1.33	1.78	0.85	0.63	0.57	0.36
Other	0.11	0.07	0.02	0.01	0.01	0.58
Indirect taxes	3.90	4.38	2.22	1.76	1.57	1.30
Sales	0.85	0.65	0.37	0.30	0.34	0.43
Import duty	0.73	1.08	0.32	0.39	0.48	0.22
Export duty	0.37	0.68	0.19	0.06	0.01	—
Excise	1.74	1.60	0.81	0.85	0.57	0.56
Other	0.21	0.37	0.54	0.17	0.17	0.10
Other revenue	6.58	4.15	1.86	2.19	1.37	1.45
Development revenue	0.17	2.18	0.19	0.06	0.05	0.02
Domestic	0.00	1.82	0.14	0.05	0.03	0.02
Foreign	0.17	0.35	0.05	0.01	0.02	—
Total revenue	12.89	13.24	5.61	5.05	3.97	3.89
Expenditure	15.52	18.83	9.14	10.28	9.55	10.66
Central	6.13	5.77	2.24	2.53	4.08	4.02
Defense	6.48	8.64	4.92	3.05	3.16	4.26
Production	1.32	2.32	1.16	3.03	1.23	1.20
Communications	0.52	0.74	0.26	0.94	0.50	0.72
Welfare	1.06	1.35	0.56	0.72	0.58	0.46
Deficit	2.62	5.60	3.54	5.23	5.58	6.76

— Not available.

Source: Bank Indonesia annual reports; national accounts; authors' computations.

Table 18A.3 Budget Items as a Percentage of GDP, 1965–1983/84

Item	1965	1966	1967	1968	1967/70	1970/71	1971/72	1972/73	1973/74
Routine revenue	7.78	9.84	13.32	12.67	14.67	17.23	18.37	18.54	20.06
Domestic revenue	3.89	4.16	7.10	7.14	8.48	10.07	10.99	11.55	12.50
Oil and gas	—	—	0.88	1.59	2.29	2.90	3.61	4.51	4.94
Other	3.89	4.16	6.22	5.56	6.19	7.17	7.38	7.05	7.56
Direct taxes	1.13	0.57	1.11	1.22	1.50	1.54	1.76	1.72	1.82
Income	0.18	0.20	0.37	0.45	0.42	0.39	0.45	0.46	0.44
Corporate	0.36	0.19	0.40	0.45	0.54	0.60	0.65	0.60	0.57
Withholding	—	—	0.08	0.30	0.53	0.54	0.63	0.59	0.73
Local development	0.01	0.16	0.25	—	—	—	—	—	—
Other	0.58	0.01	0.01	0.01	0.01	0.01	0.03	0.07	0.07
Indirect taxes	2.55	3.40	4.96	4.11	4.58	5.24	4.91	4.64	5.10
Sales	—	0.43	0.54	0.60	0.44	0.53	0.53	0.62	0.67
Import sales	—	—	—	0.29	0.55	0.65	0.58	0.54	0.66
Excise	—	0.56	0.70	0.90	0.79	1.12	1.14	1.04	0.92
Import duty	0.22	1.17	1.99	1.78	2.01	2.07	1.78	1.43	1.66
Export	—	0.62	1.25	0.66	0.26	0.73	0.72	0.64	0.89
Property	—	—	—	—	—	—	—	0.30	0.25
Other	1.34	0.36	0.21	0.15	0.12	0.13	0.18	0.13	0.15
Nontax revenue	0.21	0.19	0.15	0.23	0.11	0.38	0.71	0.68	0.64
Development revenue	—	—	2.91	1.69	3.17	3.52	3.48	3.09	2.63
Total revenue	3.89	4.16	10.01	8.84	11.65	13.59	14.47	14.64	15.13

Routine expenditure	6.82	8.27	8.26	7.14	7.54	8.42	8.96	8.57	9.21
Personnel	2.81	4.70	3.73	3.29	3.61	3.84	4.19	3.92	3.47
Rice and food allowance	—	—	—	—	—	1.32	1.14	0.90	0.87
Material	1.56	2.47	2.40	1.84	1.75	1.83	1.72	1.87	1.42
Subsidies to local governments	0.16	0.54	1.23	1.22	1.54	1.64	1.72	1.64	1.40
Amortization and interest	0.14	0.15	0.63	0.48	0.50	0.75	1.20	1.04	0.91
Domestic	0.14	0.03	0.15	0.09	0.06	0.06	0.14	0.14	0.11
Foreign	—	0.13	0.48	0.38	0.44	0.69	1.05	0.90	0.81
Other	2.14	0.40	0.27	0.33	0.13	0.36	0.13	0.10	2.00
Oil subsidy	—	—	—	—	—	—	—	—	—
Development expenditure	3.83	1.18	2.07	1.69	4.11	4.96	5.03	5.83	5.82
Administration/defense	—	—	—	—	—	2.42	2.63	2.94	2.16
Regional development	—	—	—	—	—	0.95	0.96	1.13	1.11
Other	—	—	—	—	—	—	0.37	0.28	0.55
Fertilizer subsidy	—	—	—	—	—	—	—	—	—
Project aid	—	—	—	—	—	1.21	1.16	1.22	1.47
Total expenditure	10.65	9.45	10.33	8.84	11.65	13.38	13.99	14.41	15.04
Deficit	6.76	5.29	3.23	1.70	3.17	3.31	3.00	2.86	2.54
Excluding oil	6.76	5.29	4.11	3.28	5.46	6.21	6.61	7.36	7.48

(Table continues on the following page.)

Table 18A.3 (continued)

Item	1974/75	1975/76	1976/77	1977/78	1978/79	1979/80	1980/81	1981/82	1982/83	1983/84
Routine revenue										
Domestic revenue	15.67	16.79	17.77	17.79	17.17	18.93	21.49	22.03	19.66	18.80
Oil and gas	8.55	9.35	10.00	9.81	9.29	12.04	14.75	15.57	12.94	12.40
Other	7.12	7.45	7.77	7.99	7.88	6.89	6.74	6.47	6.73	6.40
Direct taxes	2.03	2.31	2.35	2.57	2.51	2.26	2.36	2.47	2.70	2.52
Income	0.39	0.46	0.51	0.52	0.49	0.42	0.34	0.37	0.46	0.52
Corporate	0.81	0.96	0.78	0.86	0.91	0.84	0.94	1.01	1.07	0.99
Withholding	0.74	0.73	0.91	1.02	0.94	0.82	0.91	0.93	1.02	0.82
Local development	—	—	—	—	—	—	—	—	—	—
Other	0.09	0.16	0.15	0.17	0.17	0.18	0.16	0.16	0.16	0.19
Indirect taxes	4.49	4.31	4.69	4.69	4.59	4.10	3.71	3.39	3.33	3.21
Sales	0.76	0.89	0.99	1.02	0.89	0.54	0.56	0.56	0.76	0.75
Import sales	0.62	0.54	0.63	0.58	0.51	0.39	0.41	0.40	0.37	0.33
Excise	0.66	0.73	0.80	0.92	1.02	0.92	0.92	0.98	0.98	1.01
Import duty	1.44	1.30	1.57	1.44	1.19	0.90	0.94	0.97	0.83	0.73
Export	0.63	0.46	0.38	0.41	0.67	1.10	0.64	0.23	0.13	0.14
Property	0.25	0.26	0.26	0.26	0.25	0.20	0.18	0.17	0.17	0.17
Other	0.14	0.12	0.07	0.07	0.07	0.05	0.06	0.08	0.11	0.08
Nontax revenue	0.60	0.83	0.72	0.72	0.77	0.53	0.66	0.61	0.69	0.68
Development revenue	2.07	3.68	4.79	3.89	4.16	3.90	3.14	3.08	3.07	5.06
Total revenue	17.74	20.48	22.56	21.68	21.33	22.83	24.63	25.12	22.74	23.86

Routine expenditure	9.08	9.98	9.97	10.81	11.04	11.48	12.19	12.59	11.08	10.96
Personnel	3.75	4.45	3.89	4.49	4.03	4.01	4.25	4.11	3.83	3.59
Rice and food allowance	0.75	1.16	0.98	0.88	0.74	0.82	0.94	0.89	0.86	0.79
Material	1.57	2.28	2.08	1.90	1.69	1.61	1.41	1.67	1.65	1.38
Subsidies to local governments	1.80	2.13	1.91	2.41	2.10	1.89	2.05	2.18	2.08	2.02
Amortization and interest	0.66	0.59	1.16	1.15	2.15	1.93	1.65	1.68	1.94	2.74
Domestic	0.06	0.05	0.15	0.04	0.04	0.10	0.07	0.03	0.03	0.04
Foreign	0.60	0.54	1.01	1.11	2.12	1.83	1.58	1.65	1.91	2.70
Other	1.30	0.53	0.92	0.87	1.07	2.03	2.83	2.96	1.58	1.24
Oil subsidy	—	—	—	0.32	0.80	1.49	2.00	2.7	—	—
Development expenditure	8.59	10.47	12.56	10.85	10.28	11.35	12.43	12.52	11.66	12.90
Administration/defense	1.98	2.88	3.61	3.75	3.42	4.18	5.32	4.92	5.16	4.20
Regional development	1.41	1.75	1.74	1.84	1.73	1.55	1.70	2.05	1.73	1.89
Other	3.45	2.30	2.48	1.55	1.15	1.89	2.41	2.56	1.72	1.78
Fertilizer subsidy	2.03	1.01	0.66	0.16	0.33	0.35	0.60	0.67	0.67	0.42
Project aid	1.75	3.53	4.73	3.71	3.97	3.72	3.00	3.00	3.05	5.04
Total expenditure	17.67	20.45	22.53	21.67	21.32	22.83	24.62	25.11	22.73	23.86
Deficit	2.00	3.66	4.76	3.88	4.15	3.90	3.13	3.08	3.07	5.06
Excluding oil	10.55	13.00	14.76	13.68	13.44	15.94	17.88	18.64	16.00	17.46

— Not available.
Source: Bank Indonesia annual reports; national accounts; authors' computations.

Table 18A.4 Domestic and Foreign Budget as a Percentage of GDP, 1972–83

Year	Domestic			Foreign				
	Revenue	Expenditure	Balance	Revenue	Aid	Expenditure	Increase in funds[a]	Balance
1972/73	7.67	10.41	-2.74	3.89	3.09	3.99	0.22	3.21
1973/74	8.05	8.54	-0.49	4.46	2.63	6.51	0.18	0.76
1974/75	6.98	9.63	-2.66	8.69	2.07	8.03	-0.43	2.31
1975/76	7.44	12.23	-4.79	9.36	3.69	8.23	-0.09	4.73
1976/77	7.87	12.04	-4.17	9.90	4.79	10.49	2.15	6.36
1977/78	7.99	12.77	-4.78	9.81	3.89	8.90	1.24	6.04
1978/79	7.88	11.41	-3.53	9.29	4.16	9.92	1.60	5.14
1979/80	6.89	13.71	-6.82	12.04	3.90	9.12	3.44	10.27
1980/81	6.74	12.54	-5.81	14.75	3.14	12.07	3.74	9.56
1981/82	6.43	12.70	-6.26	15.60	3.08	12.41	0.35	6.62
1982/83	7.34	13.33	-5.99	14.45	2.93	11.39	-1.25	4.74

Note: Routine expenditure and all revenue are divided between domestic and foreign sectors on the basis of officially published information; development expenditures use weights derived by Booth and McCawley.
a. Set equal to the increase in government funds with the monetary system.
Source: Authors' calculations, derived from calculations of Booth and McCawley 1981, updated by Scherer 1982.

Table 18A.5 Money Stocks and Factors Affecting the Money Supply, 1953–84
(percentage of GDP)

Item	1953	1954	1955	1956	1957	1958	1959	1960
Stocks								
Currency	5.67	7.52	6.69	5.31	6.78	9.07	8.94	8.73
Demand deposits	2.47	3.41	2.77	2.28	2.32	4.34	2.88	3.53
M1	8.14	10.93	9.46	7.59	9.11	13.41	11.82	12.26
Quasi-money	—	—	—	—	—	—	—	—
M2	—	—	—	—	—	—	—	—
Changes								
Net foreign assets	-1.70	-0.27	0.80	-1.03	-0.49	0.26	4.74	1.15
Central government assets	2.67	3.33	1.21	1.42	2.78	4.35	1.14	-0.21
Assets of official entities	-0.30	0.16	0.15	-0.14	0.03	0.61	1.78	0.85
Assets of other entities	0.25	0.27	-0.95	0.54	1.07	-0.39	0.33	-0.26
Time deposits	-0.04	-0.01	-0.05	0.02	0.00	-0.01	0.04	-0.04
Other	0.08	-0.02	-0.30	-0.16	-0.74	-0.06	-6.16	1.84
M1	0.96	3.46	0.86	0.66	2.66	4.77	1.87	3.32
Currency	—	—	0.91	0.41	2.27	2.64	2.21	1.97

(Table continues on the following page.)

Table 18A.5 (continued)

Item	1961	1962	1963	1964	1965	1966	1967	1968
Stocks								
Currency	10.33	7.70	5.47	6.35	7.64	4.55	4.02	3.56
Demand deposits	4.06	2.48	2.74	3.12	3.21	2.48	2.05	1.87
M1	14.39	10.18	8.21	9.46	10.85	7.03	6.07	5.43
Quasi-money	—	—	—	—	0.34	0.11	0.27	0.57
M2	—	—	—	—	11.19	7.14	6.34	6.00
Changes								
Net foreign assets	-1.45	-0.69	-0.34	-0.14	0.08	-0.08	-1.46	0.60
Central government assets	4.98	4.00	3.82	4.85	4.87	3.99	2.82	0.14
Assets of official entities	0.67	0.96	0.73	1.15	1.68	0.97	0.77	2.68
Assets of other entities	1.54	0.42	0.33	0.47	1.54	0.89	2.14	0.31
Time deposits	-0.04	-0.03	0.00	-0.02	-0.29	-0.08	-0.22	-0.47
Other	-1.49	0.46	-0.56	-0.53	-0.09	0.53	-0.59	-0.28
M1	4.21	5.11	3.97	5.77	7.79	6.22	3.45	2.98
Currency	3.08	4.07	2.26	3.89	5.75	3.97	2.32	1.94

Item	1969/70	1970/71	1971/72[a]	1972/73	1973/74	1974/75	1975/76	1976/77
Stocks								
Currency	4.37	4.87	5.40	5.70	5.44	4.81	4.94	5.22
Demand deposits	2.94	3.02	3.85	4.68	4.69	4.37	5.76	5.88
M1	7.33	7.89	9.25	10.37	10.13	9.18	10.70	11.10
Quasi-money	1.92	2.77	4.82	4.67	5.41	4.98	6.25	6.29
M2	9.25	10.67	14.07	15.04	15.54	14.16	16.95	17.40
Changes								
Net foreign assets	-0.54	0.49	3.97	2.43	1.98	0.01	-5.66	2.72
Central government assets	-0.14	-0.55	0.42	-0.42	-0.32	0.22	0.19	-2.37
Assets of official entities	}5.21	}3.75	}3.13	}4.41	1.39	2.76	6.96	2.46
Assets of other entities					4.68	2.13	2.52	1.93
Time deposits	-0.96	-1.16	-2.34	-1.03	-2.33	-1.23	-2.08	-1.19
Other	-0.80	-0.79	-3.08	-2.07	-2.12	-1.72	1.07	-1.19
M1	2.78	1.74	2.11	3.33	3.28	2.17	3.00	2.37
Currency	1.58	1.18	1.07	1.58	1.68	1.05	0.90	1.19

(Table continues on the following page.)

Table 18A.5 (continued)

Item	1977/78	1978/79[b]	1979/80	1980/81	1981/82	1982/83[b]	1983/84
Stocks							
Currency	5.21	5.51	5.01	4.68	4.59	4.75	4.63
Demand deposits	5.41	5.76	5.72	6.27	7.64	6.93	5.86
M1	10.62	11.27	10.73	10.96	12.22	11.69	10.49
Quasi-money	5.86	5.45	5.67	5.66	6.09	7.71	10.04
M2	16.48	16.72	16.40	16.61	18.31	19.39	20.53
Changes							
Net foreign assets	2.97	3.25	7.29	4.82	-0.06	-0.03	3.65
Central government assets	-1.47	-1.17	-3.34	-3.82	-0.19	1.09	-2.39
Assets of official entities	0.29	3.92	0.71	1.13	1.23	0.60	0.36
Assets of other entities	1.84	2.54	1.58	2.73	3.47	4.21	3.07
Time deposits	-0.68	-0.77	-1.84	-1.44	-1.23	-2.36	-3.70
Other	-0.88	-5.00	-1.58	-0.43	-0.40	-2.62	-0.11
M1	1.49	2.77	2.82	2.98	2.82	0.96	0.88
Currency	0.92	1.34	1.14	0.96	0.56	0.73	0.72

— Not available.

a. After 1971/72 some items previously classified as "other" are classified as "net foreign assets."

b. Includes valuation adjustments following devaluation.

Source: Bank Indonesia reports; authors' computations.

Table 18A.6 Government Saving, Foreign Official Borrowing, and Gross Fixed Capital Formation, 1960–84

(percentage of GDP)

Year	Government saving[a]	Foreign official borrowing	Gross fixed capital formation[b]
1960	—	0.17	7.9
1961	—	0.35	10.2
1962	—	0.05	5.6
1963	—	0.01	8.2
1964	—	0.02	12.1
1965	−2.93	0.00	6.7
1966	−4.11	0.00	4.5
1967	−1.16	2.91	8.0
1968	0.00	1.69	8.8
1969/70	0.94	3.17	11.7
1970/71	1.65	3.52	13.6
1971/72	2.03	3.48	15.8
1972/73	2.98	3.09	18.8
1973/74	3.29	2.63	17.9
1974/75	6.59	2.07	16.8
1975/76	6.81	3.68	20.3
1976/77	7.80	4.79	20.7
1977/78	6.98	3.89	20.1
1978/79	6.13	4.16	20.5
1979/80	7.45	3.90	20.9
1980/81	9.30	3.14	20.9
1981/82	9.44	3.08	25.7
1982/83	8.58	3.07	22.5
1983/84	7.84	5.06	25.7

— Not available.

a. Defined as the excess of revenue (excluding foreign capital) over routine expenditure.

b. Calendar years, 1969–83.

Source: Bank Indonesia reports; national accounts; authors' computations.

19 Explaining the Outcomes

This chapter considers why the patterns of economic growth and income distribution identified in chapter 16 came about. The discussion draws on the previous historical and analytic discussions, although that material is not summarized here. Growth and distributional outcomes can be explained as resulting from the interaction of policies, initial conditions, and exogenous events. However, the policies themselves are the outcome of a political process reflecting the balance among interest groups, beliefs, and past outcomes. We begin, therefore, with the evolution of policy and then consider growth and distributional outcomes.

The Evolution of Policy

The discussion in earlier chapters underlined a paradox in the evolution of economic policy since independence. The most superficial reading of Indonesia's history demonstrates that economic policy underwent dramatic changes in detailed design. More fundamentally, the issue of whether technical economic questions were central or peripheral to the concerns of the day changed considerably over time. Also, underlying these rather violent swings was genuine progress in response to changes in the structure of the economy and external circumstances. What is somewhat less obvious is that there was a remarkable continuity in policy concerns in Indonesia, with many characteristic strands familiar throughout the period—strands that were typically opposed to each other or at least difficult to reconcile, and that waxed and waned relative to each other with the passage of time.

At times these opposing forces offset each other, producing periods of stalemate during which nobody was able to put their programs to the test. At other times one side or another was able to establish a measure of dominance over at least some aspects of policy. Here we consider briefly the origin and nature of the underlying economic ideas that have proved so resilient.

Technocrats and dirigistes alike (or, in an earlier epoch, pragmatists and revolutionaries) claimed legitimacy for their ideas by appealing to the state philosophy of Pancasila and to the constitution. This practice was facilitated by the extreme vagueness of both. Unlike *demokrasi* Pancasila, which was increasingly defined by what the regime did, the nature of *ekonomi* Pancasila was less easily resolved. This permitted a broad debate about its interpretation, constrained mainly by article 33 of the constitution of 1945, which was readopted under the aegis of Sukarno in 1959. The article, in Robert Rice's translation, states:

> 1. Economic affairs are to be organized as a joint effort based on family principles.
> 2. Branches of production which are important for the state and which control [the supply of] the basic needs of the masses are to be controlled by the state.
> 3. The land and water and natural wealth contained within are to be controlled by the state and used as much as possible for the prosperity of the populace. (Rice 1983, p. 61)[1]

These sentences are clearly open to a wide variety of interpretations, ranging from a mainstream, Western, mixed-economy formulation to a thoroughgoing socialist one. Even this does not exhaust the possibilities. A former minister remarked in 1981 that "a pancasila economic system does not represent something on the continuum between a capitalist economy and a socialist one, or a joint venture between capitalism and socialism. . . . It is an economic system which runs parallel to and besides these two major economic systems" (quoted in McCawley 1982, p. 102).

In some measure, this view appears to rest on a misconception about the nature of capitalism, or at least about the extent to which mixed economies are capable of modifying capitalist imperatives with socially defined controls. Thus there was much early disparagement of "free-fight capitalism" and advocacy of such alternative institutions as cooperatives and state enterprises. A deep-rooted suspicion of competition is one pervasive strand in Indonesian economic thinking. Regardless of how the question of asset ownership was to be resolved, it was felt that the control of economic organizations should be based on "harmonious and family principles" rather than subject to conflicting personal interests.

It is useful to digress briefly to consider the political analogue of this view—a suspicion of majority voting as a basis for democracy and a preference for making decisions by consultation and consensus. This attitude is seen in the village procedure of making decisions in a spirit of mutual cooperation known as *musyawarat*; its origins lie in a system suited to small numbers of individuals who know each other well.

Translation of this process from the village to regional and national politics poses severe problems. Reconciliation of potentially conflicting interests requires that these interests be appropriately represented, and neither adversarial nor anonymous procedures are appropriate under such a system. The premise underlying guided democracy—that representation should be handled not by political parties but by functional social groups (such as the army, peasants, unions, women, and youth)—is best seen as an attempt to tackle this conundrum.

The parallel response in the economic sphere is a distrust of anonymous market forces as a coordinating device, even when private ownership is accepted. This perception has colored the whole debate concerning the ownership, control, and organization of the means of production and the role of direct intervention in the economy. The word *control* is used twice in article 33. Opinions have differed on the extent to which effective state control presupposes state ownership. The Sukarno government took the view that the important branches of production should be owned by state enterprises and not just overseen and regulated by the state. Hatta took a different view, favoring state ownership for infrastructure and some basic industries but otherwise relying on state supervision—a position broadly adopted by the Suharto government.

However, the whole question of ownership has been complicated by three factors. First, there are at least three distinct classes of private owners: indigenous, Chinese, and foreign. Second, the behavior of private owners and the benefits accruing to them are often determined more by their relationship to the state apparatus and the system of direct controls than by their status or capability as entrepreneurs. Third, even state ownership has frequently been preempted by the phenomenon of bureaucratic capitalism, so that the division between private and public ownership becomes still more blurred.

The consequence is that ideological questions of ownership have become markedly entangled with other ideological issues like economic nationalism. This has led to a number of paradoxical alignments. Perhaps the most bizarre was the position of the Communist Party in the Sukarno era as the leading advocate for giving private business a larger role and defending it against bureaucratic exactions (Castles 1965). This stance reflected the large part played by Chinese businesses in funding the party, but it also reflected a clear perception that bureaucratic-capitalist state enterprise was not socialist.

The relatively pragmatic view of the ownership question that had evolved by the late 1980s probably reflects the fact that formal ownership was largely irrelevant to the underlying ideological issues: state ownership offered no guarantee of beneficial control or nonpartisan behavior, and private ownership offered no guarantee of efficiency or innovation. The more important issues were market structure and the system of direct controls, which we consider in turn.

The first provision of article 33 is usually interpreted to mean that cooperatives were to be the basic type of economic enterprise. Both the Sukarno and Suharto governments consistently followed a policy of promoting cooperatives in agriculture but not in the formation of large- and medium-size enterprises. Both governments—and indeed the colonial administration in the 1930s—actively discouraged competition, especially in manufacturing, by direct restrictions on investment and by quantitative restrictions on imported substitutes. The Suharto government also actively encouraged industry associations, which usually discourage competition among their members. To determine whether new investment should be allowed and imports restricted, the estimated capacity of production was compared with the quantity demanded in the country at the existing price. If capacity was at least as great as the domestic demand thus defined, the industry was closed temporarily to new investment.

This policy had all sorts of drawbacks. The industrial planners often had poor estimates of the capacity of production and quantities sold (Rice 1983). Also, the policy was based on the false premise that demand can be defined independently of price. The more nearly true this is, with highly inelastic demand, the more scope there is for protected firms to be high-cost producers or to make excessive profits. If demand is relatively elastic and there are economies of scale, this strategy has the effect of shutting out domestic producers from eventual emergence into export markets.

Although the policy was deplored by the neoclassically inclined technocrats, there does not appear to have been any great popular opposition to it (unlike the narrower issue of import monopolies, which came under increasing criticism during the early 1980s). This lack of opposition may reflect the distrust of competition and overt conflict discussed above or the sheer longevity of the policy, which had been a continuous part of the economic fabric since the 1930s. This was an area in which the technocrats could not summon their usual political support, since the authorities were direct beneficiaries of the existing system. Having no popular constituency to call upon, the technocrats were never able to make serious inroads into the problem, thus ensuring continuity on at least this dimension between the New Order and earlier periods.

In marked contrast to the issue of ownership are the adoption of a balanced budget and convertibility under the New Order. Here the break in performance with the earlier period could not be more dramatic. But even here the continuity of policy is greater than might first appear. Arndt (1967) pointed out how similar the procedure for floating the currency was in 1967 to that attempted in the reform of 1957, and he expressed only qualified optimism that it would work the second time around. The fact that it did work is perhaps more a reflection of the greater success on the budgetary front than of any significant difference in how exchange management was tackled. And, as already remarked, the early success in taming the budget deficit was more a consequence of being prepared and able to attract large official capital inflows than of any instant fiscal magic.

Even in the heart of the guided economy period, the Economic Declaration of March 1963 was not only a brave attempt to balance the budget whatever the political opposition; it also abolished many price controls, granted considerable autonomy to state enterprises, and generally moved back toward the liberal policies of the earlier period (Castles 1965). A storm of criticism ensued, but the government did not immediately bow to this pressure. However, it sank the whole policy and, in particular, any chance of budget rectification, in a reintensification of the confrontation with Malaysia.

All this suggests that it was not the desire to balance the budget and to instill some order into the foreign exchanges that distinguishes the New Order period; it was rather that both objectives were achieved and sustained. The capacity to move from the depths of crisis to fiscal discipline gave the technocrats their subsequent stature and authority, and it was this stature that permitted the policies to be maintained. Nevertheless, there are some peculiarities to note.

First, the balanced budget was in practice an extremely blurred and idiosyncratic concept. Official foreign capital flows were treated as revenue, which, as we have seen, was absolutely critical to any early hope of achieving a balanced budget after 1966. Also, any increase in government funds with the monetary system was treated as expenditure—a practice known as "investment through the banking system." During both oil booms, but particularly the second, a substantial budget surplus was thus able to masquerade as a balanced budget. In that sense, budget balance has been a myth.

Second, because revenue disproportionately accrued in foreign exchange, an overall budget balance would imply a deficit of domestic revenue over domestic expenditure, with expansionary effects on the money supply unless steps were taken to sterilize these. Given the high real growth of the economy and the relatively high income elasticity of demand for real balances in Indonesia (usually put at around 1.5), a substantial deficit would be compatible with price stability. If the underlying rationale of the balanced budget was to prevent inflation, we should expect to have seen strenuous attempts to prevent excessive monetary expansion. On the contrary, the authorities appear to have been content to take a relaxed attitude, tolerating inflation rates of 20 to 30 percent with little sign of discomfort. This is in dramatic contrast to the great fear of inflation often attributed to economies that have suffered an episode of hyperinflation.

If the balanced budget proves on closer inspection to be an extremely flexible concept consistent with a wide variety of real fiscal stances, the same cannot be said of convertibility. This is neither an opaque nor a fuzzy concept: citizens can either exchange currency freely or they cannot. For this reason, an adherence to convertibility is a relatively unforgiving macroeconomic commitment; as noted in chapter 13 it was one of the central planks in enforcing and maintaining a conservative macroeconomic posture. Indeed, the common link between these two policies is that they stipulate and embody in their different ways the idea of a sustainable configuration for the economy.

Growth and Equity Objectives

This discussion has focused on the instruments of policy rather than the objectives. We close with a brief consideration of the objectives of equity and growth. As with most developing countries, these have always figured high on Indonesia's list of objectives. From 1949 to 1953 and from 1965 to 1979 the government placed more emphasis on increasing real per capita income than on equity, whereas from 1953 to 1965 economic growth was for the most part neglected (Rice 1983). During the first part of each growth period, the emphasis was on rehabilitating the economy. In the period of the third five-year development plan, starting in 1979, equity was officially made the primary objective, with growth secondary.

Equity has been seen as a multidimensional concept throughout. In 1957 Hatta was promoting a basic-needs approach with emphasis on food, clothing, health, housing, and "appropriate" education. By the 1980s the focus was more narrowly on health and education. Although the third plan's "eight paths to equity" also stressed various dimensions of income distribution, little use was made of fiscal measures to influence these: the main instruments were budgetary expenditures and the use of selective credit. Furthermore, the interpretation of equity for policy purposes had much in common with the idea of poverty eradication. The plan had little to say on inequality as such, or on the undesirability of extremes of wealth in a poor society.

III *A Concluding Comparison*

20 *A Comparison*

From 1950 to the late 1980s Indonesian living standards rose to triple those in Nigeria, which fell absolutely. GNP per capita in 1987, on a purchasing power parity basis, was twice as high in Indonesia as in Nigeria (10.1 and 5.0 percent of the U.S. value, respectively, per World Bank 1995). Even allowing for the fragility of this type of comparison, it is evident that over the period Indonesia moved from being a poorer country than Nigeria to being a substantially richer one. The incidence of poverty declined substantially in Indonesia and increased in Nigeria. There was also a weak trend toward greater equity in Indonesia. By the end of the period Indonesia was by far the more equal society.

These outcomes did not evolve in a steady progression: both economies experienced massive domestic and external shocks. The domestic shocks—war and hyperinflation—were country specific, but the main external shocks—the temporary oil windfalls—were common to both Nigeria and Indonesia. Although growth, equity, and poverty outcomes diverged remarkably when viewed over the whole period, this is attributable to relatively brief periods after 1973 when external shocks were similar (well after the differing domestic shocks). Thus the key question is why performance of the two countries diverged during and after the oil shocks.

We start this comparison by examining policies and outcomes for income distribution and economic growth. We then compare macroeconomic performance and management, since these were important underlying determinants of the differing outcomes. We next focus on the crucial institution of markets and then turn to agriculture, where outcomes diverged more radically than in any other sector. Finally, we look at the underlying political economy question of why policies themselves—which account for much of the difference in outcomes in the two countries—differed.

Poverty and Equity

Comparing poverty and equity outcomes and attributing them to policies, exogenous shocks, and initial conditions in the countries demands extensive, reliable data. There are, however, no published data on distribution of income prior to 1992 in Nigeria, and the data that exist permit the observer to draw only qualified inferences. The story seems to be one of rising living standards, declining poverty, and increasing income equality in Indonesia, versus a drop in living standards, greater poverty, and little progress toward equity in Nigeria. Although these findings are far from robust, they appear consistent with other evidence and can be supported by an analytic account. Below we compare the data on poverty and equity outcomes; later we examine the extent to which these might be related to policy differences and why such differences may have occurred.

Outcomes Compared

We begin by comparing trends in living standards as indicated by mean per capita private consumption (tables 20.1 and 20.2). Trends in real private consumption are related to, but distinct from, trends in per capita GDP. As already noted, over the whole period there was a remarkable divergence in living standards so measured, with Indonesians increasing their living standards threefold compared with Nigerians. The comparison becomes even more remarkable when we look at specific periods. Between 1950 and 1955 living standards rose rapidly in both countries at the same rate—2.7 percent a year. From then until the mid-1960s there was stagnation in Nigeria and decline in Indonesia. Between then and 1973 there was a hiatus in Nigeria because of the civil war and a slow recovery in Indonesia. By 1973, at the start of the oil boom, both countries had recovered from their respective phases of decline and had exceeded slightly the previous peak living standard year of 1955. During the entire period, 1950–73, despite different, brief phases of decline, living standards in both countries increased by around 20 percent.

Thus all the divergence in living standards occurred after 1973, when relative performances diverged by 8 percent a year. Even within the post-1973 period it is during the oil slump rather than the oil boom that most of the differences lie. During the boom, 1973–80, living standards rose in Nigeria by 2.3 percent a year compared with 7 percent in Indonesia. During the slump, 1980–84, Indonesian living standards continued to rise, though at the slower rate of 2.7 percent, whereas Nigerian living standards declined at the annual rate of 15.2 percent. Thus it is the differing outcomes of the oil slump phase that dominate the period since 1950.

Table 20.1 Real Per Capita Private Consumption, 1950–84
(1950 = 100)

Year	Nigeria	Indonesia	Year	Nigeria	Indonesia
1950	100	100	1968	84	107
1951	104	100	1969	86	110
1952	108	109	1970	94	111
1953	108	105	1971	—	113
1954	113	110	1972	—	118
1955	114	114	1973	120	118
1956	110	—	1974	146	133
1957	110	—	1975	140	136
1958	109	—	1976	133	141
1959	106	—	1977	124	147
1960	114	101	1978	133	154
1961	108	107	1979	127	172
1962	114	112	1980	141	189
1963	115	105	1981	133	216
1964	115	103	1982	135	218
1965	105	103	1983	106	205
1966	104	99	1984	73	210
1967	88	105			

— Not available.
Source: Tables 6.1 and 16.1.

The rise in living standards in Indonesia and the decline in Nigeria would lead us to expect that the incidence of absolute poverty declined in Indonesia and rose in Nigeria. For Indonesia there is firm evidence that this indeed occurred; for Nigeria the data are too poor to investigate the matter. No inference about which country had the higher incidence of absolute poverty can be drawn, therefore, but we may safely conclude that poverty worsened in Nigeria and was substantially alleviated in Indonesia. This conclusion is secure despite the gaps in the income distribution data, because, given the trends in mean living standards, only large redistributions would upset it.

Table 20.2 Fitted Growth Rates, 1950–84
(percent)

Period	Nigeria	Indonesia	Difference
1950–84	2.0	1.6	0.4
1950–66	–0.1	0.1	0.2
1972–84	5.7	7.6	1.9

Source: Table 20.1

Table 20.3 Nutrition and Survival, Various Years

Category	1965	1973	Early 1980s
Calorie consumption per capita			
Nigeria	2,185	—	2,038
Indonesia	1,792	—	2,533
Life expectancy at birth (years)			
Nigeria	42	45	50
Indonesia	44	50	55
Infant mortality (deaths per 1,000 population)			
Nigeria	179	146	110
Indonesia	138	111	97
Child mortality (deaths per 1,000 population)			
Nigeria	33	29	21
Indonesia	20	15	12

— Not available.
Source: World Bank 1986a and 1987.

Despite the decline in private consumption in Nigeria, the provision of public services improved. Since well-being depends on both consumption and services, it may well have improved with the added services. Table 20.3 provides an indication of the consequences of these divergent trends in the consumption of public and private goods. Levels of nutrition rose in Indonesia and fell in Nigeria, reversing the ranking of the two. In both countries life expectancy increased and infant and child mortality declined. Since Nigeria started from much less favorable levels of survivorship, it is not possible to conclude which had the more satisfactory improvement.

We now consider outcomes for income distribution. In both Indonesia and Nigeria the politically dominant distributional dimension was regional. In both countries the politically most powerful region was the largest, and in both it happened to start the period as the poorest. A particularly interesting comparison is therefore the trend in the income differential between the region at the political core and the periphery (table 20.4). In Indonesia there was a clear and continuous trend over the 20 years from 1963/64 to 1983/84 for Java to gain relative to the periphery. The growth of 1.8 percent a year was sufficient to reverse the initial income ranking: by the end of our period the Javanese had a higher income than people in the periphery. For Nigeria the data are disjointed, but there is no basis to claim that the North gained relative to the other regions; after 1963 it is more likely that the opposite occurred.

The other spatial dimension of inequality we considered was urban-rural differences. In Nigeria in the first half of our period urban income, particularly among wage earners, was well above the supply price of labor from rural areas. During the 1970s and more especially in the oil slump, this differential was eroded and—by the end of our period—reversed. This trend is clear from table 20.5, which, however, makes no correction for differences in urban and rural price levels. In Indonesia there is no clear trend. We showed in chapter 18, however, that for most of the period urban income was closely pinned to the rural supply price, and so no trend should be expected.

The obvious distributional question to ask in any comparison is which country was more equitable. A national distribution of income is available for Nigeria only as of 1992. For earlier years survey data permit the distribution of cash income to be estimated separately for rural and urban areas. Since the share of subsistence income is known, we can compute bounds to the true distribution by assuming in turn that subsistence income is distributed either in proportion to cash income or perfectly equally. Part A of table 20.6 sets out the resulting comparison.

The comparison of income distributions between countries is always subject to qualification because of unknown differences in methodologies. However, the data suggest that by the end of our period, the

Table 20.4 Per Capita Income in the Periphery Relative to That in the Politically Dominant Region, Various Years
(per capita income in the core = 100)

	Nigeria[a]			
Year	All	Rural	Urban	Indonesia[b]
1950	290	—	—	—
1957	270	—	—	—
1963/64	—	108	—	119
1969/70	—	—	—	116
1976	—	—	—	100
1978	—	—	—	99
1980	—	135	—	—
1980/81	—	132	134	—
1983/84	—	184	72	83

— Not available.

a. The periphery here consists of the Western and Eastern regions; the dominant region is the North. The Western and Eastern regions have been aggregated using equal weights. Because of the absence of a usable population census, the true weights are unknown. The 1963 census implied weights very close to being equal.

b. The periphery consists of the outer islands; the dominant region is Java. The regional cost of living differential, available only for 1976, is applied to all other years.

Source: Tables 6.2 and 16.6.

Table 20.5 Urban/Rural Per Capita Nominal Expenditure Differential,
Various Years

Year	Nigeria	Indonesia
1952–54	181	—
1963/64	—	162
1970	—	167
1974/75	163	—
1976	—	203
1978	—	195
1979	151	151
1980	179	169
1981	150	179
1982	147	—
1983	139	—
1984	121	189
1985	120	—

— Not available.
Source: Tables 6.3 and 16.9.

distribution of income in both urban and rural areas had become significantly more equal in Indonesia. In almost all cases the Indonesian distribution was more equal than the most-equal bound of the Nigerian distribution. For example, in rural areas in Indonesia the poorest 40 percent
had 22.4 percent of all income; in rural Nigeria their share was between
13.4 and 22.0 percent. Differences were most marked between the top
quintiles, especially in urban areas. These broad inferences are corroborated by the more recent evidence, as part B of table 20.6 demonstrates.

National trends in the distribution of household income are measurable for Indonesia after 1962. There was a modest trend toward greater
equity. Part B of table 20.6 compares the end-period snapshots; the full
series is shown in table 16.5. The poorest 40 percent gained relative to
the mean at an annual rate of 0.3 percent. Since the mean was itself rising by 3.4 percent, nearly all the gains of the poor were the consequence
of growth rather than redistribution.

Policies

At no time during our period did the Nigerian government implement
a program focused directly on the poor. Some policies, such as universal
primary education, would have directly benefited the poor (among others), and other policies, such as construction expenditure, may have indirectly benefited the poor more than others.

Table 20.7 compares trends in the delivery of health and education services. In both countries the supply of health services increased substantially relative to the population, but there are marked differences in composition. The Nigerian government predominantly increased supplies of hospitals and doctors, whereas the Indonesian government concentrated on nurses. By the early 1980s Nigeria was considerably better supplied with hospitals than Indonesia and less well supplied with

Table 20.6   Inequality: Some Comparisons for Various Years

	Population quintile				
Category	Q1	Q2	Q3	Q4	Q5
A. National sample survey, 1983/84					
Rural					
Nigeria					
Most unequal	5.1	8.3	11.9	19.2	55.5
Most equal	10.0	12.0	14.7	19.7	43.8
Midpoint	7.6	10.2	13.3	19.5	46.8
Indonesia	9.2	13.2	18.4	21.4	37.8
Urban					
Nigeria					
Most unequal	3.9	8.1	13.0	20.7	54.3
Most equal	5.8	9.4	13.8	20.6	50.3
Midpoint	4.9	8.8	13.4	20.7	52.3
Indonesia	8.3	12.3	17.1	21.2	41.1
B. Other national sample surveys					
Nigeria					
1992	5.1	10.1	14.8	21.0	49.0
Indonesia					
1990	8.7	12.1	15.9	21.1	42.3
1963	6.9	12.5	17.0	23.4	40.2

Note: The Nigerian published data are for the distribution of income by household size. These data have been recomputed to generate per capita income shares by population quintiles. The two bounds reported above are for cash income only (most unequal) and with subsistence income (for which the mean per capita is known) assumed to be equally distributed across the population (most equal). The Indonesian data are for expenditure rather than income; however, from chapter 16 it can be seen that the two are very similar and that the income distribution is generally slightly more equal than the expenditure distribution.

Source: For part A, tables 16.10 and 16.12; Nigeria, NISH National Consumer Survey, table 25; authors' computations. For part B, World Bank 1995; table 16.5.

nurses, whereas in 1965 the position was reversed. In part this may have reflected the rent-seeking incentives in Nigeria, which favored construction projects. However, it may also have reflected prior differences in education policies. One of the significant successes of the Sukarno period was the expansion of primary education. By 1965 Indonesia had already made real progress toward universal primary education, a position not matched by Nigeria until around 1980. The Suharto government continued the expansion of education to the secondary level, and the enrollment rates Indonesia achieved by the start of the oil boom were not reached by Nigeria until the early 1980s.

Given the absence of poverty-focused policies in Nigeria, it is not surprising that there were also no policies designed to increase equity. In contrast, Indonesian governments always sought to alleviate poverty, and equity was another objective in the Sukarno era. The range of policy interventions has been considerable: price controls on food, the kerosene subsidy, the delivery of public services (both productive and for consumption), the provision of employment through rural public works, and—in the Sukarno era—an abortive land reform. These differences

Table 20.7 Health and Education Indicators, Various Years

Sector	1965	1973	Early 1980s
Health			
Nigeria			
Population per doctor	45.0	30.4	12.0
Population per nurse	5.8	5.1	2.4
Population per hospital bed	2.4	1.7	1.1
Indonesia			
Population per doctor	31.8	20.0	12.3
Population per nurse	9.3	3.0	2.1
Population per hospital bed	1.5	1.4	1.5
Education (percentage of age cohort)			
Nigeria			
Primary enrollment	32.0	37.0	92.0
Secondary enrollment	5.0	4.0	29.0
Higher enrollment	0.4	—	3.0
Indonesia			
Primary enrollment	72.0	80.0	118.0
Secondary enrollment	12.0	26.0	39.0
Higher enrollment	1.0	—	7.0

— Not available.

Source: World Bank, 1986a and 1987; Minstry of Finance, Bureau of Statistics (BPS), *Statistical Yearbook of Indonesia, 1985.*

give rise to two questions: do the differences in policy account for the differences in outcomes, and why did policies differ?

The central outcome to be addressed is why the distribution of income was by 1990 considerably more equal in Indonesia than Nigeria. Given initial conditions, Nigeria might have been expected to be the more equitable society. Indonesia had a far more limited supply of agricultural land, and both theory and evidence suggest that landownership would therefore become more concentrated in that country.

The weak trend toward equity in Indonesia indicates that either the poverty-focused policies were quantitatively minor or that growth worsened income distribution. The latter is not unlikely in the Indonesian case, because of the Dutch disease effects that might have been expected in agriculture. As discussed in chapter 14, Indonesian agriculture includes a nonfood sector that produces highly labor-intensive traded goods and a food sector that is dominated by rice. Rice is also highly labor intensive, and although it is little traded because of the government's reluctance to be dependent on imports, the domestic rice price has closely followed the world price. Agriculture thus stood to lose heavily through the general equilibrium effects of the oil boom on the real exchange rate. In turn, through its effects on the labor market, the decline of agriculture would probably have worsened the distribution of income, because it is hard to imagine oil revenue being spent on such labor-intensive production.

According to this view, the key policy initiatives that alleviated poverty in Indonesia were not necessarily those directly focused on the poor but rather those that enhanced agricultural production. The success of agriculture was the result of several factors: the overtly pro-agriculture policies, notably the desire for rice self-sufficiency; the exchange rate policy (which prevented the nonfood sector from contracting as in Nigeria); and exogenous technical progress. Thus although agriculture was not a major component of Indonesian GDP growth, its support probably accounts for the fact that GDP growth was translated so successfully into poverty reduction.

Nigeria might conceivably be the obverse of this, so that in Nigeria we observe the Indonesian counterfactual policy. Such a thesis would run as follows: an oil boom in the absence of pro-agriculture policies (and the presence of technological stagnation) causes agricultural decline, which in turn weakens the labor market, giving rise to increasing inequality. However, such a thesis—that Nigeria experienced what would have happened in Indonesia had not policies there been pro-agriculture and poverty focused—must be qualified. We have seen that there were country-specific crosscurrents in Nigeria. Cocoa farmers, who were among the rural rich, lost relative to food farmers as a result of general equilibrium effects during the oil boom. Food agriculture was largely nontradable, and labor was attracted out of the sector despite rising food prices as a result of the expansion of more attractive public employment (the phenomenon we have described as "Nigerian disease"). Both of these effects should have equalized rural incomes during the oil boom.

Additionally, recall that secondary education policies differed substantially (table 20.7). In the early 1970s, 1 in 4 teenagers was in school in Indonesia, compared with only 1 in 20 in Nigeria. Consider the consequences for the stocks of skilled workers relative to unskilled workers by the early 1980s. The wage premium for educated labor would have been higher in Nigeria than in Indonesia, and this in turn would have tended to make the urban income distribution less equal. Furthermore, during the oil slump Nigeria resorted to quantitative restrictions on trade and an overvalued currency to a far greater extent than Indonesia. As a result, there was a massive growth in rents, which by 1984 had reached 6 percent of GDP by our tentative estimates. We suggested that only about half of these were dissipated in competitive rent-seeking, so very large amounts were accruing as supranormal returns. Thus the greater inequality of the Nigerian income distribution may have reflected the greater value of rents.

We now turn to the divergent distributional trend between the dominant and the peripheral regions. The redistributive policy that both countries had in common was interregional. In both countries the transfer of oil revenue between states was massive, and in Nigeria it was the very stuff of the political process. However, whereas in Indonesia the politically dominant region succeeded in systematically raising its relative living standard, no such trend occurred in Nigeria. Three factors may explain this divergence. First, in Nigeria the capital was not in the dominant region, the North, but in the Southwest; as a result, much federal expenditure on the public sector injected income into the Southwest.[1] Second, in Indonesia the general equilibrium effects of labor market tightening in agriculture benefited Java most. Third, Java was more dominant in Indonesia than the North was in Nigeria, and so the latitude for regional preference was correspondingly greater; in Nigeria regional redistributions were continuously and fiercely contested.[2]

Economic Growth

In Nigeria GDP increased by 241 percent in real terms from 1950 to 1984; in Indonesia the increase was 438 percent. In per capita terms the increases were 23 percent and 146 percent, respectively. Part of the explanation for this enormous difference lies in the handling of the oil windfalls, discussed later in this chapter.

In table 20.8 we decompose GDP growth into its sectoral components. During the 1950s, agriculture was the main source of growth for both countries. By the 1980s in Indonesia manufacturing had taken over from agriculture, whereas in Nigeria the manufacturing growth that had occurred during the oil boom proved unsustainable. In Indonesia the oil boom did not arrest agricultural growth but, as discussed in chapter 17, was used to enhance factor productivity. In Nigeria, even during the period of agricultural growth prior to the oil boom, factor productivity did not increase (with the exception of cocoa). During the boom, labor was withdrawn from agriculture and output contracted. There was no green revolution and much less public investment in the sector.

Both countries registered a huge increase in oil output prior to the 1973 price increases. In Nigeria this was the result of exploration activities in the late 1960s. In Indonesia a substantial oil industry already

Table 20.8 GDP *Growth, 1950–84*

		Share in GDP growth[b]		
Period	*GDP growth*[a]	*Agriculture*	*Mining*	*Manufacturing*
Nigeria				
1950–60	42	60	0	12
1960–73	125	11	32	12
1973–79	23	-18	32	28
1979–84	-14	16	-83	9
1950–84	241	17	18	36
Indonesia				
1950–60[c]	50	—	—	—
1953–59	21	51	6	5
1960–73	87	30	11	12
1973–79	52	17	4	22
1979–84	36	23	0	25
1953–84[c]	358	24	4	17

— Not available.

a. Percentage increase in GDP at factor cost (constant prices) over the period.

b. Increase in sectoral GDP over the period, as a percentage of the absolute value of the increase in total GDP.

c. The 1953–59 series has been linked to the 1960–84 series and carried back to 1950 by assuming that total GDP increased between 1950 and 1953 (and each sector's GDP between 1959 and 1960) at the same rate as agricultural value added in the series of van der Eng (1993). In the first two years of the period there was considerable per capita growth from a very low level—one-quarter below the level reached in 1930. From 1952 to 1970 per capita output was roughly stable; it increased by 35 percent in the 1970s and then remained fairly stable at this higher level.

Source: Tables 9.1, 16.12, and 16.13.

Table 20.9 Domestic Investment, Selected Years, 1950–90
(percentage of GDP at current market prices)

Year	Nigeria	Indonesia
1950	7.2	9.4
1955	12.2	9.9
1960	13.2	7.9
1965	18.3	6.3
1970	14.9	13.6
1975	25.2	19.5
1980	22.2	26.6
1983	14.7	25.1
1990	14.6	36.6

Source: World Bank 1980, 1986b, and 1994b.

existed before the war. A wartime restriction on exploration was still in force when, in 1951, the oil companies were confined to their existing concessions, pending a review of the operation of mineral rights that lasted until 1960. They were in a position to develop known reserves discovered but not exploited before the war—such as the Minas oil field (Arndt 1983a)—but new exploration was not actively encouraged until the foreign investment law of 1967. Although the oil industry inevitably requires substantial investment, the driving forces for output growth in this sector were a combination of national policies (particularly those affecting exploration activities), international policies (within the OPEC cartel), and luck (exploration success).

Investment in both countries in the period started at extremely low rates (table 20.9). In Indonesia the rate of investment fell even further during the Sukarno period, reaching only 6.3 percent of GDP in 1965. Price control and the rationing of imported raw materials made the accumulation of domestic real assets extremely unattractive.[3] At the same time Nigerian economic policies—through tax and tariff incentives—actively encouraged investment, particularly in industry. In the 1960s a substantial part of investment (one-third of the total) was financed with foreign direct investment and external loans; in 1965 these were insignificant in Indonesia. As a result, over the same period that Indonesian investment was falling, in Nigeria it more than doubled. Any forecast made on the basis of these figures would have been that Nigeria, rather than Indonesia, was poised for accelerated growth.

During the oil boom, investment rates were similar in both countries. We have seen that both underwent rapid industrial growth during the boom, but that capital costs rose enormously in Nigeria, and relative to capital accumulation there was little output growth. There are three reasons for this difference. First, in Nigeria much of what was classified as investment did not represent capital accumulation but kickbacks, which often accounted for half, and sometimes far more, of total project cost. Second, there was a difference because Indonesia could still embark on industrial investment with relatively low capital intensity—investment that Nigeria had already undertaken in the 1960s. Textile investment is a case in point.

A final reason for the difference in output growth was that Nigeria attempted to convert the windfall very quickly into domestic real assets. Even without corruption the attempts of the Nigerian governments to buy more than the economy was capable of supplying—given its inflexible productive structure, shortages of technical skills and executive capacity, and limited physical ability to import and distribute foreign products—would have amounted to a reinforcement of the Dutch disease spending effect. Spending on goods and factors that were, or effectively became, nontradable resulted in rents rather than output increases. Although to some extent inevitable, this problem was much less serious in Indonesia, which adjusted spending less quickly, hoarded part of the oil revenue, invested a smaller proportion of the remainder, and scrapped the most extravagant investment projects after the Pertamina crisis. Repayment of the Pertamina debt in 1976 also fortuitously provided an effective counterinflationary way of dealing with oil surpluses.

Macroeconomic Policies

Macroeconomic policies also played a role in the divergent paths of the Indonesian and Nigerian economies. In this section we examine fiscal balances, trade and exchange rate policies, relative prices, and policy responses to the oil booms.

Fiscal Balance

Analysis of fiscal policy in earlier chapters suggested two broad conclusions. First, although fiscal management in Indonesia greatly improved in the New Order period, the absolute magnitude of the required fiscal correction was not great. Second, in Nigeria the budget showed a long-run secular tendency to deteriorate, with expenditure growing even when revenue was relatively stationary.

Table 20.10 summarizes the major budgetary components as annual averages over the periods used in discussing Indonesia (those used for Nigeria differ only in the boundary between the first and second: 1960 rather than 1957). The relative size of the average Indonesian budget deficit was remarkably constant until the late 1980s, ranging from 2.8 to 3.6 percent of GDP, except during the period of fiscal collapse, when it rose only to 4.8 percent. The period of 1951–57, generally regarded at the time as plagued by a severe deficit problem, was in retrospect characterized by a relatively small deficit. For the entire Old Order period (the years preceding the New Order) the deficit averaged 4.0 percent, whereas that for the New Order period until 1990 was only a little lower, at 3.8 percent. The crisis of the 1960s was essentially a revenue and financing crisis, not an expenditure crisis. Government spending was remarkably constant at around 12.5 percent of GDP for the quarter of a century between independence and the first oil boom.

The nature of the fiscal problem in Indonesia during 1958–66 was twofold. First, there was considerable erosion of domestic revenue, which fell from 9.8 percent during 1951–57 to 7.4 percent during 1958–66. What is more, it did not recover, with averages of 6.7 percent, 7.6 percent, and 6.8 percent during the New Order periods of 1967–73, 1974–79, and 1980–85. Second, there was a dearth of noninflationary means with which to finance a deficit. There was in any case no domestic bond market, and the policy of confrontation led to a cessation of the already limited access to international capital. In consequence, the expansion of the money stock (M1) during 1958–66 coincided with the deficit, averaging 4.8 percent of GDP (table 18A.5). Since the money stock was in any case rather small (around 10 percent of GDP), this rate of expansion was massively inflationary.

What made such a rapid fiscal recovery feasible was the relatively small scale of the underlying problem. The advent of oil revenue on a serious scale (3 percent of GDP) offset the further decline of the deficit from 4.8 to 2.8 percent. This level was comfortably covered by the resumption of development aid.

Table 20.10 Comparative Budgets, 1951–90
(annual average percentage of GDP)

	Nigeria				Indonesia			
	Revenue		Expen-		Revenue		Expen-	
Period	Total	Oil	diture[a]	Deficit	Total[b]	Oil	diture	Deficit
1951–57	10.4	—	7.7	(2.7)[c]	9.8	—	12.8	3.0
1958–66	11.6	—	11.7	0.1	7.4	—	12.2	4.8
1967–73	14.6	5.3	16.6	2.0	9.7	3.0	12.5	2.8
1974–79	25.0	19.2	25.4	0.3	17.4	9.8	21.0	3.6
1980–85	23.0	16.8	29.2	6.2	20.3	13.5	23.9	3.6
1986–90	26.0	19.7	31.9	5.8	16.6	7.4	22.0	5.4

— Not available.
a. Includes allocation of federally collected revenue to the states.
b. Excludes development receipts.
c. Parentheses indicate a surplus.
Source: Tables 8.1, 8.2, 8.3, and 18A.1.

Table 20.11 Comparative Budgets, 1973–84
(annual average percentage of GDP)

| | Nigeria | | | | Indonesia | | | |
| | Revenue | | Expen- | | Revenue | | Expen- | |
Period	Total	Oil	diture[a]	Deficit	Total[b]	Oil	diture	Deficit
1973–77	24.3	18.8	23.3	-1.0	15.7	8.2	18.9	3.2
1977–79	23.9	17.0	27.0	3.1	17.5	9.6	21.5	4.0
1979–82	26.3	20.1	31.1	4.7	20.8	14.1	24.2	3.4
1982–84	20.4	14.3	28.0	7.7	19.2	12.7	23.3	4.0

a. Includes allocation of federally collected revenue to the states.
b. Excludes development receipts.
Source: Tables 8.3 and 18A.1.

The Nigerian budgetary story from 1951 to 1973 could not be more different. In place of stationary expenditure there was a strong upward trend of around one-half of 1 percent of GDP a year. The share of government expenditure in GDP during 1967–73 was more than double that during 1951–57; it had also moved from being substantially smaller than that in Indonesia to being substantially larger. In consequence, despite the relatively rapid growth of revenue, the budget swung increasingly into deficit, with a total swing of nearly 5 percent of GDP. However, the position during 1967–73 was not particularly problematic. The average deficit was only 2 percent and was entirely attributable to the civil war. The remainder of the change was the elimination of the inappropriate and large budget surplus (2.7 percent) run during 1951–57 by the colonial authorities.

The later two periods also show a very different pattern. Nigerian government oil revenue was much higher during the first oil cycle, 1974–79—at 19.2 percent of GDP—than that for Indonesia (9.8 percent). In the second cycle, 1980–84, the gap closed, with the Nigerian government obtaining revenues of 17.1 percent and the Indonesian government, 13.9 percent. The Nigerian government ran a somewhat smaller average deficit over the whole decade (3.3 percent) than did the Indonesians (3.6 percent), but the pattern is quite different, with the Indonesian deficit stationary between the two cycles and the Nigerian deficit increasing alarmingly from near balance to 7 percent of GDP during 1980–84.

Since these were cycles, it is of interest to disaggregate them further. Table 20.11 presents similar information for four periods within the cycles, isolating the upswing phases of 1973–77 and 1979–82 from the stationary and downswing phases, 1977–79 and 1982–84. The table presents two particularly interesting features. First, the pattern of a relatively stationary deficit in Indonesia and a secularly increasing deficit in Nigeria was preserved within the periods. Second, revenue instability was much greater in Nigeria than in Indonesia, particularly during the second cycle. Thus the Nigerian government faced a more severe budgetary adjustment problem. Between 1979–82 and 1982–84 Nigeria suffered a revenue deterioration of 6 percent of GDP and achieved an expenditure reduction of 3 percent. In contrast to Nigeria, Indonesia's revenue decline was 1.6 percent and the expenditure was reduced by 0.9 percent. In each case expenditure was reduced by around half the revenue decline, but since the revenue shock was much larger in Nigeria, the deterioration in the deficit was much more severe.

The Nigerian deficit during the last decade was considerably larger (relative to GDP) than the deficit that produced hyperinflation and destroyed the Old Order in Indonesia. The reason for the spectacularly more severe domestic consequences in the Indonesian case was the lack of financing facilities—in particular, the lack of access to foreign funds. The Nigerian government was able to avoid similar consequences because it was able to cover the deficit by foreign borrowing. Of course, this large cumulate debt itself posed serious problems for subsequent macroeconomic policy.

Trade and Exchange Rate Policies

We compare trade and exchange rate policies for the years 1971–86 by means of six indicators (tables 20.12 and 20.13). As proxies for adjustment through changes in assets we show changes in reserves, capital flows classified by the IMF as "exceptional financing," and other short-term capital flows. The tables also show the nominal official exchange rate (against the SDR, or special drawing rights of the IMF), the price of nontradables relative to the price of importables as an indicator of Dutch disease, and the domestic price of imported goods relative to their c.i.f. value as a proxy for protection through tariffs and quantitative import controls. The construction of the protection index is described in appendix 20.A.

THE FIRST OIL CYCLE. In Nigeria there was, until the 1980s, no use of exceptional financing and very little change in short-term borrowing. Reserves reflected the oil cycle: from less than $0.5 billion at the beginning of our period, reserves rose to $5.6 billion at the end of 1974; they were subsequently drawn down until they amounted to less than $2 billion four years later. Indonesia, however (except for 1975, the year dominated by the Pertamina crisis), accumulated reserves throughout the 1970s. Thus the two countries differed markedly in the use of assets. The Dutch disease series are based on very different data sources and so

Table 20.12 Nigeria's Trade and Exchange Rate Policies, Selected Indicators, 1971–86

| Year | Reserves (millions of dollars)[a] | Yearly change (millions of dollars) | | | Exchange rate (SDRs per naira)[c] | Dutch disease, Pn/Pm (1972 = 100)[d] | Protection, Pd/Pw (1972 = 100)[e] |
		Reserves	Exceptional financing	Other short-term capital[b]			
1971	408	-206	n.a.	174	1.40	98.6	101.2
1972	355	53	n.a.	-92	1.40	100.0	100.0
1973	559	-204	n.a.	-49	1.26	96.5	89.7
1974	5,602	-5,043	n.a.	-239	1.33	98.6	70.5
1975	5,586	16	n.a.	-22	1.36	113.8	72.5
1976	5,180	406	n.a.	-39	1.36	125.1	85.4
1977	4,232	948	n.a.	-184	1.26	119.9	81.4
1978	1,887	2,345	n.a.	169	1.19	118.7	94.5
1979	5,548	-3,661	n.a.	10	1.35	133.8	97.8
1980	10,235	-4,687	n.a.	28	1.44	139.9	100.5
1981	3,895	6,340	57	197	1.35	137.5	98.4
1982	1,613	2,282	3,487	139	1.35	127.2	127.2
1983	990	623	2,532	-151	1.28	91.0	154.6
1984	1,462	-472	1,446	-912	1.26	80.4	245.1
1985	1,667	-56	2,179	-775	0.91	74.7	—
1986	1,081	580	441	845	0.25	59.7	213.8

— Not available.
n.a. Not applicable.
a. Total reserves, minus gold, end of year.
b. Includes payments arrears.
c. SDRs are special drawing rights of the IMF. Data are for end of year.
d. Pn is the price of nontradables; Pm is the price of importables. For 1971–81, Pn is calculated as the price deflator of GDP in "other services"; thereafter, data from table 5.13 are used.
e. Pd is the domestic price of imports; Pw is the world price of imports, calculated as the import unit value index multiplied by the exchange rate index provided by the deflator for value added in manufacturing.
Source: International Financial Statistics, various issues; table 5.13.

Table 20.13 Indonesia's Trade and Exchange Rate Policies, Selected Indicators, 1971–86

| Year | Reserves (millions of dollars)[a] | Yearly change (millions of dollars) | | | Exchange rate (SDRs per rupiah)[b] | Dutch disease, Pn/Pm (1972 = 100)[c] | Protection, Pd/Pw (1972 = 100)[d] |
		Reserves	Exceptional financing	Other short-term capital			
1971	185	-29	—	60	1.40	109.6	86.5
1972	572	-387	—	154	1.40	100.0	100.0
1973	805	-233	—	271	1.26	95.7	114.5
1974	1,490	-685	—	-87	1.24	113.0	102.4
1975	584	906	—	-1,889	1.30	125.5	73.6
1976	1,497	-913	—	-268	1.31	132.9	91.5
1977	2,509	-1,012	—	-391	1.25	150.6	90.1
1978	2,626	-117	—	121	0.78	156.9	89.1
1979	4,062	-1,436	—	-454	0.76	137.8	101.3
1980	5,392	-1,330	—	-820	0.79	148.6	103.3
1981	5,014	378	—	-290	0.84	179.4	98.6
1982	3,144	1,870	—	526	0.83	179.4	96.5
1983	3,718	-574	—	731	0.61	167.6	137.4
1984	4,773	-481	—	476	0.60	172.1	144.1
1985	4,974	-201	—	-98	0.51	n.a.	n.a.
1986	4,051	923	—	n.a.	0.31	n.a.	n.a.

— Not available.
n.a. Not applicable.
a. Total reserves, minus gold, end of year.
b. SDRs are special drawing rights of the IMF. Values are indexed to a base of 1971 = 1.40 for comparability with Nigeria. Data are for end of year.
c. Pn is the price of nontradables; Pm is the price of importables. Data for 1972–79 are the inverse of column 4 in table 14.9 (rebased to 1972); data are extended for 1980–86 with the same methodology, using the Jakarta CPI (housing) for Pn.
d. Pd is the domestic price of imports; Pw is the world price of imports.
Source: International Financial Statistics, various issues; table 14.9.

are not comparable.[4] However, both show strong evidence—in the form of a relative price increase for nontradables—of Dutch disease, and both peak at the peak of the oil windfall.

The common phenomenon of Dutch disease produced pressure to compensate the nonoil tradable sector. In Nigeria this took the form of rapidly increasing protection of import-substitute manufacturing. In Indonesia, by contrast, the intervention was through undervaluation of the exchange rate. In 1978 and then again in 1983 the rupiah was devalued. The 1978 devaluation was particularly remarkable because there was no need for it on balance of payments grounds. Rather, the objective was to enhance the competitiveness of the nonoil tradable sector. The key difference between these two strategies was that Indonesia's strategy benefited exports whereas Nigeria's strategy further handicapped them.

THE SECOND OIL CYCLE. During the second oil cycle Nigeria, as before, maintained the exchange rate, accumulated reserves during the boom (some $8.3 billion in 1979 and 1980), and—during the downturn—started using assets: $6.3 billion in 1981 alone, and another $2.2 billion in 1982. Already during 1982 reserves were falling dangerously low, and the policy was changed to borrowing, of which some $10 billion took the form of "exceptional financing." Finally, the fixed exchange rate was abandoned and there was a massive devaluation of the naira (from 1.26 SDRs per naira at the end of 1984 to only 0.25 two years later). Relative prices of nontradables declined rapidly. In reaction to the downturn, Nigeria experienced a phase of borrowing followed by trade controls; note that the protection index rose sharply. In Indonesia, by contrast, although the phase of the use of reserves (1981 and 1982) was followed by a period of borrowing, this took place on a very limited scale.

Relative Prices

The domestic relative prices of exportables, importables, and nontradables can have powerful effects on growth and distribution. They influence the sectoral allocation of investment and the functional distribution of income, especially to sector-specific factors. The two independent relative prices are jointly determined by the two sets of policies—monetary-budgetary and exchange rate–trade policies—reviewed above. It is clear that whereas the oil booms imposed some common features on the two economies, both policy responses and relative price outcomes were significantly different. This section attempts to synthesize the previous discussion of macroeconomic policy.

Throughout this synthesis we use a diagrammatic analysis developed in Bevan, Collier, and Gunning (1990). The space is defined on the two relative prices, nontradables to importables and exportables to importables, and the schedules are equilibrium loci in the nontradable and money markets. The diagram is more fully described in appendix 20.B.

THE FIRST OIL CYCLE: THE BOOM OF 1973–77. The effect of an oil boom on prices is depicted in the top panel of figure 20.1. The expansion of demand increases the demand for nontradables and so shifts the locus of equilibrium in that market (N–N) to the right (N'–N'). With unchanged monetary and exchange rate policies the M–M locus is unaltered, so that the equilibrium for the economy changes from E0 to E1. This change raises the price of nontradables relative to importables. It also involves a trade liberalization, wherein the domestic price of importables falls relative to their world price. These two price changes follow from an oil boom unless monetary and exchange rate policies are altered massively: a sufficiently large revaluation or a large monetary expansion would leave no room for trade liberalization. In neither country were monetary and exchange rate policies so deviant during this period: both countries had small exchange rate depreciations and some monetary expansion.

The actual relative price changes during the first oil boom are shown in the bottom panel of figure 20.1, the data being those of the previous section. It is apparent that price changes were similar in the two economies. There was a substantial reduction in the domestic price of importables relative to their world price and a substantial increase in the relative price of nontradables. This is entirely in accord with our a priori predictions of the effects of the windfall. Thus we may conclude that the first oil boom gave rise to powerful general equilibrium effects common to both economies.

THE FIRST OIL CYCLE: THE DOWNTURN OF 1977–79. Between 1977 and 1979 there was a modest downturn in oil prices and quantities. Recall that the policy responses diverged markedly in the two countries. In Indonesia the government devalued and deflated, running a continuous payments surplus. In Nigeria the exchange rate was maintained, public expenditure was increased and financed by money creation, and the balance of payments was allowed to go into deficit, with import controls used to contain the deficit.

The top panel of figure 20.2 illustrates the theoretical consequences of a loss of foreign exchange earnings with these different policies. The oil downturn shifts the nontradables locus back to the left, partially reversing the previous shift. The Nigerian monetary expansion shifts the monetary equilibrium locus downward to $M_n'–M_n'$, whereas the Indonesian devaluation shifts it upward to $M_i'–M_i'$. Thus for Indonesia the equilib-

Figure 20.1 The First Oil Boom, 1973–77: Effects on Prices

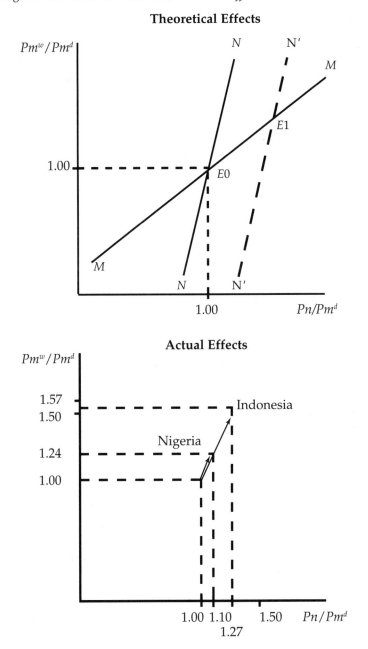

Theoretical Effects

Actual Effects

Note: Pm^w is the world price of importables, Pm^d is the domestic price of importables, Pn is the price of nontradables, and E is a point of monetary equilibrium.

rium changes from *E1* to *E2*. The equilibrium implied by Nigerian policies is at *En*. However, Nigeria did not return to equilibrium because the reserves were depleted. It thus temporarily occupied a disequilibrium such as *D2*.

The bottom panel of figure 20.2 shows what actually happened. Relative prices again changed substantially in both countries, but this time the changes were markedly divergent. Although in both economies there was some increase in protectionism, in Indonesia this was modest—less than half the level removed during the previous liberalization, whereas in Nigeria it was double the level during the initial liberalization. Furthermore, whereas in Nigeria the price of nontradables continued to rise, in Indonesia it fell. These changes are again consistent with the analysis (although not the only possible price changes implied by that analysis). They suggest that divergent general equilibrium effects were indeed generated by key differences in macroeconomic policies—devaluation and fiscal retrenchment in Indonesia were not matched in Nigeria.

THE SECOND OIL CYCLE: THE BOOM OF 1979–82. Although the economies shared the second oil boom, in Nigeria chickens were already coming home to roost from the first oil cycle. As a result, the Nigerian increase in demand was far more modest: per capita private consumption rose over the three years by 27 percent in Indonesia and only 6 percent in Nigeria. The public sector was in deficit, financed by monetary expansion. Even with this more modest growth in private demand, the Nigerian balance of payments was under severe pressure by 1982, and protection was used to defend the exchange rate (see chapter 5). As of 1982 neither economy had fully adjusted to the fall in oil volumes, leaving the balance of payments in disequilibrium deficit in both countries.

Our analytic account of the impact of the oil shock is shown in the top panel of figure 20.3. For simplicity both economies are shown as starting the period at the same point, $E2(D2)$, although this was a disequilibrium for Nigeria. The demand expansion shifts the nontradables locus rightward as previously, to $N_n'-N_n'$ for Nigeria and to $N_i'-N_i'$ for Indonesia. The equilibrium for Indonesia thus changes from $E2$ to E_i. However, as of 1982 the economy is in disequilibrium at a point such as $D3_i$ (at which the nontradables market is clearing but there is excess supply of money and a payments deficit). In Nigeria the period is characterized by a budget deficit financed by a monetary expansion, shifting the M–M locus downward to M_n'–M_n'. The equilibrium thus changes to E_n, but—as in Indonesia—there is a payments disequilibrium at a point such as $D3_n$. The changes implied by these differing income windfalls and differing monetary responses are unambiguous for Indonesia—an increase in the price of nontradables along with trade liberalization. For Nigeria the outcome depicted is rising prices for nontradables together with increased protectionism.

Figure 20.2 The Downturn of the First Oil Cycle, 1977–79: Effects on Prices

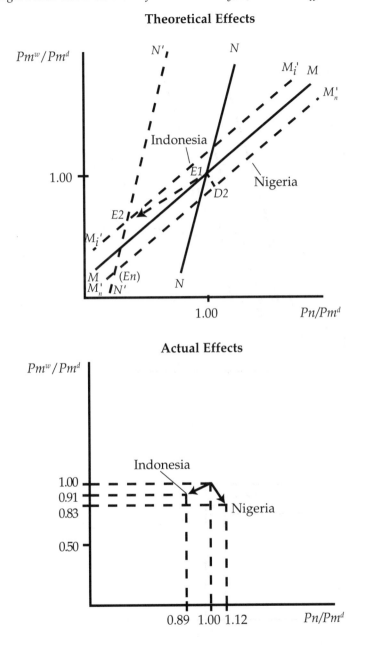

Theoretical Effects

Actual Effects

Note: Pm^w is the world price of importables, Pm^d is the domestic price of importables, Pn is the price of nontradables, E is a point of monetary equilibrium, and D is a point of disequilibrium.

Figure 20.3 The Second Oil Boom, 1979–82: Effects on Prices

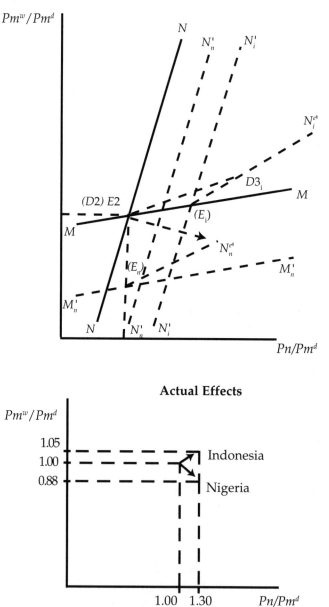

Theoretical Effects

Actual Effects

Note: Pm^w is the world price of importables, Pm^d is the domestic price of importables, Pn is the price of nontradables, E is a point of monetary equilibrium, and D is a point of disequilibrium.

The actual evolution of relative prices is shown in the bottom panel of figure 20.3. The price changes are again substantial, divergent, and consistent with our analytic account.

THE SECOND OIL CYCLE: THE OIL SLUMP OF 1982–84. From 1982 onward, foreign exchange revenue declined substantially for both economies. The decline was more pronounced in Nigeria because Indonesia was able to use the cushion of its previously accumulated reserves, whereas Nigeria had already exhausted both these and its credit opportunities. Policies also diverged, at least until 1984. In particular, in 1983 Indonesia had a major devaluation combined with fiscal retrenchment, whereas Nigeria maintained the exchange rate and continued with deficit financing, induced by the elections at the end of 1983.

The analytic account is depicted in the top panel of figure 20.4. To simplify, both economies are shown as starting the period at a common disequilibrium point, $D3$. The loss of income shifts the nontradables locus leftward to $N_i'-N_i'$ for Indonesia and to $N_n'-N_n'$ for Nigeria. The Indonesian devaluation and fiscal retrenchment shift the $M–M$ locus upward to $M_i'-M_i'$, whereas the Nigerian deficit financing shifts it downward to $M_n'-M_n'$. The resulting equilibria for the two economies are at $E4_i$ and $E4_n$. Qualitatively, these produce the same relative price changes—a fall in nontradable prices and a rise in protectionism; however, both changes are quantitatively larger for Nigeria.

The actual evolution of relative prices is shown in the bottom panel. Again they are analytically explicable. However, the most important feature is that for Nigeria the price changes are enormous. The cumulative consequences of macroeconomic policy differences gave rise to powerful and divergent general equilibrium effects that must have radically altered the distribution of income and the incentives for the sectoral allocation of investment.

Booms and Policy Responses

Both countries experienced three booms: the Korean commodity boom and the oil booms of 1973/74 and 1979/80. In neither country did the Korean boom confront the government directly with a policy problem. Unlike the oil windfalls, which largely accrued directly to the government, income from the Korean boom did not go principally to the state, although revenue from trade taxes rose. Nor did the Korean boom induce trade liberalization; recall that in Indonesia much of the 1950/51 liberalization was implemented before the government was aware of the boom. Thus in both countries the policy response was largely passive, resulting in reserve accumulation. In Nigeria this was so because the marketing boards, in keeping with their stabilization role, did not

Figure 20.4 The Slump of the Second Oil Cycle, 1982–84: Effects on Prices

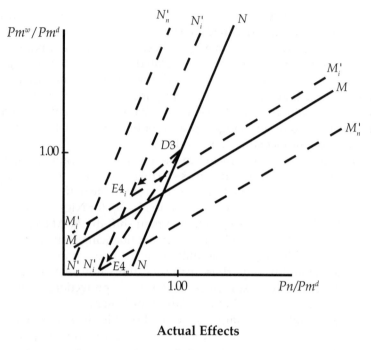

Theoretical Effects

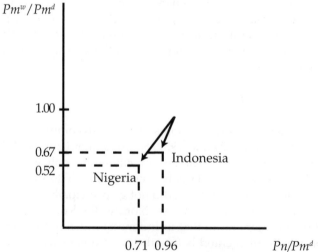

Actual Effects

Note: Pm^w is the world price of importables, *Pm^d* is the domestic price of importables, *Pn* is the price of nontradables, *E* is a point of monetary equilibrium, and *D* is a point of disequilibrium.

adjust producer prices for export crops in line with world prices. The resulting accumulation was unintentional in that the boards did not foresee the boom's magnitude. Similarly, in Indonesia the accumulation of reserves was largely unplanned, resulting from the failure to adjust import licensing quickly to increase foreign exchange availability. Although in Nigeria adjustment during the downturn was still semiautomatic (as it had been before the war)—because an independent monetary policy was impossible—Indonesia was less constrained, and the downturn resulted in a deficit in both the government budget and the balance of payments.

The oil booms enriched the governments. In addition, by that time the Indonesian government had constrained its own policy choices by its commitment to convertibility and budget balance. In Nigeria the policy response was a massive increase in federal expenditure, which doubled in 1974 and again in 1975, with heavy emphasis on capital formation. Investment absorbed 78 percent of the windfall, reflecting the commitment of the civil service to growth. The share of industrial investment increased rapidly, in particular in large projects like steel and petrochemicals. Current expenditure rose very little and actually fell as a percentage of GDP (table 20.14), and within this category the share of agriculture fell from 3 to 1 percent. Spending on education, however, increased considerably.

The Indonesian reaction differed in two respects. First, there was much less emphasis on capital formation. Our counterfactual exercises suggest that Indonesia invested only half of the windfall. Although public investment rose in Nigeria from 2.2 percent of GDP before the boom to

Table 20.14 *Public Expenditure during the Oil Cycles, Selected Years, 1971–83*
(percentage of GDP, current prices)

Country	1971	1974	1978	1980	1983
Nigeria					
Current federal expenditure	7.4	4.8	10.1	12.4	21.6
Indonesia[a]					
Routine expenditure	9.0	9.1	11.0	12.2	10.9
Personnel	4.2	3.8	4.0	4.3	3.5
Oil subsidy	—	—	0.8	2.0	—
Development expenditure	—	8.6	10.3	12.4	12.9
Fertilizer subsidy	—	2.0	0.3	0.6	0.4

— Not available.

a. Data are for 1971/72, 1974/75, 1978/79, 1980/81, and 1983/84.

Source: Tables 8.3 and 18A.1.

6.9 percent in 1974 and an astonishing 15 percent in 1978, the Indonesian share rose in the same period from 5.0 to 10.3 percent. The numbers are in many ways not quite comparable, but the difference is so large that the conclusion that Indonesia invested a much smaller proportion appears robust. The initial response in Indonesia to the increase in oil revenue was similar to the Nigerian response, although Indonesia actually aimed at a budget surplus initially; investment plans were expanded, and emphasis was placed on manufacturing investment, particularly on heavy industry, including (as in Nigeria) a Soviet-inspired plan for a steel industry.

The Pertamina crisis and intensifying Dutch disease put a severe brake on this development. Although at the start of the windfall both countries had adopted a structuralist emphasis on heavy industry, Indonesia pruned its investment plans severely in 1975, and in 1978 it chose to accumulate reserves to implement exchange rate protection rather than spend on investment projects. By contrast, Nigerian public investment accelerated.

A second—and related—difference in Indonesia's reaction to the oil booms was that the balanced budget principle, now tested for the first time, was upheld, with the effect of considerable underspending. In Nigeria the boom induced extra expenditure well in excess of the extra revenue, and there was (in addition to a planned use of reserves) a loss of control. Apart from industrial investment, Nigeria used the oil money in two principal ways: for education and for public employment. Public employment trebled between 1973 and 1981, which contributed to the agricultural decline. In Indonesia a large part of development expenditure was allocated to agriculture, in particular to irrigation rehabilitation and extension of the rainfed paddy area.[5] The food subsidy was one of the reasons for the increase in current expenditure. There was no massive expansion of the public sector, as in Nigeria.

In Nigeria revenue from the second oil boom was absorbed in large part directly by the political process. A much smaller proportion of the windfall was invested than during the first boom. The emphasis on industrial investment remained, but investment was no longer seen as valuable in itself but as a channel for patronage and kickbacks. The efficiency of investment declined dramatically. In Indonesia the response to the second oil price increase was slow. Initially, through the underspending of amounts transferred to the regions, the government ran a surplus. Subsequently the boom was used for three subsidies—on fuel, rice, and fertilizer.

During the slump, trade controls were tightened initially in both countries. In Indonesia the emerging budget problem led to drastic expenditure cutting much earlier than occurred in Nigeria. The Indonesian commitment to currency convertibility was tested in 1983 by a speculative capital outflow. The response was to maintain convertibility and devalue.

There was a further, enforced devaluation in 1986, and the government began a series of trade liberalizations. By contrast, Nigeria, through a combination of the use of reserves, borrowing, and trade controls, was able to postpone adjustment until 1986. Even then liberalization was halfhearted; it was also bitterly opposed by the academic community and subsequently reversed.

Markets

There were marked differences between the two countries in policies toward agricultural exports, production of food crops, and trade and exchange rates. Factor markets, and the role government played in these markets, were similar in the two countries. We consider product and factor markets in turn.

Product Markets

In Nigeria agricultural exports were taxed heavily through the marketing boards for much of the period. What started out as a commodity price stabilization scheme became a fiscal instrument in the mid-1950s and remained so until the reform of 1973, by which time agricultural exports had been virtually wiped out. Nothing similar occurred in Indonesia.[6] It would have been unwise—if not impossible—to implement such a policy in Indonesia in the 1950s because it would have added to secessionist pressures and later to smuggling. The geographic position of the main export regions made export taxes impractical. The ease with which agricultural exports could be smuggled was a major constraint on Indonesian trade policy, and many of the numerous policy changes and innovations can be interpreted as devices intended to make legal exporting more attractive.

In Nigeria the government had a significant effect on food crop production through the urban labor market, but its direct role in food crops was, until the 1980s, largely a policy of neglect (except for the fertilizer subsidy). By contrast, food crops—especially rice—were a major policy focus in Indonesia. At a time when agriculture was virtually ignored in Nigeria, Indonesia set up an effective extension system, promptly introduced high-yielding varieties, and supported rice production through the deliberate manipulation of the rice/fertilizer price. It should be emphasized that some aspects of Indonesian rice policy make generalization difficult. The 1972 rice riots were a principal reason for the resolve with which the policy was carried out, and it is doubtful whether the dilemma that was becoming clear in 1973 could have been resolved if the oil boom had not made it unnecessary to choose between high producer prices and low retail prices for rice. The government of Indonesia chose to allocate a significant part of the windfall to food and fertilizer subsidies (and to investment in domestic fertilizer production). In Nigeria, however, food crops were ignored, except that they enjoyed protection through import controls, having in effect become nontradables.

The Nigerian trade and exchange rate policies were relatively simple throughout the period. Quantitative restrictions were unimportant until the mid-1960s; they were introduced during the civil war and kept largely intact afterward. The exchange rate was kept stable. Declining export receipts therefore meant a loss of reserves initially and then, when that policy reached its logical limit, tighter import controls. Thus, restrictions were relaxed during 1975–77, intensified at the end of the first oil cycle, relaxed in 1980, and tightened again in 1982. Only in 1986 was the fixed exchange rate abandoned, only to be subsequently restored.

Indonesia, by contrast, underwent a bewildering succession of changes in trade and exchange rate policies. One reason is that whereas Nigerian trade and exchange rate policies were concerned mainly with the balance of payments position and inflation, Indonesian trade policies were aimed at very different objectives, such as undermining the monopoly position of the Dutch trading houses, aiding the establishment of an Indonesian entrepreneurial class, and averting secession. For much of the Sukarno period policy changes succeeded each other so quickly that it is difficult to describe what the policy stance really was. Policy was clear only in the guided economy period (detailed and very restrictive import controls) and just afterward (the liberal regime of 1965–68).

During the oil cycles, trade policy was used in Nigeria to constrain total imports. In Indonesia it was used increasingly for industrial protection; local content requirements and restrictions on foreign investment became important instruments of industrial policy. However, another reason for the changes in Indonesian trade policy is that during the 1970s a competing vision to that of import substitution gained sway— namely, that the manufacturing sector could be sufficiently competitive to export. After 1977 the Indonesians devalued frequently in response to falling export revenues, increasingly using devaluation rather than protection to compensate manufacturing for Dutch disease effects.

A final difference between the two countries is in the attachment to particular policies. Nigeria has at times been dogmatic about not using certain instruments, particularly the exchange rate. Indonesia has been remarkably flexible: the foreign exchange certificate system was changed when it was realized that it was detrimental to exports; Sukarno was willing to give up price control if that was needed to obtain foreign aid; the system of rice prices, which did not differ between locations, was quickly changed when it was realized that no trade would take place; and the complicated and highly protective system of trade controls was substantially liberalized during 1985–87.

Factor Markets

Whereas there were significant differences in macroeconomic and product market policies, factor markets were similar in the two countries. Labor markets were broadly efficient, and interventions in the capital market followed a common trajectory. Thus, differences in factor markets were not sufficient to account for the divergence in economic performance.

LABOR MARKETS. The key symptoms of labor market malfunction are unemployment, persistent wage differentials between similar workers, and very high or very low skill differentials. Respectively, these symptoms indicate idle resources, intersectoral misallocation, and intertemporal misallocation. Table 20.15 compares urban male unemployment rates. In Indonesia no trend was discernable; rates fluctuated between 3 and 7 percent. In Nigeria, by contrast, there was a pronounced U-shape. Both in the 1960s and in the mid-1980s, to the extent that survey methods are comparable, Nigeria had substantially higher unemployment than Indonesia, whereas during the peak of the oil boom the rate was lower. This pattern is consistent with the differences in macroeconomic policy, in particular with the accentuation of the boom through borrowing in Nigeria compared with its smoothing through foreign asset accumulation in Indonesia. However, the initially higher rate of unemployment in Nigeria was, of course, unrelated to boom management and was more directly the result of labor market policies.

We have shown that during the 1950s and 1960s formal sector wage employees acquired rents in Nigeria, whereas in Indonesia rents became negative. This occurred despite the fact that the Indonesian labor market was much more heavily unionized, and unions had more political influence. In Nigeria rents developed because the government chose to pay a premium to its own work force to increase its patronage, so even weak unions merely had to preserve existing relativities to extend the premium to the entire formal sector. By contrast, in Indonesia the budgetary consequences of accelerating inflation and declining real revenue meant that the government was incapable of maintaining the real wages of its employees despite a wish to do so. By the onset of the oil boom, formal sector rents were substantial in Nigeria, particularly in the public sector, but in Indonesia there was no significant wage premium.

The creation of a wage premium for unskilled workers in the formal sector in Nigeria had as a corollary a narrowing of skill differentials. As discussed in chapter 7, the observed narrowing of differentials was not a market-induced phenomenon but was generated by government wage policy. After the oil boom both governments narrowed skill differentials for their own employees, but they did so by depressing the wages of the

Table 20.15 Urban Male Unemployment Rates, 1961–86

Year	Nigeria	Indonesia
1961	—	7.4
1962	—	—
1963	14.0[a]	—
1964	—	—
1965	—	—
1966	10.4	—
1967	—	—
1968	—	—
1969	—	—
1970	—	—
1971	—	5.0
1972	—	—
1973	—	3.8
1974	5.8	—
1975	—	—
1976	4.7	6.4
1977	—	—
1978	2.3[a]	7.0
1979	4.1[a]	—
1980	1.5[a]	2.9
1981	—	—
1982	2.8[a]	5.6
1983	5.8	—
1984	6.9	—
1985	8.5	—
1986	10.4	—

— Not available.

a. Male and female rate.

Source: Tables 7.3 and 17.1.

skilled rather than raising the wages of the unskilled. As a consequence, whereas the positive rents of the unskilled were replicated in the private sector, the negative rents of the skilled were not, and so the public sector had difficulty recruiting and keeping skilled labor. The presence of public sector employment rents by the start of the oil boom in Nigeria, but not in Indonesia, in turn accounted for differences in the subsequent expansion of public sector employment. In Nigeria lobbying for state patronage was more intense because it was more attractive.

Data on public sector employment are patchy for both countries, but the civil service appears to have expanded at an annual rate of 11.3 percent in Nigeria during 1973–83, compared with only 5.5 percent in Indonesia during 1975–83. As a consequence, it seems likely that public sector overstaffing increased in Nigeria relative to Indonesia. Because the wage bill in Nigeria was being inflated so much more by employment expansion, there was correspondingly less capacity to spend on wage rates. Furthermore, Nigerian public sector employees started the oil boom with rents that were the result of temporary ad hoc circumstances and thus unsustainable. Thus both governments used the initial revenue impetus of the oil boom to reward public sector employees by doubling wages—in 1975 in Nigeria and in 1976/77 in Indonesia. But in Nigeria this wage hike was first extended to the private sector as a result of popular protest and then rapidly eroded, whereas in Indonesia further, more modest increases were offered so that by the end of the boom some wage premium had developed. At the peak of the boom both governments introduced something approaching a national minimum wage, although in Indonesia the process was decentralized and coverage was vague, so enforcement was limited. In Nigeria, in addition to limited enforcement, the wage was rapidly eroded in real terms; however, for a few years it must have had a substantial impact on labor-intensive formal sector firms, especially the plantations.

The erosion of rents in Nigeria increased the flexibility of the labor market during the 1980s when urban employment contracted substantially. Retrenched labor migrated to rural areas and entered agriculture rather than remain unemployed in the cities. By the 1980s the Indonesian labor market was also spatially well integrated as a result of improved transport. Other than the emerging public sector wage premium, there appeared to be no segmentation between urban and rural employment, or between formal and informal employment. Interestingly, the public sector pay premium of the 1980s does not appear to have been widely transmitted to the private formal sector as it was in Nigeria in the 1950s. This perhaps reflects the considerable weakening in union power that took place as a result of the regime change in the late 1960s. Had the public sector paid a wage premium in the 1950s, it seems likely that the Indonesian unions would have been able to enforce its extension.

To conclude, by the 1980s the labor market in both countries was highly responsive to market conditions. It was spatially well integrated, there were no substantial rents, and when put to the test, as happened in Nigeria, real wages were downwardly flexible in both the public and the private sectors to a degree inconceivable in most countries. Neither market was like this for the entire period: there were phases of positive or negative rents, and spatial integration was achieved only gradually as a result of improved transport. The one important institutional change was the dismantling of Indonesian unions, but this made the two markets more similar because Nigeria had never had powerful unions.

CAPITAL. Capital markets in both countries went through a trajectory of increasing controls followed by liberalization. In Indonesia, controls culminated in 1965 with the merger of all banks, including the Central Bank, into a single institution. As discussed in chapter 17, credit was allocated on a more or less arbitrary basis. In Nigeria after 1964, sector-specific credit targets and interest rate controls accumulated until the early 1980s. It is impossible to quantify the extent to which these controls misallocated capital or the deleterious consequences of such misallocation for growth. However, it is clear that during the oil boom the incremental capital-output ratio (ICOR) was radically higher in Nigeria than in Indonesia. Although this may have been partly a consequence of the financial liberalization that took place in Indonesia in 1967, the liberalization was partially reversed in 1974. Full convertibility was maintained, but domestic bank credit was subject to a variety of credit ceilings. Full convertibility enabled citizens wishing to save to gain access to the world capital market, and private holdings of foreign assets became widespread. Thus, the savings market remained liberalized after 1974, whereas the credit market did not.[7]

In the 1980s both countries embarked upon a radical liberalization of the credit market—in 1983 in Indonesia and 1986 in Nigeria. Indonesian liberalization was motivated by the desire to stimulate private savings to substitute for the decline in public investment. However, the main potential benefit was in the allocation of investment. The liberalization thus contained an element of good fortune rather like the obsession with rice self-sufficiency. The desire to maintain the aggregate investment rate owed more to a mentality of GDP growth targeting than to the macroeconomic efficiency the chosen policy reform inadvertently generated. In Nigeria the financial liberalization was part of the IMF–World Bank package. Interest rates were permitted to rise, but citizens were still not permitted legal access to foreign assets, so in an important aspect the market was more controlled than in Indonesia. Some sector-specific direction of credit also remained.

Neither government seems to have appreciated the investment allocation role of the financial system. Whereas wage rate differences generate lobbying pressures that erode rents, misallocation in the capital market is less visible and so more persistent. As a result, both countries went through a massive temporary investment boom without an adequate allocative mechanism. It is therefore not surprising that in both countries the ICORs rose substantially during the boom.

LAND. The land market is much more developed in Indonesia, probably reflecting a prolonged history of high population density. In Nigeria the land frontier is only now being reached. Land sales and tenancy have emerged, but not the extensive linkage of factor markets common in Indonesia. However, even in Nigeria land-labor ratios have been equalized across holdings as a result of factor market transactions, so there are no grounds for regarding land markets as inefficient. In both countries there have been episodes of interventionist land policies. The Sukarno regime attempted a land reform that proved abortive. In Nigeria the Land Use Decree of 1979 attempted a degree of land nationalization. The consequences appear to have been an increase in the cost of land transactions as the bureaucracy exacted rents.

Agricultural Performance

The performance of a single sector of an economy might appear to be of no consequence for overall poverty and growth. However, in both countries agriculture is significant in three respects—it includes nontradable staple foods, it dominates the nonoil export sector, and it is the income source on which a substantial majority of the poor rely. Poor performance of agriculture may therefore lead to a food security problem, an accentuated vulnerability to fluctuations in oil prices, and a less equal distribution of income.

There is no doubt that Nigerian agriculture grew substantially less rapidly than that in Indonesia. Between 1960 and 1984 value added grew by 18 percent in Nigeria and 122 percent in Indonesia. This was a far larger divergence than for GDP as a whole—growth rates were 144 percent and 280 percent, respectively. At first view this is surprising: it might be expected that because agriculture is the least dynamic sector of both economies, it would have had the narrowest difference in performance. Clearly, there is something sector specific to be explained.

We first consider food crops. There is little basis for the quantitative comparison of food production. However, using the FAO series on total food production that are available after 1962, we calculate that annual per capita production fell 0.8 percent in Nigeria and rose 1.6 percent in Indonesia between 1962 and 1985. According to the FAO data, the difference in performance has no pronounced temporal pattern, although the differential was somewhat narrower from 1972 to 1985. This is surprising because both policy changes and exogenous technological innovations put Indonesia in a more favorable position after 1972 than before. During the oil boom the Indonesian government allocated 20 percent of its budget to agriculture, compared with only 2 percent in Nigeria. In addition, the green revolution in irrigated rice cultivation enhanced Indonesia's yields, whereas no such innovation emerged suitable for Nigerian conditions. Nigeria's disadvantages as a producer, however, were offset by the substantial increase in relative food prices during the 1970s, presumably reflecting the conjunction of production failure and oil boom spending power. Policy and technology shifted the Indonesian supply curve relative to the Nigerian curve—market-clearing prices moved Nigerian production up the supply curve.

It must be emphasized, however, that in dealing with Nigerian food production data we are on fragile ground, and the FAO series for 1972–85 yield implausibly high growth. The fitted growth rate of 2.9 percent is a full percentage point above our own estimate of the maximum growth rate of the six major food crops, and that figure itself is based on taking whichever of four series for each crop showed the highest growth. Unfortunately, therefore, the only secure conclusion is that since 1962 per capita food production declined in Nigeria and rose increasingly rapidly in Indonesia. Some of this growth differential was reflected in changing trade positions: Nigeria became increasingly dependent on imports while Indonesia achieved self-sufficiency. More important, however, the growth differential resulted in different trends in the relative price of food and in per capita consumption.

Given that there was such a large divergence in outcomes and also in policies toward food production, it is tempting to attribute the outcomes to policies. However, Indonesian rice production benefited from technical progress not suitable for Nigeria. Also, the production of foods other than rice grew markedly less rapidly, in part because land and labor were redirected from other crops into rice. Thus it is not possible to quantify the effect of different policies on the outcomes.

In food production the Indonesian government had both more impetus to act than the Nigerian government, because of the political threat posed by food insecurity, and more opportunity, because of foreign technical progress in irrigated rice. In nonfood agriculture neither of these factors applied. For both countries nonfood agriculture was predominantly a foreign exchange earner; prior to the oil boom it was the dominant foreign exchange source. Technological opportunities were similar, because some of the most important crops were common to both countries. Had both governments given equal weight to agriculture in aggregate, the better opportunities in the food sector in Indonesia should have induced it to concentrate more on that sector. In turn the Nigerian government should have been more active in the promotion of nonfood agriculture, where opportunities were the same in absolute terms but better in relative terms. This makes the comparison of nonfood agriculture a much better indicator of the consequences of the policy environments.

In tables 20.16 and 20.17 we compare the growth rates of four important nonfood crops. Rubber and oil palm are common to both countries. Cocoa is the major crop in Nigeria but it has been grown only recently in Indonesia; a better comparator is coffee, a tree crop with similar economic characteristics and one that is important and long established in Indonesia. From 1950 to 1985 Indonesia had faster growth rates for oil palm and coffee but slower rates for rubber. However, once this span is broken down into shorter periods a clearer picture emerges. We consider the periods of 1950–66 (the New Order in Indonesia) and 1972–85 (the oil booms). The intervening years of 1967–72 are omitted because of the disturbance of the civil war in Nigeria and reconstruction phases in both countries.

During 1950–66 Nigeria had faster growth rates than Indonesia for oil palm and rubber and for coffee relative to cocoa. Not only was performance relatively good, growth rates were high in absolute terms. In the second period relative performance was precisely reversed: Indonesia had a substantially higher growth rate in all three crops. This precise reversal of the three pairwise rankings reflects substantial absolute changes. The final row of table 20.17 shows the change in the Nigeria-Indonesia growth rate differential between the two periods. This ranges from a low of 9 percentage points for oil palm to a high of 19 percentage points for rubber.

These large changes came about partly through an increase in the Indonesian growth rates and partly through a decrease in the Nigerian rates. That the absolute growth rate in Indonesia should be higher in the second period is remarkable in view of the expectations of Dutch disease. As we have seen, relative prices did move against the nonoil export sector. This resource reallocation effect was evidently more than offset by the enhanced GDP growth brought about by the New Order and the windfall savings from the oil boom. Nigeria offers a much clearer case of Dutch disease, with growth rates in nonfood agriculture not merely falling but turning heavily negative. The proximate reasons for output decline were the withdrawal of labor, the reduced use of fertilizer, and the failure to replace the tree stock.

Although we have confined our comparison to three crops, the extent of the divergence in performance is in fact more marked because Indonesia diversified into new crops while Nigeria became more concentrated in the three considered above. Indonesia developed its timber exports but—more dramatically for purposes of comparison—it diversified into cocoa, Nigeria's principal crop. So high was the Indonesian growth rate in this sector (more than 20 percent during 1972–85) that by the end of the 1990s Indonesia had become a larger cocoa producer than Nigeria.

The reasons for this radical difference in performance from 1972 onward are unambiguously policy related. The crops we are comparing were common to both countries, and Nigeria's long-term record prior to the oil boom was unambiguously superior to Indonesia's. Furthermore, because of the exogenously inspired opportunities that emerged in food agriculture in Indonesia but not in Nigeria, we would have expected Nigeria's superiority in nonfood crops to have been enhanced after 1972. The question is not, therefore, whether the massive deterioration in

Table 20.16 Production of Major Nonfood Crops, 1950–91
(thousands of metric tons)

Year	Oil palm Nigeria	Oil palm Indonesia	Rubber Nigeria	Rubber Indonesia	Cocoa Nigeria	Cocoa Indonesia	Coffee, Indonesia
1950	390	126	14	704	107	—	59
1951	340	121	21	828	109	—	51[a]
1952	360	146	19	761	111	—	47
1953	390	161	22	706	102	—	62
1954	440	169	21	751	91	—	58
1955	450	169	31	749	116	—	65
1956	420	166	39	697	137	—	61
1957	460	165	40	738	90	—	75
1958	410	160	52	696	143	—	78
1959	457	148	54	705	157	—	90
1960	433	138	60	640	195	—	92
1961	541	146	56	682	194	—	97
1962	509	141	60	682	179	—	111
1963	510	148	64	582	220	—	144
1964	515	161	72	649	298	—	87
1965	530	163	69	717	184	—	105
1966	508	151	71	716	267	—	116
1967	325	174	48	695	238	1	159
1968	370	188	53	730	192	2	157
1969	425	189	57	788	223	2	177
1970	488	215	59	811	300	2	185

Year							
1971	500	225	60	820	285	2	180
1972	460	269	81	819	241	2	179
1973	430	289	91	852	214	2	163
1974	485	339	90	855	297	3	161
1975	500	409	95	825	306	4	162
1976	510	456	85	845	250	4	168
1977	660	497	90	835	202	5	193
1978	670	525	58	885	160	5	223
1979	650	606	60	905	180	9	227
1980	675	650	60	919	175	9	240
1981	675	741	43	963	181	13	315
1982	700	824	45	880	160	15	265
1983	730	972	50	997	118	28	236
1984	700	1,132	58	1,041	150	33	331
1985	730	1,230	60	1,057	110	37	311
1986	760	1,351	60	1,113	100	39	361
1987	730	1,313	70	1,128	145	44	354
1988	834	1,833	68	1,235	165	49	405
1989	857	1,942	78	1,260	160	122	441
1990	900	1,937	80	1,300	155	150	391
1991	900	2,658	155	1,284	110	169	419

— Not available.
a. Estimated from estates production.
Source: FAO, various years.

415

Table 20.17 Growth of Major Nonfood Crops, 1950–85
(fitted annual growth rates, percent)

| Period | Oil palm | | | Rubber | | | Cocoa | | Coffee, | Differential between Nigerian cocoa and Indonesian coffee |
	Nigeria	Indonesia	Differential (percentage points)	Nigeria	Indonesia	Differential (percentage points)	Nigeria	Indonesia	Indonesia	(percentage points)
1950–85	1.7	6.0	–4.3	2.8	1.1	1.7	1.3	—	5.1	–3.8
1950–66	2.4	0.5	1.9	10.2	–0.9	11.1	6.4	—	5.7	0.7
1972–85	4.6	11.3	–6.7	–5.6	2.1	–7.7	–5.8	21.5	5.1	–10.9
Differential between later and earlier periods			–8.6			–18.8				–11.6

Source: Authors' calculations based on table 20.16.

Nigerian performance is attributable to policy, but rather to which policies it should be attributed. The candidates are macroeconomic policies, policies in the nonfood agriculture sector, and the general equilibrium effects of policies in other sectors.

Macroeconomic policies were compared earlier. Recall that the domestic price of nonfood agricultural output relative to importables and nontradables is influenced by the trade–exchange rate–monetary policy nexus. Differences favored the more rapid growth of nonfood agriculture in Indonesia—the exchange rate was devalued much earlier, import controls were less restrictive, and monetary policy was more conservative. Thus, the relative price symptoms of Dutch disease would be expected to be, and were, far less severe in Indonesia. Policies toward the sector also diverged. The only substantial help directed to the sector by the Nigerian government was the phasing out of export taxes. By contrast, the Indonesian government directed substantial public investment into the sector. Finally, the general equilibrium effects of public expenditure in Nigeria were to draw labor from agriculture, thereby hitting hardest the most labor-intensive agricultural crops, which happened to be the nonfood crops.

Why Policies Differed

From the early 1970s the economic performance of Nigeria and Indonesia diverged markedly. Starting from similar positions, Indonesia achieved equitable growth whereas Nigeria did not, and by the 1990s Indonesia was much the richer and more equitable society. Much of this, as we have seen, was the result of differences in policy.

During the 1970s several major economic policies began to diverge. These fall into three groups—agricultural policies, poverty-alleviating policies, and the nexus of industrial, exchange rate, and trade policies that generated the intersectoral incentive regime. The priority attached to agriculture differed radically and consistently. The Indonesian government spent heavily on the sector in both the recurrent and capital budgets. Recurrent spending was through fertilizer subsidies, extension and credit, and capital spending on irrigation. The Nigerian government had these policies in its portfolio but spent far less on them. Similarly, the Indonesian government attached more importance to poverty alleviation. Under Sukarno this took the form of policies concerned with wage earners and with small, indigenous businesspeople. Under Suharto the most serious pockets of poverty were identified through mass surveys and made the subject of targeted programs of public expenditure.

The intersectoral incentive regime was initially similar: both governments committed huge resources to import-substituting industry and reinforced these expenditures with protection. However, in Indonesia a countervailing vision gradually emerged, in which priority was given to international competitiveness. After 1974 investment in the import-substitute sector was reined in. By 1978 the government recognized a tradeoff between spending the oil windfall and the competitiveness of the nonoil export sector: the exchange rate was devalued and reserves were accumulated. After 1982 trade policy began to be significantly liberalized. The Nigerian intersectoral incentive regime became cumulatively more distorted until it was reformed in the big bang devaluation and trade liberalization of 1986—a reform that, despite delivering rapid growth, was subsequently reversed.

These policy divergences were accentuated by the oil shock. The boom enormously enhanced the spending power of both governments so that differences in spending priorities mattered more. The slump forced choices between depreciation and trade restrictions and so accelerated both the move to competitiveness in Indonesia and the antiexport bias in Nigeria.

Each of the three areas of policy divergence had significant consequences, again accentuated by the opportunities provided by the oil boom and the difficulties created by the oil slump. The agricultural growth rates were more divergent than those in any other sector: by 1984 Indonesia had attained rice self-sufficiency, a goal that had earlier appeared unattainable, whereas in Nigeria agriculture declined. The incidence of poverty declined radically in Indonesia between 1970 and 1990, and the country became considerably more egalitarian than Nigeria. Although Nigerian import-substitute manufacturing rapidly declined during the 1980s because of the growing inability of the government to finance it, Indonesian manufacturing broke into export markets and by the 1990s was a major source of employment. The policy differences had their most dramatic consequences where they reinforced each other—in the export agriculture sector. In Indonesia the sector expanded rapidly, whereas in Nigeria it contracted severely and parts of it were completely eliminated.

The three areas of policy divergence stemmed partly from persistent differences in social structure and other initial conditions and partly from chance events that occurred during the period. We focus first on the persistent differences and then examine domestic and external events that affected policy choices.

Initial Conditions

The difference in food policies of the two countries is explicable in part by their differing vulnerability to fluctuating world food prices. This vulnerability was a given in 1950. Indonesia was a large importer of its staple, rice, relative to the size of the world market, and so faced the danger that in years of poor harvest it would drive up prices against itself. Conversely, Nigeria did not have a single staple food, and the country imported on a smaller scale, mainly grains for which the world market was much larger. Thus, Indonesian governments were forced to develop policies that enhanced food supplies.

The greater priority Indonesia attached to poverty alleviation may have had roots in the very different origins of the Indonesian and Nigerian armies. The former was originally a mass army that fought for liberation from colonial rule. After the war it described itself as having a "dual function" and assumed nonmilitary tasks such as the creation of rural infrastructure. The Nigerian army was initially conventional, and although it subsequently seized a political function, it defined its political objectives both more narrowly and in line with the political parties, espousing the causes of national unity and anticorruption. Poverty alleviation was not part of this agenda. In this the Nigerian army may have reflected differing attitudes of Northern and Southern elites toward inequality. The Northern elites came from a society in which wealth was justified by hierarchy, whereas the Southern elites saw their wealth as justified by achievement.

In the same vein, the fact that the Nigerian government never focused on poverty as such surely reflected the priorities of Nigerian society: ethnic rivalry and the politics of perceived ethnic disadvantage precluded cross-ethnic interventions. By contrast in Indonesia the Javanese secured undisputed control from the late 1950s, but it was still politic to balance the interests of Java against those of the outer islands, and continued legitimacy required that the government spread wealth regionally.

The eventual difference between the two countries in reliance on the market—particularly in the degree of antiexport bias—may also have derived from differences in initial inheritance. Indonesia started the period much more oriented toward exports, having been a major plantation economy for several decades. As a result, there was a larger proexport constituency, and although during the 1950s exporting was overshadowed by the goal of import substitution, it always remained important. Also, the geography of Indonesia militated against effective export taxation since smuggling from the outer islands where export agriculture was concentrated was relatively easy. These factors combined to restrain antiexport bias more in Indonesia than in Nigeria, and each country's position became self-reinforcing. In Nigeria the nonoil export sector was politically too weak to defend itself from Dutch disease and so its power as a lobby was further diminished. By contrast, in Indonesia by the 1990s nonoil exports were a significant component of the economy and a powerful lobby.

A third factor explaining the greater readiness of the Indonesian government to liberalize markets may again arise from long-standing differences in the ruling elites. Although both countries had large, diverse populations and governments in the hands of a dominant group, the characteristics of that group differed markedly. The Javanese dominated Indonesia not only numerically but historically and culturally. By contrast, the Nigerian North had only a precarious plurality and was the most backward region educationally. Although in both cases commerce was dominated by minorities, in Indonesia that minority was the Chinese, a group too small to be a political threat to the elite, who formed a coalition with them. In Northern Nigeria, immigrants from the Southern regions made up the minority that dominated commerce. Northern elites feared that they would lose in an unrestricted commercial contest and that this might eventually lead to their political domination, and so they used the state to restrict the operation of market capitalism.

These differences—in the culture of the army and the elite and in geography and economic history—did not produce divergent outcomes during the 1950s and 1960s. Although there were growth episodes in those two decades, living standards were broadly stagnant in both countries. However, the differences are important in understanding subsequent policy divergence. Nigeria did not become independent until 1960, so the capacity of interest groups to influence policy before then was restrained. Afterward, because the government had inherited large accumulated reserves, it was able temporarily to reconcile conflicting claims. Furthermore, few developing countries adopted a market-oriented strategy prior to the 1970s. However, as international evidence on the merits of the strategy mounted during the 1970s, some countries liberalized—perhaps disposed to by their initial social and economic conditions—while others did not, again perhaps because of initial conditions. Finally, it was only after 1972 that the oil windfall presented Indonesia and Nigeria with new opportunities. Thus, differences that were unimportant in the 1950s and 1960s may have been important in the changed environment of the 1970s.

Internal Chance Events

A series of events occurred in Indonesia that cumulatively, and in conjunction with the initial conditions outlined above, triggered policy change. The first such event was the emergence of a charismatic leader with a distinctive vision. President Sukarno, at the time one of the most effective communicators in the world, conceived of and conveyed a philosophy of social cohesion. This was far from a well-articulated socioeconomic program of poverty alleviation, but it did signal clearly that the Indonesian state regarded itself as responsible for the interests of ordinary people. This in turn created expectations in the population that Sukarno was unable to fulfill and that became a legacy to Suharto. The

Suharto regime, as a counterrevolutionary government, might not have afforded poverty alleviation a high priority otherwise. However, when the Javanese poor rioted over threats to their living standards, the government responded by prioritizing poverty alleviation in general and food policy in particular.

The importance of Sukarno's role in creating public expectations of protection for the poor can be gauged by the absence of food riots in Nigeria despite much more severe increases in food prices. Nigerians' acceptance of these price hikes was not a sign of quiescence—when the government attempted to raise gasoline prices, the people invariably rioted—but they did not seem to hold the government responsible for food prices. This is dramatically illustrated by government actions during the 1983 election campaign, when the government chose to restrict rice imports to create rents for its campaign fund. Such a strategy was regarded as a net electoral asset, whereas in Indonesia it would have been suicidal.

Another chance event to which we accord primary significance is the Indonesian hyperinflation episode. Recall that this was triggered by a deterioration in the terms of trade leading to a revenue decline, which—because of the very small size of the monetary base—caused a large proportionate increase in the money supply. Both at the time and subsequently this was wrongly diagnosed as having been caused by a loss of control of public expenditure. The conjunction of the hyperinflation and its misdiagnosis produced a potent legacy, which caused the population to attach a high priority to the avoidance of inflation. The policy responses were commitments to a balanced budget and to convertibility. Whereas the balanced budget rule was more an emphasis on fiscal prudence than a precise, restraining operational procedure, convertibility introduced a powerful new restraint upon the government. For example, in 1983 there was a speculative attack on the currency that forced a devaluation of the exchange rate. Thus convertibility became a restraint mechanism against overvaluation.

The implications of the hyperinflation were, however, even more wide-ranging. The episode discredited the economic policies of the Old Order, providing an opening for the economic technocrats whose presence constituted another chance event, discussed below. Nigeria never experienced an economic crisis comparable to hyperinflation. The policy failures after 1970 caused gradually declining real expenditure without a crescendo. The nearest equivalent economic experience was the big bang devaluation of 1986, which resulted in large income transfers from the urban middle classes. The Nigerian fear of currency depreciation can be viewed as analogous to the Indonesian fear of hyperinflation. The Nigerian fear led to a delay in liberalization and made exchange rate adjustment, once it belatedly occurred, vulnerable to reversal.

During the mid-1960s a group of Indonesians trained in economics in the United States returned home. This group, known as the Berkeley mafia, was able to gain influence by offering both a critique of and an alternative to the now-discredited policies. These thinkers were attractive to the new regime, which styled itself the New Order precisely because it wanted to differentiate itself from its predecessor. At the same time that Indonesia was gaining an economic technocracy, Nigeria was losing one—the team of expatriate economic experts that had advised policymakers was disbanded. One consequence was that there was no economic appraisal of public investment projects during the oil boom. In Indonesia, too, the technocrats lost much of their influence by the early 1970s, for in both countries the arrival of the oil windfall appeared to make the dreams of public sector import-substituting investment realizable.

The final domestic event that affected policy—and reinvigorated the technocrats—was the Pertamina crisis of 1975. The state oil company had become a state within a state, borrowing massively to finance a wide array of projects unrelated to the oil sector. Its inability to roll over its borrowings triggered a public reevaluation of recklessness on a grand scale. The Berkeley mafia used this situation as it had used the hyperinflation, harnessing the outcry over the event to mount a generalized policy critique, and thereby regaining influence. The economic success of the next decade consolidated this position: between 1976 and 1984 private consumption per capita rose by 50 percent and the incidence of poverty was more than halved. It has been suggested that the inability of Pertamina to roll over its borrowings on the world capital market was the result of a preemptive intervention in the market by the Central Bank. If this is true, the technocrats and their allies brilliantly contrived the whistle-blowing crisis that led to their own recovery.

Nigeria had a close parallel to such whistle-blowing in the same year. As in Indonesia there had been gross misuse of oil money. A government report documented the high-level corruption taking place, and when President Gowon attempted to suppress the report, this attempt at cover-up was itself exposed. However, opponents of the Nigerian government used the discrediting event for a very different purpose. Gowon was toppled, and the incoming government set in process the transition back to democracy. Thus the critique was a political one targeted against the corruption of the military, rather than an economic one targeted against dirigisme. This was to become a persistent characteristic of opposition to the Nigerian military governments.

External Events

Three external events also facilitated the policy transitions that led to better growth and equity outcomes in Indonesia than in Nigeria. First, the growing success of the East Asian export-oriented economies gradually became a potential engine and role model for both economies. To an extent Nigeria harnessed this engine: in Southeast Nigeria many manufacturing businesses forged links with Taiwan-China. However, Indonesia's geographic and cultural location placed it at a considerable advantage in both respects. For example, the "high-cost economy" debate of the mid-1980s, in which Indonesian economics professionals advocated exchange rate depreciation and trade liberalization, gained some of its potency through competitiveness with neighboring countries. This stance coincided with the stance taken by Nigerian economics professionals against devaluation of the far more overvalued naira. The success of the East Asian export-orientation strategy was not seen as a pertinent role model by the Nigerian economists, let alone by the government.

The second external event, the increases in world oil prices in 1973 and 1979 and their subsequent crash, obviously generated similar shocks in both countries, but they accentuated the pace of policy divergence. Initially, the opposite occurred: the windfall caused policy convergence. The greatly enhanced ability to implement import-substitution projects reduced the influence of the Berkeley mafia and so led Indonesian policy back toward that of Nigeria. However, by the late 1970s, after the Pertamina crisis had restored the influence of the Indonesian technocrats, the windfall reinforced divergence. The extraordinary growth in Indonesian living standards between 1976 and 1984, which greatly strengthened the hand of the technocrats, could probably not have been delivered without the revenue gains from oil.

The windfall also enabled both governments to implement their now-diverging visions. Nigeria continued to concentrate on import-substituting industrial projects, whereas Indonesia reined these in and brought agriculture and poverty targeting to the fore. However, the major contribution of the oil shocks to policy divergence was the slump. In Indonesia, with the technocrats already in place and reserves already accumulated as a by-product of the exchange rate protection strategy, the shock could be moderated and liberalization continued. In Nigeria the previous borrowing amplified the shock, and the policy response was to intensify overvaluation and trade restrictions. This was the phase when both policies and outcomes diverged most rapidly.

The remaining external event was the Mexican debt crisis of 1982. Just as East Asia potentially offered a model, so Mexico potentially offered a warning. In Indonesia the reformers were already influential, and they used the Mexican crisis to reinforce their policy priorities. In Nigeria during 1982 policymakers were absorbed by the difficulty of managing a massive patronage system with rapidly declining income, and the Mexican event was insufficient to get economic policy onto the agenda.

Conclusion

The comparison of Nigeria and Indonesia provides dramatic evidence that policies matter. Over the space of only two decades Indonesia transformed itself through equitable growth. We have suggested that three areas of policy divergence account for much of this: the higher priorities afforded to agriculture and to poverty targeting in Indonesia and the gradual shift in Indonesia away from import-substituting industrialization and antiexport bias. We have explained these differences in policy by a number of underlying factors, including both differences in initial conditions and events that occurred either shortly before or during the period when the economic performance of the two countries began to diverge markedly.

The initial differences that help explain policy differences were Indonesia's greater vulnerability to the volatility of world food markets, the dual function of the Indonesian army, the country's greater export orientation historically and the constraint that easy smuggling from the outer islands placed on antiexport bias, and the greater political security and comfort with market capitalism among Indonesia's ruling elite. Since prior to the late 1960s Indonesia had neither better policy nor better performance than Nigeria, these initial differences were not decisive during that period. At the most, they became decisive only in conjunction with later events. As of the mid-1960s there was no basis for a forecast of divergence in either policies or performance; a thesis of historical determinism is therefore unsustainable.

Three events—the oil shocks, the Mexican debt crisis, and the 1975 whistle-blowing reaction to misspending—were common to both countries and so again were not in themselves decisive. They help explain policy divergence only through their interaction with either the different initial conditions or certain experiences unique to Indonesia: Sukarno's emphasis on social cohesion, the 1966 hyperinflation, the early creation of a group of economic technocrats, and the emergence of geographically proximate, externally oriented successful economies. By the late 1990s all but the first of these had belatedly been more or less replicated in Nigeria. Although Nigerian inflation did not reach the level defined as hyperinflation, the oil slump of the early 1990s, which led to a reimposition of controls (in particular, trade restrictions and exchange control) inflicted upon the Nigerians an experience similar to that of the Indonesians in the mid-1960s. Nigerian economists by the late 1990s comfortably outnumbered those in Indonesia during the period of its policy transformation. And globalization made the importance of international competitiveness at least as evident to Nigerians as the emerging East Asian economies of the 1970s had to Indonesians.

Thus Nigeria gradually accumulated a history of events not dissimilar from those that triggered policy change in Indonesia. But it did not accumulate them in the same sequence—and this evidently mattered to some extent. For example, the Mexican debt crisis of 1982 was not as useful to a future, reforming Nigerian technocracy as it was to the Indonesians at the time. And even if Indonesian events had belatedly been fully replicated in Nigeria, they might not have been sufficient to trigger policy change. Differing sequences might have made the events ineffective, or the differences in initial conditions might still have been inhibiting.

Our assessment of why Indonesia but not Nigeria escaped from stagnation after 1970 leads us to two conclusions that are hopeful for Nigeria's future. First, Nigeria is most unlikely to be locked into stagnation by its initial inheritance. The initial differences between Nigeria and Indonesia were scarcely remarkable, and a few chance events were sufficient to transform Indonesian policy. Second, although by the late 1990s Nigerian and Indonesian policy and performance had diverged, in many respects the circumstances that triggered Indonesian policy change had also occurred by then in Nigeria.

Nigeria, unfortunately, experienced one important change of circumstance between the mid-1960s and the mid-1990s that constitutes a significant handicap: it acquired a reputation for poor government and slow growth. Since such reputations exert a powerful influence on investment, they can be self-fulfilling. However, we suggest that to view Nigeria's reputation as its destiny is to misuse history. The extrapolation of the past, which is what reputation amounts to, is liable to be wrong, because policies are not deeply embedded in unchanging structures. Nigeria's reputation in the mid-1990s may be as inaccurate a forecast of its development over the next two decades as was Indonesia's in the mid-1960s.

Appendix 20A Construction of the Protection Index for Indonesia

We collected domestic wholesale prices in Jakarta of 14 imported commodities for the period 1971–84 from the Bureau of Statistics data files (table 20A.1). Changes often occur in the specification of the commodities. We have spliced the series when possible by using the data for a year in which the two series overlap, and otherwise by assuming that there was no price change between the last year of the old series and the first year of the new series. All price data were converted to 1972 = 100.

From the trade statistics we collected c.i.f. prices (in domestic currency) for imported goods, the description of which matched the 14 commodities as closely as possible. These world prices were also converted into index series (1972 = 100).

The 14 commodities were assigned to the five Standard International Trade Classification (SITC) groups shown in the table below. These five categories accounted in 1975 for 94.11 percent of the value of imports, and each was weighted according to its share in the total.

SITC group	SITC category	Weight (percent)
0	Food and live animals	12.10
3	Mineral fuels, etc.	5.38
5	Chemicals	16.93
6	Manufactured goods	22.53
7	Machinery and transport equipment	37.17
Total		94.11

Intragroup weights were calculated as follows:

• *Group 0:* For 1974–84 total imports amounted to $105.6 billion, of which rice accounted for $4.5 billion, or 4.3 percent. Thus rice was assigned a weight of 4.3, and cloves were assigned 7.8, the remainder of the group weight (12.1 – 4.3 = 7.8).

• *Group 3:* Since asphalt is the only commodity in this group, it was assigned the group weight of 5.38.

• *Group 5:* In 1975 imports of chemical and pharmaceutical products and fertilizers amounted to $119.6 and $401.3 million, respectively; the group weight was distributed over the two commodities in proportion to these imports.

• *Group 6:* Six commodities are in this group. In the absence of other information, one-sixth of the group weight was assigned to rayon. The remaining five-sixths was distributed over the other five commodities in proportion to the value of their 1975 imports: $23.1 million (paper), $69.4 million (cement), $101.1 million (iron and steel bars), $223.5 million (pipes of iron and steel), and $101.1 million (assumed value for iron angles to give commodities 7 and 8 equal weight).

- *Group 7:* The group weight was distributed over commodities 12, 13, and 14 in proportion to their 1975 import values: $528.1 million (machinery for industrial and commercial equipment), $120.9 million (motorized vehicles), and $17.5 million (internal combustion engines).

The resulting weights were adjusted for noncoverage of SITC groups 1, 2, 4, 8, and 9 by dividing them by 0.9411. This gives the weights shown in table 20A.1. Note that two commodities—generators and fertilizer—have very large weights (31 percent and 14 percent, respectively).

The indexes of world prices (Pw) and of domestic prices (Pd) shown in table 20A.2 were computed by applying the weights in table 20A.1 to the c.i.f price series and the wholesale prices of imported commodities. Our protection index is the ratio of Pd to Pw. Thus, a rise in the domestic wholesale prices of imported commodities, relative to the c.i.f. prices of the same commodities, is reflected in a rise in the protection index.

Table 20A.1 Commodities Used for the Protection Index

Commodity	Specification	Weight (percent)	SITC group
1. Cloves	Zanzibar cloves	8.288	0
2. Rice	Beras Siam 10 percent[a]	4.570	0
3. Asphalt	Not specified[b]	5.717	3
4. Fertilizer	French nitrogen fertilizer[c]	13.865	5
5. Methyl alcohol	Not specified[d]	4.135	5
6. Cement	Portland cement for 1971–76; white cement thereafter[e]	2.676	6
7. Iron angles	Besi siku[f]	3.896	6
8. Iron pipes	Besi pipa 1" x 34" x 277" after 1974[g]	8.606	6
9. Paper	Kertas HVS 60 grams	0.896	6
10. Rayon	Rayon 1.5 D x 38 millimeters[h]	3.996	6
11. Steel	Steel sheets 1/8" x 1-1/4"[i]	3.896	6
12. Engines	Not specified[j]	1.047	7
13. Generators	TS 50 generator[k]	31.297	7
14. Trucks/automobiles	Mobil pengangkut[l]	7.167	7
Total		100.000	

a. A new series starts in 1980 and was spliced to the earlier one by assuming that the increase in Sumatra prices (from Rp 152,833 per piece in 1979 to Rp 154,750 per piece in 1980) applied to Jakarta.

b. 1953 price, corrected for difference in units (ton versus 152 kilograms).

c. A new series starts in 1982 and was spliced to the earlier one by using 1982 data (Rp 59.4 in the old series is Rp 205 in the new one).

d. Medan prices for 1971–76. In 1977 the Medan price was Rp 138 and the Jakarta price, Rp 135.

e We assumed that there was no price change between 1976 and 1977.

f. New series start in 1975 (2,750 in the old series is 200 in the new one), in 1977 (188 in the old series is 500 in the new one), and in 1981 (950 in the old series is 313 in the new one).

g. The specification is unknown before 1974. The post-1974 series was spliced to the earlier one (in December 1974 the old series stands at 2,760 and the new one at 460); a third series starts in 1978 (448 in the old series is 1,750 in the new one); a fourth one in 1979 (2,600 in the old series is 2,292 in the new one); and a fifth one in 1981 (2,554 in the old series is 2,250 in the new one).

h. Except for 1983 (United States).

i. A new series starts in 1974 and was spliced to the earlier one (2,700 in the old series is 5,000 in the new series); a third series starts in 1980 (we assumed that there was no price change between 1979 and 1980).

j. New series start in 1975 (673,433 in the old series is 94.62 in the new one) and in 1984 (224.87 in the old series is 100,375 in the new one).

k. New series start in 1979 (404,900 in the old series is 536,250 in the new one) and in 1981 (550,000 in the old series is 7.5 million in the new one).

l. A new series (index 1975 = 100) starts in 1975 (813,131 in the old series is 100 in the new one); and a third series starts in 1984 (200.3 in the old series, for cars, is 7.5 million in the new series, for trucks).

Source: Authors' computations based on 1975 import data from the Bureau of Statistics.

Table 20A.2 World and Domestic Prices of Commodities Imported by Indonesia, 1971–84

(index: 1972 = 100)

Year	World price (Pw)	Domestic price (Pd)	Protection index (Pd/Pw)
1971	97.1	84.0	86.5
1972	100.0	100.0	100.0
1973	123.3	141.2	114.5
1974	179.1	183.4	102.4
1975	267.3	196.6	73.6
1976	235.4	215.3	91.5
1977	236.3	213.0	90.1
1978	246.6	219.8	89.1
1979	268.0	271.5	101.3
1980	296.0	305.6	103.3
1981	331.4	326.7	98.6
1982	327.5	316.2	96.5
1983	278.8	383.1	137.4
1984	293.2	422.6	144.1

Source: Unpublished Bureau of Statistics data for domestic prices; trade statistics for world prices.

Appendix 20B The Geometry of Open-Economy Macroeconomics

We now present a simple geometric model that relates exchange rate, trade, and monetary policies to the relative prices of nontradables to importables and of importables at world prices to importables at domestic prices.[8] The two domestic relative prices form the axes within which the diagrammatic account of the model is developed. World and domestic prices are denoted by superscripts w and d, and importables and nontradables by m and n. The vertical axis shows Pm^w/Pm^d. The world price of m is treated as an exogenous constant, so Pm^w/Pm^d varies only as a result of commercial policies such as tariffs and quotas. The horizontal axis shows Pn/Pm^d. Such commercial policies plus the exchange rate determine Pm^d. By definition, nontradable (n) goods have no world price, their domestic price being determined under market-clearing conditions by the money supply. Along any vertical line, Pn/Pm^d is constant, and so there are no substitution effects in consumption. Barring biased income effects, the pattern of demand is therefore constant. Along any horizontal line, commercial policy is being held constant, and the model reduces to the more familiar two-aggregate analysis of tradables and nontradables.

We begin by identifying in turn the loci of equilibria in the nontradables and money markets. In figure 20.1 the schedule N–N denotes such a locus for nontradables. To the left of the locus, nontradables are too cheap and are therefore in excess demand; to the right they are too dear and so are in excess supply.

The N–N locus is generally steeper than a ray through the origin. Point A in the figure denotes the relative prices that clear the market under free trade for given world prices. Points directly below A, such as B, are disequilibria, at which import restrictions have raised Pm^d but there is as yet no change in Pn/Pm. This induces a shift of resources out of exportables into the production of both importables and nontradables, causing an excess supply of the latter. To restore equilibrium in the nontradables sector, a lower relative price of nontradable goods is needed. However, the fall in Pn/Pm must stop short of the point H at which Pn/Pm^w has reverted to its value at A. At such a point the incentive for resources to shift from exportables into nontradables has been entirely eliminated while an incentive for consumption to switch into nontradables has been created. Thus it must be a point of excess demand for nontradables. Therefore, the N–N locus of equilibria must be steeper than a ray through the origin, passing through points like C.

The R–R locus represents equilibrium in the money market for given asset demand, real income, and money supply values in foreign currency. It is convenient to measure the money supply by its foreign currency value since changes in the supply of domestic currency and in the exchange rate then have equivalent effects: a doubling of the supply of domestic currency combined with a halving of the exchange rate keeps the money supply constant.

Above $R–R$ the price level is too low and there is excess supply of money; below $R–R$ the price level is too high and there is excess demand. Letting E be a point of monetary equilibrium, all points directly to the right are disequilibria. If the exchange rate and trade restrictions are unaltered, then the nominal price of importables is unchanged. Thus the only way for Pn/Pm to have risen is for Pn to have risen; with one price constant and the other increased, nominal expenditure must rise to maintain real income so that at F there is excess demand for money. A vertical move (to G) restores monetary equilibrium: the tariff rate is reduced, lowering the nominal price of importables. But since Pn/Pm^d is unchanged, the nominal price of nontradables also falls. Thus such a move represents a reduction in the price level.

Combining the two loci, we now introduce the concept of a compatible policy set that generates a sustainable equilibrium. Point $E0$ denotes such a position in which the exchange rate and trade restrictions fix Pm^d, and Pn is then determined by the money supply generated by the budget deficit. At these prices the nontradables market clears. By assumption, there is no net asset accumulation, and so the budget is in balance. The money market clears, and thus by Walras's Law the balance of payments is in equilibrium. This in turn implies that there is no change in the money supply.

The disequilibrium dynamics of the model are generated partly by endogenous changes in prices, the money supply, and investment, and partly by changes in the policy variables. Endogenous changes in prices can occur only in the nontradables sector and, unless these prices are controlled, are determined by excess supply or demand. Endogenous changes in the money supply are determined by the balance of payments and the fiscal deficit; an increase in the money supply converts some points of excess demand into excess supply and so shifts the $R–R$ locus downward. Endogenous changes in investment occur if the capital stock is gradually reallocated toward the sector in excess demand.

The impact effect of a trade liberalization is to lower the price of importables. A reduction in the supply of domestic currency with a given exchange rate lowers the money supply in units of domestic currency, which, with a given exchange rate, lowers the money supply in units of foreign currency and thereby shifts the $R–R$ locus upward. The initial prices now generate a disequilibrium. A devaluation affects both prices and the $R–R$ locus: it raises the domestic price of tradables, and by reducing the money supply in units of foreign currency, it also shifts the $R–R$ locus.

Notes

Chapter 1

1. Support for cotton, usually completely unsuccessful, emerges again and again in colonial history as the government's one main departure from laissez-faire in agriculture.

2. The Eastern and Western regions together constitute "the South."

Chapter 2

1. The currency of Nigeria was the Nigerian pound (N£) until January 1, 1973, when it was replaced by the naira (₦) at the rate N£ = ₦2.

2. Calculated from the average unit export values for groundnuts, cocoa, palm kernels, palm oil, and raw cotton (World Bank 1974, p. 214); producer prices from p. 240; and export values (used as weights) from p. 214. In 1960 these five export products accounted for two-thirds of total exports. In the case of rubber, producer prices fell by much less (31 percent) than world prices (47 percent).

3. For a discussion of the market protection hypothesis and a review of the evidence, see Kilby 1969, chapter 3.

4. The deficit continued to increase, reaching ₦130.9 million in 1966, before falling to ₦80.0. million in 1967.

Chapter 4

1. This term, despite its use of the word *disease*, describes a natural response to a boom in export earnings. If part of the increased income is to be spent on nontradable goods, the production of these goods must be increased. In a fully employed economy, this can be achieved only by switching resources out of the nonbooming tradable goods sectors, such as manufacturing or agriculture. See the later discussion in this chapter.

2. Partly, resources were diverted out of food production because prior to the boom, export crop production was considerably more rewarding than food pro-

duction (as shown in chapter 6), so such a switch might not maintain income at its preboom level.

3. Additionally, within agriculture, farmers could switch from nonfood into food crops. As a result, the labor force in the nonfood agricultural sector contracted until the marginal physical product rose enough to increase the marginal revenue product to a point broadly in line with that in food production.

Chapter 5

1. The particularly poor years of 1983 and 1984 are in part explicable by drought.

2. For investment purposes, the private sector here includes all public entities outside the federal government.

3. There was a standby arrangement with the Fund, but no drawings were made under this facility.

4. For example, in 1988 and 1989 the government lost almost a third of its foreign exchange revenue (net of debt service) in this way.

5. It is striking that both relative outputs and relative prices changed substantially. This is why aggregate output is so sensitive to the relative prices at which it is valued.

6. In neither period was the government completely free from external lobbies whose behavior constrained the attainment of government objectives.

7. After 1982 the federal government had an intrinsic advantage over the states in its ability to maintain expenditure—its control of the Central Bank.

8. The series shown in table 5.15 uses equal weights for each good. To check whether this result is sensitive to reweighting we also used the CPI middle-income wage earner weights. Using these weights, between 1983 and July 1986 the relative price of controlled goods rose by 8 percent.

Chapter 6

1. This calculation assumes a population growth rate of 3 percent and uses national accounts data reported in World Bank (1994b), annex table 2.

Chapter 7

1. This finding of a low interest rate is at variance with the extremely high rates reported by Vigo (1965) in another survey of Northern Nigeria.

2. Derived from Kilby (1969), p. 208, taking the simple average of wage differentials in Lagos, Ibadan, and Kaduna.

3. Nigeria, Ministry of Labour, *Quarterly Bulletin of Labour Statistics 1983*, table 6.1, unweighted average of textiles, printing, chemicals, iron and steel, and construction in Lagos.

4. Employment in the surveyed establishments was 859,000. Khan (1985) estimates formal sector employment in 1984 as 3.3 million.

5. To check whether this might be caused by trends in transport costs rather than crop supplies, time trends were also estimated for the Kano data and for the same subperiod of Lagos data. On both data sets there was a negative (though statistically insignificant) time trend, suggesting that the behavior of Lagos prices over the longer period was not attributable to transport costs.

6. This is only a proxy indicator because as excess supply develops, firms rely increasingly on other means of filling vacancies.

7. To the extent that return migration reduced the size of urban households and increased the size of rural households, the table overstates the deterioration of the relative position of urban households: they would have lost less in per capita terms.

8. The NISH surveys support these data, reporting a 38 percent decline in the real income of urban wage earners.

9. Ross (n.d.) suggests that given this need to maintain social bonds both within the resident community and between resident and nonresident members, large expenditures on social ceremonies become intelligible as investments to maintain rights.

10. Data already available in 1957 from the Galletti survey of cocoa farmers during the 1951 cocoa boom indicated a 40 percent savings rate, but this finding was ignored.

Chapter 8

1. This finding is based on tables 8.1 and 8.2. Table 8.4 suggests a temporary rise in the early 1960s.

2. Deflated by the 1973–84 GDP series, revenue rose in the same period by 4.7 percent to 15.4 percent, whereas oil revenue rose by more than 8 percent to 9.2 percent of GDP.

3. The supply price of agricultural labor includes the return to land and agricultural capital that the migrant forfeits by leaving. Thus the only part of GDP not covered by payments to the formal sector labor force and incomes of other workers is the return on nonagricultural capital. In the 1960s this could not have been a large component of GDP.

4. According to FOS *1985 Statistical Abstract*, table 11.4, total private consumer expenditure at domestic prices was almost ₦92.4 billion. The 1980–81 National Consumer Survey found the share of food consumption in expenditure (including subsistence) to be 74 percent in rural areas and 61 percent in urban areas. The weights for these two groups are unknown and we adopt 1:2, yielding 65 percent. Food consumption at domestic prices was therefore approximately ₦60.2 billion. The FAO food balance sheet estimates imports as providing 9 percent of total calorie intake between 1979 and 1981. If the cost at domestic prices of imports and local food is the same per calorie, then at domestic prices the cost of imported food was ₦5.4 billion. The c.i.f. cost is given in the *1985 Statistical Abstract*, table 8.3.

5. Furthermore, the Udoji award was motivated largely by the political necessity for the Gowon government to palliate hostility to continued military rule, not by the class interests or pressure of the civil servants.

Chapter 9

1. To the extent that investment requires nontradables their price will be pushed up. This increase in the price of nontradable capital costs is the counterpart of the rise in the relative prices of nontradable consumer goods emphasized in Dutch disease theory (see Collier and Gunning 1994).

2. The liberalization (but not the subsequent reversal) is discussed in Bevan, Collier, and Gunning 1992.

Chapter 10

1. The legal system used was similar to that of the feudal manor. The local people were treated as serfs, and abuses led to considerable migration out of this area in the eighteenth century.

2. An estimated 200,000 Indonesians and 15,000 Dutch died in this war.

3. The extra income could be considerable, allowing the resident of East Java (whose salary was already 25 percent above that of a Dutch cabinet minister) to more than treble his income (de Jong 1984, p. 54).

4. Compulsory growing of export crops was abolished only gradually and, in the case of coffee, not fully until 1917. Under the Agrarian Act an Indonesian who developed land became its owner (rather than the village).

5. Not all plantations were Dutch. Non-Dutch foreign investment was actively encouraged, and there was, for example, considerable American investment in rubber estates.

6. Sukarno emphasized the differences in personality rather than ideology. Typically, he thought the "best way to describe Hatta is to relate the afternoon he was en route somewhere and the only other passenger in the car was a beautiful girl. In a lonely, isolated area the tire went flat." For Sukarno, Hatta, who did not touch the girl, "was a hopeless case. We never thought alike on any issues" (Sukarno 1965, p. 119).

7. The attacks on the Chinese led to an official protest by the Chinese government.

8. The simplicity of Bahasa Indonesia contrasts with Javanese, in which three different vocabularies are used depending on the social positions of the speaker and the person addressed.

9. Sugar mills producing for export were by law prohibited from buying smallholder sugar cane. During the Depression, when rubber production had to be reduced under the International Rubber Restriction Agreement, the production of estates was cut from 220,000 to 205,000 tons, but that of smallholders was cut much more dramatically—from 300,000 to 145,000 tons (Robison 1986, pp. 26–27).

10. A few Sumatran traders managed to compete successfully with the Chinese. These traders first concentrated on trade in imported manufactured goods and moved into manufacturing in the 1950s (Robison 1986, p. 22).

11. This situation contrasts with that of Nigeria, where any secessionist region would be relatively large.

12. Indonesia's currency is the rupiah (Rp).

13. We have given the official translation of the clause. Wilopo's own translation reads: "The economy shall be organized as a joint endeavor based on the principle of the family relationship."

Chapter 11

1. Because of the increasing corruption, in 1955 the government found it necessary to announce as its first objective the restoration of the moral authority of the government.

2. Arndt (1980, p. 437, n. 16) points out that later in the same article (p. 37) Penny does not reject *homo economicus* but advances an alternative explanation for the "non-developmental response" of peasants, attributing it to an extremely high aversion to risk.

3. Such effects of trade and exchange controls are discussed by Bevan, Collier, and Gunning (1990) and by Collier and Gunning (1994 and forthcoming).

4. In 1952 the Chinese, who had owned no agricultural estates before the war, owned 19 percent of those on Java.

5. The year 1958 is included because the increase between 1956 and 1957 seems unlikely: industrial value added rises from Rp 12.5 billion to Rp 16.1 billion in 1957, followed by a fall to Rp 9.8 billion the following year.

Chapter 12

1. Exporters received a negotiable certificate to the face value of their exports. These were sold to importers who had to produce certificates to the value of their foreign exchange requirements. The (daily) rate was market determined.

2. Arndt (1966) gives a detailed account of the hyperinflation period.

Chapter 13

1. Investment in oil and gas was covered separately.

Chapter 14

1. Investment realized under the PMA (foreign) and PMDN (domestic) investment laws through 1973 was $1,131 million and $876 million, respectively. Investment in oil and gas (not covered by these two laws and largely foreign) was estimated at $4 billion.

2. One reason for the anti-Japanese emotions that surfaced in 1974 seems to be that Japanese investment was highly concentrated in textiles and other sectors where it confronted domestic competition (unlike, for example, U.S. investment, much of which was in the oil sector).

3. The 1973 level was 118; $(82–70)/(118–70) = 0.25$.

Chapter 16

1. Sources for this data were the *1968/69 Cost of Living Survey*, table 1.8, and the *1977/78 Cost of Living Survey*, table 1.8A. We assumed mean household size for those in size groups 9+ to be 10.5 and maximum expenditure to be Rp 45,000 in 1968 and Rp 360,000 in 1978.

2. McDonald claims that his data show an equalizing tendency, but there seems no good basis for such an interpretation.

3. The data show an implausibly rapid narrowing in the differential between the top and bottom quintiles.

4. In the Indonesian context "large" is more than 0.5 hectares. Some 25 percent of farm households in the six villages were in this size category.

5. See the detailed criticism of Hollinger and Tan (1956).

Chapter 17

1. The female participation rate was far higher in the 1958 survey than in subsequent surveys, which suggests that female unemployment rates might be highly noncomparable between surveys.

2. The survey is cited in Hawkins 1971, who unfortunately gives an erroneous reference for the original.

3. Series on plantation wages need to be treated with caution because most income was in kind: in 1956 in-kind payments constituted 74 percent of the estates' labor costs (Blake 1962, table VI). However, such costs were supposed to be included in the wage data reported by the plantations.

4. Because there was little change in per capita real consumption in this period, income distribution must have changed in favor of groups other than wage earners.

5. The dependency ratio is defined as that population aged under 15 and over 65, relative to those aged 15–64.

6. For example, as of 1984 the wage level in Bali was more than four times higher than that in Jogjakarta, although both were low-wage regions. Between 1977 and 1984 the minimum fell in real terms by 5.3 percent a year on Sumatra and rose at 3.6 percent a year in Jakarta (Manning and Mazumdar 1985, table AII and p. 20).

7. However, the data exclude salary supplements (both legal and illegal). For that reason, our conclusion that there was no government wage premium must be qualified. We are indebted to H. W. Arndt for this point.

8. Only two of the wage series in table 16.2 cover both years; these show real wages in 1965 to be 44 and 61 percent, respectively, of their 1973 level.

9. This was accepted by Collier (personal communication of W. Collier with P. Collier; see also Collier and others 1982).

10. A survey of 1903 found rural wage labor to be 29 percent (Booth 1983, table 11).

11. In 1965, however, there was an innovative early use of an indexed bond offered without penalty to those declaring illegally obtained or retained funds.

12. In central Java the first two categories involved better-quality land and accounted for 13 percent of the total, according to Penny and Singarimbun (1972), and 20 percent according to Utami and Ihalauw (1973).

13. Since the state trading companies could not handle import trade successfully, restrictions on private importers were relaxed, first in 1960 and then in 1963 (Robison 1986, p. 84).

14. BE certificates covered the bulk of import and export businesses and were intended to establish a free market rate (see note 1, chapter 12, for a description of the earlier version). DP exchange could be used for less essential consumer goods not on the BE list.

15. The tire and tube sector, although more than 50 years old, was defined as an infant industry and enjoyed an effective rate of protection of more than 100 percent.

16. This section on food policy draws heavily on Mears and Moeljono 1981.

17. There seems to have been a slight improvement on Java (from 1.16 to 1.22 tons), offset by decline on the outer islands (from 1.23 to 1.17 tons).

18. These figures are old series estimates; according to the new series, production in 1965 was 10.24 million tons.

Chapter 18

1. One observer who did evaluate the situation correctly was Hicks (1966), as noted by Sundrum (1973), who develops the point. Another was Mackie (1967). The indexes available tended to be downward biased by the heavy weights attached to articles, such as food items, whose prices were subject to some control.

2. Detailed tables are presented in the appendix to this chapter and serve as the sources for the text tables.

3. The procedure adopted for this period was to derive an overall GDP growth factor for the period 1952–60 and to partition this between component years, using as (geometrical) weights the growth rates in the U.N. series. These figures should be treated with the greatest caution.

4. More recently, there has been some tendency for the deficit—when aid is defined as a financing item—to creep up again, but this is misleading, given the second accounting device.

5. A similar picture emerges from table 18A.6, which shows that the contractive effect of the central government on the money supply peaked in 1980/81.

6. Later calculations by Asher and Booth, on a somewhat different basis, suggest a more substantial instability of the domestic deficit, rising to more than 10 percent of GDP in 1980/81 and 1981/82 (Asher and Booth 1992, table 2.8).

7. The drain was proportionately a much heavier burden than that suffered by most colonies. See, for example, Maddison (1985) for a comparison with India.

Chapter 19

1. Rice's article is a mine of information on the origins of economic ideas in Indonesia.

Chapter 20

1. The capital was eventually moved to the North but too late to have an effect during the period we consider.

2. In many respects intra-Javanese concerns eventually became the principal focus of national policy, and the welfare of the Javanese *padi* farmer became the litmus test for the stability of the regime. We have also seen that Java gained relative to the periphery in income distribution.

3. The data, of course, do not reflect the illegal acquisition of foreign financial assets, which reportedly happened on a large scale; to that extent, the low savings rates shown are misleading.

4. As an example of the difference in data sources, the GDP deflator for services in Nigeria contrasts with a much more disaggregated set of proxies for the prices of nontradables in Indonesia.

5. Agriculture expenditure was 10 percent in 1974/75, rising to 16 percent in 1977/78; throughout this period it was considerably more than the share received by industry.

6. Exporters, however, did suffer indirectly from the exchange rate policy. For example the dual exchange rate system in effect during the Korean boom amounted to a 33 $\frac{1}{3}$ percent export tax, but it was abandoned fairly quickly.

7. This was sufficient to overcome one of the supposed distortionary effects of financial repression on investment—the disincentive to accumulate sufficient financial assets to afford large, indivisible projects.

8. The model is more fully presented in Bevan, Collier, and Gunning (1990).

References

Aboyade, O. 1971. "The Development Process." In A. A. Ayida and H. M. A. Onitiri, eds., *Reconstruction and Development in Nigeria.* Ibadan, Nigeria: Oxford University Press.

Adedeji, Adebayo. 1969. *Nigerian Federal Finance: Its Development, Problems and Prospects.* London: Hutchinson.

Adegoye, R. O. 1983. "Procuring Loans by Pledging Cocoa Trees." In J. D. Von Pischke, D. W. Adams, and G. Donald, eds., *Rural Financial Markets in Developing Countries: Their Use and Abuse.* Baltimore: Johns Hopkins University Press.

Ahimie, P. O. 1971. "Health, Housing and Social Welfare." In A. A. Ayida and H. M. A. Onitiri, eds., *Reconstruction and Development in Nigeria.* Ibadan, Nigeria: Oxford University Press.

Akimtola-Bello, O., and A. Adedipe. 1983. "Estimating the Cost of Equity Capital to Nigerian Firms." *Nigerian Journal of Economic and Social Studies* 25 (l).

Aklilu, B., and J. R. Harris. 1980. "Migration, Employment and Earnings." In Gustav Papanek, ed., *The Indonesian Economy.* New York: Praeger.

Altaf, A. 1985. "Nigeria Labor Markets: Data Analysis and Literature Survey." World Bank, West Africa Programs Department, Washington, D.C. Processed.

Aluko, S. A. 1971. "Prices, Wages and Costs." In A. A. Ayida and H. M. A. Onitiri, eds., *Reconstruction and Development in Nigeria.* Ibadan, Nigeria: Oxford University Press.

Arndt, Heinz W. 1967. "Survey of Recent Developments." *Bulletin of Indonesian Economic Studies* 3 (October): 1–34.

————. 1970. "Survey of Recent Developments." *Bulletin of Indonesian Economic Studies* 6: 1–30.

————. 1971. "Banking in Hyperinflation and Stabilization." In Bruce Glassburner, ed., *The Economy of Indonesia: Selected Readings.* Ithaca, N.Y.: Cornell University Press.

————. 1974. "Survey of Recent Developments." *Bulletin of Indonesian Economic Studies* 10: 1–34.

————. 1975. "Krakatau Steel, PT." *Bulletin of Indonesian Economic Studies* 11: 122–26.

————. 1978. "Survey of Recent Developments." *Bulletin of Indonesian Economic Studies* 14 (3): 1–28.

————. 1979. "Monetary Policy Instruments in Indonesia." *Bulletin of Indonesian Economic Studies* 15 (3): 107–22.

————. 1980. "Growth and Equity Objectives in Economic Thought about Indonesia." In Ross G. Garnaut and Peter T. McCawley, eds., *Indonesia: Dualism, Growth and Poverty.* Canberra: Research School of Pacific Studies, Australian National University.

————. 1981. "Survey of Recent Developments." *Bulletin of Indonesian Economic Studies* 17 (3): 1–24.

————. 1983b. "Survey of Recent Developments." *Bulletin of Indonesian Economic Studies* 19 (2): 1–26.

Arndt, Heinz W., and C. Ross. 1970. "The New National Income Estimates." *Bulletin of Indonesian Economic Studies* 6: 33–60.

Arndt, Heinz W., and N. Suwidjana. 1981. "The Jakarta Dollar Market." *Bulletin of Indonesian Economic Studies* 17 (2): 35–64.

Asher, M. G., and Anne Booth. 1992. "Fiscal Policy." In Anne Booth, ed., *The Oil Boom and After: Indonesian Economic Policy and Performance in the Soeharto Era.* Oxford: Oxford University Press.

Bank Indonesia. Various years. *Annual Report.* Jakarta.

Bank Indonesia. Various issues. *Indonesia Financial Statistics.* Jakarta.

Bates, R. 1983. *Essays on the Political Economy of Rural Africa.* New York: Cambridge University Press.

Bauer, P. T. 1954. *West Africa Trade.* Columbia University Press, Cambridge.

Bauer, P. T., and F. W. Parish. 1952. "The Reduction of Fluctuations in the Incomes of Primary Producers." *Economic Journal* 62: 750–80.

Becker, Gary. 1983. "A Theory of Competition among Pressure Groups for Political Influence." *Quarterly Journal of Economics* 98 (3): 371–400.

Berry, S. S. 1975. *Cocoa, Custom and Socio-Economic Change in Rural Western Nigeria.* London: Oxford University Press.

Bevan, David L., Paul Collier, and Jan Willem Gunning. 1989. *Peasants and Governments.* Oxford: Oxford University Press (Clarendon).

————. 1990. *Controlled Open Economies.* Oxford: Oxford University Press (Clarendon).

————. 1992. *Nigeria: Policy Responses to Shocks, 1970–90.* San Francisco: ICS Press.

Bienen, Henry. 1984. *Oil Revenues and Policy Choice in Nigeria.* World Bank Staff Working Paper 592. Washington, D.C.

Bienen, Henry, and Martin Fitton. 1978. In Keith Panter-Brick, ed., *Soldiers and Oil: The Political Transformation of Nigeria.* London: Frank Cass.

Blake, D. 1962. "Labour Shortage and Unemployment in North East Sumatra." *Ekonomi dan Keuancan Indonesia* 15 (1/12).

Boeke, J. H. 1953. *Economics and Economic Policy of Dual Societies as Exemplified by Indonesia.* Haarlem, Netherlands: Tjeenk Willink.

Bolnick, B. 1982. "Concessional Credit for Small Scale Enterprise." *Bulletin of Indonesian Economic Studies* 18 (2): 65–85.

Booth, Anne. 1977. "Interprovincial Comparisons of Taxable Capacity, Tax Effort and Developing Needs in Indonesia." *Malayan Economic Review* 22 (1).

———. 1983. "Income Distribution in Indonesia: Trends and Determinants." Department of Economics, Australian National University, Canberra. Processed.

———. 1985a. "Accommodating a Growing Population in Javanese Agriculture." *Bulletin of Indonesian Economic Studies* 21: 115–45.

———. 1985b. "Efforts to Decentralize Fiscal Policy: Problems of Taxable Capacity, Tax Effort and Revenue Sharing." In C. MacAndrews, ed., *Central Government and Local Development in Indonesia.* Singapore: Oxford University Press.

———, ed. 1992. *The Oil Boom and After: Indonesian Economic Policy and Performance in the Soeharto Era.* Oxford: Oxford University Press.

Booth, Anne, and Bruce Glassburner. 1975. "Survey of Recent Developments." *Bulletin of Indonesian Economic Studies* 11 (l): 1–40.

Booth, Anne, and Peter McCawley, eds. 1981. *The Indonesian Economy during the Soeharto Era.* Kuala Lumpur: Oxford University Press.

Booth, Anne, and R. M. Sundrum. 1981. "Income Distribution." In Anne Booth and Peter McCawley, eds., *The Indonesian Economy during the Soeharto Era.* Kuala Lumpur: Oxford University Press.

Booth, Anne, and A. Tyabji. 1979. "Survey of Recent Developments." *Bulletin of Indonesian Economic Studies* 15 (2): 1–44.

Bousquet, G. H. 1940. *A French View of the Netherlands Indies.* London: Oxford University Press.

Brand, W. 1968. "The Manpower Situation in Indonesia." *Bulletin of Indonesian Economic Studies* 9 (11): 48–72.

Bretton, H. L. 1962. *Power and Stability in Nigeria: The Politics of Decolonization.* New York: Praeger.

Brown, C. V. 1966. *The Nigerian Banking System.* London: Allen and Unwin.

Byerlee, Dirk, C. K. Eicher, C. Liedholm, and D. S. C. Spencer. 1977. "Rural Employment in Tropical Africa: Summary of Findings." African Rural Economy Program Working Paper 20. Department of Agricultural Economics, Michigan State University, East Lansing.

Caldwell, J. C. 1982. *Theory of Fertility Decline.* London: Academic Press.

Castles, L. 1965. "Socialism and Private Business: The Latest Phase." *Bulletin of Indonesian Economic Studies* 1: 13–45.

CBN (Central Bank of Nigeria). 1983. *Nigeria's Flow of Funds, 1970–78.* Lagos.

———.1990. *Statistical Bulletin* (December).

———. Various years. *Annual Report and Statement of Accounts.* Lagos.

———. Various issues. *Economic and Financial Review.* Lagos.

Central Planning Office. 1974. *Guidelines for the Third National Development Plan, 1975–80.* Lagos.

Central Statistical Bureau. Various issues. *Indicator Economics.* Jakarta.

Cohen, J. M. 1980. "Land Tenure and Rural Development." In R. H. Bates and M. F. Lofchies, eds., *Agricultural Development in Africa.* New York: Praeger.

Cohen, R. 1974. *Labour and Politics in Nigeria.* London: Heinemaan.

Collier, Paul. 1983. "Oil and Inequality in Nigeria." In D. Ghai and S. Radwan, eds., *Agrarian Policies and Rural Poverty in Africa.* Geneva: International Labour Office.

———. 1986. "An Analysis of the Nigerian Labour Market." DRD Discussion Paper 155. World Bank, Development Research Department, Washington, D.C.

Collier, Paul, and Jan Willem Gunning. 1994. "Trade and Development: Protection, Shocks and Liberalization." In D. Greenaway and L. A. Winters, eds., *Surveys in International Trade.* Oxford: Blackwell.

—————. Forthcoming. *Trade Shocks in Developing Countries.* Oxford: Oxford University Press.

Collier, Paul, and Deepak Lal. 1986. *Labour and Poverty in Kenya, 1900–1980.* Oxford: Oxford University Press.

Collier, W., G. Wiradi, and Soentoro. 1973. "Recent Changes in Rice Harvesting Methods: Some Serious Social Implications." *Bulletin of Indonesian Economic Studies* 9 (2): 36–45.

Collier, W., and others. 1982. "Acceleration of Rural Development in Java." *Bulletin of Indonesian Economic Studies* 18 (3): 84–101.

Corden, W. Max. 1984. "Booming Sector and Dutch Disease Economics: Survey and Consolidation." *Oxford Economic Papers* 36 (3): 359–80.

Crawford, E. W. 1982. "A Simulation Study of Constraints on Traditional Farming Systems in Northern Nigeria." MSU International Development Paper 2. Department of Agricultural Economics, Michigan State University, East Lansing.

Dapice, D. 1980. "Income Distribution 1970–77: A Comment." *Bulletin of Indonesian Economic Studies* 16 (1): 86–91.

—————. 1983. "Dealing with the 1980s: Indonesia and the World Economy." Tufts University, Medford, Mass. Processed.

Daroesman, R. 1981. "Survey of Recent Developments." *Bulletin of Indonesian Economic Studies* 17 (2): 1–41.

de Jong, L. 1984. *The Kingdom of the Netherlands in the Second World War* (in Dutch). Vol. 11A, Part 1. The Hague: Government Printers.

Dick, Howard. 1979. "Survey of Recent Developments." *Bulletin of Indonesian Economic Studies* 15 (1): 1–44.

—————. 1982. "Survey of Recent Developments." *Bulletin of Indonesian Economic Studies* 18 (1): 1–38.

Dina, I. O. 1971. "Fiscal Measures." In A. A. Ayida and H. M. A. Onitiri, eds., *Reconstruction and Development in Nigeria.* Ibadan, Nigeria: Oxford University Press.

Emmerson, D. K. 1983. "Regime Survival in Indonesia: Questions for an Old New Order." University of Wisconsin, Madison. Processed.

Fajana, F. O. 1975. "The Evolution of Skill Wage Differentials in a Developing Economy: The Nigerian Experience." *The Developing Economies* 13 (2): 150–67.

—————. 1977. "Import Licencing in Nigeria." *Development and Change* 8: 509–22.

FAO (Food and Agriculture Organization of the United Nations). Various years. *Production Yearbook.* Rome.

Feith, Herbert. 1963. "The Dynamics of Guided Democracy." In R. T. McVey, ed., *Indonesia.* New Haven, Conn.: Human Relations Area Files Press.

Feith, Herbert, and L. Castles, eds. 1970. *Indonesian Political Thinking 1945–1965.* Ithaca, N.Y.: Cornell University Press.

Forrest, T. 1981. "Agricultural Policies in Nigeria 1900–78." In J. Heyer, P. Roberts, and G. Williams, eds., *Rural Development in Tropical Africa.* London: Macmillan.

————.1986. "The Political Economic of Civil Rule and the Economic Crisis in Nigeria 1979–84." *Review of African Political Economy* 35.

FOS (Federal Office of Statistics). 1963. *Urban Consumer Surveys in Nigeria.* Lagos: Government Printer.

————. 1966. *Rural Economic Survey of Nigeria: Rural Composition Enquiry for Western State 1965/66.* Lagos: Government Printer.

————. Various years (a). *Annual Abstract of Statistics.* Lagos: Government Printer.

————. Various years (b). *General Household Survey.* Lagos: Government Printer.

————. Various years (c). *Labourforce Survey.* Lagos: Government Printer.

————. Various years (d). *Report of National Consumer Survey.* Lagos: Government Printer.

————. Various years (e) *Report of Urban Household Surveys.* Lagos: Government Printer.

————. Various years (f). *Rural Economic Survey of Nigeria.* Lagos: Government Printer.

————. Various years (g). *Statistical Abstract.* Lagos: Government Printer.

Furnivall, J .S. 1944. *Netherlands India: A Study of Plural Economy.* Cambridge: Cambridge University Press.

Galletti, R., K. D. S. Baldwin, and I. O. Dina. 1956. *Nigerian Cocoa Farmers.* London: Oxford University Press.

Garnaut, Ross. 1979. "Survey of Recent Developments." *Bulletin of Indonesian Economic Studies* 15 (3): 1–62.

Geertz, Clifford. 1963. *Agricultural Involution in Java.* Berkeley: University of California Press.

Gelb, Alan. 1985. "Adjustments to Windfall Gains: A Comparative Analysis of Oil Exporting Countries." World Bank, Public Information Center, Washington, D.C.

Gelb, Alan, and associates. 1988. *Oil Windfalls: Blessing or Curse?* New York: Oxford University Press.

Glassburner, Bruce. 1971a. "Economic Policy-Making in Indonesia, 1950–57." In Bruce Glassburner, ed., *The Economy of Indonesia: Selected Readings.* Ithaca, N.Y.: Cornell University Press.

————, ed. 1971b. *The Economy of Indonesia: Selected Readings.* Ithaca, N.Y.: Cornell University Press.

————. 1979. "Government Budget and Fiscal Policies." *Ekonomi dan Keuangan Indonesia* 27.

————. 1986. "Survey of Recent Developments." *Bulletin of Indonesian Economic Studies* 22 (1): 1–33.

Glassburner, Bruce, and Mark Poffenberger. 1983. "Survey of Recent Developments." *Bulletin of Indonesian Economic Studies* 19 (3): 1–27.

Goddard, A. D., J. C. Fine, and D. W. Norman. 1971. "A Socio-Economic Survey of Three Villages in the Sokoto Close-Settled Zone." Samuru Miscellaneous Papers 37 and 65. Zaria, Nigeria.

Graaff, J. de V. 1984. "Economic Theory and the Economy of Palanpur." *Oxford Economic Papers* 36 (3): 327–35.

Gray, Clive S. 1982. "Survey of Recent Developments." *Bulletin of Indonesian Economic Studies* 18 (3): 1–51.

Grenville, Stephen. 1973. "Survey of Recent Developments." *Bulletin of Indonesian Economic Studies* 9 (1): 1–29.

————. 1974. "Survey of Recent Developments." *Bulletin of Indonesian Economic Studies* 10 (1): 1–32.

————. 1977. "Survey of Recent Developments." *Bulletin of Indonesian Economic Studies* 13 (1): 1–32.

————. 1981. "Monetary Policy and the Formal Financial Sector." In Anne Booth and Peter McCawley, eds., *The Indonesian Economy during the Soeharto Era.* Kuala Lumpur: Oxford University Press.

Harris, J. R., and M. P. Todaro. 1970. "Migration, Unemployment and Development: A Two Sector Analysis." *American Economic Review* 60: 126–42.

Hart, G. 1986. *Power, Labor and Livelihood.* Berkeley: University of California Press.

Hawkins, E. D. 1971. "Labor in Developing Countries: Indonesia." In Bruce Glassburner, ed., *The Economy of Indonesia: Selected Readings.* Ithaca, N.Y.: Cornell University Press.

Hayami, Y., and A. Hafid. 1979. "Rice Harvesting and Welfare in Rural Java." *Bulletin of Indonesian Economic Studies* 15: 95–112.

Healey, D. T. 1981. "Survey of Recent Developments." *Bulletin of Indonesian Economic Studies* 17 (1): 1–35.

Helleiner, G. K. 1966. *Peasant Agriculture, Government and Economic Growth in Nigeria.* Homewood, Ill.: Irwin (for the Yale Economics Growth Center).

Higgins, B. 1984. "Jan Boeke and the Doctrine of 'the Little Push.'" *Bulletin of Indonesian Economic Studies* 20 (3): 55–69.

Hill, H. 1992. "The Economy, a Qualified Success." Department of Economics, Research School of Pacific Studies, Australian National University, Canberra. Processed.

Hollinger, W. C., and A. D. Tan. 1956. "The National Income of Indonesia, 1951–1952: A Critical Commentary on the Neumark Estimates, (I) and (II)." *Ekonomi dan Keuangan Indonesia.*

Hopkins, A. G. 1973. *An Economic History of West Africa.* London: Longman.

Horsnell, P., and P. Collier. 1986. "Migration and the Rural Labour Market in Nigeria." Institute of Economics and Statistics, Oxford University, Oxford. Processed.

Hughes, G. A., and I. Islam. 1981. "Inequality in Indonesia: A Decomposition Analysis." *Bulletin of Indonesian Economic Studies* 17 (2): 42–71.

ILO (International Labour Office). 1981. *First Things First.* Addis Ababa.

IMF (International Monetary Fund). Various years. *Government Finance Statistics.* Washington, D.C.

————. Various years. *International Financial Statistics.* Washington, D.C.

Indonesia. 1974. *The Second Five-Year Development Plan (1974/75–1978/79).* Jakarta: Government Printer.

Indonesia, Ministry of Finance, Bureau of Statistics (BPS). 1971. *1969/70 Cost of Living Survey.* Jakarta.

Indonesia, Minstry of Finance, Bureau of Statistics (BPS), Various years. *Statistical Abstract.* Jakarta.

————. Various years. *Statistical Pocket Book of Indonesia.* Jakarta.

————. *Statistical Yearbook of Indonesia, 1985.* Jakarta.

Isicher, Elizabeth, with a contribution by Peter Uche Isicher. 1983. *A History of Nigeria.* London: Longman.

Islam, I., and H. Khan. 1986. "Spatial Patterns of Inequality and Poverty in Indonesia." *Bulletin of Indonesian Economic Studies* 22: 80–102.

Ismael, J. E. 1980. "Money and Credit in Indonesia, 1966–1969." *Economics and Finance in Indonesia* 28: 97–103.

Jamal, V. 1985. "Poverty and Inequality in Nigeria." International Labour Organisation, Geneva. Processed.

Keyfitz, N. 1985. "Development in an East Javanese Village, 1953 and 1985." *Population and Development Review* 11 (4): 695–719.

Khan, A. R. 1986. "Wages and Employment in Nigeria." World Bank, Public Information Center, Washington, D.C. Processed.

Kilby, P. 1969. *Industrialisation in an Open Economy: Nigeria, 1945–66.* Cambridge: Cambridge University Press.

King, D. Y., and P. D. Weldon. 1977. "Income Distribution and Levels of Living in Java 1963–70." *Economic Development and Cultural Change* 25: 699–711.

Kirk-Greene, A. H. M. 1971. *Crisis and Conflict in Nigeria: A Documentary Source Book.* London: Oxford Universtiy Press.

Kirk-Greene, A., and D. Rimmer. 1981. *Nigeria since 1970: A Political and Economic Outline.* London: Hodder and Stoughton.

Koehn, P. H., and A. Y. Aliyu. 1982. "Local Autonomy and Inter-Governmental Relations in Nigeria." Local Government Research Series 2. Department of Local Government Studies, Institute of Administration, Ahmadu Bello University, Lagos.

Kosut, H., ed. 1967. *Indonesia: The Sukarno Years.* New York: Facts on File.

Legge, J. D. 1972. *Sukarno: A Political Biography.* Sydney: Allen and Unwin.

Leiserson, M. 1979. "Employment and Income Distribution in Indonesia." Report 2378-IND. World Bank, Public Information Center, Washington, D.C.

Lerche, D. 1974. "Taxation and Tax Administration in Developing Countries with Special Reference to Indonesia." Jakarta. Processed.

————. 1983. "Paradox and the Residual Factor in Indonesian Taxation." *Ekonomi dan Keuancan Indonesia* 21 (4).

Lewis, W. A. 1967. *Reflections on Nigeria's Economic Growth.* Paris: OECD Development Centre.

Lluch, C., and D. Mazumdar. 1985. *Indonesia: Wages and Employment.* Washington, D.C.: World Bank.

Longhurst, R. 1980. "Work, Nutrition and Child Malnutrition in a Northern Nigerian Village." Ph.D. dissertation. University of Sussex, U.K.

Luckham, Robin. 1971. *The Nigerian Military: A Sociological Analysis of Authority and Revolt, 1960–67.* Cambridge: Cambridge University Press.

Mackie, J. A. C. 1967. "Problems of the Indonesian Inflation." Monograph series. Department of Asian Studies, Cornell University, Ithaca, N.Y.

————. 1971. "The Indonesian Economy, 1950–1963." In Bruce Glassburner, ed., *The Economy of Indonesia: Selected Readings.* Ithaca, N.Y.: Cornell University Press.

————. 1983. "Property and Power in New Order Indonesia." Australian National University, Canberra. Processed.

Maddison, A. 1985. "Dutch Income in and from Indonesia 1700–1938." Australian National University, Canberra. Processed.

Manning, C. 1979. "Wage Differentials and Labor Market Segmentation in Indonesia Manufacturing." Ph.D. thesis. Australian National University, Canberra.

————. 1986. "The Green Revolution, Employment and Economic Change in Rural Java." Flinders University. Processed.

Manning, C., and D. Mazumdar. 1985. "Indonesian Labor Markets: An Overview." DRD Discussion Paper. World Bank, Development Research Department, Washington, D.C.

Matlon, P. J. 1977. "The Size Distribution, Structure and Determinants of Personal Income among Farmers in the North of Nigeria." Ph.D. thesis. Cornell University, Ithaca, N.Y.

McCawley, Peter. 1981. "The Growth of the Industrial Section." In Anne Booth and Peter McCawley, eds., *The Indonesian Economy during the Soeharto Era.* Kuala Lumpur: Oxford University Press.

————. 1982. "The Economics of Ekonomi Pancasila." *Bulletin of Indonesian Economic Studies* 18 (1): 102–9.

————. 1983. "Survey of Recent Developments." *Bulletin of Indonesian Economic Studies* 19 (1): 1–31.

McDonald, P. 1980. "The Equality of Distribution of Child Mortality, Java-Bali, 1950–76." *Bulletin of Indonesian Economic Studies* 16 (3): 115–19.

Mears, L. A., and S. Moeljono. 1981. "Food Policy." In Anne Booth and Peter McCawley, eds., *The Indonesian Economy during the Soeharto Era.* Kuala Lumpur: Oxford University Press.

Miners, M. J. 1971. *The Nigerian Army 1956.* London: Methuen.

————. 1981. *1977/78 Cost of Living Survey.* Jakarta.

Muljatno. 1960. "Perhituntgan Pendapatan National Indonesia untuk tahun 1953 dan 1954." *Economics and Finance in Indonesia* 13: 162–216.

Myrdal, Gunnar. 1956. *An International Economy: Problems and Prospects.* Harper: New York.

Nasution, Anwar. 1986. "Instruments of Monetary Policy in Indonesia after the 1983 Banking Disregulation." University of Indonesia, Jakarta. Processed.

Nelson, H. D., and others. 1972. *Area Handbook for Nigeria.* Washington, D.C.: U.S. Government Printing Office.

Neumark, S. D. 1954. "The National Income of Indonesia, 1951–1952." *Ekonomi dan Keuangan* (June).

Nigeria. 1962. *Nigerian Development Plan 1962–68.* Lagos: Government Printer.

————. Various issues. *Government Finance Statistics Yearbook.* Lagos: Government Printer.

Nigeria, Ministry of Labour, Department of Statistics. Various issues. *Quarterly Bulletin of Labour Statistics.* Lagos.

Norman, D. W. 1971. "An Economic Survey of Three Villages in Zaria Province." Samuru Miscellaneous Papers 19 and 38. Zaria, Nigeria.

Ogunsanwo. 1986. "Government Policy, Growth and Distribution in Nigeria." Rutgers University, New Brunswick, N.J. Processed.

Okigbo, P. N. C. 1962. *Nigerian National Accounts.* Lagos: Federal Ministry of Economic Development.

Olaloku, F. A., ed. 1979. *Structure of the Nigerian Economy.* Lagos: University of Lagos Press.

Olatunbosun, D. 1975. *Nigeria's Neglected Rural Majority.* Ibadan, Nigeria: Oxford University Press.

Olatunbosun, D., and H. M. A. Onitiri, eds. 1974. *The Marketing Board System: Proceedings of an International Conference.* Ibadan, Nigeria: Nigeria Institute of Social and Economic Research.

Olson, M. 1965. *The Logic of Collective Action.* Cambridge, Mass.: Harvard University Press.

Olunsanya, P. O., and D. E. Pursell. 1981. *The Prospects of Economic Development in Nigeria—under Conditions of Rapid Population Growth.* Ibadan, Nigeria: Nigerian Institute of Social and Economic Research.

Oluwasanmi, H. A. 1971. "Agricultural and Rural Development." In A. A. Ayida and H. M. A. Onitiri, eds., *Reconstruction and Development in Nigeria.* Ibadan, Nigeria: Oxford University Press.

Onitiri, H. M. A. 1971. "Nigeria's External Trade, Balance of Payments and Capital Movements 1959–1968." In A. A. Ayida and H. M. A. Onitiri, eds., *Reconstruction and Development in Nigeria.* Ibadan, Nigeria: Oxford University Press.

Onoh, J. K. 1980. *The Foundations of Nigeria's Financial Infrastructure.* London: Croom Helm.

Osoba, A. M. 1987. "The Political Economy of Poverty, Equity and Growth in Nigeria: The Industrial Perspective." Nigerian Institute of Social and Economic Research, Ibadan. Processed.

Oyejide, T. A. 1986. "The Effects of Trade and Exchange Rate Policies on Agriculture in Nigeria." Research Report 55. International Food Policy Research Institute, Washington, D.C.

————. 1991. "Trade Shock, Oil Boom and the Nigerian Economy, 1973–83." Department of Economics, University of Ibadan, Nigeria. Processed.

Oyovbaise, S. Egike. 1978. "The Politics of Revenue Allocation." In Keith Panter-Brick, ed., *Soldiers and Oil: The Political Transformation of Nigeria.* London: Frank Cass.

Paauw, Douglas S. 1960. *Financing Economic Development: The Indonesian Case.* Glencoe, Ill.: Free Press.

Papanek, Gustav, ed. 1980. *The Indonesian Economy.* New York: Praeger.

Papanek, Gustav F., and D. Dowsett. 1975. "The Cost of Living, 1938–73." *Ekonomi dan Keuangan Indonesia* 23 (2).

Partadireja. 1974. "Rural Credit: The IJON System." *Bulletin of Indonesian Economic Studies* 10 (3): 54–71.

Pearson, S. R. 1970. "Nigerian Petroleum: Implications for Medium-Term Planning." In C. K. Eicher and C. Liedholm, eds., *Growth and Development of the Nigerian Economy.* East Lansing: Michigan State University Press.

Penny, D. H. 1966. "The Economics of Peasant Agriculture: The Indonesian Case." *Bulletin of Indonesian Economic Studies* 5 (October): 22–44.

Penny, D. H., and M. Singarimbun. 1972. "A Case Study of Rural Poverty." *Bulletin of Indonesian Economic Studies* 8 (1): 79–88.

Polak, J. 1942. "The National Income of the Netherlands Indies in 1921–1939." Institute of Pacific Relations, New York. Processed.

Posthumus. 1972. "The Inter-Governmental Group on Indonesia." *Bulletin of Indonesian Economic Studies* 8 (2): 55–66.

Rao, V. V. B. 1984. "Poverty in Indonesia, 1970–80." World Bank, East Asia and Pacific Region, Washington, D.C.

Reid, A. J. S. 1980. "The Origins of Poverty in Indonesia." In R. G. Garnaut and P. T. McCawley, eds., *Indonesia: Dualism, Growth and Poverty.* Canberra: Research School of Pacific Studies, Australian National University.

Rice, R. C. 1983. "The Origin of Basic Economic Ideas and Their Impact on 'New Order' Policies." *Bulletin of Indonesian Economic Studies* 19 (2): 60–82.

Rice, R. C., and D. Lim. 1976. "Survey of Recent Developments." *Bulletin of Indonesian Economic Studies* 12 (2): 1–29.

Rimmer, D. 1978. "Elements of Political Economy." In Keith Panter-Brick, ed., *Soldiers and Oil: The Political Transformation of Nigeria.* London: Frank Cass.

Robison, Richard. 1986. *Indonesia: The Rise of Capital.* Sydney: Allen and Unwin.

Roepstorff, T. 1985. "Industrial Development in Indonesia: Performance and Prospects." *Bulletin of Indonesian Economic Studies* 21: 32–61.

Ronohadiwirjo, S. 1969. "Agricultural Credit Structures in Rice Producing Areas: A Case Study in Karawang, West Java." Ph.D. dissertation. IPB, Bogor, Indonesia.

Rosendale, Phyllis. 1975. "The Indonesian Terms of Trade, 1950–1973." *Bulletin of Indonesian Economic Studies* 11: 50–80.

————. 1981. "The Balance of Payments." In Anne Booth and Peter McCawley, eds., *The Indonesian Economy during the Soeharto Era.* Kuala Lumpur: Oxford University Press.

Ross, P. J. n.d. "Land as a Right to Membership: Land Tenure Dynamics in a Peripheral Area of the Kano Close-Settled Zone." Processed.

"S." 1946. "Our Nationalism and Its Substance." Reprinted in Herbert Feith and L. Castles, eds., 1970, *Indonesian Political Thinking 1945–1965.* Ithaca, N.Y.: Cornell University Press.

Sadli, M. 1970. "Development Policies for the Private Sector of Indonesia." Processed.

Scherer, P. 1982. "Survey of Recent Developments." *Bulletin of Indonesian Economic Studies* 18 (2): 1–34.

Schmitt, H. 1962. "Foreign Capital and Social Conflict in Indonesia." *Economic Development and Cultural Change* 10.

Sen, Amartya. 1981. *Poverty and Famines.* Oxford: Oxford University Press.

Shaw, G. 1980. "Intergovenmental Fiscal Relations." In Gustav Papanek, ed., *The Indonesian Economy.* New York: Praeger.

Shenton, R. W. 1986. *The Development of Capitalism in Northern Nigeria.* London: James Currey.

Smythe, H. H., and M. M. Smythe. 1960. *The New Nigerian Elite.* Stanford, Calif.: Stanford University Press.

Soehoed, A. R. 1980. "Japan and the Development of the Indonesian Manufacturing Sector." Address by Indonesia's Minister of Industry to the Eighth Japan-Indonesia Conference, Tokyo. Cited in T. K. Wie, "Regulating Foreign Direct Investment in the Manufacturing Sector: A Case Study of Indonesia." Revised draft. Processed.

Stewart, Francis. 1985. *Colonial Indonesia/Nigeria in 1985.* P.A.I.S.

Stolper, W. F. 1966. *Planning without Facts: Lessons in Resource Allocation from Nigeria's Development.* Cambridge, Mass.: Harvard University Press.

Suebsaeng, P. 1984. "Employment and Salaries in the Nigerian Civil Service."

Sukarno. 1965. *Sukarno: An Autobiography. As Told to Cindy Adams.* New York: Bobbs-Merrill.

Sundrum, R. M. 1973. "Money Supply and Prices: A Reinterpretation." *Bulletin of Indonesian Economic Studies* 9 (3): 73–86.

————. 1979. "Income Distribution 1970–76." *Bulletin of Indonesian Economic Studies* 15 (1): 137–41.

Turner, Teresa. 1978. "Commercial Capitalism and the 1975 Coup." In Keith Panter-Brick, ed., *Soldiers and Oil: The Political Transformation of Nigeria.* London: Frank Cass.

United Nations. 1960. *Yearbook of National Accounts Statistics.* New York.

Utami, W., and J. Ihalauw. 1973. "Some Consequences of Small Farm Size." *Bulletin of Indonesian Economic Studies* 9 (2): 46–56.

van der Eng, P. 1993. "Agricultural Growth in Indonesia since 1880." Ph.D. thesis. University of Groningen, Netherlands.

Vigo, A. 1965. "A Survey of Agricultural Credit in the Northern Region of Nigeria." Ministry of Agriculture, Kaduna. Processed.

Warr, Peter. 1980. "Survey of Recent Developments." *Bulletin of Indonesian Economic Studies* 16 (3): 1–31.

———. 1986. "Indonesia's Other Dutch Disease." In J. P. Neary and Sweder van Wijnbergen, eds., *National Resources and the Macroeconomy.* Oxford: Blackwell.

Wells, J. C. 1970. "Issues in Agricultural Policy during the 1962–68 Nigerian Development Plan." In C. K. Eicher, and C. Liedholm, eds., *Growth and Development of the Nigerian Economy.* East Lansing: Michigan State University Press.

White, V. 1976. "Population, Employment and Involution in a Javanese Village." *Development and Change* 7.

Wie, T. K. 1984. "Subcontracting in the Engineering Subsector in Indonesia: Preliminary Survey." Draft.

———. 1986a. "Development Problems of a Resource-Rich Country: The Indonesian Economy since 1966." Processed.

———. 1986b. "Regulating Foreign Direct Investment in the Manufacturing Sector: A Case Study of Indonesia." Revised draft.

Wie, T. K., and K. Yoshihara. 1986. "Foreign and Domestic Capital in Indonesian Industrialization." Processed.

Wijaya, Hesti, and N. H. Sturgess. 1979. "Land Leasing in East Java." *Bulletin of Indonesian Economic Studies* 15 (2): 75–93.

Wilopo, and Nitisastro Widjojo. 1959. *The Socioeconomic Basis of the Indonesian State: On the Interpretation of Paragraph 1, Article 33 of the Provisional Constitution of the Republic of Indonesia.* Translation Series, Modern Indonesia Project. Ithaca, N.Y.: Cornell University Press.

World Bank. 1974. *Nigeria: Options for Long-Term Development.* Baltimore: Johns Hopkins University Press.

———. 1980. *World Tables 1980.* Baltimore: Johns Hopkins University Press.

———. 1983. "Indonesia, Policies, for Growth with Lower Oil Prices." Report 4274-IND. Public Information Center, Washington, D.C.

———. 1984. "Nigeria: Agricultural Pricing Policy." Public Information Center, Washington, D.C. Processed.

———. 1986a. *Social Indicators of Development 1986.* Washington, D.C.

———. 1986b. *World Tables 1986.* Baltimore: Johns Hopkins University Press.

———. 1987. *World Development Report 1987: Industrialization and Foreign Trade.* New York: Oxford University Press.

———. 1990. "Indonesia: Strategy for a Sustained Reduction in Poverty." Public Information Center, Washington, D.C. Processed.

————. 1994a. "Nigeria Structural Adjustment Program." Public Information Center, Washington, D.C. Processed.

————. 1994b. *World Tables 1994.* Baltimore: Johns Hopkins University Press.

————. 1995. *World Development Report 1995: Workers in an Integrating World.* New York: Oxford University Press.

Zainu'ddin, A. 1968. *A Short History of Indonesia.* Melbourne: Cassell.

Index